# Addison-Wesley

# Science Insights
## Exploring Matter and Energy

## Authors

**Michael DiSpezio, M.A.**
Science Consultant
North Falmouth,
Massachusetts

**Marilyn Linner-Luebe, M.S.**
Former Science Teacher
Fulton High School,
Fulton, Illinois

**Marylin Lisowski, Ph.D.**
Professor of Education
Eastern Illinois University
Charleston, Illinois

**Bobbie Sparks, M.A.**
K–12 Science Consultant
Harris County Department
   of Education
Houston, Texas

**Gerald Skoog, Ed.D.**
Professor and Chairperson
Curriculum and Instruction
Texas Tech University
Lubbock, Texas

## Addison-Wesley Publishing Company

Menlo Park, California • Reading, Massachusetts • New York
Don Mills, Ontario • Wokingham, England • Amsterdam • Bonn
Paris • Milan • Madrid • Sydney • Singapore • Tokyo
Seoul • Taipei • Mexico City • San Juan

## Content Reviewers

**Farzan Abdolsalami**
Assistant Professor
Trinity University
San Antonio, Texas

**Randall Bryson**
Middle School Science
    Coordinator
Durham Academy
Durham, North Carolina

**John Caferella**
Science Programs Supervisor
Community School District 10
Bronx, New York

**Catherine K. Carlson**
Science Department
    Chairperson
Parkhill/Richardson
    Intermediate School District
Dallas, Texas

**Anita Gerlach**
Chemistry/Physics Teacher
Santa Fe High School
Santa Fe, New Mexico

**Karen G. Jennings**
Chemistry Instructor
Lane Technical High School
Chicago, Illinois

**George Moore**
Science Coordinator
Midwest City Public Schools
Midwest City, Oklahoma

**Gary J. Vitta**
Superintendent of Schools
West Essex Regional Schools
North Caldwell, New Jersey

**Miriam R. Weiss**
Director of
    Science/Technology
Community School District 11
Bronx, New York

**Richard A. Williams**
Chemistry Instructor
Winter Haven High School
Winter Haven, Florida

## Multicultural Reviewers

**William Bray**
Stanford University
Stanford, California

**Gloriane Hirata**
San Jose Unified School
    District
San Jose, California

**Joseph A. Jefferson**
Ronald McNair School
East Palo Alto, California

**Martha Luna**
McKinley Middle School
Redwood City, California

**Peggy P. Moore**
Garnet Robertson
    Intermediate
Daly City, California

**Steven Oshita**
Crocker Middle School
Burlingame, California

**Modesto Tamez**
Exploratorium
San Francisco, California

Front cover photographs: NASA (Earth), Jeff Foott/Bruce Coleman Inc. (honeycomb), K. Murakami/Tom Stack & Associates (integrated chip wafer), Gareth Hopson for Addison-Wesley (geode).

Back cover photograph: K. Murakami/Tom Stack & Associates (integrated chip wafer).

ISBN    0-201-44597-2

1 2 3 4 5 6 7 8 9 10 —DO—99 98 97 96 95

# Contents

*Chapter 1  Studying Science*                                    2–29

**1.1  Science Skills and Methods**                                  3
    Science and Society  *Science Communities*                    10
**1.2  Measuring With Scientific Units**                            11
    Science and You  *Designer Fit*                               16
**1.3  Graphing**                                                  17
    Science and Society  *Take a Second Look*                     20
**1.4  Science Tools and Technology**                              21
    Science and Technology  *Prehistoric Tech*                    24
    *Activity 1*  *How do you make a microbalance?*               26

*Chapter 2  Motion and Energy*                                  30–53

**2.1  Motion**                                                    31
    Science and Technology  *Air Navigation*                      38
**2.2  Acceleration**                                              39
    Science and Society  *Skid-Mark Evidence*                     44
**2.3  Energy of Motion**                                          45
    Science and Technology  *Great Potential*                     49
    *Activity 2*  *How can you change the speed of a rocket?*     50

*Chapter 3  Forces and Motion*                                  54–83

**3.1  Forces, Motion, and Gravity**                               55
    Science and You  *Strikeout Forces*                           59
**3.2  First Law of Motion**                                       60
    Science and Technology  *Friction Control*                    63
**3.3  Second Law of Motion**                                      64
    Science and Society  *More Miles for the Size*                69
**3.4  Third Law of Motion**                                       70
    Science and Technology *From Fireworks to Outer Space*        72
**3.5  Universal Forces**                                          73
    Science and Technology  *Reading Your Heartbeat*              79
    *Activity 3*  *Do heavier objects fall faster than light objects?*  80

*Chapter 4  Forces in Fluids*                                  84–105

**4.1  Fluid Pressure**                                            85
    Science and Technology  *Putting on the Brakes*               90
**4.2  Buoyancy**                                                  91
    Science and Technology  *Making Steel Float*                  95
    *Activity 4*  *How can you control an object's buoyancy?*     96
**4.3  Forces in Moving Fluids**                                   97
    Science and Society  *Kite Flying*                           102

## Unit 1
## Forces, Motion, and Energy

page 1

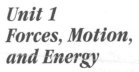

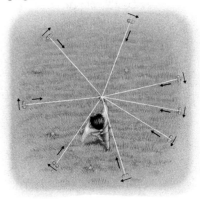

Unit 2
*Particles of Matter*

page 132

## Chapter 5  Work, Machines, and Energy     106–129

| 5.1 | **Work and Power** | 107 |
| | Science and You  *Your Electric Bill* | 111 |
| 5.2 | **Work and Machines** | 112 |
| | Science and Society  *Energy Efficiency* | 115 |
| 5.3 | **Simple and Compound Machines** | 116 |
| | Science and Technology  *Travel by Bicycle* | 121 |
| 5.4 | **Energy and Its Forms** | 122 |
| | Science and You  *Energy Conversions in Your Body* | 125 |
| | *Activity 5*  *How does the rate of energy change affect work?* | 126 |
| | **Science and Literature** "The Boy Who Reversed Himself" | 130 |

## Chapter 6  Properties of Matter     134–155

| 6.1 | **Matter** | 135 |
| | Science and Technology  *Enhancing the Stone* | 139 |
| 6.2 | **Phases of Matter** | 140 |
| | Science and You  *Packaging Liquids* | 146 |
| 6.3 | **Changes in Matter** | 147 |
| | Science and You  *Haircuts and Permanents* | 151 |
| | *Activity 6*  *What is the evidence for a chemical change?* | 152 |

## Chapter 7  Atoms, Elements, Compounds, and Mixtures     156–181

| 7.1 | **Structure of the Atom** | 157 |
| | Science and Technology  *Tracking Subatomic Particles* | 163 |
| 7.2 | **Elements** | 164 |
| | Science and You  *Trace Elements in Your Body* | 167 |
| 7.3 | **Compounds** | 168 |
| | Science and Society  *The Origins of Pharmacy* | 172 |
| 7.4 | **Mixtures** | 174 |
| | Science and You  *Hard Water or Soft Water* | 177 |
| | *Activity 7*  *What makes a soap bubble last?* | 178 |

## Chapter 8  Introduction to the Periodic Table  182–203

| 8.1 | **The Modern Periodic Table** | 183 |
| | Science and and Technology  *Synthetic Elements* | 188 |
| 8.2 | **Metals** | 189 |
| | Science and Technology  *Making Alloys* | 193 |
| 8.3 | **Nonmetals and Metalloids** | 194 |
| | Science and Technology  *Uses of Noble Gases* | 198 |
| | *Activity 8*  *What elements can you find in your kitchen?* | 200 |
| | *Science and Literature*  "Invitation to the Game" | 204 |

## Chapter 9   Heat                                    208–229

**9.1   Heat Energy**                                      209
Science and Technology   *A Cool Engine*                  212
**9.2   Transfer of Heat**                                213
Science and You   *Food Calories and Energy*              220
*Activity 9   How do you measure the transfer of heat?*   221
**9.3   Heat and Matter**                                 222
Science and Society   *Food for Tomorrow*                 226


## Chapter 10   Using Heat                             230–251

**10.1   Heating Technology**                             231
Science and You   *Weatherize Your Home*                  237
*Activity 10   What materials make the best
  heat insulators?*                                       238
**10.2   Cooling Technology**                             239
Science and Society   *CFCs and the Ozone Layer*          243
**10.3   Heat Engines**                                   244
Science and Society   *Combustion Waste*                  248
*Science and Literature*   *"Child of the Owl"*           252


## Chapter 11   Electricity                            256–285

**11.1   Electric Charges**                               257
Science and You   *Your Electric Nerves*                  259
*Activity 11   Which material has the greatest
  force of attraction?*                                   260
**11.2   Static Electricity**                             261
Science and You   *Fabric Softeners and Hair
  Conditioners*                                           266
**11.3   Electric Current**                               267
Science and Technology   *Electric Plastics*              273
**11.4   Electric Circuits**                              274
Science and Society   *Efficient Energy Use*              278
**11.5   Electric Power and Safety**                      279
Science and You   *Electric Safety and Your Body*         282


## Chapter 12   Magnetism                              286–307

**12.1   Magnets and Magnetism**                          287
Science and You   *The Helpful Compass*                   292
**12.2   Electricity to Magnetism**                       293
Science and Technology   *Electric Cars*                  298
*Activity 12   Does the number of electric coils
  affect magnetic force?*                                 299
**12.3   Magnetism to Electricity**                       300
Science and Technology   *Generators for Bikes*           304

*Unit 3*
*Heat*

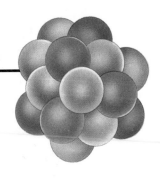

page 206

*Unit 4*
*Electricity and*
*Electromagnetism*

page 254

v

## Chapter 13   Electronics
308–329

**13.1   Electronic Devices** 309
Science and Society   *Smart Cards* 314
**13.2   Audio and Video Electronics** 315
Science and Technology   *CD-ROM* 320
*Activity 13   How are dots used to make pictures?* 321
**13.3   Computers** 322
Science and You   *Laptops: The Book of the Future* 326
***Science and Literature***
   "Genie With the Light Blue Hair" 330

## Unit 5
## Waves, Sound, and Light

page 332

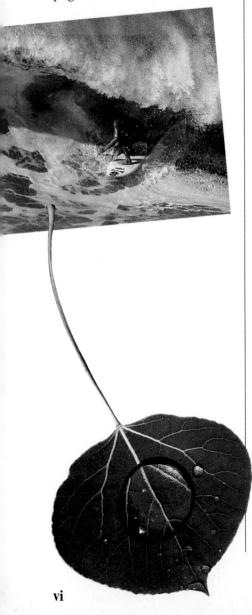

## Chapter 14   Waves
334–357

**14.1: Nature of Waves** 335
Science and Society   *Surfing* 339
*Activity 14   How does the water surface move
   when waves pass?* 340
**14.2   Wave Properties** 341
Science and Society   *Earthquake-Proof Buildings* 347
**14.3   Wave Interactions** 348
Science and Technology
   *Computer Models of Waveforms* 353

## Chapter 15   Sound
358–383

**15.1   Wave Model of Sound** 359
Science and You   *Listening Through Your Bones* 365
**15.2   Properties of Sound** 366
Science and Technology   *Sound-Effects Machines* 371
**15.3   Sound-Wave Interactions** 372
Science and Technology   *Acoustics—Sound Control* 379
*Activity 15   How do sound waves reflect?* 380

## Chapter 16   Using Sound
384–407

**16.1   How You Hear** 385
Science and You   *Hearing Protectors* 388
**16.2   Sounds You Hear** 390
Science and Society   *Noise Pollution* 396
*Activity 16   What musical instruments can be made
   from common materials?* 397
**16.3   Sound Technology** 398
Science and Technology   *High-Tech Hearing Aids* 404

## Chapter 17   Light
408–431

**17.1   Nature of Light** 409
Science and Society   *Light Cures SADness* 414
*Activity 17   Does light travel in a straight line?* 415
**17.2   The Electromagnetic Spectrum** 416
Science and Technology   *Using a Microwave Oven* 421
**17.3   Light and Color** 422
Science and Technology   *Four-Color Printing* 428

## Chapter 18   Using Light     432–461

**18.1   Light Sources**     433
Science and Society  *Energy-Saving Light Bulbs*     436
**18.2   Vision**     437
Science and You  *Living Without Light*     440
**18.3   Reflection and Mirrors**     441
Science and Technology  *Super Telescopes*     444
**18.4   Refraction and Lenses**     445
Science and Technology  *Correcting Your Vision*     448
*Activity 18*  *Is a convex hand lens like an eye?*     450
**18.5   Light Technology**     451
Science and Society  *New Communications Age*     458
***Science and Literature***  "Blue Tights"     462

## Chapter 19   Chemical Bonding     466–487

**19.1   Atoms and Bonding**     467
Science and Technology  *Designer Molecules*     470
**19.2   Ionic Bonds**     471
Science and You  *Trading in Ions*     477
**19.3   Covalent Bonds**     478
Science and You  *A Sticky Problem*     482
*Activity 19*  *How do ionic and covalent bonds differ?*     484

## Unit 6
## Interactions of Matter

page 464

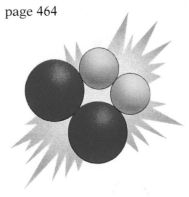

## Chapter 20   Chemical Reactions     488–513

**20.1   Characteristics of Chemical Reactions**     489
Science and You
   *Chemistry Celebration: The Fourth of July*     493
**20.2   Chemical Equations**     494
Science and Society
   *Chain Reactions in the Ozone Layer*     498
**20.3   Types of Chemical Reactions**     499
Science and You  *How Antacids Work*     502
**20.4   Energy and Reaction Rate**     503
Science and Technology
   *Catalytic Converters and Smog Reduction*     509
*Activity 20*  *How do some everyday substances
   react chemically?*     510

## Chapter 21   Solution Chemistry     514–535

**21.1   Solutions**     515
Science and You  *Kitchen Solutions*     521
**21.2   Suspensions and Colloids**     522
Science and Technology  *Smooth and Creamy Foods*     526
**21.3   Acids, Bases, and Salts**     527
Science and You  *The pH of Your Blood*     531
*Activity 21*  *What's an acid and what's a base?*     532

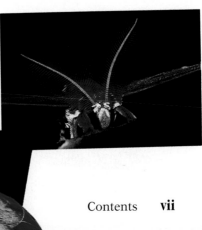

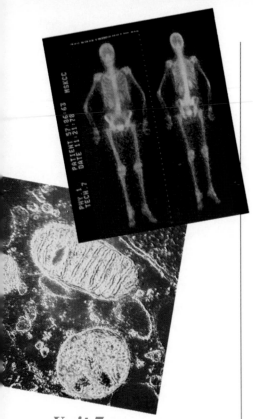

**Chapter 22  Carbon Compounds and the Chemistry of Life**                    536–559

22.1  **A World of Carbon**                             537
Science and Technology  *Presto! Plastics!*            543
*Activity 22*  *How can you capture a scent?*          544
22.2  **Food Chemistry**                               545
Science and You  *Essential Vitamins?*                549
22.3  **Energy in Living Things**                      551
Science and You  *Your Body's Energy Budget*          556

**Chapter 23  Nuclear Chemistry**                      560–577

23.1  **Radioactivity**                                561
Science and Technology  *Radiation Detectors*         564
23.2  **Radioactive Decay**                            565
Science and Technology  *Nuclear Medicine*            569
*Activity 23*  *How can you make a model
of radioactive decay?*                                570
23.3  **Energy from the Nucleus**                      571
Science and Society  *Nuclear Waste*                  574
*Science and Literature*  "Mother and Daughter"       578

*Unit 7*
*Technology and
Resources*

page 580

**Chapter 24  Energy Use and Technology**              582–603

24.1  **Generating and Using Electric Power**          583
Science and You  *Energy Cost of Your Lunch*          588
24.2  **Alternative Energy Technologies**              589
Science and Technology  *The Hydrogen Stove*          594
*Activity 24*  *How do you make a solar hot-dog cooker?*  595
24.3  **Energy Conservation Decisions**                596
Science and Society  *Saving Energy by Recycling*     600

**Chapter 25  Chemical Technology**                    604–631

25.1  **Petroleum Fuels**                              605
Science and Society  *Petroleum Reserves*             608
25.2  **Petrochemical Products**                       609
Science and You  *Plastic Recycling*                  613
25.3  **Materials Science**                            614
Science and Technology  *Ceramic Engines*             619
*Activity 25*  *How can the properties of
a polymer be changed?*                                620
25.4  **Technology and the Environment**               621
Science and Society  *River on Fire!*                 628
*Science and Literature*  "M. C. Higgins the Great"   632

**Data Bank**                                          634–643
**Math Appendix with Practice Problems**               644–647
**Glossary**                                           648–655
**Index**                                              656–670
**Acknowledgments**                                    671–672

# Features

## *Career Corner*

What Careers Use Scientific Skills and
  Knowledge? ...................................... 24
Mechanical Engineer ................................ 114
Chef .................................................... 150
Machinist .............................................. 190
Refrigeration Technician ........................... 241
Electrician ............................................. 272
Optician ................................................ 449
Quality-Control Chemist ........................... 507
Food Scientist ........................................ 549
Electrical Engineer .................................. 593

## *Historical Notebook*

Motion Changes with the Times .................. 37
Boat Design in Polynesia ........................... 94
Understanding Heat ................................. 210
Magnetism in Ancient Times ..................... 289
Incident at Tacoma Narrows Bridge .......... 378
History of Musical Instruments ................. 394
Color and Impressionism .......................... 427
Ceramic Pottery ..................................... 617

## *Consider This*
### Decision Making Skills

Should Seat Belts and Air Bags
  Be Required? ..................................... 67
Should Fluoride Be Added
  to Public Water Supplies? ..................... 172
Should Cars Use Solar-
  Powered Engines? .............................. 247
Should People Avoid Low-level
  Magnetic Fields? ................................ 295

Do Computer Networks Invade
  Your Privacy? .................................... 319
Should Breakwaters and Wave
  Barriers Be Built? ............................... 353
Should There Be More Regulation
  of Noise Pollution? ............................. 388
Should Office Buildings Leave Lights
  on at Night? ...................................... 454
Stricter Regulations for Food Additives? ... 482
Should the pH of Lakes Be Adjusted? ........ 530
Should New Nuclear Power Plants
  Be Built? .......................................... 573
Are Biodegradable Plastics Good
  for the Environment? ........................... 612

## *Science and Literature*

"The Boy Who Reversed Himself" .............. 130
"Invitation to the Game" ........................... 204
"Child of the Owl" .................................. 252
"Genie With the Light Blue Hair" .............. 330
"Blue Tights" ......................................... 462
"Mother and Daughter" ............................ 578
"M. C. Higgins the Great" ......................... 632

# Hands-On Science

## Activities

Activity 1 ............................................. 26
  *How do you make a microbalance?*
Activity 2 ............................................. 50
  *How can you changes the speed of a rocket?*
Activity 3 ............................................. 80
  *Do heavier objects fall faster than light objects?*
Activity 4 ............................................. 96
  *How can you control an object's buoyancy?*
Activity 5 ............................................. 126
  *How does the rate of energy change affect work?*
Activity 6 ............................................. 152
  *What is the evidence for a chemical change?*
Activity 7 ............................................. 178
  *What makes a soap bubble last?*
Activity 8 ............................................. 200
  *What elements can you find in your kitchen?*
Activity 9 ............................................. 221
  *How do you measure the transfer of heat?*
Activity 10 ........................................... 238
  *What materials make the best heat insulators?*
Activity 11 ........................................... 260
  *Which material has the greatest force of attraction?*
Activity 12 ........................................... 299
  *Does the number of electric coils affect magnetic force?*
Activity 13 ........................................... 321
  *How are dots used to make pictures?*
Activity 14 ........................................... 340
  *How does the water surface move when waves pass?*
Activity 15 ........................................... 380
  *How do sound waves reflect?*
Activity 16 ........................................... 397
  *What musical instruments can be made from common materials?*
Activity 17 ........................................... 415
  *Does light travel in a straight line?*
Activity 18 ........................................... 450
  *Is a convex hand lens like an eye?*
Activity 19 ........................................... 484
  *How do ionic and covalent bonds differ?*

Activity 20 ........................................... 510
  *How do some everyday substances react chemically?*
Activity 21 ........................................... 532
  *What's an acid and what's a base?*
Activity 22 ........................................... 544
  *How can you capture a scent?*
Activity 23 ........................................... 570
  *How can you make a model of radio-active decay?*
Activity 24 ........................................... 595
  *How do you make a solar hot-dog cooker?*
Activity 25 ........................................... 620
  *How can the properties of a polymer be changed?*

## SkillBuilder Activity

### Problem Solving/Process Skills

What Kind of Graph .......................... 18
  *Making a Graph*
A Racer's Accelerations .................... 41
  *Calculating*
Force in Newtons .............................. 57
  *Measuring*
Paper Airplane Design ...................... 99
  *Making a Model*
The Hat-Removal Machine ................ 120
  *Classifying*
Going Through a Phase .................... 145
  *Predicting*
Model of an Atom ............................. 162
  *Making Models*
Atomic Mass ..................................... 198
  *Making a Graph*
Melting Points .................................. 224
  *Interpreting Data*
Reading Electric Meters .................. 280
  *Observing*
Flowcharting ..................................... 325
  *Making Models*
The Center of an Earthquake ......... 345
  *Interpreting Data*
Musical Bottles ................................. 363
  *Inferring*
Polarized Sunglasses ....................... 411
  *Comparing, Controlling Variables*
Properties of Ionic Solids .............. 476
  *Observing*
Writing Chemical Equations ........... 497
  *Calculating*

**SkillBuilder Activities Continued**

Soluble of Insoluble? ................................... 520
  *Interpreting Data*
The Best Light for Photosynthesis ............. 554
  *Interpreting Data*
Your Annual Radiation Dose ...................... 563
  *Estimating*
A Risk-Benefit Analysis ............................ 597
  *Analyzing*

## Skills WarmUp Activities

Sense of Place ................................................. 3
  *Communicating*
Finger Ruler ................................................. 11
  *Measuring*
Graph of Choice ........................................... 17
  *Classifying*
School Tools ................................................. 21
  *Observing*
Point of Reference ...................................... 31
  *Observing*
Pacing Yourself ........................................... 39
  *Inferring*
Matter vs. Energy ....................................... 45
  *Classifying*
Know Your Strength ..................................... 55
  *Comparing*
Balloon Moves ............................................. 70
  *Observing*
Common Forces ........................................... 73
  *Reasoning*
Fluid Air ...................................................... 85
  *Inferring*
Sink or Float? .............................................. 91
  *Predicting*
Flying Paper ................................................ 97
  *Observing*
Work Is . . . ............................................... 107
  *Defining Operationally*
Lifting a Lawnmower ................................ 112
  *Inferring*
Working Toward School ............................ 116
  *Classifying*

Energy on TV ............................................ 122
  *Inferring*
Likenesses ................................................. 135
  *Observing*
Alike and Different .................................... 140
  *Comparing*
It's in the Bag ............................................ 147
  *Hypothesizing*
Matter of Life and Non-Life ...................... 157
  *Classifying*
It's Elemental ............................................ 164
  *Communicating*
Compound Familiarity .............................. 168
  *Communicating*
Banana Split .............................................. 174
  *Comparing*
Metals and Their Uses .............................. 183
  *Collecting Data*
Testing Your Metals .................................. 189
  *Predicting*
Nonmetals .................................................. 194
  *Inferring*
Cold Hands, Warm Face? .......................... 209
  *Observing*
Spooning .................................................... 213
  *Hypothesizing*
Running a Temperature ............................. 222
  *Modeling*
Heat Changes ............................................ 231
  *Classifying*
Cooling Systems ........................................ 239
  *Inferring*
Transportation .......................................... 244
  *Inferring*
Simply Shocking ....................................... 257
  *Comparing*
Keeping Current ........................................ 261
  *Predicting*
All Electric Household .............................. 267
  *Generalizing*
Switch Back ............................................... 274
  *Observing*

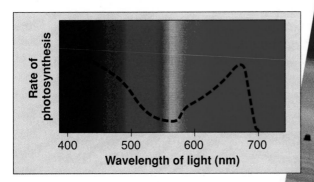

*Skills WarmUp Activities Continued*

High Energy Users ........................ 279
  *Interpreting Data*
Magnetic Materials ........................ 287
  *Classifying*
Motoring ........................ 293
  *Classifying*
Minimal Electricity ........................ 300
  *Inferring*
Elevator Operator ........................ 309
  *Classifying*
Audio/Video ........................ 315
  *Estimating*
Long Multiplication ........................ 322
  *Relating Concepts*
Do the Wave ........................ 335
  *Making a Model*
Hum Tickler ........................ 341
  *Inferring*
Making Waves ........................ 348
  *Observing*
Thwang! ........................ 359
  *Observing*
Let It Rip ........................ 366
  *Predicting*
Sound Cup ........................ 372
  *Inferring*
Hear! Hear! ........................385
  *Observing*
Musical Listing ........................ 390
  *Classifying*
Silent Noise? ........................ 398
  *Inferring*
Thin Light ........................ 409
  *Generalizing*
Light Through Glass ........................ 416
  *Observing*
Up Close ........................ 422
  *Observing*
Reflecting on Light ........................ 433
  *Comparing*
How Much Can You See ........................ 437
  *Observing*
ECNALUBMA ........................ 441
  *Inferring*

Glasses Survey ........................ 445
  *Calculating*
Lenses and Mirrors ........................ 451
  *Classifying*
Oil vs. Salt ........................ 467
  *Classifying*
Shell Diagram ........................ 471
  *Making a Model*
Like Salt? ........................ 478
  *Contrasting*
New Substances ........................ 489
  *Inferring*
Secret Code ........................ 494
  *Communicating*
Coinage Molecules ........................ 499
  *Making a Model*
Match Wits ........................ 503
  *Hypothesizing*
Solutions ........................ 515
  *Defining Operationally*
Mixing it Up ........................ 522
  *Classifying*
Lemons and Vinegar ........................ 527
  *Comparing*
Substance of Life ........................ 537
  *Comparing*
Food Processing ........................ 545
  *ommunicating*
Plants vs. Animals ........................ 551
  *Comparing*
Radiant Things ........................ 561
  *Classifying*
Nuclear Changes ........................ 565
  *Inferring*
Wording Energy ........................ 571
  *Communicating*
Energy Sources ........................ 583
  *Inferring*
New Energy Source ........................ 589
  *Observing*
Energy Map ........................ 596
  *Observing*

### Skills WarmUp Activities Continued

Oil and Water Don't Mix ............................ 605
*Hypothesizing*
Petroleum Products .................................... 609
*Classifying*
Building Materials ...................................... 614
*Classifying*
Separating Refuse ...................................... 621
*Classifying*

## Skills WorkOut Activities

Index Patterns ............................................ 5
*Interpreting Data*
So Big, So Small ........................................ 15
*Estimating*
Sunlight Travel Time .................................. 37
*Calculating*
Speed from Skids ....................................... 44
*Interpreting Data*
Mass vs. Weight ......................................... 56
*Calculating*
Free Fall ..................................................... 58
*Comparing*
Gas Usage .................................................. 69
*Collecting Data*
Fluid Pressure ............................................ 86
*Comparing*
Clay Float .................................................. 93
*Hypothesizing*
More or Less Work .................................... 108
*Predicting*
Dividing the Water .................................... 138
*Making a Model*
Phasing In .................................................. 142
*Classifying*
Kinds of Changes ...................................... 149
*Defining Operationally*
Radioactivity .............................................. 161
*Researching*

State Symbols ............................................ 166
*Inferring*
Atoms in the Body ..................................... 167
*Graphing*
Ions and Oranges ...................................... 170
*Making a Model*
Mixtures ..................................................... 177
*Classifying*
Metals vs. Nonmetals ................................ 193
*Classifying*
Potato Under Glass .................................... 226
*Observing*
Hot Pursuit ................................................ 237
*Observing*
Blowing Hot and Cold ............................... 241
*Classifying*
Clean Air Actions ...................................... 248
*Reasoning*
Electric Bits ............................................... 259
*Observing*
Electric Comb ............................................ 266
*Hypothesizing*
Usage of Electricity ................................... 269
*Interpreting Data*
Devices and Current .................................. 273
*Collecting Data*
Circuit Town .............................................. 276
*Making Models*
Flashlight ................................................... 277
*Hypothesizing*
Auto Fuse ................................................... 282
*Predicting*
Compass ..................................................... 291
*Making a Model*
Charting the Course ................................... 304
*Organizing Data*
Dopey Devices ........................................... 312
*Communicating*
Sound Sources ........................................... 317
*Observing*
Prime Programs ......................................... 326
*Collecting Data*
Spring Waves ............................................. 337
*Comparing*

**Skills WorkOut Activities Continued**

Wave Barriers ............................................. 350
  *Observing*
Listening Outside ...................................... 365
  *Generalizing*
Sound Device ............................................ 371
  *Making a Model*
Listening Day and Night ........................... 375
  *Observing*
Sound Instruments ................................... 391
  *Observing*
Noise ........................................................ 395
  *Classifying*
Light ........................................................ 412
  *Making a Model*
Traveling Light ......................................... 414
  *Estimating*
Tracking Lighting ..................................... 436
  *Collecting Data*
Eyes ......................................................... 439
  *Comparing*
Learning the Angles ................................. 444
  *Predicting*
Methane Model ......................................... 479
  *Making a Model*
Reaction Model ......................................... 491
  *Making a Model*
The Right Equation ................................... 495
  *Communicating*
Reaction Type .......................................... 502
  *Classifying*
Catalysts .................................................. 508
  *Hypothesizing*
Water's Properties .................................... 517
  *Observing*
Heavy on the Mayo ................................... 526
  *Observing*
Plastic ..................................................... 543
  *Applying*
Vitamins .................................................. 550
  *Making a Table*
Stable Nuclei ........................................... 562
  *Interpreting Data*
Cost of Food Processing ........................... 588
  *Calculating*
Hydrogen as Fuel ..................................... 594
  *Hypothesizing*
Energy Distribution .................................. 599
  *Graphing*
Washable? ................................................ 612
  *Observing*
Material Witness ...................................... 618
  *Collecting Data*

## Integrated Science Activity Links

Life Science ........................................ 5
Astronomy .......................................... 14
Life Science ........................................ 44
Life Science ........................................ 66
Oceanography ..................................... 89
Life Science ........................................ 92
Geology ............................................. 112
Life Science ....................................... 143
Health ............................................... 176
Life Science ....................................... 190
Geology ............................................. 225
Geology ............................................. 247
Physical Science ................................. 264
Health ............................................... 295
Astronomy .......................................... 311
Meteorology ....................................... 318
Oceanography ..................................... 335
Life Science ....................................... 343
Life Science ....................................... 362
Life Science ....................................... 373
Physical Science ................................. 393
Life Science ....................................... 423
Astronomy .......................................... 448
Astronomy .......................................... 475
Environmental Science ......................... 481
Life Science ....................................... 496
Life Science ....................................... 507
Life Science ....................................... 516
Earth Science ..................................... 520
Environmental Science ......................... 539
Environmental Science ......................... 555
Physical Science ................................. 574
Astronomy .......................................... 587
Environmental Science ......................... 610

# Concept Mapping...

Reading a science textbook is not like reading a magazine or a story. You may not need to work hard to understand a story. You may not need to remember a story for a long time, either. But when you read science, you are reading to learn something new. You will need to think about what you read. You will also need to remember as much as you can. You may just *read* a story, but you will need to *study* your textbook.

## Build a Concept Map

One way to help you study and remember what you have learned is to organize the information in the chapter visually. You can do this by making concept maps. In a concept map, the main ideas are identified by a word or phrase enclosed in a box. When these boxes are linked, you can better understand the meanings of the ideas by seeing how the concepts are connected to one another. To build a concept map, follow the steps below.

### Identify

1. Identify the concepts to be mapped. They may come from a short section of your book, directions from an activity, or a vocabulary list. List the concepts on a separate sheet of paper or on small cards.

### Decide

2. Decide which concept is the main idea. Look for ways to classify the remaining concepts. You may want to list or rank the concepts from the most general to the most specific. For example, "energy resources" is general, and then "renewable" and "conserved" are more specific concepts.

### Organize

3. Place the most general concept at the top of your map. Link that concept to the other concepts. Draw a circle or square around each concept.

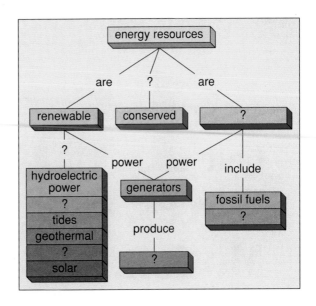

### Choose

4. Pick linking words for your map that identify relationships between the concepts. Linking words should not be the concepts themselves. Label all lines with linking words that explain how each pair of concepts relate to one another.

### Create

5. Start making your map by branching one or two general concepts from your main concept. Add other, more specific, concepts to the general ones as you progress. Try to branch out. Add two or more concepts to each concept already on the map.

### Connect

6. Make cross-links between two concepts that are already on the map. Label all cross-links with words that explain how the concepts are related. Use arrows to show the direction of the relationship.

As you build a concept map, you are doing two things. First, you are automatically reviewing what you already know. Second, you are learning more. Once you have a completed map, you can use it to study and test yourself.

You will often find that several different maps can be made from the same group of concepts.

# Unit 1

# Forces, Motion, and Energy

## *Chapters*

1 Studying Science
2 Motion and Energy
3 Forces and Motion
4 Forces in Fluids
5 Work, Machines, and Energy

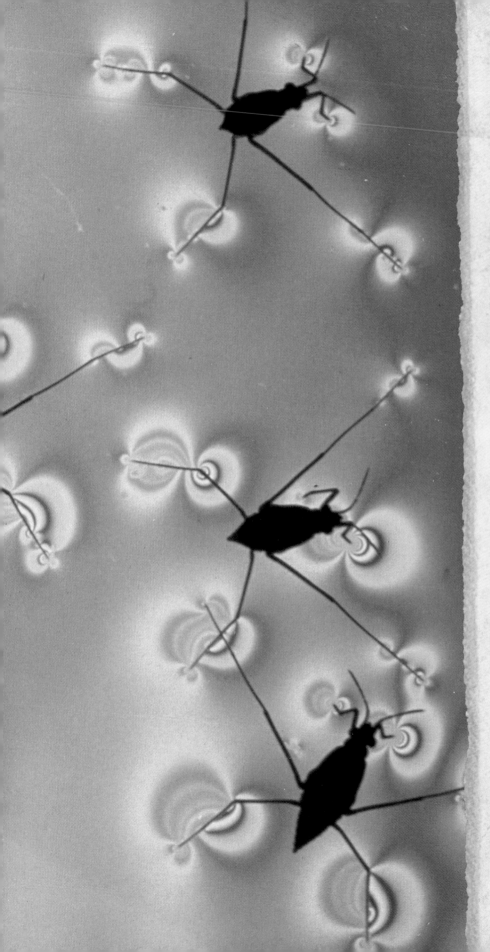

# Data Bank

Use the information on pages 634 to 643 to answer the questions about topics explored in this unit.

## *Interpreting Data*

Which city has the highest average maximum daily temperature in July: New York City, Salina Cruz, or San Diego?

## *Comparing*

In 15 minutes, how much farther can a cheetah travel than a hawk moth?

## *Predicting*

Assuming normal breathing was possible, would it be harder to walk on Earth, Venus, or Jupiter?

The photograph to the left shows how the legs of the water striders put stress on the water surface. Why doesn't the water strider sink?

1

# Chapter 1

# Studying Science

## Chapter Sections

**1.1** Science Skills and Methods

**1.2** Measuring with Scientific Units

**1.3** Graphing

**1.4** Science Tools and Technology

## What do you see?

66 This is petrified wood. It is a piece of a tree that over many years has slowly lost its inner material and has been replaced by minerals from the earth. It is as hard as rock and is made of many colors which are the minerals. By using carbon-14 dating you could probably find out its exact age.99

*Mike Monsilovich*
*Indiana Area Junior High*
*Indiana, Pennsylvania*

To find out more about the photograph, look on page 28.
As you read this chapter, you will learn about science and how to study matter and energy.

# 1.1 Science Skills and Methods

## Objectives

▶ **Identify** and **use** science skills.

▶ **Describe** a controlled experiment.

▶ **Apply** a scientific method.

▶ **Make a model** of a safety symbol.

What is science? If you look up the definition of the word science in a dictionary or in a science book, you will see words that give you clues. These words are *knowledge*, *skills*, *experiment*, and *systemize*. *Systemize* means "to organize in an orderly way." Science is a way to gather and organize information about the natural world. When you do science, you gather information about the thing you want to study by using such skills as observing and experimenting. You organize the information in an orderly way so that you can figure out its meaning. Science is also a collection of facts about the natural world around you.

## Science Skills

To gather information, or **data**, you use many different skills. These skills are sometimes called science process skills. As you read about science process skills, you'll discover that they're not mysterious or difficult. Science process skills aren't reserved for science classes. In fact, you already use many of these skills every day!

**Observe** The most direct way to gain knowledge about something in nature is to observe it. When you observe, you use one or more of your senses to get information about your surroundings. Your senses are sight, touch, taste, smell, and hearing. Your ability to observe can be extended by using tools such as microscopes, telescopes, thermometers, and rulers. Look at the objects in Figure 1.1. List as many observations as you can about each object. Which sense did you use most often?

**Figure 1.1 ▲**
Do you think the people who design new skateboards and roller blades use science skills?

**Figure 1.2** ▲

What can you infer about these symbols?

**Infer**  When you suggest a possible explanation for an observation, you make an inference, or you infer. You often can make more than one inference to explain the same observation. You probably can infer several things about the drawings in Figure 1.2. For example, you could infer that the drawings represent safety hazards, or precautions you should take. Most likely, you could also infer that one of the drawings represents fire. The shape and color of the symbol help you to infer its meaning. You use your past experience to associate fire with the shape of the symbol.

**Estimate**  When you estimate, you make a careful guess. Estimating skills are used to gather information when exact measurements aren't needed. Perhaps getting exact measurements is impossible or too time consuming. You base estimates on the knowledge you already have about many things. You can estimate many things including speed, distance, size, or time.

**Measure**  When you need exact information about an observation, you measure. Measurements describe an observation exactly by comparing it to standard units. Measurements include both a number and a unit. The number of things in a group, the size of an object, the speed of a car, and your height and weight are all things you can measure.

**Predict**  When you predict, you state what you think might happen in the future. Predictions are based on past experiences and observations. Therefore, you can state how and why something will occur. Predictions always include reasons why.

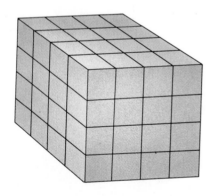

**Figure 1.3**

Estimate the number of blocks in the cube above and the number of crystals in the photograph. Count the number of blocks and crystals for a more exact measurement. Compare your numbers. ▶

◀ **Figure 1.4**
What are some different ways to classify these rocks?

**Classify**   When you classify, you group things together based on how they are alike. You can group things in many different ways. You group things by size, color, shape, texture, or any other characteristic. In science, chemical substances are classified by how they react with other substances. Rocks are classified by how they form. Living things, or organisms, are classified into groups that share common ancestors.

**Hypothesize**   When you state a hypothesis (hy PAHTH uh sihs), or hypothesize, you suggest an answer to a problem. Your answer is based on information that you know. Think of a hypothesis as an explanation or an idea that states why something may always occur. Once you state a hypothesis, you can test it by observing, studying, or experimenting. Your observations, research, or the results of experiments should support your hypothesis. If they don't, you need to think about your hypothesis again and state a new one.

**Record and Organize**   Careful record keeping is a important part of science. During activities and investigations, you should record all your observations, measurements, predictions, and so on. Often you want to organize the data you collect in some way. You can record and organize data in a number of ways, such as using tables, charts, graphs, diagrams, and flow charts.

**Analyze**   After data are recorded and organized, you need to analyze it. When you analyze data, you look for trends or patterns. You also look to see whether or not your data support your inference, prediction, or hypothesis.

**Life Science**
**L I N K**

List the following organisms: lizard, whale, tiger, snake, cat, alligator, and lion. Write at least two physical characteristics of each organism. Classify these organisms according to their characteristics.

**1.** Divide the organisms into two groups, based on similar characteristics.

**2.** Then divide each of those groups into two groups, again based on characteristics.

How is classification the same in all sciences?

**A C T I V I T Y**

▼ **ACTIVITY**
**Interpreting Data**

*Index Patterns*

Examine the index of this book. How is the data organized? Can you uncover any patterns among entries? Why aren't the entries made according to the numerical order of the page numbers?

**SKILLS WORKOUT**

# Safety Skills

Your science classroom must be a safe place in which to work and to learn. When you are in the laboratory, always follow these general safety guidelines.

▶ Do not chew gum, eat, or drink in the laboratory.

▶ Read carefully through the activity before you begin. Reread each procedure before you do it.

▶ Clean up your laboratory work area after you complete each activity.

Study the guidelines in Table 1.1. By following these guidelines, you can help make your science laboratory a safe place.

## Table 1.1  Laboratory Safety

 **Plant Safety**
▶ Use caution when collecting or handling plants.
▶ Do not eat or taste any unfamiliar plant or plant parts.
▶ If you are allergic to pollen, do not work with plants or plant parts without a gauze face mask.

 **Eye Safety**
▶ Wear your laboratory safety goggles when you are working with chemicals, open flame, or any substances that may be harmful to your eyes.
▶ Know how to use the emergency eyewash system. If chemicals get into your eyes, flush them out with plenty of water. Inform your teacher.

 **Heating Safety**
▶ Turn off heat sources when they are not in use.
▶ Point test tubes away from yourself and others when heating substances in them.
▶ Use the proper procedures when lighting a Bunsen burner.
▶ To avoid burns, do not handle heated glassware or materials directly. Use tongs, test-tube holders, or heat-resistant gloves or mitts.

 **Clothing Protection**
▶ Wear your laboratory apron. It will help protect your clothing from stains or damage.

 **Poison**
▶ Do not mix any chemicals unless directed to do so in a procedure or by your teacher.
▶ Inform your teacher immediately if you spill chemicals or get any chemicals on your skin or in your eyes.
▶ Never taste any chemicals or substances unless directed to do so by your teacher.
▶ Keep your hands away from your face when working with chemicals.

 **Animal Safety**
▶ Handle live animals with care. If you are bitten or scratched by an animal, inform your teacher.
▶ Do not bring wild animals into the classroom.
▶ Do not cause pain, discomfort, or injury to an animal. Be sure any animals kept for observations are given the proper food, water, and living space.
▶ Wear gloves when handling live animals. Always wash your hands with soap and water after handling live animals.

 **Fire Safety**
▶ Tie back long hair when working near an open flame. Confine loose clothing.
▶ Do not reach across an open flame.
▶ Know the location and proper use of fire blankets and fire extinguishers.

 **Glassware Safety**
▶ Check glassware for chips or cracks. Broken, cracked, or chipped glassware should be disposed of properly.
▶ Do not force glass tubing into rubber stoppers. Follow your teacher's instructions.
▶ Clean all glassware and air dry them.

 **Electrical Safety**
▶ Use care when using electrical equipment.
▶ Check all electrical equipment for worn cords or loose plugs before using them.
▶ Keep your work area dry.
▶ Do not overload electric circuits.

 **Sharp Objects**
▶ Be careful when using knives, scalpels, or scissors.
▶ Always cut in the direction away from your body.
▶ Inform your teacher immediately if you or your partner is cut.

# Experiments

What's the best way to learn about something? If you said to ask questions, you're on the right track. Every day you ask questions to get information. In science, you also learn by asking questions and getting answers. A good way to get answers in science is to do experiments.

How would you begin your experiments? When you carefully plan a series of activities, steps, or procedures, you are off to a good start. Experiments need to be carefully designed to

▶ observe how something behaves.

▶ investigate an observation.

▶ test an idea, prediction, hypothesis, or even an inference.

▶ get an answer to a question.

When you plan and design an experiment, be sure that the experiment can be repeated exactly. If your experiment is well planned, anyone can repeat the experiment and get the same results. Scientists repeat experiments to check their data and conclusions.

Most experiments are **controlled experiments**. A controlled experiment has two test groups—the control group and the experimental group. The control group is a standard by which any change can be measured. In the experimental group, all the factors except one are kept the same as those in the control group. The factors that are kept the same are **constants**. The factor that is changed by the person doing the experiment is the **variable**. Read the captions describing the controlled experiment shown in Figure 1.5. What is the variable?

**Figure 1.5 A Controlled Experiment ▼**

**Hypothesis:** Adding salt to water will increase the temperature at which water boils.

Each beaker has the same amount of distilled water.

Each beaker of water was heated at the same setting.

Salt was added to the experimental beaker.

The water in both beakers was stirred for one minute.

A thermometer measured the temperature of boiling water in both beakers.

The unsalted water boiled at 100°C. The salted water boiled at a higher temperature. Do the observations support the hypothesis? Write a conclusion.

# Methods of Science

Does science have one method to approach any problem, experiment, or issue? The answer is both yes and no. You may know the phrase *scientific method* used to describe how scientists find out about the natural world. This method refers to systemized testing of ideas, inferences, predictions, and hypotheses.

The best method for studying science is not a rigid set of steps like those in a cooking recipe. Many different ways are used to study, investigate, and think about scientific problems. An exchange of ideas and information is also part of scientific methods.

To help you think about scientific methods, read Figures 1.6 and 1.7. They show a model for designing and planning an experiment and a model for decision making. This model will help you as you do the activities in this book as well as in your everyday life.

**Figure 1.6   Designing and Planning an Experiment** ▼

**State the Problem**
What do you want to find out? State the problem as a question.

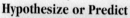

**Hypothesize or Predict**
What do you think may happen? What information from past experiences or observations are you using to state your hypothesis or make your prediction?

**Conclude**
State your conclusion based on your data. Your data should either support your conclusion or lead you to another hypothesis. Have any new questions or problems come up?

**Plan Your Experiment**
Do you need a control? If so, what is the variable? What are the constants? Write a step-by-step procedure that another person could easily follow. Your experiment must be able to be repeated exactly the way you did it.

**Analyze Data**
Do you see any trends or patterns in the data? Do the data support your hypothesis or prediction? Do you need more information?

**Record and Organize Data**
How will you record and organize your data? Will you use tables and graphs? Will you include diagrams and drawings?

**Gather Data**
How will you gather your data? Will you observe, estimate, or measure? Any other ways?

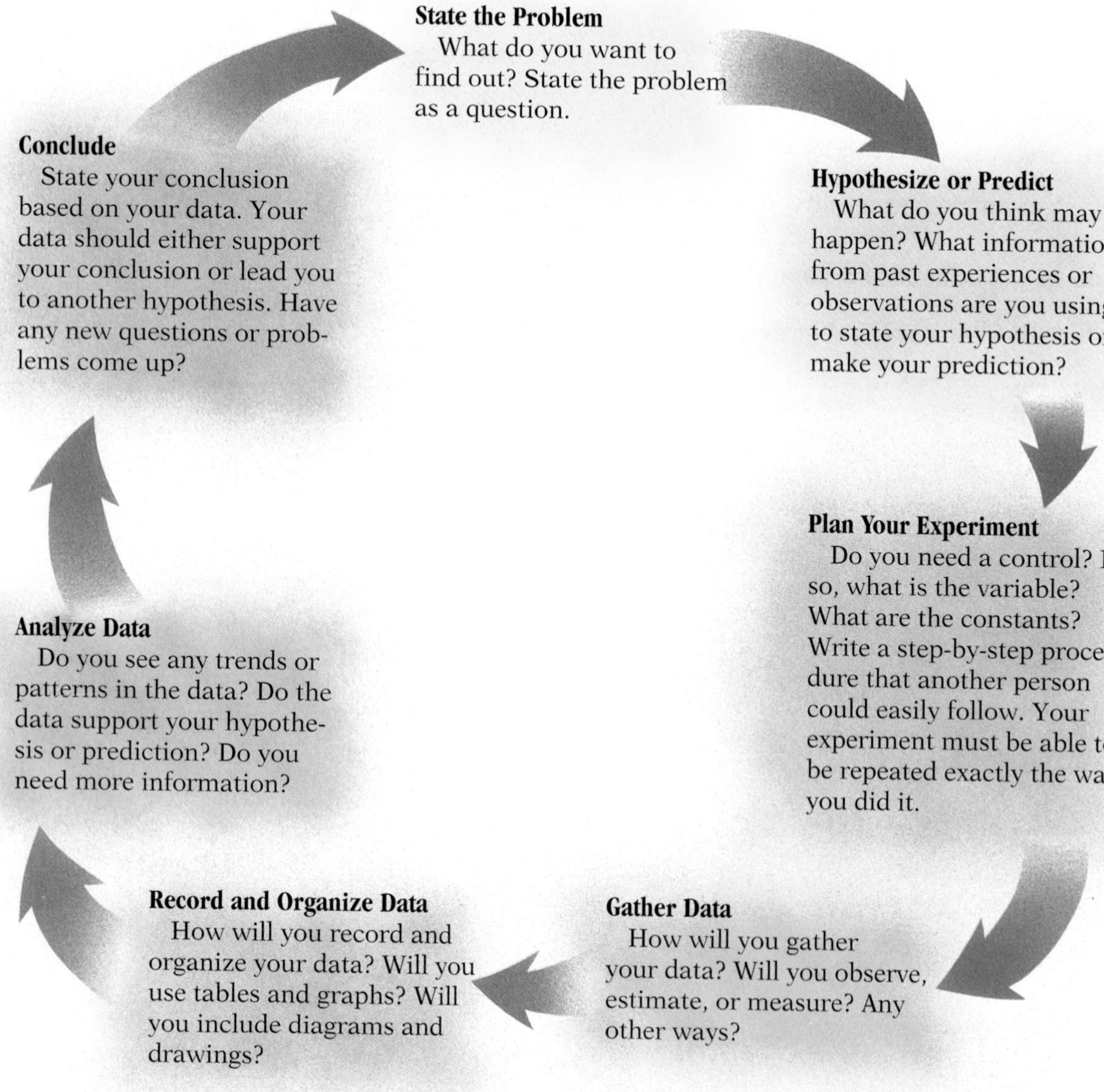

**Figure 1.7   Decision Making** ▼

**Write About It**
Research information about the issue. Write about each point of view. Remember that most issues have at least two points of view.

**Think About It**
Do you clearly understand the issue? State the issue in your own words. What are the different points of view about the issue?

**Organize It**
Organize the information so that you can see what information supports the different points of view.

**Analyze and Evaluate It**
Evaluate the points of view. What solutions and reasons are given for each point of view? What are the possible results of each point of view?

**Conclude**
Write a conclusion that expresses your opinion. Be sure that you support your conclusion with data.

**Decide About It**
Do you need more information? If so, complete more research.

## Facts, Theories, and Laws

In science, a fact is an agreement about many observations made by qualified scientists. Science facts are always based on observations, studies, and repeated tests and experiments.

Many related science facts can lead to a scientific theory. A scientific theory is an idea that explains why and how something happens. Scientific theories are used to make predictions.

When predictions based on a scientific theory occur, the theory can become a scientific law. Scientific laws are sometimes stated in mathematical terms. Although scientific theories and laws have been tested, they can change. As new hypotheses are tested, theories are often redefined.

## Models in Science

Did you ever notice the tiny parts on a model car or airplane? Even the wheels and lights are scaled to fit on these small copies. There is a mathematical ratio between the measurements of the parts on the model and those on the real object. Suppose a model airplane is built to a scale of 1 centimeter (cm) to 1 meter (m). Each centimeter on the model equals 1 m on the airplane.

There are many types of scale models. Some models are drawings, such as diagrams and maps. Often models are built from real materials and are working models of the real object. Mental models are used to imagine what something would look like. All models are plans from which real objects can be built.

## Science and Society  *Science Communities*

In many pictures of scientists, you often see the scientist working alone in a laboratory. Nothing could be further from the truth! Science is done by people working together, not by individuals working alone.

A research group is the basic unit of a science community. Each research group is made up of people who share an interest and knowledge in the same problem. Each person works on a different piece of the scientific puzzle being studied. Group members hold discussions, plan experiments, and share their knowledge and ideas with each other, as shown in Figure 1.8.

Researchers form a worldwide scientific community based on common interests. They form a network that shares information and holds national and international meetings. They contribute to each other's research by repeating experiments and reviewing published articles.

The large scientific community includes organizations such as research institutes, industrial laboratories, university science departments, and government science agencies. These organizations provide places for scientists to form research groups. Many organizations are an important part of the scientific community. Libraries and companies that make technical equipment provide many services and tools. Museums and schools teach the public about science and prepare students for science careers. Your science class is part of the world scientific community!

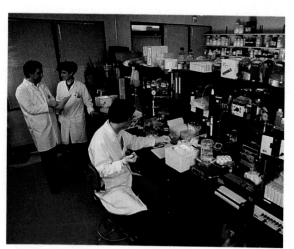

**Figure 1.8** ▲

These scientists are part of a research group. Why do you think scientists work together?

---

## Check and Explain

1. Identify three skills and explain how you used them today.

2. Explain why a control is necessary in an experiment.

3. **Apply**  How would you use scientific methods to decide if a chemical plant should be located near a river?

4. **Model**  Design a safety symbol to use in your school.

# 1.2 Measuring with Scientific Units

## Objectives

▶ **Identify** the base units used in the SI system.

▶ **Explain** the use of scientific notation.

▶ **Compare** volume, mass, and density.

▶ **Measure** length, mass, and temperature using SI units.

D id you know that your feet get bigger during the day? Although this may be hard to believe, it's true. When you are standing or sitting, the earth's gravity pulls blood and other body fluids down to your feet. By the end of the day, your feet are slightly bigger. People discovered this change by making and comparing measurements of foot length and width.

You describe measurements in terms of numbers and units. The system of measurement used throughout most of the world today is the *Système International d'Unités*, or SI. It is also called the metric system.

The basic SI units are shown in Table 1.2. Unlike other systems of measurement, SI units are based on multiples of ten. Calculations are made by multiplying or dividing by ten. To change quantities, you simply move the decimal point. Prefixes such as *kilo-* or *centi-* indicate units larger or smaller than the basic SI units. These prefixes are shown in Table 1.3.

**Table 1.2  SI Units**

| Measure | Unit/Symbol |
|---|---|
| Length | Meter/m |
| Mass | Gram/g |
| Area | Square meter/ $m^2$ |
| Volume | Liter/L, cubic centimeter/$cm^3$ |
| Temperature | Degrees Celsius/°C |
| Time | Second/s |

**Table 1.3  Prefixes Used in SI**

| Measurement | Unit | Symbol |
|---|---|---|
| kilo | 1,000 | k |
| hecto- | 100 | h |
| deca- | 10 | da |
| deci- | 1/10 | d |
| centi- | 1/100 | c |
| milli- | 1/1,000 | m |
| micro- | 1/1 000 000 | µ |

## Length

The basic SI unit of length is the **meter** (m). One meter is about the distance between a doorknob and the floor. The SI measuring tool that you'll be using in class is a metric ruler.

A ruler is divided into smaller units. Notice that the metric ruler in Figure 1.9 is marked in units called centimeters (cm). A centimeter is 1/100 of a meter. Your little finger is about 1 cm across. Each centimeter is divided into ten smaller units called millimeters (mm). A dime is about 1 mm thick.

To measure long distances, units of 1,000 meters are used. These units are called kilometers (km). If you walk or run two and one-half times around a stadium track, you travel about 1 km.

## Volume

Take a deep breath. As your lungs fill with air, you can feel your chest expand. This change in your lung size is an increase in **volume**. Volume is the amount of space that something occupies.

The basic SI unit of volume is the **cubic meter** ($m^3$). One cubic meter is the space occupied by a box 1 m × 1 m × 1 m. To measure smaller volumes, the cubic centimeter ($cm^3$) is used. A convenient unit for everyday use is the **liter** (L). In the United States, soft drinks come in plastic 2-L containers.

A graduated cylinder is used to measure liquid volumes. Look at the cylinder in Figure 1.10. The units marked on its scale are milliliters (mL). There are about 20 drops of water in each 1 mL.

In a graduated cylinder, the liquid surface curves downward to form a *meniscus* (mehn IHS kus). To measure liquid volume accurately, read the scale at eye level at the lowest part of the meniscus.

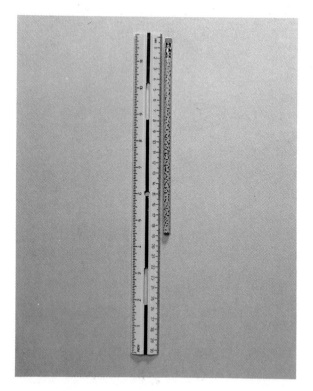

**Figure 1.9** ▲
You will measure many distances that are less than 1 meter. The numbers to the right on this metric ruler represent centimeters.

**Figure 1.10** ▲
You can measure liquid volume with a graduated cylinder. To read, observe the surface level of the liquid at eye level.

## Mass and Weight

Did you know that an object weighs slightly less at the equator than it does at the north and south poles? That's because an object's weight depends upon the force of gravity. Because gravity is measurably less at the equator, things weigh less there.

Although the weight of an object varies with the force of gravity, its **mass** does not. Mass is the amount of matter that an object contains. An object's mass always stays the same no matter where the measurement is taken.

The basic SI unit of mass is the **kilogram** (kg). In the laboratory, you will use a unit equal to 1/1,000 kg, called a gram (g). The cap of a pen has a mass of about 1 g.

To determine an object's mass, you use a tool called a balance, similar to the one shown in Figure 1.11. A balance allows you to compare an unknown mass with a known mass. When the arm of the balance is level, the two masses are equal.

## Density

Mass is related to another important quantity called **density**. Density tells you how much matter is packed into a given volume of space. The units of density are grams of matter per cubic centimeter ($g/cm^3$). For example, steel has a density of 7.8 $g/cm^3$. This means that each $cm^3$ of steel contains 7.8 g of matter. Oak wood has a density of 0.9 $g/cm^3$. This means that each cubic centimeter of oak contains 0.9 grams of matter.

Density is a characteristic that can be used to identify a substance. Also, an object's density determines whether it will float or sink in water. Water has a density of 1 $g/cm^3$. Materials with densities greater than 1 $g/cm^3$ will sink in water. Materials with densities less than 1 $g/cm^3$ will float. What do you think happens when an object with a density of 1 $g/cm^3$ is put into water?

**Figure 1.11** ▲
The kilogram is the basic unit for mass in the metric system. What unit would you use to measure the mass of an eraser?

**Figure 1.12** ▲
The number of cc, or mL, the water level rises is equal to the volume of the submerged object, which has an irregular shape.

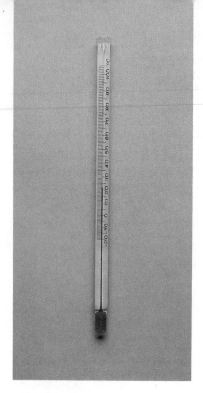

**Figure 1.13 ▲**
On the Celsius scale, water freezes at 0°C and boils at 100°C.

**Astronomy**
**L I N K**

Large quantities are often described as "astronomical." This description is related to the huge distances between objects in space.

**1.** Find the distance of each of the planets in the solar system from the sun, in km.

**2.** Write each number in scientific notation.

What do all of these numbers have in common?

**A C T I V I T Y**

## Temperature

When you are healthy, your normal body temperature is about 98.6 degrees Fahrenheit (F). On the Celsius scale, which is used internationally and in science, your normal body temperature measures about 37 degrees Celsius, or 37°C.

Temperature is measured with a thermometer like the one in Figure 1.13. Most classroom thermometers are made from a thin glass tube that is filled with a liquid. As the liquid heats up, it expands and moves up the tube. The sides of the glass tube are marked in Celsius degrees. Two important reference marks on the Celsius scale are the boiling point of water, which is 100°C, and the freezing point of water, which is 0°C.

## Time

The basic SI unit of time is the second (s). Amounts of time less than one second are measured in milliseconds (ms). One ms is 1/1,000 of one s. You probably know other units of time, such as minutes, hours, days, and years. There are 60 seconds in a minute, 60 minutes in an hour, 24 hours in a day, and 365 days in a year. These units have been adopted into the SI system and unlike other units are not based on multiples of ten.

## Scientific Notation

Suppose you want to write the distance between two stars. It might be 20 000 000 000 000 km. The diameter of a microscopic organism could be about 0.000001 mm. Scientists often work with very long numbers. To save time, they write these numbers in **scientific notation**.

In scientific notation, a number is written as the product of two numbers. The first number is between 1 and 10. The second number is 10 and has a small number, called an exponent (ehks POHN uhnt), written above it. For example, 20 000 000 000 000 km is written $2 \times 10^{13}$ km. The exponent tells you that the decimal point is really 13 places to the right of the 2.

How would you write 0.000001 mm? In scientific notation, the diameter of the organism would be written $1 \times 10^{-6}$ mm. The negative exponent (–6) tells you how many decimal places there are to the *left* of the first number, or 1.

# Unit Calculations and Measurements

When you do calculations involving measurements, you must keep careful track of the units. You also need to check your answers to be sure they make sense. This process is so important that it has been given the name *dimensional analysis*.

Sometimes you need to convert one unit to another. A fraction, called a conversion factor, shows how one kind of unit relates to another. The measurement on the top of the conversion factor equals the measurement on the bottom. For example, 100 cm equals 1 m. You can write: 1 m/100 cm or 100 cm/1 m.

To convert a measurement, you multiply the measurement by the appropriate conversion factor. For example, suppose your friend's height is 170 cm. How many meters is 170 cm?

First write down the value given. Write the conversion factor with the unit you want on top. Then multiply:

## ▼ ACTIVITY

### Estimating

*So Big, So Small*

List some things that you think are so big or so small that scientific notation would be needed to write their measurements. Give reasons why scientific notation would be useful to express the measurements for these objects.

**SKILLS WORKOUT**

---

## Sample Problems

1. How do you write $2.79 \times 10^{-4}$ mm as a standard numeral?

   **Plan** The negative sign on the exponent means you move the decimal point to the left.

   **Gather Data** The number is $2.79 \times 10^{-4}$ mm.

   **Solve** Move the decimal point four spaces to the left. Compare your result to the correct answer: 0.000279 mm.

2. How would you convert 250 mL into L?

   **Plan** The conversion factor must relate to both the units mL and L.

   **Gather Data** 250 mL = ? L    1,000 mL = 1 L

   **Solve** Arrange the conversion factor with L on top. Cancel like units. Then multiply.

   $$250 \text{ mL} \times \frac{1 \text{ L}}{1,000 \text{ mL}} = \frac{250 \text{ L}}{1,000} = 0.25 \text{ L}$$

## Practice Problems

1. Write the following measurements in scientific notation:

   a. 1 000 000 000 000 000 000 000 km

   b. 45 000 000 000 L

   c. 0.00000000000000001 mm

   d. 0.000000000372 mg

2. Write the following measurements as standard numerals:

   a. $9.46 \times 10^{12}$ km

   b. $3 \times 10^{10}$ cm/sec

   c. $1.5 \times 10^{-5}$ mm

   d. $2.6 \times 10^{-11}$ m

3. Do the following unit conversions:

   a. 10 m to km

   b. 2,000 g to kg

   c. 10 kg to mg

170 cm × 1 m/100 cm. The next step is to cancel out like units, in this case, cm. The equation will be 170 × 1 m/100. The last step is to multiply and divide. The answer is 1.7 m. Work through the practice problems to better understand how to use dimensional analysis and conversion factors.

**Table 1.4**
**Standard Garment Sizes**

| Size (cm) | | | |
|---|---|---|---|
| Teen Boys | Small | Medium | Large |
| Chest | 81 | 89 | 93 |
| Waist | 69 | 74 | 76 |
| Hip | 83 | 90 | 94 |
| Neck | 35 | 37 | 38 |
| Sleeve | 74 | 79 | 81 |

| Size (cm) | | | |
|---|---|---|---|
| Misses | Small | Medium | Large |
| Bust | 83 | 91 | 102 |
| Waist | 64 | 71 | 81 |
| Hip | 88 | 97 | 107 |
| Back Waist | 41 | 42 | 43 |

## Science and You  *Designer Fit*

Do you like to shop in a mall? All the items you see there were designed and constructed to exact measurements. Exact measurements make it possible for industries to use standardized sizes. Designers use standard sizes so that manufacturing and using products will be easier.

The diameter of the jack for the headphone in your personal stereo is standardized. Any brand of headphone can be plugged into your personal stereo and it will work. Any brand of AA dry cells will work in your personal stereo because dry cells are standardized also.

When you shop for clothing, you know that certain sizes will fit you because clothing sizes are standardized. Table 1.4 shows the standard for determining clothing sizes for boys and misses. Clothing sizes are based on data collected about human body measurements. The data are based on a certain range of sizes for most of the population. The international clothing industry uses this information to set size standards.

## Check and Explain

1. Identify the basic SI units for length, volume, mass, density, temperature, and time. How are amounts much larger and smaller than the basic units named?

2. Explain why scientific notation is used in science and math.

3. **Compare** Explain how volume, mass, and density relate to each other.

4. **Measure** Using the appropriate SI measuring tools and SI units, measure the length and mass of a classroom object and the room temperature.

# 1.3 Graphing

## Objectives

▶ **Describe** three types of graphs.

▶ **Identify** the parts of a line graph.

▶ **Analyze** data and plan a graph.

▶ **Classify** data by how it can be graphed.

You've probably seen many different kinds of graphs in newspapers, magazines, and even on television news reports. What is a graph? Basically a graph is a picture of data. You can think of a graph as a picture of a data table. Some data tables contain a lot of information. It may take some time to figure out what all the data means. However, a graph makes it easier to understand this information.

Graphs show numerical data in diagram form. Graphs are useful tools for presenting information. They make it easy to identify trends and patterns quickly, sometimes at a glance.

## Kinds of Graphs

Three kinds of graphs are circle graphs, bar graphs, and line graphs. All three types let you compare numerical data. Each kind of graph, however, shows numerical data in a different way. Each is most useful for showing different kinds of data.

**Circle Graphs**  If you think of how a pie is cut into pieces, you have a mental model of a circle graph. A circle graph is a circle divided into parts. This kind of graph makes it easy to compare how one part relates to the whole amount. You can see quickly what fraction, percentage, share, or proportion of the whole each part represents.

Look at the circle graph in Figure 1.14. At a glance, you can tell what percent of oxygen gas is present in air. How does the percentage of oxygen gas compare to the percentage of nitrogen gas? You can use a series of circle graphs to show change over time.

**Gases in Air**

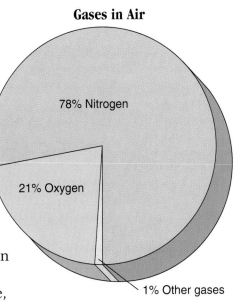

78% Nitrogen

21% Oxygen

1% Other gases

**Figure 1.14** ▲
What two gases make up most of the air? Which of the two is there more of?

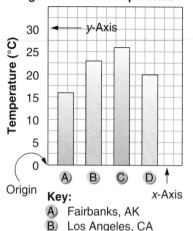

**Highest Annual Temperature**

**Figure 1.15** ▲
Which city has the highest yearly temperature? Which has the lowest?

**Bar Graphs** The wide columns on a bar graph are used to compare measurements, such as weight, height, and length, about groups or individual items. Bar graphs also let you compare quantities and change over time. The bar graph in Figure 1.15 shows the highest yearly temperatures in four North American cities. You can easily see which city is the hottest and which is the coolest.

Notice that the bar graph is drawn on graph paper. At the left side of the graph, a scale shows temperature in degrees Celsius. The label for each column is shown at the bottom of the graph. The labels on this graph are letters keyed to the names of the cities.

When you make a bar graph, you need to decide on the scale by looking at the highest and lowest numbers in your data. On this graph, the scale ranges from 0°C to 30°C. Notice that the scale includes values larger than the hottest temperature. Also, each numbered division is equal to 5°C. All bar graphs have a scale and equally numbered divisions.

## *SkillBuilder*  *Making a Graph*

## *What Kind of Graph*

When you make a graph, the first step is to determine what kind of graph to use. What you want to show and the kind of data you have determine which graph is the most useful. A circle graph is useful for showing parts or proportions of a whole. A bar graph is useful for comparing quantities and change over time. A line graph is good for comparing two sets of data or for showing changes and trends over time. Study the data tables at the right before answering the following questions.

1. What kind of graph would you use for the data table showing the composition of concrete? Explain your choice.

2. What kind of graph would you use for the data table showing U.S. population changes since 1910? Explain your choice.

3. Identify the scales you would use on the *x*- and *y*-axes on your graph for question 2.

| Composition of Concrete | |
|---|---|
| **Substance** | **Percentage** |
| Sand | 33 |
| Aggregate | 43 |
| Cement | 16 |
| Water | 8 |

| U.S. Population by Year | |
|---|---|
| **Year** | **Population** |
| 1910 | 91,972,266 |
| 1930 | 122,775,046 |
| 1950 | 150,697,361 |
| 1970 | 203,302,031 |
| 1990 | 248,709,873 |

4. Make a graph for each data table shown. For each graph, use labels, scales, and titles as needed.

Write a short report on the two types of graphs you have prepared. Give examples of other possible data that could be shown with each type of graph.

**Line Graphs** One of the most useful graphs is the line graph. Line graphs let you compare two or more sets of numerical data. They also show change and patterns, or trends in data. This type of graph can help you answer "if-then" questions by showing how one variable changes in relation to another. One common use of a line graph is to show how a variable changes over time.

Look at the growth data for the twins Rosa and Raul in Table 1.5. The variable in the first column is age in years. The second and third columns list height measurements in centimeters taken each year from age 5 to age 18. A graph of the data in Table 1.5 shows how the height of the twins Rosa and Raul changed over the years.

Look at the graph in Figure 1.16. The horizontal line on the bottom of the graph is the *x*-axis. The vertical line is the *y*-axis. The point where the *x*- and *y*-axes meet is called the origin. To make a graph of Table 1.5, use the years from 5 to 18 as *x*-values. Mark a scale showing height in centimeters on the *y*-axis.

To build a line graph of each data set, you place a dot on the graph for each pair of *x*- and *y*-values. For example, for Rosa's data set, the first *x*-value is age 5, and the *y*-value is 45 cm. The dot for this data is placed directly across from the *y*-value and directly above the *x*-value.

When all the data are presented as points on the graph, draw a line to connect all the points as shown in Figure 1.16. This line is called a *curve*. Notice that the curve shows the growth pattern of Rosa to her adult height. Raul's data are added to the graph in the same way. Study the graph. You can see that between certain years Rosa or Raul grew much more rapidly than between other years.

**Table 1.5  Growth Data**

| Age (Years) | Height (cm) Rosa | Raul |
|:---:|:---:|:---:|
| 5 | 45 | 60 |
| 6 | 60 | 70 |
| 7 | 68 | 80 |
| 8 | 79 | 90 |
| 9 | 85 | 100 |
| 10 | 95 | 105 |
| 11 | 105 | 109 |
| 12 | 118 | 110 |
| 13 | 123 | 115 |
| 14 | 148 | 123 |
| 15 | 148 | 123 |
| 16 | 148 | 133 |
| 17 | 148 | 160 |
| 18 | 148 | 160 |

**Growth Data for Raul and Rosa**

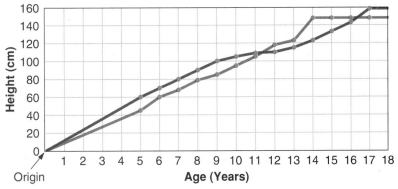

Key:
Rosa
Raul

◀ **Figure 1.16**
Compare and contrast Raul and Rosa's growth patterns. Who is taller at age 8? At age 14?

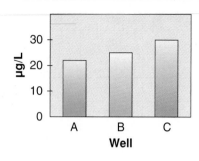

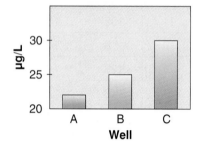

**Figure 1.17** ▲

Always study data carefully. Information displayed in graphs and tables may be misleading.

You often see graphs in newspapers, in magazines, and on television. For example, if you were reading a magazine article that compared how many people quit smoking cigarettes each year since 1975, you would probably find a graph. Graphs are an effective tool for showing trends and patterns at a glance. If the same information were presented in a data table, it would take more time to analyze it and you still might not see the pattern.

Although graphs are easy to understand, they can sometimes give you a false impression. Graphs are often used to sway public opinion. Look at the pair of bar graphs in Figure 1.17. Both graphs show the amount of a chemical found in the water samples from three wells. The same information was put on two different graphs. Which graph gives you the impression that the contamination in well C is twice that of well A?

Study the graphs carefully. Compare the scales on the y-axis of both graphs. The graph on the top shows a spread of 30 $\mu$g/L. The graph on the bottom shows a spread of only 10 $\mu$g/L. Yet both graphs show exactly the same data! Which graph is the most effective for comparing the chemical in the three wells? Which graph gives the most realistic picture of the chemical in the wells?

## Check and Explain

1. Name three kinds of graphs. Describe each kind.

2. Make a drawing of a simple line graph and label its parts. Show your data in a table.

3. **Analyze** The highest annual temperatures of four cities are shown in a bar graph on page 18. If the lowest temperatures are –5, 15, 18, –3 degrees Celsius, what scale would you use on the bar graph? What would be the equal divisions?

4. **Classify** What kind of graph would you use if you wanted to show what proportion of your time you spent sleeping, eating, going to school, working, playing, and watching television? Give reasons for your choice.

# 1.4 Science Tools and Technology

## Objectives

▶ **Describe** the connections in science.

▶ **Give examples** of technological tools.

▶ **Compare** science and technology.

▶ **Infer** why tools influence science research.

 **ACTIVITY**

**Observing**

*School Tools*

Identify three examples of tools used in your classroom. Explain how each is used. Are the tools used for every-day activities, scientific investigations, or both?

**SKILLS WARMUP**

Have you ever wondered what your fingernails are made of? Why a light turns on when you flip a switch? How television and radio signals reach your home? These questions all involve matter and energy. Physical science is the study of matter and energy and how they affect each other. Matter is the "stuff" that everything in the universe is made of. Energy causes matter to interact.

## Connections in Science

The study of matter can be identified as two connected sciences, chemistry and physics. Chemistry is the study of matter and its changes. Chemistry can explain why a cake rises, how acid rain forms, and how your body uses food. Physics is the study of energy and how it affects matter. Physics can explain how a bicycle and telephone work, how birds and airplanes fly, and why stars shine.

Science has many divisions. For example, biochemistry is the chemistry of living things. The study of energy and matter in stars is called astrophysics. Geophysics is the physics of the earth, its atmosphere, and its oceans.

Science research explores why and how things happen in the natural world. Technology is the use of science principles to help solve practical problems. Sometimes technology is referred to as *applied science*. Engineering is an applied science based on physical science principles. It focuses on using and developing technology.

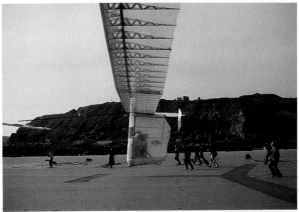

**Figure 1.18 ▲**
The *Gossamer Albatross* is a human-powered airplane. Which science can explain its ability to fly?

## Tools and Technology

Because the physical world includes objects you can see or touch, many physical science discoveries were made using simple tools. For example, the speed of light was measured with rotating mirrors on two mountaintops. The newest physical science research often involves things that are too far away or too small to be detected by the unaided senses. Some of the tools that make it possible to observe these things are shown here.

### Computer

◄ The rapid calculations done by a computer can help people identify things that are too tiny or too distant to see. A computer can help a chemist see the structure of a chemical. Physicists can test their hypotheses with computer models. Engineers use computers to test designs.

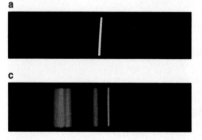
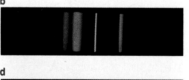
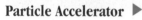
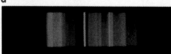

### Spectroscope

◄ The spectrogram produced by a spectroscope indicates what kind of matter makes up a star or other object in space.

### Particle Accelerator ▶

To study how matter and energy interact, physicists "shoot" tiny particles of matter at a larger particle in a particle accelerator. When the tiny particles hit the larger particle at high speed, energy is transferred and the larger particle may break apart.

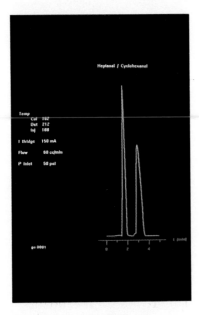

## Gas Chromatograph ▲

A gas chromatograph (kroh MA toh GRAF) is an important tool for chemists. An unknown substance is injected into a heating chamber. The different kinds of matter in the substance vaporize, one by one, and travel through the machine's tubing. As it travels, each substance "peaks" on an attached recorder or computer. The height of the peaks is used to identify each substance.

## Electrophoresis Gel ▶

Biochemists use electricity to separate the proteins and nucleic acids that make up living things. A sample of a living material is placed on an electrophoresis (ee LEHK troh for EE sihs) gel layer. The gel layer is put into a liquid that conducts electricity.

As electricity separates the proteins or nucleic acids, a pattern of bands forms. Pure substances can be isolated from a single band, or the band pattern can be used for identification.

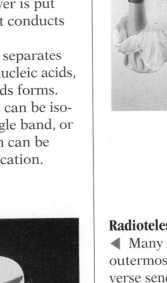

## Radiotelescope

◀ Many objects in the outermost part of the universe send out radio waves. Instruments called radio telescopes receive these waves. Astrophysicists use radiotelescopes to "listen" to outer space.

## Wind Tunnel ▶

To study the effects of moving fluids such as water or air, high winds are sent through a wind tunnel. Engineers use wind tunnels to test different designs and materials under extreme conditions.

# Career Corner

## What Careers Use Scientific Skills and Knowledge?

Many different careers require some use of science. Artists and musicians, as well as building contractors and marine biologists, use science knowledge and skills in their work. The table at the right shows some branches of science and several careers related to each branch.

Each major branch of science includes a large body of knowledge. The main sciences can be divided into more specialized branches. For example, mechanics is a specialized branch of physics. Physiology is a specialized branch of biology.

### Careers in Science

| Branch | Study | Careers |
|---|---|---|
| Biology | All living things | Animal trainer, environmental specialist, food scientist |
| Chemistry | Different substances and the changes they undergo | Chef, food scientist, chemist, materials scientist |
| Mechanics | The action of forces on objects | Mechanical engineer, machinist, construction worker |
| Physics | Properties, changes, and interactions of matter and energy | Electrician, civil engineer, materials scientist, physical therapist |
| Physiology | Functions and life processes of living things | P.E. teacher, optician, physician, physical therapist |

## Science and Technology  *Prehistoric Tech*

When you hear the word *technology*, you probably think of computers, lasers, compact disks, or other modern inventions. Actually, technology based on the principles of physical science is ancient. The stone tools made about 1.9 million years ago in Africa are one example.

The technology in a stone ax is a simple machine called a wedge. Because a wedge is wide at one end and narrow at the other, it can be used to exert a strong force on a small area. The force applied to a wedge is transferred to the narrow edge. As a result, an ax cuts easily through many materials.

The development of this ancient technology probably started with an observation. Ancient people may have observed that wedge-shaped stones cut their feet or foot coverings. When they needed to cut something, they probably remembered the sharp stones and used one for cutting. When natural wedge-shaped stones

◀ **Figure 1.19**
A gold ring of Pharaoh Ramses II (1290-1224 B.C.), and a stone cutting tool made by *Homo habilis.*

were not available, they experimented with making their own. Perhaps they discovered how to make an even better cutting tool, like the one in Figure 1.19. A stone hand ax like this one, made by *Homo habilis,* could cut through wood, animal hide, or bone.

Between 1.6 and 0.4 million years ago, people learned to control and use fire for cooking and heating. Many other technologies became possible once fire was controlled. Metals such as iron, silver, and gold could be obtained by heating rocks that contained ores. Bowls made of clay could be fired into waterproof containers and used as cooking pots. Precious metals could be worked into jewelry.

## Check and Explain

1. What are two connected sciences that study matter and energy? Give examples of topics studied by each science.

2. Describe a tool used by scientists to study something too far away to see. Describe a tool used to study something too tiny to see.

3. **Compare** How are science and technology different? How are they alike?

4. **Infer** How might the kind of tools available influence science research?

# Activity 1   *How do you make a microbalance?*

***Skills***   Measure; Model; Collect Data

## Task 1   Prelab Prep

1.  Collect the following items: hole punch, 2 jumbo plastic straws, single-size cereal box (or other small box), scissors, 3 wooden depressors, toothpick, glue, needle, masking tape, and pencil.
2.  Gather small items to test your scale, such as a blade of grass, rice grain, staple, or thread.
3.  Prepare your "disk-units" for measuring mass. Use the hole punch to make 10 to 15 plastic disks from one straw. These are your standard masses (50 mg each).

## Task 2   Data Record

1.  Prepare a three-column data table. Label the columns as follows: *Object, Mass in Disks, Mass in Milligrams.*
2.  You will measure and record the mass of each item in disk-units. Then, convert and record the mass of each item in milligrams.

## Task 3   Procedure

1.  Close the top of the cereal box. Cut out the front of the box. **Caution! Handle sharp objects with care.** It should look like a miniature shoebox without a lid. Make two parallel cuts about 0.5 cm deep in each long edge of the box. Fit one depressor into each of these cuts as shown in the figure at right.
2.  Cut off a small section of straw no longer than $3/4$ the width of the box. Cut a section out of one end to form a small scoop.
3.  Glue a portion of the toothpick into the other end of the straw. The toothpick will act as a pointer on the scale as shown in the figure at the right.
4.  Push the needle through the straw at a point between the middle and the toothpick end.

5.  Balance the needle and straw on the depressors. If the straw doesn't balance, reposition the needle in the straw until it does balance.
6.  Use tape to fasten the last depressor to the balance as shown. This is the scale.
7.  Add one plastic disk at a time to the scoop. With a pencil, mark the position of the toothpick's tip on the scale after each disk is added. These marks are 50-mg calibrations.
8.  Use the calibrated balance to determine the mass of each small item you gathered. Record the mass of each item.

## Task 4   Analysis

1.  What would you have to do to use your balance after moving it to a new location? Explain.
2.  What variables could affect the accuracy of your balance?

## Task 5   Conclusion

Write a report explaining how your balance worked. Discuss your data.

## *Extension*

Explain why your balance is only good for measuring very small masses. What can you infer about balance design and manufacturing processes from your model?

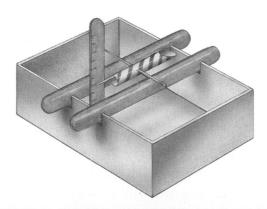

# Chapter 1 Review

## Concept Summary

### 1.1 Science Skills and Methods

▶ Scientists use many skills. They observe, infer, estimate, measure, predict, classify, hypothesize, record, organize, and analyze.

▶ Scientists perform experiments to gather data about nature.

▶ Scientific theories and laws may change.

▶ Scientists use models to represent the part of nature they study.

### 1.2 Measuring with Scientific Units

▶ Scientists measure length, volume, mass, density, temperature, and time with standard SI units.

▶ Scientific notation is used to express very large and very small numbers.

### 1.3 Graphing

▶ Circle graphs show how parts of something make up a whole.

▶ Bar graphs compare one aspect of several different things.

▶ Line graphs show data defined by two variables.

### 1.4 Science Tools and Technology

▶ Technology applies science principles to solve problems.

▶ Matter and energy are studied in two connected sciences, chemistry and physics. Other divisions of these sciences extend into the areas of life science and earth science.

▶ Scientists use tools, both simple and complex, to gather data about the world.

## Chapter Vocabulary

| | | | |
|---|---|---|---|
| data (1.1) | variable (1.1) | cubic meter (1.2) | kilogram (1.2) |
| controlled experiment (1.1) | meter (1.2) | liter (1.2) | density (1.2) |
| constant (1.1) | volume (1.2) | mass (1.2) | scientific notation (1.2) |

## Check Your Vocabulary

Use the vocabulary words above to complete the following sentences correctly.

1. Many drink containers use the SI unit ____ to measure their volume.

2. Very large or very small numbers are written using ____.

3. In a controlled experiment, a factor that is kept the same is a ____.

4. Scientists use science process skills to gather ____, or information.

5. The kilogram and gram are units of ____.

6. The factor that is changed by a person doing a controlled experiment is the ____.

7. A space 1m × 1m × 1m is one ____.

8. The ratio of an object's mass to its volume is the object's ____.

9. To do a ____, you must have two test groups, an experimental group and a control group.

10. The distance between a doorknob and the floor is about one ____.

11. In SI, the unit used to measure mass is ____.

12. The amount of space matter occupies is its ____.

## Write Your Vocabulary

Write sentences using each vocabulary word above. Show that you know what each word means.

# Chapter 1 Review

## Check Your Knowledge

Answer the following in complete sentences.

1. What are the basic units of length, volume, mass, and temperature in the metric system?

2. Without placing an object in water, how can you determine if it will float?

3. What is the function of a control in an experiment?

4. What instrument would you use to measure the following?

   a. The volume of water in a jar

   b. The width of this book

   c. The temperature of the ocean

   d. The amount of time it takes to run 100 m.

5. How do scientists protect their eyes during laboratory activities?

6. What is a wind tunnel used for?

Determine whether each statement is true or false. Write *true* if it is true. If it is false, change the underlined term(s) to make the statement true.

7. <u>Circle</u> graphs have *x*- and *y*-axes.

8. To measure volume in a graduated cylinder, you read the level of the <u>lowest</u> point of the meniscus.

9. SI units are based on multiples of <u>100</u>.

10. Scientific facts <u>never</u> change.

11. A number written in scientific notation is a <u>two-part</u> expression.

12. A conversion factor is written as a <u>fraction</u>.

13. <u>Computers</u> help scientists calculate rapidly, test hypotheses, or see the structure of a chemical.

## Check Your Understanding

Apply the concepts you have learned to answer each question.

1. Why must all parts of a circle graph add up to 100 percent?

2. **Application**   Which skill or skills could you apply to each statement? Explain.

   a. There are heavy dark clouds in the sky. It's going to rain.

   b. The mailbox is empty—either I didn't get mail today or the letter carrier has not delivered the mail.

   c. The container can hold 2 L of milk.

3. In an experiment on how temperature affects the rate at which sugar dissolves, what factor(s) should remain constant? What factor(s) will vary?

4. **Application**   What kind of graph—circle, bar, or line—would you use to show each of the following kinds of data?

   a. The percentage of students in your class with brown eyes.

   b. The height of a tree in the park on January 1 for the past 15 years.

5. **Mystery Photo**   The photograph on page 2 shows petrified wood. Petrified wood is a fossil formed when minerals replace natural wood fibers. Read Mike's response on page 2. List the science skills he uses to answer the question, "What do you see?"

6. Write each number below in scientific notation.

   a. 0.000 000 9

   b. 13 000 000 000

7. Write each number expressed below as a standard numeral.

   a. $2.3 \times 10^{-4}$

   b. $7 \times 10^{6}$

## Develop Your Skills

Use the skills you have developed in this chapter to complete each activity.

1. **Calculate**  Complete the following metric conversions.

   a. 1 kg = _____ g

   b. 2 L = _____ mL

   c. 10 dm = _____ mm

2. **Interpret Data**  The circle graph below shows land use in the United States.

   a. What portion of land is farmland?

   b. The amount of forestland is how many times greater than the amount of urban area?

**Land Use in the United States**

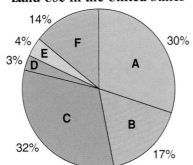

**Key:**
A = Grassland and pasture
B = Farmland
C = Forestland
D = National and state parks
E = Urban areas
F = Other

3. **Data Bank**  Use the information on page 637 to answer the following questions:

   a. In what month was the highest average temperature for 2 cities? The lowest average temperature?

   b. What city has the most variable weather in a year? How can you tell?

## Make Connections

1. **Link the Concepts**  Below is a concept map showing how some of the main concepts in this chapter link together. Only part of the map is filled in. Copy the map. Using words and ideas from the chapter, complete the map.

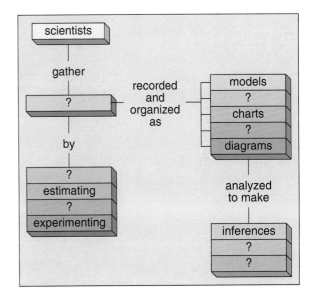

2. **Science and Art**  Choose a common symbol that you have seen. Develop a new symbol that shows the same idea.

3. **Science and Social Studies**  Many of the modern methods of science are based on the ideas or work of scientists who lived many centuries ago. Find out the names of some important scientists who lived before the 1800s. Choose one and write a report about her or his contributions to science.

4. **Science and Technology**  Research newspaper and magazine articles dealing with the scientific debate surrounding cold fusion. Explain how communication and controlled experimentation are important in this issue.

# Chapter 2

# Motion and Energy

## Chapter Sections

2.1    Motion

2.2    Acceleration

2.3    Energy of Motion

## What do you see?

" It looks like a maze with people carrying lights through the maze. The photographer left the shutter open on the camera and exposed the film for a long time causing the moving lights to become lines. The standing people have potential energy, while the 'moving' lines have kinetic energy. "

*Jim Emmons*
*El Toro High School*
*El Toro, California*

To find out more about the photograph, look on page 52. As you read this chapter, you will learn about motion and energy.

# 2.1 Motion

## Objectives

▶ **Compare** frames of reference.

▶ **Distinguish** between speed and velocity.

▶ **Calculate** when a moving object will arrive at a given point.

▶ **Make a graph** to solve a distance-time problem.

▼ **ACTIVITY**

**Observing**

*Point of Reference*

Select an object in the classroom or in the school yard as a reference point. Describe the motion of objects or people in relation to the reference point chosen.

**SKILLS WARMUP**

I magine you are traveling across the ocean on a ship. You see another ship getting closer, as shown in Figure 2.1. Are both ships moving or is only the ship you are on moving? To figure out what's happening, you need to know more about the motion of each ship. For example, you need to know if the other ship is moving. If you know how fast and in what direction the ships are moving, you can figure out the motion of the two ships.

## Frame of Reference

It isn't always easy to decide when objects are moving. Clues are often given by looking at other objects in your surroundings. Normally you think of walls or signs as not moving, or as being stationary. You judge motion in relation to these apparently stationary objects. When you do this, you use the walls or signs as a *frame of reference*. A frame of reference is a place or object that you assume is fixed. You observe how objects move in relation to that frame of reference.

Frames of reference also move relative to each other, which may cause confusion. Suppose you are seated on a bus that is parked close to another bus. The bus next to you starts to move forward. You may think your bus is moving backward. You are fooled into thinking you are moving. However, this time your frame of reference is moving.

Motion depends on the observer's frame of reference. From your frame of reference, you're not moving as you sit and read this book. To an observer in outer space, you are a passenger on a planet moving around the sun. You are moving over 100 times faster than a jet plane!

**Figure 2.1** ▲
What do these photographs tell you about the motion of the ship?

**An Earth Event**  You use the earth's surface as your frame of reference most of the time. However, you experience moving frames of reference when you ride in a vehicle, such as a car, a bus, or an elevator. If the vehicle moves at a constant speed, events in that frame of reference occur just as if you were not moving. For example, suppose you toss an apple to your friend as you both ride in a moving car.  The apple lands in her lap just as it would if you were both sitting on a bench. To an observer who is not in your moving frame of reference, such an event actually looks quite different.

**Figure 2.2**
**Frames of Reference** ▼

Two persons with the same frame of reference see the motion of an object the same way. Both boys on the bus see the ball drop straight down.

Two persons with different frames of reference see an object's motion differently. To a bystander, the ball moves in two directions— forward with the bus and down toward its floor.

**A Space Event** Objects in space can be used as a frame of reference, just as they are on the earth. An object used as a frame of reference in space could be a planet, moon, star, or a space vessel. To an observer in space, the earth's shape is very different from the one you experience every day. You experience the earth as a flat, nonmoving surface. From outer space, the earth appears as a rotating sphere revolving around the sun.

Away from the earth's surface and the pull of the earth's gravity, directions such as "up" and "down" are no longer relative. Events that seem impossible on the earth can occur in space.

During a space walk, the astronaut would see another astronaut outside the shuttle as upside down or floating. She may find it difficult to determine whether she is moving or if the astronaut outside the shuttle is moving.

Using the shuttle as a frame of reference in space, the earth is a rotating sphere beneath the astronauts.

Astronauts have a different frame of reference to the sun than you do. Every earth day they witness 16 sunsets behind the earth!

33

**Figure 2.3** ▶

How can you tell that the cyclist is moving and the road sign is in a fixed position?

## Measuring Motion

How would you describe the motion taking place in Figure 2.3? Although you can see that a cyclist passed a road sign, you don't really have much information about the cyclist's motion. To describe the motion further, you measure the cyclist's **speed**. Speed is the distance an object travels in a certain amount of time. To calculate its speed, you divide the distance the bike travels by the time it travels.

$$\text{speed} = \frac{\text{distance}}{\text{time}}$$

Speed is usually expressed in kilometers per hour (km/h). If the cyclist rode her bike 8 km to school in 20 min, you can calculate her speed in km/h as follows:

$$\text{speed} = \frac{8 \text{ km}}{20 \text{ min}} \times \frac{60 \text{ min}}{1 \text{ h}} = \frac{24 \text{ km}}{\text{h}}$$

An object's speed doesn't indicate all there is to know about its motion. The direction of motion is also important. The speed and the direction of an object's motion are called **velocity** (vuh LAHS uh tee). For example, the cyclist's velocity might be 24 km/h south. People often use the word *speed* when they mean *velocity*. Since a moving object always travels in some direction, velocity is a more accurate term for describing motion.

Wind is often described in terms of its velocity. What would be the velocity of the wind in Figure 2.4 if it blows at 40 km/h? Meteorologists use wind-velocity measurements to help predict weather.

**Figure 2.4**

This weather vane indicates wind direction. Which direction is the wind blowing? ▼

## Constant Speed

A moving object that doesn't change its speed travels at constant speed. Constant speed means equal distances are covered in an equal amount of time. Suppose you and a friend want to run around a track at constant speed for half an hour. How can you check to see if your speed is constant? You can use a stopwatch to measure how long it takes to run each lap. Your measurement can be even more accurate if you measure how long it takes to travel very short distances of equal length. If all the times are the same, your speed must be constant.

Look at the graph in Figure 2.5. Notice that in 2 s the runner ran 20 m and in 4 s, she ran 40 m. Her speed was constant at 10 m/s. On the graph, the curve for constant speed appears as a straight line. At this speed, she will run 100 m in 10 s.

The steepness of the curve indicates how fast the runner is moving. A greater speed has a steeper line. Suppose another runner ran the 100 m in 12 s. How would her speed curve look on the graph?

## Average Speed

A marathon course usually winds through city streets and up and down hills. Because the conditions of the course change, marathon runners can't keep a constant speed during a 42-km race.

A distance-time graph for a marathon runner is shown in Figure 2.6. Notice that the curve representing speed isn't straight. The graph shows that the runner traveled 10 km in the first hour and less than 5 km in the second hour. If a runner has changing speeds, what is his speed during the entire race?

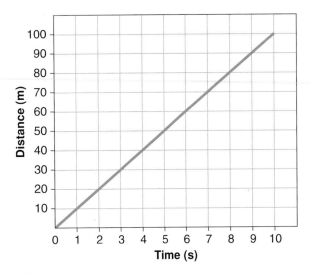

**Figure 2.5** ▲
A distance-time graph of constant speed forms a straight line.

**Figure 2.6**
A distance-time graph of a marathon shows that the runner's speed changed several times. ▼

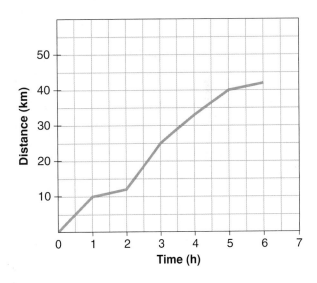

To find the speed of the runner during the entire race, you need to calculate his *average* speed. Average speed is equal to the total distance of the course divided by the runner's total time. What was the average speed of the marathon runner?

1. A group of teens traveled 150 km by car to a beach resort. If the driving time was 2 h, what was the average speed their vehicle traveled during the trip?

**Plan** To find the average speed, divide the distance by the time.

**Gather Data** distance = 150 km; time = 2 h

**Solve** $\text{speed} = \dfrac{\text{distance}}{\text{time}}$

$$\text{speed} = \frac{150\ km}{2\ h} = \frac{75\ km}{h}$$

2. The teens used a map like the one shown below. The sun would be setting in an hour and a half. They wanted to reach home before dark. If they drove at 90 km/h, how far could they travel in 1.5 h?

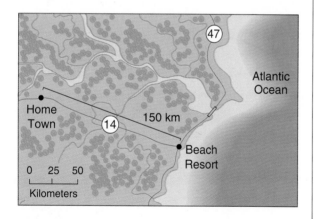

**Plan** To determine the distance the group could travel, multiply the speed of the car by the time remaining before dark.

**Gather Data** $\text{speed} = \dfrac{90\ km}{h}$; time = 1.5 h

**Solve** distance = speed × time

$$\text{distance} = \frac{90\ km}{\cancel{h}} \times 1.5\ \cancel{h} = 135\ km$$

1. A kayak races 100 m in 50 s. What is its speed?

2. At the speed of 2.5 m/s, how many seconds will it take the kayak to run a 4,500 m course? What is the speed of the kayak in kilometers per hour?

3. When a kayak races downstream, its speed is clocked at 3 m/s. How far does the kayak travel in 35 s? In 1 h?

4. The river in problem 3 was flowing downstream at a velocity of 1.5 m/s. How fast was the kayak being paddled? In order to travel upstream at a speed of 1.0 m/s, how fast must the kayak be paddled?

5. A family backpacking at Yosemite National Park took 5 h to climb a mountain trail 7.5 km long. What was the family's average speed?

6. When it was time to leave the park, the family could only drive at 60 km/h in the mountains. How long would it take them to travel the 270 km to their home? How fast would they have to travel to make the trip in 3 h?

## Relativity and Space-Time

You know that observations of motion depend on your frame of reference. Experiments with light show that the speed of light is always the same, regardless of the motion of the light source or the motion of the observer! To understand this, think about a rocket docked on the earth and another rocket traveling directly toward the sun at great speed. The light from the sun reaches each rocket at the same speed of 300 000 000 m/s.

The constant speed of light is the basis of Albert Einstein's special theory of relativity. He reasoned that space and time are connected into one whole, called space-time. You are constantly traveling through this combination of space and time. When you stand still, you travel only through time. When you move, you travel through space and time. If you could move at close to the speed of light, you would travel quickly through space and slowly through time.

### ▼ ACTIVITY

**Calculating**

*Sunlight Travel Time*

The sun is 149 million km from the earth. If light travels 300 000 000 m/s, how many minutes does it take light from the sun to reach the earth? If you see the sun set at 5:21 p.m., what time did the sunlight actually leave the sun?

**SKILLS WORKOUT**

## *Historical Notebook*

### *Motion Changes with the Times*

About 2,300 years ago, philosophers in China wrote about motion in a book called the *Mo Ching*. They wrote: "Motion stops due to an opposing force. If there is no opposing force, the motion will never stop."

About the same time, the Greek philosopher Aristotle wrote that horizontal motion was "unnatural." He thought that a push or a pull was needed to start and to keep something in horizontal motion. He also thought heavy objects fall at a faster rate, or acceleration, than lighter objects do. Aristotle's ideas about motion were widely accepted for more than 1,900 years.

During the 1500s, Galileo questioned the ideas of Aristotle. He reasoned that if two bricks of the same mass fall at the same rate, side-by-side, they ought to fall at the same rate even when cemented together. In 1589, according to an often-repeated, unverified story, Galileo did an experiment from the Leaning Tower in Pisa, Italy. Galileo is supposed to have dropped two cannonballs of different masses at the same time from the top of the tower. Both cannonballs reached the ground at about the same time. Whether he actually did the experiment or not, his reasoning was correct.

Galileo also did experiments that showed that an object moving horizontally continues to move at the same speed unless a force opposes it. Galileo's experiments confirmed the ideas stated thousands of years earlier in the *Mo Ching*.

1.  Design an experiment to test Aristotle's hypothesis that heavy objects fall faster than lighter objects.

2.  How did Galileo's experiments support the philosophers' ideas on motion in the *Mo Ching*?

## Science and Technology *Flight*

You and everything on the earth move with the planet. The earth makes one complete rotation every 24 hours. You can observe this motion as the sun appears to move across the sky each day. The sun may seem to be moving, but it's actually you on the earth that is moving! Locations near the equator move faster than those near the north and south poles. A point on the equator has to travel 40 000 km to make one complete rotation. In contrast, a point at the north or south poles does not move during one rotation.

The earth's rotation creates patterns of wind over its surface. The effect of these winds on airplane flight must be taken into account by pilots and navigators. The winds blow west to east over most of the United States. Westbound planes usually fly into the wind, while eastbound planes fly with the wind. Look at Figure 2.7. Which plane will arrive first? The plane flying from Los Angeles to New York travels east—the same direction as the prevailing winds. The eastbound plane flies faster due to the wind and will arrive first.

At Cape Canaveral in Florida, the earth turns toward the east at about 1,470 km/h. Rockets and space shuttles are launched from this site toward the east, in the same direction that the earth rotates. Because the speed of the earth's rotation adds to the launch speed, the rocket can reach its orbital velocity in less time.

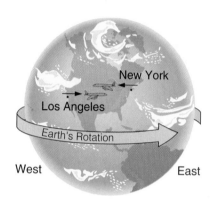

**Figure 2.7** ▲

Both planes will cover the same number of miles between New York and Los Angeles. If the departure time is the same for both planes, which one will reach its destination first?

## Check and Explain

1. How is a frame of reference used to determine the motion of an object? Give two examples.

2. How is the velocity of a bird in flight different from its speed?

3. **Calculate** How long does it take a migrating whale traveling at 20 km/h to travel 400 km?

4. **Make a Graph** At noon, a cyclist starts riding at a constant speed of 10 km/h. Make a graph that shows the distance traveled every hour until 5:00 p.m. What time would the cyclist reach a destination 50 km away?

# 2.2 Acceleration

## Objectives

▶ **Define operationally** the acceleration of an object.

▶ **Relate** motion in a circle to acceleration.

▶ **Contrast** acceleration and constant speed.

▶ **Make a graph** showing acceleration.

▼ **ACTIVITY**

### Inferring

*Pacing Yourself*

**1.** Choose an exercise, such as running in place.

**2.** Begin at a slow pace. Increase to a medium pace. Then increase to a fast pace.

As you increase the pace of exercising, what do you think happens to the rate of your heartbeat and your use of oxygen?

**SKILLS WARMUP**

Imagine you are competing as a speed skater at the Winter Olympics. You feel the excitement mount as you wait for the signal to begin the race. You are off to a fast start on the open stretch of ice. You gain speed with every stride. You think nothing can stop you. As you approach the curve, you slow down to keep your balance during the change in direction. Then once more you speed up to keep your lead.

During practice, you learned that three changes in speed were the key to winning the race: speed up whenever possible, slow down with control when necessary, and change direction as smoothly as possible. When you mastered these three things, you were ready to compete.

## Change in Velocity

You experience changes in velocity many times every day. Each time you take a step, you change the velocity of your body. When you write, the velocity of your hand moving across the paper changes. You are probably most familiar with the velocity changes of a moving bus or car. For example, a moving bus changes direction and speed when it turns a corner or pulls over to the curb. To let off passengers or to pick them up, the bus slows to a stop. The bus then starts up again.

In real-life situations, the rate at which a velocity change occurs is very important. For example, if a velocity change occurs too quickly on a moving bus, the passengers can be thrown from their seats. If the velocity changes are slower, they get a smooth, even ride. The rate at which velocity changes occur is called **acceleration**.

**Figure 2.8** ▲
To move around the curve, in what direction will the skater next place her right foot?

To calculate acceleration, you divide the change in velocity by the amount of time. Since you divide velocity in units of meters per second (m/s) by the time in seconds (s), the units for acceleration are meters per second per second, or meters per second squared (m/s²).

$$\text{acceleration} = \frac{\textbf{final velocity} - \textbf{starting velocity}}{\textbf{time}}$$

Suppose you ride a bike on a straight path to school at a velocity of 4 m/s. As you get closer, you hear the school bell. In 3 s, you speed up to 10 m/s. How would you calculate your acceleration? First, calculate the change in velocity, and then divide by the time involved.

$$\text{change in velocity} = \textbf{final velocity} - \textbf{starting velocity}$$
$$= \frac{10m}{s} - \frac{4m}{s} = \frac{6m}{s}$$

$$\text{acceleration} = \frac{\textbf{change in velocity}}{\textbf{time}} = \frac{\frac{6m}{s}}{3s} = \frac{\frac{2m}{s}}{s} = \frac{2m}{s^2}$$

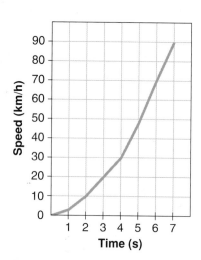

**Figure 2.9** ▲
How many seconds did the car travel at a constant positive acceleration?

**Positive Acceleration**   To think about positive acceleration, imagine a car waiting at a stoplight. It is temporarily motionless. The light turns from red to green, the driver steps on the accelerator, and the car speeds up. As the car moves faster, you feel the change in motion as your body is pushed back against the seat. The car's speedometer shows an increase in speed.

A distance-time graph of positive acceleration is shown in Figure 2.9. How does this graph differ from the constant-speed graph shown in Figure 2.5? The curve on the constant-speed graph is a straight line because equal distances were traveled in each unit of time. The curve for positive acceleration is not a straight line because the distance covered is not the same for each unit of time. Notice how the curve changes. Each second the car moved faster until it reached a maximum constant speed.

**Negative Acceleration**   To think about negative acceleration, imagine a car slowing down. The car's velocity decreases over a certain amount of time. This type of velocity change is also called **deceleration**.

You can graph negative acceleration just as you graph positive acceleration. The graph in Figure 2.10 shows negative acceleration. How does the curve differ from the curve for positive acceleration? How is it similar?

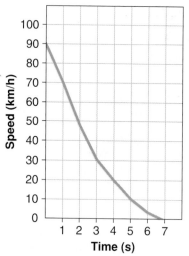

**Figure 2.10** ▲
The graph shows the negative acceleration of an automobile. During what 3 second interval did the car decelerate fastest?

Anyone who drives a car has to make sure its brakes are working properly so the car will decelerate quickly. Suppose the driver of a car moving at 80 km/h brakes suddenly. If the car comes to a full stop after moving only 40 m, an accident may safely be avoided. If it stops after moving 52 m, it may not!

**Change in Direction**   Turning the steering wheel of a moving car changes the direction of the car. Whenever direction of a moving object changes, the velocity of the object changes. Any change in velocity is acceleration—even if the speed of the object remains the same.

Look at Figure 2.11. In what two locations must the automobiles change velocity? When you ride on a swing, you experience oscillating motion. The swing continuously changes speed, and the direction of its motion reverses in a repeating pattern.

**Figure 2.11** ▲
Each change in direction represents a change in velocity.

# SkillBuilder Calculating

## A Racer's Acceleration

Suppose you are driving a car in a race. You know that your car must be able to accelerate quickly. Suppose that one second after the start of the race you traveled 5 m; at 2 seconds, you traveled 20 m; at 3 seconds, you pass the 45-m mark; and at 4 seconds, you reach the 80-m mark. Apply the acceleration formula to calculate your acceleration at 4 seconds. Use the information in the table to the right to make a line graph that shows your acceleration.

1. What information do you need to calculate acceleration?

2. Calculate your acceleration over the first 2 seconds. Explain your answer.

3. What does each data point on your graph indicate?

4. What information does the graph supply?

| Time and Distance | |
|---|---|
| **Time (s)** | **Distance (m)** |
| 0 | 0 |
| 1 | 5 |
| 2 | 20 |
| 3 | 45 |
| 4 | 80 |

5. Another car in the race accelerates at a speed of 18 m/s². After 4 seconds, would the car be ahead or behind your car?

Write a short paragraph comparing the information on an acceleration graph to an acceleration calculation.

# Sample Problem

A cheetah can move from 0 km/min to 3 km/min in 2 s. What is the cheetah's acceleration?

**Plan** To determine the acceleration of the cheetah. First calculate the change in velocity in units of m/s. Next divide by the time required in seconds.

**Gather Data**

$$\text{starting velocity} = \frac{0 \text{ km}}{\text{min}} = \frac{0 \text{ m}}{\text{s}}$$

$$\text{final velocity} = \frac{3 \text{ km}}{\text{min}}$$

$$= \frac{3000 \text{ m}}{1 \text{ min}} \times \frac{1 \text{ min}}{60 \text{ s}} = \frac{50 \text{ m}}{\text{s}}$$

$$\text{time} = 2 \text{ s}$$

**Solve** $\text{acceleration} = \dfrac{\text{change in velocity}}{\text{time}}$

$$\text{change in velocity} = \frac{50 \text{ m}}{\text{s}} - \frac{0 \text{ m}}{\text{s}} = \frac{50 \text{ m}}{\text{s}}$$

$$\text{acceleration} = \frac{\dfrac{50 \text{ m}}{\text{s}}}{2 \text{ s}} = \frac{25 \text{ m}}{\text{s}^2}$$

# Practice Problems

1. The velocity of water flowing over Lava Falls is 12 m/s. After going over the falls, the water slows to 6 m/s in 3 s. What is the acceleration of the water?

2. The winner of a track race ran at a speed of 10 m/s. As shown on the graph below, the runner took 3 s to slow down and come to a complete stop. What was the runner's acceleration?

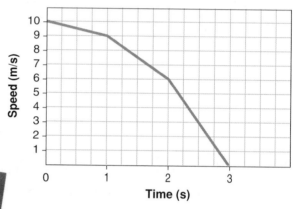

3. A speedboat goes from 4 m/s to 12 m/s in 4 s. What is the speedboat's acceleration? During the next 6 s, the speed of the boat increases to 18 m/s. How much did the speedboat's acceleration change?

4. A light breeze blows at 6 km/h. After 1 h the breeze becomes a strong wind that is traveling at 120 km/h. What is the acceleration of the wind?

**Figure 2.12** ▲
The people on this amusement-park ride experience centripetal acceleration.

## Motion in a Circle

The amusement-park ride shown in Figure 2.12 moves in a circle. At some point, the ride moves at a constant speed. However, at constant speed the ride is still accelerating! Recall that acceleration is a change in velocity that results from speeding up, slowing down, or changing direction. An object moving in a circle or a curve is constantly changing direction. Therefore, the object is accelerating. Acceleration caused by motion in a circle is called **centripetal** (sehn TRIHP uh tuhl) **acceleration**.

When you go around a sharp curve in a car, you experience centripetal acceleration. Your body tends to keep going in a straight line, but your seat belt pushes you toward the center of the curve. You change direction of motion every second. Centripetal acceleration is toward the center of the circle.

To see how centripetal acceleration works, try this. Fasten a small, rubber eraser to the end of a string. Watch what happens when you twirl the eraser around on the string, as shown in Figure 2.13. The tension on the string pulls the eraser toward the center of its path and keeps it from flying off in a straight line. The velocity continuously changes, so the eraser can't follow a straight path.

**Figure 2.13** ▲
What would happen to the eraser if the girl let go of the string? Why?

## ▼ ACTIVITY

### Interpreting Data

*Speed from Skids*

The skid length from a car involved in an accident was measured at 59.4 m. The car's drag factor was 0.80. How fast was the car going? Refer to Table 2.1 for help in calculating the speed of the car.

### SKILLS WORKOUT

### Life Science

### LINK

When a car crashes head-on, it slows down quickly. Without seatbelts, the people in the car will continue to move through space at the same speed the car was traveling. At 50 km/h, the force necessary to slow a person down and prevent injury is about 14 times a person's weight.

**1.** Weigh yourself in pounds.

**2.** Convert your weight in pounds to the force you exert in newtons by multiplying it by 4.448.

**3.** Calculate the force necessary to slow you down in a collision at 50 km/h.

### ACTIVITY

## Science and Society *Skid-Mark Evidence*

Police and insurance investigators use skid marks to determine the velocity of cars at the time of an accident. With a table similar to the one below, they can determine how far a vehicle slides before stopping completely. A car slides farther on wet or oily pavement than it does on dry pavement. In Table 2.1, the total of all the factors that affect deceleration is expressed as the "drag factor." The drag factor is shown as a decimal at the top of the table. The skid length is shown in the column at the left.

**Table 2.1   Distance Needed to Stop**

| Drag Factor | 0.60 | 0.65 | 0.70 | 0.75 | 0.80 |
|---|---|---|---|---|---|
| Skid Length (m) | Speed (km/hr) | | | | |
| 53.3 | 90 | 93 | 98 | 101 | 104 |
| 54.9 | 92 | 95 | 98 | 103 | 106 |
| 56.4 | 93 | 97 | 100 | 104 | 108 |
| 57.9 | 93 | 98 | 101 | 105 | 109 |
| 59.4 | 95 | 100 | 103 | 106 | 109 |

The investigator locates the length of the skid mark in the left column. He then locates the drag factor column across the top of the table. The row for the skid length meets the drag factor column at a number that tells the speed of the car at the time of the accident!

## Check and Explain

1. What three factors can change when an object accelerates?

2. Explain how centripetal force affects a person on a playground swing.

3. **Compare and Contrast**  Compare the acceleration of a car with its motion at constant speed.

4. **Make a Graph**  Make a speed-time graph to show an acceleration of 10 m/s² for 6 s. How much did the boat's speed increase between 2 s and 6 s?

# 2.3 Energy of Motion

## Objectives

▶ **Define** energy.

▶ **Explain** the law of conservation of energy.

▶ **Compare** and **contrast** potential energy and kinetic energy.

▶ **Infer** the gravitational potential energy of everyday objects.

A bird swoops down from a tree to pick up crumbs you tossed out for it. You are almost knocked over as your dog chases a cat across the yard. Fortunately, you recover in time to race inside to answer the telephone. In each example, changes in motion take place. Identify the changes in motion that occur in Figure 2.14.

Changes in motion occur constantly in the world around you. Cars move on busy highways. Tons of rock hurtle down mountainsides. Underground water is brought to the surface for crop irrigation. What gives the cars, rocks, and water the ability to move?

## Energy and Change

A car won't run without the energy it obtains from burning gasoline. Your body can't move unless you have energy from food. Any change in motion requires **energy**. Energy

◀ **Figure 2.14**
What are the energy sources for the motion changes shown in this photograph?

is the ability to do work. When work is done, a change occurs. You might say that energy is the source of change.

An unwound spring in a music box has no energy with which to make sound. Suppose you wind the spring into a tight coil. As the spring unwinds, it releases energy that causes a cylinder inside the music box to rotate. Steel pins on the rotating cylinder pluck metal teeth that make sounds.

The archer in Figure 2.15 uses energy to pull the bow's string toward her to change the string's position. When she lets go, energy in the tight string transfers to the arrow, and the arrow moves forward. The changes in the music box and in the bow-and-arrow involve two types of energy—potential energy and kinetic energy.

**Potential Energy**   Stored energy has the ability to do work and is called **potential energy**. Potential energy is associated with position. For example, when the spring in the music box is wound up, its position changes. Energy is stored in the spring, so the spring has potential energy. When the archer's bow is drawn, the change in the position of the bow gives it potential energy. Potential energy is usually written P.E.

Substances that can be burned also contain potential energy. For example, energy from the sun is stored in gasoline, wood, and plants. When these substances are burned, their potential energy is released.

You use potential energy many times a day. The food you carry to school in your lunch has potential energy. As your body digests food, it releases its potential energy. You use this energy to move. Name some other kinds of potential energy you use.

**Kinetic Energy**   A flying arrow and a moving bus have the same type of energy. They have energy of motion. Energy of motion is called **kinetic** (kih NEHT ihk) **energy**. Kinetic energy is written K.E.

The amount of kinetic energy depends on the moving object's mass and speed. To calculate kinetic energy, you multiply one half of the object's mass by the square of its velocity.

$$\text{kinetic energy} = \frac{\text{mass} \times \text{velocity}^2}{2}$$

$$\text{K.E.} = \frac{mv^2}{2}$$

Do you have more kinetic energy when you walk up stairs or when you run? By looking at the equation, you see that kinetic energy depends on an object's velocity. When you run, you move faster than when you walk up stairs. Your mass does not change. Therefore, you have more kinetic energy when you run.

Mass also affects kinetic energy, as shown in Figure 2.16. A bowling ball and a basketball travel at the same velocity. The speed of the two balls is the same, but the bowling ball has more mass and thus more kinetic energy.

**Figure 2.16** ▲
If the mass of the bowling ball is 4 kg and its velocity is 45 m/s, how much kinetic energy does it have?

**Conservation of Energy**   Potential energy and kinetic energy can change from one into the other. The wrecking ball in Figure 2.17 changes potential energy into kinetic energy during each swing. When the ball is stopped at the top, it has all potential energy and no kinetic energy. When the ball is released, its potential energy changes to kinetic energy. When it makes contact, the kinetic energy of the heavy ball transfers to the building, breaking the structure apart.

A child uses kinetic energy to wind the spring in a mechanical toy. Each turn of the key puts more tension on the spring, and adds potential energy. When the spring can't be wound further, the child releases the toy. The potential energy in the toy's spring changes to kinetic energy as the toy moves about.

Because potential and kinetic energy change from one kind to the other, energy isn't created or destroyed. This is known as the *law of conservation of energy*. Energy can change into other forms of potential or kinetic energy. Energy can transfer to another object, increasing the object's kinetic energy. However, the total amount of energy always remains the same.

**Figure 2.17** ▲
At what point does the wrecking ball have the greatest amount of kinetic energy?

## Gravity and Energy

Think about a rock perched at the top of a steep cliff. Does the rock have energy? Recall that energy causes change. What changes could the rock cause if it falls?

What kind of energy does the rock have? You may infer that the rock has potential energy because of its position. Once over the cliff's edge, the force of gravity pulls the rock downward. The rock's energy is due to both its position on the cliff and the force of gravity. This type of energy is called gravitational potential energy (G.P.E). Gravitational potential energy depends on an object's weight and the distance it falls before stopping completely.

As a rock begins to fall, some of its gravitational potential energy changes to kinetic energy. Because of the force of gravity, a rock speeds up as it falls. Its kinetic energy increases because more of its gravitational potential energy changes into kinetic energy. As the rock hits bottom, it has maximum kinetic energy and zero gravitational potential energy. Which would receive greater damage when hit by the falling rock: a tree near the top of the cliff or one at the bottom? Explain how kinetic energy can break rock into smaller pieces.

The rock at the top of the hill has potential energy because of its position. This same rock has no kinetic energy because it's not moving.

The falling rock still has some potential energy, but some of its potential energy has changed to kinetic energy. As the rock loses potential energy, it gains kinetic energy.

A fallen rock has lost all its potential energy. It no longer has a position from which to fall. The fallen rock has no kinetic energy because it has stopped moving.

◀ Figure 2.18
Energy Conversion
in a Rockslide

## Science and Technology *Great Potential*

Around 4,600 years ago, the people of ancient Egypt began to use the potential energy of water stored behind dams. The largest of these dams was 97 m wide, 14 m high, and 55 m thick. Its core was made of impermeable clay, and the mass of the rock fill on each side totaled 90,000 metric tons. The ancient Egyptians originally built dams for flood protection. They also released water over the dam's spillway, changing potential energy into the kinetic energy of flowing water. Workers used the flowing water in transport canals to move construction materials to build the pyramids and other ancient monuments.

Other ancient people used the energy of falling water. Over 2,000 years ago in Greece, people used the kinetic energy of falling water to turn water wheels. The kinetic energy of the turning wheel was used to grind grain into flour. The water wheels used in China about 3,000 years ago were similar to the water wheels used by the Greeks.

Today people use the energy from falling water to produce electricity. Typically, enough water is stored behind a dam to produce continuous power. As the water falls, its potential energy changes to kinetic energy. The kinetic energy makes the turbines rotate. The rotating turbines generate electricity.

You can see in Figure 2.19 that water flows through channels or pipes from a height of 15 m to 30 m to water turbines below the dam. Notice the high, vertical drop of the water. The higher the dam, the more potential energy the water has.

**Figure 2.19** ▲
How is the water wheel like the dam?

## Check and Explain

1. What is energy?

2. How is an arrow shot from a bow an example of the law of conservation of energy?

3. **Compare and Contrast** How are potential energy and kinetic energy different? How are they similar?

4. **Infer** A person on a trampoline can go higher with each bounce. Explain how gravity affects the amount of energy available for each succeeding jump.

# Activity 2   *How can you change the speed of a rocket?*

***Skills***   Control Variables; Collect Data; Calculate

## Task 1   Prelab Prep
1. Collect the following items: fishing line, scissors, tape, balloon, straw, meter stick, watch to measure seconds, pencil, paper.
2. Cut a length of fishing line the width of the classroom. Attach one end of the fishing line to a table or chair. Inflate the balloon.
3. With tape, attach the balloon to the straw, as shown in the drawing. Deflate the balloon.

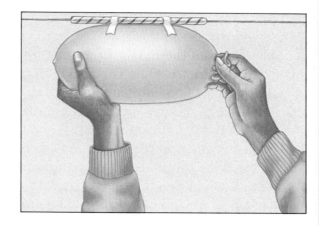

## Task 2   Data Record
1. On a separate sheet of paper, draw a table like the one shown.
2. Record all data collected. Double check all your calculations.

### Table 2.2   Speed Measurements

| Trial | Variable Changed | Distance (m) | Time (s) | Speed (m/s) |
|-------|------------------|--------------|----------|-------------|
| 1     |                  |              |          |             |
| 2     |                  |              |          |             |
| 3     |                  |              |          |             |

## Task 3   Procedure
1. Hold the straw so the neck of the balloon faces you. Thread the free end of the fishing line through the straw.
2. Measure the distance from the end of the balloon to the attached end of the fishing line. Record the distance in meters.
3. Inflate the balloon. Pinch shut the neck of the balloon. Hold one end of the fishing line.
4. Release the inflated balloon. Record the time in seconds it takes for the balloon to reach the other end of the fishing line.
5. Calculate the speed of the balloon. Record the speed in your data table.
6. Change the mass of the balloon, the amount of air in the balloon, or the slope of the fishing line. Record each variable you change.
7. Repeat steps 3 and 4. Record the speed for each trial in your table.

## Task 4   Analysis
1. What variables did you change on your balloon rocket?
2. Which variable caused the lowest speed?
3. Which variable caused the greatest speed?

## Task 5   Conclusion
Write a paragraph describing how the speed of a balloon rocket is affected by the balloon's mass, amount of air, and slope of movement.

### *Extension*
Calculate the speed of the balloon if it moved half as fast as the fastest speed. Change one variable at a time until your balloon rocket travels at half its fastest speed.

### *Everyday Application*
Apply the results of your findings to discuss how a jet airplane might control its flight speed and the angle of a climb.

# Chapter 2 Review

## Concept Summary

### 2.1 Motion

▶ The motion of an object varies depending upon the frame of reference of the observer.

▶ The distance an object moves in a certain amount of time is its speed. Speed = distance/time. The speed and direction of an object are its velocity.

▶ An object moving at constant speed travels the same distance in each unit of time. A distance-time graph of constant speed has a straight line curve.

▶ If the object's speed varies with time, the curve on a distance-time graph doesn't form a straight line. An object's average speed is calculated by dividing the distance traveled by the total amount of time.

### 2.2 Acceleration

▶ Acceleration is a change in velocity caused by speeding up, slowing down, or changing direction.

▶ An object moving in a circle changes direction, so it accelerates. This is called centripetal acceleration.

### 2.3 Energy of Motion

▶ Energy is the ability to do work and to cause change.

▶ Energy of position or stored energy is potential energy.

▶ Energy of motion is kinetic energy.

▶ Potential and kinetic energy can change from one to the other. The law of the conservation of energy states that energy is not created or destroyed.

## Chapter Vocabulary

speed (2.1)                    deceleration (2.2)                    potential energy (2.3)

velocity (2.1)                 centripetal acceleration (2.2)        kinetic energy (2.3)

acceleration (2.2)             energy (2.3)

## Check Your Vocabulary

Use the vocabulary words above to complete the following sentences correctly.

1. A cup resting on a table has ____ .

2. The distance you travel in a certain amount of time is called ____ .

3. An object that speeds up, slows down, or changes direction is undergoing ____ .

4. A crawling baby has ____ .

5. The speed and direction of motion of an object is its ____ .

6. When you ride on a merry-go-round, you experience ____

7. The slowing down of a galloping horse is ____ .

8. The ability to do work and cause change is ____ .

Pair each numbered word with a vocabulary term. Explain in a complete sentence how the words are related.

1. Circle            6. Position

2. Direction         7. Motion

3. Change            8. Time

4. Slower            9. Rate

5. Work             10. Transfer

## Write Your Vocabulary

Write sentences using the vocabulary words above. Show that you know what each word means.

# Chapter 2 Review

## Check Your Knowledge

Answer the following in complete sentences.

1. How do you calculate the speed of a moving object?

2. What information do you need to describe a moving object's velocity?

3. What is a frame of reference? Give two examples.

4. How are constant speed and average speed different?

5. Give examples of three different kinds of acceleration.

6. What causes changes in motion?

7. Can energy be destroyed? Explain.

8. What is space-time?

Choose the answer that best completes each sentence.

9. The rate of velocity change is called (constant speed, average speed, acceleration, centripetal acceleration).

10. An object's motion depends on the observer's (mass, velocity, energy, frame of reference).

11. Potential energy is due to an object's (weight, position, motion, mass).

12. To determine the speed of a moving object, divide the distance it travels by (mass, time, acceleration, deceleration).

13. The kinetic energy of a moving object depends on the object's mass and (energy, weight, speed, gravity).

14. To calculate acceleration, divide the (starting velocity, change in velocity, final velocity, rate of change) by the time in seconds.

## Check Your Understanding

Apply the concepts you have learned to answer each question.

1. The space shuttle orbits the earth. A communications satellite passes beneath it in a lower orbit. Describe this event from the frame of reference of the earth, the space shuttle, and the satellite.

2. **Calculate** World-class athletes can run 10 000 m in 30 min. What is their average speed in meters per second?

3. The acceleration of a moving object is $-4$ m/s$^2$. Explain what is happening to the object's motion.

4. **Application** A plane takes off from Miami, headed for Toronto, Canada, which is located due north; the plane heads northeast. Why? What direction does the plane take on its return trip?

5. **Critical Thinking** A skateboarder at the top of a steep hill coasts downhill and makes it to the top of the next hill.

   a. Draw a picture of what happened.

   b. Analyze this event in terms of potential and kinetic energy. Label your drawing using these terms.

6. **Mystery Photo** The photograph on page 30 shows a time exposure of a people maze, as seen from above. As people walk through the maze, their flashlights form lines of light on the photograph.

   a. Each line of light represents the path of one person's journey through the maze. Select one path and describe the person's journey in terms of velocity and acceleration.

   b. Identify areas where motion slows or stops completely.

## Develop Your Skills

Use the skills you have developed in this chapter to complete each activity.

1. **Interpret Data** The distance-time graph below shows the motion of three cyclists.

   a. What does each line on the graph represent?

   b. Which cyclist traveled the most distance? The least distance?

   c. Which cyclist traveled at the greatest speed? The slowest speed? At constant speed?

   d. Which cyclist had a flat tire? How do you know?

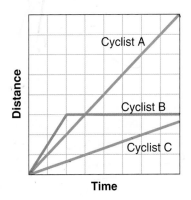

2. **Data Bank** Use the information on page 638 to answer the following questions.

   a. How far can a honeybee travel in 30 min?

   b. A jack rabbit runs at top speed to a hiding place 600 m away. How long does it take to get there?

   c. If a running human reaches top speed in 10 s, what is the acceleration? If the swimming human reaches top speed in the same amount of time, what is the acceleration? Compare the accelerations and explain any differences.

## Make Connections

1. **Link the Concepts** Below is a concept map showing how some of the main concepts in the chapter link together. Only parts of the map are filled in. Copy the map. Using words and ideas from the chapter, complete the map.

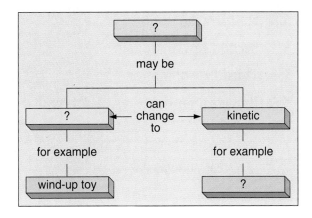

2. **Science and Social Studies** Before the invention of modern navigational instruments, people from many different cultures traveled the open ocean. As a group project, research the navigation methods of several different seafaring cultures. Give a class presentation on your findings.

3. **Science and Math** With a friend, measure a distance of 100 m. Time each other as you each run and walk that distance. Calculate each other's speed in meters per second.

4. **Science and Art** Sculptures that have moving parts are called kinetic sculptures. Design your own kinetic sculpture and describe its motion.

5. **Science and You** Plan a trip to a location 4,800 km east of your home. Research how much time the entire trip will take. What will be your average speed?

# Chapter 3 Forces and Motion

## Chapter Sections

**3.1** Forces, Motion, and Gravity

**3.2** First Law of Motion

**3.3** Second Law of Motion

**3.4** Third Law of Motion

**3.5** Universal Forces

## What do you see?

❝The photograph looks like a Ferris wheel. It looks like it's going really fast because of the blurred lines and colors. It also almost looks like rings belonging to a planet. But because of the ladder coming out of the center, it isn't.❞

*Meike Lampe*
*North Mid High School*
*Edmond, Oklahoma*

To find out more about the photograph, look on page 82. As you read this chapter, you will learn about forces and motion.

# 3.1 Forces, Motion, and Gravity

## Objectives

▶ **Identify** some forces that act in everyday situations.

▶ **Determine** the force of gravity in SI units.

▶ **Generalize** about how friction affects motion.

▶ **Observe** projectile motion in everyday objects.

▼ **ACTIVITY**

**Comparing**

*Know Your Strength*

Explain the difference in the amount of strength you use to lift a bag of groceries, to hold an apple, and to push a heavy box of books.

**SKILLS WARMUP**

**M**oving in a 76-m circle probably sounds like something you have never done. Actually, if you have ever ridden on a Ferris wheel, that is exactly what you were doing. Part of the thrill of the ride is stopping 76 m in the air. However, you knew the wheel would return you to the ground.

A Ferris wheel is driven by the motor attached to it. The motor applies energy to the huge wheel. Energy provides the push that starts the Ferris wheel moving and keeps the wheel in motion. Energy is also needed to stop the wheel.

## Forces Around You

When you walk into the wind, you can feel it push against you. When you ride in a car, you push against the seat as the car turns a corner. You are constantly affected by some kind of **force**. A force is a push or pull that starts, stops, or changes the direction of an object.

Force transfers energy to an object. To push the wheelbarrow, the man in Figure 3.1 must first apply force to lift it. He must then apply force in another direction to push the wheelbarrow. He applies a different amount of force to each handle as he pushes the wheelbarrow around the corner in order to keep it from tipping over. To determine the amount of force needed to move an object, you need to know the mass and acceleration of the object.

Other forces are acting on the man and the wheelbarrow. In order to maintain his balance, the man's muscles apply forces that keep him from falling over. Identify the forces on the wheelbarrow if all the plants were moved to the front. How would the force that's applied by the man change, if the load were three-10 kg sacks of sand?

**Figure 3.1** ▲
How do the forces on the wheelbarrow handles change after the man turns the corner?

## Force and Gravity

The amount and direction of most forces can be measured. A spring scale is one kind of instrument used to measure force. The spring scale, shown below,  measures the force of gravity on an object. A spring scale attached to an object measures how much force you use to lift the object. The amount of force needed to move an object depends on the mass of the object. More force is needed to move a large mass than to move a small mass.

The SI unit for force is called a **newton**. The newton is named for Sir Isaac Newton, the scientist who explained how force and motion are related. One newton (N) is the amount of force needed to cause a 1-kg mass to accelerate at a rate of 1 m per second for each second of motion. This is about the same as the force a small mouse sitting on a table exerts on the table. You write one newton as

$$N = 1 \text{ kg} \times \frac{1 \text{ m}}{\text{sec}^2}$$

The weight of an object depends on the force that pulls the object toward the earth. You know this force as gravity. Since the force of gravity on the earth is 9.8 m/s², the weight of a 1-kg object is 9.8 N.

**Figure 3.2
Force of Gravity Measurement** ▼

The force of gravity on an object is measured by attaching it to a spring scale.

Objects with a large amount of mass stretch the spring farther than do objects with less mass. The force of gravity exerted on an object is called the weight of the object.

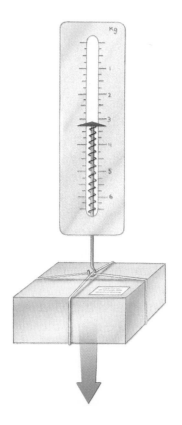

Weight is measured in newtons. Some spring scales are calibrated to show the force of gravity in newtons.

The spring scale shows that gravity is a downward force. It also shows that weight is the downward force of gravity on an object.

## Falling Objects

If you drop a feather and a coin at exactly the same time from a second story window, which one will reach the ground first? You might predict that the coin will be first. Recall that the acceleration of gravity is 9.8 m/s². If no other force acts on them, both the feather and the coin should accelerate at 9.8 m/s² for every second they fall. However, you know this is not what actually happens.

What kind of force might act differently on the feather and the coin? Look at Figure 3.3. Both objects are falling through air. When an object moves through air, its motion is opposed by the force of **friction**. Friction occurs when the surfaces of any kind of matter move past each other.

Friction from the air affects the motion of a falling object by acting against the force of gravity. A falling object gains speed until the force from air friction, which acts upward, equals the downward force of gravity. When the upward and downward forces are equal, the object

**Figure 3.3** ▲
What forces are acting on both objects that affect the speed of the falling feather and the coin?

## *SkillBuilder* *Measuring*

### *Force in Newtons*

You have some idea of how much force to apply to lift a medium-size apple. Your idea allows you to estimate its weight, or force, in newtons. Although every apple doesn't exert the same amount of force, an average apple exerts a force of about 1 N. Use an apple as a standard to estimate in newtons the weight of other objects.

1. Make a chart like the one shown to record your predictions and measurements.

2. Collect 5 small common objects about the size of an apple or smaller. Lift each object and predict how much each one weighs in newtons. Record your predictions on the chart.

3. Attach a string to an object and hang it from a spring scale that measures in newtons. Weigh the object and record your measurement.

| Measurement in Newtons | | |
|---|---|---|
| Object | Predicted Force (N) | Measured Force (N) |
| 1 | | |
| 2 | | |
| 3 | | |
| 4 | | |
| 5 | | |

4. Repeat step 3 for each object.

5. How did your predictions compare with the actual measurements? Explain any differences.

Write a short paragraph discussing how this method of measurement could be useful in some kind of everyday situation.

reaches **terminal velocity**. At terminal velocity, an object's velocity becomes constant.

All falling objects reach terminal velocity if given enough time. However, the time required to reach terminal velocity varies. Dense objects with little surface area, such as coins, must fall for several seconds before reaching terminal velocity. Less dense objects with a lot of surface area, such as a feather, reach terminal velocity much faster. The average velocity of a falling coin is greater than that of a feather. Therefore, the coin reaches the ground before the feather does. How would changing the shape of an object affect its terminal velocity?

## Projectile Motion

If you throw a ball for your dog to fetch, the ball follows a curved path to the ground. This path is called *projectile motion*. Look at Figure 3.4. When the ball is thrown, it moves horizontally.

The ball also responds to the force of gravity. The ball's projectile motion is a combination of the downward force of gravity and the horizontal motion of velocity. This combination of horizontal and vertical motion causes the ball to follow a curved path.

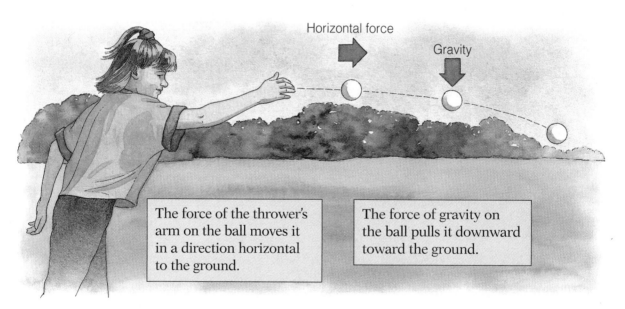

Horizontal force

Gravity

The force of the thrower's arm on the ball moves it in a direction horizontal to the ground.

The force of gravity on the ball pulls it downward toward the ground.

**Figure 3.4** ▲

If the girl throws the ball harder, the ball will go farther horizontally. Does the distance the ball drops change if the ball is thrown harder? Explain.

## Science and You *The Curve Ball*

Anyone who is familiar with baseball has probably heard of a curve ball. A pitcher throws a curve ball to confuse the batter because the path of a curve ball is difficult to judge, and the batter frequently swings and misses. Curve balls, which appear to "break" as they approach the batter, are often referred to as "breaking balls."

What causes a curve ball to break away from the normal path of a pitched ball? The answer becomes clear once you study the forces that are acting on the ball. First, the pitcher applies a force to get the ball moving. Then, as the ball travels through the air, the force of gravity acts on it. These forces combine to produce the gradually arcing path taken by most thrown objects.

Why does a curve ball "break"? A curve ball "breaks" because it has an additional force acting on it. The ball is thrown so it spins as it travels through the air. The spin produces an unbalanced air-pressure force around the ball, causing it to break away from its normal path. The batter judges the path of the ball and swings to hit it. However, it is difficult for the batter to see the spin on the incoming baseball. Instead of hitting the ball, the batter misses it completely! The unexpected spin on the ball has fooled the batter.

**Figure 3.5 ▲**
Here, a picher has just thrown a curve ball. You can see the ball on its way to the batter.

## Check and Explain

1. Give two examples of forces.

2. Describe how you can use a spring scale to measure the force of gravity on an object.

3. **Generalize** How does friction affect a flat sheet of paper falling through air? How would friction affect a crumpled ball of paper? Make a generalization about friction and falling objects.

4. **Observe** Place two coins next to each other on the edge of a table. Push both coins off the table at the same time. Apply more force to one of the coins. Which coin hits the ground first? Why?

**Arm in Arm**

Suppose two students are arm wrestling, and neither can bring the other's arm down. What can you infer about the forces being exerted?

# 3.2 First Law of Motion

## Objectives

▶ **State** Newton's first law of motion.

▶ **Identify** inertia and explain how to overcome it.

▶ **Define operationally** how friction occurs in an everyday situation.

▶ **Observe** Newton's first law of motion.

Suppose you decide to listen to your favorite cassette on the tape player. When you look through the stack of tapes, you notice the cassette you want is at the bottom. You grasp the cassette and yank on it quickly. To your surprise, the rest of the stack doesn't fall over. The tapes remain in a vertical stack. The only tape that really moved horizontally was the one you yanked on.

## Inertia

As early as the fourth century B.C., people in China knew about laws of motion. However, their knowledge did not spread outside of China. Newton is recognized as the first person to state laws about the relationship between motion and forces.

Newton observed that an object at rest stays at rest until an outside force causes it to move. He also observed that an object in motion continues to move in the same direction until a force stops it or changes its direction. Newton stated his observations as the first law of motion.

> An object at rest will remain at rest and an object in motion will remain in motion unless acted upon by an outside force.

**Objects at Rest** When you sit in a chair, many forces act on your body. The pressure of the atmosphere pushes on you and gravity pulls you toward the earth. You sit comfortably, because your body pushes onward with equal force against the atmospheric pressure. Your chair pushes up against the force of gravity to keep you from falling to the ground. All the forces acting on you are balanced.

**Figure 3.6**

Why do the disc boxes at the top of the stack stay in place when the girl pulls out the lower one?

▼

As you sit, your body obeys Newton's first law of motion. Your body is at rest, and it will remain at rest until some outside force moves it. Your body resists change. You have **inertia** (ihn ER shuh).

The word *inertia* comes from the Latin word *iners*, meaning "idle." Inertia is the tendency of an object to resist any change in motion. To overcome your inertia and move out of the chair, you must apply some kind of force to your body. The force you apply to overcome inertia must be greater than the forces that are acting on your body.

**Objects in Motion**   The first law of motion and inertia also applies to objects in motion. For example, when you pedal a bike, you accelerate to make the bike move forward. Notice in Figure 3.7 that the rider is no longer pedaling. However, because of their inertia, the bike and the rider keep moving forward in the same direction. Inertia can be overcome only by the application of some type of force. The bike will slow as forces of air resistance and friction act on it. Other forces could result from pushing the pedals, turning the handlebars, or using the brake.

## Friction

What would the world be like if every object set into motion continued to move until it hit another object? The bus would go right past the bus stop. A kicked soccer ball would continue to bounce. Fortunately when matter rubs against other matter, the motion creates friction. Friction works in the opposite direction to the force of motion.

Newton's first law states that objects in motion tend to stay in motion unless they are acted upon by an outside force. Friction is an outside force that resists motion when two surfaces come in contact. The surfaces can be between two objects or between an object and air or water.

Recall the falling feather and coin as they moved through air. It was the upward force of friction from the air that slowed the feather. Friction is present whenever objects slide, roll, or rub against a surface. For example, if you kick a soccer ball on flat ground, friction between the ball and the ground slows and stops the ball.

**Figure 3.7** ▲

What would happen to the rider if the bike slowed to a complete stop? What force would be acting on the rider?

# Types of Friction

Friction affects every object on the earth. When you slide a box across the floor, the force of friction opposes your effort. Without friction, you wouldn't be able to walk without slipping and falling down. You wouldn't be able to write because your pencil would slip off the page. Friction even affects boats and airplanes as they move through fluids, such as water or air.

## Sliding Friction

When two solid surfaces slide over each other, sliding friction acts between them. The weight of the object and the type of surface it moves over determine the amount of sliding friction present between the two objects. A heavy object exerts more pressure on the surface it slides over, so the sliding friction will be greater.

Sliding friction keeps the baseball player from passing the base. Which kind of surface causes less sliding friction, a smooth surface or a rough one? ▼

## Fluid Friction ▲

Air, water, and oil are all fluids. When the boat in the photo sails through the water, fluid friction from both the air and the water opposes its motion. Fluid friction also occurs when an object falls through the air.

## Rolling Friction ▶

When an object rolls over a surface, the friction produced is called rolling friction. The force needed to overcome rolling friction is much less than that needed to overcome sliding friction.

The tread on a tire affects the amount of rolling friction to be overcome. Which tire in the photograph will create more rolling friction?

## Science and Technology *Friction Control*

Friction keeps tires on the road, and it slows down a tossed ball. Friction also slows down motion inside a machine. As machine parts rub against one another, friction causes them to wear out. Worn-out parts can be expensive and dangerous. Too much friction between the moving parts in a car can cause it to breakdown.

Several techniques are used to reduce friction in machine parts. One technique is to use ball bearings. A ball bearing is a smooth, round ball. It is placed between two surfaces in a machine. The ball rolls as the surfaces move past each other. Friction is directed onto the very small surface that contacts the rolling ball rather than directly onto the two larger surfaces. Friction is reduced because there is less area in contact with a rolling ball.

Imagine two books rubbing against one another. The book covers will wear away because of friction. If you place several marbles between the two books, they can still slide past one another. The marbles reduce friction, so the covers will not wear as quickly.

Usually ball bearings are used in sets. Some are sealed into a part. Some are greased to reduce friction even more. You probably use something that has ball bearings in it. Roller skate and skateboard wheels, bicycles, and car parts all use ball bearings to reduce friction.

Another method of controlling friction is to use fluids. The fluid can be a liquid film or a gas, such as air, trapped between the machine parts. The fluid keeps surfaces from making direct contact and reduces friction. The oil in a car engine reduces wear on the engine parts.

**Figure 3.8** ▲
Why do you think these ball bearings are set inside the casing?

## Check and Explain

1. What is Newton's first law of motion?

2. Explain how a dog overcomes inertia when it gets up after napping on the floor.

3. **Define Operationally** Explain how friction works to keep bicycle tires from sliding on the road.

4. **Observe** Identify two examples each of an object at rest and of an object in motion. Use examples of things in your school. Explain how Newton's first law applies to each example.

# ▼ ACTIVITY

# 3.3 Second Law of Motion

## Objectives

▶ **State** Newton's second law of motion.

▶ **Calculate** the force of a moving object by using information about its mass and acceleration.

▶ **Identify** the relationship between momentum, mass, and velocity.

▶ **Make a model** to show how force acts during circular motion.

Suppose you are sitting in a rowboat on a sandy beach. Your friends get behind the boat and push it toward the water. The force of their push and the force of friction of the sand on the boat act against each other. Your friends push with a greater force than the friction force of the sand. The boat moves because the two opposing forces are unbalanced. When two opposing forces are unbalanced, the combined, or net, force is determined by subtracting the small force from the large one.

## Accelerated Motion

The two skateboarders in Figure 3.9 wait for a signal to begin racing. When they hear the signal, both racers start to move at the same time. Assuming that they both use the same amount of force, Maria, the smaller racer, accelerates faster than Christine, the larger racer. Although Newton never saw either racer, he explained why this happens.

Since Christine has more body mass, she accelerates more slowly than Maria. Christine must use more force to match Maria's acceleration. Newton understood that force, mass, and acceleration are related. He showed that the motion of an object changes, or accelerates, when a force acts on it. If you know the mass and the acceleration of an object, you can determine its force. This relationship is stated in Newton's second law of motion.

**Figure 3.9** ▲
Assuming both girls apply equal force, why will Maria accelerate faster?

The net force on an object equals its mass times its acceleration.

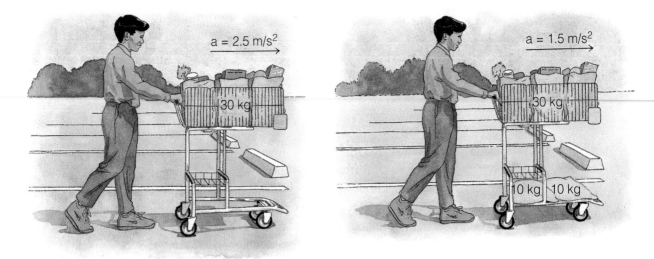

**Figure 3.10** ▲
What would have to happen for both carts to have the same acceleration?

## Force, Mass, and Acceleration

A direct relationship exists between force (f), mass (m), and acceleration (a). The boy in Figure 3.10 applies the same amount of force to both carts. Notice that each cart has a different acceleration. Because more mass was added to the cart on the right, it's acceleration is less.

A change in force also affects acceleration. Suppose the boy applies more force to the second cart. If the mass doesn't change, the acceleration of the cart will increase. If both carts have the same acceleration how much force must be added to the cart on the right?

Newton's second law can also be applied to the amount of gas needed to accelerate a car. A car with a large amount of mass requires a large force to accelerate. Since this force is supplied by gas, a large car requires more gas to accelerate than a small one does.

## Graphing Acceleration

Graphs can help you understand relationships between force and acceleration and between mass and acceleration. Look at the graph in Figure 3.11. The graph shows the relationship between force and acceleration during a dog-sled race. Notice that as the force the dogs apply to the sled increases, the acceleration of the sled also increases. In most dog-sled races, more than one dog pulls a sled. How would each dog affect the acceleration of the sled?

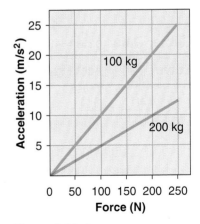

**Figure 3.11** ▲
How does the acceleration of the 200 kg sled compare to the acceleration of the 100 kg sled?

The graph also shows the effect of force and mass on acceleration. One sled has a load with a 100-kg mass. The load on the other sled has a mass of 200 kg. Compare the slope of the two curves. How does mass affect the acceleration of each sled?

## Using Newton's Second Law

Imagine that you are trying to push a stalled car. Your friends come to help. Your force, plus that of your friends, causes the car to move. As you apply more force, the car accelerates. However, if people get into the car, the total mass of the car increases, and the car slows down.

Even without doing calculations, Newton's second law helps you understand how force, mass, and acceleration are related. Recall Newton's formula for the second law of motion.

$$\text{force} = \text{mass} \times \text{acceleration}$$

$$\text{acceleration} = \frac{\text{force}}{\text{mass}}$$

## Sample Problem

A dog has a mass of 20 kg. If the dog is pushed across the ice with a force of 40 N, what is its acceleration?

**Plan** Use Newton's second law to find the acceleration.

$$\text{force} = \text{mass} \times \text{acceleration}$$

**Gather Data** force = 40 N    mass = 20 kg

**Solve** $\dfrac{\text{force}}{\text{mass}} = \text{acceleration}$

$$\frac{40 \text{ N}}{20 \text{ kg}} = \frac{2 \text{ N}}{\text{kg}}$$

Since 1 N is the amount of force that accelerates a 1–kg mass by 1 m/s$^2$,

$1 \text{ N} = 1 \text{ kg} \times 1 \text{ m/s}^2$. Therefore,

$1 \text{ m/s}^2 = 1 \text{ N}/1 \text{ kg} = 1 \text{ N/kg}$

The unit m/s$^2$ equals the unit N/kg, so acceleration of the dog is 2 m/s$^2$.

## Practice Problems

1.  Suppose a student pushes a cart of groceries with a 40-kg mass. How much force does he use if the cart accelerates 2.5 m/s$^2$? What units are used in the answer? Show how to convert to those units in your calculation.

2.  A bag of charcoal has a mass of 10 kg. Two bags were added to the cart of groceries mentioned in problem 1. If the student pushes with a force of 90 N, what is the acceleration of the cart? Show how to convert to the correct units in your calculation.

3.  If the acceleration of the cart with the added mass of the two bags of charcoal is increased to 2.5 m/s$^2$, how much additional force must be applied to the cart? Show how to convert to the correct units in your calculation.

## Momentum

A rolling marble can be stopped more easily than a bowling ball moving at the same velocity. Both objects have inertia of motion, or **momentum**. However, the bowling ball has more momentum than the marble. The momentum of a moving object is related to its mass and velocity. A moving object has a large momentum if it has a large mass, a large velocity, or both. The formula for momentum is

$$\textbf{momentum} = \textbf{mass} \times \textbf{velocity}$$

Momentum doesn't change unless the velocity or mass changes. However, momentum can transfer from one object to another. For example, when a ball rolling across a pool table hits another ball, the momentum of the first ball transfers to the second ball. Maintaining and transferring momentum is called *the law of the conservation of momentum.*

## Consider This

### Should Seat Belts and Air Bags Be Required?

Insurance companies and lawmakers are working hard to increase the use of seat belts and to require air bags in new cars. Most states already require seat belts to be worn.

**Consider Some Issues** When a moving car stops quickly, the passengers move forward toward the windshield. Seat belts change the forces of motion and prevent the passenger from moving.

During an accident, air bags fill the space between the passenger and the windshield. Air bags dissipate energy over a longer time than seatbelts.

When the time of impact is increased, the acceleration of the passenger is decreased. Thus the chance of injury is greatly reduced.

For some people, seat belts are inconvenient or uncomfortable. They feel seat belt laws interfere with their freedom of choice. These people believe that if they drive safely, seat belts are unnecessary.

While air bags increase the cost of new cars, consumers have been willing to absorb the additional cost.

**Think About It** Does the risk of personal injury outweigh the inconvenience of using seat belts and the cost increase of air bags?

**Write About It** Write a paper stating your position on the use of seat belts and air bags.

## Forces in Circular Motion

You learned that an object moving in a circle has centripetal acceleration. If you twirl an eraser on a string, the tension on the string pulls the eraser toward the center, causing a continuous change in direction. The inward tension on the string is *centripetal force*. Centripetal force is any force that causes an object to follow a circular path. Look at Figure 3.12. How does centripetal force apply to the cars to keep them moving around a curved track?

**Figure 3.12
Centripetal Force** ▼

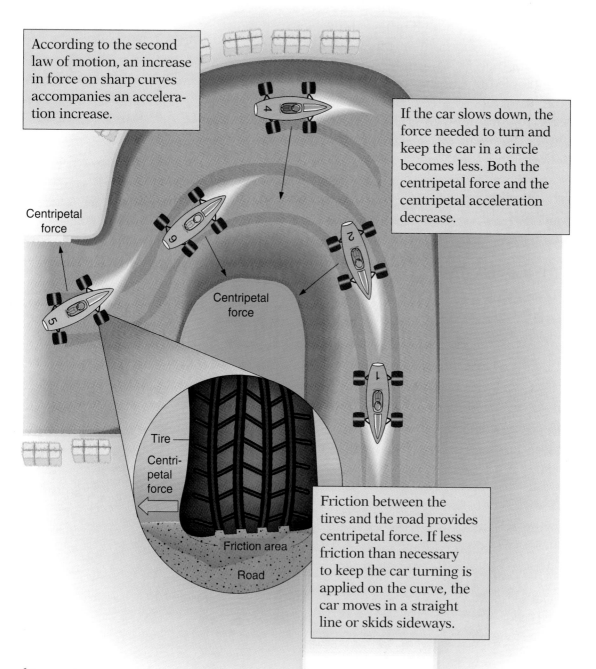

According to the second law of motion, an increase in force on sharp curves accompanies an acceleration increase.

If the car slows down, the force needed to turn and keep the car in a circle becomes less. Both the centripetal force and the centripetal acceleration decrease.

Centripetal force

Centripetal force

Tire

Centripetal force

Friction area

Road

Friction between the tires and the road provides centripetal force. If less friction than necessary to keep the car turning is applied on the curve, the car moves in a straight line or skids sideways.

**Science and Society** *More Miles for the Size*

When gasoline cost less than fifty cents a gallon, many people had large cars that got low gas mileage. Some people liked the feel of a large car on the road. Others thought large cars were more comfortable and luxurious.

When the price of gasoline suddenly increased in the 1970s, people began calling the large cars "gas guzzlers." Small cars became more economical and more practical. Soon there were fewer large cars on the highways. Why would the size of the car affect gas mileage?

Gas mileage is the number of kilometers a car travels for each liter of gasoline the engine uses. The second law of motion explains why a large car uses more gasoline than a small one. Consider how much force is needed for a car with a mass of 1,000 kg to accelerate 3 m/s². You know that force is equal to mass times acceleration; therefore, 1,000 kg × 3 m/s² = 3,000 N. How does this compare with the force needed for an 800-kg car? It takes more energy to move a car with a mass of 1,000 kg than it does to move one with a mass of 800 kg.

Gasoline is used much faster in the larger car. Gasoline is made from oil, which is being used at a rapid rate. It makes sense to conserve oil resources. In addition, gasoline exhaust causes air pollution. Driving a car with better gas mileage benefits air quality.

Efforts are being made to develop cars that use other types of fuel, such as alcohol and solar power. The resources for these fuels are renewable. For example, plant fiber is used to make alcohol that is suitable for automobile engines. Solar-powered cars are practical in areas that have the most exposure to the sun.

## Check and Explain

1. How does a change in the force applied to an object affect its acceleration?

2. If an eagle and a bumble bee are both traveling at 16 km/hr, which has more momentum? Explain.

3. **Calculate** A 28-kg meteor hits the surface of the moon at 130 km/s. What is the meteor's momentum?

4. **Make a Model** Develop a model to illustrate the force needed to keep an object moving in a circle.

*Balloon Moves*

Blow up a balloon. Hold the balloon with the opening downward and let go. In what direction does the balloon move? Blow up the balloon again. Hold the balloon horizontally. In what direction does the balloon move when you let go? Explain why both balloons don't move in the same direction.

**SKILLS WARMUP**

**Figure 3.13**
Look carefully at the photo. Where is the interaction of forces the greatest on the rockets? ▼

# 3.4 Third Law of Motion

## Objectives

▶ **Describe** Newton's third law of motion.

▶ **Distinguish** between balanced and unbalanced forces.

▶ **Predict** how forces interact in everyday situations.

▶ **Infer** how the third law of motion is applied.

Suppose you are watching the liftoff of a space shuttle. You hear a deafening roar and see burning gases shooting from the exhaust vents of the rockets. At that moment, the space-shuttle system moves slowly upward. You can infer from Figure 3.13 that the force for the liftoff comes from the burning gases pushing against the shuttle rockets. Why does the shuttle system move in the opposite direction of the gases?

## Equal and Opposite Forces

The forces on the space shuttle are similar to the forces in a collision between two tennis balls. When the balls collide, they are propelled in opposite directions. The rockets of the space shuttle force burning gases downward through the exhaust vents. In response to these downward forces, the shuttle system moves upward. The motion of the space shuttle demonstrates Newton's third law of motion.

> When one object exerts a force upon a second object, the second object exerts an equal and opposite force upon the first object.

An easy way to understand the third law of motion is to say that every action has an equal and opposite reaction. You can see equal and opposite forces interact when you blow up a balloon and then let it go. Air shoots out of the neck of the balloon as it moves in the opposite direction. The force propelling the balloon is equal and opposite to the force of the air leaving the balloon.

**Balanced and Unbalanced Forces**  Notice what happens in Figure 3.14 when the diver jumps down on a diving board. The board springs back and forces the diver into the air. The action force exerted on the board by the diver causes a reaction force by the board on the diver. The force of the diver on the board is equal and opposite to the force exerted by the diving board.

These interacting forces are unbalanced and differ from the forces you studied in Newton's first law. Recall that no acceleration occurs when the forces are balanced. If the diver stands quietly on the diving board, all the forces on the diver and the board are balanced. Neither the diver nor the board accelerates.

**Observing Newton's Third Law**  The crew team in Figure 3.15 uses Newton's third law of motion to move its boat. When an oar is put into the water, the water exerts an equal force on both sides of the oar. However, when the members pull on their oars, the surface of the flat side of the oars pushes against the water. The water pushes back on the oars with an equal and opposite force. The boat moves in the opposite direction of the oars with a force that is equal to that of the oars as they push against the water. The boat moves because the forces against it are unbalanced.

**Figure 3.14** ▲
How will the force of the diving board affect the diver's performance?

**Figure 3.15** ▲
Why do you think it's important for all the crew members to pull on their oars at the same time?

# Science and Technology
## *From Fireworks to Outer Space*

About 500 years before Newton, the Chinese were putting his third law of motion into practice. They were making rockets! The Chinese invented the rocket around A.D.1150.

Whenever you see a fireworks display, you see one of the first uses of rocket technology. The ancient Chinese developed fireworks for religious festivals. The bright lights and bursting sound were said to "make the devils jump." Beginning in the thirteenth century, the Chinese used rockets extensively. The rockets burned an explosive black powder that propelled them into the air.

All rockets require fuel that produces rapidly expanding gases. The gases exert a large amount of force against the inside of the rocket. The expanding gases escape out the back of the rocket. The force of the escaping gases thrusts the rocket forward. A large amount of thrust is needed to propel a rocket into space.

Rocket fuels became very important as space exploration and technology developed. Rockets burn fuel very rapidly. Liquid fuels that work well in automobile or ship engines are heavy and can't be used in space rockets. Also fuel needs oxygen to burn. There is no oxygen in outer space. Some rockets carry an oxygen supply into space. Modern space rockets also use solid fuels, which when mixed together, release oxygen and burn.

**Figure 3.16** ▲

The shape, color, and size of a fireworks display depends on the chemicals used to make them.

## Check and Explain

1. What is Newton's third law of motion?

2. Explain how unbalanced forces are important in a tennis game.

3. **Predict**   What are the action and reaction forces acting when someone jumps from a canoe to a riverbank? Explain why the jumper often falls into the water.

4. **Infer**   Explain how Newton's third law of motion is at work when you walk.

# 3.5 Universal Forces

## Objectives

▶ **Identify** the four universal forces.

▶ **Describe** how each universal force affects everyday experiences.

▶ **Generalize** on the importance of universal forces.

▶ **Classify** everyday forces according to the types of universal forces.

I f you travelled through the universe, you would experience many kinds of forces. On the most distant planets, you would be subjected to the same four forces that exist all around you on the earth. These four forces—gravitational, electromagnetic, strong and weak nuclear force—are called the **universal forces**. Table 3.1 compares the strength of the universal forces.

## Gravitational Force

Objects of any size are pulled toward each other by gravitational force. You don't notice the gravitational force between small objects because it is the weakest of the universal forces. The strength of gravitational force depends on the amount of mass in an object and the distance between objects. Planets, stars, and galaxies are so large that their gravitational force affects other objects in space.

Gravity keeps the planets in orbit around the sun and the stars in orbit in their galaxies. The gravitational force of the earth on the moon keeps the moon in its orbit around the earth. The gravitational force of the moon on the earth causes the ocean tides to rise and fall.

**Table 3.1   Universal Forces**

| Force | Relative Strength | Acts Upon |
|-------|-------------------|-----------|
| Gravitational | 1 | All matter |
| Weak nuclear | $10^{27}$ | Nucleus |
| Electromagnetic | $10^{38}$ | Charged particles |
| Strong nuclear | $10^{40}$ | Quarks |

◀ **Table 3.1**
Look at the difference between the electromagnetic force and the force of gravity. What would happen to objects on the earth if the force of gravity was as strong as the electromagnetic force?

# Gravity and the Solar System

Newton proposed that the sun exerts a gravitational force on the earth and its moon, as well as on all the other planets. Gravitational force keeps the earth and other objects in the solar system in orbit around the sun. Each planet moves in an elliptical orbit around the sun.

**Figure 3.17**
**The Planets in the Solar System** ▼

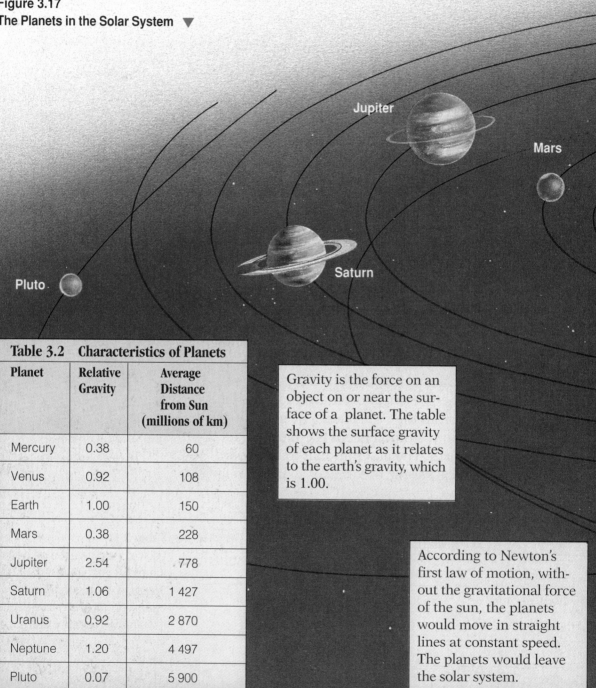

| Table 3.2 | Characteristics of Planets | |
|-----------|---------------------------|---|
| **Planet** | **Relative Gravity** | **Average Distance from Sun (millions of km)** |
| Mercury | 0.38 | 60 |
| Venus | 0.92 | 108 |
| Earth | 1.00 | 150 |
| Mars | 0.38 | 228 |
| Jupiter | 2.54 | 778 |
| Saturn | 1.06 | 1 427 |
| Uranus | 0.92 | 2 870 |
| Neptune | 1.20 | 4 497 |
| Pluto | 0.07 | 5 900 |

Gravity is the force on an object on or near the surface of a planet. The table shows the surface gravity of each planet as it relates to the earth's gravity, which is 1.00.

According to Newton's first law of motion, without the gravitational force of the sun, the planets would move in straight lines at constant speed. The planets would leave the solar system.

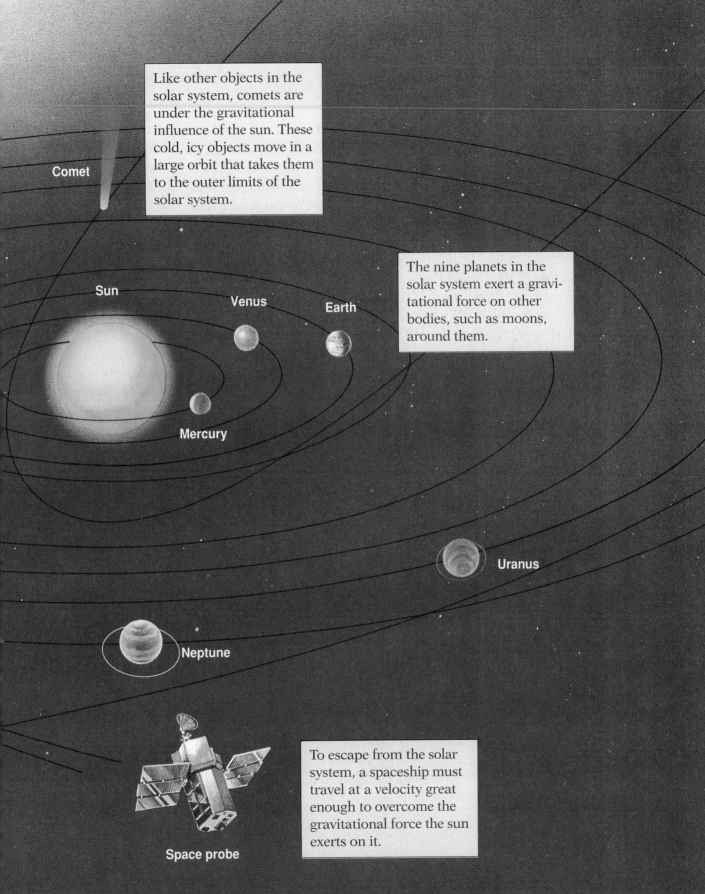

Comet

Like other objects in the solar system, comets are under the gravitational influence of the sun. These cold, icy objects move in a large orbit that takes them to the outer limits of the solar system.

Sun

Venus

Earth

The nine planets in the solar system exert a gravitational force on other bodies, such as moons, around them.

Mercury

Uranus

Neptune

To escape from the solar system, a spaceship must travel at a velocity great enough to overcome the gravitational force the sun exerts on it.

Space probe

**Law of Universal Gravitation** Newton's law of universal gravitation states that every object in the universe attracts every other object. For example, the earth's gravitational force on your body pulls you toward the ground. That's why you don't float in the air.

The gravitational force between two objects depends on the mass of each object and on the distance between them. If the mass of both objects is very small, the gravitational force between them is extremely small. For example, the gravitational force between two buildings is too small to measure. However, the gravitational force between the earth and the moon is easily measured, because both objects have a large amount of mass.

Gravitational force is also affected by distance. The gravitational force between your school and Neptune is too small to measure because Neptune is very far away. However, because the distance between a vase on a table and the earth is short, the gravitational force is large and can be measured.

**The Earth-Moon System** Newton realized the gravitational force that applies to objects on the earth also applies to the moon. He proposed that the moon travels around the earth because the earth pulls on the moon.

Newton also predicted that objects on the moon would weigh less than they do on the earth. Because the mass of the moon is one sixth the mass of the earth, Newton reasoned that the force of gravity on the moon would be less. The astronauts who visited the moon proved Newton's theory correct. If you weigh 490N on the earth, you weigh about one sixth of 490N, or 81.5N, on the moon.

The earth and the moon are affected by each other's gravitational force. As the moon orbits the earth, the moon pulls on the surface waters of the earth. The gravitational pull of the moon causes the ocean waters nearest the moon to bulge. You know these bulges as tides.

**Figure 3.18**

The combined gravitation force of the sun and the moon (top) produces large spring tides. Small neap tides (bottom) occur when the gravitational force of the moon and the earth is at right angles. ▼

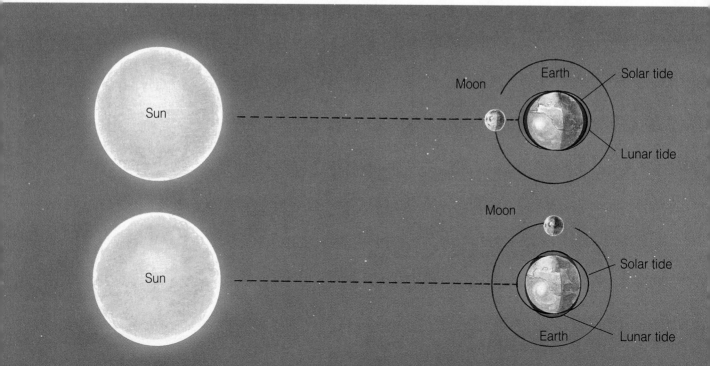

◀ **Figure 3.19**
The electric force not only lights this city, it also helped to build it. How is electricity used in construction?

## Electromagnetic Forces

Electromagnetic forces are really two different forces that are closely related—electric force and magnetic force. Both of these forces may attact or repel.

Electric force exists between charged particles. Objects with different charges attract each other, and objects with the same charge repel each other. The electric force is much stronger than the gravitational force.

You are constantly being affected by electric force. Electric force causes some objects to come together and others to stay apart. It holds together the particles that make up all matter—the foods you eat, the clothes you wear, and everything around you.

You can't actually see the strength of the electric force. You can only see what it does. Electric force causes static cling in your dryer. It creates lightning during a thunderstorm. The electric force creates electricity. Think of how electricity affects your daily life.

Magnetic force is similar to electric force. The magnetic force acts between two magnets. Magnetic force attracts or repels just as electric force attracts and repels.

You are probably familiar with the magnetic force. A magnet in a refrigerator door attracts the door toward the rest of the refrigerator. Very large magnets can lift an automobile. Magnets move the maglev train in Figure 3.20 along its track.

Magnetic force and electric force interact in motors and other devices. For example, carbon granules in the receiver of your telephone change the sound of your voice into electric signals. These electric signals travel through the wires from your home to that of your friend. A magnet in your friend's telephone receiver changes the electric signals back into the sound of your voice.

**Figure 3.20**
The magnets moving this train can be seen along the outer edges of the track. ▼

# Nuclear Forces

All matter is made of tiny particles called atoms. An atom is composed of electrons orbiting around a nucleus of protons and neutrons. Electric forces keep electrons in orbit around the nucleus. The forces that hold the particles in the nucleus together are **nuclear forces**.

One type of nuclear force is called the *strong force*. Protons and neutrons are made of even smaller particles called quarks. The strong force holds the nuclear particles together by holding the quarks together. The strong force exists over very short distances. When the nuclear strong force breaks, it releases a great amount of energy. The energy of this nuclear strong force can produce electricity, or it can produce a nuclear explosion.

The other type of nuclear force is the *weak force*. The weak force holds together the particles within neutrons and protons. In neutrons, the weak force is easily overcome, and the neutrons decay to form new atoms. Nuclei that decay in this way are called radioactive. Measurement of radioactive decay is used to reveal the age of ancient artifacts, such as the one shown in Figure 3.21. Some kinds of nuclear decay release harmful radiation that can affect people and the environment. Safe, permanent disposal of radioactive materials is a worldwide problem.

**Figure 3.21** ▲
With special equipment, the scientist is able to determine the amount of radioactive elements in the Ice-age carving. A formula applied to his results will reveal the age of the carving.

**Figure 3.22** ▶
Burying radioactive materials in pits like this one is a temporary means of disposal.

## Science and Technology
### *Reading Your Heartbeat*

The cells of your nervous system carry nerve impulses. These impulses pass through nerve cells as an electric charge. Usually electric activity is measured with an electric meter. Perhaps you have watched someone use such a meter to test the electric charge in a battery.

Electric activity in your body can be measured in a similar way. Your heartbeats begin with an electric impulse passing through the heart's muscle cells. The electric current generated in the heart spreads throughout your body. When a machine called an electrocardiograph is attached to your skin, the electric current can be picked up and recorded.

The graph in Figure 3.23 is called an electrocardiogram, or EKG reading. EKG readings have three distinct waves. Each wave shows electric activity increasing then decreasing in different parts of the heart. Doctors use EKG readings to detect abnormal heartbeats.

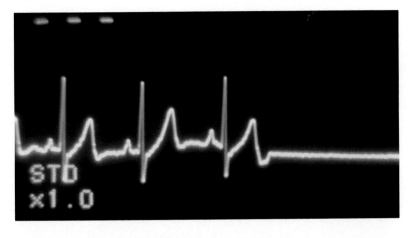

◀ **Figure 3.23**
The top of the wave on the electrocardiogram indicates when the heart muscle contracts. What area indicates that the heart muscle is at rest?

## Check and Explain

1. Name the four universal forces.

2. Explain how each universal force might apply when you warm food in an oven.

3. **Generalize**  State why the gravitational force is important to every object in the universe.

4. **Classify**  List the activities taking place in your classroom. Classify each activity according to the universal force that applies to it.

# Activity 3 Do heavier objects fall faster than lighter objects?

**Skills** Predict; Observe; Infer

## Task 1 Prelab Prep
1. Collect the following items: 2 metal or wood grooved ramps of equal length, clay, ruler, steel ball and aluminum ball with the same diameter, and 2 books.
2. Determine which ball has more mass.

## Task 2 Data Record
1. On a separate sheet of paper, draw the data table shown.
2. Predict which ball will take the least amount of time to roll down one of the ramps. Record your prediction.
3. Record your observations about the speed of the two balls in the data table.

### Table 3.3 Trial Observations

| Ramp A Trial | Which ball reaches bottom first? | |
| --- | --- | --- |
| | Prediction | Actual |
| 1 | | |
| 2 | | |
| 3 | | |

| Ramp B Trial | | |
| --- | --- | --- |
| 1 | | |
| 2 | | |
| 3 | | |

## Task 3 Procedure
1. Set up the two ramps, *A* and *B*, side-by-side. Raise one end of each ramp 5 cm. Support the raised end with a book.
2. With the clay, make a stop at the bottom of each ramp.
3. Place one ball at the top of each ramp. Hold the balls in place with the ruler.
4. Release the balls at the same time by quickly raising the ruler. Listen for the sound of the metal balls striking the clay stop. In your data table, record which ball reached the bottom first.
5. Repeat steps 2 and 3 two more times. Record your results.
6. Reverse the balls used on each of the ramps in order to control for differences in your ramps. Repeat steps 2 and 3 three times. Record your results.

## Task 4 Analysis
1. Does one ball consistently reach the end of the ramp before the other ball? If so, which one?
2. Which ball has more mass?
3. Identify the variables in this activity.
4. Why was it important to release each of the balls on both ramps?
5. What forces act on the balls as they roll down the ramp?

## Task 5 Conclusion
Write a short paragraph explaining what happens when objects of different masses fall at the same time.

## Everyday Application
Suppose you want to move some very heavy boxes and some lightweight boxes down a ramp. Explain how this activity might help you to decide which boxes to move down the ramp.

## Extension
If you dropped a table-tennis ball and a steel ball from 3 m above the floor, would there be a difference in their falling time? Try it. Explain your observations.

# Chapter 3 Review

## Concept Summary

### 3.1 Forces, Motion, and Gravity
▶ Forces give energy to an object.
▶ Gravity determines weight.
▶ The SI unit for force is the newton.
▶ Friction is a force that opposes motion.

### 3.2 First Law of Motion
▶ Newton's first law of motion states an object at rest stays at rest and an object in motion stays in motion unless acted on by an outside force.
▶ The inertia of a resting or moving object can be overcome by an outside force.
▶ The types of friction include sliding, rolling, and fluid friction.

### 3.3 Second Law of Motion
▶ Newton's second law of motion states that force equals mass times acceleration.

▶ The acceleration of an object is directly affected by any change in its mass or in the force applied to it.

### 3.4 Third Law of Motion
▶ Newton's third law of motion states that for every action exerted on an object an equal and opposite reaction results.
▶ When the forces on an object are unbalanced, motion occurs.

### 3.5 Universal Forces
▶ The four universal forces are gravity, electric, magnetic, and nuclear.
▶ Gravitational force is the attraction between objects in the universe.
▶ Electric force and magnetic force depends on the charges of objects.

## Chapter Vocabulary

| | | | |
|---|---|---|---|
| force (3.1) | friction (3.1) | inertia (3.2) | universal forces (3.5) |
| newton (3.1) | terminal velocity (3.1) | momentum (3.3) | nuclear forces (3.5) |

## Check Your Vocabulary

Use the vocabulary words above to complete the following sentences correctly.

1. The force that opposes motion is ___ .
2. When the upward and downward forces on a falling object are equal, the object reaches ___ .
3. When your body is at rest, you have ___ .
4. A push or pull that starts or stops the motion of an object or changes its direction is called a(n) ___ .
5. Gravitation, electric, magnetic, and strong and weak nuclear forces are ___ .
6. The forces that hold together the particles in the nucleus of an atom are called ___ .
7. The SI unit for force is ___ .

Identify the word or term in each group that does not belong. Explain why it does not belong with the group.

8. universal force, magnetic force, gravitational force
9. weak force, strong force, sliding force
10. electric, magnetic, centripetal
11. sliding, rolling, momentum
12. terminal velocity, constant acceleration, friction

## Write Your Vocabulary

Write sentences using the vocabulary words above. Show that you know what each word means.

# Chapter 3 Review

## Check Your Knowledge

Answer the following in complete sentences.

1. What is terminal velocity?

2. Calculate the acceleration of a 70-kg mass on a swing if you push it with a 40-N force.

3. How does the force of gravity from the moon affect the earth?

4. What is centripetal force?

5. How is gravity related to the weight of an object?

6. What causes a ball to follow a curved path when you throw it?

7. List three different kinds of force you use when you ride your bike.

Determine whether each statement is true or false. Write *true* if it is true. If it is false, change the underlined word to make the statement true.

8. According to the second law of motion, force is equal to mass times <u>speed</u>.

9. The forces that hold the <u>atom</u> together are the nuclear forces.

10. Newton's <u>third</u> law of motion could be called the law of inertia.

11. According to Newton's second law, acceleration <u>decreases</u> as mass increases.

12. <u>Momentum</u> can transfer from one object to another object.

13. The electric force and the <u>magnetic</u> force are both a result of charged particles.

14. The acceleration of the earth's gravity is <u>9.8m/s²</u>.

## Check Your Understanding

Apply the concepts you have learned to answer each question.

1. Why do objects fall toward the surface of the earth?

2. Predict how a toy car moving over sandpaper will accelerate compared to the same car moving over marble? Explain the reason for your prediction.

3. Explain how the acceleration of a mass changes if the force applied to it increases or decreases.

4. What would happen if the chair you are sitting on disappeared? Explain.

5. Calculate the momentum of a 5-kg fish swimming at 400 m/hr. Which would have more momentum: a 5-kg fish swimming at 400 m/hr or a 25-kg fish at rest?

6. Give an example of each type of friction: sliding friction, rolling friction, and fluid friction.

7. **Application**   A handball is hit hard against a concrete wall. Use Newton's third law of motion to explain what happens and why.

8. In what way are electric force and magnetic force similar?

9. **Application**   If the surface gravity of Jupiter is 2.54, Earth 1.00, Pluto 0.23, and Saturn 1.06, which planet has the most mass? Explain your reasoning.

10. **Mystery Photo**   The curved lines of light in the photograph on page 54 are from a Ferris wheel moving in a circle. What force is acting on the Ferris wheel to keep it moving in a circle? What is the source of this force? If this force were removed, what would happen to the motion?

## Develop Your Skills

Use the skills you have developed in this chapter to complete each activity.

1. **Interpret Data**  The graph below shows data about four objects dropped to the ground from the same height at the same time.

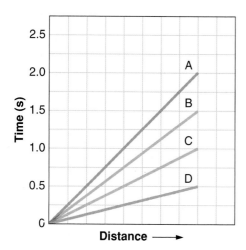

a. Which object fell fastest? Slowest?

b. Suppose object A and C have the same mass. Which object experiences the most fluid friction?

2. **Data Bank**  Use the information on page 636 to answer the following questions.

a. Imagine you jumped straight up on each of the solar-system bodies listed in the table. On which planet or moon would you jump the highest?

b. On which solar-system body would you jump the least distance?

c. Why does the distance you could jump vary with each planet?

3. **Design an Experiment**  There are many ways to reduce friction in moving parts, such as using oils, greases, air flow, water, and ball bearings. Design an experiment to test which friction-reducing method works best.

## Make Connections

1. **Link the Concepts**  Below is a concept map showing how some of the main concepts in this chapter link together. Only parts of the map are filled in. Copy the map. Using words and ideas from the chapter, complete the map.

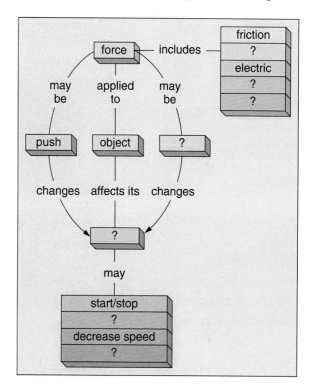

2. **Science and P.E.**  Identify the types of friction that take place during a softball game. Explain how each type of friction you identify applies to the softball game.

3. **Science and Art**  Using pictures from magazines, make a collage that illustrates Newton's third law of motion.

4. **Science and You**  Use your weight on the earth to determine your weight on the moon, on Jupiter, on Saturn, and on Pluto.

# Chapter 4    Forces in Fluids

## Chapter Sections

**4.1** Fluid Pressure

**4.2** Buoyancy

**4.3** Forces in Moving Fluids

## What do you see?

❝Water is going down the drain. It is moving like this because there is a hole in the sink and it is pulling the rest of the water. If I were in the middle of this, I would be pulled down the drain.❞

*Emily McCormick*
*Barnstable School*
*Hyannis, Massachusetts*

To find out more about the photograph, look on page 104. As you read this chapter, you will learn about forces at work in fluids.

# 4.1 Fluid Pressure

## Objectives

▶ **Define** pressure and explain how it is measured.

▶ **Identify** examples of fluid pressure.

▶ **Predict** the effects of fluid pressure in land and water environments.

**W**hat tools do you need to fix a flat tire on a bicycle? One of the tools you probably need is an air pump. By attaching the air pump to the tire stem, you form a passageway for air to flow into the tire. Air is a **fluid**. A fluid is any substance that can flow. People often think of fluids as liquids, such as water or oil. But a gas, like air, is also a fluid.

As you operate the air pump, the tire fills with air. You observe the tire expand and become firmer. How do you know when the tire has enough air? By squeezing the tire, you can judge the amount of air it contains. If the tire feels soft, you keep on pumping. If the tire feels too hard, you let out some air.

## Pressure

When you squeeze a bicycle tire, you feel an opposing force. The force comes from billions of air particles striking the inside of the tire. Look at Figure 4.1. The air particles inside the tire are in constant motion. As they move about, the air particles collide with the tire's walls. The force of all the collisions spreads over the tire's inner surface, pushing the wall of the tire outward.

A force exerted on a surface is called **pressure**. To calculate pressure, you divide the force by the area over which it is applied.

$$\text{pressure} = \frac{\text{force}}{\text{area}}$$

Remember force is measured in newtons. When you divide force (N) by area in square meters ($m^2$), you get an answer in units of newtons per square meter ($N/m^2$). The official SI unit of pressure, the pascal (Pa), is equal to $1\ N/m^2$.

**Figure 4.1**
Air particles pushing against the tire's inner surface produce pressure. What happens if you put too much air in the tire? ▶

## ▼ ACTIVITY

### Comparing

**Fluid Pressure**

Collect the following items: a milk carton, a pin, and tape.

**1.** Using the pin, make three small holes at different levels in the milk carton.

**2.** Tape the holes closed, and fill the carton with water.

**3.** Place the carton over a sink and remove the tape. Compare the flow of water from each hole.

### SKILLS WORKOUT

**Figure 4.2**
**Atmospheric Pressure** ▼

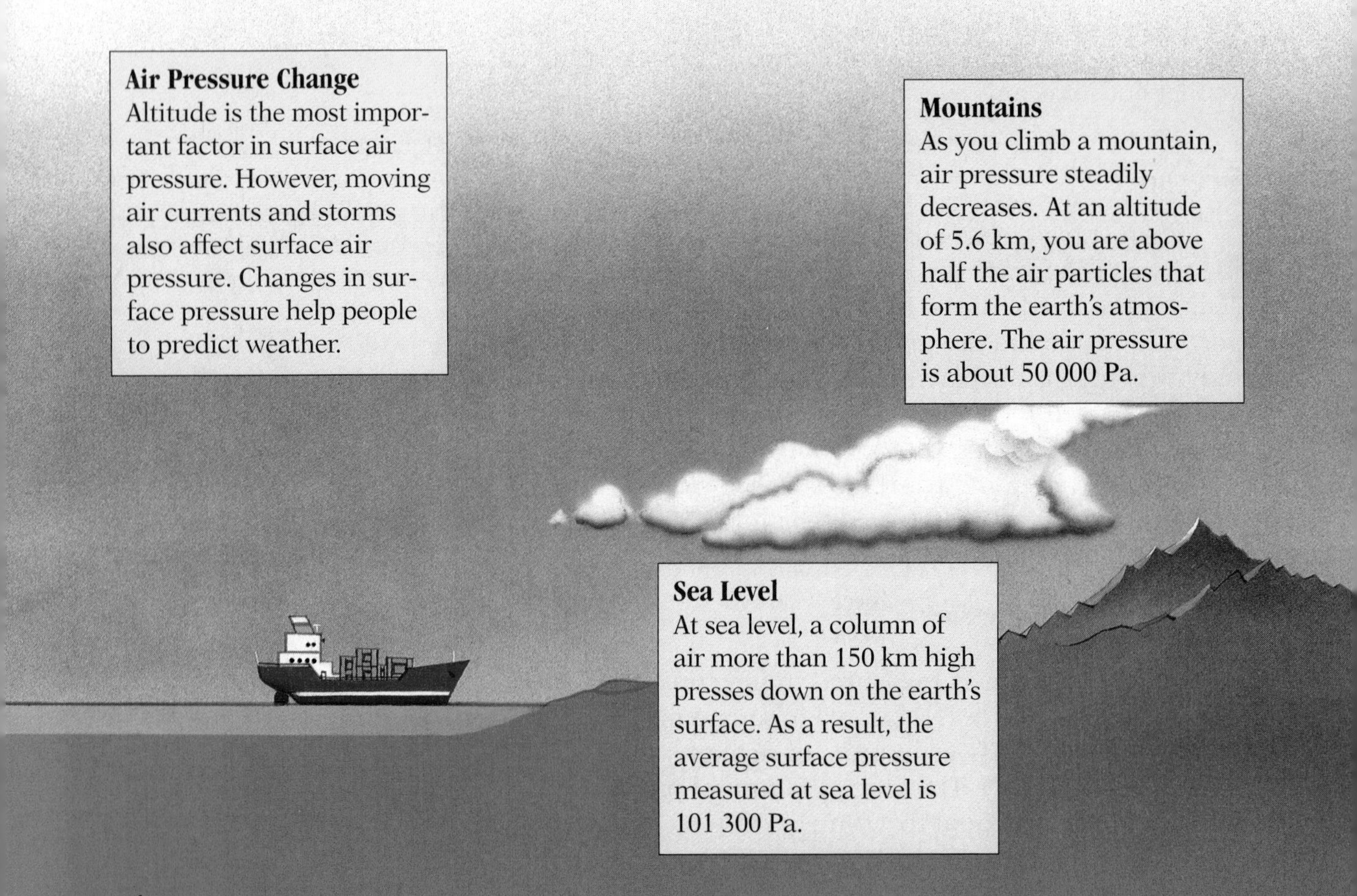

## Fluid Pressure in the Environment

Do you ever feel your ears "pop" when you ride in a plane or elevator? Or feel a sharp ear pain when you swim underwater? These experiences result from fluid pressure in the environment. Air and water are the most common fluids on the earth's surface. As you move up or down in air or water, the pressure around you changes. The change may be too small for you to notice. However, your eardrums sometimes detect small pressure changes.

**Pressure and the Atmosphere**   You live at the bottom of an ocean of air, the atmosphere. The air that makes up the earth's atmosphere is a mixture of gas particles. The gas particles are pulled toward the earth by the force of gravity. The weight of air causes atmospheric pressure.

Air exerts a downward force on the earth's surface. Over the earth's entire surface, the average pressure produced by the atmosphere is about 100 000 Pa. Look at Figure 4.2. It describes pressure conditions at different locations on or near the earth's surface.

**Air Pressure Change**
Altitude is the most important factor in surface air pressure. However, moving air currents and storms also affect surface air pressure. Changes in surface pressure help people to predict weather.

**Mountains**
As you climb a mountain, air pressure steadily decreases. At an altitude of 5.6 km, you are above half the air particles that form the earth's atmosphere. The air pressure is about 50 000 Pa.

**Sea Level**
At sea level, a column of air more than 150 km high presses down on the earth's surface. As a result, the average surface pressure measured at sea level is 101 300 Pa.

Imagine an area measuring one square meter (1 m$^2$). Such an area has about enough room for you and your school desk. Above you and your desk is a column of air about 150 km high. The force of the column of air pressing down on each square meter of the earth's surface is nearly equal to the weight of a school bus! Why aren't you crushed by this great force? Although you can't feel it, air pressure does push down on you. But the pressure of the fluids inside your body pushes on you with the same amount of force. The forces on your body are balanced.

If you travel upward in the air column, the air pressure around you changes. The air column above you gets shorter, and the air gets thinner. Since fewer gas particles are around you and above you, the air pressure is lower. Eventually, you rise to an altitude that has almost no air or other gas particles. The absence of matter is called a vacuum. Space is a near vacuum, which begins at an altitude of about 150 km above the earth's surface.

150 km

50 km

**Edge of Space**
At an altitude of 150 km, air contains so few gas particles that the pressure approaches zero. Beyond 150 km is space. Space contains about one hydrogen molecule per cubic centimeter.

**Ozone Layer**
A layer of ozone gas at an altitude of 20–50 km shields the earth against harmful ultraviolet radiation. The air pressure in the ozone layer is less than 100 Pa.

20 km

11 km

6 km

**Aircraft**
Jet aircraft travel at an altitude of 11 km. The air pressure there is only about 25 000 Pa. People can't survive breathing such thin air, so high-flying aircraft have pressurized cabins.

0 km

**Pressure and the Ocean** Suppose you take a trip beneath the ocean's surface. You bring along a pressure gauge to compare the water pressure at different depths. The drumlike membrane of a pressure gauge responds to pressure changes much as your eardrum does. As the pressure outside the container changes, the membrane moves. A dial attached to the membrane records the pressure in pascals.

Using your gauge, you observe that pressure at the water's surface is equal to about 100 000 Pa. Your gauge shows the air pressure at sea level. When you place your gauge 1 cm beneath the water's surface, you observe a pressure increase of about 100 Pa. As you go deeper into the water, the pressure increases. More particles of matter are above and around the gauge.

The particles that make up water are packed more closely together than the particles in air. Water is denser than air. So, water exerts more force per unit area than air does. How do you think the pressure will change as you go to the bottom?

**Figure 4.3**
**Water Pressure Beneath the Ocean** ▼

**Intertidal Zone**
Near shore, the water level changes with the tides. Organisms living here experience constant changes in water pressure. In one day, the pressure can vary as much as 200 000 Pa!

**Continental Shelf**
The shelf is a nearly level extension of the continent. The shelf is up to 200 m deep. Organisms living on the deepest part of the shelf must withstand water pressure of 2 million Pa.

If you continue to descend in the ocean, the water pressure builds rapidly. At a depth of about 10 m, your gauge indicates an increase of about 100 000 Pa. A water column 10 m high exerts as much pressure as all of the earth's atmosphere! The total pressure is equal to the air and water pressure combined. So, at 10 m, the pressure is about 200 000 Pa, twice the pressure at sea level.

Marine organisms, like those in Figure 4.3, have adapted to withstand the water pressure where they live. Most of these organisms have water-saturated tissues that enclose air spaces that aren't easily compressed. Deep-water organisms live at great pressures without being crushed, but they can't survive a trip to the low-pressure surface. What do you think happens to tissues of the fish?

The viperfish is one deep-water organism that can adjust to depths. During the day, it stays at depths of 1.5 km to 2.5 km where water pressure ranges from 15 to 25 million Pa. At night, it moves up to a depth of 500 meters to feed where prey is more plentiful and water pressure is about 5 million Pa.

## Oceanography
### L I N K

Collect the following items: an 8-oz milk carton, a half-gallon milk carton, scissors.

**1.** Make a hole in each milk carton about 2 cm from the bottom.

**2.** Working over a sink, cover the holes in each carton with one finger.

**3.** Have a partner fill each carton with water to about 5-cm deep.

**4.** Take your fingers away from the holes. Which stream goes farther? Explain.

### A C T I V I T Y

**Mid-ocean**
At depths of up to 1 km, the sea floor supports many kinds of organisms. They withstand a pressure of 10 million Pa.

**Trench**
The trenches are the deepest parts of the sea. At depths of more than 11 km, pressures exceed 100 million Pa. A variety of organisms are able to live in the deepest ocean.

0 km

6 km

**Figure 4.4** ▶
Follow the path of force through the brake system. What happens if there is a break in the fluid line?

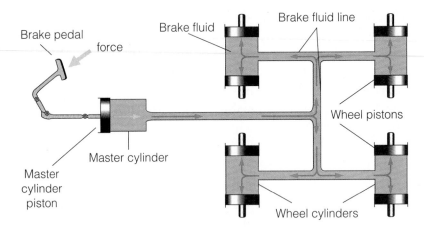

Brake pedal
force
Brake fluid
Brake fluid line
Master cylinder
Master cylinder piston
Wheel pistons
Wheel cylinders

## Science and Technology
*Putting on the Brakes*

A car's braking system uses fluid pressure to allow a driver to stop a moving car with just one foot! Study Figure 4.4. The driver puts on the brakes by applying a pushing force to the brake pedal. The brake pedal moves a metal rod attached to a piston. A piston is a "plug" that can slide snugly inside a cylinder, or tube. As the piston slides into the master cylinder, it presses on the fluid inside. Under pressure, the fluid exits the cylinder and flows into the brake line. The high-pressure fluid then moves evenly throughout the system.

The brake line connects the master cylinder to a smaller cylinder near the hub of each wheel. Pressurized fluid from the brake line enters each wheel cylinder through a small opening. Within each cylinder, the high-pressure fluid pushes against the pistons. The pistons move forcefully out of the cylinders, pushing a brake pad against the spinning car wheel. The friction between the brake pad and the wheel slows the car down.

## Check and Explain

1. What is fluid pressure?

2. Give two examples of fluid pressure.

3. **Reason and Conclude** An automobile tire has "200 kPa" written on its side. What does this mean?

4. **Predict** What changes in both air and water pressure occur on your body as you leap from a diving board?

# 4.2 Buoyancy

## Objectives

▶ **Explain** buoyant force.

▶ **Compare** and **contrast** density and buoyancy.

▶ **Predict** whether an object will float in water.

T hink about a hot air balloon. These colorful craft seem to float effortlessly through the skies. Why can they do this? You may have heard them described as being "lighter than air."

These balloons take advantage of the fact that hot air is less dense than cool air. The hot air balloon rises, carrying a basket filled with passengers up into the sky.

From what you learned about forces, you probably know that the rising motion of the balloon is caused by unbalanced forces. The air beneath the balloon exerts more force on it than the air above. When the balloon reaches an altitude where the forces are equal, it stops rising.

## Buoyant Force

What force makes an object float in air or in water? Look at the iceberg in Figure 4.5. Two forces act on the iceberg. The downward force is gravity. Recall that the force gravity exerts on an object is equal to the object's weight. The upward force acting on the iceberg is the **buoyant force**. The buoyant force opposes gravity.

If the weight of a submerged object is greater than the buoyant force, the object will sink. If the weight is equal to the buoyant force, the submerged object will remain at any level, like a fish does. If the weight is less than the buoyant force, the object will rise to the surface and float. Is the weight of the iceberg greater, the same, or less than its buoyant force?

To understand buoyant force, think about what happens to the water level in a glass when you add an ice cube. The ice pushes away, or displaces, some of the water. The weight of the water that is displaced is equal to the buoyant force. The greater the volume displaced, the

▼ **ACTIVITY**

| Predicting |

*Sink or Float?*

Collect the following items: a cup, an eraser, a pencil, a piece of paper, and a pushpin.

**1.** Predict whether each object will sink or float in water. Then test your predictions.

**2.** Fill the cup with water.

**3.** Place each object in the cup of water.

Were your predictions correct?

**SKILLS WARMUP**

Force of gravity

Buoyant force

**Figure 4.5** ▲
Why is most of the iceberg's mass under water?

**Figure 4.6** ▲

The volume of each of these three cubes is the same. Why is each cube at a different level in the water?

greater the buoyant force. The strength of the buoyant force depends upon the object's displaced volume.

Study the three examples in Figure 4.6. In one example, the buoyant force acting upon the block is greater than the downward force of gravity. These unbalanced forces result in an upward force that causes the block to float.

The second example shows the strength of the forces reversed. The block's weight is greater than the buoyant force. A downward force results, and the block sinks.

If the downward force of gravity equals the upward buoyant force, no movement occurs. The forces balance each other, as in the third example. The object is neutrally buoyant and remains at a fixed depth.

## Archimedes' Principle

More than 2,000 years ago, the Greek mathematician and inventor Archimedes observed a relationship between the buoyant force and the fluid displaced by an object. According to legend, when he stepped into his bathtub, he noticed that the water level rose. He later reasoned that the weight of the fluid displaced would be equal to the buoyant force. For example, if an object immersed in water displaces a volume of water that weighs 4.9 N, then a buoyant force of 4.9 N acts on the object.

Archimedes' principle applies to all fluids, including air. At sea level, one cubic meter ($1 \text{ m}^3$) of air has a weight of about 12 N. So, a balloon that occupies $1 \text{ m}^3$ has a buoyant force of 12 N acting upon it.

## Density and Buoyancy

To predict whether an object will sink or float, you need to consider its density. Recall that mass measures how much matter an object contains. To find the density of an object, you divide its mass by its volume. The density of a substance is one of its properties. The density of liquid water is 1 $g/cm^3$. The density of solid steel is 7.8 $g/cm^3$. Cooking oil's density is 0.82 $g/cm^3$. Balsa wood has a density of about 0.12 $g/cm^3$.

Any object with a density greater than 1 $g/cm^3$ will sink in water. For example, a steel bolt sinks because the bolt's density is greater than that of water. The weight of the steel is greater than the buoyant force of the water it displaces. But an object with a density less than 1 $g/cm^3$ will float in water. For example, a block of balsa wood floats because the wood's density is less than that of water. The buoyant force that the water exerts on the wood is greater than the wood's weight.

Buoyancy can also be observed between fluids of different densities. The density of cooking oil is less than the density of water. When you combine oil and water, the oil floats in a layer at the mixture's surface. You can see what happens when you combine substances with different densities in Figure 4.7. Which substance is the least dense? Which substance is the most dense?

**Figure 4.7**
**Density Differences** ▼

Balsa wood 0.12 $g/cm^3$

Ethyl alcohol 0.79 $g/cm^3$

Cooking oil 0.82 $g/cm^3$

Polyethylene plastic 0.92 $g/cm^3$

Colored water 1.0 $g/cm^3$

Neoprene® rubber 1.23 $g/cm^3$

Corn syrup 1.38 $g/cm^3$

Steel 7.8 $g/cm^3$

Balsa wood has the lowest density of all the substances, so it floats at the top. The other materials arrange themselves in order of density.

Liquids form layers. Each solid floats at the top of a denser liquid layer.

Steel and corn syrup have the highest densities. They rest on the bottom.

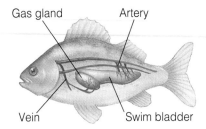

**Figure 4.8** ▲

How does its swim bladder help the fish rise or sink in the water?

Gas gland   Artery

Vein   Swim bladder

What can you say about objects that don't float? They are too dense. To float, you need to reduce an object's density. Since density is weight divided by volume, you can reduce the weight while keeping the volume the same. Or, you can increase the volume while keeping the weight the same. The purpose of a life jacket is to increase volume while adding very little to a person's weight.

Many types of bony fishes change the density of their bodies to help them rise and sink in their water environment. Look at the diagram of a bony fish in Figure 4.8. These fishes have a balloonlike organ, the swim bladder. An inflated swim bladder increases the fish's volume. This lowers the density of the fish's body relative to the surrounding water. So, the fish rises. To move downward, the fish increases the density of its body by deflating the swim bladder. A gas gland helps control the movement of gases between the fish's bloodstream and the swim bladder.

## *Historical Notebook*

### *Boat Design in Polynesia*

For thousands of years, the people of the South Pacific have built a special type of boat, an outrigger. The boat's main body, or hull, is long and narrow like a canoe. The hull usually attaches to one or two logs alongside. The crew sits within the hull and propels the boat using paddles like you would in a canoe.

Another Polynesian boat design consists of two hulls joined by a central platform. Sails are mounted on the central platform. The double-hulled design is very stable, so these boats can sail in strong winds. While sailing downwind, the long, narrow hulls rise in the water. The boat sails very fast because there is less hull surface in contact with the water. Ancient Polynesians used these double-hulled voyaging canoes to colonize islands in a vast area of the South Pacific. The Hawaiian Islands were colonized by these early explorers about 1000 A.D.

1. Compare an outrigger to a canoe. Explain how they are alike and how they are different.

2. Research the water routes traveled by the ancient Polynesians. Make a map of their travels across the Pacific.

3. Make models of an outrigger and a double-hulled voyaging canoe. Locate and identify the forces acting on each boat.

## Science and Technology
*Making Steel Float*

What happens when you drop a steel nail into water? The nail sinks. The density of steel is greater than the density of water. So why does a steel ocean liner float?

Ship designers know that flotation depends upon the craft's average density. Both the steel hull and the air trapped in the hull must be considered. A ship with a large volume of trapped air has an average density less than the density of water. As a result, the heavy steel ship floats easily.

The density difference between a craft and water can vary. Look at the ships in Figure 4.9. If the density difference is large, the craft extends high above the water's surface like the ship on the right does. A high-floating craft tends to rock and is easily capsized. The rocking motion can make the passengers seasick. If the density difference is small, the hull may not extend very far above the surface. High waves are likely to swamp the craft.

**Figure 4.9** ▲
Why is the ship on the right higher in the water than the ship on the left?

A submarine is designed to have nearly the same density as ocean water. When special tanks, called ballast tanks, fill with ocean water, the weight of the submarine increases. The submarine's average density increases also, so the craft sinks. When air replaces the ocean water in the ballast tanks, the submarine's density decreases, and the submarine rises.

## Check and Explain

1. Describe the forces acting on a floating object.

2. What is Archimedes' principle?

3. **Compare and Contrast** How are density and buoyancy similar? How are they different?

4. **Predict** Which items will float in water: canoe, flower petal, brick, or roller skate? Explain.

# *Activity 4*  *How can you control an object's buoyancy?*

***Skills*** Observe; Infer

## Task 1  Prelab Prep
Collect the following: a glass dropper, 1-L plastic soda bottle with a screw cap, and water.

## Task 2  Data Record
1. Draw two outlines of a dropper.
2. Label the first outline *Dropper Before Squeeze*. Label the second outline *Dropper After Squeeze*.
3. Record your observations about the dropper next to your drawings.

## Task 3  Procedure
1. Add water to the soda bottle almost up to the bottle's neck.
2. Fill the dropper about halfway with water. Gently place the dropper into the soda bottle.
3. If the dropper sinks, remove it from the bottle. Empty some of the water from the dropper. Repeat steps 1 and 2 until the dropper just floats at the water's surface, as shown in the figure below.

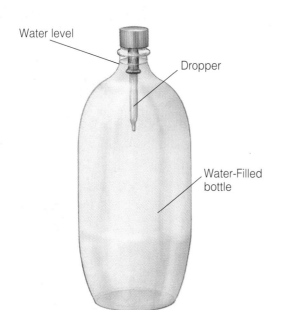

Water level

Dropper

Water-Filled bottle

4. Carefully fill the soda bottle to the top with water.
5. Screw on the cap tightly. Be careful to trap as little air as possible.
6. Squeeze the body of the soda bottle. Observe what happens to the dropper. Release your grip and observe the dropper.
7. Using the drawings created in the Data Record, draw the size of the air bubble in the dropper before you squeezed the bottle.
8. Draw the size of the dropper's air bubble after you squeezed the bottle.
9. Record your observations next to each of the outlines.

## Task 4  Analysis
1. What happened to the dropper when you squeezed the bottle?
2. How did the air bubble trapped inside the dropper change when the container was squeezed?
3. What happened to the dropper when you released your grip?

## Task 5  Conclusion
Explain how the forces applied to the bottle and the air bubble in the dropper controlled the dropper's buoyancy.

### *Extension*
Repeat this activity. This time screw on the container cap without filling the bottle to the top. How does this affect the behavior of the dropper? Explain your observations.

### *Everyday Application*
Get your parent's permission to carefully remove the lid to the tank behind your toilet. You will see a rubber float about the size of a softball. Push this float under water and observe what happens. What is the float's function?

# 4.3 Forces in Moving Fluids

## Objectives

▶ **Describe** Bernoulli's principle.

▶ **Explain** how airplanes and birds fly.

▶ **Generalize** about things that fly.

▶ **Infer** how an object's shape affects its movement through a fluid.

Imagine flying an airplane! As the plane moves through the sky, what holds it up? You know that as you fly the plane, you must make sure that it maintains a certain speed. You know that if the plane slows down or stalls, it can't stay up. Somehow the speed of the plane is connected to the force that keeps the plane in the air.

Your airplane moves through a fluid, air. Its motion through the fluid creates unbalanced forces. As the plane moves, air rushes over and under the wings. The plane's wings create forces that hold it up.

## Pressure Differences in Moving Fluids

Look at the student blowing across the top of a sheet of paper in Figure 4.10. Just as the force of moving air keeps a plane in the sky, the paper rises due to the force of the moving air created by the blowing action.

When a fluid moves, its pressure drops. As the student blows across the paper, he creates a low-pressure region above it. The air beneath the paper is not affected by the blowing. Its pressure remains the same. The pressure is greater on the bottom of the paper. The unbalanced pressures produce an upward force on the paper. When the boy stops blowing, the air above the paper returns to its original pressure. The pressure on both sides of the paper is the same, so it sinks.

In the 1700s, Swiss scientist Daniel Bernoulli studied the relationship between moving fluids and pressure. He observed that as the speed of a fluid increases, the pressure in the fluid decreases. This concept is called Bernoulli's principle.

**Figure 4.10**
Blowing across the paper creates a low pressure area above it. Why does the paper rise upward? ▼

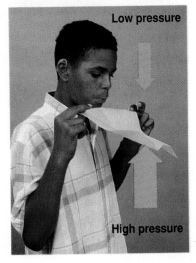

Low pressure

High pressure

# Using Pressure Differences for Flight

Notice the special shape of the cross section of an airplane wing in Figure 4.11. This shape is called an **airfoil**. An airfoil has a curved upper surface and a relatively flat-bottom surface.

An airfoil's design uses Bernoulli's principle. As air moves past an airfoil, the airfoil's shape creates a pressure difference. The air that moves over the upper curved surface has farther to travel. So, air moving over the upper surface must move faster than air moving across the lower surface to reach the back edge of the wing at the same time. As a result, a low-pressure area is created on the wing's upper surface.

The difference between the pressure on the airfoil's upper and lower surfaces results in an upward force, called **lift**. When the lift is greater than the plane's weight, the plane rises. When the lift is less than the plane's weight, the plane sinks. When the lift and the plane's weight are equal, the plane levels off.

Both propellers and jet engines produce a force that moves the plane and its airfoil-shaped wings forward. The force that pushes the plane forward is

**Figure 4.11**
**How an Airplane Flies** ▼

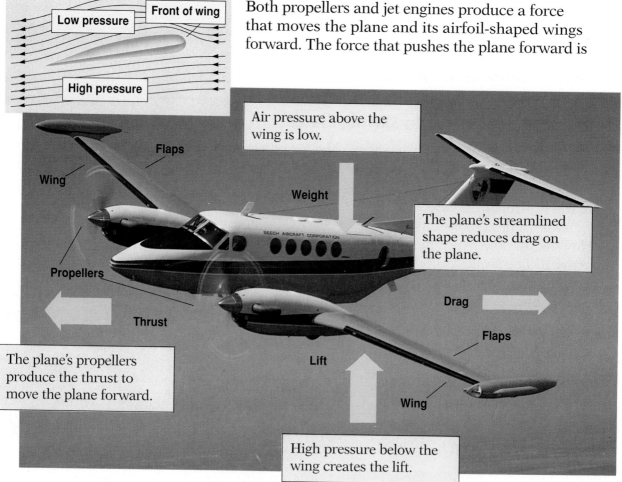

Low pressure

Front of wing

High pressure

Air pressure above the wing is low.

Flaps

Wing

Weight

The plane's streamlined shape reduces drag on the plane.

Propellers

BEECH AIRCRAFT CORPORATION

Drag

Thrust

Flaps

The plane's propellers produce the thrust to move the plane forward.

Lift

Wing

High pressure below the wing creates the lift.

called **thrust**. The shape and movement of the propeller blades produce thrust. As the blades spin, they create a low-pressure region in front of the propeller and a high-pressure region behind it. Like the pressure difference that creates lift, this pressure difference produces a directional force. In this case, the force pushes the plane forward. Jet engines take in air, compress it, and then forcefully expel the heated air to produce thrust.

The forward motion of an aircraft is slowed by an opposing force called **drag**. Like friction, drag opposes the movement of objects. Disturbances in the flow of air or other fluids increase drag. By designing streamlined aircraft, drag is reduced.

Before landing, the pilot lowers the aircraft's hinged wing parts called the flaps. As the flaps drop, the shape of the wings changes. The drag and lift of the wings change. By changing the wings' characteristics, the pilot can control the plane's speed and direction.

## *SkillBuilder* *Making a Model*

### *Paper Airplane Design*

Paper airplanes must develop lift to stay aloft. To extend their time aloft, paper airplanes also need a streamlined shape that produces little drag.

Make a paper airplane following the design shown. Copy the table below. To test for lift, launch your airplane. Measure the distance it traveled. Record the distance in your table. Decide how to alter your plane to increase the lift. Make adjustments to your plane. Test for lift and record the distance. Continue to adjust, launch, and record distances for two more trials. Answer the questions below about your airplane.

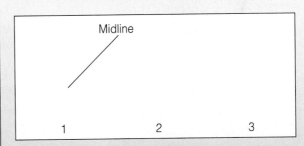

1. Which adjustment most affected the lift of your plane?

2. Discuss how you could adjust your plane to increase drag.

3. Draw your plane and label the forces affecting your plane when it flies.

4. Compare the forces of gravity and lift affecting your plane.

**Testing for Lift on a Paper Airplane**

| Trial | Adjustment | Distance Flown (m) |
|-------|-----------|--------------------|
| 1 | | |
| 2 | | |
| 3 | | |

# Bird Flight

Have you ever held a bird? If so, maybe you discovered how little the bird weighed. Low body weight is an important adaptation for flight. If you examine a bird's skeleton, you will discover that many bones aren't solid! Although they are long and sturdy, bird bones have pockets of air to make them light.

Feathers are another important adaptation for flight. Feathers are lightweight and stiff. Firmly attached to the skin, these structures form a streamlined body covering, which can withstand the stresses of flight.

Like the wing of an airplane, a bird's wing is an airfoil. Look at Figure 4.12. The wing has a curved upper surface and a flat underside. Air passing over and under the bird's wing creates the lift.

The wings of a bird can also produce thrust. A bird can flap its wings when flying. During each flap, the wing tips twist and push air behind the bird propelling the bird forward. Birds such as hawks, hummingbirds, and gulls use lift and thrust to produce distinctive flying patterns.

**Figure 4.12** ▼
How is the way a bird flies similar to the way a plane flies? How is it different?

**Hawks** Hawks are adapted for soaring flight. These birds need to use very little effort to remain aloft. They just extend their large wings and glide on the lift produced by passing air currents.

Hawks often fly in a circular path. As shown in Figure 4.13, they circle within a rising column of warm air, a thermal. By staying in a thermal, the birds rise without flapping their wings. They take advantage of the warm air moving upward. Only when they leave the thermal, do they flap their wings.

**Figure 4.13** ▲
How does soaring help hawks and other soaring birds catch their prey?

Hawks are adapted for flying in moving air currents. A hawk's broad wing presents a large lift surface to the passing air. Feathers at the end of the hawk's wing tips spread out in a fingerlike pattern. Because this arrangement reduces drag, less effort is needed for staying aloft. To change directions, the hawk twists some of the extended feathers, changing its wing shape.

**Hummingbirds** Look at Figure 4.14. The hummingbird has a unique flying style. With wing movements too rapid to see, this tiny bird can dart in any direction. Like a helicopter, it can remain stationary over a fixed point. The hummingbird can even fly backward!

The hummingbird's wings and body are adapted for flapping flight. Powerful muscles flap the wings back and forth at a rate of nearly 100 times per second. The rapid movement produces the humming sound from which these birds get their name. A hummingbird can easily twist its short, triangular wings to propel itself in any direction.

To maintain such a high flapping rate, a hummingbird's muscles need a large energy supply. To meet this demand, hummingbirds feed on flower nectar, a concentrated sugar solution.

**Figure 4.14**
The rapid movement of a hummingbird's wings allows it to stay aloft without the lift generated by forward thrust. ▼

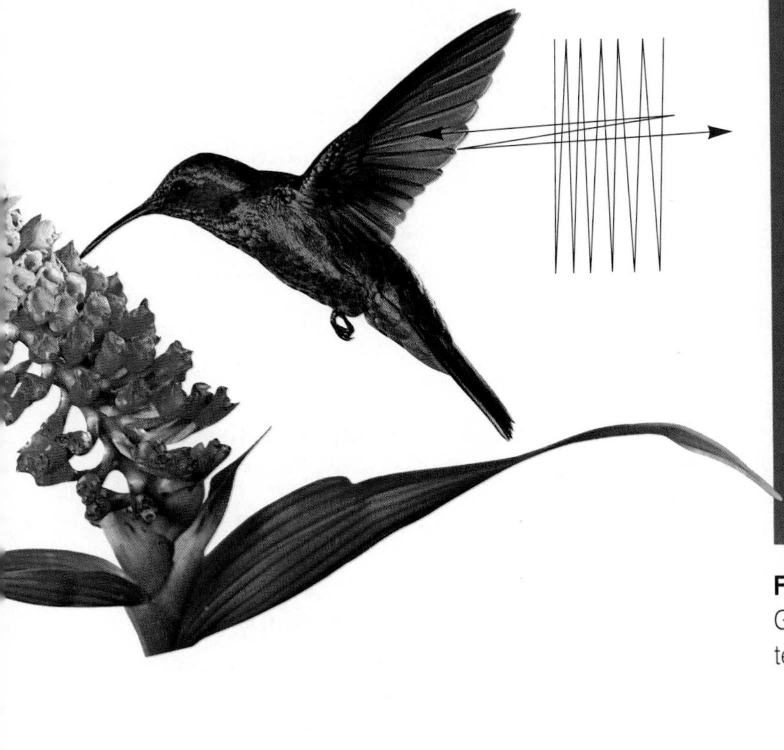

**Gulls** The wings and body of a gull are adapted for flight that is a combination of gliding and flapping. Figure 4.15 shows the gull's flying pattern.

On a windless day, a gull uses its powerful flight muscles to flap its wings. The flapping produces thrust, which propels the bird forward. Air passing over the extended wings produces lift to raise the bird high in the air.

On a windy day, a gull uses updrafts and stays aloft with little effort. The gull simply extends its long, slender, pointed wings. Like the narrow wings of a glider, the gull's outstretched wings generate lift from the passing air. The streamlined wings cut through the air with very little drag. If the wind blows fast enough, the gull can remain motionless over the ground without flapping its wings. Once out of the updraft, however, the gull must flap its wings to stay aloft.

**Figure 4.15** ▲
Gulls are known to range over thousands of kilometers. How does their flying style make this possible?

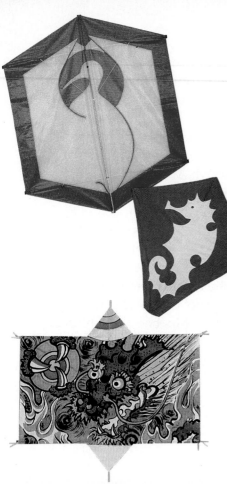

**Figure 4.16 ▲**

In addition to kites like the ones shown, the word *kite* also refers to a type of soaring bird and to the highest sails on a ship. How are all these objects similar?

## Science and Society *Kite Flying*

Ancient people from cultures all around the world built working kites and gliders. In China, kites shaped like birds, butterflies, and dragons were in use 2,500 years ago. Some of these ancient kites had airfoil-shaped wings. In Egypt, working model gliders more than 2,200 years old have been found. In Central America, the ancient Maya built giant, round kites for festivals.

Kite flying is still a popular activity. Every year in the city of Hamamatsu, Japan, hundreds of people fly kites during the annual kite-flying festival. In the United States, children and adults fly kites year round from windy hills, beaches, city parks, and open fields. Even the modern sport of hang gliding is based on kite technology. Participants strap themselves into a harness hanging below a large kite. They use the kite to ride thermals, like soaring birds do.

Kites are usually made from lightweight materials, such as wood, bamboo, paper, and fabric. Kites of all shapes and sizes stay aloft because of differences in air pressure. Air passes over the kite's upper surface, developing lift. When the lift is greater than the kite's weight, the kite rises. The air passing over the kite must be moving fast enough to create sufficient lift. So, kites fly best on windy days.

Some kites are made with two strings attached to their frames to give the people flying the kites greater control. Pulling more on one string than the other changes the shape of the kite's surface. This change affects the forces on the kite, causing it to move. A person can make the kite move to the left or right, or make it dive and then rise again.

## Check and Explain

1. What is Bernoulli's principle?

2. How do airplanes fly? What does airplane flight have in common with bird flight?

3. **Generalize** Write a general statement about all things that can fly.

4. **Infer** What characteristics of an object's shape affect how it moves through a fluid?

# Chapter 4 Review

## Concept Summary

### 4.1 Fluid Pressure

▶ Fluids are any substances that flow, such as water and air.

▶ When fluids apply a force to an area, it is called pressure. Pressure is measured in newtons per square meter ($N/m^2$) or pascals (Pa).

▶ Since the environment is made of air and water, fluid pressure exists everywhere.

### 4.2 Buoyancy

▶ The downward force on an object in a fluid is the force of gravity. The force of gravity on an object is equal to the object's weight.

▶ The force that pushes up on an object in a fluid is the buoyant force.

▶ The buoyant force on an object is equal to the weight of the fluid that is displaced by the object. This relationship is called Archimedes' principle.

▶ Density is the amount of matter in a certain volume. The average density of an object affects its buoyancy.

### 4.3 Forces in Moving Fluids

▶ Bernoulli's principle states that the faster a fluid moves, the lower the fluid's pressure is.

▶ An airfoil's shape creates a low-pressure area above it and a high-pressure area below it. The difference generates lift.

▶ The forces involved in flight are lift, weight, the forward force called thrust, and the rearward force called drag.

▶ Birds and aircraft use pressure differences, low body weight, and streamlined shapes to aid in flight.

## Chapter Vocabulary

| | | | |
|---|---|---|---|
| fluid (4.1) | buoyant force (4.2) | lift (4.3) | drag (4.3) |
| pressure (4.1) | airfoil (4.3) | thrust (4.3) | |

## Check Your Vocabulary

Use the vocabulary words above to complete the following sentences correctly.

1. Planes, birds, and boats are streamlined to reduce _____ .

2. The _____ on an object is equal to the weight of the fluid the object displaces.

3. Force per unit area is _____ .

4. The shape of an airplane wing is a(n) _____ .

5. Any substance that can flow is a(n) _____ .

6. The force that moves a plane forward is _____ .

7. As air moves over an airfoil, _____ is generated.

Pair each numbered word with a vocabulary term. Explain in a sentence how the words are related.

8. Friction
9. Wing
10. Float
11. Pascal
12. Flow
13. Up
14. Forward
15. Area
16. Pressure
17. Sink

## Write Your Vocabulary

Write sentences using the vocabulary words above. Show that you know what each word means.

# Chapter 4 Review

## Check Your Knowledge

Answer the following in complete sentences.

1. What is a fluid?

2. Explain what pressure is and how it is measured.

3. Explain how air pressure varies from place to place on the earth's surface.

4. Describe the forces acting on a floating object.

5. How does density affect buoyancy?

6. What happens to the pressure as a fluid moves faster? Slower?

7. Describe an airfoil.

8. What are the forces involved in airplane flight?

Choose the answer that best completes each sentence.

9. The motion of air particles inside a bicycle tire produces (friction, pressure, heat, kinetic energy).

10. Air and water are (substances, fluids, mixtures, liquids).

11. To calculate pressure, you divide the force by the (volume, weight, area, length).

12. As you travel upward in the earth's atmosphere, the pressure (increases, stays the same, decreases, inflates).

13. The SI unit of pressure, the pascal, is equal to one ($g/cm^3$, $N/m^3$, $N/m^2$, J).

14. To fly, an airplane must have sufficient (buoyant force, thrust, drag, lift).

15. According to Bernoulli's principle, the pressure in a fluid increases if the fluid (moves faster, moves slower, changes density, flows downward).

## Check Your Understanding

1. **Application** When you get into a filled bathtub, the water level changes. Explain what happens and why.

2. Which is less dense? Ice or water? Explain your answer.

3. Why aren't you crushed by the column of air above you?

4. Why do your ears "pop" when you move to a higher or lower altitude?

5. **Critical Thinking** How are a bird's wings like airplane wings? How are they different?

6. How does the buoyant force that acts on a fish compare to the weight of the fish?

7. **Mystery Photo** The photograph on page 84 shows a whirlpool of water.

   a. Name two common fluids on the earth's surface.

   b. Which has the greater density, air or water?

   c. Which has greater pressure acting on it—a rock in 5 m of water or a rock 5 m above sea level?

8. **Application** Is there more pressure at the bottom of a bathtub of water 30 cm deep or at the bottom of a pitcher of water 35 cm deep?

9. **Application** When you let go of an air-filled balloon, it sinks. When you let go of a helium-filled balloon, it rises. Why?

10. **Extension** A diver at 10 m below the water surface goes to twice this depth. How much more water pressure is exerted on her ears?

## Develop Your Skills

Use the skills you have developed in this chapter to complete each activity.

1. **Interpret Data** The drawings below show the forces acting on three different blocks placed in the same fluid.

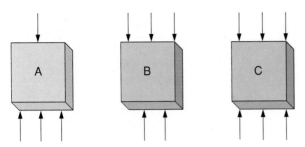

a. Which block(s) will sink? Why?

b. Which block(s) will float? Why?

c. For which block is the buoyant force equal to its weight?

d. Judging from the buoyant force acting on them, rank the blocks from heaviest to lightest. Explain your ranking.

2. **Experiment** Try to float an egg in water. Then dissolve salt in the water until the egg floats. How does the density of an egg compare to tap water? To salt water?

3. **Data Bank** Use the information on page 638 to answer the following questions.

a. Compare the speeds of a sailfish and a spine-tailed swift. Which is faster, the fish or the bird? Which must move through a denser fluid?

b. Compare the speed, in water, of a human and a dolphin. Explain the difference using the words *streamlined* and *drag*.

## Make Connections

1. **Link the Concepts** Below is a concept map showing how some of the main concepts in this chapter link together. Only parts of the map are filled in. Copy the map. Using words and ideas from the chapter, complete the map.

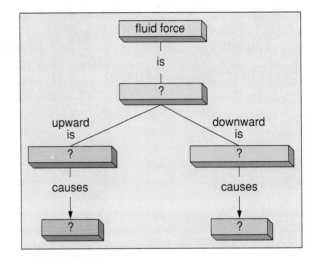

2. **Science and Language Arts** The word *pressure* is used often in everyday life. Make a list of those situations in which pressure is used. Write a report comparing the everyday meaning of the word to its scientific meaning.

3. **Science and Technology** Ships and other watercraft have specialized designs suited for their specific uses. Do a research project on ship and boat design. Use models, photographs, or diagrams to compare similarities and differences. Present your findings in an oral report or class display.

4. **Science and You** Why is your blood pressure measured in your upper arm, on a level with your heart? Is the blood pressure in your legs greater? Research the effects that high blood pressure can have on your body and how the condition can be prevented.

# Chapter 5

# Work, Machines, and Energy

## Chapter Sections

5.1 Work and Power

5.2 Work and Machines

5.3 Simple and Compound Machines

5.4 Energy and Its Forms

## What do you see?

❝I see gears that could be in a wristwatch or even a factory. They are used to move things by turning and interlocking their little teeth on the circumference. By working together, they use less energy to complete their work.❞

*Marie Fridman*
*Bair Middle School*
*Sunrise, Florida*

To find out more about the photograph, look on page 128.
As you read this chapter, you will learn about work, machines, and energy.

# 5.1 Work and Power

## Objectives

▶ **Describe** the conditions which must be met to do work.

▶ **Distinguish** between work and power.

▶ **Calculate** work and power.

▶ **Interpret data** from a sample electric bill.

What does the word *work* make you think of? You probably think of tasks that you would rather not do. For example, you might think it is work to rake leaves in your front yard or run laps around a school track.

Your idea of work might be quite different from another person's idea. If you enjoy being outside, you might like to rake leaves. If you are a member of a sports team, you might like to run. In everyday life, the word *work* means different things to different people. But in science, work has a specific meaning. In science, work relates to forces, motion, and energy.

**Figure 5.1**
The boy is doing work. How is he meeting the two conditions which are necessary for work to be done? ▼

## Work

Two conditions must be met in order for **work** to be done on an object:

▶ The object moves.

▶ A force must act on the object in the direction the object moves.

When you rake leaves, as the boy is doing in Figure 5.1, you do work. You apply a force against the leaves and they move. Most people push the rake downward and pull horizontally. The force directed downward doesn't do any work because it doesn't make the leaves move. Only the horizontal force that moves the leaves does work.

When you run laps around a track you do work. Your legs apply a force against the track to move your body forward. As a result, you move a certain distance around the track. The amount of work you do depends only on force and distance. How much time it takes to do work is not involved.

**Figure 5.2** ▲
The downward force does not
do work. Only the force applied
in the same direction the lawn
mower moves does work.

Energy is needed to rake leaves or to do any kind of
work. In fact, energy is defined as the ability to do work.
Are you doing work right now?

  Can you think of a situation when you use energy
but do not do work? When an Olympic weight-lifter
presses a barbell over his head, he must hold it there
until the judges say he can put it down. If the weight-
lifter holds the barbell perfectly still while it is over his
head, is he doing work? The answer is no. He is applying
force against the barbell, but he is not moving the force
through a distance. For work to be done, a force must
move an object through a distance.

## Measuring Work

  Imagine that you earn money by mowing your neighbors' lawns like the girl in Figure 5.2. What factors would
you consider when deciding how much to charge? You
might vary your fee according to the size of the lawn
being mowed. It takes a large amount of work to mow a
large lawn. The farther the lawn mower is pushed, the
greater is the amount of work done.

  To determine the amount of work done, you use a
mathematical formula. The formula relates work to force
and distance. Two measurements are needed to use this
formula. One measurement is the amount of force exerted
in the direction of motion. The other measurement is
the distance moved. Multiplying the force measurement
by the distance measurement gives you the amount of
work done.

$$\text{work} = \text{force} \times \text{distance}$$
$$W = Fd$$

  The amount of force exerted on an object is measured
in newtons. The distance the object moves is measured
in meters. As a result, the unit for work is sometimes
called the newton meter (Nm). Another word for the
Newton meter is the **joule** (JOOL). One joule (J) equals
the work done by a force of 1 N that moves an object a
distance of 1 m.

  The joule is a unit that is also used to measure energy.
Lifting a glass of water from a counter top to your mouth,
for example, would require you to use about 1 J of energy
and to perform about 1 J of work. As you can see, energy
and work are related.

## Power

Imagine that you and a friend each mow a lawn of equal size. You both use the same force and push the lawn mowers the same distance. You and your friend do equal amounts of work. However, you finish the job 20 min faster than your friend. To do this you had to use a greater amount of **power**. Power is the rate at which work is done. To calculate power, you divide the amount of work done by the time it took to do the work.

$$\text{power} = \frac{\text{work}}{\text{time}}$$

When the work is in joules and the time in seconds the power is in joules per second (J/s). Another name for a joule per second is the **watt** (W). One watt is equal to one J/s. One watt is about the amount of power it takes for you to lift a glass of water one meter in one second. One hundred joules of work done in one second is equal to one hundred watts of power. Study Figure 5.3 and compare the power involved in each situation.

The SI unit of power was named for James Watt, a Scottish engineer. Watt coined the term "horsepower" (hp), which is used to rate electric motors and gasoline engines. He defined one horsepower as the amount of work a horse could do in one second. One horsepower is equal to 745.56 W.

◀ **Figure 5.3**
The backhoe has more power than a person with a shovel. Why?

## Sample Problems

1. Rita mows lawns on the weekends. If she uses 15 N of force to move a lawn mower a distance of 10 m, how much work does Rita do?

   **Plan**  To find the amount of work done, multiply the force by the distance.

   **Gather data**  The force is 15 N, the distance is 10 m.

   **Solve**  Work = force × distance
   = 15 N × 10 m
   = 150 Nm = 150 J

2. How much work did Joe do when he used 30 N of force to pull a table a distance of 3 m?

   **Plan**  To find the amount of work done, multiply the force by the distance.

   **Gather data**  The force is 30 N. The distance is 3 m.

   **Solve**  Work = force × distance
   = 30 N × 3m
   = 90 Nm = 90 J

3. You run up several flights of stairs in 1.5 min. If the work you do is equal to 450 J, how much power do you use?

   **Plan**  Divide the amount of work done by the time it took to do it. Since time is given in minutes, it needs to be converted to seconds before you divide by it.

   **Gather data**  The work done was 450 J. The time was 1.5 min. There are 60 s in 1 min.

   **Solve**  1.5 min × 60 s = 90 s

   $$power = \frac{work}{time}$$

   $$= \frac{450 \text{ J}}{90 \text{ s}}$$

   = 5 J/s = 5 W

## Practice Problems

1. How much work is done by a force of 60 N that moves an object 6 m?

2. In preparing for a classroom activity, two students work together to push a desk a distance of 4.2 m. The combined force they used to complete the task was 20 N. How much work did they do together?

3. Five students exert a combined force of 500 N to lift a heavy crate a distance of 2 m off the ground. How much work did the students exert together in lifting the crate?

4. Nancy stores her holiday decorations in the garage rafters. She uses a ladder to lift a 50 N box 3 m off the ground. How much work does she do?

5. A cat weighing 40 N jumps 2 m onto a fence. How much work does the cat do?

6. Two students decide to go rowing on the weekend. They row the boat for 14 min and together do 1680 J of work. How much power did they exert?

7. How much power would a forklift need to raise a 500 N load 1.5 m high in 10 s? How much power would be needed to do the same work in 5 s?

8. Calculate the "leg power" of a 400 N sprinter who runs a kilometer in 3.7 min.

9. The same 400 N sprinter from question 8 can run 100 m in 20 s. How much leg power is used?

10. The power of a 350 N runner is 5000 W. The runner took 1 min and 10 s to run the course. How long was the course?

## Science and You  *Your Electric Bill*

Your electric meter is read each month. The bill you receive may contain information about gas usage, as the bill does in Figure 5.4. To check the accuracy of the electric part of the bill, study the following items:

A. The amount of electricity you used that month.

B. Baseline, or Lifeline Allowance. This is the amount of electricity you can buy at the cheapest rate.

C. Lifeline usage. The amount of your Lifeline Allowance you actually used.

D. The cheapest electricity rate. This rate applies only for your Lifeline Allowance.

E. The rate you pay for electricity that is over your Lifeline Allowance.

Calculate your own bill using items A-E.

1. If A is smaller than B, multiply A and D. The product is the cost of the electricity. Then, you can skip steps 2-4 below.

2. If A is larger than B, multiply C and D.

3. Subtract C from A. Multiply the difference by E.

4. Add the products from steps 2 and 3. This sum, along with any taxes and service charge, is the amount you owe for electricity.

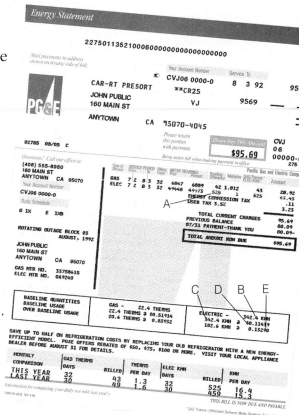

**Figure 5.4** ▲
It is a good idea to check the accuracy of your electric bill each month.

---

## Check and Explain

1. Suppose you tried to move a large boulder by pushing it, but it didn't move. Did you do work? Explain.

2. How are work and power similar? How are they different?

3. **Calculate**  How many watts of power are represented by a sprinter weighing 500 N who runs a kilometer in 4.3 min? How much work did he do?

4. **Interpret Data**  Use Figure 5.4 to determine the charge for electricity (not counting tax and the service charge).

*Lifting a Lawn Mower*

You have been asked to load a lawn mower onto the bed of a pickup truck. The lawn mower is too heavy to lift directly. How will you move the lawn mower onto the truck?

**SKILLS WARMUP**

# 5.2 Work and Machines

## Objectives

▶ **Explain** how machines make work easier.

▶ **Calculate** mechanical advantage.

▶ **Infer** the relationship between energy use and mechanical efficiency.

Suppose your music teacher is preparing for a concert. He needs to move a piano from the third floor music room to the first floor gym. The piano fits easily through the classroom door. From there, the instrument would have to be carried down three flights of stairs. The piano is very heavy. Another way to move the piano is out the music room's large window. For the second method to work, a device is needed to gently lower the instrument down to the ground. The teacher asks the class for suggestions on how to accomplish the task. How would you plan to move the piano?

## Machines

You and your classmates probably have many different ideas about how to move a piano. More than likely your plans are similar in one way. They probably involve using a **machine**. A machine is a device that makes work easier. Machines make work easier by changing the direction or the size of the force needed to do work.

Two forces are involved when you use a machine. The force applied *to* the machine is called the *effort force*. For example, when you push down on a screwdriver to remove the lid from a can of paint, you apply effort force to the screwdriver. The force opposing the effort force is the *resistance force*. The lid on the paint can is the resistance, or opposing, force. Often, resistance is the weight of the object.

Ropes and pulleys, boards with wheels, and ramps are examples of machines that might make moving the piano easier. A rope and pulley can reduce the amount of force needed to raise or lower the piano. A flat board with wheels reduces the amount of force needed to push the piano across the floor. A ramp reduces the

### Geology

**L I N K**

Early humans made and used stone tools. Many of these tools were simple machines. Although working with stone takes great force, you can model the making of a stone tool. Collect the following items: scissors, pieces of chalk.

**1.** Break a few pieces of chalk in half.

**2.** Use your scissors to carve the pieces into wedge shapes.

Would chalk be a good material for real stone tools? Explain.

**A C T I V I T Y**

amount of force needed to move the piano down three flights of stairs.

Machines can't save work. A machine lets you apply less force to overcome a resistance. However, you must apply the force over a greater distance. A bicycle and a doorknob are other examples of machines.

## Mechanical Advantage

Most machines multiply the force of your efforts. The number of times a machine multiplies an effort force is its **mechanical advantage** (M.A.). A machine with an M.A. of 2 doubles your effort force. As a result, you only have to use half of the effort force needed to do the same amount of work without a machine.

Machines can also change the direction of a force. A machine that only changes the direction of a force has an M.A of 1. An M.A. of 1, however, does not change the force you have to apply. Machines with an M.A. less than 1 increase the distance or speed of motion.

To find out a machine's mechanical advantage, divide the resistance force by the effort force.

**Figure 5.5** ▲
A screwdriver can be used as a lever to open a can of paint. Identify the forces being applied.

$$\text{M.A.} = \frac{\text{resistance force}}{\text{effort force}}$$

For example, if you can lift a 300 N object by applying only 20 N of force to a lever, the M.A. of the lever is 15.

## *Sample Problem*

Jill likes to work on old automobiles. She has constructed a pulley system to help her lift the engine out of the car. She can lift a 600-N engine by applying only 150 N of force. What is the M.A. of her pulley system?

**Plan**  Divide the resistance force by the effort force to find M.A.

**Gather data**  The resistance force is 600 N. The effort force is 150 N.

**Solve**  M.A. = $\frac{600 \text{ N}}{150 \text{ N}}$ = 4

## *Practice Problems*

1. John works at a construction site. The foreman told him that with a particular crowbar he needs 50 N of force to lift 500 N. What is the M.A. of the crowbar?

2. A smaller crowbar is available to John. It has an M.A. of 5. How much force will John need to apply to the smaller crowbar to lift the same concrete block?

3. You use 50 N of force to push a crate up a ramp. The crate puts 200 N of friction force on the ramp. What's the M.A. of the ramp?

## Mechanical Efficiency

Machines make it easier to do work. However, the amount of work put into a machine, or *work input*, is always greater than the amount of work done by the machine, or *work output*. Work input is always greater than work output because some of the work put into the machine is used to overcome friction.

The **mechanical efficiency** of a machine compares its work output with the work input. In general:

$$\text{mechanical efficiency} = \frac{\text{work output}}{\text{work input}} \times 100\%$$

Because the work output is always less than the work input, the mechanical efficiency of a machine is always less than 100%. The efficiency of a machine, such as a bicycle or automobile, can be increased by keeping its parts clean and well lubricated. Such measures help reduce friction which results in higher efficiency.

## *Career Corner*  *Mechanical Engineer*

### Who Designs Machines?

Suppose you visited a bike store, and noticed a moped display. A sign read that the moped was "new and improved." You wondered how this moped was different from previous models. The moped's improvements were probably made by a mechanical engineer.

Mechanical engineers explore ways to produce and use mechanical power. They design and test all types of machines. Some mechanical engineers do research and design new types of machines. Other mechanical engineers work to improve existing machines, like the moped.

Mechanical engineers work on a wide variety of machines. Automobiles, air conditioners, heating systems, and industrial equipment are examples of machines developed and improved by mechanical engineers.

To be a mechanical engineer, you should be curious about how things work. You also should be able to find creative ways of solving problems. Mechanical engineers need a strong background in math and science. Most mechanical engineers have a four-year college degree. You can learn more about this profession by writing to the American Society of Mechanical Engineers, 345 E. 47th Street, New York, NY 10017.

# Science and Society
## Energy Efficiency

Have you ever seen a commercial for a new, more energy-efficient model of a refrigerator or other household appliance? Such machines use less energy and therefore cost less to operate. Automobiles and household appliances often have labels that tell the buyer how energy-efficient the product is. An example of these labels is shown in Figure 5.6. Consumers who use this information to choose energy-efficient products can save money. They also help conserve energy resources.

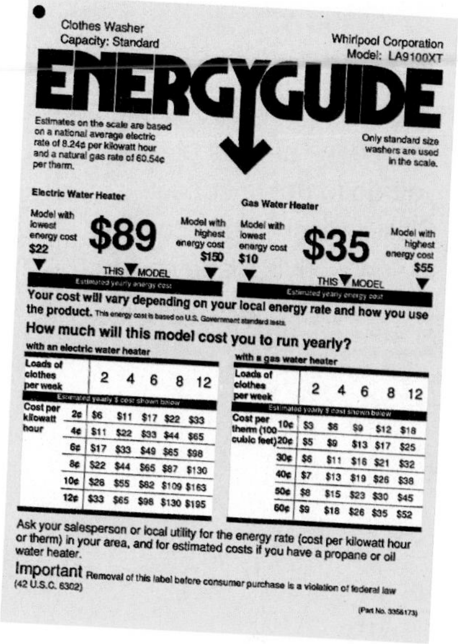

Design improvements and advanced technology help to make many appliances more energy efficient. But in spite of the improvements, no machine is 100% efficient. Some of the work put into any machine is used to overcome friction between the machine's moving parts. Since friction produces heat, the work used to overcome friction is lost as waste heat energy.

In general, the more moving parts a machine has, the lower its mechanical efficiency is. A machine with only a few moving parts can be up to 98% efficient. Such a machine uses 98% of the energy it takes in to do useful work. It loses only 2% as waste heat.

Only about 30% of the energy produced by burning gasoline in an auto engine does useful work. About 35% of the energy is lost as heat to the cooling system. The remaining 35% is lost as heat in the exhaust gases. The amount of gas the car uses depends on the efficiency of the engine. How might car engines become more energy efficient?

**Figure 5.6** ▲

This label is an estimation of the yearly energy cost of using a particular model washing machine.

## Check and Explain

1. How do machines make work easier?

2. You apply 20 N of force to a machine consisting of pulleys that can lift 80 N of bricks. What is the M.A. of the machine?

3. **Analyze**  A refrigerator that is 78% efficient costs more than a similar appliance that is only 46% efficient. The salesperson tells the consumer that the more expensive appliance will save money. Explain.

4. **Infer**  How does properly maintaining your bicycle increase its mechanical efficiency?

*Working Toward School*

List some ways you can reduce the amount of work you do to get to school. Classify each one according to how work is made easier.

**SKILLS WARMUP**

# 5.3 Simple and Compound Machines

## Objectives

▶ **Explain** how six simple machines make work easier.

▶ **Classify** the simple machines in a compound machine you are familiar with.

▶ **Predict** the mechanical advantages of simple machines.

Machines are almost everywhere you look. How many can you see around you? Below are two groups of devices.

Group 1: Ramp, bottle opener, pulley, wheelbarrow

Group 2: Car, escalator, lawn mower, hair dryer

Which group of items contains machines? All devices in both groups make work easier. Each changes the size or direction of a force applied to it. Therefore, every device in both groups is a machine. The devices in Group 1 are examples of **simple machines**. Simple machines do work with one movement. There are six types of simple machines: the inclined plane, wedge, screw, lever, wheel and axle, and pulley.

## Inclined Plane

A simple machine that has a sloping surface is an *inclined plane*. The ramp shown in Figure 5.7 is an inclined plane. You use less force to pull the crate up a ramp than if you lifted it vertically. In exchange for using less force, you must pull the crate a greater distance. An inclined plane will not change the amount of work. It reduces the effort force.

A *wedge* is an inclined plane that can move. An ax is a wedge. The resistance force required to split a log is great. The effort force driving the ax into the log is less, but it must be applied over a greater distance.

A *screw* is also an inclined plane. Many car jacks are screws. A great many turns are needed to move a car jack a short distance. However, the car jack produces a far greater force than the force needed to turn it.

**Figure 5.7**

A ramp makes moving a heavy crate easier. ▼

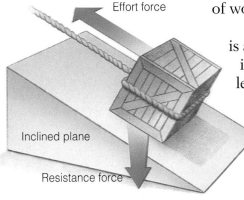

Effort force

Inclined plane

Resistance force

# Levers

A balance, a wheelbarrow, and a shovel are all machines. They all have a straight part that moves when a force is applied. And they all have one point that does not move. The fixed point is called the *fulcrum*. Machines that do work by moving around a fixed point are called levers. The three classes of levers are shown below. Levers are classified according to the location of the fulcrum, the effort force, and the resistance force.

**First Class Lever**   A balance like the one shown is an example of a first class lever. The fulcrum is always between the effort force and the resistance force. First class levers multiply the effort force and also change its direction.

A crowbar is a first class lever. A large resistance force is required to pull nails from boards. This force can be achieved when a small effort force is applied to a long crowbar. However, no work is saved. The effort force applied to the crowbar moves farther than the resistance force. Other examples of first class levers include a pair of shears and a teeter-totter or seesaw.

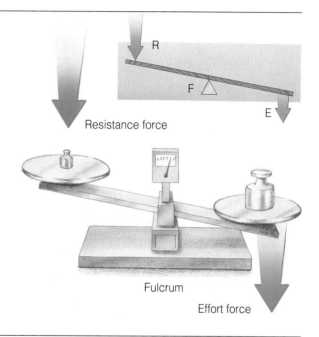

Resistance force

Fulcrum

Effort force

**Second Class Lever**   A wheelbarrow is an example of a second class lever. The resistance force is between the fulcrum and the effort force. Notice in the picture to the right that in second class levers, the distance from the fulcrum to the resistance force is less than the distance from the fulcrum to the effort force. When you lift the handles of the wheelbarrow, you apply less force than the weight of the load. In return, you have to move the handles a greater distance than the load is raised. Second class levers multiply the effort force without changing its direction. Examples of second class levers include bottle openers, doors, and some nutcrackers.

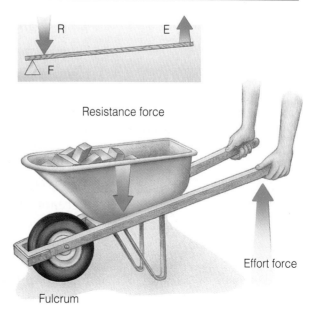

Resistance force

Fulcrum

Effort force

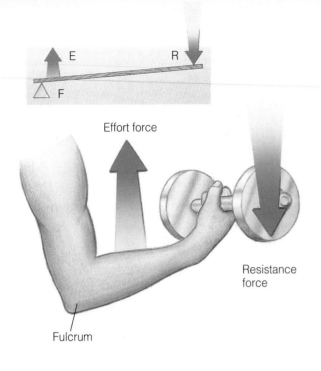

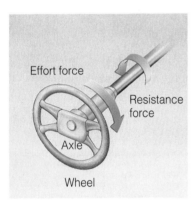

**Third Class Lever** Your forearm is an example of a third class lever. The effort force is between the fulcrum and the resistance force. When a weight lifter curls a dumbbell upward, his forearm pivots at the elbow. His elbow is the fulcrum. The biceps muscle is attached to the forearm just below the elbow. When the biceps muscle contracts, the effort force is applied to the attachment point on the forearm. When you use a third class lever, the effort force is greater than the resistance force. The mechanical advantage is less than one. The reason for using a third class lever is to increase the distance moved, not to reduce the force. Examples include a rake and a fishing pole.

## M.A. of Levers

The mechanical advantage of a lever is calculated by dividing the effort distance by the resistance distance.

$$\text{M.A.} = \frac{\text{distance of the effort force from the fulcrum}}{\text{distance of the resistance force from the fulcrum}}$$

The M.A. of first and second class levers is usually greater than 1. The M.A. of third class levers is less than 1. Third class levers do not multiply force.

## Wheel and Axle

The steering mechanism on a car, like the one shown in Figure 5.8, is an example of a wheel and axle. This type of simple machine consists of two circular objects called a wheel and an axle. The wheel has a larger radius than the axle does. The radius is the distance from the center of the wheel to the edge. An effort force applied at the wheel is multiplied at the axle to overcome a resistance force. The effort force applied to the wheel moves over a greater distance than the resistance force does. The mechanical advantage of a wheel and axle is equal to the radius of the wheel divided by the radius of the axle. The M.A. of a wheel and axle is always greater than 1. Examples include a door knob, a Ferris wheel, and a wheelchair.

**Figure 5.8** ▲
The effort force applied to the wheel overcomes the resistance force of the axle.

## Pulleys

Window blinds are raised and lowered using pulleys. A *pulley* is a rope wrapped around a grooved wheel. The two main types of pulleys are called fixed pulleys, and movable pulleys.

Look at Figure 5.9. A fixed pulley is attached to a stationary structure. The mechanical advantage of a fixed pulley is 1 because it does not multiply the effort force. A fixed pulley can make lifting an object easier by changing the direction of the effort force. Why is it easier for you to pull down than it is for you to lift?

A movable pulley is hung on a rope and hooked to a resistance. The movable pulley in Figure 5.10 is hung from a fixed pulley. As you pull on one end of the rope, the resistance and the movable pulley move together. Movable pulleys can multiply your effort force. They have a M.A. of 2. Notice that this pulley system also changes the direction of force.

When two or more pulleys are used together, a pulley system is formed. Compare the pulley systems in Figures 5.10 and 5.11. Each consists of a fixed and movable pulley. Notice, however, that the two pulley systems differ in the number of rope segments that support the resistance force. As a result, they do not have the same mechanical advantage.

The pulley system in Figure 5.11 has a M.A. of 3. The system in Figure 5.10 has a M.A. of 2. The mechanical advantage of a pulley or pulley system is equal to the number of rope segments pulling up on the resistance force. What is the direction of force in Figure 5.11?

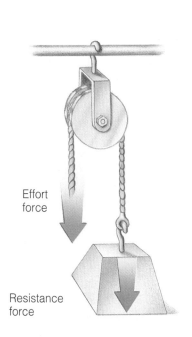

**Figure 5.9** ▲
This fixed pulley has one rope segment supporting the resistance force. It has a M.A. of 1.

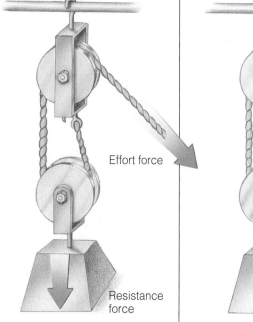

**Figure 5.10** ▲
This 2-pulley system has 2 rope segments supporting the resistance force. It has a M.A. of 2.

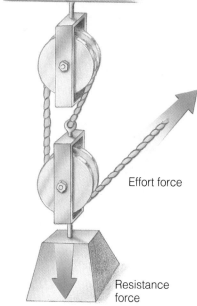

**Figure 5.11** ▲
This 2-pulley system has 3 rope segments supporting the resistance force. It has a M.A. of 3.

## Compound Machines

Some household appliances, some bicycles, and many mechanical devices that you use every day are compound machines. A **compound machine** is a system of two or more simple machines. The mechanical advantage of a compound machine is much greater than that of a simple machine. The combination of simple machines in the compound machine multiplies the total mechanical advantage.

Look at the compound machine in Figure 5.12. What simple machines do you see? If you look carefully, you can find wheels and axles and inclined planes.

Take a close look at other mechanical devices that you use every day. Identify the simple machines that they contain. All of the simple machines in a compound machine work together as a system to accomplish a task. What types of machines are in a stapler, a pair of scissors, and a tape dispenser?

**Figure 5.12** ▲
How many simple machines are there in this pencil sharpener?

## *SkillBuilder* *Classifying*

### *The Hat-Removal Machine*

The Hat-Removal Machine below is similar to all compound machines. Compound machines are made up of a number of simple machines working together as a system. Identify the various simple machines that make up the Hat-Removal Machine.

a.   inclined plane

b.   wheel and axle

c.   pulley

d.   lever

1.   Describe how the Hat-Removal Machine contains each of the following simple machines:

2.   Design and draw a compound machine. Give your machine a name, and label each simple machine in it.

## Science and Technology  *Travel by Bicycle*

In the late 1800s, a bicycle called the "ordinary" was the most efficient and inexpensive way to travel. The rider sat above a huge front wheel. Each time the pedals completed a turn, so did the big wheel. The ordinary was dangerous because riders often fell off. Designers found that by adding simple machines to the bicycle they could reduce the size of the front wheel and increase its performance.

Each pedal on a modern ten-speed bicycle moves in a circle like a wheel, and is part of a wheel and axle. The axle is a front sprocket. The bicycle chain transfers the force to a rear sprocket attached to the rear wheel. The rear sprocket is the effort wheel of the rear wheel and axle system. As the rear sprocket turns, it causes the rear wheel to turn. The turning rear wheel overcomes the force of friction between the tires and the road. What other simple machines does a bicycle contain?

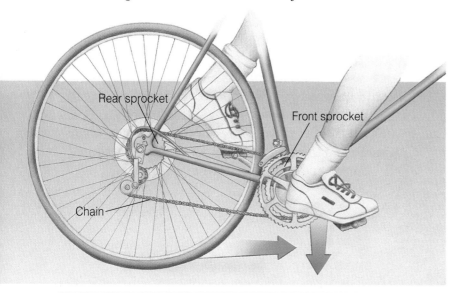

Rear sprocket

Front sprocket

Chain

◀ **Figure 5.13**
The simple machines on a well-maintained bicycle form a compound machine with a very high mechanical efficiency.

## Check and Explain

1. Name six simple machines. Explain how each works.

2. What simple machines make up a crank-type pencil sharpener?

3. **Classify**  Choose a compound machine you are familiar with. What simple machines does it contain?

4. **Predict**  What is the M.A. of a pulley system that uses four rope segments to support the resistance force?

▼ ACTIVITY

### Inferring

*Energy on TV*

Explain how a television set changes energy from one form to other forms. Compare your explanation with that of a classmate.

**SKILLS WARMUP**

# 5.4 Energy and Its Forms

## Objectives

▶ **Name** and **describe** five forms of energy.

▶ **Give examples** of energy conversions.

▶ **Describe** the Law of Conservation of Mass and Energy.

▶ **Infer** the role of energy conversions in an everyday situation.

As you learned in the previous section, machines can make your work easier. You would not try to pull a nail out of a board without a crowbar or cut a lawn without a lawn mower.

Despite their usefulness, machines have limitations. Machines can't save work or energy. The amount of work you get out of a machine can never be greater than the amount of work or energy put into it. The work a lawn mower engine does is less than the energy in the gasoline that is burned. Most of the energy is converted to heat, due to friction between moving parts in the motor.

Work and energy are related. Energy is the ability to do work. Both work and energy are measured in joules. Energy has many forms. In some way, all of these forms are related to each other. Energy can be converted from one form to another.

**Figure 5.14**
A windmill is a compound machine that uses mechanical energy to do work. ▼

Drive shaft powers water pump

## Mechanical Energy

Mechanical energy is the energy of the movement or the position of an object. The mechanical energy of a moving object is also called its kinetic energy. The mechanical energy of an object due to its position is also called *potential energy*.

Wind and moving water have mechanical energy. Not only do they move, they also can move objects. For thousands of years people have used the wind's mechanical energy to do work. Windmills like the one in Figure 5.14 use the wind's mechanical energy to operate a water pump or to generate electricity. Wheels turned by moving water were used to grind grain into flour.

## Nuclear Energy

All matter is made up of particles called atoms. A great amount of energy is stored in an atom's core, or nucleus. This energy, called nuclear energy, is released when an atomic nucleus breaks apart, or when a new nucleus forms. Look at Figure 5.15. The sun's energy is a result of nuclear reactions like these. Nuclear power plants use energy from nuclear reactions to generate electricity.

## Chemical Energy

Chemical bonds between atoms hold substances together. Look at Figure 5.16. In a car engine, chemical bonds between atoms in gasoline are broken. Breaking these bonds releases large amounts of energy. In a car engine, the chemical reaction is controlled so that the energy can be used to do useful work. Chemical energy is the energy stored in the bonds between atoms.

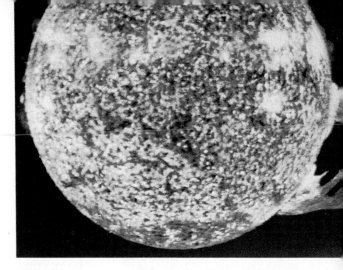

**Figure 5.15 ▲**
The sun has great amounts of nuclear, heat, and electromagnetic energy.

## Electromagnetic Energy

Atoms are made of even smaller particles. One of these smaller particles is the electron. In an atom, electrons carry an electric charge. Have you ever gotten a mild shock after walking across a carpet and touching a metal doorknob? The shock you felt was caused by this charge. When electrons flow through conducting material, a moving charge is formed. This moving charge is electricity, a form of electromagnetic energy. Light is another form of electromagnetic energy.

## Heat Energy

When something is colder than its surroundings, it will warm up. When a substance becomes warmer, its particles move faster. The kinetic energy of the particles increases. Contact between different substances, such as cold water and warmer air, will transfer this kinetic motion. The fast-moving particles of air collide with the slower moving water particles, increasing their motion. Energy flows from the warm air to the cool water. Heat is the energy that flows from a warm substance to a cooler one.

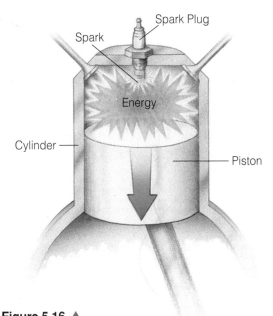

**Figure 5.16 ▲**
Energy released from gasoline drives the piston that moves the car wheels.

Spark Plug
Spark
Energy
Cylinder
Piston

## Energy Conversions

What happens when you strike a match? You hear the match head scratch against the striking strip. A puff of smoke rises. The match head changes color and a small yellow and blue flame appears. The burning match gives off light that you can see and heat that you can feel.

Look at Figure 5.17. Think about this series of events in terms of energy. How does energy change from one form to another as you light the match? When you move the match head against the striking strip, particles in the match head begin to move faster. As this happens, mechanical energy changes to heat energy. The heat energy causes a chemical change to begin. The match head begins to change color and release stored chemical energy. The chemical energy changes into heat energy and light energy.

In the world around you, energy is constantly changing from one form to another. A toaster changes electrical energy to heat energy. Power plants use generators to change mechanical, chemical, or nuclear energy into electric energy. Your body changes the chemical energy in food to kinetic energy and heat. By changing from one form to another, energy is recycled throughout the world.

## The Law of Conservation of Mass and Energy

In each of the energy conversions you have just read about, the total amount of energy remained the same. As energy changes from one form to another, it is never created or destroyed. This fact has been observed to be true in so many different situations that it has become a scientific law. According to the *Law of Conservation of Mass and Energy*, the amount of mass and energy in the universe is always the same.

This scientific law was once thought of as two separate laws, one for energy and one for mass. Today, one law includes mass and energy together because nuclear reactions were observed where matter was transformed directly into energy, and energy into matter. Albert Einstein predicted the relationship between matter and energy. He expressed it in mathematical form as:

$$E = mc^2$$
$$\text{Energy} = \text{mass} \times (\text{the speed of light})^2$$

**Figure 5.17** ▲

Striking a match involves mechanical, chemical, heat, and light energy.

## Science and You
### *Energy Conversions in Your Body*

As you read the words on this page, energy is changing from one form to another right in your own body! At this minute, your digestive system is hard at work breaking down the food you ate for breakfast or lunch. As digestion takes place, a new supply of chemical energy is released that can do work in your body.

Chemical energy in your body changes to mechanical energy every time you move a muscle to do work. You use mechanical energy for all your daily activities such as walking, talking, and writing. Chemical energy from your food is used also to build or repair body tissues. In this case, the chemical energy from your food is stored again as chemical energy in new body tissues.

Some of the chemical energy from your food is changed into heat energy. This heat energy helps to keep your body temperature at about 37°C. When the surrounding air is less than 37°C, your body must generate heat energy to maintain your body temperature.

The thermogram in the margin shows how heat is distributed over your body's surface. When your body temperature is more than 37°C, your body must release heat energy so that your body temperature doesn't get too high. Your body transports water to the surface of your skin where it can evaporate, releasing heat energy and cooling your body.

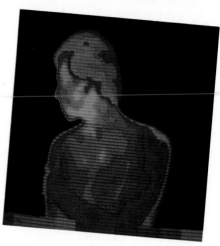

**Figure 5.18** ▲
This thermogram of a person shows the warmest areas in red. Compare the warmest and coolest areas.

## Check and Explain

1. What are five forms of energy? Give an example of each form.

2. Describe the energy conversions that occur in each of the following situations:

   a. an automobile driving down a road

   b. an athlete running around a track

3. **Communicate**  State the *Law of Conservation of Mass and Energy*. Explain its meaning in your own words.

4. **Infer**  Usually, a person will perspire when they exercise. How might this be triggered by energy changing form?

# Activity 5 *How does the rate of energy change affect work?*

*Skills*   Observe; Measure; Infer

## Task 1   Prelab Prep
Collect the following items: 1 hot plate, 1 tea kettle, water, 1 toy car, 2 plastic straws, small piece of cloth, scissors, and tape. You will need to set up the activity near an electrical outlet.

## Task 2   Data Record
1.  Copy the data table below on a separate sheet of paper.

**Table 5.1   Trial Measurements**

| Trial Run | Distance Car Traveled |
|-----------|----------------------|
| 1         |                      |
| 2         |                      |

## Task 3   Procedure
1.  Place the hot plate where the cord will be able to reach an electric outlet. Do not plug it in, yet.
2.  Fill the tea kettle with water. Place it on top of the hot plate.
3.  Cut the cloth so its width is approximately equal to the width of the toy car.
4.  Tape each edge of the cloth to the straws. The cloth should look like a volleyball net.
5.  Place the car in front of the tea kettle. Hold the bottom of the straws on either side of the car. Position the straws so that the cloth lies directly in front of the spout of the tea kettle. To do this, you may have to cut a section off the bottom of each straw. When the cloth is at spout level, tape the straws to the sides of the car.
6.  Plug in the hot plate. Wait and observe.
7.  When the car has stopped moving, unplug the hot plate. Use the meter stick to measure the distance the car moved. Record the data under Trial Run 1 in the data table.

8.  Refill the tea kettle to the same volume of water as you used in Trial Run 1. Plug in the hot plate.
9.  Once you hear the kettle start to whistle or when you see steam, *carefully* place the car in front of the spout. Be sure that the cloth "sail" is directly in front of the spout, exactly as it was at the beginning of Trial Run 1! **CAUTION! Be careful not to put your hand or arm in front of the spout. Steam can burn your skin.**
10. When the car has stopped moving, unplug the hot plate. Use the meter stick to measure the distance the car moved.
11. Record the data under Trial Run 2 in the data table.

## Task 4   Analysis
1.  In which trial did the car move the greatest distance?
2.  What variable was different between the two trial runs?
3.  In which trial run was the car's "sail" hit with the greatest force?
4.  Was work done in this activity? Explain your answer.

## Task 5   Conclusion
Identify the various ways energy changed form in this activity. In this activity, you observed energy change forms. Explain how the rate at which the change occurred affected the amount of work done?

# Chapter 5 Review

## Concept Summary

### 5.1 Work and Power
▶ Work is done on an object when the object moves in the direction of a force acting on it. No work is done when the object does not move. Work is equal to force times distance.
▶ Power is the rate at which work is done. Power is equal to work divided by time required to do work.

### 5.2 Work and Machines
▶ A machine is a device that helps do work. Machines change the size or direction of the force used to do work.
▶ The mechanical advantage of a machine equals the resistance force divided by the effort force.
▶ The mechanical efficiency of a machine is a comparison of work output to work input. Because of friction, no machine can be 100 percent efficient.

### 5.3 Simple and Compound Machines
▶ The six kinds of simple machines are inclined planes, wedges, screws, levers, wheels and axles, and pulleys.
▶ A compound machine is a combination of two or more simple machines working together as a system.

### 5.4 Energy and Its Forms
▶ Mechanical energy is due to the position of something (potential energy) or the movement of something (kinetic energy).
▶ Forms of energy are mechanical, nuclear, heat, chemical, and electromagnetic.
▶ Energy can change from one form to another.
▶ The *Law of Conservation of Mass and Energy* states that the total amount of mass and energy in the universe is constant. Energy and mass can't be created or destroyed.

## Chapter Vocabulary

| | | |
|---|---|---|
| work (5.1) | watt (5.1) | mechanical efficiency (5.2) |
| joule (5.1) | machine (5.2) | simple machine (5.3) |
| power (5.1) | mechanical advantage (5.2) | compound machine (5.3) |

## Check Your Vocabulary

Use the vocabulary words above to complete the following sentences

1. The _____ is a unit used to measure work.

2. A lever is an example of a(n) _____ .

3. The _____ is a unit used to measure power.

4. A device that helps do work is a(n) _____ .

5. To calculate _____ , you divide the amount of work done by the time it took to do the work.

6. The _____ of a machine compares its work output with the work input.

7. A machine with a(n) _____ of two doubles the force applied to the machine.

8. The product of force and distance is called _____ .

9. A system using simple machines, such as levers and pulleys working together, makes up a(n) _____ .

## Write Your Vocabulary

Write sentences using each vocabulary word above. Show that you know what each word means.

# Chapter 5 Review

## Check Your Knowledge

Answer the following in complete sentences.

1. What two conditions must be met for work to be done on an object?

2. What units are used to measure work and power?

3. How do machines make work easier?

4. What is the difference between a simple machine and a compound machine?

5. What is the equation that relates matter and energy? Use words to describe the meaning of this equation.

6. Describe a series of energy conversions involving at least three forms of energy.

Determine whether each statement is true or false. Write *true* if it is true. If it is false, change the underlined term to make the statement true.

7. Work relates force and <u>simple machines</u>.

8. Power is the rate at which <u>work</u> is done.

9. The number of times a machine multiplies a force is the machine's <u>mechanical efficiency</u>.

10. The mechanical efficiency of a machine is always <u>less</u> than 100 percent.

11. A machine that works with one movement is a <u>simple machine</u>.

12. A combination of <u>complex</u> machines is a compound machine.

13. <u>Energy</u> can be converted from one form to another.

14. A <u>wedge</u> is a type of inclined plane.

## Check Your Understanding

Apply the concepts you have learned to answer each question.

1. **Application** You push against a car, but the car doesn't move. Has work been done? Explain.

2. Work is needed to lift a barbell. How many times more work is needed to lift the barbell three times as high?

3. **Critical Thinking** To open a swinging door, you usually push on the part of the door farthest from the hinges. Use you knowledge of levers to explain why it would be harder to open the door if you pushed on the the center of the door.

4. **Application** Describe at least three energy conversions that take place in a moving automobile.

5. If it takes 10 s for you to do 1000 J of work, what is your power output?

6. **Mystery Photo** The photograph on page 106 shows the gears of a watch. Explain how these gears help do work. Use the terms *force* and *distance* in your answer. Is this a simple machine or a compound machine? Explain.

7. Which has the greater mechanical advantage, a ramp that is 10 m long and 2 m high or a ramp that is 5 m long and 2 m high?

8. **Application** A person slides a box 10 m across a floor. The floor exerts a friction force on the box of 40 N.

   a. Draw a picture of this situation.

   b. Label the effort force, resistance force, and distance.

   c. How much work was done?

## Develop Your Skills

Use the skills you have developed in this chapter to complete each activity.

1. **Interpret Data**  Three crates, each weighing 200 N, are pushed down a hallway. The amount of work done on each crate is shown on the bar graph below.

   a. What factor(s) could account for the differences in the amount of work done on each crate?

   b. Suppose each crate was pushed for 2 min. To which crate was the least power applied?

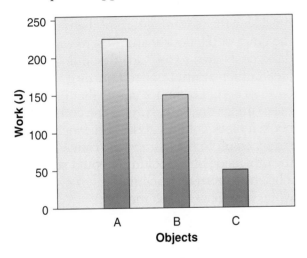

2. **Calculate**  How many joules of work are done on an object when a force of 10 N pushes it a distance of 10 m?

3. **Data Bank**  Use the information on page 638 to answer the following questions.

   a. What machine has the highest mechanical efficiency? The lowest?

   b. What machine(s) have a mechanical efficiency less than 50 percent?

## Make Connections

1. **Link the Concepts**  Make a concept map to show how the following concepts from this chapter link together: work, force, distance, energy, object, simple machines, and compound machines.

2. **Science and Social Studies**  James Watt was a Scottish engineer. He built a fast, efficient steam engine in the 1760s. The SI unit for power is named for him. The joule and the newton are also named for scientists from the past. Find out as much as you can about James Prescott Joule and Isaac Newton. When did they live? What were their occupations? What did they invent or discover?

3. **Science and Technology**  The earliest bicycles were very different in design from modern ones. They had no gears or steering systems. Pedals were not added until 1861. Research the development of the modern bicycle. Draw diagrams of bicycles from the past that show its evolution. Label your drawings with the names of simple machines that are part of each machine.

4. **Science and You**  The energy required for maintaining life comes from the chemically-stored potential energy in food. During digestion this is changed into other forms of energy. What happens to a person whose work output is less than the energy taken in? What happens when the person's work output is greater than the energy taken in? Can an undernourished person perform extra work without extra food? Explain your answers.

# Science and Literature Connection

**O**mar took the end of the coil of rope, squatted down and tied it firmly around one of the legs of my desk.

"Why are you doing that?"

"So we can find our way back, in case we get lost [in the fourth dimension]." He stood up and hooked a strap from his harness around one of my belt loops. "Take my hand, Laura." He reached out his left hand, and I took it with my right. His hand was unpleasantly moist. "We won't go far. We'll just look around your room. But still, no matter what happens, you must *not* let go of my hand. You got that, Laura? Do *not* let go."

"Why not? What about this strap?"

"Straps can get unhooked. And if we ever got separated, you could easily get lost. And you might never find your way back. And I might never be able to find you. It's big out there, and it's complicated. If I lost you . . . It's too terrible to even think about. Do you promise not to let go?"

"Yes, yes, I promise."

He squeezed my hand. "Here we go."

Omar bent his knees and lifted his arms like a plump little Superman preparing to take off. I did the same. His face reddened and a vein stood out on his forehead. He tilted over in a sideways direction. Then his body was stretching out at an impossible angle. He rippled and pulsated like a reflection in a distorting mirror. He grunted.

The floor lurched and tilted away. I closed my eyes. It was like falling down an unexpected stairway in the darkness. Dizziness slammed through me. My stomach jumped. My fingers loosened and began to slip away from Omar's.

He gripped my hand harder. We weren't

### The Boy Who Reversed Himself

*The following excerpts are from the novel* The Boy Who Reversed Himself *by William Sleator*

falling. The dizziness stopped.

"Open your eyes, Laura," Omar said.

I opened them. Instantly I squeezed them shut, moaning, dizzier than before.

"Take it slow, Laura. Try not to move your head. You'll get used to it."

Cautiously, my heart pounding, I opened my eyes again.

My bedroom floor hung directly above me. I saw the woven pattern of the rag rug, the grain of the floorboards. There was a dark, dusty area to one side that didn't look familiar, until I noticed the dim cover of an old romance comic that had fallen under my desk. Next to the comic book, a black column about three inches stretched off to the left and the right. On the other side of the column I could see a bright pattern of blue-and-white octagons. It took me a

moment to realize it was the bathroom floor.

"Keep your eyes fixed in one place, Laura," Omar said, invisible beside me. "You okay?"

"But nothing makes sense! I can hardly tell what I'm looking at."

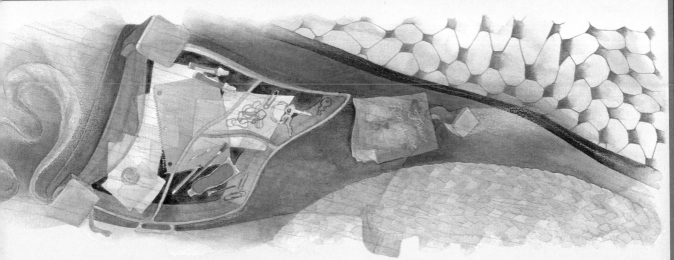

"That's because you don't have 4-D eyes, so you can only see a 3-D cross section of 4-D space. When you move your eyes, you'll see a different section. You have to learn how to put them all together. Now, move your head just a little bit."

I turned my head about an inch. There was a confusing moment of things rushing past. Then another picture stabilized. . . .

I saw a confusing jumble of objects in separate compartments, heavily outlined by shadows. I began to recognize pencils and rubber bands and keys, an old school work-book from last year, a pyramidlike shape of many layers that seemed to be a pile of paper viewed from some peculiar angle. And what was that wrinkled red oval thing with a thin black edge? A tube of red paint, seen from the inside and the outside at the same time.

I lifted my hand to take the tube of paint out of the desk. In the flashlight beam, I saw white bones enclosed in layered strips of pink, thin branching wires with blue liquid coursing through them.

"My hand!" I whispered. "I can see the inside of my hand!"

## Skills in Science

### Reading Skills in Science

1. **Find Context Clues** Identify the two main characters in the selection.

2. **Find the Main Idea** What is the main idea of the selection?

### Writing Skills in Science

1. **Compare and Contrast** Describe how Laura's perspective of her room is different in four dimensions than it is in three.

2. **Predict** What do you think the picture being stabilized at the end of the reading might be? Identify the lines on which you based your prediction.

### Activities

**Communicate** Illustrate the difference between the second and third dimensions by creating a model of each dimension.

**Collect Data** Use reference materials to learn about techniques artists use to create a three-dimensional effect on a two-dimensional medium.

### Where to Read More

*A Wrinkle in Time* by Madeline L'Engle. New York: Farrar, 1962. Meg and her brother travel through time and space to the planet of Camazotz in search of their scientist father.

# Unit 2

## Particles of Matter

### Chapters

**6** Properties of Matter

**7** Atoms, Elements, Compounds, and Mixtures

**8** Introduction to the Periodic Table

# Data Bank

Use the information on pages 634 to 643 to answer the questions about topics explored in this unit.

## Observing

List three patterns in the placement of the elements in the modern periodic table.

## Comparing

Which element has the highest density: helium, iron, oxygen, or uranium?

## Generalizing

Make a general statement about the relationship between atomic mass and atomic number.

## Interpreting Data

How does the amount of iron in the earth's crust compare to the amount of silicon?

The photograph to the left shows downtown Chicago at night. What are some kinds of matter used in these buildings?

# Chapter 6

# Properties of Matter

## Chapter Sections

6.1 Matter

6.2 Phases of Matter

6.3 Changes in Matter

## What do you see?

"As I look at the picture, I see many different designs. One design is an overhead view of different colored palm trees. The trees are very close together. I also see flowers in full bloom with soft crevices deep in their petals. The flowers are blowing in the wind. Or, I see many shapes of windmills spinning rapidly. Turning the picture causes the shapes to look like rocks or shells artistically arranged."

*LaToya Cobbins*
*Sullivan High School*
*Chicago, Illinois*

To find out more about the photograph, look on page 154. As you read this chapter, you will learn about matter, phases of matter, and changes in matter.

# 6.1 Matter

## Objectives

▶ **Define** matter and describe its major properties.

▶ **Explain** how the arrangement of particles in a substance may determine its properties.

▶ **Classify** kinds of matter based on their properties.

▶ **Make a model** illustrating the particle model of matter.

Imagine you are an astronaut approaching the earth from space. At first the earth appears as a distant blue and white sphere. As you get closer, you see the shapes of continents. Then rivers, mountains, highways, and cities come into view. When you near the surface, you see cars on the highways, houses in the cities, and beaches by the ocean. If you land on a beach, you see sand and waves. Looking closer, you see even the individual grains of sand that make up the beach. Do you think the grains of sand are made of things that are still smaller?

## Particle Model of Matter

Grains of sand and everything else you see, hear, smell, touch, and taste are made of **matter**. Matter is anything that has mass and takes up space. Matter exists in many shapes, colors, textures, and forms. Water, rocks, living things, and stars are all made of matter.

To understand matter, you need to take a closer look at it. As an astronaut approaches the earth from outer space, the features of the planet's surface become more visible. Similarly, as you examine matter more closely, more of its parts are revealed.

All forms of matter are made up of tiny particles that are in constant motion. This idea is known as the **particle model** of matter. The particles that make up matter are much too small to see. Even the tiniest speck of matter contains huge numbers of particles. Particles vary in their size, shape, arrangement, motion, and individual properties. These factors help explain the properties of matter.

**Figure 6.1** ▲
The closer you get to something, the more you can observe about the parts that make it up. What can you observe about the earth when standing on its surface that you can't observe from outer space?

# Properties of Matter

Investigating the properties of a sample of matter gives you important clues about its nature and composition, or makeup. Each of the many kinds of matter in the universe has characteristics that help to identify it. These characteristics are known as properties. Knowing the properties of a sample of matter can help you to classify it with other substances.

Some properties such as mass, volume, and density are common to all matter. These properties can be measured by using the methods described in Chapter 1. You can observe many other properties of matter using your senses. Some properties that are easily observed include color, texture, odor, luster, and transparency.

These common rocks are similar, but they have different textures. The dark-colored slate has a smooth, fine-grained texture. The speckled granite has a coarse, large-grained texture. How do you think each rock would feel if you could touch it? ▼

▲ These leaves appear green because they reflect green light back to your eyes. All objects that appear green, whether living or nonliving, reflect green light.

Most metals, such as copper, silver, and gold, have a shiny appearance, or luster. ▼

Many other properties of matter can be observed by using simple tests and measurements. These properties include hardness, resistance to breakage, and the ability to dissolve in water. Various kinds of matter also differ in how they interact with other substances, and how they are affected by temperature changes.

Baking soda reacts strongly with vinegar, and less strongly with water. Baking soda is used in cooking to make quick breads rise. ▼

▲ Some types of matter, including iron, nickel, and cobalt, are affected by magnetic fields. This lodestone contains permanently magnetized iron.

Electricity flows easily through the copper in the center of these wires. Copper is a conductor. In contrast, the plastic covering the wires does not conduct electricity at all. Plastic is an insulator. ▼

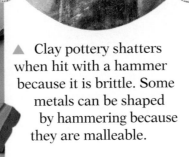

▲ Clay pottery shatters when hit with a hammer because it is brittle. Some metals can be shaped by hammering because they are malleable.

# ▼ ACTIVITY

## Making a Model

### Dividing the Water

How many times can the water in a glass be divided in two? Develop a mental model of what would happen if you halved the volume over and over again until you were left with the smallest particle that was still water. How small would it be? What would it look like if you could see it?

## SKILLS WORKOUT

**Figure 6.2**

Diamond, graphite, and soot have different properties because the arrangement of their carbon particles differs. ▼

# Explaining Matter's Properties

Why is matter so varied? What gives each kind of matter its special properties? The properties of any kind of matter are determined in part by the way its particles are arranged.

Look at Figure 6.2 below. Diamond, graphite, and soot are made up of identical particles of carbon, even though they are very different substances. These three kinds of matter are different because their carbon particles are arranged differently. Notice that the particles making up the diamond form a rigid, three-dimensional framework. All the particles are held together strongly. Graphite particles, in contrast, form layers. The layers are held together so weakly that they slide past one another, making graphite very soft. The particles in soot are randomly arranged and held together weakly.

Many other properties of matter are determined by the characteristics of the particles themselves. For example, particles that reflect green light give a substance the property of being green in color. The particles in baking soda, not their arrangement, account for how it reacts in vinegar.

The motion of the particles in matter is also important. The speed of particle movement changes with temperature. As the temperature increases, the speed of the particles in matter increases. Particle movement determines whether a substance will be a solid, liquid, or gas.

Graphite

Diamond

Soot

## Science and Technology
### *Enhancing the Stone*

Throughout history, gemstones have been heated to make them look clearer and to deepen their color. The ancient Romans heated agate, a variety of quartz, to enhance its color. In Sri Lanka, the current method for heating rubies dates back to about the year 1240.

Clear, deeply colored gems are very valuable. The color of any gemstone depends on the type and amount of particles present in the stone. So, if you can increase the number of certain kinds of particles present in a gem, you may be able to increase its value.

Not only heating, but other specialized techniques can heighten the clarity and color of gems. In one technique, colorless sapphires are packed in metal oxide powders. These precious packages are heated above 2,000°C for 25 days. During this process, the gemstones absorb particles from the metal oxides. The gems that result, shown in Figure 6.3, are polished to a deep, clear blue. Unfortunately, the gems are not completely transformed by this process. If you cut one in half, the inside is still colorless!

**Figure 6.3** ▲
Gems such as sapphires begin as uncut stones (left). Before they become finished gems (center) they may go through a heating process (right).

## Check and Explain

1. Define matter and give three examples of matter.

2. Make a list of ten objects in your classroom and name at least one physical property for each object.

3. **Classify**  Organize ten different objects by grouping them by physical properties. Describe the properties on which you based your classification.

4. **Make a Model**  Choose one property of matter and draw a diagram to show an arrangement of particles that could determine the property.

▼ **ACTIVITY**

### Comparing

*Alike and Different*

How are ice, steam, and water alike? How are they different? Make a table and list their similar and different properties. Compare your table with that of a classmate.

**SKILLS WARMUP**

# 6.2 Phases of Matter

## Objectives

▶ **Give examples** of solids, liquids, and gases.

▶ **Relate** the particle model to solids, liquids, and gases.

▶ **Make models** illustrating the gas laws.

Imagine that you and your classmates represent particles of matter. During class, everyone is seated at desks in neatly arranged rows. This arrangement of students is like the arrangement of particles in a solid. You can move in your seats while at your desks, just as particles in a solid move about a fixed point.

At the end of class, you get up from your desks and move freely toward the door of the classroom. This close, but unorganized, movement resembles the motion of particles in a liquid. Finally, as you and your class-mates leave the classroom, you travel in many different directions through the school grounds. This movement is similar to the way particles of a gas spread out to fill a space.

## Familiar Phases of Matter

The three most familiar states of matter are solid, liquid, and gas. Each of these states of matter is called a phase. Like the students described above, particles of matter in each phase are arranged differently and have different ranges of motion.

**Figure 6.4**

In each phase of matter, the particles move about in a different way. ▼

Solid                Liquid                Gas

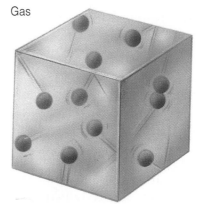

## Solids

The shape and volume of a rock are the same whether you put the rock in a shoe box or on a rock pile. When matter has a definite shape and a definite volume, it is a **solid**. A solid has these characteristics because of its closely packed particles. The particles can move slightly, but they do not change positions.

Most solids occur as crystals. Salt, bones, diamonds, computer chips, and snowflakes are all made up of crystals. Particles in a crystal are arranged in a regular, orderly way.

At some temperature, a solid substance melts to form a liquid. When the temperature of the melted substance is lowered, it becomes a solid again.

Materials such as glass, hard candy, and candle wax appear to be solid, but the arrangement of their particles is less regular. These materials are sometimes called amorphous (uh MOR fuhs) solids.

**Figure 6.5** ▲
A quartz crystal is a typical solid. Why do its shape and volume remain the same?

## Liquids

Matter with a definite volume, but no definite shape, is a **liquid**. Particles in a liquid behave something like bird seed in a sack. Like the bird seed, the liquid particles easily slide over each other. As a result, a liquid will take the shape of its container.

Look at Figure 6.6. It shows that the particles in a liquid are close together, but move enough so they do not stay in fixed positions. The particles flow freely past one another. Some liquids, like water, flow quickly. Other liquids, such as syrup, molasses, or motor oil, flow more slowly because the particles tend to stick together.

In most liquids at room temperature, some of the particles move fast and can escape into the air. This process, called evaporation, forms a vapor or gas. The opposite of evaporation is condensation (KAHN duhn SAY shuhn). When condensation occurs, a gas forms a liquid.

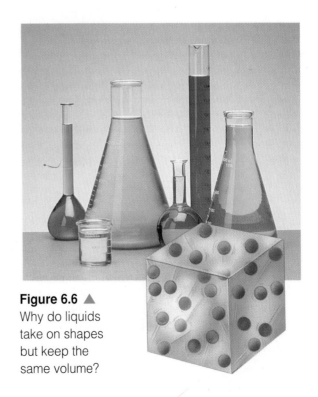

**Figure 6.6** ▲
Why do liquids take on shapes but keep the same volume?

*Phasing In*

Make a list of the things you used today that were in the gas phase. Then make lists of things you used that were solids and liquids. Did you use the same substance in two different phases? How is this possible?

## Gases

Matter that has no definite shape and no definite volume is a **gas**. Like a liquid, a gas will take the shape of any container. Unlike a liquid, a gas expands to fill whatever space is available. The scent of a flower and the odor of a rotten egg come from gases that can fill a room.

The air is made up of several different gases. Although air is invisible, you can feel the effect of gas particles striking you when the wind blows. Gases fill balloons, propel rockets, and enable your cells to release energy from nutrients.

Look at the gas particles shown in Figure 6.7. Notice that the particles do not stick to one another. They move in straight lines, flying all over. They change direction only when they strike the walls of their containers or bump into other particles. The particles in a gas move very far apart.

**Figure 6.7** ▶

How do you know that a blown-up balloon contains matter?

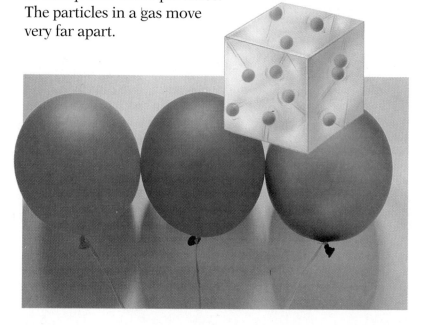

Unlike the particles in a solid or liquid, each gas particle is mostly unaffected by its neighbors. Only temperature and pressure can affect the way the particles move and the volume they occupy. Because each gas particle is independent of other gas particles, the behavior of gases can be described by general laws. These laws, called gas laws, hold true for a wide range of temperatures and pressures. However, at very high or very low temperatures or pressures, gases behave differently than the gas laws predict.

**Boyle's Law**   A gas sealed in a container has a certain pressure. Recall that pressure is the force created by particles striking the walls of a container. You have seen the effect of pressure on the rubber walls of balloons like those in Figure 6.7. The walls of the balloons are pushed out by the constant bumping of the gas particles trapped inside.

What happens to the pressure exerted by a gas when the volume of its container is changed? If you squeeze a gas into a smaller space, its particles will strike the walls of the container more often. The pressure on the walls will increase. If you increase the space, the gas particles strike the container's walls less often and the pressure will decrease. This relationship between pressure and volume is called *Boyle's Law*. It was discovered by Robert Boyle, a British scientist who lived in the 1600s.

Boyle's Law states that if a sample of gas is kept at a constant temperature, decreasing its volume will increase the pressure the gas exerts. Boyle's Law can be tested using a cylinder with a movable piston like the one shown in Figure 6.8. Data on pressure and volume can be used to construct a graph similar to the one you see below. What inferences can you make from the shape of the curve?

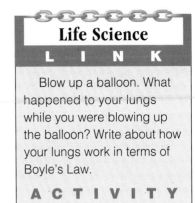

**Life Science**

**L I N K**

Blow up a balloon. What happened to your lungs while you were blowing up the balloon? Write about how your lungs work in terms of Boyle's Law.

**A C T I V I T Y**

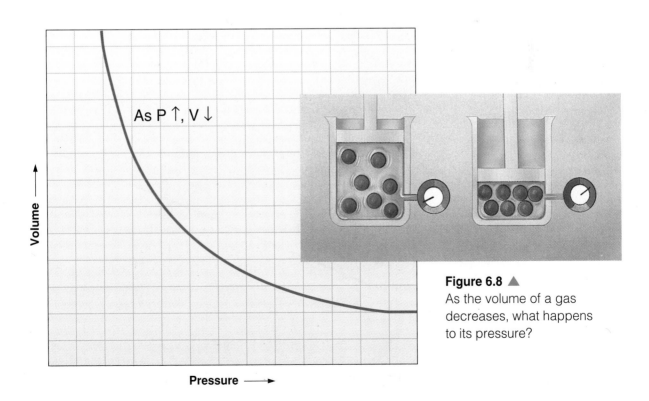

As P ↑, V ↓

Volume ⟶

Pressure ⟶

**Figure 6.8** ▲
As the volume of a gas decreases, what happens to its pressure?

**Charles' Law** The relationship between the temperature of a gas and its volume was first described in the late 1700s by a French scientist named Jacques Charles. According to *Charles' Law*, if a sample of gas is kept at constant pressure, its volume increases as the temperature increases. The graph in Figure 6.9 shows this relationship. Many products in spray cans, such as whipped cream and paint, contain gas at a fairly high pressure. Their labels warn you to keep them away from heat or fire. Why?

Adding heat energy to a gas causes the gas particles to move faster. When the particles move faster, they strike the walls of their container harder and more often. If the container walls aren't flexible, as in a can of whipped cream, the pressure of the gas will increase. Since the can will withstand only so much pressure, the result could be explosive and dangerous!

However, if a gas in a container with flexible walls is heated, the volume of the gas will increase. You can see the volume increase in the balloons in Figure 6.9. Cooling a gas causes the reverse to happen. The volume of the gas decreases. Have you noticed what happens to the air in sealed bags of food you put in the refrigerator?

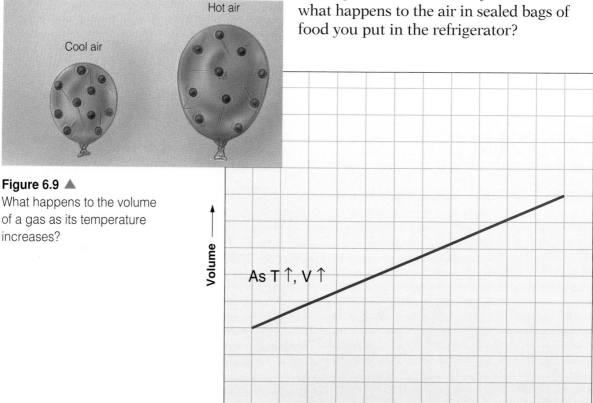

**Figure 6.9** ▲
What happens to the volume of a gas as its temperature increases?

## Plasmas

At very high temperatures, over 1 000 000°C, gas particles break down, forming a **plasma** (PLAZ muh) phase. Temperatures high enough to form plasmas exist naturally only in stars. Plasma, called the fourth phase of matter, is the most common phase of matter in the universe. The sun and other active stars are made up mostly of plasmas. These plasmas are formed from the gases hydrogen and helium.

Plasmas have unusual properties that gases do not have. For example, plasmas conduct electricity. Also, they are affected by magnetic fields. On earth, plasmas can be manufactured and studied only in special laboratories. These laboratories must be able to handle the extreme temperatures at which plasmas exist. No solid substance can contain plasma. Therefore, super-heated plasma is created and confined within a strong magnetic field, called a "magnetic bottle."

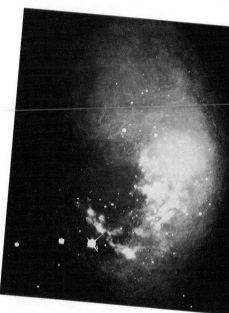

**Figure 6.10** ▲
Matter in the plasma phase makes up much of the universe.

# *SkillBuilder* Predicting

## *Going Through a Phase*

When you make ice cubes in an ice cube tray, the ice cubes take up more space than the water you poured into the tray. Based on this observation, predict what will happen in the following situation.

Two identical cups are filled with the same mass of water. One cup is placed in the freezer. The water in the other cup is kept at room temperature. After the water freezes, its mass is measured again. The masses of the cup of water and the cup of ice are compared. Are they the same or different? Try the experiment yourself:

1. Fill two plastic cups with 100 mL of water each. Using a balance, adjust the amount of water in the cups (a dropper can be used) until the two cups are the same in mass. Record this mass in a data table like the one shown.

2. Place one of the cups in the freezer overnight. Predict what will happen to the mass of the water when ice forms.

3. The next day, measure the mass of the cup of water and the cup of ice. Record your observations.

4. How did your prediction match your observations?

Write a paragraph describing the differences you observed when water changed from the liquid phase to the solid phase.

|  | **Starting mass** | **Treatment** | **Ending mass** |
|---|---|---|---|
| Cup A |  | None |  |
| Cup B |  | Frozen |  |

**Figure 6.11** ▲

Can you tell which of these containers holds the most liquid?

## Science and You *Packaging Liquids*

When you shop for a liquid product, such as a mouthwash, how do you decide which product gives you the most mouthwash for your money? One way is to compare the shape and size of bottles. If you have tried this comparison, however, you may have discovered that appearances can fool you.

Bottles can be designed to fool your eye and make you think that containers hold more liquid than they actually do. Sometimes, unusual shapes with indentations are used to make bottles appear larger. You know that a liquid takes the shape of its container. But shape and volume have a complex relationship that is difficult to determine just by observation. As a result, it is hard to tell how much liquid is present by comparing the containers.

A better way to tell how much of a product is in a container is to read the label. The law requires that labels tell you the volume of liquid you are purchasing. Usually this measurement is given in liters or milliliters. By determining the cost per unit volume of several different brands, you can decide which product is the most economical. You divide the price by the volume. For example, a 0.5-liter bottle of mouthwash costing $2.50 is $5.00 per liter. Is this a better buy than mouthwash costing $3.00 for 0.6 liters?

## Check and Explain

1. List two examples each of a solid, a liquid, and a gas.

2. Draw a diagram to show the spacing of particles in a solid, a liquid, and a gas.

3. **Find Causes** If you take a bicycle trip on a hot summer day, would you expect your tire pressure to be higher at the beginning or at the end of the trip? Explain.

4. **Make a Model** Place a balloon filled with air in a container of ice water and observe its volume. Then place the balloon into a container of very warm water. Make a table to record your observations of the volume of the balloon at room temperature, in the ice water, and in the very warm water. Explain how this illustrates Charles' Law.

# 6.3 Changes in Matter

## Objectives

▶ **Give examples** of physical and chemical changes.

▶ **Compare** and **contrast** physical and chemical changes.

▶ **Interpret data** about a phase change.

If you hang your wet washcloth in the bathroom, it will dry. If you forget to clean your paintbrush and the paint dries, the paintbrush becomes hard and useless. The drying washcloth and the hardening paint are examples of changes in matter. The water in the washcloth and also in the paint changed to water vapor in the air. As the water in the paint changed to water vapor, the paint hardened. The small particles in the paint joined together to form long chainlike particles. This change made the paint form a hard, shiny film on the brush.

## Physical Changes in Matter

If you break a piece of glass, the shape of the glass changes. However, the fragments of glass contain the same particles and have the same properties as the original piece of glass. If you cut and sand a piece of wood to make a model, only the size and shape of the wood changes. When you freeze water into an ice cube and then let it melt, the liquid that remains is still water.

When matter undergoes a change in size, shape, or phase, it is a **physical change**. Physical changes do not change the particles that make up matter. The arrangement of the particles, however, may be moved around during a physical change.

Are you causing a physical change when you mix salt and water? A mixture of salt and water can be compared to a mixture of nails and screws. You can separate a mixture of nails and screws by hand. In a similar way, a mixture of pebbles and sand can be separated with a strainer. If you make a mixture of salt and water, the particles are too small for you to separate by hand or strainer. However, the water can be boiled away, leaving the salt behind.

**Figure 6.12** ▲
What physical change will occur as the warm sun strikes these icicles?

Because the particles in a mixture do not change and can be easily separated, making a mixture is also an example of a physical change.

Physical changes help shape the earth's surface. The weathering and erosion of rocks involves many kinds of physical changes. For example, rocks are broken apart by the repeated freezing and thawing of water in the cracks, as shown in Figure 6.13. Heat from the sun also breaks rocks into smaller pieces. The outer layer of rock expands as it gets hot in the sun. As the rock cools quickly at night, its outer layer shrinks and cracks.

The pieces of rock produced by these weathering processes are then carried away by gravity, water, and wind. These forms of erosion grind and break the rock pieces into even smaller bits. The sand grains that result have the same kinds of particles as the rocks they came from.

**Figure 6.13**
Rocks are physically changed by processes such as ice wedging.
▼

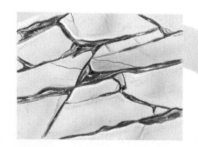

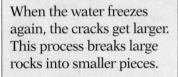

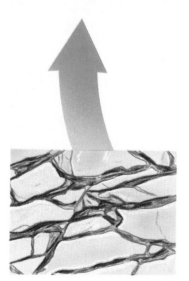

When the water freezes again, the cracks get larger. This process breaks large rocks into smaller pieces.

As water in the cracks of the rock freezes and expands, it forces the sides of the crack outward. The cracks become wider and deeper.

The ice thaws when the rock is warmed by the sun. More water fills the larger cracks.

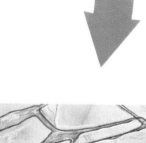

## Chemical Changes in Matter

Have you seen matter undergo a change that was not just a physical change? If you leave an iron nail outside, it will rust. When you compare the rust with the iron nail, you will find that both the nail and the rust have different properties. The color and hardness of rust and iron are different. Rust is a new substance, resulting from a **chemical change** in the iron nail. In a chemical change, particles of one substance are changed in some way to form particles of a new substance that has new and different properties.

**Evidence of Chemical Changes**  How do you know when a chemical change has occurred? Look at the photographs below to see different kinds of evidence for chemical changes. The production of heat or light, the appearance of gas bubbles, and the formation of a solid all indicate that a chemical change has taken place.

▼ **ACTIVITY**

**Defining Operationally**

*Kinds of Changes*

Think about what happens to a newspaper when it burns. Identify any physical changes or chemical changes that take place in the newspaper. Explain how you would know whether each change is a physical change or chemical one.

**SKILLS WORKOUT**

▲ What evidence of chemical change do you see on the surface of this plant? What kind of substance is being given off by the chemical change?

◀ To produce the glow of light below its head, a chemical change occurs inside the body of the firefly. What other kinds of chemical changes produce light?

▲ If you polished a spot on the Statue of Liberty, you would find a bright orange metal color. The blue-green color you see here is caused by a chemical change.

How can you tell a chemical change from a physical change? One way is to observe whether the matter that has changed can be changed back to the original form by physical means. Any change in phase, for example, can be reversed. Ice can melt to form water, and water can freeze to form ice. Usually only physical changes can be reversed.

**Chemical Changes in Rocks** The earth's surface is shaped by chemical changes as well as physical changes. Gases in the atmosphere and water combine with minerals in rocks to create new substances. These chemical changes weaken rocks so that they chip, crack, and break apart more easily. Chemical weathering happens to rocks all over the earth's surface. Chemical changes work together with physical changes to weather and erode the earth's surface. These changes in matter help to shape mountains and plains, and to form soil.

## Career Corner *Chef*

### Who Causes Physical and Chemical Changes in Food?

A chef is responsible for the preparation of food in the kitchen of a restaurant or institution. In a large kitchen, the chef supervises the work of cooks who may each be in charge of one type of food preparation. In small restaurants, one or two chefs, often the owners, prepare all the food themselves.

Think of a kitchen as a laboratory. A chef, like a chemist, separates, mixes, measures, and heats various substances. A chef must know how to cause the right kinds of chemical and physical changes in food.

The preparation of many dishes involves changing food products physically. For example, when a chef chops onions or chiles, only the size and shape of the vegetables change.

When a chef cooks food, it is often changed chemically. Heat breaks down large food particles into smaller ones. The cooked dish usually has very different properties from the properties of the starting ingredients. For example, when the chef cooks an egg, chemical changes occur. The color of the egg yolk and the egg white change. The texture of the egg changes as well.

If you want to be a chef, you can learn the required skills at a culinary school or in some community colleges. You may also be able to train on the job. For more information, write to the National Institute for the Food Service Industry.

## Science and You *Haircuts and Permanents*

When you change your hairstyle, you may be making use of physical or chemical changes. Cutting your hair is a physical change. The hair itself has not been changed, only the length of the hair shafts. However, permanent waves and hair relaxers cause chemical changes in your hair.

Each hair shaft is made of ropelike bundles of protein fibers produced by your hair follicles. These bundles are held together by chemical bonds. The bonds hold the shape of each shaft of hair by preventing the bundles from moving.

A substance called thioglycolic (THY oh gly KAH lihk) acid can break the bonds holding the bundles together. It is the active ingredient of most permanent wave solutions. After thioglycolic acid has been applied, the fiber bundles can slide past one another. The hair becomes soft and stretchable. At this point, straight hair can be made curly, by wrapping it around rollers. Curly hair can be made straight by stretching and combing. After styling, the fiber bundles are bonded back together in their new positions using a hardening solution of hydrogen peroxide.

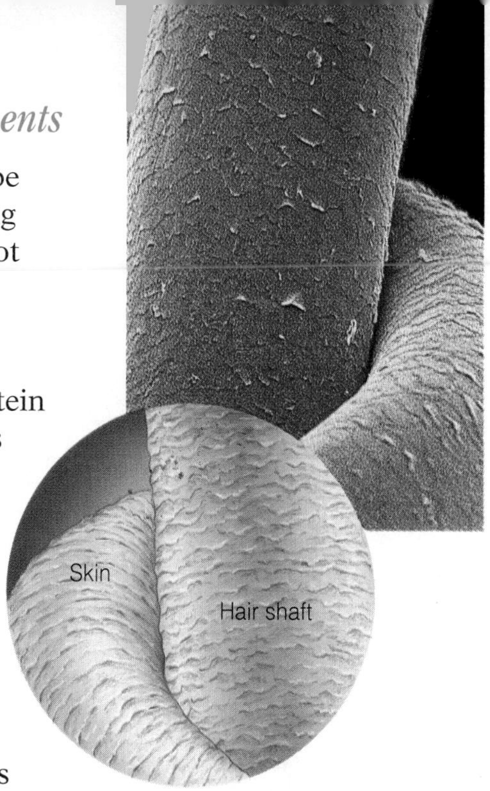

Skin

Hair shaft

**Figure 6.14** ▲
Making straight hair curly or curly hair straight requires chemical changes affecting the hair's structure.

## Check and Explain

1. Give three examples of physical changes and three examples of chemical changes.

2. Explain how to distinguish between a chemical change and a physical change.

3. **Classify**   Identify each of the following as a chemical or a physical change.

   a. Oxygen gas is liquefied.

   b. Liquid oxygen is burned to power a space shuttle.

   c. Liquid oxygen evaporates.

   d. Space shuttle passengers breathe oxygen gas.

4. **Interpret Data**   A student measured the temperature of a recently melted ice cube at 0°C. After freezing the water back into an ice cube, she found that its temperature was the same. Explain why the temperature remained the same.

# Activity 6 *What is the evidence for a chemical change?*

***Skills*** Observe; Measure; Infer; Interpret Data

## Task 1 Prelab Prep
Gather the following materials: 1 teaspoon baking soda, 1 teaspoon calcium chloride, 10 mL phenol red solution, a vial with a lid, and 1 liter-sized self-locking plastic bag.

## Task 2 Data Record
1. On a separate sheet of paper, draw the data table shown.
2. Record your observations about the properties of each of the substances in the data table.

## Task 3 Procedure
1. Put 1 teaspoon of baking soda (NaHCO₃) into the self-locking plastic bag. **CAUTION! Wear gloves, a laboratory apron, and goggles when using these chemicals.**
2. Put 1 teaspoon of calcium chloride (CaCl₂) into the bag with the baking soda and mix the two substances.
3. Measure 10 mL of phenol red solution and pour it into the vial.
4. Place the vial into the self-locking plastic bag so that it is standing upright in the dry powder.
5. Carefully seal the self-locking plastic bag, taking care not to spill the contents of the vial.

6. From the outside, work with the bag and its contents so that you spill the phenol red solution in the vial into the baking soda and calcium chloride. Be careful not to unseal the bag.
7. Hold the bag in your hands and observe any changes. **CAUTION! Wash your hands after the activity.**

## Task 4 Analysis
1. Describe any changes in the properties of the substances in the bag.
2. What is the evidence that a chemical change has taken place?
3. What is the evidence that a physical change has taken place?

## Task 5 Conclusion
Have the substances in the bag gone through a physical change or a chemical change? Write a paragraph explaining your answer.

## *Everyday Application*
Describe how you could make an emergency hand-warmer.

## *Extension*
Hypothesize which of the substances in this activity caused heat energy to be released. Write out the procedures that you would use to test your hypothesis.

**Table 6.1 Observations**

| Substance | Before mixing | After mixing |
|---|---|---|
| | Properties | Properties of mixture |
| Baking powder | | |
| Calcium chloride | | |
| Phenol red | | |

# Chapter 6 Review

## Concept Summary

### 6.1 Matter

▶ Matter is anything that has mass and takes up space.

▶ All forms of matter are made up of tiny, constantly moving particles.

▶ Matter has properties that can be observed and measured.

▶ The properties of matter are determined in part by the arrangement of the particles that make it up, and in part by the properties of the particles themselves.

### 6.2 Phases of Matter

▶ A solid has a definite shape and a definite volume.

▶ A liquid has a definite volume but no definite shape.

▶ A gas has neither a definite shape nor a definite volume.

▶ According to Boyle's Law, a decrease in the volume of a certain amount of gas will result in an increase in its pressure.

▶ According to Charles' Law, an increase in the temperature of a certain amount of gas will result in an increase in its volume.

### 6.3 Changes in Matter

▶ A physical change is a change in the size, shape, or phase of matter.

▶ A chemical change occurs when new kinds of particles are created.

▶ Chemical changes may produce heat or light, create bubbles of gas, or form a new solid.

## Chapter Vocabulary

matter (6.1)

particle model (6.1)

solid (6.2)

liquid (6.2)

gas (6.2)

plasma (6.2)

physical change (6.3)

chemical change (6.3)

## Check Your Vocabulary

Use the vocabulary words above to complete the following sentences correctly.

1. Matter with a definite volume but no definite shape is a ____ .

2. The evaporation of a liquid into a gas is an example of a ____ .

3. Everything you can see or touch is made up of ____ .

4. Matter in the ____ phase fills whatever space is available to it.

5. The ____ of matter describes matter as made up of tiny, constantly moving particles.

6. Matter in the ____ phase can be held in your hand.

7. Stars are made up mainly of ____ .

8. If you combine two kinds of matter and heat is produced, you know a ____ has taken place.

Explain the difference between the terms in each pair.

9. Gas, plasma.

10. Physical change, chemical change.

11. Phase change, weathering.

12. Gas, air.

13. Particle model, phase change.

## Write Your Vocabulary

Write sentences for each of the vocabulary words in the list. Show that you know what each word means.

# Chapter 6 *Review*

## Check Your Knowledge

Answer the following in complete sentences.

1. What are the four phases of matter?

2. Give an example of a chemical change. What is one way of knowing that a chemical change has occurred?

3. Choose a kind of matter you can see right now. List five of its properties.

4. Why do diamonds and graphite have different properties?

5. What is the opposite of condensation?

6. What is ice wedging?

7. Describe the movement of the particles in a solid.

Choose the answer that best completes each sentence.

8. The phase change from solid to liquid is called (melting, boiling, freezing, evaporation).

9. One of the properties common to all matter is (luster, electrical conductivity, density, transparency).

10. If the temperature of a gas is increased, its (mass, density, volume, weight) will increase also.

11. Breaking a balloon is an example of a (phase change, physical change, chemical change, temperature change).

12. Chemical weathering occurs when the minerals in rocks are (heated, broken apart, frozen, chemically changed).

13. The particles of matter move slowest in a (solid, liquid, gas, plasma).

## Check Your Understanding

Apply the concepts you have learned to answer each question.

1. Contrast the movement of particles in solids, liquids, and gases.

2. **Critical Thinking** According to Charles' Law, the volume of a gas decreases as its temperature is decreased. Is there a temperature at which the volume of a sample of gas will reach zero? Explain.

3. Do all kinds of matter exist in all three phases? Give reasons for your answer.

4. **Mystery Photo** The photograph on page 134 shows the crystalline structure of aspirin. Look closely at the photograph. What evidence do you see that the aspirin has particles arranged as crystals?

5. **Classify** For each of the following, tell whether it involves a physical change or a chemical change.

   a. Burning wood

   b. Shaking up a soft drink

   c. Digesting food

   d. Boiling water

   e. Writing with a pencil

   f. Putting mousse on your hair

6. **Extension** Some kinds of matter change directly from a solid to a gas at a certain temperature. Solid carbon dioxide, or "dry ice," is an example of matter that does not go through a liquid phase. Using the particle model, develop an explanation for this behavior.

7. **Application** When you inflate a bicycle tire, you force a large volume of air into a small space. If you release some air from a fully inflated tire, will it be warm or cold? Explain how Charles' Law helps you make this prediction.

## Develop Your Skills

Use the skills you have developed in this chapter to complete each activity.

1. **Interpret Data**  The table below contains data from an experiment in which the pressure of a sample of gas was measured at various volumes.

   a. For which volumes are pressure measurements given?

   b. When the volume was reduced from 50 cm$^3$ to 31 cm$^3$, by how much did the pressure increase?

   c. Estimate the pressure at 25 cm$^3$. How could you make a reasonably accurate prediction without doing any calculations?

| Volume (cm$^3$) | Pressure (Pa) |
|:---:|:---:|
| 50 | 67,000 |
| 31 | 108,000 |
| 21 | 159,000 |
| 15 | 222,000 |

2. **Graph**  Use the data in the table above to draw a line graph. If you were not sure how to answer question 1b above, read it again after you have completed the graph.

3. **Data Bank**  Use the information on page 641 to answer the following questions.

   a. What is the melting point of gold?

   b. At room temperature (25°C) is bromine a solid, liquid, or gas?

4. **Calculate**  Look again at the table in question 1 above. Multiply each volume by its corresponding pressure measurement. What do you notice?

## Make Connections

1. **Link the Concepts**  Below is a concept map showing how some of the main concepts in this chapter link together. Only parts of the map are filled in. Copy the map. Using words and ideas from the chapter, complete the map.

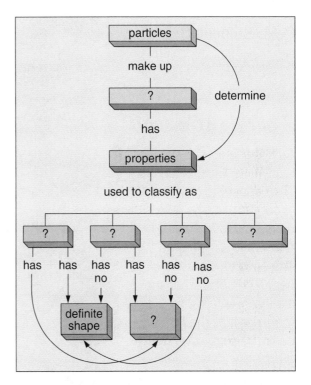

2. **Science and History**  The idea that matter is made up of tiny particles is very old. An ancient Greek scientist named Democritus was one of the first to propose a particle theory. Research Democritus and his ideas about matter. How did the method he used to reach his conclusions differ from modern scientific method?

3. **Science and Geometry**  Crystals exist in seven different basic shapes, called systems. Research these seven crystal systems. Discover the name of each one and make a drawing of it.

# Chapter 7

# Atoms, Elements, Compounds, and Mixtures

## Chapter Sections

7.1 Structure of the Atom

7.2 Elements

7.3 Compounds

7.4 Mixtures

## What do you see?

66 This photograph contains many different substances. They appear to be different minerals, perhaps gold or iron pyrite (commonly referred to as 'fool's gold'). The conglomerate in the center contains other substances. There is also a large rock, perhaps the rim of a basin, as suggested by the dampness of the specimens. These are all made of basic elements and compounds. 99

*Chad Henderson*
*Woodford County School*
*Versailles, Kentucky*

To find out more about the photograph, look on page 180. As you read this chapter, you will learn about atoms, elements, compounds, and mixtures.

**156**

# 7.1 Structure of the Atom

## Objectives

▶ **Summarize** how models of the atom have changed.

▶ **Name** and **describe** the parts of the atom.

▶ **Calculate** the numbers of protons, neutrons, and electrons in an atom given its mass number.

Y ou have learned that all matter in the universe is made up of tiny particles. A glass of water, for example, has many water particles, each too small to see. If you could see them, what would they look like? What makes them different from the particles of other kinds of matter?

## Atoms and Elements

Water particles can actually be divided into even smaller units. The pieces of matter that result from dividing a water particle are no longer water. They are examples of the most basic units of matter called **atoms**. Atoms can't be broken down into smaller pieces by any common methods of separating matter.

Atoms are the building blocks of the universe. As with other sets of building blocks, there are different kinds of atoms. Scientists have identified nearly 100 different kinds of naturally-occurring atoms. Each kind has unique properties and is called an **element**. An atom of an element can't be broken down and retain its properties.

Look at Figure 7.1. The particles of matter can be made of single atoms, two or more atoms of the same element, or two or more atoms of different elements. You can see that a water particle is made up of three atoms, two of hydrogen and one of oxygen.

## Models of the Atom

All atoms share the same basic structure. During the past 200 years, scientists have proposed different models for this structure. Each model was the best one for its time. With new observations or experiments, however, the model had to be changed.

Particle of helium
1 atom of 1 element

Particle of oxygen
2 atoms of 1 element

Particle of water
3 atoms of 2 elements

**Figure 7.1** ▲
Some atoms exist alone as separate particles. Other atoms form particles by joining together in groups of two or more.

**Dalton's Model**   In the early 1800s, John Dalton performed experiments with gases. His results convinced him that matter was made up of tiny, indivisible particles.

Dalton observed, for example, that the same amounts of hydrogen and oxygen always combined to form a given amount of water. He reasoned that each element must be made of its own unique kind of particle and that these particles combine in simple ways. Dalton called these basic particles atoms and pictured them as tiny, solid spheres.

Based on his experiments, Dalton developed a theory of the structure of matter. His theory contained four main concepts.

▶ All matter is composed of tiny, indivisible particles called atoms.

▶ Atoms of each element are exactly alike.

▶ Atoms of different elements have different masses.

▶ Atoms of different elements can join to form compounds.

**Thomson's Model**   At the end of the 1800s, J. J. Thomson discovered that atoms were not just simple, solid spheres. They contained even smaller, *sub*atomic particles. The subatomic particles Thomson discovered were very small and negatively charged. Thomson called them **electrons**.

Thomson discovered electrons while experimenting with a glass vacuum tube containing metal electrodes. When he connected the tube to a source of high-voltage electricity, glowing green "rays" appeared inside. Thomson discovered that electric charges bent the rays. The rays, he inferred, had to be made of charged particles.

Thomson knew that atoms are electrically neutral. Therefore, he reasoned, an atom must contain enough positive charge to balance the negative charge of the electrons. Thomson developed an atomic model in which electrons were stuck into a positively charged sphere, like chocolate chips in cookie dough. A positive charge in the substance of the sphere balanced the electrons' charge.

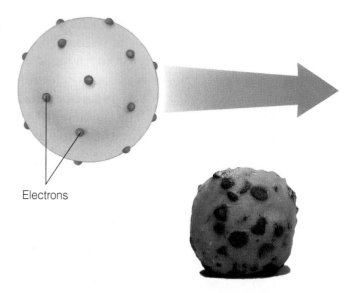

Electrons

In the early 1800s, John Dalton proposed the first scientific theory about atoms. In this model, atoms were solid spheres.

J. J. Thomson discovered the first subatomic particle, the electron. He imagined electrons to be stuck in the atom's surface.

**Rutherford's Model** By the early 1900s, scientists knew that the positive charge of an atom comes from subatomic particles called **protons**. A proton is a positive particle with a mass much greater than that of an electron. At that time, scientists hypothesized that electrons and protons were evenly scattered throughout an atom.

In 1911, Ernest Rutherford set out to test this theory. He aimed a beam of positively charged particles at a sheet of gold foil only a few atoms thick. Most of the particles passed straight through the foil. To Rutherford's surprise, however, some particles bounced back. The only explanation for this result was that the particles had struck objects larger than single protons.

Rutherford reasoned that the protons are concentrated in a small area at the center of the atom. He called this region the **nucleus** (NOO klee uhs). According to this model, an atom is mostly empty space. The nucleus is tiny compared to the whole atom, but it contains nearly all the atom's mass.

**Bohr's Model** Niels Bohr modified Rutherford's model in 1913. He proposed that each electron in an atom has a fixed amount of energy. This energy keeps an electron moving around the nucleus within a specific region called an *energy level*. In Bohr's model, energy levels surround the nucleus in rings or shells, like the layers of an onion.

The energy levels in Bohr's model can be compared to the rungs of a ladder. Moving out from the nucleus, each energy level is like a higher rung on the ladder. By absorbing or releasing a specific amount of energy, an electron can move from one energy level to another just as you can climb up or down a ladder. And just as you can't be between rungs on a ladder, an electron can't be between energy levels.

Bohr's model has been called the planetary model. It compares electrons to planets and the nucleus to the sun. The energy levels occupied by electrons are like the orbits of planets at different distances from the sun.

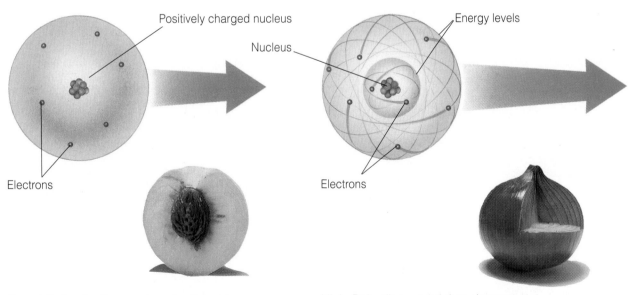

Ernest Rutherford's experiments showed that an atom's mass is concentrated in the nucleus.

Niels Bohr discovered that electrons surround the nucleus in specific regions called energy levels.

**Electron Cloud Model** Each atomic model offered new ideas and information about the nature of matter. Today scientists know that electrons do not actually orbit the nucleus as in Bohr's planetary model. The electron cloud model is now used to describe atoms. In this model, electrons dart about within an energy level in an ever-changing path. Most of this path falls into a region called an electron cloud. At any given time, there is a high probability that the electron exists in the electron cloud.

The idea of an electron cloud is not so strange. You have probably seen the blur of a fan when it spins at high speed. The fast-moving blades appear to fill the space between them, just as fast-moving electrons seem to fill the space around the nucleus. The paths of an atom's electrons account for nearly all of its volume. If the nucleus of an atom was the size of a marble on the 50-yard line of a football field, the electron cloud would extend to the end zones!

## Inside the Nucleus

As scientists learned more about atomic structure, they found that the nucleus is more complicated than they had thought. In 1932, James Chadwick showed that most atomic nuclei contain a third kind of subatomic particle, called a **neutron** (NOO trahn). A neutron has about the same mass as a proton but has no electrical charge.

An atomic nucleus is a positively charged, tightly-packed cluster of protons and neutrons. If you remember that like electric charges repel each other, you may wonder how protons can be packed so tightly into the nucleus. The answer is that the electric force repelling the protons is overwhelmed by a much stronger force that holds the neutrons and protons together. It is called the strong force, one of the four universal forces that operate in nature. The strong force actually gets stronger as the distance between particles increases.

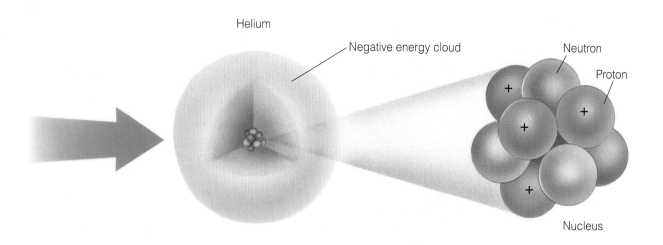

Helium

Negative energy cloud

Neutron

Proton

Nucleus

In the atomic model accepted today, the rapid and random motion of electrons creates an electron cloud around the nucleus.

The nucleus is known to be made up of both protons and neutrons, held together by the strong force.

## Atomic Numbers and Isotopes

All atoms of an element contain the same number of protons. This number, called the *atomic number*, identifies an element. Sodium, for example, has an atomic number of 11. If all iron atoms contain 26 protons, what is the atomic number of iron?

The atomic number also represents the number of electrons in an atom. Remember that an atom is electrically neutral. Thus the number of negative particles must equal the number of positive particles.

As you may recall, Dalton hypothesized that all atoms of an element are exactly alike. Today scientists know that he was not completely correct. Atoms of the same element do have the same number of protons and electrons, but they may differ in the number of neutrons they contain. Atoms of the same element with different numbers of neutrons are called **isotopes** (EYE suh TOHPS).

For each element, only a limited number of different isotopes are possible. Figure 7.2 shows two of several possible isotopes of carbon. Some elements have isotopes that exist in nature but are unstable. These unstable isotopes are called radioactive isotopes. The structures of their nuclei may change suddenly.

## ▼ ACTIVITY

### Researching

*Radioactivity*

Find out about the medical uses of radioactive isotopes. What properties do they have that make them useful in medicine?

**SKILLS WORKOUT**

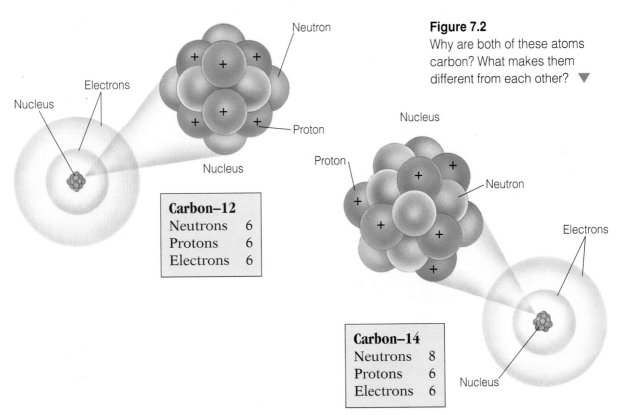

**Figure 7.2**
Why are both of these atoms carbon? What makes them different from each other? ▼

**Carbon–12**
Neutrons 6
Protons 6
Electrons 6

**Carbon–14**
Neutrons 8
Protons 6
Electrons 6

## Mass Number and Atomic Mass

Almost every atom contains one or more neutrons in its nucleus. The number of neutrons does not affect the charge of an atom, but it does affect its mass. The total number of protons and neutrons in an atom is called its *mass number*. This number is usually written with a hyphen after the element's name. For example, a helium atom with 2 protons and 1 neutron is called helium-3. The mass number helps to distinguish one isotope from another. What is the difference between carbon-12 and carbon-14?

Scientists also have a way of describing the actual mass of an atom. Since the mass of a single atom is so small, a special unit of measurement, called the *atomic mass unit*, is used to describe its mass. Atomic mass units are abbreviated as *amu*. An atomic mass unit is defined as $\frac{1}{12}$ the mass of a carbon-12 atom. An atom of hydrogen-1 has a mass of approximately 1 amu.

## *SkillBuilder*  *Making Models*

### *Model of an Atom*

You can use a simple pinwheel as a model of an atom. To construct a pinwheel, follow the steps below.

1.  Draw an 8 cm square on a piece of construction paper. Cut out the square.

2.  Make four diagonal cuts to within 1 cm of the center of the square. Draw a bold **X** on one point of the pinwheel.

3.  Bend the paper to form a pinwheel as shown. Use a straight pin to fasten the pinwheel to one end of a plastic soda straw.

Blow on the pinwheel and observe its motion. Watch the **X** as the pinwheel moves. Then answer the following questions:

1.  Can you see the blades of the pinwheel when it spins rapidly?

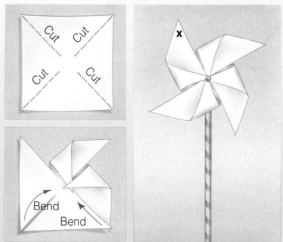

2.  Can you describe the location of the **X** at any point in time when the pinwheel is spinning rapidly?

Based on your observations, write a short paragraph explaining the relationship between the spinning pinwheel, the **X**, and the electron cloud model of the atom.

Recall that most elements have more than one naturally occurring isotope. A sample of one of these elements, therefore, will contain atoms with different atomic masses! How can scientists describe an element's mass? This measurement is given as an average. When the relative amounts of each isotope in a sample of an element are known, an average atomic mass for that element can be calculated. For example, copper is 69.1 percent copper-63 and 30.9 percent copper-65, giving it an average atomic mass of 63.6 amu.

## Science and Technology
### *Tracking Subatomic Particles*

How can you study particles too small for you to see? Scientists at Fermi National Accelerator Laboratory near Chicago, Illinois use a machine, called an accelerator, to smash atoms and release atomic particles. Devices attached to the accelerator detect these particles.

The simplest particle detector is a bubble chamber. It is a large, sealed metal cylinder with a glass window containing supercold liquid hydrogen. When subatomic particles from the accelerator pass through the bubble chamber, they cause the cold liquid to boil. A line of bubbles, called a track, marks each particle's path. The tracks are recorded on photographs.

A track tells a lot about a particle. For example, the direction a track curves in a magnetic field tells what kind of charge it has, and the amount of curve indicates its mass and energy. Learning about these particles allows scientists to understand more about matter.

**Figure 7.3 ▲**
Photographs of the tracks left by subatomic particles in a bubble chamber are magnified for study by scientists.

## Check and Explain

1. What does an atomic number tell you about an element?

2. Describe one way each atomic model after Dalton's improved on earlier models.

3. **Compare and Contrast**  How are an atom's nucleus and its electron cloud different? Alike?

4. **Calculate**  The atomic number of oxygen is 8. How many protons, neutrons, and electrons are in oxygen-16? Oxygen-17? Oxygen-18?

*It's Elemental*

Choose five elements you are familiar with. For each, describe as many uses as you can.

# 7.2 Elements

## Objectives

▶ **Describe** what elements are.

▶ **Give examples** of common elements.

▶ **Make a model** that relates the particle model to a familiar property of matter.

High in the Rocky Mountains or on the streets of New York City, the oxygen in the air you breathe is the same. The air is different, but the oxygen atoms in both places have the same properties. All oxygen atoms have eight protons and eight electrons.

Oxygen is an element. As you have learned, elements are the basic kinds of matter in the universe. If you compare atoms to the bricks used to construct a building, then learning about the elements is like finding out what kinds of bricks are available.

## Elements and Matter

An element is a substance made of just one kind of atom. You may recall that many kinds of matter can be broken down or changed into other kinds of matter by chemical changes. An element, however, cannot be broken down or changed by chemical means.

Even though all matter is made up of elements, only a few elements exist in nature in their pure form. You may remember that the oxygen and nitrogen in air are elements. Diamond is a natural form of the element carbon. Occasionally pure deposits of silver, gold, or copper are found. However, most elements in nature are combined with other elements.

You would probably not recognize many elements in their pure form because you rarely see them this way. Take sodium, for example. Although many common substances contain sodium, the only place you are likely to see pure sodium is in a chemistry laboratory.

Of the more than 100 known chemical elements, only about 30 play an important role in your daily life. About 18 elements do not occur in nature. They are created in laboratories and known as synthetic elements.

**Table 7.1**

| Elements in the Earth's Atmosphere | |
|---|---|
| **Element** | **Percent** |
| Nitrogen | 78 |
| Oxygen | 21 |
| Argon | 0.9 |
| Other | 0.1 |

## Properties of Elements

The same properties used to describe matter in general can be used to describe the elements in their pure forms. These properties include luster, texture, color, density, and the ability to conduct electricity. Elements differ in how they react with other elements. Most elements are solids, but some are gases and others are liquids.

### Helium

At room temperature, helium is a colorless, odorless gas. The only element less dense than helium is hydrogen. Because helium has a very low density, it is used to inflate balloons and blimps. ▼

### Iron ▲

Pure iron is a silvery-white metal. Like copper, it can be drawn into wires or rolled into sheets. Iron is one of the few metals that can be magnetized. In a moist environment, iron atoms combine easily with oxygen atoms to form the substance called rust. You can see rust on these iron bolts.

### Copper

Copper is a useful metal because it conducts heat and electricity well. It can also be shaped in many different ways. Copper can be drawn into wires, rolled into sheets, or hammered into different shapes. When polished, this reddish metal has a shiny luster. ▶

### Mercury

Mercury is the only metal that is a liquid at room temperature. Because the metal and its vapor are poisonous, mercury must be handled carefully. It is used in some thermometers because it expands and contracts with heat changes. ▼

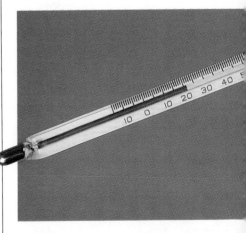

### Sulfur

Pure sulfur is a yellow solid. It is one of the few elements that exists free in nature. Pure sulfur is often deposited around volcanic vents. When it burns, sulfur combines with oxygen to form a toxic gas called sulfur dioxide. ▼

## Chemical Symbols

### State Symbols

Chemical symbols are similar to the two-letter abbreviations for each of the 50 states. Make a list of as many state abbreviations as you can, writing the full name of the state next to each one. Study the list and decide what rules were followed to create the abbreviations. Use the same set of rules to create two-letter abbreviations for all of your classmates' first names.

Instead of labeling your papers with the complete date, you may use symbols to abbreviate it. For instance, you may write 7/10/96 to indicate July 10, 1996. To simplify their work, chemists use symbols to represent the names of elements. The symbol of an element also represents the atom of that element.

A chemical symbol is one or two letters taken from the name of the element. In some cases, the symbol is derived from the element's name in a language other than English. For example, the symbol for gold, Au, comes from *aurum*, the Latin word for gold. Latin words are also the basis for the symbols of such common elements as copper, silver, iron, lead, and tin.

Chemical symbols are useful for two reasons. First, they are shorter to write and to work with than the names of elements. Second, the symbols form a kind of universal chemical shorthand. Ca means calcium to chemists in Japan, Mexico, Kenya, India, and everywhere else.

**Table 7.2   Some Elements: Their Sources and Uses**

| | Element Name, Symbol | Source | Common Uses |
|---|---|---|---|
| | Sodium, Na | Mineral: halite | ▸ Sodium vapor lamps<br>▸ Compounds used in synthetic fibers, petroleum products, and paper pulp |
| | Strontium, Sr | Minerals: celestite, strontianite | ▸ Compounds used to make red color in fireworks and flares, to extract sugar from molasses, and in paint driers |
| | Magnesium, Mg | Minerals: magnesite, brucite, dolomite | ▸ Photoflash bulbs<br>▸ Alloys used for spacecraft, auto parts, aircraft, tools<br>▸ Compounds used in dyeing cloth and making medicines |
| | Iodine, I | Nitrate deposits in Chile, Bolivia (occurs as sodium iodate or periodate) | ▸ Mild antiseptic (tincture of iodine)<br>▸ Compounds used in iodized salt and photographic film |

## Science and You
*Trace Elements in Your Body*

Iron is just one of many elements that are found in your body. Your body needs iron to make hemoglobin, the part of your blood that carries oxygen throughout the body. Because your body contains only a small amount of iron, it is called a trace element. Other trace elements in your body include zinc, copper, iodine, fluorine, cobalt, and chromium.

How scarce are these elements in your body? One way to picture this is to think in terms of individual atoms. It is estimated that the human body contains some 10 trillion cells. A single cell has room for about 90 trillion atoms. Thus the number of atoms in the body is about $2 \times 10^{27}$, or 2 followed by 27 zeros! Of every billion atoms in your body, only 38,000 atoms are iron and 1,500 atoms are zinc. And the numbers get smaller! Out of each billion atoms, there are just 170 copper atoms, 125 fluorine atoms, 20 iodine atoms, and 5 cobalt atoms.

To look at it another way, a human body contains about 3 to 5 grams of iron. This is about the mass of one nickel coin. There are just a few hundred micrograms of chromium in your body. One microgram is one-millionth of 1 gram. The dot of ink at the end of this sentence has a mass of about 4 micrograms.

You get supplies of these elements naturally in the food you eat. Even though they make up only a small part of your body, trace elements are important for your body's proper functioning. Lack of iodine, for example, can cause a serious condition called goiter.

▼ **ACTIVITY**

**Graphing**

*Atoms in the Body*

Make a bar graph comparing the numbers of iron, copper, fluorine, and iodine atoms for every billion atoms in the body.

**SKILLS WORKOUT**

## Check and Explain

1. Tell what an element is in your own words.

2. Name at least three properties that can be used to describe an element.

3. **Reason and Conclude**  Write several statements that support the conclusion that the properties of a sample of an element are the properties of its atoms.

4. **Make a Model**  On paper, draw a diagram of iron atoms in solid iron.

*Compound Familiarity*

On a piece of paper, write the names of all the compounds you are familiar with. Share your list with a classmate and discuss your reasons for thinking each item is a compound.

**SKILLS WARMUP**

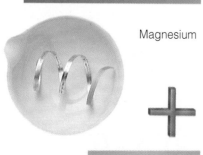

Magnesium

Chlorine

Magnesium
chloride

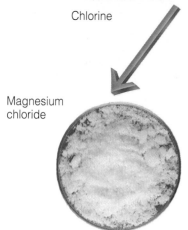

**Figure 7.4** ▲
Two different elements can combine to form a compound.

# 7.3 Compounds

## Objectives

▶ **Describe** the properties of a compound.

▶ **Give examples** of common compounds.

▶ **Define operationally** the composition of a compound by writing its chemical formula.

Nearly all the products you use are made of more than one element. The clothes you wear, the food you eat for breakfast, and the toothpaste you use to brush your teeth are all combinations of elements. You can add any number of items to this list, such as the paper and ink used to print this book and the sports equipment you use in physical education class. Almost everything you can think of is made up of some combination of elements.

## Defining Compounds

The atoms of most elements are reactive. They do not exist alone in nature. They tend to combine with the atoms of other reactive elements to form **compounds**. A compound is a substance made of two or more elements, chemically combined.

There are millions of compounds in, on, and around the earth. Many compounds are found in living things. Compounds also make up most of the nonliving world. You may know that water is a compound. Rocks and soil are made up of many different compounds.

How are compounds formed? Many are created by geologic processes deep in the earth. Some compounds are formed when an element combines with one of the gaseous elements in the air. Also living things create many compounds. An organism must manufacture compounds to stay alive. Plants, for example, are always making the compound glucose.

Many products you buy are made of compounds that aren't found in the natural world. For example, if you look at the list of ingredients on food packages you will probably see some compounds you don't recognize. People create these compounds in factories and chemical plants.

# Properties of Compounds

The properties of a compound are different from those of the elements that make it up. Hydrogen and oxygen are both gases, but they combine to form water. A compound also has a definite composition. The elements that make it up always combine in a specific proportion. Carbon *di*oxide is two parts oxygen and one part carbon. Carbon *mon*oxide is made of equal amounts of the two elements. The properties of the compounds described below are the result of unique combinations of elements.

### Sodium Chloride

This compound of sodium and chlorine is a white solid with a salty taste. By contrast, the element sodium is a soft, silvery metal that reacts explosively with water. Chlorine is a greenish yellow poisonous gas. ▼

### Propane ▶

This compound is a gas at room temperature. You may have used liquid propane as fuel. Propane molecules are made of three atoms of carbon and eight atoms of hydrogen.

### Silicon Dioxide ▲

This compound makes up a large part of many rocks and minerals. It is made of one silicon atom and two oxygen atoms. Because silicon dioxide resists chemical breakdown better than other compounds in rocks, most grains of sand are almost 100 percent silicon dioxide.

### Calcium Carbonate

Three elements—calcium, carbon, and oxygen—make up calcium carbonate. Limestone is one of its many natural forms. Calcium carbonate dissolves when it comes in contact with an acid. Caves can be formed when parts of limestone bedrock are slowly dissolved through this process. ▼

Oxygen       Oxygen
Carbon

**Figure 7.5** ▲
The molecular compound carbon dioxide normally exists as a gas. At a very low temperature, however, it freezes, forming the solid called dry ice.

# Types of Compounds

Compounds differ in the kinds of atoms that make them up. Compounds also differ in the way the atoms are joined. Compounds can be classified into two groups based on how their atoms are bonded, or joined to each other.

**Molecular Compounds** What do you call a single particle of water? It is a **molecule** (MAHL ih KYOOL). A molecule is a particle of matter made up of two or more atoms held together by the sharing of electrons. A compound made up of molecules is a molecular compound.

Most liquids and gases are molecular compounds. Examples include carbon dioxide, and ammonia. Although many compounds are molecules, some molecules are not compounds. Oxygen gas, for example, exists as molecules formed by two oxygen atoms.

**Ionic Compounds** In many compounds, the elements exist not as atoms but as **ions** (EYE ahnz). An ion is a charged particle formed when an atom or a group of atoms gains or loses one or more electrons. A positive ion has lost one or more electrons, and a negative ion has gained one or more electrons.

An ionic compound is a combination of positive and negative ions. The ions are held together by electrical attraction. Most ionic compounds are solids. In ionic compounds that are solids, the ions are arranged in a regular three-dimensional crystal structure. A good example is copper sulfate, shown in Figure 7.6. Ionic compounds are usually soluble in water. When melted or dissolved in water, they conduct electricity.

 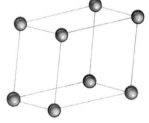

**Figure 7.6** ▲
Ionic compounds such as copper sulfate exist as solid crystals. Ions in these crystals form a characteristic three-dimensional shape.

## Formulas of Compounds

What you see in Figure 7.7 may look like an unfamiliar language. They are chemical formulas. A chemical formula is a combination of symbols and numbers that represent the composition of a compound. The symbols show the kinds of atoms in the compound. The numbers, called subscripts, show the number of each kind of atom. When more than one atom of an element is present in a compound, a subscript is written to the right and below the element's symbol. If there is only one atom of the element, no subscript is used.

How do you write a formula for a compound? First you need to know what it is made of. A molecule of carbon dioxide, for example, has one atom of carbon and two atoms of oxygen. To write the formula for this compound, begin by writing the symbol for carbon: C. Because the molecule has only one carbon atom, you do not need to write a subscript after the C. Now write the symbol for oxygen: O. Because there are two atoms of oxygen, write a small 2 below and to the right of the oxygen symbol. The formula is $CO_2$.

Here are the formulas for several of the compounds described on page 169.

| | |
|---|---|
| Calcium carbonate | $CaCO_3$ |
| Sodium chloride | $NaCl$ |
| Propane | $C_3H_8$ |
| Silicon dioxide | $SiO_2$ |

**Figure 7.7**
**Writing Formulas for Compounds**
▼

H is the symbol for hydrogen.

O is the symbol for oxygen.

N is the symbol for nitrogen.

H is the symbol for hydrogen.

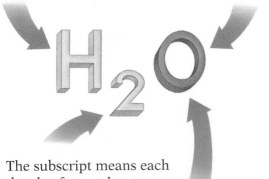

The subscript means each molecule of water has two atoms of hydrogen.

No subscript after oxygen means each molecule of water has only one atom of oxygen.

No subscript after nitrogen means each molecule of ammonia has only one atom of nitrogen.

The subscript means each molecule of ammonia has three hydrogen atoms.

# Consider This

## Should Fluoride Be Added to Public Water Supplies?

In the 1930s, U.S. health officials noticed a link between tooth decay in children and the amount of fluorine in drinking water. To lower the amount of tooth decay, sodium fluoride was added to public water supplies starting in 1945. Today more than 60 percent of the people in the United States drink fluoridated water.

**Consider Some Issues**
Studies have shown that water fluoridation does prevent tooth decay and poses no risk to human health.

Adding fluoride to public water, however, takes away a person's freedom of choice. People who want fluoride can get it in other ways. Fluoride is available in products such as toothpaste and in treatments at the dentist. Some people, however, cannot afford fluoride products or treatments.

Large amounts of fluoride may cause cancer. In one study, a few rats given large amounts of fluoride in drinking water got bone cancer. However, no human studies have linked fluoride with cancer.

**Think About It** Do you think fluoridation of water is necessary to prevent tooth decay? How do the benefits compare with the risks?

**Write About It** Write a paper stating your position for or against adding fluoride to public water supplies. Include the reasons for choosing your position.

## Science and Society
### The Origins of Pharmacy

For thousands of years, humans have treated sick people with natural compounds from plants and animals. Every culture has a heritage of using natural medicines, and in many places, they are still used. To treat snakebite, for example, some tribes in Africa use plants containing ouabain (WAH bayn), a heart stimulant, and strychnine (STRIHK nin), a nerve tonic. Other cultures use the bark of willow trees to treat rheumatism. The bark contains salicylic acid, the active ingredient in aspirin.

People have specialized in making drugs and medicines for a long time. As long ago as 3600 B.C., Egyptian physicians wrote prescriptions on stone tablets. These records show they used about 1,000 different animal, plant, and mineral products in treating illness.

**Figure 7.8**
What is the job of a pharmacist today?

In Europe, early physicians and other healers made their own medicines, using a process called compounding. True pharmacists, called apothecaries, sold medicine in Europe at least as far back as the twelfth century. The walls of an apothecary shop were lined with jars of herbs. The apothecaries measured out the herbs and then ground them into powder with a mortar and pestle. To temper the medicinal taste, they added honey and spices.

During the Industrial Revolution, machines began to replace the hand tools used by apothecaries. New technology allowed the large-scale manufacture of drugs. In industrialized countries today, most prescriptions are for manufactured drugs. Filling these prescriptions involves just counting and labeling. Pharmacists still learn methods of compounding, but their main job is to advise patients about how and when to take medication. They also warn patients about common side effects and substances to avoid while taking the medication.

## Check and Explain

1. Explain why compounds are more common than pure elements.

2. Name three compounds and describe their properties.

3. **Compare and Contrast** List ways in which ionic and molecular compounds are alike and ways in which they are different.

4. **Define Operationally** Write the chemical formula for a molecule that has 12 carbon atoms, 22 hydrogen atoms, and 11 oxygen atoms.

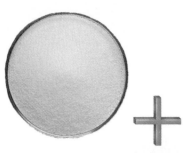
*Banana Split*

Describe how eating a mixture of ice cream, bananas, and hot fudge is different from eating all of these ingredients separately. What does this tell you about mixtures?

**SKILLS WARMUP**

# 7.4 Mixtures

## Objectives

▶ **Compare** and **contrast** mixtures and compounds.

▶ **Distinguish** between homogeneous and heterogeneous mixtures.

▶ **Define operationally** a method for separating a mixture.

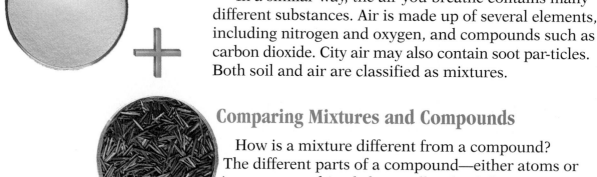

I f you look closely at a sample of garden soil, you will see that the soil particles are not all alike. They may be different sizes and colors. You may also find plant roots and bits of decaying plant and animal matter.

In a similar way, the air you breathe contains many different substances. Air is made up of several elements, including nitrogen and oxygen, and compounds such as carbon dioxide. City air may also contain soot par-ticles. Both soil and air are classified as mixtures.

## Comparing Mixtures and Compounds

How is a mixture different from a compound? The different parts of a compound—either atoms or ions—are combined chemically. The different parts of a mixture, in contrast, are simply mixed together. Also, mixtures and compounds differ in other ways:

▶ The makeup, or composition, of a mixture can vary. The composition of a compound, on the other hand, is constant.

▶ The components of a mixture keep their original properties. You can still taste the sodium chloride dissolved in sea water, for example. A compound, however, has properties different from the elements that make it up.

▶ Because the components of a mixture are not com-bined chemically, they can usually be separated by physical means. Distillation and filtering are exam-ples of physical means used to separate mixtures. In contrast, the elements in a compound must usually be separated by chemical means, such as the addition of heat energy.

**Figure 7.9** ▲
When two substances are mixed without chemically combining, they form a mixture.

## Properties of Mixtures

Mixtures can be made up of any number of different compounds or elements. The substances that make up a mixture determine the mixture's properties. Ketchup, for example, is made of tomatoes, sugar, salt, vinegar, and other ingredients. Its taste is a combination of the flavors of these ingredients. The sweetness comes from the sugar and the tanginess from the vinegar. The tomatoes also add flavor to the ketchup. Ingredients also determine a mixture's texture, shape, and form.

**Seasoning Mix** ▲

At home, you may use seasoning mixes. The product shown here is a mixture of 14 herbs and spices. This particular blend of ingredients was chosen because someone liked its flavor. If you tasted the mix, could you identify some of the ingredients?

**Iron and Aluminum Nails**

Suppose you have a mixture of iron and aluminum nails. How could you easily separate the two kinds of nails? If you remember that iron is magnetic, you probably know the answer. ▼

**Chocolate Milk** ▲

Chocolate milk is more than just a mixture of milk and chocolate. Milk and chocolate are each themselves mixtures of many compounds. Milk contains more than 60 compounds. The chocolate flavor is a blend of about 300 flavor compounds!

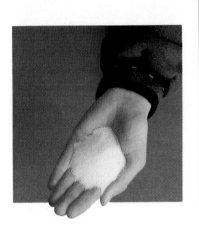

◀ **Iodized Table Salt**

Iodized table salt is a mixture of sodium chloride and potassium iodide. Like sodium chloride, potassium iodide is safe to eat and tastes salty. It supplies you with iodine, which your thyroid gland needs to function properly.

## Types of Mixtures

To make grape juice from concentrate, you stir the concentrate into water. If the water and the concentrate are completely mixed, every sip tastes exactly like every other sip. The drink is a **homogeneous** (HOH moh JEE nee uhs) **mixture**. All parts of a homogeneous mixture contain the same amount of each component. Most mixtures formed by dissolving a compound in a liquid are homogeneous mixtures. Perfume is a homogeneous mixture of dozens of fragrance compounds dissolved in alcohol.

As you can see, the ingredients of the seasoning mix on page 175 are not evenly mixed. One part of the mixture has more of certain kinds of spices than another part. This is a **heterogeneous** (HEHT ur oh JEE nee uhs) **mixture**. Not every part of a heterogeneous mixture has the same composition. Can you think of another example of a heterogeneous mixture?

Different metals can be combined to form a special kind of mixture, called an alloy. An alloy is made by heating two or more metals until they melt together, and then cooling the mixture. All coins are made of alloys. Pennies made before 1982 are a mixture of copper and zinc, an alloy you can see in Figure 7.12. Is an alloy a homogeneous or a heterogeneous mixture?

**Figure 7.10** ▲
When you make fruit juice from concentrate, you create a homogeneous mixture.

**Figure 7.11** ▲
Shells mixed with sand on a beach form a heterogeneous mixture.

**Figure 7.12** ▲
An alloy is a homogeneous mixture of a metal and another metal or nonmetal.

## Science and You  *Hard Water or Soft Water*

When you turn on a faucet, the water that comes out is not pure $H_2O$. Tap water usually contains many dissolved substances. Water that contains a high concentration of dissolved calcium and magnesium compounds is called hard water.

Well water, or ground water, is usually harder than surface water from a lake or reservoir. This is because water dissolves substances as it moves down through soil and bedrock. Rainwater is the best example of naturally soft water because it has few opportunities to dissolve other substances.

Hard water can cause several problems. Sometimes it has an unpleasant taste. Hard water also hinders the cleaning action of soaps. The compounds in hard water react with soap, forming a scum that sticks to bathtubs, dishes, clothes, and skin. Suds will not form until all of these compounds have been used up to make the scum. This means that cleaning in hard water uses up more soap. Synthetic detergents help solve the scum problem, but you still have to use more detergent to clean effectively with hard water than you do with soft water.

Another problem with hard water is that it can leave scaly deposits that build up in hot water heaters and plumbing systems. The buildups can eventually block the flow of water. Many people in areas with hard water use an ion-exchange water softener to remove the calcium and magnesium compounds. The water softener replaces the unwanted compounds with sodium chloride. A water softener creates softer water, but the water tastes saltier.

## ACTIVITY

### Classifying

*Mixtures*

At the top of a piece of paper, write the words *homogeneous* and *heterogeneous*. Then put each of the following mixtures under the correct heading: fruit salad, ink, cement, pancake syrup, toothpaste, and blood. Add to the appropriate column any other mixtures you can think of.

**SKILLS WORKOUT**

---

## Check and Explain

1. Name and describe both a homogeneous mixture and a heterogeneous mixture. How do they differ?

2. Is lemonade an element, a compound, or a mixture? Explain your answer.

3. **Compare and Contrast**  How are mixtures and compounds alike? How are they different?

4. **Define Operationally**  Write down a numbered set of instructions for separating a mixture of table salt and sand.

# *Activity 7* *What makes a soap bubble last?*

**Skills**   Measure; Observe; Infer; Interpret Data

## Task 1  Prelab Prep

1. Collect the following items: 4 jars, measuring cup, liquid dishwashing detergent, glycerin, warm water, labels, coat hanger, watch to measure seconds.
2. Bend a wire coat hanger into a loop about an inch in diameter. Leave a handle about 6-inches long.
3. Prepare the following labels: No glycerin; 7.5 mL glycerin; 15 mL glycerin; 22.5 mL glycerin.

## Task 2  Data Record

On a separate sheet of paper, draw the data table shown below. Use the table to record your observations.

## Task 3  Procedure

1. To each jar, add 15 mL liquid dishwashing detergent and 120 mL warm water. Then add glycerin to each jar as indicated on the labels. Gently stir the mixture in each jar to mix it well.
2. Dip the loop into the jar containing no glycerin and gently wave it through the air to make a bubble. Use the watch to time how long the bubble lasts before bursting. Make two more bubbles with this mixture and time each one.
3. Repeat step 2 for the other three mixtures.

## Task 4  Analysis

1. What is the variable in this activity?
2. For each mixture, calculate the average time a bubble lasted. Add all the times for that mixture and then divide by three.
3. Why is it better to average three different time measurements than to test each mixture only once?
4. Which mixture produced the longest-lasting bubbles?
5. List the mixtures you tested in order of performance, starting with the one that produced the longest-lasting bubbles.

## Task 5  Conclusion

Write a short paragraph comparing the performance of the bubble mixtures you tested. Make a hypothesis to explain the differences you observed.

## *Everyday Application*

Try to find out how commercial bubble mixtures are made. What characteristics other than long-lasting bubbles would influence your choice of a mixture?

## *Extension*

How might you use your data to create a mixture that makes even longer-lasting bubbles?

**Table 7.3   Bubble Data from Various Mixtures**

| Mixture | Length of Time Bubble Lasted | | | |
|---|---|---|---|---|
| | 1 | 2 | 3 | Average |
| No glycerin | | | | |
| 7.5 mL glycerin | | | | |
| 15 mL glycerin | | | | |
| 22.5 mL glycerin | | | | |

# Chapter 7 Review

## Concept Summary

### 7.1 Structure of the Atom

▶ Atoms are the basic units of matter. There are nearly 100 different kinds of atoms in nature; each is called an element.

▶ Atoms are made up of a nucleus surrounded by a cloud of electrons at different energy levels. The nucleus contains protons and neutrons.

▶ Atoms of the same element have the same number of protons, but different isotopes of the element have different numbers of neutrons.

▶ The total number of protons and neutrons in an atom is its mass number.

### 7.2 Elements

▶ An element is a substance made of just one kind of atom.

▶ Elements differ in their properties.

▶ Each element can be represented with a one- or two-letter chemical symbol.

### 7.3 Compounds

▶ A compound is a substance made of two or more elements chemically combined.

▶ The properties of a compound differ from the properties of the elements that make it up.

▶ Some compounds exist as molecules; others are ionic compounds.

▶ The makeup of a compound can be described by a chemical formula.

### 7.4 Mixtures

▶ A mixture is formed when two or more different substances are mixed but not chemically combined.

▶ Each part of a mixture keeps its original properties and can be separated from the others by physical means.

▶ Mixtures can be homogeneous or heterogeneous.

## Chapter Vocabulary

| | | | |
|---|---|---|---|
| atom (7.1) | proton (7.1) | isotope (7.1) | ion (7.3) |
| element (7.1) | nucleus (7.1) | compound (7.3) | homogeneous mixture (7.4) |
| electron (7.1) | neutron (7.1) | molecule (7.3) | heterogeneous mixture (7.4) |

## Check Your Vocabulary

Use the vocabulary words above to complete the following sentences correctly.

1. When the atoms of a compound share electrons, it is a _____ .

2. All of a _____ has the same composition.

3. Every _____ contains a nucleus.

4. Atoms with the same number of protons but different numbers of neutrons are _____ .

5. When an atom loses an electron, it becomes a positive _____ .

6. Protons and neutrons make up the _____ .

7. An atom's _____ have different energy levels.

8. The subatomic particle called a(n) _____ has a positive charge.

9. Oxygen is an example of a(n) _____ .

10. A substance made up of two or more elements is a _____ .

11. If you add black beads to a box of white beads, you create a _____ .

12. A subatomic particle with no charge is a _____ .

## Write Your Vocabulary

Write sentences using each of the vocabulary terms above. Show that you know what each word means.

# Chapter 7 Review

## Check Your Knowledge

Answer the following in complete sentences.

1. What are the subatomic particles that make up an atom? Compare the charge and mass of each.

2. What is the difference between an element and a compound?

3. Give examples of four different mixtures and classify each as homogeneous or heterogeneous.

4. Write the chemical formula for a compound containing six carbon atoms and six hydrogen atoms.

5. Name three elements and list one property of each.

6. What is an atomic mass unit?

7. Why is the atomic mass of an element an average?

Determine whether each statement is true or false. Write *true* if it is true. If it is false, change the underlined word(s) to make the statement true.

8. An ion is a <u>subatomic particle</u> that has gained or lost an electron.

9. Zinc-64 and zinc-66 are different <u>elements</u>.

10. The compound written as $KNO_3$ has <u>three</u> atoms of oxygen.

11. Protons and <u>electrons</u> make up the nucleus.

12. There are about <u>100</u> naturally-occurring elements.

13. When you dissolve sugar in water, you create a <u>compound</u>.

14. <u>Dalton</u> proposed the planetary model of the atom.

## Check Your Understanding

Apply the concepts you have learned to answer each question.

1. Give an example of a heterogeneous mixture that could be turned into a homogeneous mixture. Describe how the change could be carried out.

2. **Infer** Several of the compounds you learned about in this chapter have names that end in the word *oxide*. Based on what you know about the makeup of these compounds, infer what *oxide* means.

3. **Mystery Photo** The photograph on page 156 shows gold nuggets and rocks. Is the gold an element, a compound, or a mixture? How can you tell? Is the rock in the lower right an element, a compound, or a mixture? What visual evidence do you have to support your answer?

4. **Summarize** Review the four concepts that make up Dalton's theory of matter. Compare them to what is known today about atomic structure. What was correct about Dalton's ideas? What was incorrect?

5. **Compare and Contrast** How is an atom different from an element?

6. **Predict** Describe what would happen if all the atoms making up a car were packed together so that the nuclei touched each other.

7. **Application** A certain compound is a solid at room temperature and conducts electricity when dissolved in water. Is it most likely an ionic compound or a molecular compound? Why?

## Develop Your Skills

Use the skills you have developed in this chapter to complete each activity.

1. **Interpret Data** The table below shows the atomic number, number of neutrons, and mass number for three isotopes of hydrogen.

   a. Which hydrogen isotope has the most neutrons?

   b. What information tells you that protium, deuterium, and tritium are isotopes rather than three different elements?

| Isotope | Atomic Number | Neutrons | Mass Number |
|---------|---------------|----------|-------------|
| Protium | 1 | 0 | 1 |
| Deuterium | 1 | 1 | 2 |
| Tritium | 1 | 2 | 3 |

2. **Graph** Construct a circle graph showing the data in the table below.

| Isotope | Percent of All Zinc |
|---------|--------------------|
| Zinc–64 | 50 |
| Zinc–66 | 27 |
| Zinc–67 | 4 |
| Zinc–68 | 19 |

3. **Data Bank** Use the information on page 641 to answer the following questions.

   a. What is the atomic mass of iron?

   b. What is one element with a density higher than that of iron?

## Make Connections

1. **Link the Concepts** Below is a concept map showing how some of the main concepts in this chapter link together. Only parts of the map are filled in. Copy the map. Using words and ideas from the chapter, complete the map.

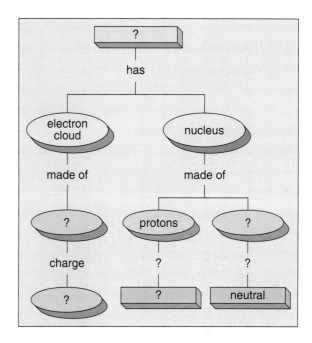

2. **Science and Technology** Scientists have discovered many subatomic particles in addition to protons, neutrons, and electrons. Read about the branch of science called particle physics and find out what these other subatomic particles are.

3. **Science and Social Studies** Throughout history, people in different cultures have thought of matter as being made of a few kinds of basic substances or energies. The ancient Chinese, for example, considered everything to be some combination of wood, fire, earth, metal, and water. Research this philosophy and find out more about the meaning given to these five "elements."

# Chapter 8

# Introduction to the Periodic Table

## Chapter Sections

**8.1** The Modern Periodic Table

**8.2** Metals

**8.3** Nonmetals and Metalloids

## What do you see?

*"I see a 'neon' sign. The tubes have noble gases in them. They have different colors because they contain different gases. The signs work by passing electricity through the noble gases. This produces colored light."*

*Ben Barrett-Nisbet*
*Tuckahoe Middle School*
*Richmond, Virginia*

To find out more about the photograph, look on page 202. As you read this chapter, you will learn about the noble gases and the other elements in the periodic table.

# 8.1 The Modern Periodic Table

## Objectives

▶ **Describe** the kinds of information provided by the periodic table.

▶ **Explain** the structure of the periodic table in terms of the periods and groups.

▶ **Generalize** about the properties of metals, nonmetals, and metalloids on the periodic table.

▶ **Organize** data to develop a table of atomic masses.

Imagine looking for the answer to a homework question in a book with no table of contents! You would have to thumb through the book—page by page. Why is it easier to find information in a book with a table of contents? Data that have been organized are easier to find, compare, and interpret. What other tables have you used? How did each of these tables help you find or use information?

## Developing the Modern Periodic Table

One kind of table you use often is a calendar. Look at the calendar in Figure 8.1. Think of the calendar as a grid made up of horizontal rows and vertical columns. Each column represents a different day of the week. Each day is repeated in every row through the whole month. In the calendar in Figure 8.1, for example, Monday is repeated five times. This arrangement of the days in the month is **periodic**. Things that are periodic have a regular, repeating pattern.

Like the days of the month, the chemical elements can be arranged in a way that shows a repeating, or periodic, pattern. The chemical properties of the elements repeat as the elements increase in atomic number. A table that shows these patterns in the elements' properties is called a periodic table. Look at the modern periodic table of the elements on pages 186–187. How does it resemble a calendar? What do you think the vertical columns represent?

In 1869, a Russian chemist named Dmitri Mendeleev (MEN duh LAY uhf) created the first periodic table of the elements. At that time, chemists had identified about 70

| June | | | | | | |
| S | M | T | W | Th | F | S |
|---|---|---|---|---|---|---|
| | | 1 | 2 | 3 | 4 | 5 | 6 |
| 7 | 8 | 9 | 10 | 11 | 12 | 13 |
| 14 | 15 | 16 | 17 | 18 | 19 | 20 |
| 21 | 22 | 23 | 24 | 25 | 26 | 27 |
| 28 | 29 | 30 | | | | |

**Figure 8.1 ▲**
How are the days of a month organized in a calendar?

elements. Mendeleev spent years collecting information about the properties of these elements.

Mendeleev wrote each element's name, atomic mass, and properties on a card. He ordered the cards from lowest to highest atomic mass and pinned them to his laboratory wall. He grouped elements that had similar properties and put these cards in rows along the wall. Mendeleev's project took up so much time and thought, his friends called it the "game of patience."

Arranging the elements in this way, Mendeleev ran into several problems. Certain elements could not be put into groups with similar properties and at the same time stay in order of increasing atomic mass. Mendeleev had to ignore the atomic masses of the elements. Also, there were spaces where no element seemed to fit, so Mendeleev put question marks in these spaces.

Look at Mendeleev's table in Figure 8.3. It shows how he arranged the cards. Mendeleev predicted the properties of

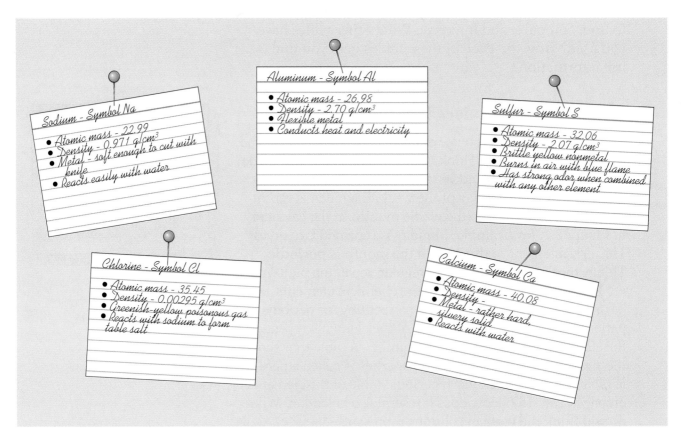

**Figure 8.2** ▲

Mendeleev discovered how to organize the elements in his periodic table by making an information card for each element.

```
                              Ti=50      Zr=90      ?=180.
                              V=51       Nb=94      Ta=182.
                              Cr=52      Mo=96      W=186.
                              Mn=55      Rh=104,4   Pt=197,4
                              Fe=56      Ru=104,4   Ir=198.
                        Ni=Co=59         Pl=106,6,  Os=199.
  H=1                         Cu=63,4    Ag=108     Hg=200.
         Be=9,4    Mg=24      Zn=65,2    Cd=112
         B=11      Al=27,4    ?=68       Ur=116     Au=197?
         C=12      Si=28      ?=70       Sn=118
         N=14      P=31       As=75      Sb=122     Bi=210
         O=16      S=32       Se=79,4    Te=128?
         F=19      Cl=35,5    Br=80      I=127
  Li=7   Na=23     K=39       Rb=85,4    Cs=133     Tl=204
                   Ca=40      Sr=57,6    Ba=137     Pb=207.
                   ?=45       Ce=92
                   ?Er=56     La=94
                   ?Yt=60     Di=95
                   ?In=75,6   Th=118?
```

**Figure 8.3 ▲**

Turn Mendeleev's periodic table so the left side is the top. How does it compare to the modern periodic table on the next two pages? Can you guess which elements go where Mendeleev left question marks?

elements that would be discovered to fill in the blank spaces. One element he left space for, gallium, was discovered in 1875. The discovery of elements that were predicted by the blank spaces in the table established the value of Mendeleev's periodic table.

After Mendeleev's death, a British physicist named Henry Moseley carried on Mendeleev's work. Moseley arranged the elements in order of increasing atomic number instead of atomic mass. He discovered that the pattern had no irregularities. The position of an element in the modern periodic table is related to its atomic number and the arrangement of electrons in its energy levels.

# The Modern Periodic Table

On these pages, you will tour the modern periodic table. During this tour, you will learn more about the structure of the table and the patterns that make it useful. As you will see, the periodic table is an important tool in the study of chemistry.

**Figure 8.4**
**Periodic Table of the Elements** ▶

## Group

Vertical columns are called groups. Elements within a group may have many similar properties. Their properties are similar because they have a similar arrangement of electrons.

## Group number

Groups of elements are identified by numbers from 1 to 18, beginning at the left side of the table.

## Period

The seven horizontal rows are called periods. Elements 57–71 and 89–103 fit into periods 6 and 7. The elements in a period are not alike. As you move from left to right in a period, elements range from metals to nonmetals.

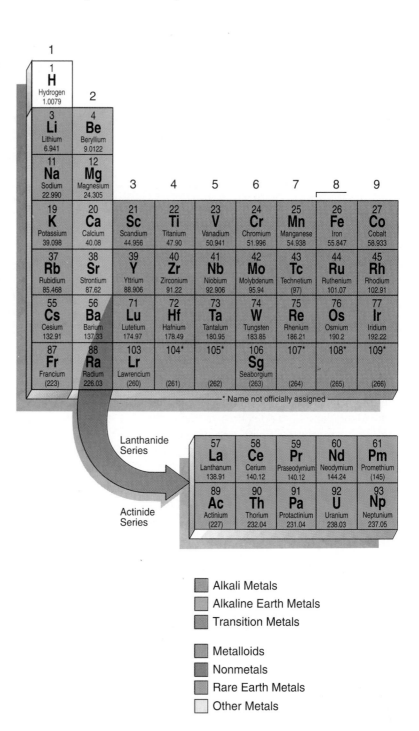

Alkali Metals
Alkaline Earth Metals
Transition Metals

Metalloids
Nonmetals
Rare Earth Metals
Other Metals

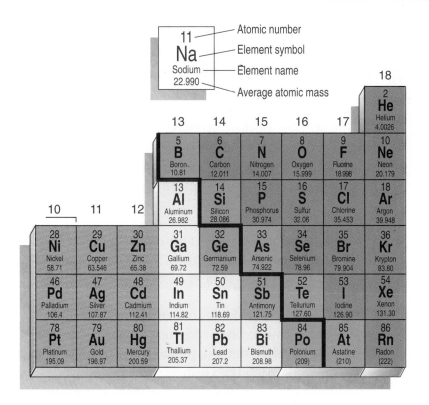

**Nonmetals**

Nonmetals occupy the upper right hand corner of the periodic table. All of these elements, except hydrogen, are to the right of the zigzag line.

**Metals**

About 80 percent of the known elements are metals. They occupy the large area to the left of the zigzag line in the periodic table.

**Metalloids**

Elements that have properties of both metals and nonmetals are **metalloids**. In the periodic table, metalloids border both sides of the zigzag line that separates the metals from the nonmetals.

**Rare Earth Metals**

These two rows of elements are separated from the rest of the table to make it a more convenient size.

## Science and Technology  *Synthetic Elements*

What do the elements neptunium, plutonium, einsteinium, and mendelevium have in common? None of them are found in nature. How, then, can they exist?

All of these elements, and many others, are synthetic. Synthetic elements must be manufactured in laboratories.

Synthetic elements are also known as "transuranium elements," meaning "beyond uranium." They are "beyond uranium" because they have an atomic number greater than 92, the atomic number of uranium. The first transuranium elements were made in the 1940s, when scientists bombarded uranium with neutrons. The bombardment changed the atomic number of uranium. Since no two elements have the same atomic number, a new element was formed!

The first transuranium element had an atomic number of 93 and was named neptunium. In the solar system, the planet Neptune is next to Uranus. Uranium was named after Uranus, so neptunium was named after Neptune. Some of the other names of the synthetic elements may sound familiar to you. Einsteinium, for example, was named after the physicist Albert Einstein. Who do you think mendelevium was named after?

Transuranium elements have many uses. For example, promethium, like all transuranium elements, is radioactive. Its radioactivity makes it useful as an electric power source for artificial hearts and pacemakers. Americium is used in smoke detectors. It has properties that help make an electric connection when smoke is present.

**Figure 8.5** ▲
This device, called a pacemaker, helps people with irregular heartbeats. It is powered by the synthetic element promethium.

## Check and Explain

1. How is the periodic table like a calendar? What do the columns and rows on the periodic table represent?

2. What did Moseley discover that influenced the organization of the modern periodic table?

3. **Generalize**  What change occurs in the properties of elements as you move across a period from left to right?

4. **Organize Data**  Find the atomic masses of the elements in Group 2. Use this data to make a table.

# 8.2 Metals

## Objectives

▶ **Describe** common properties of metals.

▶ **Generalize** about the trend in Groups 13 through 16.

▶ **Classify** metals using the periodic table.

▼ **ACTIVITY**

### Predicting

*Testing Your Metals*

Predict whether elements with the following properties are metals: Element A is a black, brittle solid. Element B conducts an electric current. Element C has a silvery, shiny surface. Element D is a gas. Element E can be stretched into wire.

**SKILLS WARMUP**

Try to imagine a world without metals. What products would disappear from your home or school? Many items, such as pipes, file cabinets, and wire, are made mostly of metal. Products, such as thermostats and telephones, contain important metal parts that are hidden. Transportation would be different, too, since cars, bikes, and airplanes are mostly metal. The properties of metals make them very useful substances.

## Properties of Metals

Metals share many of the same properties. Observe the metals in Figure 8.6. What visible properties do they have in common? Most metals are silvery or gray in color. When polished, they usually have a surface that reflects light, a quality called **luster**. Luster is one of the properties of metals.

Metals also have properties that you *can't* see. For example, metals conduct heat and electricity. These properties make metals useful materials to use in making cooking utensils and wire.

Most metals are hard and have high melting points, but there are many exceptions. For example, pure gold and pure silver are relatively soft, so they are not often used alone in jewelry and coins. Gold and silver are combined with other metals to make them more durable. A few metals, such as gallium, have melting points that aren't much higher than room temperature. One metal, mercury, is actually a liquid at room temperature.

One of the most useful properties of metals is **malleability** (MAL ee uh BIHL uh tee). Materials that are malleable can be flattened, bent, and shaped without breaking. Aluminum, for example, can be flattened into foil by heavy rollers. Most metals are also *ductile*—they can be pulled into wire. To make wire, a metal is pulled, or drawn, through a tiny hole called a die.

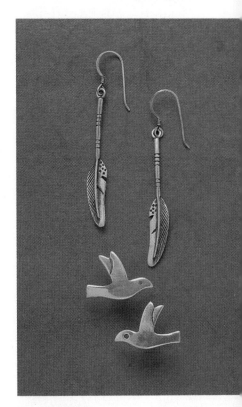

**Figure 8.6** ▲
What are some of the properties of metals that make them useful for jewelry?

Why do metals share all these properties? Recall that atoms have their electrons arranged in different energy levels. The electrons in the highest energy level are most important, because they determine an element's properties. Although metals have very different total numbers of electrons, most have from one to three electrons in the highest energy level. This low number of outer electrons is what gives metals their properties.

A metal atom gives up its outer electrons very easily. They are not held tightly by the nucleus. When many metal atoms are combined, they all share their outer electrons. These electrons move in a "cloud" around the metal atoms. As a result, a metal can change shape without breaking. The metal atoms slide past each other. They are held together, but not locked into a particular structure. This behavior makes metals ductile and malleable. And they conduct electricity because the electrons are free to move.

## Career Corner  Machinist

### Who Makes Machines and Tools?

Machinists are highly skilled workers who operate machine tools such as drill presses and lathes. Machinists work with metals such as steel, aluminum, and brass. To form these metals into precise shapes, a machinist must understand their properties. Metals vary in their melting point, strength, malleability, and hardness.

Many of the metal parts and tools machinists make are used to build engines and other machinery. Machinists cut precision gears. They make tools and dies for cutting and shaping metal.

Machinists may work in small machine shops where parts and tools are made to order for customers. Many machinists work in large industrial machine shops.

To be a machinist, you should enjoy working with your hands. You must also have the patience it takes to do highly accurate work. High school courses in math, mechanical drawing, and shop are useful background classes for becoming a machinist.

A high school graduate can become a machinist by completing a four-year apprenticeship program. These programs often include both on-the-job and classroom training. You can also qualify as a machinist by attending a technical college that offers programs in advanced machining skills.

## Alkali Metals

Group 1 in the periodic table on pages 186–187 contains six elements known as the alkali (AL kuh LY) metals. The alkali metals are very reactive, which means they combine easily with other elements, as you can see in Figure 8.7. They all have just one electron in the highest energy level of their atoms. Because this electron is so easily lost, alkali metals are found in nature only as positively-charged ions. They combine with negatively-charged ions to form salts. Table salt is made of sodium ions and ions of the element chlorine.

In pure form, all of the alkali metals have similar properties. For example, they are so soft that they can be cut easily with a knife. They have low densities and melt at low temperatures. Cesium, in fact, will melt on a hot day.

## Alkaline Earth Metals

Look to the right of the alkali metals in the periodic table. The six elements in Group 2 are called the alkaline earth metals. Alkaline earth metals are reactive, but they are not as reactive as the alkali metals. Alkaline earth metal atoms have two electrons in the highest energy level. Like the alkali metals, they occur in nature as ions combined with other elements.

Magnesium and calcium are common alkaline earth metals. Calcium compounds make up much of your bones and teeth. These elements are also used to make building materials, such as cement. The shells of sea animals also contain calcium. You may be familiar with the compound magnesium hydroxide. It's also called milk of magnesia, and is used to soothe upset stomachs.

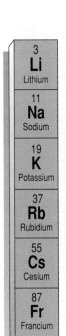

**Figure 8.7** ▲
Alkali metals are always found in compounds because they are so reactive.

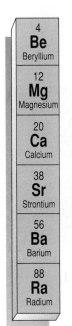

**Figure 8.8** ▲
Alkaline earth metals are a major part of objects such as sea shells and magnesium wheels.

## Transition Metals

Locate the transition metals in the periodic table using the color key. Most transition metals are shiny. They have high melting points and are good conductors of heat and electricity. Because of the arrangement of their outer electrons, transition metals are much less reactive than the alkali or alkaline earth metals. They can, however, combine with other elements.

Groups of transition metals share similar properties. Neighboring elements in the same period may also have like properties. For example, iron, cobalt, and nickel are the only metals with magnetic properties.

Transition metals are often found in **ores**. Ores are minerals containing relatively large amounts of metal compounds. Zinc comes from an ore called sphalerite (SFAL uh RYT). Hematite and magnetite ores are very rich in iron.

## Rare-Earth Metals

The elements located in the two separate rows at the bottom of the periodic table are the rare-earth metals. The lanthanide series, elements 58–71, follows lanthanum in Period 6. The actinide series, elements 90–103, follows actinium in Period 7. Except for element 61, all of the lanthanides occur in nature. Most of the actinides, however, are synthetic, or made in laboratories.

Lanthanides are found in certain special ores. They are called "rare-earths" because they occur only in small amounts in the earth's crust. Pure lanthanides look like steel and have steel-like properties. Tiny amounts of pure lanthanides are used in lasers. Certain lanthanide compounds create the red color in color televisions.

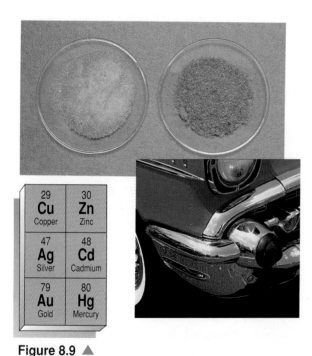

**Figure 8.9** ▲
Transition metals make up most metal objects. Some form colorful compounds.

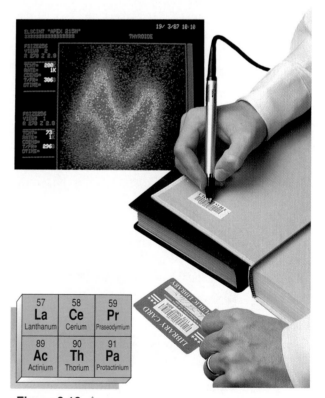

**Figure 8.10** ▲
Rare earth metals have properties that make them useful in certain special devices.

## Science and Technology *Making Alloys*

Almost every metal product you use is made of some kind of alloy. An *alloy* is a material formed by mixing a metal with other metals or nonmetals. Brass is an alloy of two metals, copper and zinc. Steel is an alloy made with a metal, iron, and a nonmetal, carbon. Adding different amounts of these elements or others can change the properties of steel. For example, more carbon makes a harder steel.

Steel-making is not a new process. In the second century B.C., the Chinese developed a process for making steel from cast iron. When iron is melted and reformed, it contains carbon. To make steel, the Chinese removed just enough of the carbon to create the right proportion of carbon and iron.

Alloyed metals create materials with just the right combination of properties for a particular use. For example, airplane bodies need a material that is both light and strong. Aluminum is lightweight, but it is also soft, and bends easily. Steel is hard, but it is very heavy. An alloy of aluminum with copper, magnesium, and other metals, however, has the right mixture of properties for an airplane body. The alloy is both strong and lightweight.

You may know that silver and gold jewelry is often made of alloys, because alloys are less expensive than the pure metals. Cost is not the only reason. Other metals, such as copper, are added to make these soft metals more durable. The percentage of gold in a piece of jewelry varies. Twenty-four-karat gold is pure gold, while fourteen-karat gold contains $^{14}\!/_{24}$ gold and $^{10}\!/_{24}$ other metals.

## ▼ ACTIVITY

### Classifying

*Metals vs. Nonmetals*

Write the words *metal* and *nonmetal* at the top of a piece of paper. Place each of the following items in the correct column: gold chain, aluminum foil, charcoal, iron nail, copper wire, and gas in a neon sign.

**SKILLS WORKOUT**

**Figure 8.11** ▲
The alloy bronze has been used for making metal objects for thousands of years.

## Check and Explain

1. What properties do most metals have in common? What gives metals these properties?

2. Why do the alkali metals and alkaline earth metals exist in nature as ions?

3. **Infer** Where might you find calcium in your school?

4. **Classify** Use the periodic table to determine the groups of the following elements: barium, cesium, chromium, lithium, mercury, and uranium.

*Nonmetals*

Nonmetals have properties that are different from those of metals. List some of the properties of metals. Use your list to infer what the properties of nonmetals might be.

**SKILLS WARMUP**

# 8.3 Nonmetals and Metalloids

## Objectives

▶ **Identify** the groups containing nonmetals and metalloids.

▶ **Explain** why nonmetals have different properties than metals.

▶ **List** the nonmetals essential to life.

▶ **Communicate** in a chart the different properties of metals, nonmetals, and metalloids.

**D**id you know your life depends on nonmetals? Look to the right of the zigzag line in the periodic table. In Periods 2 and 3, locate carbon, nitrogen, oxygen, sulfur, and phosphorus. These five nonmetals make up much of your body. Together with hydrogen, they form fats, carbohydrates, proteins, and nucleic acids—the building blocks of living things.

Metalloids also play an important role in daily life. For example, silicon is used to make computer chips. These chips are used in computers, watches, calculators, and even cars.

## Properties of Nonmetals and Metalloids

Unlike metals, nonmetals do not have luster and are poor conductors of heat and electricity. Solid nonmetals are usually dull and brittle. They are neither malleable nor ductile. Many nonmetals are gases at room temperature.

Compared to metals, most nonmetals have many electrons in their highest energy levels. These electrons are held tightly by the nucleus. As a result, the electrons are not free to move around. The atoms of many nonmetals tend to accept electrons from other elements. Many form negatively-charged ions.

Metalloids have properties of both metals and nonmetals. All the metalloids are shiny solids, but they do not have as much luster as the metals. Most metalloids conduct heat and electricity, but not as well as metals do. Some metalloids, such as silicon, are semiconductors. A semiconductor conducts electricity when small amounts of certain substances are added.

**Figure 8.12** ▲

Computer chips are made from wafers of the metalloid silicon, a semiconductor.

## Boron Group

The only element in Group 13 that is not a metal is boron. Boron is a brittle, black metalloid. It is used to make boric acid, a mild antiseptic. Boron is also part of borax, a compound used in laundry products as a water softener.

Below boron in the periodic table is aluminum. Aluminum has many uses because it is light, soft, and easy to cut. It also conducts heat and electricity very well. Aluminum is used to make soft drink cans, bicycles, aircraft parts, and cooking utensils. The properties of aluminum also make it very useful in many kinds of building materials.

Aluminum is the most abundant metal in the earth's crust. However, extracting aluminum from bauxite, its major ore, requires great amounts of energy. The other elements in the boron group are the uncommon metals gallium, indium, and thallium.

**Figure 8.13** ▲
Aluminum is used to make baseball bats. Your body heat will melt the metal gallium.

## Carbon Group

How is the lead in your pencil like a diamond? Both are made of carbon. Carbon is the only nonmetal in Group 14. It has two common forms: graphite and diamond. Graphite makes up much of the "lead" in your pencil. Carbon is unique because it can form an unlimited number of different compounds. Most of the compounds found in living things contain carbon.

Silicon and germanium are metalloids. The silicon compounds in rocks and soil make up 60 percent of the earth's crust. Many minerals, like the agate in Figure 8.14 are made of natural silicon components.

Tin and lead are both metals. Tin is obtained from cassiterite ore, and lead from galena. "Tin" cans are steel food containers lined with tin. Lead and its compounds are poisonous.

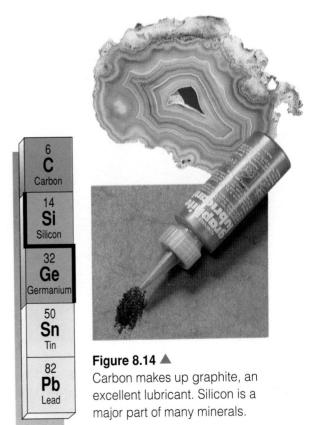

**Figure 8.14** ▲
Carbon makes up graphite, an excellent lubricant. Silicon is a major part of many minerals.

## Nitrogen Group

About 80 percent of the air is nitrogen, a nonmetal in Group 15. You breathe in nitrogen molecules with every breath. Pure nitrogen is a gas that does not combine easily with other elements. Nitrogen is one of the elements essential to life. Living things need nitrogen compounds to make proteins. If its temperature is lowered to -210°C, nitrogen gas becomes a liquid.

Phosphorus is another nonmetal element in Group 15 that living things need. It is in bones, teeth, and DNA. Phosphorus reacts very easily with other elements. Even the friction from cutting it can make white phosphorus ignite. You may be familiar with the red phosphorus you see in Figure 8.15.

Arsenic and antimony are metalloids. Arsenic compounds are used as a pesticide. One use of antimony is to harden and strengthen lead.

**Figure 8.15** ▲
Phosphorus is used to make matches. Liquid nitrogen will instantly freeze a rose.

## Oxygen Group

Oxygen, one of the most important elements on the earth, is also the most abundant. In combination with other elements, it makes up about 20 percent of air, 60 percent of the mass of the human body, and 50 percent of the mass of the earth's crust. Most oxygen is combined with silicon in silicate rocks in the earth's crust. Oxygen is also produced by plants during photosynthesis.

Sulfur is a nonmetal. Texas and Louisiana have large underground deposits of nearly pure sulfur. Major uses of sulfur include making rubber and sulfuric acid.

Selenium is a nonmetal that conducts electricity in the presence of sunlight. Because of this property, selenium is used in light meters, solar cells, and photocopiers.

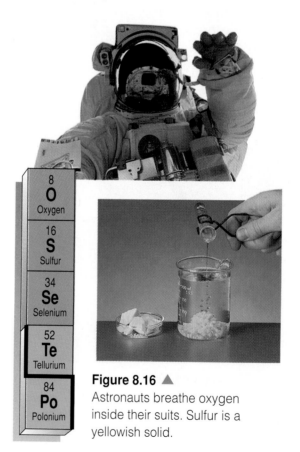

**Figure 8.16** ▲
Astronauts breathe oxygen inside their suits. Sulfur is a yellowish solid.

## Halogens

The elements in Group 17 are called **halogens**. Most of the food you eat contains a halogen compound. You call it table salt. Halogen means "salt-former." Halogens combine with metals to form salts. Sodium chloride, or table salt, is a halogen compound with many uses. Your body needs sodium chloride to conduct nerve impulses.

Fluorine is the most reactive of all nonmetals. It comes from a mineral called fluorspar. Fluoride toothpaste is made with fluorine. You are probably familiar with another use of fluorine: it is combined with other nonmetals to make the nonstick coatings on pans.

Chlorine, bromine, iodine, and astatine are the other halogens. Chlorine is a green gas. Bromine is the only nonmetal that is liquid at room temperature.

## Noble Gases and Hydrogen

Group 18 contains six colorless gases. They are called noble gases, because they don't readily combine with other elements. All the noble gases exist in the earth's atmosphere.

Neon, argon, krypton, and xenon can be removed from air. You have probably seen neon and other noble gases in advertising signs. Helium is the second lightest gas. Since it is lighter than air, helium is used to fill balloons and blimps.

Hydrogen is set apart from other elements in the periodic table because its properties do not fit any single group. Although its physical properties resemble those of helium, hydrogen reacts easily with other elements. In some chemical reactions hydrogen acts like a metal; in others it acts like a nonmetal.

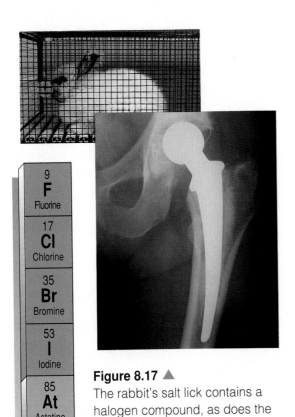

**Figure 8.17** ▲
The rabbit's salt lick contains a halogen compound, as does the plastic hip replacement.

| 9 |
|---|
| **F** |
| Fluorine |

| 17 |
|---|
| **Cl** |
| Chlorine |

| 35 |
|---|
| **Br** |
| Bromine |

| 53 |
|---|
| **I** |
| Iodine |

| 85 |
|---|
| **At** |
| Astatine |

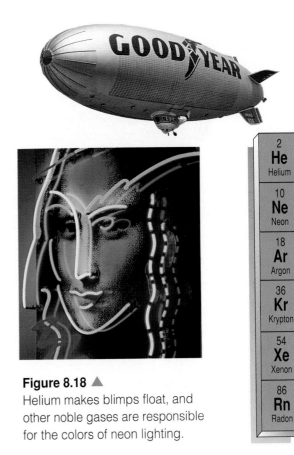

**Figure 8.18** ▲
Helium makes blimps float, and other noble gases are responsible for the colors of neon lighting.

| 2 |
|---|
| **He** |
| Helium |

| 10 |
|---|
| **Ne** |
| Neon |

| 18 |
|---|
| **Ar** |
| Argon |

| 36 |
|---|
| **Kr** |
| Krypton |

| 54 |
|---|
| **Xe** |
| Xenon |

| 86 |
|---|
| **Rn** |
| Radon |

## Science and Technology *Uses of Noble Gases*

The most important property of a noble gas is that it doesn't readily combine with other elements. It is chemically inactive. This property is useful in manufacturing processes that use reactive elements. Forming the microscopic patterns in an integrated circuit, for example, requires a carefully controlled series of chemical reactions. A protective layer of helium or argon gas prevents reactions with oxygen that would interfere with the procedure.

Each noble gas has special properties that make it useful for certain purposes. Helium, for example, has a very low density. Many times a day, hundreds of helium-filled weather balloons rise into the air. They carry instruments that record temperature, humidity, and pressure readings from various levels of the atmosphere. This information is sent back to weather stations. These measurements help meteorologists prepare long-range weather forecasts.

## SkillBuilder *Making a Graph*

### Atomic Mass

How is atomic mass related to atomic number? The best way to understand this relationship is to plot the atomic mass and atomic number of each element on a graph.

First, set up a graph like the one to the right. Look in the periodic table in the Data Bank to find out the range of numbers you will need to use for the atomic mass of elements 1 to 20, hydrogen to calcium. Write this scale of numbers on the *y*-axis of the graph.

Plot each element from hydrogen to calcium as a point on the graph, using the data in the periodic table. Connect the points with a line.

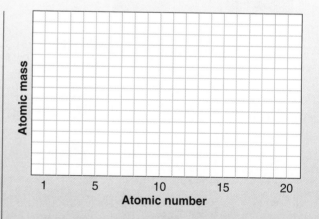

1. What does your curve look like? What does it tell you about the relationship between atomic number and atomic mass?

2. Are there any points on your graph that seem out of place compared to the others? Explain.

3. What do you think your graph would look like if you plotted all the elements up to uranium?

Use your graph to explain in a short paragraph why the periodic table is arranged by increasing atomic number instead of increasing atomic mass. How does your graph support your explanation?

◀ **Figure 8.19**
Krypton gas is used in the lights marking airport runways.

People with asthma or other breathing problems may be treated with a mixture of helium and oxygen. Helium atoms are small and light. The helium-oxygen mixture can be pumped in and out of the lungs more easily than air can. A helium-oxygen mixture is also used in the breathing tanks of deep-sea divers.

Krypton and xenon gases are used in high intensity light bulbs because they conduct very little heat away from the filament. The filament gets hotter and glows brighter than ordinary bulbs do. Airport landing strips are lined with powerful krypton bulbs. Bulbs made with these denser noble gases also last longer because they slow down evaporation of the metal filament. A longer-lasting filament means a longer-lasting bulb.

Electronic photoflash units also contain krypton, xenon, or both. Passing an electric current through the gas produces a brilliant flash of light. One electric photoflash unit can produce thousands of flashes.

## Check and Explain

1. List the groups containing nonmetals and metalloids.

2. What nonmetals are essential to life? What is the importance of each?

3. **Generalize** What trend do you notice in the elements as you move down Groups 13, 14, 15, and 16?

4. **Communicate** Identify ten metal objects in your school. List each item on a chart under metals, nonmetals, and metalloids. Share your chart with the class.

# Activity 8 *What elements can you find in your kitchen?*

*Skills*  Classify; Collect Data; Interpret Data

## Task 1  Data Record

On a separate sheet of paper, copy the table shown on this page. You will use it to record the data you discover in your search for elements.

## Task 2  Procedure

1. Find at least five common cooking or baking products that are made up of one or a few simple chemical compounds. You may include the following: sugar, baking soda, baking powder, vinegar, and vanilla extract (vanillin).
2. Use the dictionary to determine the elements that make up the compounds in these products. To do this, you may have to practice your detective skills. For example, if you look up *sugar* in the dictionary, it will tell you that sucrose is one kind of sugar. Then if you look up *sucrose*, you will find its chemical formula.
3. In your data table, write down all the chemical formulas that you find in your dictionary search.
4. Use the periodic table to determine the full name of each element listed in the chemical formulas. Write down the names of the elements in your table.

## Task 3  Analysis

1. What element occurred most often in the products you examined? What are the properties of this element? Why do you think the element is a part of so many different compounds?
2. Did you find any elements that are metals in their pure form? What products contain them?
3. Did you find two or more compounds that were made up of the same elements? If so, how do the products that contain them differ from one another?
4. Can two compounds have the same chemical formula but be different substances? Why or why not?
5. What elements are you *not* likely to find in cooking and baking products? Why?

## Task 4  Conclusion

Write a paragraph summarizing what you have discovered about the chemical elements in your kitchen. Use the periodic table to identify the family and group of each element.

## *Extension*

Discover which elements make up other kinds of common household products, such as ammonia, rubbing alcohol, and chlorine bleach. Make another table to record your findings.

## Table 8.1  Elements in Your Kitchen

| Product | Compound | Chemical Formula | Elements |
|---------|----------|------------------|----------|
|  |  |  |  |
|  |  |  |  |
|  |  |  |  |
|  |  |  |  |
|  |  |  |  |

# Chapter 8 Review

## Concept Summary

### 8.1 The Modern Periodic Table

▶ The Russian scientist Dmitri Mendeleev developed the first periodic table in 1869.

▶ The periodic table is a systematic arrangement of the elements. The elements are arranged by atomic number and properties.

▶ The modern periodic table has numbered groups in vertical columns and periods in horizontal rows.

▶ Elements in the table are divided into metals, nonmetals, and metalloids.

### 8.2 Metals

▶ Common properties of metals include luster, ability to conduct heat and electricity, malleability, and ductility.

▶ Metals vary in their hardness, melting point, and reactivity.

▶ When metal atoms are grouped together, their electrons are free to move. This structure accounts for the properties of metals.

▶ The groups of metals include the alkali metals, alkaline earth metals, transition metals, and rare-earth metals.

### 8.3 Nonmetals and Metalloids

▶ Nonmetals have properties that are opposite those of metals.

▶ Metalloids are elements that have properties of both metals and nonmetals.

▶ The nonmetals and metalloids are found in the boron group, carbon group, nitrogen group, oxygen group, halogens, and noble gases.

▶ The nonmetal hydrogen is in a group of its own.

## Chapter Vocabulary

| | | |
|---|---|---|
| periodic (8.1) | luster (8.2) | ore (8.2) |
| metalloid (8.1) | malleability (8.2) | halogen (8.3) |

## Check Your Vocabulary

Use the vocabulary words above to complete the following sentences correctly.

1. The elements that combine with metals to form salts are called ____.

2. A pattern that repeats is called ____.

3. The shininess of a metal's surface is a property called ____.

4. A mineral that contains relatively large amounts of one or more metal compounds is called a(n) ____.

5. Elements that have properties of both metals and nonmetals are ____.

6. Some metals have ____, a property that allows them to be shaped without breaking.

Explain the difference between the words in each pair.

7. Metalloid, nonmetal
8. Ore, metal
9. Halogen, noble gas
10. Malleability, ductility

## Write Your Vocabulary

Write sentences for each vocabulary word from the list. Show that you know what each word means.

# Chapter 8 Review

## Check Your Knowledge

Answer the following in complete sentences.

1. How are the groups on the periodic table identified?

2. Describe three properties of metals.

3. What are the four groups of metals? Name one example from each group.

4. What are the properties of nonmetals? Give two examples of each property.

5. What makes carbon unique? Identify the two common forms of carbon.

6. What is the most abundant element on Earth?

7. How did Henry Moseley's discovery influence the arrangement of the atoms in the modern periodic table?

Choose the answer that best completes each sentence.

8. About 80 percent of the known elements are (nonmetals, metalloids, metals, transuranium elements).

9. Materials that are (malleable, ductile, soft, ores) can be bent and shaped without breaking.

10. Metalloids have properties of (nonmetals, metals, metals and nonmetals, gases).

11. Pure alkaline earth metals are (negatively charged, stable, radioactive, reactive).

12. The elements carbon, nitrogen, oxygen, sulfur, and phosphorus are (poisonous, essential to life, metals, alloys).

13. The most reactive of all the metals are the (alkali, alkaline earth, transition, rare-earth) metals.

## Check Your Understanding

Apply the concepts you have learned to answer each question.

1. **Application** What important property of metals makes wire-making possible? How are wires made?

2. Why are pure alkali metals usually kept away from air or water?

3. **Critical Thinking** Pure calcium is brittle. How can calcium compounds be used as building materials?

4. **Mystery Photo** The photograph on page 182 shows tubes filled with different noble gases. The tubes are often called "neon lights" and are used for signs or lighting. The tubes give off light when electricity is passed through them. The color of the light depends upon the gases filling the tube. When energized, helium produces a yellowish light, argon a lavender light, krypton a whitish light, xenon a blue light, and neon an orange-red light.

   a. What are the colors of the noble gases?

   b. Where are the noble gases on Earth?

5. Why are the elements in Group 17 called halogens?

6. How is a period identified in the periodic table of the elements? How many elements are in each period?

7. Why are cooking utensils often made of metals such as iron, stainless steel, aluminum, and copper?

8. Why are lanthanides and actinides called rare-earth metals? Where are they located in the modern periodic table? Give one example of how rare-earth metals are used.

## Develop Your Skills

Use the skills you have developed in this chapter to complete each activity.

1. **Interpret Data** The chart below shows the number of elements discovered during different historical periods.

   a. During which period were the most elements discovered?

   b. How did Mendeleev's work fit into the pattern of element discovery? Could a periodic table have been constructed before 1800? Explain.

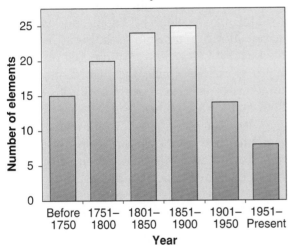

**Discovery of Elements**

2. **Data Bank** Use the information on page 643 to answer the following questions.

   a. What are the first, second, and third most common elements in the earth's crust?

   b. What percentage of the earth's crust is potassium?

3. **Hypothesize** How would the placement of the elements in the periodic table change if they were arranged by increasing atomic mass instead of increasing atomic number?

## Make Connections

1. **Link the Concepts** Construct a concept map that shows how the following concepts in this chapter link together: element, periodic table, chemical property, atomic number, period, group, alkali metal, alkaline earth metal, halogen, noble gas.

2. **Science and Language Arts** The expression "in the limelight" is directly related to an alkaline earth metal: calcium. Research the relationship of calcium to the expression, and write a brief report. Hint: calcium oxide is also known as "quicklime." Investigate properties of calcium and how calcium oxide is formed.

3. **Science and Social Studies** Large areas of the ocean floor are covered with nodules, or lumps, of the metal manganese. No particular country owns the oceans. Should manganese nodules be harvested? If so, who should harvest them? Research the issue and write a report on how manganese nodules could be harvested, who might benefit, and how to decide which countries should get to harvest them.

4. **Science and Technology** Research the elements and alloys used in making jet planes and jet engines. What special properties make each kind of metal just the right one for the job?

5. **Science and History** People called alchemists built a foundation for modern chemistry many hundreds of years ago. Find out more about the alchemists, what they believed, and what they did. Compare them to modern scientists.

# Science and Literature Connection

It was an extraordinary place. The surface of the water was very still, reflecting the sky in blinding blue-white, like a sheet of molten metal. What we had thought was a froth of wavelets along the shore had no movement. Like a frozen foam. It wasn't until we got close that we could see the waves were really a thick deposit of salty crystals. From a distance they reflected the sun as dazzling white, although as we got closer we could see that the white was streaked with garish shades of yellow, orange, and green.

"Let's swim," I suggested. "I've always wanted to swim in a real lake, haven't you?"

"Great idea!" Scylla began to unlace her boots.

"No, don't!" Alden's voice was sharp. "It's salt. Like the Dead Sea. So full of minerals that nothing can live in it."

"People swim in the sea, don't they? That's salty."

"Not like this. This is a chemical soup. It'll itch and burn. And we don't have enough fresh water to wash it off."

## Invitation to the Game

*The following excerpts are from the novel*
Invitation to the Game
*by Monica Hughes*

It was so tantalizing. I bent down, not quite believing Alden, touched the water and licked my fingers. My tongue burned and my mouth watered. I spat and spat. The obnoxious taste reminded me of the salts they used to give us at school for upset stomachs. . . .

We walked steadily, in a rhythm that we could keep up for hours if we needed to. The air was clean and spicy, and we strode along, arms swinging, breathing deeply, not talking very much, just enjoying the sense of space and incredible, unaccustomed freedom. Until Paul stumbled and sprawled headlong.

"Are you all right? What happened?"

"I tripped over something. Something heavy and hard, too. I can feel it through my boot." He hopped on one foot.

We knelt and scuffed back grass and sand. Just beneath the surface was an extraordinary, bubbly mass of metal, greenish above the surface, pinky-gold beneath. Together we tugged at it and finally pulled it free.

"Copper!" exclaimed Katie, after spitting

on the lump and rubbing it clean. "Native copper!"

"Then there are people here? Do you suppose they're friendly?" I looked anxiously around. The grass that fringed the dry riverbed was at least a yard high. It would be possible for a person to hide in it and creep closer and closer. . . .

Katie laughed. "Native copper just means copper occurring naturally on the surface, not having to be mined and smelted. If there are many big lumps around, it's really a sign that the country's uninhabited. Copper's so valuable, so easy to shape, that it would have all been picked up and used by now if there were people here."

I stopped looking over my shoulder every few minutes. I'd read so many adventures about Africa—and this place *felt* like Africa—that I was expecting anything to happen. . . .

---

## Skills in Science

### Reading Skills in Science

1. **Classify**   Identify one element, one compound, and one mixture referred to, either directly or indirectly.

2. **Infer**   What are the yellow, orange, and green streaks in the crystals along the shore of the lake?

### Writing Skills in Science

1. **Compare and Contrast**   The narrator and Scylla react differently than Alden does when they see the lake. Explain how and why their initial perspective is different from Alden's.

2. **Communicate**   Imagine you are one of the explorers in the wilderness. What are three ways you could use the native copper? Be specific.

### Activities

**Collect Data**   Research the Dead Sea and the Great Salt Lake. Identify life forms and minerals present in each one. How are these lakes used by people?

**Communicate**   Research early Native-American, Chinese, or Egyptian uses of copper. Describe a common usage in writing, or draw a picture of an ancient copper tool.

### Where to Read More

*The Meteorite Craters* by Willy Ley. New York: Weybright and Talley, Inc., 1964. An in-depth study of impact craters.

*Rocks and Minerals* by Herbert Zim and Paul Shaffer. New York: Golden Press, 1957. This field guide identifies substances in your own backyard!

# Unit 3

# Heat

## Chapters

**9** Heat

**10** Using Heat

# Data Bank

Use the information on pages 634 to 643 to answer the questions about topics explored in this unit.

## *Classifying*

What air pollutants are produced by transportation?

## *Inferring*

Which animal would be most likely to survive in a cold environment: an ascaphus frog, a domestic rabbit, or a lungless salamander?

## *Calculating*

What percent of the normal body temperature of a Canada jay is the normal body temperature of a human?

The photograph to the left shows steam given off by a lake heated from beneath the earth's surface. How do you think the deposits around the lake were formed?

# Chapter 9 Heat

## Chapter Sections

**9.1** Heat Energy

**9.2** Transfer of Heat

**9.3** Heat and Matter

## What do you see?

❝I see a hand coming down to type on a keyboard. I think this waffle-looking thing is a keyboard. The colors indicate the heat of the hand and keyboard and the differences in heat given off by them. There are hot areas (in red) and cold areas (in blue) and other areas in between.❞

*Stephanie Donihoo*
*North Garland High School*
*Garland, Texas*

To find out more about the photograph, look on page 228. As you read this chapter, you will learn about heat energy.

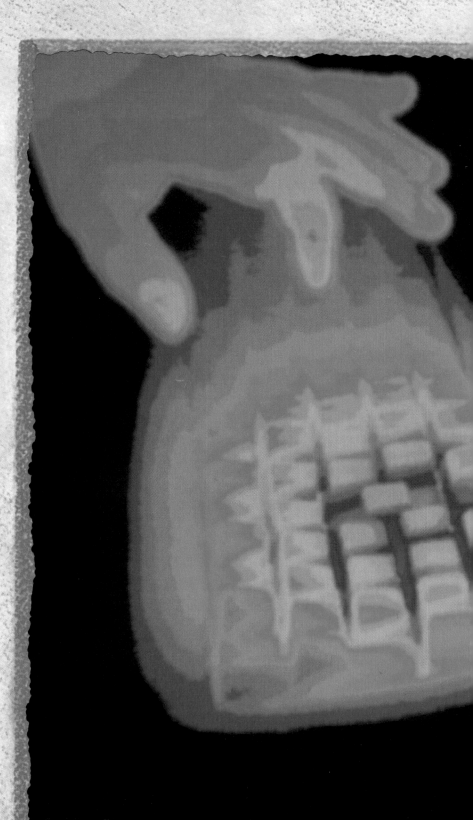

# 9.1 Heat Energy

## Objectives

▶ **Relate** heat energy to moving molecules.

▶ **Distinguish** between the Celsius and Kelvin temperature scales.

▶ **Compare** temperature, internal energy, and heat energy.

▶ **Define operationally** a temperature change.

Y ou meet your friends for a game of basketball on a cool autumn day. While playing, you feel hot and take off your sweatshirt. During a break, you go for a drink. The ice in your soft drink is partially melted. You take a drink. It is still cold. If this were summer, the heat would have made the drink warm by now. You feel chilly and put your sweatshirt on again. You experience heat all the time, and you use words such as *hot*, *cold*, and *heat* often. In science, heat has a different and very specific meaning.

## Molecules in Motion

Recall that all matter is made of molecules that are in constant motion. The gas molecules that make up air move freely all around you. Molecules of water move about in a container. The molecules in your chair constantly move back and forth, or vibrate. Matter that moves has kinetic energy. The measurement of the *average* kinetic energy of the molecules in a substance is called **temperature**.

If two objects with different temperatures come into contact, energy flows from the object with the higher temperature to the one with the lower temperature. Energy that is transferred from one substance to another is called **heat energy**. Heat is energy that flows between objects that have different temperatures. The official SI unit of heat is the joule.

When heat energy transfers to a substance, it adds to the **internal energy** of the substance. Internal energy is the total amount of energy a substance contains. Most of the internal energy of a substance is kinetic energy.

**Figure 9.1** ▲
What happens to the temperature of the water that cools the runner?

## Measuring Temperature

You probably think about how hot or cold something is in terms of its temperature. When the temperature of a substance is high, its molecules are moving rapidly. Imagine that you fill a bucket and a teacup with water from a bathtub. The temperature of the water is the same in each container, because temperature is a measure of the *average* movement of the molecules in a substance. Volume doesn't affect temperature.

You measure temperature with a thermometer. Most thermometers are thin glass tubes connected to a reservoir of liquid mercury or colored alcohol. A numbered scale is marked on the outside of the tube. As a thermometer heats up, the molecules in its liquid begin to move faster and farther apart. The liquid expands and rises in the tube. The scale indicates the temperature reading. In SI, two different scales are used for temperature readings; the Celsius scale and the Kelvin scale.

## Historical Notebook

### Understanding Heat

Two hundred years ago, most scientists thought that heat was an invisible, weightless substance. They called the substance caloric. People believed the hotter an object was, the more caloric it contained. It was thought that a piece of matter contained a specific amount of heat.

In 1798, the American-born scientist Benjamin Thompson, better known as Count Rumford, questioned the caloric theory of heat. Count Rumford observed the hole-drilling process in cannon barrels in Munich, Germany. He saw that heat was produced as long as the cutting tool moved through the cannon.

Water was used to cool the cutting tool and the cannon as the hole was drilled. The water got boiling hot! As you can see in the picture above, water is still sometimes used to cool cutting tools. Rumford noticed that no heat or matter was added during the drilling. Since matter cannot be

created out of nothing, he reasoned that heat could not be a material substance. Rumford hypothesized that the energy used to turn the drill was being transformed into heat. He concluded that heat, therefore, must be a form of energy. Rumford's theory was confirmed forty years later by the British scientist James Prescott Joule.

**Celsius Temperature Scale** In the metric system, the Celsius scale is commonly used to measure temperature. The Celsius scale was developed by Anders Celsius, a Swedish astronomer. Celsius temperature is also referred to as centigrade temperature.

Look at the Celsius thermometer in Figure 9.2. Find normal body temperature. Was it lower or higher than you expected? Normally, your body temperature changes several tenths of a degree during the day.

**Kelvin Temperature Scale** Another SI temperature scale is called the **Kelvin** scale. The Kelvin scale, also called the absolute scale, is named for its originator, Lord Kelvin. Kelvin thermometers are used primarily in the physical sciences.

The Kelvin scale is based on the amount of energy in a substance. It is used to measure the temperature of supercold substances. The Kelvin scale identifies the temperature where molecules in a substance are so cold they don't move. They have no kinetic energy. This temperature is called **absolute zero**.

Compare the Celsius and Kelvin thermometers in Figure 9.2. Notice that 0 K equals –273°C. You can convert the Celsius temperature of an object to the Kelvin temperature by adding 273. Since the boiling point of water is 100°C, the boiling point of water on the Kelvin scale is 100 plus 273, or 373 K. What is the freezing point of water on the Kelvin scale?

The Kelvin temperature scale is used in science because it relates directly to energy. For example, 1 $cm^3$ of a substance at 200 K has twice the kinetic energy of 1 $cm^3$ of the same substance at 100 K.

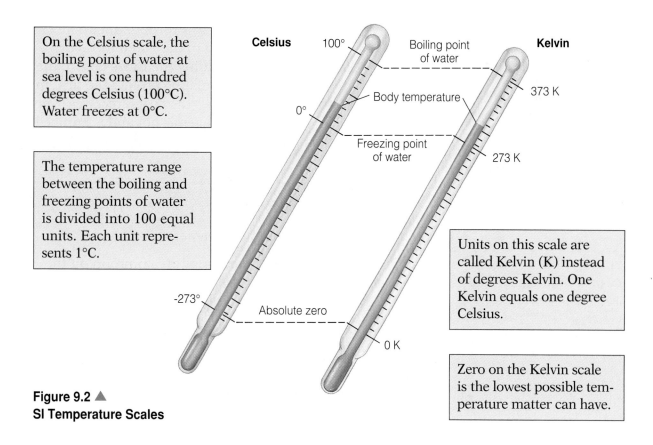

On the Celsius scale, the boiling point of water at sea level is one hundred degrees Celsius (100°C). Water freezes at 0°C.

The temperature range between the boiling and freezing points of water is divided into 100 equal units. Each unit represents 1°C.

Celsius    100°    Boiling point of water    **Kelvin**

0°    Body temperature    373 K

Freezing point of water    273 K

-273°    Absolute zero

0 K

Units on this scale are called Kelvin (K) instead of degrees Kelvin. One Kelvin equals one degree Celsius.

Zero on the Kelvin scale is the lowest possible temperature matter can have.

**Figure 9.2 ▲**
**SI Temperature Scales**

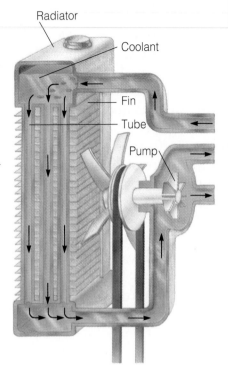

Radiator

Coolant

Fin

Tube

Pump

**Figure 9.3** ▲

A radiator is part of a car's cooling system. What happens when a car's radiator is broken?

## Science and Technology *A Cool Engine*

What liquid does a car need to run properly? Most people answer "gasoline." However, another liquid—water—is just as vital to a car's performance.

Large amounts of heat are given off when gasoline is burned in the cylinders of an engine. Also, an engine contains many moving parts that rub against each other. Even though oil lubricates engine parts, enough friction still exists to produce heat. Because excessive heat can seriously damage the engine, cars have a cooling system that controls engine temperature.

A car's cooling system consists of a radiator, hoses, and channels that are filled with a mixture of water and antifreeze, called a coolant. The channels carry the coolant through the engine block. The engine block contains the cylinders and other moving parts that get hot when the engine is running.

A pump circulates the coolant through the engine. Heat is transferred to the coolant as it flows over hot engine parts. The heated coolant then moves away from the engine and through the hoses to the car's radiator.

Look at the radiator in Figure 9.3. Follow the path of the coolant as it moves through the radiator. Inside the radiator, the heated coolant passes through metal tubes. Heat transfers from the coolant to the metal tubes by conduction. Metal fins surrounding the tubes absorb the heat and transfer it into air circulating around the fins. In this way, the coolant mixture loses the heat it receives from the engine. The coolant is no longer as hot and is pumped back to the engine where the cycle starts over again!

## Check and Explain

1. How are heat and moving molecules related?

2. Negative temperature readings are common on the Celsius scale. Explain why you don't get a negative reading on the Kelvin scale.

3. **Compare** How do the temperature, internal energy, and heat energy in a cup of hot tea change overnight?

4. **Define Operationally** Suppose you put some hot water in the refrigerator for two hours. Explain what happens to the molecules of water.

# 9.2 Transfer of Heat

## Objectives

▶ **Identify** three ways heat is transferred.

▶ **Explain** how heat transfer is measured.

▶ **Calculate** the amount of heat transferred between two substances.

▶ **Infer** how heat transfer affects climate.

H ave you ever cooked food in a cast-iron skillet? You probably used a pot holder to insulate your hand from the heat of the skillet's handle. Did you wonder why the handle was hot even though it didn't come in direct contact with the burner? Heat energy is transferred from the bottom of the skillet, up through the sides, and into the handle by the process of conduction. Heat is also transferred by convection and radiation.

## Conduction

Heat energy flows from a warm substance to a cool substance. When solid substances are in contact, heat energy transfers by **conduction**. Conduction is the transfer of heat energy throughout a substance, or when one substance comes in contact with another.

When you put the lower part of a spoon in boiling water, heat transfers from the boiling water to the cool spoon. The spoon's molecules that are in contact with the water move more rapidly and collide with the molecules in the upper portion of the spoon. Through a continuous series of collisions, heat energy transfers throughout the entire spoon. The hot spoon handle is evidence that heat energy has been transferred.

Some materials conduct heat better than others. For example, a cloth pot holder conducts heat poorly. It is an insulator. Wood, plastic, and glass are also insulators. Look at Figure 9.4. The sun heats the wood door and the metal doorknob on the outside. Soon, the inside doorknob gets hot also. Why doesn't the inside of the door get hot?

### Hypothesizing

*Spooning*

Collect the following items: an all-metal spoon, a metal spoon with a plastic handle, and a mug of boiling water.

**1.** Place the two spoons in the mug of boiling water.

**2.** Gently touch the handles of the spoons after two minutes. Touch the handles again after five minutes.

Write a hypothesis to explain what you observe. How could you test your hypothesis further?

**SKILLS WARMUP**

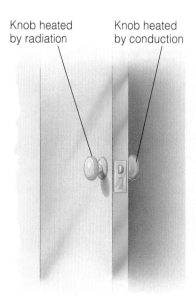

Knob heated by radiation    Knob heated by conduction

**Figure 9.4** ▲

Which methods of heat transfer contribute to heating the inside doorknob?

## Convection

Air in contact with a wood-burning stove spreads out to warm an entire room. Water boils when heated in a pan. These are examples of heat transfer by a process called **convection**. Convection is the transfer of heat energy by the movement of a fluid, such as a liquid or a gas.

Heat energy flows through a fluid in a pattern called a convection current. Convection currents form because heated fluid expands and is less dense than surrounding fluid, which is cooler. The difference in the density causes warm fluid to rise and cooler fluid to sink. The result is a convection current that moves heat energy through the fluid.

If you have ever boiled water, then you have observed convection currents in a liquid. Convection currents cause the rolling motion of gently boiling water. The water at the bottom of the pan heats up. The heated water molecules move faster, spread apart, and become less dense. They rise to the surface. Cooler, denser water at the top moves downward toward the bottom of the pan. This water then heats up and rises. Convection currents continue to form as long as there is a heat source.

To understand how convection currents form in a gas, think about how heat moves in an oven. Look at the convection currents that circulate hot air in the oven in Figure 9.5. Trace the movement of the convection currents with your finger.

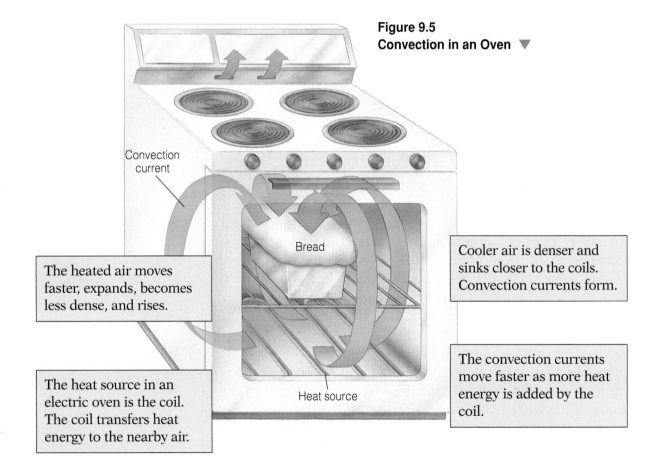

**Figure 9.5
Convection in an Oven** ▼

Convection current

The heated air moves faster, expands, becomes less dense, and rises.

Bread

Cooler air is denser and sinks closer to the coils. Convection currents form.

The heat source in an electric oven is the coil. The coil transfers heat energy to the nearby air.

Heat source

The convection currents move faster as more heat energy is added by the coil.

## Radiation

Every time you feel the sun warm your skin, you experience **radiation.** Both the sun and fire give off radiation. Radiation is the transfer of energy by infrared waves. When infrared waves strike your skin, the molecules in your skin vibrate faster and become warmer. Radiation can move energy over long distances.

Radiation differs from conduction and convection because matter isn't needed to transfer energy by radiation. Recall that conduction depends on the collision between the molecules of a substance. Convection depends on the expansion of a fluid when molecules collide. However, radiation can occur in a vacuum, where no molecules of matter are present.

Any form of energy that is transferred by radiation is called radiant energy. Radiant energy and radiation shouldn't be confused with harmful radioactivity, or nuclear radiation. All rays from the sun are forms of radiant energy that transfer by radiation. When any object gets hot, it gives off radiant energy. For example, if you move your hand close to a fire or hot electric coil, you can feel radiant energy.

Matter can reflect or absorb radiant energy. Look at Figure 9.6. Most of the sun's radiant energy that reaches the earth is in the form of light. Observe that the earth and its atmosphere reflect and absorb radiant energy from the sun. When radiant energy is absorbed, it is later re-radiated as heat. The heat increases the temperature of the atmosphere.

**Figure 9.6    Solar Radiation** ▼

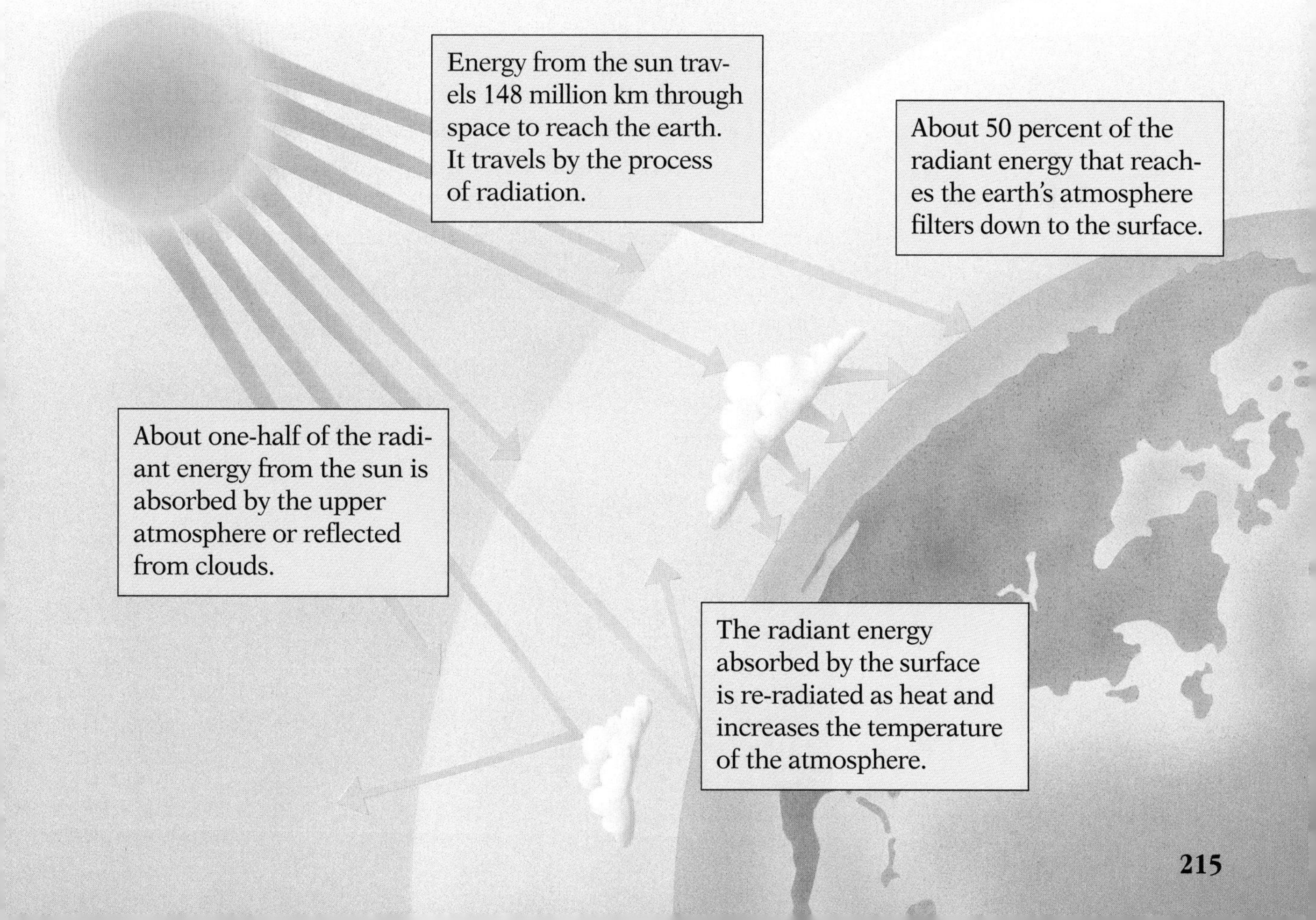

Energy from the sun travels 148 million km through space to reach the earth. It travels by the process of radiation.

About 50 percent of the radiant energy that reaches the earth's atmosphere filters down to the surface.

About one-half of the radiant energy from the sun is absorbed by the upper atmosphere or reflected from clouds.

The radiant energy absorbed by the surface is re-radiated as heat and increases the temperature of the atmosphere.

## Table 9.1  Specific Heats

| Substance | Specific Heat (J/kg°C) |
|---|---|
| Water | 4186 |
| Wood | 1750 |
| Air | 1000 |
| Aluminum | 899 |
| Carbon (graphite) | 711 |
| Sand | 664 |
| Iron | 443 |
| Copper | 385 |
| Tin | 213 |
| Gold | 130 |

## Measuring Heat Transfer

Think about a hot fruit pie just out of the oven. You nibble a bit of the crust that is cool enough to eat. But what about the fruit filling? The filling is so hot that it will burn your mouth! You know that both the crust and the filling were heated at the same temperature for the same amount of time. Why is the filling so much hotter? Substances differ in the way they absorb heat energy. When the filling absorbs heat, its temperature increases. More heat energy would have to be added to the crust to raise it to the same temperature as the filling.

**Specific Heat**   Just like the pie crust and the filling, heat energy affects substances differently. Each substance requires a different amount of heat to raise its temperature 1°C. The amount of heat 1 g of a substance must absorb to raise its temperature 1°C is called the **specific heat** of the substance. Specific heat can be used to identify a substance.

Look at Table 9.1 to compare the specific heat of some common substances. For example, the specific heat of copper is lower than the specific heat of water. When an equal amount of heat is applied to both copper and water, the temperature of the copper will be higher than the temperature of the water. Less heat energy is needed to raise the temperature of 1 kg of copper than is needed to raise the temperature of 1 kg of water. The items in Figure 9.7 are made of different metals. Use Table 9.1 to compare their specific heat. Which metal has the lowest specific heat?

**Figure 9.7** ▶
These items are made of aluminum, copper, and tin. What is the specific heat of each metal?

**Calories** You know that the official SI unit of heat is the joule. Another unit still commonly used to measure heat is the **calorie**. One calorie equals 4.186 J. One calorie is the amount of heat needed to raise the temperature of 1 g of water 1°C. Five calories of heat are needed to raise the temperature of 1 g of water 5°C.

Scientists in the 1700s thought that heat was an invisible substance they called *caloric* (kuh LOR ihk). Today's word *calorie* comes from the word caloric. A device called the calorimeter was invented to measure the amount of heat given off when a substance is burned. The calorimeter is still used today.

Look at the calorimeter in Figure 9.8. A thick layer of insulation surrounds the

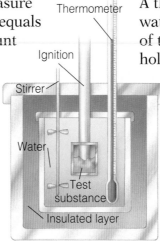

**Figure 9.8** ▲
**A Calorimeter**

device to prevent heat loss from the large, water-filled chamber. A thermometer measures the water temperature. In the center of the calorimeter, a chamber holds the substance being tested. The test substance is ignited and burned.

As heat energy flows out of the substance and into the water, the water temperature rises. The amount of heat gained by the water equals the amount of heat lost by the substance being tested. To calculate this amount of heat, multiply the mass of the water times the specific heat of the water times the temperature change of the water. How would you convert the heat into calories?

## Sample Problem

How much heat is needed to raise the temperature of 0.5 kg of aluminum from 15°C to 20°C?

**Plan** Multiply the mass by the specific heat by the change in temperature.

**Gather Data**
   a. Specific heat = 899 J/kg°C (See Table 9.1)
   b. Mass = 0.5 kg
   c. The temperature difference is
      20°C − 15°C = 5°C

**Solve** Heat = mass × specific heat × change in temperature

   heat = 0.5 kg × 899 J/kg°C × 5°C
   heat = 2247.5 J

## Practice Problems

1. How much heat is needed to raise the temperature of 0.02 kg of iron from 20°C to 30°C?

2. How much heat is needed to raise the temperature of 5 g of gold from 15°C to 25°C?

3. How much heat is given off by 30 g of tin as it cools from 90°C to 20°C?

4. On a hot stove burner, the temperature of a 500 g aluminum pan increases 120°C. How much heat was added?

5. You receive an unknown substance. A note with the substance says that to increase the temperature of 100 g of the substance 1°C, about 21.5 J of heat is needed. What is the unknown substance?

## Heat Transfer and Climate

Imagine that you win a vacation to any place in the world. Where would you like to go? You'd probably like a location that has a climate quite different from your own. You might pick a warm, tropical climate, where you could swim any day of the year. Perhaps you'd prefer to go to a cold, snowy place, where you could ski in July!

Think about places on the earth that have different climates. For example, you know that if you travel to a region near the equator, the weather will probably be hot and humid. You know if you head to the far north, it will probably be cold and snowy. Why do different locations on the earth's surface have different types of climates? The differences in weather conditions are due to the transfer of heat energy. The heat-transfer processes of conduction, convection, and radiation all play a role in determining weather and climate.

**Solar Radiation** Heat energy from the sun reaches the earth by radiation. As the earth moves around the sun, some places receive more solar radiation than others. Solar radiation is the most intense when the sun is directly overhead.

**Figure 9.9 Heat and Climate** ▼

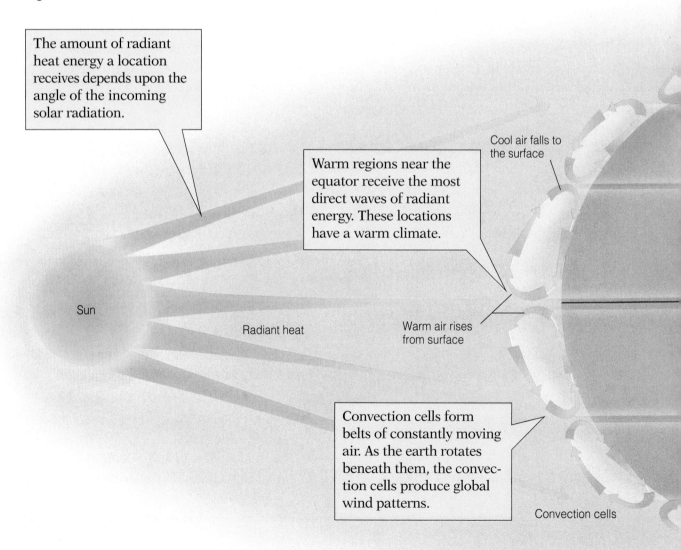

The amount of radiant heat energy a location receives depends upon the angle of the incoming solar radiation.

Warm regions near the equator receive the most direct waves of radiant energy. These locations have a warm climate.

Cool air falls to the surface

Sun

Radiant heat

Warm air rises from surface

Convection cells form belts of constantly moving air. As the earth rotates beneath them, the convection cells produce global wind patterns.

Convection cells

At the extreme northern or southern latitudes, solar radiation strikes the earth at a low angle. The sun's rays must travel a long distance through the atmosphere to reach the surface. As a result, northern and southern latitudes receive less solar radiation than the equator does. The climate at these latitudes is cool.

**Heat in the Atmosphere**   Radiant energy from the sun warms the earth's surface. The earth's surface transfers heat to the air by conduction. Actually, the air around you is warmed by the earth, which is heated by the sun.

Convection currents form as air is heated by the earth's surface. Warm air expands and rises. It displaces the cool, dense air at higher elevations. The dense air sinks.

The warm rising air carries moisture to higher elevations. As the air cools, the moisture condenses and falls to the earth as rain or snow. Convection currents in the atmosphere are called convection cells. Convection cells are responsible for the wind and rain patterns over the earth's surface. Look at Figure 9.9 to see how radiation, conduction, and convection affect climate.

Areas of sparse growth, called tundra, are located in the region near the North Pole.

Equator

Lush rain forests grow in the sunny, wet climate near the equator.

Convection cells

## Science and You *Food Calories and Energy*

Diet! Exercise! Calories! You hear these words used together all the time. Radio, television, and magazines carry ads for products that will help you to consume fewer calories or to burn them off. But what does the calorie, a unit of heat, have to do with diet and exercise?

To determine the amount of heat energy available in food, it is burned in a calorimeter. Do you know what unit is used to measure the heat energy released? If you said the *calorie*, you wouldn't be quite right. A calorie is too small a quantity to conveniently measure the energy in food. A chocolate chip cookie has 75 000 calories!

Instead of writing 75 000 calories, nutritionists write 75 Calories. Notice that *Calorie* is written with a capital C. When a capital C is used, it refers to a *food* Calorie, which is 1,000 calories, or a kilocalorie. The unit *Calorie* is always used when referring to the energy in food.

Your body uses food energy to perform all your activities, to maintain your body temperature, and to function. Compare the energy requirements for the activities in Table 9.2. Even when you do absolutely nothing, your body gives off heat at a rate of about 1,200 Calories each day!

If you reduce your Calorie intake by dieting, your body still needs energy in order to function properly. Otherwise, your body gets energy by breaking down its own tissues. Your body will break down both fat and muscle tissue to use as energy when your food intake is inadequate.

**Table 9.2   Calorie Use**

| Activity | Calories per Minute |
|----------|---------------------|
| Running | 13.0 |
| Swimming | 8.0 |
| Dancing | 6.5 |
| Bicycling | 6.0 |
| Walking | 3.5 |
| Resting | 0.8 |

## Check and Explain

1. What are three ways heat can be transferred? Describe how each occurs.

2. What evidence indicates heat transfers either into or out of a substance? How can it be measured?

3. **Calculate**  The specific heat of copper is 385 J/kg°C. How much heat is needed to raise the temperature of 20 g of copper from 25°C to 40°C?

4. **Infer**  What would happen to the weather if the earth turned "on its side" so that the equator and poles switched places?

# Activity 9  *How do you measure the transfer of heat?*

***Skills***  Measure; Calculate; infer

## Task 1 Prelab Prep
1. Collect the following items: 2 plastic foam cups, pen, pencil, graduated cylinder, Celsius thermometer, tongs, Bunsen burner, bolt, nut, large paperclip, clock that can measure seconds.
2. With the pen, number the cups *1* and *2*.

## Task 2 Data Record
1. On a separate sheet of paper, draw a data table like the one shown.
2. Notice that the column titled *Mass of water* is shown in grams (g). Recall that 1 mL of water has a mass of 1 g. You will need to measure 75 mL, or 75 g, of water with the graduated cylinder.
3. Record the initial water temperature in column $T_i$. Record the highest temperature in column $T_f$. Subtract $T_i$ from $T_f$.
4. To calculate the heat transferred to the water, use the following formula: heat = mass of the water x temperature change x specific heat. The specific heat of water is 4186 J/kg × °C.

## Task 3  Procedure
1. Measure 75 mL of tap water with a graduated cylinder and pour it into the cup labeled *1*.
2. With a sharp pencil, make a small hole in the side of cup *2* near the rim. Gently ease a thermometer through the hole. Place cup *2* upside down over cup *1* so the rims meet. Adjust the thermometer bulb so it is completely submerged in the water in cup *1*. Hold the thermometer in place.
3. Light the Bunsen burner. **CAUTION! Tie back loose hair and clothing around an open flame.**
4. Record the temperature of the water, $T_i$, in your data table.
5. With the tongs hold the bolt in the flame for 10 s. **CAUTION! metal objects will become very hot. Use tongs.**
6. Lift cup *2* and gently drop the bolt into the water in cup *1*. Immediately replace cup *2*. Keep the thermometer bulb in the water.
7. Record the highest temperature, $T_f$, in your data table.
8. Replace the water in cup *1* with fresh tap water. Repeat steps 4–7 using the nut, and again using the paperclip.

## Task 4 Analysis
1. Why did the temperature of the water rise?
2. How did the amount of heat transferred from each object differ? Why?

## Task 5 Conclusion
A set of keys near a portable heater gets hot. How would you apply the method used in this activity to determine how much heat energy was transferred to the keys?

## Table 9.3   Heat Transfer

| Heated object | Mass of water (g) | $T_i$ (°C) | $T_f$ (°C) | Temperature change $T_f$–$T_i$ (°C) | Heat transferred (J) |
|---|---|---|---|---|---|
| bolt | 75 | | | | |
| nut | 75 | | | | |
| paperclip | 75 | | | | |

## ▼ ACTIVITY

### Modeling

*Running a Temperature*

**1.** Draw three pictures showing objects undergoing temperature changes.

**2.** Beneath each picture, write "temperature increasing" or "temperature decreasing."

**3.** Use arrows to show whether heat is moving into or out of the object.

**SKILLS WARMUP**

# 9.3 Heat and Matter

## Objectives

▶ **Describe** the role of heat in phase changes.

▶ **Identify** three examples of thermal expansion.

▶ **Generalize** about what occurs at the boiling point or melting point of a substance.

▶ **Interpret data** to identify an unknown substance by its boiling point.

Sandra packed a picnic lunch to take to the beach. She put a container of yogurt, some carrot sticks, an apple, and a bottle of juice in a small cooler. Sandra then placed some ice cubes in the cooler. What do Sandra's actions tell you about the temperature conditions she expected at the beach? Suppose Sandra was going to spend the day snow skiing. How would the way she packed her lunch be different?

## Heat and Phase Changes

Recall that matter can change phases from solid to liquid to gas. When heat sufficiently increases the motion of molecules in a substance, a phase change occurs. Look at Figure 9.10 to see how heat affects the temperature and the phases of water.

When heat is applied to ice, the water molecules in the ice vibrate faster. The ice melts as it changes from a solid to a liquid. The temperature doesn't change until all the ice melts. When all the ice is melted, additional heat causes the temperature of liquid water to rise again until it reaches 100°C. At 100°C, a phase change occurs and the water evaporates, or changes to its gaseous phase.

Phase changes also occur when heat leaves matter. For example, water vapor in the air condenses, or changes from a gas to a liquid, on the outside of a glass of ice water. Condensation occurs because the temperature of the water vapor decreases when it comes in contact with the cold glass. The water vapor undergoes a phase change and becomes a liquid. What kind of phase change occurs when you make ice cubes in your freezer?

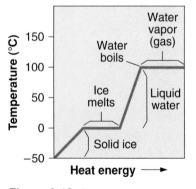

**Figure 9.10** ▲

Notice that during phase changes, heat is added without an increase in temperature.

# Boiling Point

Think about what happens when you heat a beaker of water. After a time, the liquid water enters the gas phase. This change occurs when the water reaches its **boiling point**. The boiling point is the temperature at which a substance changes from a liquid phase to a gas phase.

In order for a substance to reach its boiling point, it must gain heat energy. Study Figure 9.11. How did the water molecules in the beaker gain heat energy to reach the boiling point?

As the molecules in the liquid gain heat energy, their motion increases. The amount of internal energy in the liquid also increases. Eventually, the molecules have so much energy that they break free of the liquid surface and move away as a gas. In Figure 9.11, water molecules rise from the beaker as steam.

Every substance has its own boiling point. You know that water boils at 100°C. The chemical element fluorine boils at about -188°C. Nitrogen boils at about -196°C. The boiling point of copper is 2,595°C. Since air pressure affects boiling, standard boiling-point measurements are made at sea level.

**Table 9.4   Boiling Point of Common Substances**

| Substance | °C at Sea Level |
|---|---|
| Mercury | 356.9 |
| Water | 100.0 |
| Isopropyl alcohol | 82.5 |
| Acetone | 56.5 |
| Ether | 35.0 |
| Oxygen | −183.0 |
| Nitrogen | −195.8 |

**Figure 9.11
Liquid-Gas Phase Change ▼**

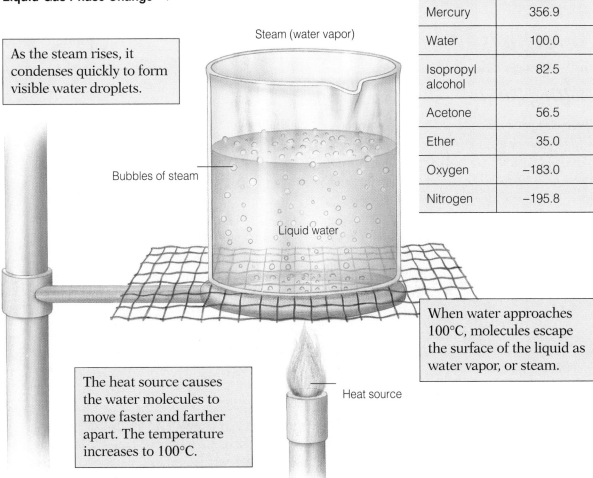

As the steam rises, it condenses quickly to form visible water droplets.

Steam (water vapor)

Bubbles of steam

Liquid water

When water approaches 100°C, molecules escape the surface of the liquid as water vapor, or steam.

The heat source causes the water molecules to move faster and farther apart. The temperature increases to 100°C.

Heat source

## Table 9.5 Melting Point of Common Substances

| Substance | Melting Point °C |
|-----------|------------------|
| Iron | 1,535.0 |
| Silver | 960.5 |
| Aluminum | 660.0 |
| Tin | 232.0 |
| Polyethylene plastic | 85.0 |
| Phosphorus | 44.0 |
| Water (Ice) | 0.0 |
| Mercury | –39.0 |
| Oxygen | –218.4 |

## Melting Point

What happens to ice cream on a very hot day? If you don't eat it quickly, the ice cream changes phase—from a solid to a liquid. This occurs when the ice cream reaches its **melting point**. The melting point is the temperature at which a solid becomes a liquid. Heat energy moves from the warm air to the ice cream. The molecules in the ice cream move about more rapidly and the solid ice cream becomes a liquid.

You know the melting point of ice is 0°C. The freezing point of water is also 0°C. For any substance, the melting point and freezing point are always at the same temperature. If heat energy is applied to ice, at 0°C the ice will melt. If liquid water is cooled to 0°C, it will freeze.

Every substance has its own melting point. Melting point is an important physical property of a substance. Look at Table 9.5. Scientists use melting-point tables to help identify unknown substances.

## *SkillBuilder* Interpreting Data

### Melting Points

The melting point of a substance is a physical property that can be used to identify the substance. Most substances have a melting point that is different than the melting point of other substances. The bar graph at the right shows the melting point of five unknown substances. Study the graph. Use the graph and Table 9.5 above to answer the following questions.

1. What substance does each bar in the graph represent? Copy the graph on a sheet of paper and label each bar with the correct substance.

2. Which substances would be solid at 600°C? Which would be liquid?

3. Which substances would be solid at 200°C? Which would be liquid?

4. At what temperature would all the substances be liquids?

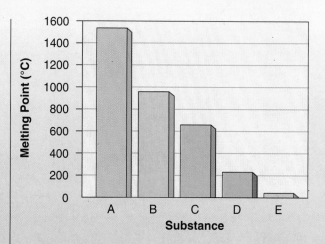

5. At what temperature would all the substances be solids?

6. Explain why the vertical axis of the graph could also have been labeled "Freezing point (°C)"?

## Thermal Expansion

As heat energy flows into a substance, molecules vibrate and move about more rapidly. As the molecules move away from each other, the substance expands. An increase in the volume of a substance due to heat is called **thermal expansion**. Thermal expansion occurs in solids, liquids, and gases.

You have observed thermal expansion in different types of matter. Perhaps you have run hot water over the top of a glass jar to loosen the metal lid. The lid expands and is easy to remove!

Have you ever filled a pot to the brim with water and heated it on a stove? If so, you may have wondered why the water spilled over the top of the pot when it got hot. The water overflowed because of thermal expansion.

When you inflate a bicycle tire, you leave room for the thermal expansion of the air inside the tire. Heat energy caused by friction between the tire and the road causes the gas to expand. After a long ride an over-inflated tire may burst.

### Geology LINK

Rainwater in the cracks of rocks can freeze, expand, and crack the rock. Collect the following items: a straw, waterproof clay, and a glass of water.

**1.** Suck water into the straw. Hold your finger over one end. Plug the other end with a piece of clay.

**2.** Plug the unplugged end.

**3.** Place the straw in the freezer for several hours.

What changes do you notice? Relate the weathering of rocks to thermal expansion.

**ACTIVITY**

### Expansion in Solids
The concrete and metal in bridges and freeways expand in the hot sun. To prevent the road from buckling or breaking, engineers build gaps, called expansion joints, between segments of the road. ▼

### Expansion in Liquids ▲
Most liquids expand when heated. There is one exception to this rule, however. Between 4°C and 0°C, water expands as it cools. Why should you not put an unopened soft drink can in the freezer?

### Expansion in Gases
The bladder of the football below expanded and split the seam. The ball was over-inflated and left in the sun on a hot day. Can you think of other examples of thermal expansion in gases? ▼

Since ancient times, people all over the world have looked for ways to preserve food for future use. Some methods developed by ancient people are still in use today. To preserve food, it must be changed in some way to prevent spoilage by bacteria and mold.

Methods using heat were probably among the first used in food preservation. For example, one ancient method was to dry foods in the sun. Heat energy from the sun evaporated the water from the food. As the water evaporated, the food became drier. The sugar and protein in the food became more concentrated. Mold and bacteria couldn't grow in the food because these organisms need a moist environment to survive. Another ancient method was to dry meat in hot smoke from a fire. This method of smoking meat is still used.

People who lived in cold climates were able to freeze their food by simply keeping it outdoors. The water in the food turned to solid ice. Most bacteria and molds can't grow at 0°C. When thawed, the food wasn't spoiled. Today, electric refrigerators and freezers slow or prevent the growth of bacteria in food.

In the early 1800s, canning was invented. Canning involves packing and sealing food in sterile containers that are heated in boiling water for 20 to 30 minutes. The heat kills any harmful bacteria present in the food. How was the food in your lunch preserved?

## ACTIVITY

### Observing

*Potato Under Glass*

Collect the following items: a slice of potato, a paper towel, and a glass.

**1.** Place a slice of potato on a paper towel beneath an upside-down glass on a sunny windowsill.

**2.** Don't disturb the potato for one hour.

What happens? Explain your observations.

**SKILLS WORKOUT**

## Check and Explain

1. How does heat energy cause matter to change phases?

2. Explain how heat can crack concrete driveways and sidewalks. How are driveways and sidewalks constructed to prevent cracking?

3. **Generalize** Explain what happens to the molecules in a substance at its melting point and at its boiling point.

4. **Interpret Data** You test the melting point of two unknown solids. Substance 1 begins to melt at 44°C. Substance 2 begins to melt at 85°C. Use Table 9.5 to identify each substance.

# Chapter 9 Review

## Concept Summary

### 9.1 Heat Energy

▶ Energy that is absorbed, given up, or transferred from one substance to another is called heat energy. Heat is measured in Joules.

▶ Internal energy is the total amount of energy a substance contains.

▶ Temperature measures the average kinetic energy of the molecules in a substance.

▶ Temperature is measured on the Celsius and Kelvin scales.

### 9.2 Transfer of Heat

▶ Heat transfer can occur by conduction, convection, or radiation.

▶ Heat transfer is measured as a temperature change in a substance.

▶ Specific heat is the amount of heat needed to raise the temperature of 1 kg of a substance 1°C.

▶ The amount of heat transferred to an object equals the object's mass times its specific heat times the temperature change.

### 9.3 Heat and Matter

▶ Adding heat energy increases the motion of a substance's molecules.

▶ At the boiling point, molecules in a liquid become a gas.

▶ At the melting point, the molecules of a solid become a liquid.

▶ Thermal expansion occurs when heat causes the molecules of a substance to spread out.

## Chapter Vocabulary

| | | | |
|---|---|---|---|
| temperature (9.1) | absolute zero (9.1) | specific heat (9.2) | melting point (9.3) |
| heat energy (9.1) | conduction (9.2) | calorie (9.2) | thermal expansion (9.3) |
| internal energy (9.1) | convection (9.2) | boiling point (9.3) | |
| Kelvin (9.1) | radiation (9.2) | | |

## Check Your Vocabulary

Use the vocabulary words above to complete the following sentences correctly.

1. Energy transfers in a vacuum by _____ .

2. At its _____ , a substance changes from liquid to gas.

3. The amount of heat needed to raise the temperature of 1 kg of a substance 1°C is its _____ .

4. Heat transfer caused by density differences in a fluid is called _____ .

5. The _____ of a substance includes all the energy it contains.

6. One _____ is equal to 1°C.

7. At _____ , the molecules of a substance have no kinetic energy.

8. When a hot object is in contact with a cool one, heat moves by _____ .

9. The _____ is a unit used to measure heat.

10. When objects are in contact, _____ flows to the cooler object.

11. A substance changes from solid to liquid at its _____ .

12. Cracks in cement are caused by _____ .

13. The Celsius scale measures _____ .

## Write Your Vocabulary

Write sentences using the vocabulary words above. Show that you know what each word means.

# Chapter 9 Review

## Check Your Knowledge

Answer the following in complete sentences.

1. What is heat?

2. What happens to molecules in a substance when it gets hotter? When it gets colder?

3. How do you know when heat has been transferred?

4. What is absolute zero?

5. What is the SI unit for heat?

6. What does it mean when one substance has a lower specific heat than another substance?

7. What energy-transfer process can take place when no matter is present?

8. What is thermal expansion?

Determine whether each statement is true or false. Write *true* if it is true. If it is false, change the underlined term(s) so that it is true.

9. The Celsius scale is used to measure <u>heat</u>.

10. When a substance gets hotter, its molecules move <u>faster</u>.

11. The <u>boiling point</u> of water at sea level is defined as 100°C.

12. The melting point of a substance is the same as its <u>freezing point</u>.

13. A temperature reading of 0 K is <u>warmer</u> than 0°C.

14. When the same amount of heat is applied, a substance with greater specific heat will get hot <u>faster</u> than one with a lower specific heat.

15. A <u>Calorie</u> is equal to one kilocalorie.

## Check Your Understanding

Apply the concepts you have learned to answer each question.

1. Summarize how heat-transfer processes affect the earth's climate.

2. What is the difference between conduction and radiation?

3. How are the Celsius and Kelvin temperature scales similar and different?

4. Draw a diagram of a convection current. Label the diagram to explain what is taking place.

5. Explain why convection doesn't occur in outer space.

6. **Critical Thinking** Two substances are heated to the same temperature. Substance A has a specific heat of 380 J/kg°C. Substance B has a specific heat of 664 J/kg°C. Which substance requires more heat energy? Explain.

7. **Mystery Photo** The photograph on page 208 shows a hand and a computer keyboard as seen by heat-sensitive thermography imaging. The different colors show the varying amounts of heat in the different parts of the objects. Blue indicates the least amount of heat. Magenta, a pinkish-red color, indicates the greatest amount of heat.

   a. What parts are the coolest? Give a possible explanation.

   b. What parts are the hottest? Give a possible explanation.

8. Which has more internal energy: 1 g of ice or 1 g of liquid water?

9. On a winter morning why is a metal lawn sprinkler colder than the rubber garden hose to which it is attached?

## Develop Your Skills

Use the skills you have developed in this chapter to complete each activity.

1. **Interpreting Data** The graph below compares the temperatures at which phase changes occur for various substances.

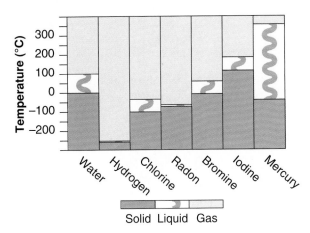

a. Which substance has the lowest melting point? The highest melting point?

b. Which substance has the lowest boiling point? The highest boiling point?

c. Two Viking spacecraft have landed on the planet Mars. The highest temperature recorded was −21°C in summer. The lowest temperature recorded, during winter, was −124°C. Describe the phase or phases in which each substance would exist on Mars within this temperature range.

2. **Data Bank** The illustration on page 640 shows the normal body temperatures of various animals.

a. Which animal has the highest body temperature? Which has the lowest?

b. At rest, which animal probably uses the most calories per gram of body weight? Which animal uses the least? Explain.

## Make Connections

1. **Link the Concepts** Below is a concept map showing how some of the main concepts in this chapter link together. Only part of the map is filled in. Finish the map, using words and ideas you find on the previous pages.

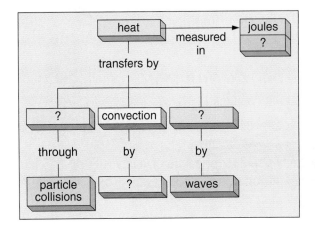

2. **Science and Literature** The climate in the location where a story takes place often affects the mood of the story. Write a short story where the temperature affects the mood, or the feeling, of the story.

3. **Science and Art** Artists, such as metal sculptors, jewelry makers, and potters use heat to shape their materials. Do library research on the processes each kind of artist uses. Write a report discussing the role of heat for each artist.

4. **Science and Technology** The process of distillation takes advantage of a substance's unique boiling point to separate it from other substances. In the library, research the distillation process for water or oil. Prepare a labeled diagram to illustrate the process.

5. **Science and Mathematics** The temperature of a 5 g tin medal increases 5°C as you hold it inside your fist. How much heat transferred to the medal?

# Chapter 10 Using Heat

## Chapter Sections

10.1 Heating Technology

10.2 Cooling Technology

10.3 Heat Engines

## What do you see?

66 What I think I see in the picture is some sort of electrical wire or wires. People may use this for a light or a television or any kind of electrical appliance. It works well because it is small and convenient. 99

*Erin Fargo*
*Highland Park School*
*St. Paul, Minnesota*

To find out more about the photograph, look on page 250. As you read this chapter, you will learn about how people use heat.

# 10.1 Heating Technology

## Objectives

▶ **Identify** five types of central heating systems.

▶ **Compare** active and passive solar heating systems.

▶ **Infer** why a material makes a good insulator.

▶ **Analyze** central heating systems to determine the best one for a particular geographic location.

What was the weather like this morning on your way to school? Maybe it was so cold outside that you bundled up in many layers of clothing and a heavy coat. Perhaps it was warm enough for you to go without a jacket.

Once you're inside your school, the weather outside is less important. The temperature inside most buildings is maintained at a comfortable level. Heating and air-conditioning systems control the environment inside a building. These systems keep the indoor temperature within a comfortable range by transferring heat energy into or out of the building.

## Central Heating Systems

The temperature inside your school, your home, or a local store stays warm on a cold day because of a central heating system. A **central heating system** generates heat from a central location. A network of wires, pipes, ducts, and vents transfers the heat from the heat source to different locations throughout the building.

Central heating systems use forced-air, hot-water, steam, radiant, or heat-pump networks. Although these systems differ in the way they distribute heat, they share common traits. For example, most central heating systems use some type of fuel to provide heat energy.

In addition, a thermostat is used to control a central heating system. The thermostat turns on the heating system when the air reaches a preselected low temperature. The thermostat also shuts off the system at a preselected high temperature. Look at Figure 10.1 to see how a thermostat works.

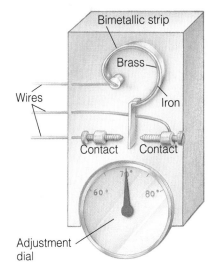

**Figure 10.1** ▲
Metals in a bimetallic strip expand at different rates when heated. The strip bends and turns the heat switch off or on.

**Forced-Air Heating** A common type of central heating system is forced-air heating, shown in Figure 10.2. In this system, air is heated inside a furnace. The warm air moves from the furnace to the walls of the building. The warm air travels through a network of connected passages called ducts. The ducts connect to outlets, or registers, in individual rooms.

When warm air enters a room, it rises and creates a convection current. As the warm air moves through the room, heat energy is lost. The air cools, sinks, and passes through a cold-air register in the room. The register connects to a duct that carries the cool air toward a blower. The blower draws the air through a filter and back into the furnace. The air is reheated and circulated again through the system.

**Hot-Water Heating** Like forced-air heating, hot-water heating also creates convection currents. In this type of central heating system, the furnace heats water. The hot water is pumped through a network of pipes. The pipes lead to metal radiators in individual rooms. The heat from the water transfers to the metal in the radiators.

Heat energy moves from the radiator and warms the surrounding air by conduction. The warm air rises, creating convection currents in the room. The water inside the radiator cools as heat energy is lost to the air. Pipes carry the cool water back to the furnace, where it is reheated and recirculated through the pipes. Study the movement of hot water and heat energy in the hot-water heating system shown in Figure 10.3.

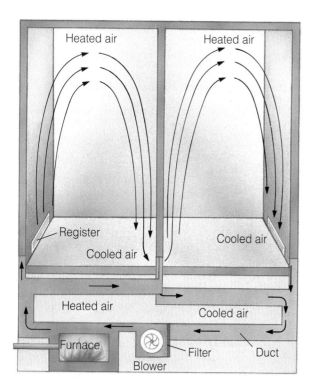

**Figure 10.2** ▲
In a forced-air heating system, air is warmed by burning fuel in a furnace. Trace the flow of warm air through the system.

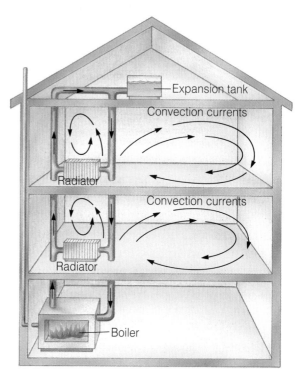

**Figure 10.3** ▲
In a hot-water heating system, water is warmed by burning fuel in a furnace. Compare the hot-water system to the forced-air system.

**Steam Heating** At high temperatures, water changes into steam. Steam heat uses water in both the gas and liquid phases. The steam heating system shown in Figure 10.4 is similar to a hot-water heating system. Both of these systems use water. In a steam heating system, water is heated in a tank, or boiler, above the furnace until steam forms. Instead of using the hot water, steam is pumped through the network of pipes. The pipes connect to radiators in each room.

The steam heats the metal in the radiators. Heat energy transfers from the radiator to warm the air in the room. As the steam in the radiator loses heat energy, it condenses to form liquid water. The cooled water returns to the furnace through another pipe. The water is then reheated to form steam, and the process is repeated.

**Radiant Heating** Hot water and electric wires radiate heat. Both are used in radiant heating systems. A hot-water radiant system is shown in Figure 10.5. In this system, water is heated in a furnace and then pumped through pipes embedded in the concrete floor of a room. Heat energy radiates from the pipes and warms the floor. In an electric radiant system, an electric current moves through wires in the floor, walls, or ceiling of a room. Heat energy radiates from the wires and warms the concrete floor.

Radiant heating systems are generally used to heat individual rooms. Heat radiating from the floor surface warms a room evenly. Usually, there is little temperature difference between the floor and ceiling of a room warmed with a radiant heating system.

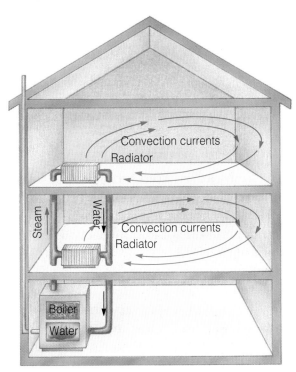

**Figure 10.4** ▲
Locate the water in the steam heating system. Follow the flow of steam from the boiler through the system.

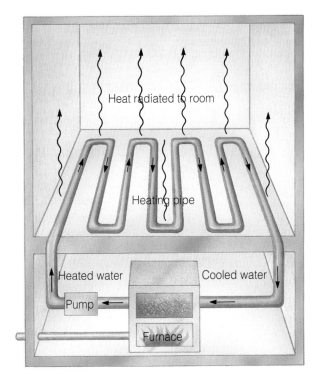

**Figure 10.5** ▲
In a radiant heating system, the heat source can be hot water or electricity. Which type is shown in this picture?

**Heat Pumps** Even on cold days, the outside environment can supply enough heat energy to warm a building. A heat pump collects the heat energy with a network of coiled pipes on the outside of the building. Heat from the air or ground evaporates the liquid inside the coils. The vapor moves through pipes to a condenser inside the building. The condenser uses pressure to raise the vapor temperature further. The heated vapor warms the surrounding air. The warm air moves through the building in the same way forced-air heat does. As the vapor in the condenser loses heat, it condenses to a liquid. The liquid returns to the unit outside the building and the process is repeated.

**Figure 10.6**
During winter, the heat pump collects heat from the outside. In summer, a heat pump is reversed to draw heat from the inside. ▼

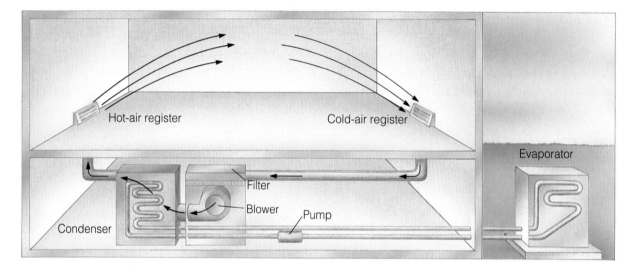

Hot-air register  Cold-air register  Evaporator  Filter  Blower  Pump  Condenser

## Solar Heating Systems

Solar heating systems differ from most central heating systems in an important way. They use a renewable energy source. Forced-air, hot-water, steam, and radiant heating systems all depend on some nonrenewable fuel to produce heat. Fossil fuels such as oil, natural gas, and coal are the fuels most commonly used to heat buildings. A typical central heating system uses large amounts of one of these fossil fuels every day.

A solar heating system doesn't need to use any fossil fuel. A solar heating system uses heat energy from the sun. As long as the sun shines, solar heating has a free, unlimited energy source. There are two types of solar heating systems in use today: active solar heating and passive solar heating. These systems differ in the way solar energy is captured and used to heat a structure.

**Active Solar Heating** A solar collector consists of a glass sheet, a black metal panel, and pipes for carrying liquid. In active solar heating, solar collectors are carefully positioned to receive direct sunlight. Sunlight is absorbed well by the color black, and the glass prevents the heat from escaping. The energy collected heats a liquid moving through the pipes. The hot liquid warms a tank of water. Hot water from the tank is pumped through pipes inside the walls of a building, as shown in Figure 10.7.

Active solar heating must have energy from the sun. On cloudy days and at night, the sun's energy doesn't reach the solar collectors. Therefore, buildings with active solar heating must have some type of backup heating system.

**Passive Solar Heating** You have probably warmed your home with passive solar heating and never knew it! Every time you raise a shade or open a curtain to let sunlight shine through a window, you start your own passive solar heating system. Solar energy streams through the glass and warms the objects in the room. The warm objects transfer heat into the air by conduction. Some buildings take advantage of passive solar heat by installing large windows and skylights in locations that receive the maximum amount of direct sunlight.

Another passive solar heating method is shown in Figure 10.8. A solar greenhouse is attached to a building. The sun's rays pass through the glass to heat the walls and floor of the greenhouse. This heat warms the room connected to the greenhouse.

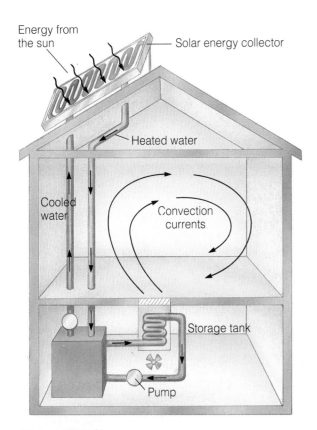

**Figure 10.7** ▲
Follow the path of heat energy as it moves through this solar heating system.

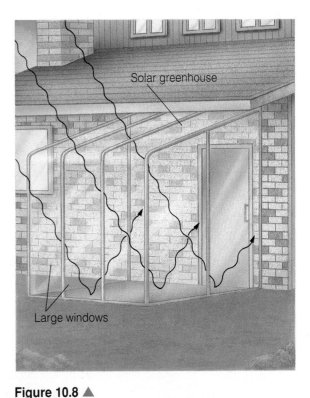

**Figure 10.8** ▲
Heat energy from the sun builds up inside a solar greenhouse, warming the wall and the room.

## Insulation

All heating systems use heat transfer to move heat where it's needed. Heat moves from a place of high heat concentration to a place of low heat concentration. However, heat transfer can be a problem. The heat tends to flow out of a heated building. To keep the inside of a building warm, people need a way to stop the flow of heat to the outside. The best way to do this is to use **insulation** (IHN suh LAY shuhn). Insulation is a substance that slows the movement of heat. Materials commonly used for insulation include fiberglass, cellulose, metal foil, and some types of plastic foam.

Insulation materials vary in the amount of heat transfer that occurs through them. Every insulation material is assigned an **R-value**. An R-value is a measurement of a material's ability to stop heat flow. The higher a material's R-value, the greater is its ability to trap heat energy. For example, a layer of fiberglass insulation like the one shown in Figure 10.9 has a higher R-value than a single pane of glass.

When a building is constructed, insulation is placed in the areas where heat is most likely to escape. Usually, these areas are the ceilings, attic floor, and the outside walls. Insulation around doors and windows, called weather stripping, prevents heat loss through air leaks. A well-insulated building conserves heat energy.

**Figure 10.9** ▲

Fiberglass insulation has many tiny spaces to trap heat within a building's walls or ceilings.

**Figure 10.10**

Insulation is placed in areas where heat might escape. Where would you put insulation in this house? ▼

## Science and You  *Weatherize Your Home*

Many homes waste heat energy. Heat leaks through small openings, such as cracks around windows and under doors. Drafts are a sure sign of escaping heat.

You can test the energy efficiency of your home by going on a "heat-escape hunt." Begin by examining your doors for heat loss. Hold a thin sheet of paper in front of the place where the door meets the floor. Observe the paper to see if it moves. If the paper moves toward you, air is blowing in. The draft is probably created by a space underneath the door. You may also be able to see light coming in. If light and air enter your home through this opening, then heat energy also leaves your home through this space.

You can minimize energy loss by insulating the opening beneath the door. You could use newspaper for insulation by rolling the newspaper, wrapping it in a towel, and placing it against the doorsill. You could also try using other materials for insulation. What materials do you think might make good insulation?

Next examine the windows of your home. Look carefully for any cracks or openings along the window frames. Some people cover their windows with sheets of plastic during winter to reduce heat loss. Storm doors and storm windows used during winter prevent some heat loss. If you find any openings around the windows, design ways to block the flow of heat to the outside. The result of your work will be a home that is more energy efficient and less costly to heat!

## ▼ ACTIVITY

### Observing

*Hot Pursuit*

Conduct a "heat-escape hunt" in your home or classroom. Record the places where you find heat escaping. Design a device that could prevent heat loss from these openings.

**SKILLS WORKOUT**

## Check and Explain

1. List five kinds of central heating systems. Briefly describe how each system works.

2. What are two types of solar heating systems? How are they different? How are they alike?

3. **Infer**  Why is winter clothing often made of wool? What criteria do fabrics need to meet to keep you warm in winter?

4. **Analyze**  Which one of the heating systems discussed in this section is best suited to a warm, sunny climate? Explain your answer.

# Activity 10  *What materials make the best heat insulators?*

***Skills***  Observe; Predict; Interpret Data

## Task 1  Prelab Prep

1. Collect the following items: marking pen, 2 identical plastic containers with lids, 2 coffee cans, 2 ice cubes, and 2 graduated cylinders. *NOTE: Each coffee can should be large enough to hold 1 plastic container.*
2. Choose two insulating materials. Possible insulating materials include newspaper, sponges, sawdust, packaging materials, and aluminum foil.
3. Label one container *A* and the other container *B*. Label one coffee can *A* and the other coffee can *B*.

## Task 2  Data Record

1. On a separate sheet of paper, draw the data table shown.
2. Predict which material will be the best insulator. Record your prediction in the table.

## Task 3  Procedure

1. Place an ice cube in each plastic container.
2. Place each plastic container in the coffee can with the same letter.
3. Pack a different insulating material in the coffee can around each plastic container. As you finish packing each coffee can, record the time in your data table.
4. Record in the data table the type of material placed in each coffee can.
5. After ten minutes, remove the plastic container from each can.

6. Pour any water present from container *A* into a graduated cylinder. Measure the amount of water from the melted ice and record it in the data table. Repeat the process for container *B*.
7. Return the containers to their appropriate cans. Repack the cans with the same insulating materials.
8. Repeat steps 5, 6, and 7 for each time span noted in the data table.

## Task 4  Analysis

1. Which ice cube turned to liquid water first?
2. What packing material surrounded the container holding this ice cube?
3. Which of the packing materials you tested is the better insulator?

## Task 5  Conclusion

Write a short paragraph identifying the type of materials that make good insulation. In what situation do you think the insulation you used would be most effective?

## *Everyday Application*

Use your findings to invent a device you could use to keep soup hot on a cold winter day. Make a diagram of your device to show how it slows down the transfer of heat energy.

## *Extension*

Construct a line graph of your data for each insulating material. Place the time in minutes on the *x*-axis, and the amount of water in mL on the *y*-axis. Which set of data produces a curve? Explain.

## Table 10.1  Insulation Materials

| | Insulation Material | Time Began | Amount of Water (mL) after: | | | | |
| --- | --- | --- | --- | --- | --- | --- | --- |
| | | | 10 min | 20 min | 30 min | 40 min | 50 min |
| Can A | | | | | | | |
| Can B | | | | | | | |

# 10.2 Cooling Technology

## Objectives

▶ **Explain** how a cooling system works.

▶ **Discuss** the role of evaporation in refrigeration.

▶ **Compare** and **contrast** heating systems and cooling systems.

▶ **Infer** how your body is similar to other cooling systems.

In the early 1900s, people used iceboxes to keep food cold. An icebox was a large insulated wood box with two compartments. A large block of ice was placed in the top compartment and food items were put in the bottom compartment.

The early icebox worked on a simple principle. As warm air rose from the bottom compartment, the air lost heat energy to the block of ice. The cool, dense air sank from the ice to the bottom compartment. The cool air absorbed heat energy from the food. Until the ice melted, the food items remained chilled through a continuous pattern of heat-energy transfer.

Since the invention of the early icebox, refrigeration technology has advanced a great deal. Refrigerators, freezers, and air conditioners now cool enclosed areas. The structure of these modern cooling devices is quite different from that of the icebox.

## Principles of Cooling Systems

All cooling systems remove heat energy from an enclosed space. A substance with a low boiling point, called a coolant, is used to absorb heat energy. Depending upon where it is located in the system, the coolant may be either a liquid or a gas. As the liquid coolant absorbs heat, its molecules move more rapidly. When the liquid reaches its boiling point, it evaporates. Recall that when a liquid evaporates, it becomes a gas. For the liquid coolant to evaporate, its temperature must increase. The heat source for evaporating the coolant comes from the enclosed space. As heat flows out of the enclosed space, the space and any objects inside it lose heat energy.

## Your Body's Cooling System

You get hot when you're involved in strenuous physical activity, or when the weather is hot. Whenever your internal temperature gets too high, your body's cooling system goes into action. You perspire. Your body's cooling system works on the same principle that a refrigerator or air conditioner does. Your body transfers heat energy through evaporation.

Your brain controls your body temperature much as a thermostat controls room temperature. When your body temperature rises, your brain sends a message to your skin's sweat glands. The message triggers the sweat glands to produce sweat. Sweat is secreted through tiny holes in the skin, called pores, onto your skin surface. Heat is transferred from your skin to the watery sweat and the water evaporates into the air around you.

Evaporation needs energy to occur. The energy is supplied by the heat from your body. As the excess heat is removed from your body, you begin to feel cooler. After the water in the sweat evaporates, salts and other substances are left behind on the surface of your skin. Your skin may feel sticky and taste salty when you are no longer sweating.

**Figure 10.11**
**The Cooling System of the Human Body** ▼

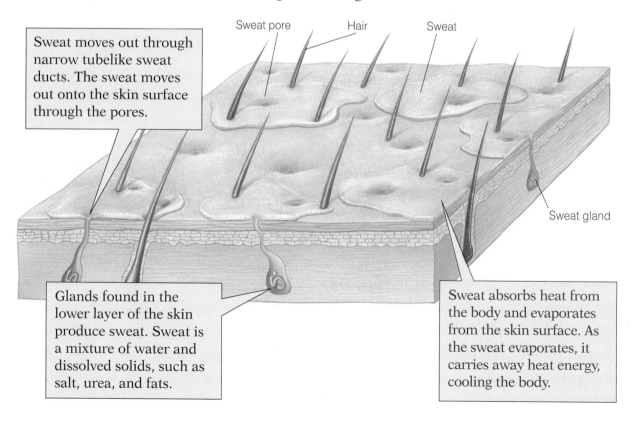

Sweat moves out through narrow tubelike sweat ducts. The sweat moves out onto the skin surface through the pores.

Sweat pore    Hair    Sweat

Sweat gland

Glands found in the lower layer of the skin produce sweat. Sweat is a mixture of water and dissolved solids, such as salt, urea, and fats.

Sweat absorbs heat from the body and evaporates from the skin surface. As the sweat evaporates, it carries away heat energy, cooling the body.

## Use of Refrigerants

You know that a cooling system works by evaporation. Cooling systems are most efficient if they use a chemical that evaporates easily at low temperatures. These chemicals, called **refrigerants**, are used in air-conditioners for automobiles, homes, and office buildings. They are also used in freezers and refrigerators. Refrigerants are pumped throughout a cooling system. As they change phase from liquid to gas, they remove heat from the enclosed space to the outside air.

Air, water, ammonia, and carbon dioxide are examples of natural refrigerants. However, most cooling systems use manufactured chemicals called fluorocarbons. Fluorocarbons are good refrigerants because they evaporate at a low temperature and are nonflammable, nontoxic, noncorrosive, and odorless. However, fluorocarbons are harmful to the ozone in the upper atmosphere if not handled properly.

## ▼ ACTIVITY

### Classifying

*Blowing Hot and Cold*

Review the heating systems described in Section 10.1. List the traits of each system. Identify the system that is most similar to an air-conditioner cooling system.

**SKILLS WORKOUT**

## *Career Corner*  *Refrigeration Technician*

### *Who Makes Sure That Frozen Foods Stay Frozen?*

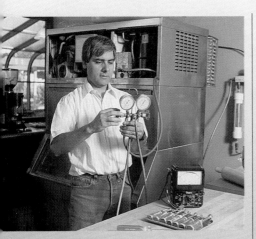

You pick up a gallon of ice cream from the frozen-food section of a local grocery store. Thanks to the work of a refrigeration technician, the ice cream is frozen.

Some refrigeration technicians fix broken cooling systems. These technicians are called troubleshooters. They generally repair equipment for a single manufacturer.

Other refrigeration technicians assist engineers in designing and installing cooling systems. This may involve calculating the cooling capability of a system, preparing designs for a system, or installing test systems. Refrigeration technicians are employed by companies that manufacture cooling systems or by dealers who market, install, and service these systems.

The ability to work well with your hands and to handle complex equipment are important skills for a refrigeration technician to have. A high-school diploma is needed. A concentration on math and science courses is important.

Many refrigeration technicians complete two-year training programs at a college or technical school. They also serve an apprenticeship. If you would like to learn more about a career as a refrigeration technician, you can write to the Air-Conditioning and Refrigeration Institute, 1815 N. Fort Myer Dr., Arlington, VA 22209.

## Cooling Systems at Work

Study the refrigerator shown in Figure 10.12. The basic parts of a refrigerator are the compressor, condenser coils, freezer unit, storage tank, and refrigerant. How do these parts work to cool the inside of the refrigerator? A refrigerator repeatedly evaporates and condenses a refrigerant. The refrigerant moves through the system and transfers heat from inside the refrigerator to the outside room. Although a refrigerator cools the food inside, it actually heats the room where it is located.

**Figure 10.12**
**The Cooling System of a Refrigerator** ▼

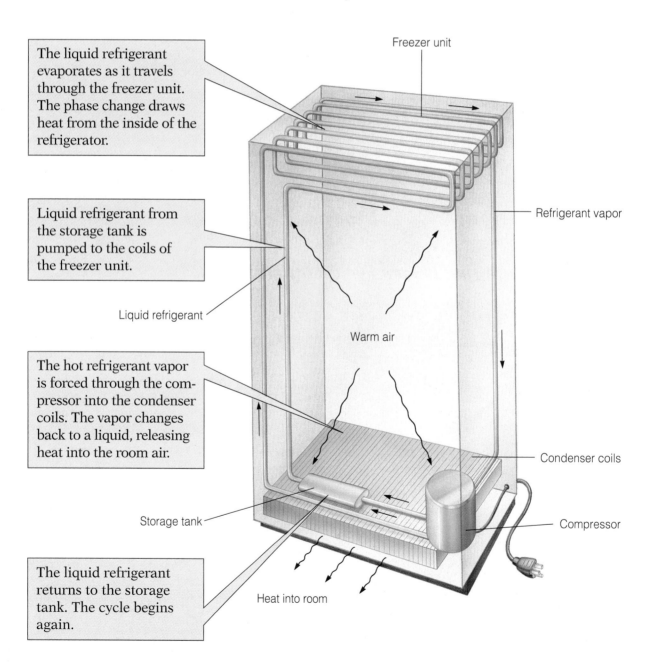

The liquid refrigerant evaporates as it travels through the freezer unit. The phase change draws heat from the inside of the refrigerator.

Liquid refrigerant from the storage tank is pumped to the coils of the freezer unit.

The hot refrigerant vapor is forced through the compressor into the condenser coils. The vapor changes back to a liquid, releasing heat into the room air.

The liquid refrigerant returns to the storage tank. The cycle begins again.

Freezer unit

Refrigerant vapor

Liquid refrigerant

Warm air

Condenser coils

Storage tank

Compressor

Heat into room

## Science and Society
### *CFCs and the Ozone Layer*

Many cooling systems use special chemicals called chlorofluorocarbons, or CFCs. Chlorofluorocarbons contain the elements carbon, chlorine, and fluorine. One property of these chemicals is their ability to rapidly absorb large amounts of heat energy. Another property is their ability to change phase easily. These properties make CFCs good refrigerants.

During the early 1970s, scientists began to express concern about the effect CFCs have on the atmosphere. Investigations indicated that soon after CFCs enter the atmosphere, they are broken down by radiation from the sun. The free chlorine that is released reacts with ozone molecules in the upper atmosphere. This reaction reduces the amount of ozone.

Ozone protects life on the earth from harmful radiation from the sun. Overexposure to this harmful radiation causes sunburn, skin cancer, and cataracts. People were concerned because this protective layer of ozone was disappearing.

In 1990, an international treaty signed by many countries limited the use of products that use CFCs. This limitation includes the chemicals used in cooling systems and in aerosol cans. The treaty reflects a global effort to protect the environment.

**Table 10.2   Commonly Used CFCs**

| Generic Name | Use | Chemical Name | Chemical Formula |
|---|---|---|---|
| Freon-11 | Aerosol propellants | Trichlorofluoromethane | $CCl_3F$ |
| Freon-12 | Refrigerators, air conditioners, freezers | Dichlorodifluoromethane | $CCl_2F_2$ |

## Check and Explain

1. Draw and label a diagram of a refrigerator to explain how a cooling system works.

2. What is the role of evaporation in a refrigeration system?

3. **Compare and Contrast**   How are heating and cooling systems alike? How are they different?

4. **Infer**   How is your body's cooling system similar to the cooling system in a refrigerator?

*Transportation*

List as many methods of transporting goods and people as possible. Identify those that use some type of engine. Think about what transportation would be like if the engine hadn't ever been invented. How might your daily life be different?

**SKILLS WARMUP**

# 10.3 Heat Engines

## Objectives

▶ **Explain** how two kinds of heat engines work.

▶ **Identify** the parts of an internal-combustion engine.

▶ **Compare** and **contrast** internal- and external-combustion engines.

▶ **Classify** motors according to their types of heat engines.

Insert a key into the ignition of a car, pump the gas pedal, turn the key, and the car starts. Shift into gear, press on the gas pedal, and the car moves. You've probably watched this sequence of activities many times. But do you know what occurs under the hood to make the car move? Inside the car's engine, chemical energy changes to heat energy. The heat energy is then changed into mechanical energy that moves the car down the road.

## How Heat Engines Work

Heat energy is changed into mechanical energy by a heat engine. Most motor vehicles, such as cars, buses, and trucks, are powered by heat engines. Heat engines also power some airplanes.

Many heat engines use fuel. The most commonly used fuels are gasoline and diesel fuel. Heat engines that use fuel have enclosed tubes called cylinders. Fuel enters the cylinder as a vapor or a liquid. A spark or temperature change causes the fuel to ignite. When the fuel is ignited, the explosion causes a piston in the cylinder to move. The piston is attached to a rod. The rod moves to transfer mechanical energy from the piston to the wheels or propeller.

There are two main types of heat engine. The difference between the two types is where the fuel burns, or where **combustion** occurs. Combustion is any type of chemical reaction with oxygen that can give off heat or light. In an internal-combustion engine, such as an automobile engine, gasoline or diesel fuel burns directly inside the cylinders. In an external-combustion engine, such as a steam engine, fuel burns outside the cylinders.

**Internal-Combustion Engine** Some cars, motor scooters, and snowmobiles have gasoline engines. Most tractors, large trucks, buses, and construction equipment have diesel engines. Although the engine structure and type of fuel may differ, all of these machines are powered by internal-combustion engines. All internal-combustion engines burn fuel inside the engine to change heat energy into mechanical energy. A four-stroke gasoline engine is shown in Figure 10.13.

**Figure 10.13**
**How a Gasoline Engine Works**
▼

**1.** Before entering the intake valve, gasoline is vaporized and mixed with air in the carburetor. Gasoline must be mixed with air to burn.

**3.** The second stroke is called the compression stroke. The upward-moving piston compresses the gasoline-air mixture. Both valves are closed to prevent the mixture from escaping.

**6.** In the fourth stroke, or exhaust stroke, the exhaust valve opens. The piston moves up forcing out the waste gases. The exhaust valve closes, and the cycle begins again.

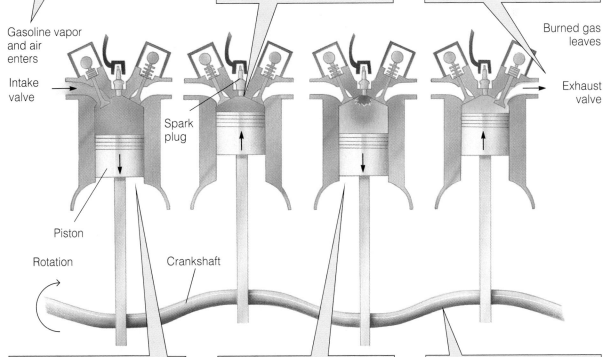

Gasoline vapor and air enters

Intake valve

Spark plug

Burned gas leaves

Exhaust valve

Piston

Rotation

Crankshaft

**2.** The cycle begins with the first stroke, called the intake stroke. The gasoline-air mixture moves through the intake valve into the cylinder.

**4.** The third stroke is the power stroke. The spark plug ignites the compressed gasoline-air mixture. An explosion occurs. The gases in the cylinder expand, forcing the piston down.

**5.** The kinetic energy of the moving piston transfers to the crankshaft. The crankshaft turns a wheel to do work.

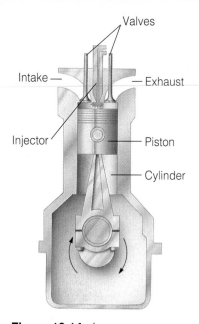

**Figure 10.14** ▲

A diesel engine has no spark plug or carburetor. Compare the fuel flow through a diesel engine and a gasoline engine.

**Figure 10.15**
**How a Steam Engine Works** ▼

Diesel and gasoline engines are both internal-combustion engines. Look at the cylinder of a diesel engine in Figure 10.14. In a diesel engine, air is drawn into the cylinders. During the compression cycle, the injector sprays diesel fuel. As the diesel fuel is compressed, the temperature increases enough to ignite the fuel. The gases expand and push on the piston to produce mechanical energy.

**External-Combustion Engine** Unlike diesel and gasoline engines, the fuel in an external-combustion engine burns outside the engine. A steam engine is an example of an external-combustion engine. In a steam engine, water heated in a boiler changes to steam. The steam piped into the engine forces the piston to move back and forth inside the cylinder. The moving piston is connected to a flywheel that does work. Look at Figure 10.15.

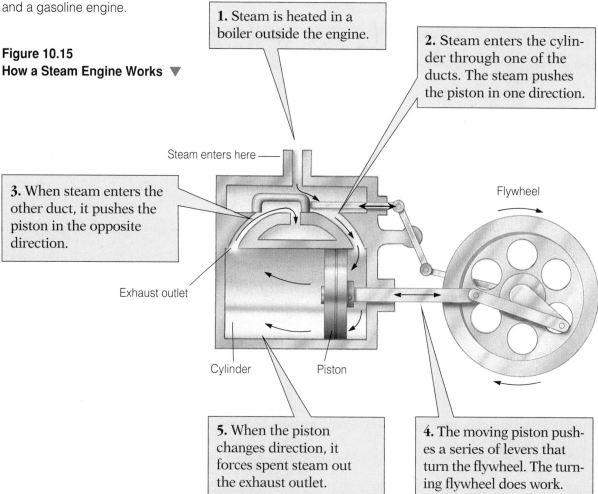

**1.** Steam is heated in a boiler outside the engine.

**2.** Steam enters the cylinder through one of the ducts. The steam pushes the piston in one direction.

**3.** When steam enters the other duct, it pushes the piston in the opposite direction.

**5.** When the piston changes direction, it forces spent steam out the exhaust outlet.

**4.** The moving piston pushes a series of levers that turn the flywheel. The turning flywheel does work.

A steam engine like the one shown was improved by James Watt in the 1700s. Watt's steam engine was responsible for starting the Industrial Revolution. The engine powered trains and factory machines.

## Use of Turbines

Years ago, most steam engines contained pistons that moved up and down in cylinders. Steam piped into the cylinders caused the motion of the pistons. The mechanical energy of the pistons moved parts on the machine, enabling it to do work. However, modern steam engines have a different design. The pistons on modern steam engines have been replaced with turbines.

A **turbine** is a set of curved blades mounted on a long shaft. When steam strikes the turbine blades, the shaft rotates. The mechanical energy of the rotating shaft is used to turn objects, such as ship propellers or electric generators.

# Consider This

## Should Cars Use Solar-Powered Engines?

Waste gases from automobile engines are major contributors to air pollution. To reduce air pollution and conserve fossil fuels, engineers are studying the use of sunlight to "fuel" automobiles. Solar cells on the automobile convert sunlight to electricity. As sunlight strikes a solar cell, it triggers the movement of electrons within the cell to produce an electric current. This electric current is used to power the car's engine.

**Consider Some Issues** The sun is a source of unlimited, free energy. Solar-powered engines don't release harmful pollutants into the atmosphere.

Sunlight isn't always available. A backup system is needed to power an automobile on cloudy days and at night. In addition, the cost of producing a solar-powered engine is quite high.

Solar-powered engines aren't as powerful as gasoline engines. Therefore, solar cars are slower and smaller than cars with gasoline engines.

**Think About It** Would you be willing to buy a solar-powered automobile that may not be large or powerful but that doesn't pollute the air? Would

the extra cost be worth it? Why or why not?

**Write About It** Write a paper stating your position for or against using solar-powered cars. Include your reasons for choosing your position.

A turbine needs a continuous flow of fluid to turn the shaft. Often this fluid is steam. However, falling water also moves turbines, such as those in hydroelectric power plants. High-pressure gases are also used to drive turbines. Gas turbines are used in jet engines.

## Science and Society  *Combustion Waste*

All heat engines burn some kind of fuel. These burning fuels produce waste products in the form of gases and small particles. A major source of air pollution is the exhaust from automobiles. Exhaust fumes carry waste gases, such as carbon monoxide, hydrocarbons, and nitrogen oxides. During this century, the levels of these air pollutants have increased drastically from automobile use.

Central heating systems used in most homes and offices release pollutants into the atmosphere. Heat engines used in electric power plants and in industrial plants also contribute to the air-pollution problem. As more heat engines are used, air-pollution problems continue to get worse.

Each year in the United States, air-pollution costs are about $16 billion for health care, building maintenance, and damage to the environment. Air pollution causes eye irritations and respiratory problems. People with asthma, young children, and elderly people suffer the most from health problems related to air pollution.

▼ **ACTIVITY**

**Reasoning**

*Clean Air Actions*

Make a list of the ways that air pollution could be reduced. Explain how each of the ideas on your list would help to solve the air-pollution problem.

**SKILLS WORKOUT**

## Check and Explain

1. Why are internal- and external-combustion engines called "heat" engines?

2. List the major parts of an internal-combustion engine. Explain the function of each part.

3. **Compare and Contrast**  Describe the similarities and the differences between internal- and external-combustion engines.

4. **Classify**  Classify each of the following according to the type of engine it has: lawn mower, locomotive, heavy road equipment, motor scooter, submarine, and automobile.

# Chapter 10 Review

## Concept Summary

### 10.1 Heating Technology
▶ Central heating systems generate heat from a central location and are controlled by a thermostat.
▶ Some common types of central heating systems include forced air, hot water, steam, radiant, and heat pumps.
▶ Active and passive solar heating use energy supplied by the sun.
▶ Insulation in a building stops the flow of heat to the outside.

### 10.2 Cooling Technology
▶ Cooling systems use evaporation and condensation to transfer heat.
▶ Your body is cooled by sweat, which absorbs heat as it evaporates from your skin.

▶ The basic parts of a refrigerator include the compressor, condenser coils, storage tank, and refrigerant.
▶ Refrigerants evaporate at low temperatures to remove heat from an enclosed space.

### 10.3 Heat Engines
▶ Heat engines burn fuel to convert heat energy into mechanical energy.
▶ A heat engine can be an internal-combustion or an external-combustion engine.
▶ Internal-combustion engines are either gasoline or diesel engines.
▶ The most common external-combustion engine is the steam engine.

---

## Chapter Vocabulary

central heating system (10.1)          R-value (10.1)          combustion (10.3)
insulation (10.1)          refrigerant (10.2)          turbine (10.3)

---

## Check Your Vocabulary

Use the vocabulary words above to complete the following sentences correctly.

1. The greater the ability to trap heat energy, the higher the material's _____.

2. A chemical reaction with oxygen that produces heat or light is called _____.

3. Heat that is generated in one location and distributed by a network of wires, pipes, ducts and vents is a(n) _____.

4. A chemical that changes phase from liquid to gas at a low temperature is used as a(n) _____.

5. Substances, such as fiberglass, that slow the flow of heat are called _____.

6. A set of blades on a shaft used to produce mechanical energy is a(n) _____.

Identify the word or term in each group that doesn't belong. Explain why it doesn't belong with the group.

7. plastics, fiberglass, air

8. combustion, evaporation, condensation

9. forced-air heating, steam heating, passive solar heating

10. ammonia, carbon dioxide, metal foil

11. gasoline engine, steam engine, diesel engine

## Write Your Vocabulary

Write sentences using the vocabulary words above. Show that you know what each word means.

# Chapter 10 Review

## Check Your Knowledge

Answer the following in complete sentences.

1. What are two types of solar heating systems?

2. What are two examples of internal-combustion engines?

3. What are the parts of a refrigerator?

4. Describe the cycle of a four-stroke internal-combustion engine.

5. What fluids are used to power turbines?

6. List the parts of a steam engine.

7. Where is insulation most commonly located in buildings?

Choose the answer that best completes each sentence.

8. When the air reaches a preselected low temperature the (thermostat, heat pump, compressor, condenser) turns on the central heating system.

9. Warm air spreads throughout a room by (conduction, radiation, convection, evaporation) currents.

10. Heat always flows from an area of high concentration to an area of (equal, high, low, deep) concentration.

11. In some heat engines, mechanical energy is transferred to the crankshaft by the movement of the (cylinder, spark plug, piston, carburetor).

12. Modern steam engines replaced pistons with (turbines, propellers, generators, cylinders).

13. The refrigerant most commonly used in cooling systems is (water, air, carbon dioxide, fluorocarbons).

## Check Your Understanding

Apply the concepts you have learned to answer each question.

1. How is a refrigerator like a heat pump?

2. **Critical Thinking**   Heat always moves from a warm body to a cool body. How does this fact explain how a cooling system works?

3. **Application**   What type of heating system would you choose for a building located in northern Alaska? In southern Texas? Explain your choice for each location.

4. **Extension**   How does the way an icebox cools food differ from the way an electric refrigerator cools food?

5. Explain how your body's cooling system works.

6. How is a diesel engine different from a gasoline engine?

7. List two features that are common to all heat engines.

8. **Mystery Photo**   The photograph on page 230 is a closeup view of fiberglass. The magnified fiberglass threads look very similar to small wires. The space between the threads traps air. Trapped air conducts heat extremely slowly. This makes fiberglass a good insulator. Make a list of other materials that could trap air to make good insulators. Evaluate the materials on your list for safety and cost as potential building insulators.

9. **Critical Thinking**   Based on the principles of cooling systems, explain how an air-conditioning system works. You may use drawings or diagrams to explain your answer.

# Develop Your Skills

Use the skills you have developed in this chapter to complete each activity.

1. **Interpret Data** The table below shows data about the R-value for four selected building materials.
   a. Which building material has the greatest R-value?
   b. Which building material is the poorest insulator?
   c. Which house is better insulated: one with double windows or one with single windows?

### R-value for Building Materials

| Material | R-value |
|---|---|
| Concrete wall | 8.00 |
| Hardwood floor | 0.71 |
| Single window | 1.00 |
| Double window | 2.00 |

2. **Data Bank** Use the table on page 640 to answer the following questions.

   a. What is the major source of air pollution in the United States?
   b. What is the second major source of air pollution?
   c. Nitrogen oxides and hydrocarbons are the major causes of smog. What is the major source of these two pollutants? Where is this source of pollution likely to be the most concentrated?

3. **Make a Model** Design a model of a building that uses passive solar heating to its full potential. Label the direction that the front of the building faces.

# Make Connections

1. **Link the Concepts** Below is a concept map showing how some of the main concepts in this chapter link together. Only part of the map is filled in. Finish the map, using words and ideas from the chapter.

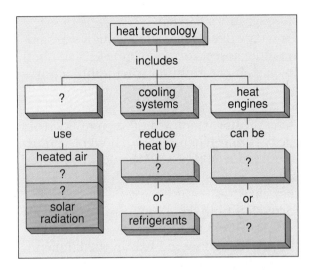

2. **Science and Society** Conduct a survey to find out the type of heating system used for homes in your area. Survey at least ten homes in different locations.

3. **Science and Social Studies** The invention of the steam engine helped start the Industrial Revolution. Use the library to research the Industrial Revolution. Find out what role the steam engine played during this time. Do you think the Industrial Revolution would have occurred without the invention of the steam engine? Why?

4. **Science and Technology** Most gasoline engines are four-stroke engines. However, there are also two-stroke engines. Find out how a two-stroke engine works. Compare the flow of fuel in a two-stroke engine to a four-stroke engine. You may use drawings for your comparison.

# Science and Literature Connection

## Child of the Owl

*The following excerpts are from the novel* Child of the Owl *by Lawrence Yep*

I started to wash the rice like Paw-Paw had told me, though it took half an hour. Once I'd bought the wrong kind, getting short-grain rice when Paw-Paw liked Texas long, which she said was the closest to good Chinese rice. I had to wash it carefully, pouring it into a pot and then adding water and swirling it around with my hand, then pouring off the excess water which would turn milky from the washing. Then repeat the whole thing about a dozen times till the water I poured out was almost clear—which wasn't all that easy to see since we only had a dinky forty-watt bulb dangling from the kitchen ceiling. That way the rice never stuck. . . .

Anyway, so there I was in the kitchen in practically all the clothes I had, and I still didn't feel any warmer. The water in the pots hadn't boiled yet. I had hot water coming out of the tap to warm my hands but you couldn't wash the rice for too long in hot water or it would start to cook and by the time it came off the stove it would be as mushy as that cruddy [instant] rice. Though I started out using lukewarm water, it got cold fast in the frigid air and my hands got as cold as the water.

To [heck] with it, I thought. I could turn off the oven before she got back. So I got a book of Paw-Paw's matches and opened the oven. Then I lit a match and turned the gas on, putting the match near the little hole and hearing the soft explosion of gas igniting. Finally I twisted the gas up to three hundred fifty and went back humming to the kitchen sink to finish washing the rice.

I did that for the next few days without getting caught. Now five will get you two

that I normally stay awake during the daytime. I usually never nap, but there was something that Friday about how the rainwater dripped from the fire escapes and the heat filled the place. After I had put the rice on, I started to do my homework but somehow all the little numbers began to run around on the page and I was asleep.

The next thing I knew, there was an acrid smell in the air and the banging of pots. A cloud of steam came from the kitchen. I ran to the door and saw Paw-Paw there, still in her scarf and coat, holding our cast-iron pot under the faucet. The pot was so hot that it made the water turn into steam.

I glanced at the stove. Paw-Paw had turned off both the burners and the oven. "It's . . . it's a good thing that

the pot wasn't aluminum. It would have warped like crazy."

"Yes?" Paw-Paw said absently. With a big spoon she scraped the burnt rice out onto a newspaper and wrapped it up into a neat bundle. Then she set the cooling pot on the sink and reached for [a scouring] pad. In the same tight-lipped silence, she began to scrub out the burn marks from the pot, only she wasn't having too much luck.

"Did I ruin the pot, Paw-Paw?". . .

Paw-Paw glanced at me. Then she turned her eyes back to the pot and went on scrubbing. I went back into the other room and sat down on the bed and tried to read my arithmetic book, only the numbers kept on blurring. Paw-Paw came out

a moment later, wiping her hands on a dish towel. She sat down on the bed beside me. "When I came in and saw you with your head lying on the table and the stove door open, I thought you were dead. I thought I'd lost you."

I kept my eyes on the page of the book. "Really?" I mumbled. I felt ashamed.

"Yes, really." Paw-Paw hesitated at saying any more. Like me, she didn't like to talk about her own feelings. Even so she decided to go on. "Respect differences, cherish the things you share in common." She took my hands and felt them. "But you are cold." Looking worried, she rubbed them between her warm palms. "Well, if you're sure you won't kill us or explode the stove, I guess we could light it."

## Skills in Science

### Reading Skills in Science

1. **Find the Main Idea** Why did the narrator light the oven?

2. **Find Context Clues** What caused the acrid smell in the air?

### Writing Skills in Science

1. **Reason by Analogy** The narrator says she had on "practically all" of her clothes trying to keep warm. How are clothes like insulation in a house? Use your knowledge of heat transfer to explain how clothes keep you warm.

2. **Communicate** A number of events were due to the evaporation or condensation of water. These concepts are difficult for young children to understand. Write a speech explaining one of these concepts to a kindergarten class. Be sure to include a demonstration!

3. **Define operationally** The narrator described how the rice should be prepared before boiling it. Describe the procedure she used.

### Activities

**Communicate** Make a poster showing how turning on the stove resulted in burning the rice. Illustrate the transfer of heat throughout the process.

**Reason and Conclude** Research information on cotton, wool, linen, and polyester fabrics. Rank these fabrics according to how warm they keep you. Give reasons for your ranking.

**Predicting** What do you think the substance rinsed from the rice is? To find out, rinse some rice thoroughly only once, catching the milky water in a pan. Boil the milky water. Describe what happens. Let the water mixture cool. Describe the cool mixture. Use a cookbook or other source to find out why rice that is not rinsed sticks together.

### Where to Read More

*Chemistry for Every Kid* by Janice Van Cleave. New York: John Wiley and Sons, 1989. This book contains 101 chemistry experiments that use household materials.

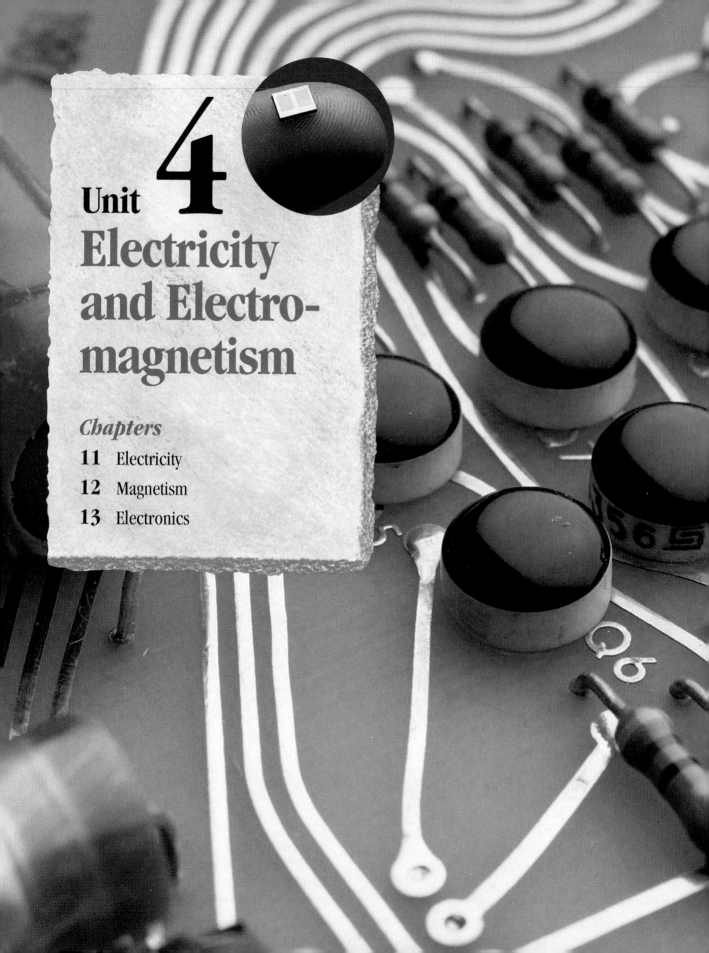

# Unit 4
# Electricity and Electro-magnetism

*Chapters*

**11**  Electricity
**12**  Magnetism
**13**  Electronics

# Data Bank

Use the information on pages 634 to 643 to answer the questions about topics explored in this unit.

## Calculating

How many years ago was the first general-purpose computer developed?

## Classifying

List in order, five metals that are the best conductors of electricity.

## Inferring

If the compass needle is always attracted to 0°, in what direction must you turn your compass to find geographic north?

## Interpreting Data

What is the magnetic declination of the compass in your state?

The photograph to the left is a circuit board. Tiny silicon chips, resistors, and transistors are connected in the circuit. What electronic devices use circuit boards?

## Chapter Sections

11.1   Electric Charges

11.2   Static Electricity

11.3   Electric Current

11.4   Electric Circuits

11.5   Electric Power and
       Safety

## What do you see?

❝I see a light bulb with many winding wires and electricity creating light. The part in the middle that's glass is there to hold the wires together. The electricity can't go through the glass.❞

*Dawn Schoffelman*
*Axtell Park Middle School*
*Sioux Falls, South Dakota*

To find out more about the photograph, look on page 284. As you read this chapter, you will learn about electricity.

# 11.1 Electric Charges

## Objectives

▶ **Identify** two forces that result from electric charges.

▶ **Explain** why objects attract and repel each other.

▶ **Communicate** how a positively charged object can be used to determine the charge on another object.

▶ **Infer** how electric charges behave in everyday situations.

Perhaps you have noticed that occasionally, when you comb your hair with a plastic comb, your hair becomes attracted to the comb, as in Figure 11.1. Sometimes you get a shock if you walk across a rug and then touch a metal doorknob. Each of these reactions occurs because of electric charge.

## Charge and Force

You learned that all matter is made of atoms that contain electrons, neutrons, and protons. Recall that protons and electrons in atoms have an electric **charge**. Electrons have a negative charge, and protons have a positive charge. Neutrons have no electric charge.

When the atoms in an object have more electrons than protons, the total charge of the object is negative. When the atoms in an object have more protons than electrons, the total charge of the object is positive. When an object has an equal number of protons and electrons, the object has no charge. It is neutral. Neutrons have no effect on the total charge of an object because neutrons have no charge.

The positive and negative electric charges in objects can produce a force between the objects. Objects are forced together, or attracted, when their charges are different. An object with a positive charge is attracted to an object with a negative charge. When objects have the same electric charge, they are pushed apart, or repelled. For example, two negatively charged objects repel each other. You can predict whether objects will attract or repel each other by remembering that unlike charges attract and like charges repel.

**Figure 11.1**
Do the comb and the girl's hair have like or unlike charges? How do you know? ▼

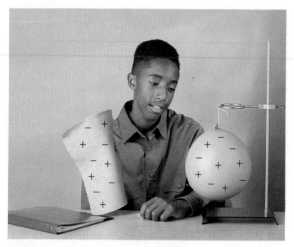

**Figure 11.2 ▲**
The cloth and the balloon are both neutral objects. They are neither attracted nor repelled.

**Figure 11.3 ▲**
Vigorous rubbing by the cloth changes the charge of both objects.

**Figure 11.4 ▲**
Notice the change in the position of the string holding the balloon. The balloon moved from its original position toward the cloth.

**Force of Attraction** The cloth and the balloon in Figure 11.2 are both neutral objects. The atoms in each object have an equal number of protons and electrons. When two neutral objects are rubbed together, electrons will leave one object and move onto the other. The objects are no longer neutral. The total, or net, charge of each object will become either positive or negative.

When the cloth rubs against the balloon as in Figure 11.3, some electrons in the cloth move to the balloon. Since the balloon now has more electrons, its net charge is negative. Since the cloth loses electrons, its net charge is now positive. Because unlike charges attract, the positively-charged cloth attracts the negatively-charged balloon, as you can see in Figure 11.4.

**Force of Repulsion** Imagine a second balloon is rubbed with the cloth. How will this balloon react to the negatively-charged balloon shown in Figure 11.4 when they are brought near each other? As the second balloon is rubbed with the cloth, more electrons leave the cloth and move onto the balloon. The second balloon now has more electrons than it has protons. Like the first balloon, its net charge is negative. When the balloons are brought near each other, they will repel, or push apart. This force of repulsion occurs because the objects have like charges. Why do you think the hairs on your head stand away from each other when you comb your hair? What is the charge of the comb?

## Electric Field

How close do you think two charged objects must be in order to be affected by each other? The forces of attraction and repulsion depend on the electric field around each object. An electric field is the region surrounding a charged object. Electric fields affect each other. The strongest part of the field is the area closest to the charged object. The weakest part of the field is the area farthest from the charged object. An object with a large amount of charge has a bigger electric field than an object with a small amount of charge.

### Science and You    *Your Electric Nerves*

How do you know to let go of a hot object? Your body uses electric signals to communicate with your brain. Even though the net charge of your body is neutral, some parts have positive or negative charges. For example, the outside of a nerve cell has a positive charge, and the inside of the nerve cell has a negative charge. These charges are separated by a membrane that covers the nerve cell.

If you touch a hot pan, negative charges on the inside of the nerve cells pass through the membrane. The net electric charge on each side of the membrane changes. A continuous change of electric charge moves along the length of the nerve, producing an electric signal, or impulse. This impulse travels to your spinal cord. A reflex from your spinal cord sends another impulse to your hand. Your muscles respond, and you drop the hot pan.

## Check and Explain

1. Name the two types of forces that can result from electric charges.

2. You bring two balloons together and they repel. Explain what happens in terms of charges.

3. **Communicate**  How can a negatively charged comb be used to determine the charge of an object?

4. **Infer**  Why does the television screen attract dust after the screen has been wiped clean?

# Activity 11 *Which material has the greatest force of attraction?*

***Skills*** Observe; Infer; Predict

## Task 1 Prelab Prep
Collect the following items: 2 balloons; two 6-cm pieces of string; a piece of flannel cloth; a cotton ball; a piece of polyester cloth; and a piece of wool cloth.

## Task 2 Data Record
1. Make a data table like the one shown.
2. As you carry out the procedure, fill in your data table. Indicate whether you did or did not rub the objects together, the force you observe between the objects, and the strength of this force (weak, medium or strong).

## Task 3 Procedure
1. Blow up the balloons and tie the end in a knot. Attach a string to each balloon. Gently rub the two balloons against each other for about 30 s. Hold each balloon by its string and bring the two balloons together. Record your observations.
2. Rub one of the balloons with the flannel cloth for about 30 s. Move the flannel cloth near the balloon. Record your observations.
3. Place a cotton ball next to the balloon you rubbed with the flannel cloth. Record your observations.
4. Place the polyester cloth next to the same balloon. Record your observations.

5. Rub the second balloon with the wool cloth for 30 s. Move the wool cloth near the balloon. Record your observations.
6. Place the cotton ball near the balloon you rubbed with the wool cloth. Record your observations.
7. Place the polyester cloth near the balloon you rubbed with the wool cloth. Record your observations.
8. Bring the two balloons near each other. Record your observations.

## Task 4 Analysis
1. What objects were the most attracted to each other?
2. What objects were the most repelled by each other?
3. Hypothesize why the force of attraction to the balloon was greater for some materials than it was for others.
4. What happened to the charge of the second balloon? Explain why.

## Task 5 Conclusion
Cotton and wool are natural materials. Based on your observations, which of these natural materials gives up electrons more easily? Give reasons why this might occur. Explain how the amount of electrons given up, affects the force of attraction or repulsion between objects. Discuss the amount and direction of force you observed between objects.

**Table 11.1   Force between Objects**

| Objects | Rubbed/Not rubbed | Force observed | Strength of force |
|---------|-------------------|----------------|-------------------|
| 1 | | | |
| 2 | | | |
| 3 | | | |
| 4 | | | |
| 5 | | | |
| 6 | | | |

# 11.2 Static Electricity

## Objectives

▶ **Identify** three ways static charge can build up.

▶ **Explain** what causes lightning.

▶ **Compare** electric conductors and insulators.

▶ **Infer** why lightning can be dangerous.

### Predicting

*Keeping Current*

List five different kinds of matter in your classroom. Predict which materials would conduct electric current. What do these materials have in common?

**SKILLS WARMUP**

**H**ave you ever wondered what causes lightning or why some storms produce more lightning than others? Actually, lightning and the shock that you might get from a metal doorknob are alike. Both are caused by static electricity.

All electricity is energy that results from the movement of electrons. The electricity used by the lights in your classroom consists of charges that continuously flow through a wire. Static electricity, however, consists of electric charges at rest. The electrons that cause static electricity can move from one object to another, and then remain at rest. The word *static* means not moving, or stationary. When electrons gather in one location, a build-up of static electricity results.

## Static Build-up

A neutral object builds up an electric charge by gaining or losing electrons. An electroscope, like the one shown in Figure 11.5, is used to observe static electric charges. The electroscope is made with a glass flask and a metal rod with a knob at the top. A rubber stopper holds the metal rod in place and keeps it from touching the glass. The metal rod has a pair of thin, metal leaves at the bottom. A charged object placed on or near the knob causes the metal leaves at the bottom of the metal rod to attract or repel each other.

Movement of static electricity depends on the forces of attraction and repulsion and the way charges act in different materials. To understand static electricity, you must understand how electric charges build up on an object. The build-up of static charge can be caused by friction, conduction, or induction.

**Figure 11.5**

Why do you think it is important that the metal rod does not touch the glass flask? ▼

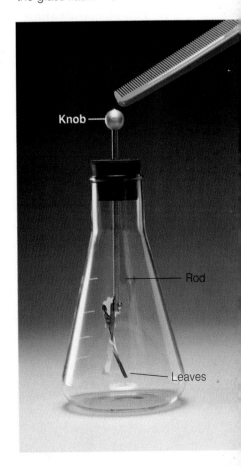

Knob

Rod

Leaves

**Friction** Charging by friction occurs when objects rub together and electrons move from the surface of one object to the surface of the other. Friction separates electrons from the surface of an object whose atoms hold electrons loosely. Once separated, the electrons move onto another object. The movement of electrons from the cloth to the balloon shown in Figure 11.3 resulted from charging by friction. The balloon receives and holds electrons from the cloth.

**Conduction** Charging by **conduction** occurs when electrons are transferred from one material to another by direct contact. An electroscope can be charged by conduction, as shown in Figure 11.7. When the knob of the electroscope is touched with a negatively-charged ruler, electrons move from the ruler to the knob. The electrons then move down the rod to the leaves. Each leaf becomes negative and repels the other. Conduction causes the small electric shock you feel when you rub your shoes on a carpet and touch metal. The shock you feel occurs when electrons move from you to the metal.

**Induction** When charges on an object are rearranged without physical contact, charging by **induction** occurs. Look at Figure 11.8. A negatively-charged object is near, but not touching, the knob of the electroscope. The electrons inside the electroscope are repelled by the negative charge of the object. Electrons move from the knob and move down the rod to the leaves. The leaves become negatively charged and the knob is positively charged. Because the object didn't touch the knob of the electroscope or give up any electrons, it remains negatively charged.

**Figure 11.6** ▲
The leaves of this electroscope are neutral. The leaves do not repel, or spread apart.

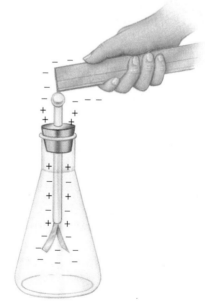

**Figure 11.7** ▲
This electroscope has been charged by conduction, which involves direct contact.

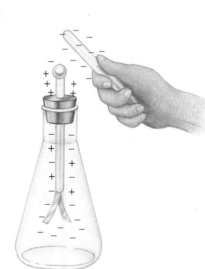

**Figure 11.8** ▲
Charging by induction doesn't involve direct contact between the negative object and the knob.

**Conductors** A material through which electric charges move easily is called a **conductor**. Most metals are good conductors. Recall that metals have a crystalline structure. Electrons in metal crystals are free to move through the crystalline structure. Good conductors have a large number of freely-moving electrons. Gold, silver, copper, aluminum, and mercury are the best conductors of electricity.

Metals that are good conductors can be useful. For example, copper and aluminum are used in electric wiring and telephone lines. Besides electrons, heat also moves easily through conductors. For this reason, some metals used for wires are also used to make cooking pots and pans.

Other materials are also good conductors. For example, the acid used in a car battery conducts electric charges. Water is also a good conductor. To prevent an electric shock, you should handle electrical appliances carefully around water.

**Insulators** A material through which electric charges can't move easily is called an **insulator**. Electrons move extremely slowly through good insulators. Electrons are tightly bound to the atoms in good insulating materials. The electrons are not free to move around. If substances were arranged according to how well they conduct electricity, the conductors would be at the top of the list and the insulators would be at the bottom.

Materials such as wood, ceramic, rubber, glass, and plastic are electric insulators. You are probably aware that wires used in electric wiring, such as lamp cords, are covered with rubber or plastic. Rubber and plastic are insulators and prevent electric charges inside the wire from flowing to the outside of the wire.

Charges don't flow easily through insulators. But charges do collect on their surfaces. The electrons that build up on the surface of an insulator tend to remain there as a static charge.

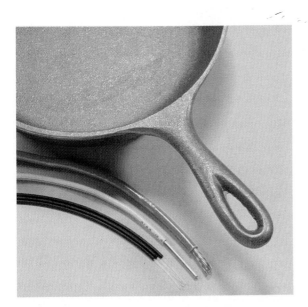

**Figure 11.9** ▲
Why is it an advantage that these objects are good conductors? Explain.

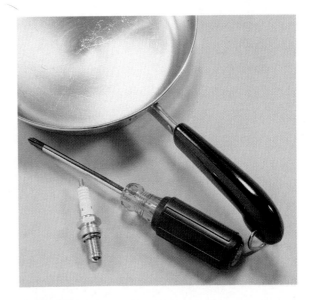

**Figure 11.10** ▲
Identify three insulators in this photograph. How is an insulator important to each object?

**Physical Science LINK**

Electric sparks similar to lightning are used to ignite gasoline in automobile engines. You can generate your own small electric spark. You need a carpeted area near a metal door knob.

**1.** Rub your shoes back and forth on the carpet.

**2.** Slowly bring your hand close to the door knob until you touch it.

What happens? List other devices that use sparks.

**ACTIVITY**

## Lightning

Electrons that build up as static charge on the surface of an object don't remain on the object forever. Eventually, the electrons leave the object. The electrons may move to the surface of another object, or they may move onto molecules in the air. The loss of static electricity by an object that occurs when electrons move is called a static discharge.

A static discharge may occur slowly and quietly. However, static discharge may also occur rapidly, converting electric energy into sound, light, and heat energy. The lightning you see during a thunderstorm is caused by the discharge of static electricity.

During a storm, water molecules and particles of matter in clouds are rubbed together by the wind. As they move, the water molecules and particles become charged by friction. As a result, areas of positive and negative charges form in the clouds.

**Figure 11.11**
**Lightning Formation and Discharge**

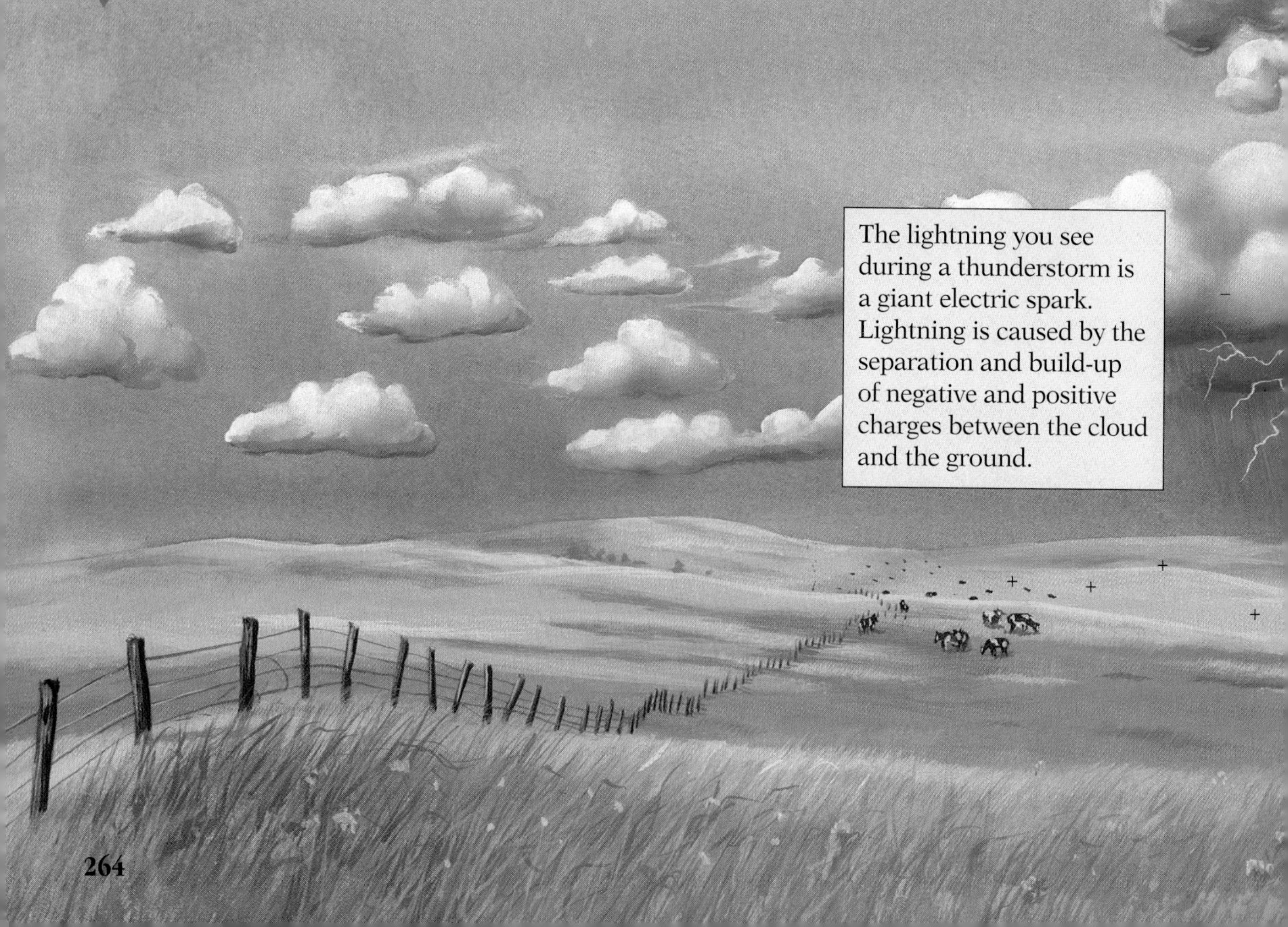

The lightning you see during a thunderstorm is a giant electric spark. Lightning is caused by the separation and build-up of negative and positive charges between the cloud and the ground.

Powerful convective currents in the thundercloud concentrate negative charges at the lower part of the cloud. The upper part of the cloud has mostly positive charges.

Lightning occurs within the thundercloud when a large charge difference exists between the positive charge at the top of cloud and the negative charge at the bottom of the cloud.

The negative charge in the bottom of the cloud will induce a positive charge in the objects on the ground below it.

Lightning rods protect buildings by conducting an electric charge from the cloud directly to the ground.

Do your clothes stick together when you take them out of the dryer? Does your hair follow the comb or brush instead of lying flat? Both of these problems are caused by static electricity.

As clothes tumble in the dryer, they build up negative charges on the surfaces of the cloth. Clothes made of synthetic materials, wool, or silk tend to pick up large amounts of negative charge. Some fabrics lose electrons and become positively charged. Some fabrics remain neutral and don't pick up a charge.

Clothes that have a positive charge attract clothes that have an opposite charge. This force of attraction causes the clothes to stick together, even after they are removed from the dryer. The electrically charged fabric will cling to other objects as well.

Perhaps you brush your hair as you dry it with an electric dryer. Friction causes electrons from the brush to build up on your hair, and it becomes negatively charged. The negative charges on your hair repel, and your hair won't stay flat. It flies everywhere.

Fortunately, modern science is able to help. Fabric softeners and hair conditioners were developed to deal with these problems. These products lubricate surfaces with a waxy or soapy substance. A thin coating of these products reduces the friction between the cloth or hair surfaces during the drying process. The reduced electron buildup controls the amount of static electricity.

## Check and Explain

1.  Name three different ways static charges can build up on an object.

2.  Explain how lightning and a shock from static electricity are related to each other.

3.  **Compare and Contrast**  How do conductors and insulators of electricity differ? Identify three materials that are good conductors and three materials that are good insulators.

4.  **Infer**  Why is it dangerous to swim or to be out in a boat during a thunderstorm?

# 11.3 Electric Current

## Objectives

▶ **Identify** three sources of electric current.

▶ **Distinguish** between current, voltage, and resistance.

▶ **Calculate** resistance using Ohm's law.

▶ **Predict** how the resistance of a wire changes with wire temperature, length, thickness, and type of material.

W hat would your life be like without electricity? Electricity supplies the energy needed to operate your household appliances, calculator, and radio. You know that electrons at rest produce static electricity. However, electrons in a wire move, or flow. These moving electrons are called **electric current**.

## Sources of Electric Current

Electric current flows through a closed, continuous path, called a **circuit**. A source of electrons is needed to produce electric current in the wire of the circuit. To keep electric current moving, the electron source must also provide a difference in the charges present at each end of the wire. One end of the wire must be negatively charged. The other end must be positively charged. The difference in the charges at each end of the wire is called potential difference, or **voltage**.

The potential difference gives electrons energy to move from the negative end of the wire toward the positive end. A device that produces the potential difference needed to move electrons through a circuit is an energy source. Electrochemical cells and thermocouples are sources of electric current.

**Electrochemical Cells** Electricity can be generated by a chemical reaction. An electrochemical cell changes chemical energy into electric energy. The two kinds of electrochemical cells are wet cells and dry cells, often referred to as batteries. Actually, a battery is several electrochemical cells working together as a source of electric current.

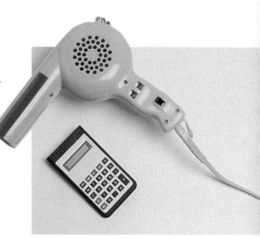

**Figure 11.11** ▲
Which of these electrical devices would be most difficult for you to live without? Explain.

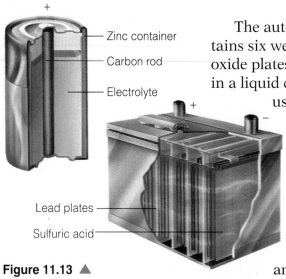

Zinc container

Carbon rod

Electrolyte

Lead plates

Sulfuric acid

**Figure 11.13** ▲

How is the dry cell (top) different from the wet cell battery (bottom)?

The automobile battery, shown in Figure 11.13, contains six wet cells. A wet cell contains lead and lead oxide plates called electrodes. The plates are immersed in a liquid conductor, called an electrolyte. Car batteries use sulfuric acid as an electrolyte. As the lead and lead oxide react with the acid, electrons are released. Electrons move from the negative lead electrode to the positive lead oxide electrode. When wires are connected to the electrodes, electrons flow through the wires. Dry cells work in much the same way as wet cells. Look at the top left side of Figure 11.13. The electrodes in a dry cell are made of zinc and carbon. The electrolyte is usually a dry base, such as ammonium chloride. It is the dry base that gives the dry cell its name.

**Thermocouples**   Differences in temperature are also used to generate electric current with a device called a *thermocouple*. It consists of a copper wire and an iron wire with the ends of the wires joined together to form a loop. Look at Figure 11.14. An electric current is produced when one iron-copper junction is heated and the other one is cooled. As the temperature difference between the two junctions increases, more electricity is generated. Thermocouples are used in the temperature gauge of an automobile. One end of the thermocouple is inside the engine and the other end is outside. As the temperature inside the engine changes, the current flowing through the gauge changes. The gauge shows the change in engine temperature.

Thermocouples are also used as a safety device in furnaces and ovens to control the gas flow to the pilot light. One iron-copper junction of the thermocouple is placed near the pilot light and gets hot. The other is placed some distance away and remains cool. The temperature difference between the two junctions produces a current that operates a switch to the gas. If the pilot light flame blows out, the wire junctions reach the same temperature. The electric current stops, and the gas shuts off.

**Figure 11.14**

Thermocouples are used to control temperature in car engines and as safety devices in gas furnaces and ovens. ▼

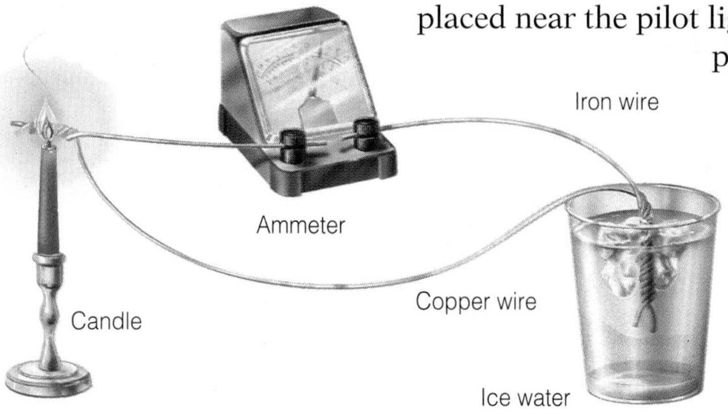

Iron wire

Ammeter

Candle

Copper wire

Ice water

## Types of Current

When an electrochemical cell is connected to a circuit, it causes a steady flow of electric current. Current that flows from an electrochemical cell source moves in one direction. Electrons that flow in the same direction in a wire produce direct current, or DC.

Electrons don't have to move in only one direction to provide electric energy. Current can change direction. The electrons in a wire are made to move first in one direction and then in the other. Electrons that flow in different directions in a wire produce an alternating current, or AC. The electricity in your home is alternating current. For alternating current in the U.S., electrons change direction about 120 times each second.

## ACTIVITY

### Interpreting Data

*Usage of Electricity*

Obtain a copy of the last electric bill that came to your home. Find the following information on the bill: kilowatt-hours of energy used and the charge per kWh. How does the rate change as you use more electricity?

### SKILLS WORKOUT

**Figure 11.15**
The electricity supplied to your home reverses direction as it moves through the wire. ▼

## Electric Current Measurement

Accurate measurement and control of electric current are important. Electric wires and appliances are built to handle only a certain amount of electric current. When too much current is present, wires get hot and can cause a fire. If an appliance does not receive enough electricity, it will operate too slowly or not at all. Often the appliance is damaged if it receives too much or too little current.

Each month your family receives an electric bill. It shows how much electricity your family used during a certain period. The electric bill also shows the unit cost of the electricity and the total cost to your family. During what months does your family use the most electricity? Why?

**Flow Rate**   The rate at which electric current flows through a wire can be compared to water flowing through a hose. The flow rate of water depends on how much water is coming out of the end of the hose. Electric-current flow rate is determined in much the same way. The number of electrons that pass a specific point in a circuit in one second indicates the flow rate of electric current. The flow rate increases as the number of electrons passing a point each second increases. If fewer electrons pass a specific point each second, the rate of current flow decreases.

The symbol for current is the capital letter *I*. In the SI system, the unit measure for current is amperes (AM peerz). Amperes are written as "amps," or as the letter "A."

An instrument called an ammeter can be connected to an electric circuit to measure the flow rate of electric current. You can see how an ammeter is connected to a circuit. Look at Figure 11.16.

**Voltage**   Electrons need an energy source to force them through a wire. Recall that the dry cell is an electron source. The energy to move electrons depends on the potential difference between the positive and negative terminals of a dry cell. The positive terminal of a dry cell has high potential. The negative terminal has low potential. The difference between high and low potential is the voltage of the dry cell.

Voltage is the amount of electric energy available to move charges. The higher the voltage, the more work the electrons can do. High-voltage dry cells are required for electric devices that use large amounts of energy. Some electric devices require more than one dry cell to operate. Why?

Voltage is measured in the SI system in volts. The symbol for volt is the capital letter "V." Voltage is measured with an instrument called a voltmeter. Notice how the voltmeter is connected to the circuit in Figure 11.17.

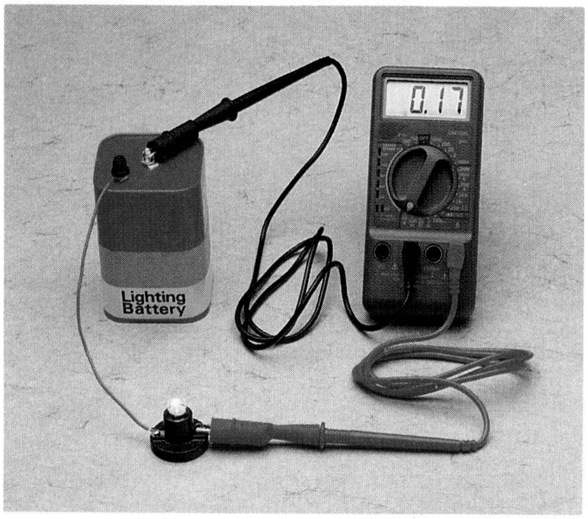

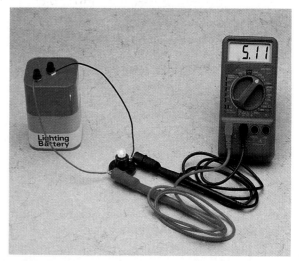

**Figure 11.16** ▲
An ammeter measures the amount of current in a circuit. The ammeter will also indicate if there is a break in the circuit. How would an electrician use an ammeter?

**Figure 11.17** ▲
The same device used in Figure 11.16 to measure current can also measure voltage, after some adjustments are made. A device that measures the voltage in a circuit is called a voltmeter.

**Resistance** Electrons flow easily through a copper wire to the filament in a light bulb. However, when electrons reach the filament, its resistance is so great that the electric energy is converted into heat and light energy. The force opposing the flow of electrons through the filament is called **resistance**. Good conductors have low resistance. Poor conductors, called resistors, have a high resistance.

A wire's resistance depends on the material from which it is made and its length, thickness, and temperature. Metals, such as copper and aluminum, have relatively low resistance. Long wires have more resistance than do short wires. Thin wires have greater resistance than do thick wires. An increase in temperature also increases the resistance of a material. A long, thin, hot, wire would have more resistance than a short, thick, cold one.

The symbol for resistance is the capital letter R. The SI unit of resistance is the ohm (OHM), and its symbol is Ω, the Greek capital letter "omega." Resistance force can be measured by connecting an ohm meter to a circuit, as shown in Figure 11.18.

## Ohm's Law

A German schoolteacher named Georg Ohm related electric current to voltage and resistance. Ohm experimented by keeping the type of material in a wire the same length, thickness, and temperature and changing only the voltage of the circuit. He discovered that when he divided the voltage (V) of the circuit by the current (I) he always got the same number. Ohm identified this number as resistance. The relationship among current, voltage, and resistance is known as Ohm's law. Ohm's law states that the current in a circuit is equal to the voltage divided by the resistance. Ohm's law is written:

$$I = \frac{V}{R}$$

If you know the voltage and the resistance of a circuit, you can find current by using this formula: $I = V/R$. If you know the current and the resistance of a circuit, you can find the voltage by solving this form of Ohm's law: $V = IR$. To find the resistance, use the formula $R = V/I$.

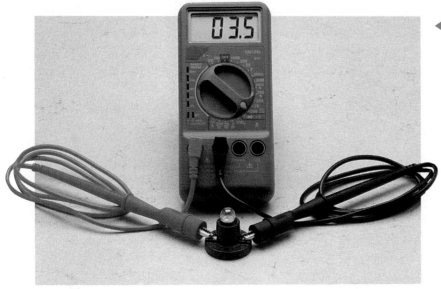

◀ **Figure 11.18**
An ohm meter has its own power source. This ohm meter is measuring the amount of resistance in the light bulb.

The current in a closed circuit measures 60 amps. The resistance through a clock connected in the circuit is 2 ohms. What is the voltage in the circuit?

$V = IR = (60 \text{ amps}) \times (2 \text{ ohm}) = 120 \text{ V}$

**Plan**  To find the voltage, multiply the current by the resistance.

**Gather data**  The current is 60 A, the resistance is 2 ohms.

**Solve**  Voltage = current x resistance
$$= 60 \text{ A} \times 2 \text{ ohms}$$
$$= 120 \text{ V}$$

1.  The electric current in a hair dryer measures 11 amps. The resistance of the dryer is 20 ohms. What is the voltage?

2.  Two dry cells in a flashlight produce 24 V. The dry cells carry a current of 3 amps. What is the resistance of the flashlight?

3.  The resistance in a radio is 10 ohms. The electric current passing through the radio measures 21 amps. What is the voltage?

4.  The dry cells in a portable radio produce 12 V. The dry cells carry a current of 0.6 amps. How much resistance does the radio produce?

# Career Corner  Electrician

## Who Installs and Repairs Electrical Systems?

A person who installs, repairs, or maintains electric devices and systems is an electrician. Electricians can work in construction, building maintenance, or repair work. Some electricians work outdoors, and others work indoors. Most electricians work in both environments.

Electricians working in construction follow blueprints. A blueprint is a plan that shows the size and type of wiring. It also shows where to install wiring, circuit breakers, and other electric parts.

Maintenance electricians repair and maintain electric systems in factories, homes, and office buildings. Some have their own shops. Others work for large companies, cities, utility companies or commercial buildings.

All electricians must understand electric circuits, wiring, motors, generators, and transformers. They also need to know about building codes and safety. To start, most electricians serve an apprenticeship under an experienced electrician. Some electricians learn the trade through correspondence or special training courses.

Mathematics, wood shop, mechanical drawing, and physics are some courses you need to take in high school to become an electrician. Most jobs require electricians to be licensed.

## Science and Technology  *Electric Plastics*

You may know that plastics are used as electric insulators. However, scientists today are developing plastics that can conduct electricity. The research that led to this new use of plastics occurred by accident during the early 1970s. While working on polymers, a student at the Tokyo Institute of Technology discovered a way to change plastics that are nonconductors into electrical conductors.

Recall that some materials conduct electricity because their electrons are free to move. The electrons in plastics don't move easily. However, by adding a few extra atoms to some plastics, the activity of the electrons can be increased. The process of adding atoms to a material to increase electron activity is called *doping*.

Think of the uses for plastics that conduct electricity! A thin plastic film in window glass could screen out heat or keep it in at the flip of a switch. Conducting plastic could be woven into cloth and used to make covers that would act as lightning rods for large structures that do not have lightning rods. Electric cars that require large batteries would be much lighter and more efficient if their batteries were made of plastic.

Unfortunately, the conducting plastics developed so far don't carry electricity as well as metals do. However, scientists continue to experiment with plastics. They are learning more about the relationship between the chemical structure of plastic and its electric properties.

### ▼ ACTIVITY

**Collecting Data**

*Devices and Current*

Look at the information on six electric devices you own. Write down how many amperes each device uses. Compare the items on your list with those of a classmate. Which devices use the most current? Which ones use the least?

**SKILLS WORKOUT**

## Check and Explain

1. Name three common sources of electric current. Name a use for each source.

2. Explain how current, voltage, and resistance relate to one another. Identify the symbol for each term.

3. **Calculate** Use Ohm's law to find the resistance of a radio that uses a 9-V battery and carries a current of 3 amps.

4. **Predict** Will a long, thin copper wire at a high temperature have a lower or greater resistance than a short, thick copper wire at a low temperature? Explain.

*Switch Back*

Locate a wall switch in your home. Use a lamp to determine which outlets in the room are controlled by the switch. How many outlets does the switch control?

# 11.4 Electric Circuits

## Objectives

▶ **Identify** the parts of a circuit.

▶ **Trace** the path of electrons through two types of circuits.

▶ **Compare** series and parallel circuits.

▶ **Predict** how circuits are wired in your home.

What happens when the connection in a water hose comes apart? The hose is connected to a water source, and pressure forces water through the hose. A break in the hose keeps water from moving to the end of the hose. An electric circuit is similar to a hose in several ways. An electric circuit requires a source of electrons and voltage to force the electrons along the circuit. If there is a break in an electric circuit, the electrons stop moving.

## Parts of a Circuit

Suppose you rode your bike along a path around a lake, beginning and ending at the same spot. You would complete a circuit. An electric circuit is similar to the bike path. It is a complete, closed path through which electrons travel. In a circuit that uses a dry cell as its electron source, the path of electrons begins in a wire attached to the negative terminal.

For work to be done by the flowing electrons, there must be a resistor connected in the circuit. A resistor is a device that uses electric energy to do work. Machines, computers, lights, appliances, and motors are examples of resistors. A wire connected from the resistor to the positive terminal completes the circuit. A circuit may have a switch to open and close the circuit. When the switch is open, or off, the path is broken and electrons can't flow through the circuit. In order to picture what a circuit looks like, electrical engineers draw circuit diagrams. A circuit diagram is shown in Figure 11.19. Notice that symbols are used to represent each part of the circuit.

**Figure 11.19**

Beneath this circuit diagram is a key which tells you what each symbol means. ▼

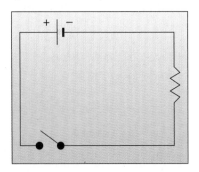

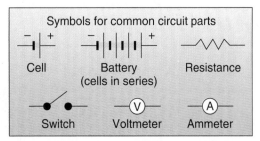

Symbols for common circuit parts

Cell

Battery (cells in series)

Resistance

Switch

Voltmeter

Ammeter

## Path of a Circuit

A simple circuit containing the basic parts of a circuit is shown in Figure 11.20. Locate the negative, or minus, terminal of the dry cell and place your finger on it. Trace the path of current by moving your finger along the wire and over each object in the circuit until you reach the positive terminal of the dry cell. By tracing this path, you can see that current from the dry cell flows through the wires, the switch, the bell, and back to the dry cell. What happens to the flow of electrons when the switch is opened? On what object is work done?

**Figure 11.20
The Path of a Current
in a Circuit ▼**

The dry cell is the electron source for the circuit. The dry cell also provides the potential difference, or voltage, needed to move electrons through the circuit.

The bell in the circuit is a resistor. The electric current moving through the bell causes the bell's clapper to move back and forth, and the bell rings.

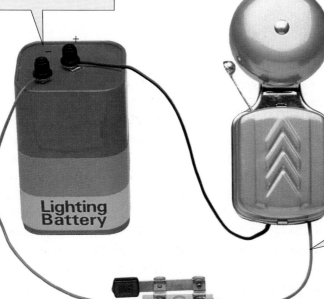

The wires provide the path through which electrons flow from the negative terminal of the dry cell, through the resistor, and to the positive terminal of the dry cell.

When the switch is closed, the metal strip attached to the insulated handle makes contact with the metal strips on the switch. The circuit is complete and electrons can flow.

When the switch is open, the metal strip connected to the insulated handle doesn't make contact with the metal strips on the switch. The circuit is broken.

How many lights turn on in your classroom when you flip the switch? You know that each light is a resistor in the circuit. Most electric circuits contain more than one resistor that uses electric energy. The resistors in a circuit can be connected in two ways. They can be connected in series or in parallel. How the parts of the circuit are connected affects the voltage and the current in the circuit.

**Series Circuits**   Suppose you want to connect two resistors, a light, and a bell in a circuit. One way to connect these resistors is to make sure that all of the current that flows through the light also flows through the bell. A circuit in which the current must pass through all the resistors is a series circuit.

All the resistors in a series circuit lie along a single path. Look at the light bulbs connected in series in Figure 11.21. Notice that the dry cell is connected by wires to all of the bulbs. The path the current travels begins at the negative terminal, passes through each light bulb, and continues back to the positive terminal.

The amount of current in a series circuit is the same at all parts of the circuit. The total resistance in the circuit changes if resistors are added or taken away. Because the same amount of current passes through each of the light bulbs in a series circuit, one bulb will be as bright as any other. If another bulb is added to the circuit, all the lights will be dimmer because the same amount of current has to do more work. What will happen if one of the bulbs is removed from the circuit?

What happens to the current if one of the bulbs burns out? If current can't pass through one bulb in a series, the path of the current is broken and the current stops. If one light goes out, all the lights go out. If you had a long string of lights connected in series, how would you find out which bulb was burned out?

**Figure 11.21**

Use this photo to explain why lights in a series circuit all go out when one goes out. ▼

**Parallel Circuits**   One way to prevent all the lights in a circuit from going out at the same time is to connect them in a parallel circuit. The electrons in a parallel circuit can travel through more than one path. Each path is separate. If there's a break in one path in the circuit, electrons can still flow through the other paths and maintain a complete circuit.

Look at the light bulbs in the parallel circuit in Figure 11.22. Notice that each bulb in the diagram is on a separate path. Part of the current available from the voltage source flows along each path and through each light bulb. How does this differ from the way in which light bulbs connected in a series receive current?

Each bulb in the circuit draws only the amount of current it needs to overcome the resistance in the bulb. As a result, each bulb will light to its full brightness. The total resistance in a parallel circuit depends on the resistances in the paths of the circuit.

What happens if one of the bulbs in Figure 11.22 burns out? Each bulb is located along its own path. Electrons will stop flowing through one bulb and continue to pass through to the others. If one bulb goes out, the others remain lit. Switches can be placed along each path in the circuit. Then, the bulb in each path can be turned on or off without affecting the others.

The electric circuits in buildings are connected in parallel. Circuits in a building carry different amounts of current. For example, a circuit used for a clothes dryer will carry more current than a circuit used for small appliances.

Parallel circuits in your home allow each light or appliance to use the amount of current it needs to work. A parallel circuit also prevents all the lights or appliances from shutting off when one of them stops working. Wall switches make it possible to use only one light or appliance at a time. Electric devices that require different amounts of currents can be used at the same time. Each device uses only the amount of current it needs.

**Figure 11.22**
The circuits in your home are connected in parallel. What is the advantage of parallel wiring? ▼

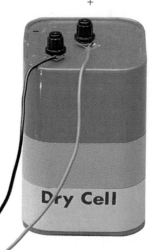

## Science and Society   *Efficient Energy Use*

Are you aware that some things are being done to improve the energy efficiency of the products you use? For example, guidelines set by the federal government limit the amount of energy new appliances can use. These limits are much smaller than the amount of electricity permitted in older appliances. How does using energy efficiently help to save money and the environment?

Replacing old appliances with the new energy-efficient models reduces household electricity use. Each time you use less electricity, more electricity is available for someone else. When less energy is needed to make electricity, nonrenewable resources like coal and oil are conserved. The whole environment benefits.

Many electric companies have time-of-day and peak-load pricing programs. In these programs, energy used during heavy-usage time periods costs more money. Many people save money by using less energy during peak-load periods.

There are many ways you can conserve energy at home. For example, planting trees around your home provides shade and reduces the energy needed to cool your home in summer. Trees also reduce the chilling effect cold winter winds have on buildings. Doubling the insulation in your home, installing double-pane windows, and adding weather stripping around doors can further reduce cooling and heating costs.

## Check and Explain

1. Name and describe three parts of a circuit.

2. Draw a simple circuit. Label your drawing with arrows to trace the path of electrons through the circuit.

3. **Compare and Contrast**   How does the path of electrons differ between a circuit connected in series and one connected in parallel?

4. **Predict**   The outlets in the circuits in homes are connected in parallel. Draw a picture of a room in a home. Predict how the circuit in the room is laid out so that some of the switches in the circuit are on, while others are not. Draw the path of the circuit.

# 11.5 Electric Power and Safety

## Objectives

▶ **Calculate** electric power and energy.

▶ **Apply** safety guidelines for household use of electricity.

▶ **Calculate** the amount of electricity used by an appliance.

▶ **Infer** about the proper use of safety devices.

Electricity is useful because it changes easily into other forms of energy. For example, a toaster changes electricity into heat energy. An electric typewriter changes electric energy into mechanical energy. Each of these devices makes work easier.

## Electric Power and Energy

The rate at which electricity does work or provides energy is called electric power. The amount of electric power a device uses to do work is determined by its resistance. The amount of power used by different appliances is shown in Table 11.2.

You can calculate power (P) if you know the voltage (V) an appliance uses and the current ($I$) in the circuit. Use the formula

$$P = V \times I$$

In SI, the unit for power is joules per second (J/s), or watts (W). Recall that voltage is measured in volts (V), and that current is measured in amperes, (amps or A).

The energy (E) an appliance uses is equal to power (P) multiplied by time (t). The formula for energy is written

$$E = P \times t$$

Power is measured in watts (W). Time is in hours (h).

The SI unit for energy is the joule. However, sometimes energy is measured with a unit called a watt-hour. Because a watt-hour is a very small unit of energy, electric companies measure electric energy in 1,000 watt-hours, or kilowatt-hours (kWh). Kilowatt-hour meters measure the electricity used in your home.

**Table 11.2**
**Power Used by**
**Common Appliances**

| Appliance | Power (watts) |
| --- | --- |
| Refrigerator with freezer | 600 |
| Dishwasher | 2,300 |
| Clock | 3 |
| Microwave oven | 1,450 |
| Color television | 200 |
| Toaster | 1,100 |
| Lamp | 100 |
| Hair dryer | 1,000 |
| Range/oven | 2,600 |
| Radio | 100 |

## Sample Problem

A light bulb has a current of 0.5 amps and is connected to a 120-V source. What is the power of the light bulb? How much energy does it use in 1 hr?

**Plan** To find power, multiply the voltage by the current. To find energy use, multiply power by time.

**Gather data** The voltage is 120 V. The current is 0.5 amps.

**Solve** $P = V \times I$
$= 120 \text{ V} \times 0.5 \text{ amps}$
$= 60 \text{ W}$
$E = 60 \text{ W} \times 1 \text{ h} = 60 \text{ Wh}$

## Practice Problems

1. An automobile headlight draws 30 amps from a 12-V battery. How much power is used?

2. How much energy is required to operate the headlight from question 1 for 3 h?

3. How much electric energy would the headlight from question 1 need in order to operate for 6 h?

4. Calculate the power used by a fan operating at 120 V and 3 amps.

5. How much electric energy would the fan from question 4 need to operate for 5 h?

# SkillBuilder  *Observing*

## Reading Electric Meters

An electric meter registers the number of kilowatt-hours of electricity used in your home. You can determine the amount of electricity used during a time period by taking two readings, and subtracting the numbers. The amount of electricity (measured in kWh), used during the time period is the difference between the two meter readings. To take each reading, follow the steps below. Look at one of the three kilowatt-hour meters shown to the right.

1. Notice that the numbers on the dials are marked in opposite directions. One dial rotates clockwise. The next rotates counterclockwise.

2. The dials are read from right to left as follows: The first dial on the right reads from 0 to 10, the next dial reads from 0 to 100 by tens, the third reads from 0 to 1,000 by

hundreds, and the dial at the left reads from 0 to 10,000 by thousands.

3. Any pointer that is between two numbers on a dial is read as the lower number. For practice, read meter A. The dial on the right reads 2. The next dial reads 40. The next dial reads 600. The dial to the left reads 3,000. Add these 4 dial readings. Meter A reads 3,642 kWh.

4. Read meters B and C.

## Electric Safety

Electricity is useful, but it can also be dangerous. Each year, many people are seriously injured or killed from shocks or fire caused by electricity. Most appliances and buildings have safety features built into them.

Many appliances are equipped with a "ground" wire on the plug. The ground wire prevents electric shocks from the outside of the appliance. Look at Figure 11.23. The rounded third prong of a three-way electric plug is attached to the ground wire. It constantly moves static electricity from the appliance to the ground.

Broken wires or water can cause electric appliances to short-circuit. A short circuit occurs when electricity takes a short path and bypasses the resistors in the circuit. As a result, the resistance in the circuit is less, and the current in the wire increases. The increased current can produce enough heat to melt wires and start a fire, or cause a serious electric shock.

Overloading a circuit also may cause a fire. A circuit can become overloaded if too many electric devices are plugged into it. Each added electric device increases the electric current flowing through the wire. When the electric current load is greater than the capacity of the wire, the wire is overloaded.

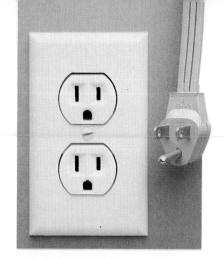

**Figure 11.23** ▲
How does the large prong at the bottom of the plug protect the appliance?

## Circuit Protectors

Fuses and circuit breakers, like those shown in Figure 11.24, protect against overloaded circuits. A number on the fuse indicates the maximum current that will flow through it. When the current goes above the maximum, the metal in the fuse melts. The circuit is broken, and the flow of electrons stops. Resistors must be removed from the circuit, and the fuse must be replaced. A special type of fuse, called a ground-fault interrupter is used with electrical appliances located near water.

Circuit breakers are often used instead of fuses. A circuit breaker is a switch that opens automatically when electric current in a circuit reaches its maximum. When the switch opens, it breaks the flow of electrons in the circuit. Circuit breakers can be reset when the switch is closed again.

**Figure 11.24** ▲
The top photo shows fuses and the bottom photo shows circuit breakers. Which kind of circuit protector is used in your home?

## Science and You
### *Electric Safety and Your Body*

Your body can conduct electricity. Electricity from an appliance can pass through you. If your hand comes in contact with the current in a circuit, a potential difference might exist between the charges in your hand and the ground. As a result, current flows from your hand, through your body, and into the ground. You can be seriously injured from the current that passes through your body.

If you are holding an object that is conducting electricity, the current is redirected through your body due to the potential difference between the object and the ground. Electric energy causes your muscles to contract and you may not be able to release the object. As long as there is a difference in the amount of charge between you and the ground, current will continue. When the current stops, so will the muscle contraction.

Water is an excellent conductor of electricity. If your body is wet, the overall resistance of your body is lower. As a result, your body will conduct current more easily. Why do you think appliances have warnings against using them in a tub or shower?

You can take safety measures to avoid receiving electric shocks. For example, safety devices, such as ground-fault interrupters, are placed in pool areas and bathrooms where water might be present. A ground-fault interrupter is a fast-acting fuse. This device carries current to the ground if it senses that current is bypassing an appliance.

## ACTIVITY

### Predicting

*Auto Fuse*

Most automobiles have fuses. What electric devices on an automobile might be protected with a fuse?

**SKILLS WORKOUT**

## Check and Explain

1.  A radio has a current of 10 amps from a 120-V source. What is the power of the radio?

2.  What can you do to minimize the risk of an electric shock or fire in your home caused by electricity?

3.  **Calculate**   A tape player operates on 120 V and 6 amps. How much power does it use? How much energy does it use if you operate it for 60 s?

4.  **Infer**   Why it is important to use the correct fuse in a circuit?

# Chapter 11 Review

## Concept Summary

### 11.1 Electric Charges

▶ Protons and electrons have electric charges that can produce forces of attraction or repulsion between matter.

▶ Like charges repel. Unlike charges attract.

▶ An electric field is the region around charged particles.

### 11.2 Static Electricity

▶ The buildup of charges is called static electricity.

▶ Electric charge can be caused by friction, conduction, or induction.

▶ Electrons flow easily through conductors. Electrons don't flow easily through insulators.

### 11.3 Electric Current

▶ Current flows through a closed continuous path called a circuit.

▶ Voltage is the amount of energy available to move charges.

▶ Resistance is the force opposing the flow of electrons.

▶ Ohm's law states that current equals voltage divided by resistance.

### 11.4 Electric Circuits

▶ A device that uses electric energy to do work is a resistor.

▶ A series circuit has only one path for current.

▶ A parallel circuit has more than one path for current.

### 11.5 Electric Power and Safety

▶ Electric power equals voltage multiplied by current.

▶ Fuses and circuit breakers protect circuits from overloading.

## Chapter Vocabulary

| | | |
|---|---|---|
| charge (11.1) | conductor (11.2) | circuit (11.3) |
| conduction (11.2) | insulator (11.2) | voltage (11.3) |
| induction (11.2) | electric current (11.3) | resistance (11.3) |

## Check Your Vocabulary

Use the vocabulary words above to complete the following sentences correctly.

1. The movement of charges, or electrons, through a circuit is ____ .

2. A material that allows electrons to move through it easily is a(n) ____ .

3. A complete, closed path through which electrons can travel is a(n) ____ .

4. The force opposing the flow of electrons through a material is ____ .

5. Plastics, glass, and wood are examples of an electric ____ .

6. The difference in the charges at each end of a circuit is ____ .

7. Charge caused by ____ occurs when charges move from one object to another through direct contact.

8. An object is charged by ____ when no contact is made with the charging object.

9. A proton has a positive electric ____ .

## Write Your Vocabulary

Write sentences using the vocabulary words above. Show that you know what each word means.

# Chapter 11 Review

## Check Your Knowledge

Choose the answer that best completes each sentence.

1. A positive charge will repel a (positive charge, negative charge).

2. An instrument that is used to detect charges is a(n) (voltmeter, ammeter, electroscope).

3. An example of a good conductor is (copper, glass, wood).

4. Lightning occurs as a result of a discharge of (resistance, static charges, amperes).

5. The closed, continuous path through which electrons can flow is a(n) (circuit, resistor, charge).

Determine whether each statement is true or false. Write *true* if it is true. If it is false, change the underlined word(s) to make the statement true.

6. Ohm's law states that current in a circuit is equal to voltage divided by <u>charge</u>.

7. The Greek letter omega, $\Omega$, is the symbol for <u>resistance</u>.

8. A dry cell uses a(n) <u>acid</u> as its electrolyte.

9. Fuses and circuit breakers protect a circuit from <u>short-circuiting</u>.

10. A material that resists the flow of electrons well is a(n) <u>insulator</u>.

11. The strongest part of an electric field is the area <u>farthest</u> from the charge.

12. A thermocouple uses differences in <u>temperature</u> to generate electricity.

## Check Your Understanding

Apply the concepts you have learned to answer each question.

1. If you know the charge of one object, how could you use it to determine the charge of a second object?

2. **Explain** What causes lightning?

3. How can you determine the current if you know the voltage and resistance of a circuit?

4. A home used 5,500 watt-hours of electricity. How many kilowatt-hours is this?

5. Why is an appliance considered a resistor?

6. **Critical Thinking** The knob of an electroscope is neutral. An object with a negative charge is brought near the knob without touching it. The leaves of the electroscope separate. Explain why. After the leaves separate, what is the charge of the object that was brought near the electroscope? What is the charge of the knob?

7. **Mystery Photo** The photograph on page 256 shows the filament in a light bulb. When electric current flows through the filament, it heats up and gives off light. Does the filament conduct or resist the flow of electrons? Explain your answer.

8. What is the power of a light bulb that has a current of 0.3 amps and is connected to a 120-V source?

## Develop Your Skills

Use the skills you have learned in this chapter to complete each activity.

**1. Interpret Data** The diagram below shows electric devices connected in a circuit and the location of each one in the circuit.

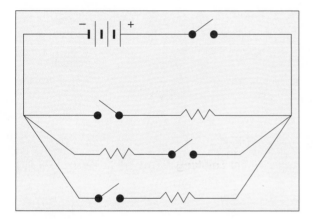

a. What is this diagram called?

b. What kind of circuit is shown in the diagram?

c. How many resistors are shown in this circuit?

**2. Data Bank** Use the information on page 639 to answer the following questions.

a. Which metal has the most resistance?

b. Which metal has the least resistance?

c. Arrange the metals in the table from most to least resistance.

**3. Design an Experiment** Lemon juice can be used as an electrolyte to conduct a current. Design an experiment to show this fact. Describe the problem, materials, procedure, expected results, and conclusion.

## Make Connections

**1. Link the Concepts** Below is a concept map showing how some of the main concepts of this chapter link together. Only part of the map is filled in. Finish the map, using words and ideas you find on the previous pages.

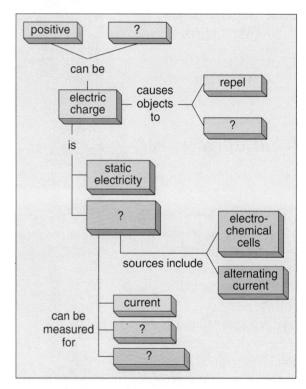

**2. Science and Social Studies** Petroleum is the most commonly used fuel for generating electricity. Research how electricity is generated in other countries. Identify the energy source for the electricity and the country in which the source is used.

**3. Science and Math** Locate the electric meter for your home. Read the meter every Monday for one month. Identify how much electricity your family used during each one-week period. How did the energy use change from week to week?

# Chapter 12 Magnetism

## Chapter Sections

**12.1** Magnets and Magnetism

**12.2** Electricity to Magnetism

**12.3** Magnetism to Electricity

## What do you see?

❝I see a circle with a lot of different blobs of color and two round dark balls at the side. I think it is an ultrasound of a brain with the dark balls at the side as eyes. I think it is a brain because of the shape and the eyes. They made this image by ultrasound or a radar or something of that sort. This method is helpful because they don't have to cut a person open to view certain parts like the brain.❞

*Tim Carey*
*Stivers Middle School*
*Dayton, Ohio*

To find out more about the photograph, look on page 306. As you read this chapter, you will learn about magnets and magnetism.

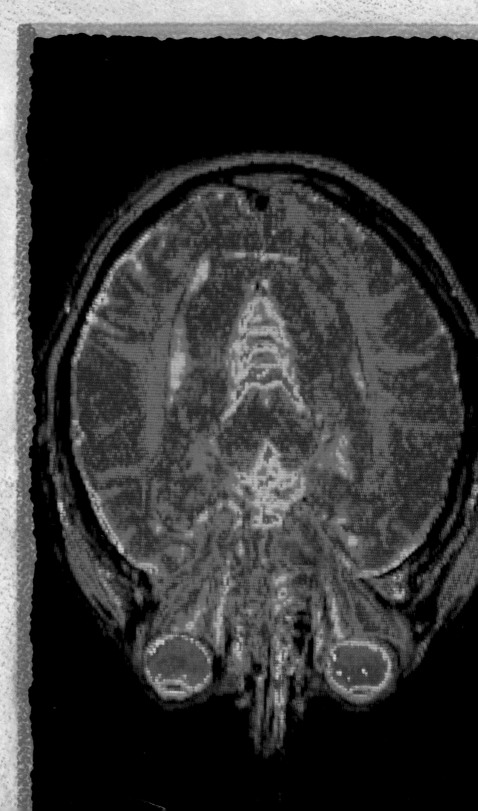

# 12.1 Magnets and Magnetism

## Objectives

▶ **Describe** two properties of magnets.

▶ **Explain** how a material can become magnetized.

▶ **Infer** how the earth is like a magnet.

▶ **Predict** how a material might become magnetic.

What do doorbells, telephones, electric motors, radios, and televisions have in common? All of these everyday devices use magnets in order to operate. Magnets create a force called magnetism. You may use the force of magnetism to hold notes on a refrigerator door. The cluster of metal pieces in Figure 12.1 is held together magnetically. The force of magnetism can lift something as small as a paper clip or as large as an automobile!

Many everyday items use magnetism in ways that you may not suspect. For example, magnetism is used to record and play back audio cassettes and videotapes. Credit cards and subway tickets have magnetic strips that carry information. Computers store information on disks coated with magnetic material.

Magnetism is a universal force like gravity or the strong and weak forces inside the nucleus of an atom. But what causes magnetic force? The properties of magnets can help you to understand what magnetism is and how it works.

**Figure 12.1** ▲
What universal force is holding together the pieces of this metal sculpture?

## Properties of Magnets

To investigate the properties of magnets, you can experiment with two bar magnets by hanging each one from a string. When you bring the hanging magnets together, you can observe magnetic force operating in one of two ways.

▶ The ends of the magnets attract each other and the magnets stick together.

▶ The ends of the magnets repel each other and the magnets move apart.

**Magnetic Poles**   The force around each end of a bar magnet differs. If you allow the magnet to hang freely, one end always points north. The north-seeking end of a bar magnet is labeled *North*, and the other end is labeled *South*. The ends of a magnet are the **magnetic poles**. The magnetic force in the magnet is strongest at the magnetic poles.

Notice the position of the hanging magnet in Figure 12.2. When two north poles or two south poles are brought near each other, they repel. However, if the north and south magnetic poles are brought near each other, they will attract. Some substances that aren't magnets are attracted to either magnetic pole.

The force of magnetic poles behaves like the force of electric charges. Recall that unlike charges attract, and like charges repel. However, magnetic poles can't be separated from each other like electric charges can. If you break a magnet in half, each piece is still a complete magnet with its own north pole and south pole.

**Magnetic Field**   You know that the magnetic force of a magnet is strongest at its poles. However, the magnetic force is not restricted to the area around the poles. Magnetic force exists around the entire magnet. The magnetic region around the magnet is called the **magnetic field**.

The lines around the magnet in Figure 12.3 show its magnetic field. These lines, called magnetic field lines, extend from one pole to the other. The arrows indicate the direction of magnetic force and the location of the magnetic field around the magnet. The magnetic field at the center of the magnet is weaker than it is at the poles.

Although the magnetic field is invisible, you can see its effect around a magnet by placing a piece of paper on top of the magnet and then sprinkling iron filings over the paper. The iron filings form a pattern similar to the magnetic field lines shown in Figure 12.3

If you were to place a piece of metal near the magnet, it would be most attracted to either the north or south pole. However, the metal would also be attracted by the magnetic field around the magnet.  What do you think happens if you place the entire magnet in a dish of iron filings?

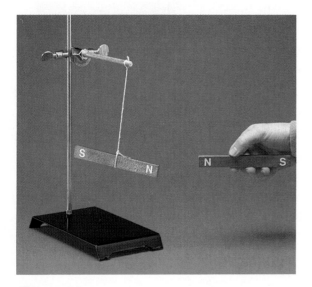

**Figure 12.2 ▲**
Two north poles will repel. What happens when poles with unlike charges are brought together?

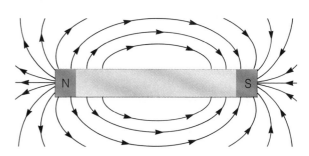

**Figure 12.3 ▲**
All magnetic material has a magnetic field around it. Identify the magnetic field in the drawing.

## Magnetic Materials

Why are some materials magnetic and others not magnetic? The electrons of all atoms spin as they move about the nucleus. A spinning electron produces a magnetic field with both a north and a south pole. Each atom acts like a tiny magnet. In most materials, the magnetic fields of individual atoms cancel each other, so the materials aren't magnetic.

In materials like iron, cobalt, and nickel, the magnetic field of each individual atom is so strong that the atoms group together. The poles line up in the same direction in microscopic magnetic regions, called **magnetic domains**. When all the domains are arranged with their poles in the same direction, the iron bar becomes a **permanent magnet**. When the domains are arranged randomly, the iron bar is not magnetized. Look at Figure 12.4. Notice how the arrangement of the magnetic domains differs in the two iron bars.

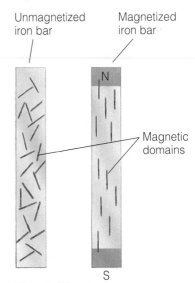

Unmagnetized iron bar

Magnetized iron bar

Magnetic domains

**Figure 12.4** ▲
How can you tell which iron bar is magnetized?

# Historical Notebook

## Magnetism in Ancient Times

More than 2,000 years ago, people in Asia discovered that certain black metallic rocks attracted iron. The Greeks and Arabs called these rocks *lodestones*, meaning "leading stone." When hung, these stones always pointed in the same direction. Later lodestone was renamed *magnetite* for the district of Magnesia which is located in present-day Turkey.

People in China also knew about the properties of magnetite. They discovered that when a small, flat piece of iron was rubbed over magnetite, it became magnetized. The magnetized iron pointed in a north-south direction when it hung by a silken thread. These pieces of magnetized iron were the first compasses.

Chinese builders first used compasses for geomacy, a technique used to align houses and cities harmoniously with the forces of the earth. By the tenth century, the Chinese were using com-

passes to navigate ships. European and Arabic navigators probably acquired the compass from the Chinese around the twelfth century.

1.  Use your library to find out why the compass was important to twelfth century navigators.

2.  Could a piece of magnetite be used as a compass? Explain.

# Earth as a Magnet

If you hang a magnet by a string, the north-seeking pole will always point north because the earth itself is a huge magnet. The magnetic field around a bar magnet is a good model for the earth's magnetic field. Imagine that a giant bar magnet extends from the North Pole to the South Pole. Magnetic field lines around the earth are like the magnetic field lines around a bar magnet.

An instrument that takes advantage of the earth's magnetic field is the **compass**. A compass has a magnetized needle in it that turns freely. Because the magnetized needle always aligns with the earth's magnetic field, a compass is used to determine direction.

Recall that the earth turns on its axis.

The North Pole and South Pole of the earth's axis are referred to as geographic poles. The geographic North Pole, sometimes called *true north*, is located in a different place from the magnetic north pole.

Notice in Figure 12.5 that the magnetic north pole is in Canada, about 1,400 km from the geographic North Pole. The magnetic south pole is in Antartica, about 2,750 km from the geographic South Pole. The angle between magnetic north and true north is called the *magnetic declination*.

Evidence suggests that the earth's magnetic field is caused by the movement of molten metals near the earth's core. Measurements show that the earth's magnetic poles change position over time. Changes in the flow of the molten metals inside the earth may cause the magnetic poles to move.

**Figure 12.5**
**The Earth's Magnetic Field** ▼

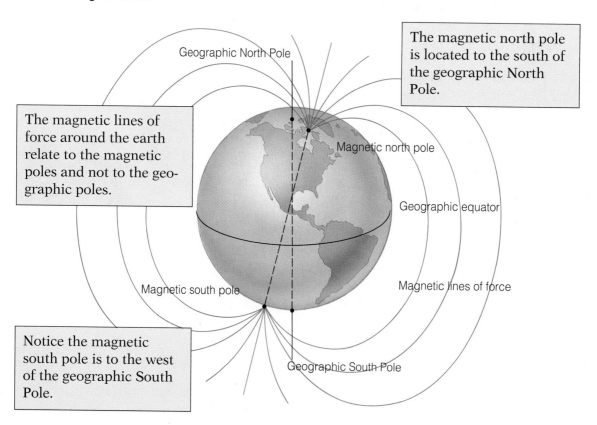

The magnetic lines of force around the earth relate to the magnetic poles and not to the geographic poles.

Geographic North Pole

The magnetic north pole is located to the south of the geographic North Pole.

Magnetic north pole

Geographic equator

Magnetic south pole

Magnetic lines of force

Notice the magnetic south pole is to the west of the geographic South Pole.

Geographic South Pole

## Magnetic Effects

The most visible effect of the earth's magnetic field is a colorful light display, called an aurora, like the one shown in Figure 12.6. An aurora hangs like a curtain of light stretching over the polar regions of the earth. Since the earth's magnetic field is strongest near the poles, charged particles given off by the sun collect there. Collisions between the charged particles and other particles in the upper atmosphere create glowing lights. The lights are called the *aurora borealis* (the northern lights) or the *aurora australis* (the southern lights). The color of an aurora depends on the kind of atoms in the atmosphere.

Another effect is disturbances in the earth's magnetic field, called magnetic storms, which interfere with compass needles and radio and television waves. Magnetic storms occur when solar flares produce charged particles that become trapped in the earth's magnetic field. The trapped particles follow corkscrew paths around the earth's magnetic field lines, causing temporary changes in the magnetic field.

The earth's magnetic field also affects living things. Tiny pieces of the magnetic mineral magnetite have been found in the brains of pigeons, bees, bacteria, and other organisms that use the magnetic field to help them sense direction. This discovery demonstrates how magnetic fields are important.

▼ **ACTIVITY**

**Making a Model**

*Compass*

Construct a model compass to see the earth's magnetic field in action. Collect the following items: a steel sewing needle, a bar magnet, and a piece of thread.

**1.** Stroke the needle in one direction with a bar magnet for ten minutes.

**2.** Tie a thread at the midpoint of the needle and suspend the needle from the thread.

Where is north and south?

**SKILLS WORKOUT**

◀ **Figure 12.6**
This photo shows the aurora borealis, or northern lights. What causes the aurora?

Imagine you're lost in the woods. Because the sun isn't visible, you don't know which direction is north. How can you find your way out? A compass can help.

Since a compass needle always points north and south, you align the needle with the *North* marking on the compass case. You can read the compass markings to locate the direction you want to go. As you walk in that direction, you check the compass now and then to be sure that you're still going the right way. Soon you're out of the woods!

Sometimes people give directions to a place by telling you to turn north on one street and east on another instead of telling you to turn left or right. If you aren't familiar with the area, you may have trouble following these directions. If you have a compass, it's much easier to reach your destination.

Although compasses may look different, they all work the same way. A pointer, or needle, inside the compass is a magnet that aligns with the earth's magnetic field. This small magnet balances on a sharp point or floats in a liquid.

Look at Figure 12.7. The large markings on every compass indicate north, south, east, and west. The smaller markings around the edge are the 360 degrees of a circle with the needle at the center. The degree markings precisely identify direction and are important to navigators on ships and aircraft.

**Figure 12.7** ▲

How would a compass be useful if you hiked through a very dense wooded area like the one shown above?

## Check and Explain

1. What are two properties of magnets and their magnetic fields?

2. Explain why some pieces of iron act as magnets and other pieces of iron don't.

3. **Infer** You know that on the earth, the north pole of a hanging magnet always points north. What does this tell you about the earth as a magnet? Explain.

4. **Predict** Explain how the atoms in metals create the magnetic domains in a magnetized material. Based on your answer, predict what would happen if a metal is melted and all its atoms are able to float freely.

# 12.2 Electricity to Magnetism

## Objectives

▶ **Relate** electricity to magnetism.

▶ **Explain** how an electric motor works.

▶ **Compare** and **contrast** electric motors and galvanometers.

▶ **Predict** how the direction of the current affects a motor.

You can dry your hair with an electric dryer and wash your clothes in a washing machine because electricity and magnetism are related! The relationship between electricity and magnetism is called *electromagnetism* (ee LEK troh MAG nuh TIHZ uhm). How are these two forces related?

Recall that iron makes a good permanent magnet because its spinning electrons group together. Moving electric charges produce a magnetic field. Electric currents also produce magnetic fields. Whenever charges move, they produce magnetic effects. The electric motors in electric clothes dryers and washing machines rely on electromagnetism to work.

## Electromagnetism

For centuries, people thought electricity and magnetism were completely unrelated. However, in 1820, Hans Christian Oersted, a Danish physicist, made an interesting observation. He noticed that when a compass was brought near electric current, the compass needle no longer pointed north! It turned 90 degrees.

Oersted discovered that the compass needle turned in the opposite direction when he reversed the current. When the wire was disconnected, as in Figure 12.8, it no longer affected the compass. The compass needle turned to the north. Oersted knew the point of a compass needle would follow a magnet. He hypothesized that when an electric current flowed through it, the wire acted like a magnet. Somehow electricity could produce magnetism.

**Figure 12.8**

What happens to the compasses when the wires are connected to the battery? ▼

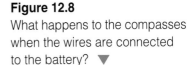
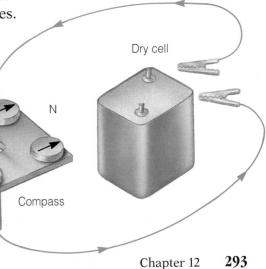

Dry cell

N

Compass

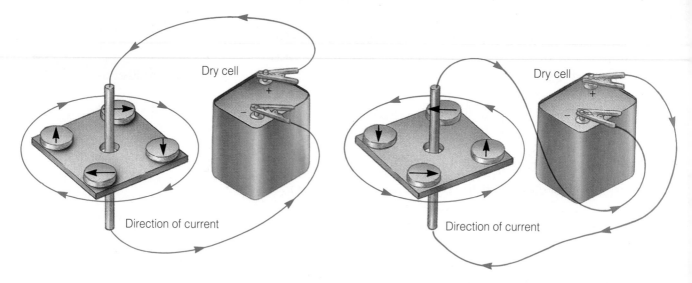

**Figure 12.9 ▲**

The compasses above detect the magnetic field in the electric current. Why do the compass directions reverse when the wires are reversed?

To see how the magnetic force produced by an electric current behaves, look at the compasses in Figure 12.9. The circular pattern of the compass needles shows the magnetic field around the current-carrying wire. When the electric current flows *down* the wire, the magnetic field exerts a force in a clockwise direction. When the electric current flows *up* the wire, the magnetic field exerts a force in a counterclockwise direction.

## Electromagnets

Oersted's discovery was responsible for the invention of new tools based on the principles of electromagnetism. For example, soon after Oersted's experiments, scientists learned to build powerful magnets that could be turned on and off. The first such magnet consisted of a coil of current-carrying wire. When a bar of soft iron is placed inside the wire coil, the magnetic force increases. A simple example of this device, called an **electromagnet**, is shown in Figure 12.10.

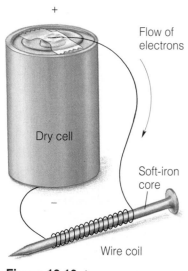

+

Flow of electrons

Dry cell

Soft-iron core

Wire coil

**Figure 12.10 ▲**

What effect does the number of coils have on the strength of the electromagnet?

The strength of an electromagnet depends on the number of turns in the coil and the size of the iron core. The greater the number of turns the coil has, the stronger is the magnetic field it can produce. The greater the size of the soft-iron core, the stronger the magnet is. How could you change the magnetic strength of an electromagnet?

When the magnet is turned on, an electric current flows through the wire coil, creating a magnetic field around the coil. The magnetic domains in the soft-iron core align with the magnetic field of the coil. The soft-iron core becomes magnetized. The shape of the magnetic field around an electromagnet is similar to the shape of the magnetic field around a bar magnet.

One end of the soft-iron core is a north pole, and the other end is a south pole. The magnetic field of the magnetized soft-iron core combines with the magnetic field of the wire coil. The combined magnetic fields create a very strong magnet.

The soft iron used for the core of an electromagnet isn't really "soft." Pure iron is referred to as soft iron. It is easy to magnetize, but soft iron loses its magnetism quickly when the electric current stops. In contrast, "hard" iron, or steel, remains magnetized for a long time. Why do you think steel might be unsuitable for making an electromagnet? Recall that material is magnetized when all of its domains line up in the same direction. The domains in steel are more resistant to change than the domains in soft iron.

### Health Science LINK

Electromagnetic fields may be harmful to your health. Using a TV and a compass, you will determine if an electromagnetic field is present.

**1.** Place the compass on the television. Turn the television on and observe.

**2.** Place the compass 1 m away from the television. Observe the result.

What happened? Explain why some health officials advise keeping a distance from electromagnetic fields.

**A C T I V I T Y**

## Consider This

### Should People Avoid Low-level Magnetic Fields?

Appliances, such as electric blankets, dishwashers, computers, and televisions, all have an electric field around them. The electric fields, created by alternating electric current, are low-frequency current. They are called ELF, for extremely low frequency electromagnetic fields.

Groups concerned about the safety of ELF fields recommend that people stay at least 1 m away from computer and television screens. However, all electric devices produce ELF fields. People are surrounded by electric wiring and electric devices at home, school, and work. The effects of long-term exposure to ELF fields are still unknown.

**Consider Some Issues**

People studying disease patterns in human populations have noticed a possible relationship between ELF fields and an increase in cancer.

Groups of people exposed daily to ELF fields have a higher-than-normal rate of brain cancer and leukemia. The groups studied include electricians, telephone-line workers, and people who live near high-voltage power lines. The higher cancer rates don't prove that ELF fields cause cancer. Many other unknown factors could be involved.

Some physicists think that ELF fields are too weak to affect the human body. They feel the studies don't prove that ELF fields cause cancer and more research is needed.

**Think About It**   How might a possible health risk from ELF fields affect the use of electric appliances? How might ELF fields affect where people live?

**Write About It**   Write a short paper arguing for or against avoiding ELF fields. Explain your reasons.

## Uses for Electromagnetism

You probably use items every day that contain electromagnets. Any appliance with an electric motor uses an electromagnet to convert electric energy to energy of motion. An electromagnet exerts a magnetic force that can make things move. Vacuum cleaners, tape recorders, and hair dryers all contain electromagnets.

**Electric Motors** A simple direct current, or DC, electric motor like the one in Figure 12.11, contains an electromagnet, a permanent magnet, and a commutator. An electromagnet, called an armature, is placed in the magnetic field of the permanent magnet.

When current flows through the electromagnet, its poles repel the like poles of the permanent magnet. When the direction of the current changes, the poles on the electromagnet reverse, and the electromagnet spins. The armature turns a drive shaft that does work.

The commutator is a split metal ring that acts as a switch. The commutator reverses the current in the electromagnet. Electric current enters the electromagnet through brushes that touch the spinning commutator rings.

**Figure 12.11**
**Simple Electric Motor** ▼

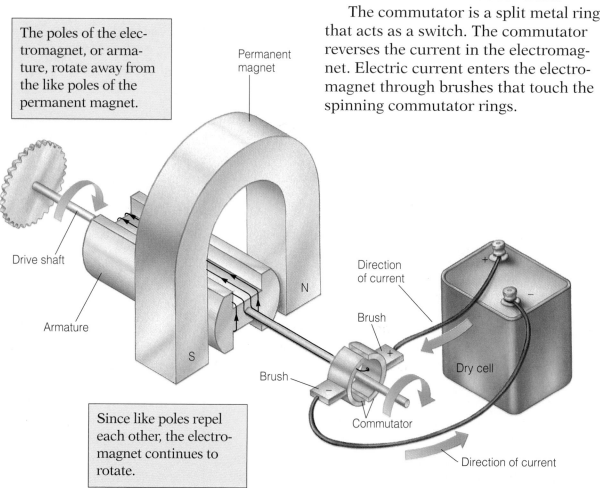

The poles of the electromagnet, or armature, rotate away from the like poles of the permanent magnet.

Permanent magnet

Drive shaft

Armature

N

S

Direction of current

Brush

Brush

Commutator

Dry cell

Direction of current

Since like poles repel each other, the electromagnet continues to rotate.

Every time the commutator makes a half turn, current direction changes.

**Figure 12.12**
**How a Meter Measures Current** ▽

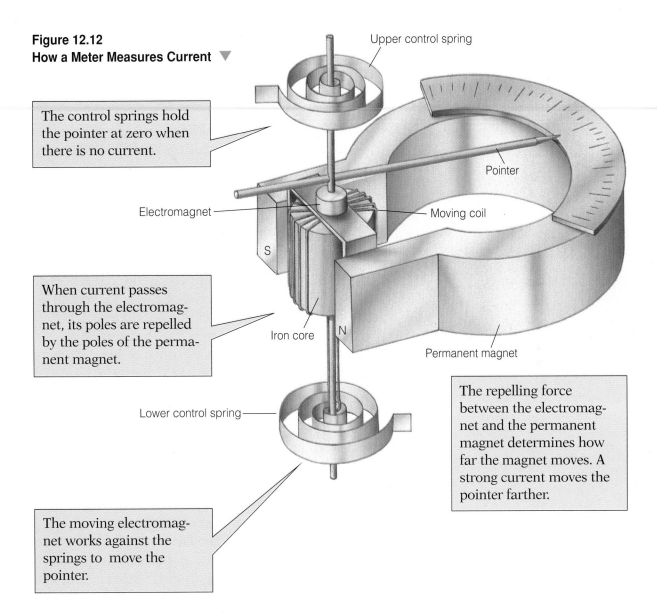

Upper control spring

The control springs hold the pointer at zero when there is no current.

Pointer

Electromagnet

Moving coil

S

When current passes through the electromagnet, its poles are repelled by the poles of the permanent magnet.

Iron core

N

Permanent magnet

Lower control spring

The repelling force between the electromagnet and the permanent magnet determines how far the magnet moves. A strong current moves the pointer farther.

The moving electromagnet works against the springs to move the pointer.

**Current Meters** The response of magnetic forces between an electromagnet and a permanent magnet is used in various kinds of meters, such as voltmeters, ammeters, and galvanometers (GAL vuh NAH muh turs). All these devices, called current meters, measure electric current.

A galvanometer, like the one shown in Figure 12.12, measures small amounts of electric current passing through a resistor. The two springs connected to the rod through the electromagnet control the pointer of the galvanometer. When an electric current

passes through the electromagnet, the poles of the electromagnet respond to the poles of the permanent magnet. If the poles are alike, they repel and force the pointer in one direction or the other.

The galvanometer's scale has equally spaced markings on either side of the zero. The direction of the current through the electromagnet determines whether the pointer moves to the right or to the left of center. The pointer's position away from zero indicates how much current is traveling through the wire coil. How are current meters used?

## Science and Technology *Electric Cars*

Someday you might go to an electric recharging station instead of a gasoline station to refuel your automobile! Instead of kilometers per liter, you would measure your fuel consumption in kilometers per kilowatt. Your electric car of the future could look like the one in Figure 12.13.

Electric cars aren't a new idea. Some of the earliest cars were electric. However, cars with gasoline engines replaced electric cars because gasoline engines provide more power per unit weight than electric motors. Also, at that time, gasoline was both abundant and cheap. Today the reduction of fossil-fuel reserves, the cost of gasoline, and air pollution make electric cars a good idea.

People want an electric car that travels as fast and as far as a gasoline-powered car. Older electric cars required heavy DC batteries to power inefficient DC motors. Also, because the windshield wipers, starter, radio, and lights all use direct current, older test models of electric cars needed more DC batteries. To solve the problem, engineers are working to develop an efficient, lightweight electric car.

The new electric cars could use newly-developed alternating-current, or AC, motors with lightweight moving parts. Since batteries produce direct current, a "power inverter" will change the DC power to AC power. A newly designed electronic power inverter has a mass of only 27 kg instead of the 136 kg of older power inverters. Many other ideas are being developed and tested to make the electric car the car of your future.

**Figure 12.13** ▲
What effect does the weight of the batteries have on the efficiency of an electric car?

## Check and Explain

1.  Name three things Oersted discovered about the relationship between electricity and magnetism.

2.  Explain how an electric motor works.

3.  **Compare and Contrast** How is the operation of a galvanometer similar to that of an electric motor?

4.  **Predict** What would happen if the current in the electro-magnet of an electric motor didn't change direction?

# Activity 12  *Does the number of coils affect magnetic force?*

***Skills***  Predict; Infer; Observe; Graph; Interpret Data

## Task 1  Prelab Prep
Collect the following items: 2 m insulated electric wire, 1 box of paper clips, 1 large iron nail, one 6-V dry cell, and tape.

## Task 2  Data Record
1. Prepare a table like the one shown.
2. Record the number of paper clips the electromagnet attracted for each number of coils.

**Table 12.1**

| Number of Coils | Number of Paper Clips |
|---|---|
| 10 | |
| 15 | |
| 20 | |
| 25 | |

3. Prepare a graph to show how magnetic force changes as the number of coils in the electromagnet increases. Put the number of coils on the *x*-axis and the number of paper clips on the *y*-axis.

## Task 3  Procedure
1. Remove about 2 cm of insulation from the ends of the electric wire.
2. Place a pile of paper clips on the table.
3. Wind the electric wire around the iron nail 10 times. The coils should be close together. You can use the diagram in Figure 12.10 as an example.
4. Connect the ends of the electric wire to the dry cell with tape. Pick up as many paper clips as possible with the electromagnet.
5. Count and record the number of paper clips picked up. Disconnect the dry cell.

6. Wind 5 more loops of wire around the nail to make 15 loops. Repeat steps 4 and 5.
7. Repeat steps 4 and 5 with 20 and 25 loops of wire around the nail.

## Task 4  Analysis
1. How many coils around the nail picked up the largest number of paper clips? The smallest number of paper clips?

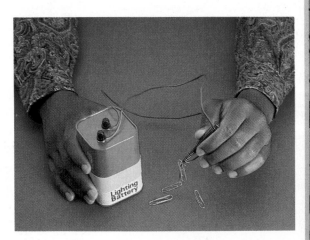

2. How does changing the number of coils affect the magnetic force of the electromagnet?
3. What does the graph tell you about the relationship between the number of coils and the strength of the electromagnet?

## Task 5  Conclusion
Write a short paragraph describing how the strength of the electromagnet depends on the number of coils wound around the nail. Explain what effect the number of coils would have on the magnetic field around the electromagnet also.

## Extension

To find out more about how to change the electromagnet's strength, use a bigger or smaller nail and observe what happens. Add a second dry cell and test the strength of the electromagnet.

# 12.3 Magnetism to Electricity

## Objectives

▶ **Describe** how magnetism is used to produce electricity.

▶ **Identify** two uses of electromagnetic induction.

▶ **Compare** and **contrast** the energy conversions in a generator with those in an electric motor.

▶ **Predict** the conditions under which a transformer will operate.

Think about what happens when you turn on an electric light. You simply flick a switch, and a room is filled with light. You know that light uses electricity, but do you know how electricity it uses is produced?

You learned that electric current can produce a magnetic field. Did you know that a magnetic field can produce electricity? The electric power that operates your lights comes from a generator that changes magnetic force into electricity. Electricity moves through wires like those shown in Figure 12.14 to supply energy to electric clocks, motors, and appliances. Actually, most electric devices in today's world depend on the electricity produced by magnetism.

**Figure 12.14** ▲
This tower is part of a network that supplies power to many homes and buildings. How does this tower compare to the power poles near your home?

## Induction of Electric Current

After Oersted showed that an electric current can produce magnetic fields, scientists began to wonder if they could reverse the process. They hypothesized that magnetic fields could somehow produce electric currents. Two scientists, Joseph Henry of the United States and Michael Faraday of England, worked independently to test this hypothesis.

Henry and Faraday both learned that when they placed a strong magnet next to a wire coil, a brief surge of current existed in the coil. However, if they moved the magnet in and out of the coil, current flowed through the coil. As long as the magnet was moving, the current would continue to flow. This process of inducing a current by moving a magnetic field through a wire coil without touching it is known as **electromagnetic induction**.

# Electromagnetic Induction

To observe the process of electromagnetic induction, look at Figure 12.15. As the magnet moves through the wire coil, it induces an electric current. The direction of the magnet's motion affects the direction of the electric current.

Electromagnetic induction occurs any time motion takes place between the wire and the magnetic field. The results are the same when the wire moves, when the magnetic field moves, or when both move. The speed of the motion affects the strength of the electric current. A weak current is produced when the movement of the wire or the magnetic field is slow. A strong current is produced when the movement is fast. The number of loops in the wire coil also affects the strength of the current. If two wire coils with different numbers of loops are moved through the same magnetic field, the current will be stronger in the coil with the larger number of loops.

Any changing magnetic field will induce a current. For example, changing current in an electric circuit induces current to flow in a nearby circuit that isn't connected to it. A steady current won't do this. Why do you think the current must be changing?

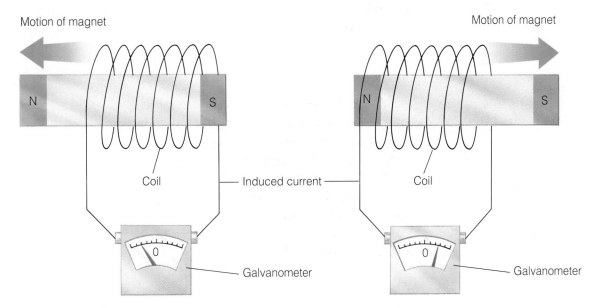

**Figure 12.15** ▲
Look at the needle and direction of the magnet in the art above. How do the galvanometer needles in each figure relate to the direction of the magnets?

# Uses of Electromagnetic Induction

Because a moving magnetic field induces current in a wire coil, it is possible to build many useful devices. For example, generators use electromagnetic induction to make electric power that you use in your home and school. Transformers use electromagnetic induction to change the voltage and current between different locations.

**Generators**   One of the most common devices that uses electromagnetic induction is an electric generator. Any device that creates an electric current by turning a coil of wire through a magnetic field is a *generator*. A generator changes mechanical energy into electric energy. A simple AC generator has an armature, permanent magnet, and slip rings. Study the generator in Figure 12.16.

**Figure 12.16
Simple AC Generator** ▼

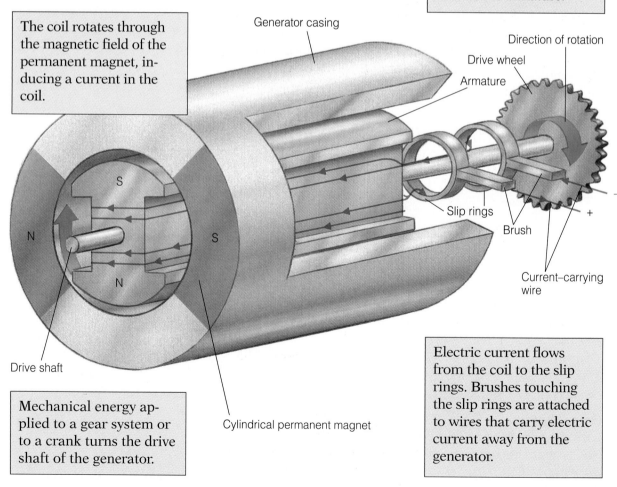

The armature contains an electromagnet and is free to spin on a drive shaft. A permanent magnet surrounds the armature.

The coil rotates through the magnetic field of the permanent magnet, inducing a current in the coil.

Generator casing

Direction of rotation

Drive wheel

Armature

Slip rings

Brush

Current–carrying wire

Drive shaft

Cylindrical permanent magnet

Mechanical energy applied to a gear system or to a crank turns the drive shaft of the generator.

Electric current flows from the coil to the slip rings. Brushes touching the slip rings are attached to wires that carry electric current away from the generator.

**Transformers** Transformers use electromagnetic induction to change the voltage and current in a circuit. Look at Figures 12.17 and 12.18. Step-up transformers increase the voltage and decrease the current. Step-down transformers reduce the voltage and increase the current.

Transformers adjust the voltage for appliances that use voltages greater or smaller than the 120 volts supplied by electric companies in the United States. Transformers also make it possible to send power over long distances through power lines.

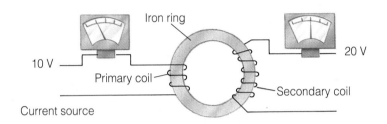

**Figure 12.17**
This is called a step-up transformer. How is the amount of current in the primary coil different from the amount of current in the secondary coil?

As current moves through a wire, the wire gets hot. When heat is lost, energy is lost. Less energy is lost as heat when voltage is high and current is low. Power companies avoid the loss of power by sending high-voltage electricity along power lines. However, the voltage needed in your home is less than the voltage in the power line. Step-down transformers reduce the voltage in the lines connected to your home.

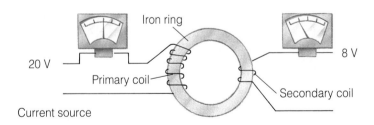

**Figure 12.18**
This is called a step-down transformer. How is the amount of current in the primary coil different from the amount of current in the secondary coil?

A transformer has a primary coil wound around one portion of a soft iron core. The primary coil is connected to the power source. A secondary coil winds around an opposite portion of the soft iron core. The wire from the secondary coil connects to the wiring in your home.

As current in the primary coil alternates and changes, it induces a magnetic field in the soft-iron core. The changing magnetic field induces a current in the secondary coil. When the current in the circuit changes, the voltage also changes.

*Charting the Course*

A flowchart is like a map of the steps involved in a process. Boxes, each with one step, are connected by lines to show the process. Create a flowchart of the energy conversions that take place as you pedal a bicycle to operate a generator light.

**SKILLS WORKOUT**

**Figure 12.19** ▲
How does a small bike generator convert your energy into light?

When you ride a bike, you can generate enough energy to light your path! A small generator attached to a bicycle wheel can use the wheel's rotation to produce enough electricity to light a lamp. Where do you think this mechanical energy comes from?

The light bulb's energy source is the food you eat. Food contains stored energy. Your body converts the food to chemical energy that moves your leg muscles. Your muscles move your legs, transferring mechanical energy to the pedals of the bicycle. Mechanical energy transfers from the pedals to the gears that turn the bike's rear wheel. Mechanical energy from the turning wheels transfers to the generator's drive shaft. A permanent magnet on the drive shaft induces an electric current in the coil. This electric current supplies the energy that lights the bulb in the lamp.

In the evening, when you ride a bicycle with the generator against the wheel, you probably notice that the bicycle is more difficult to pedal. Your observation agrees with the principles of energy conservation. The work you do to supply current to the light bulb increases the amount of energy you need to pedal the bicycle.

You might also notice that the faster you pedal, the brighter the generator light becomes. The light gets brighter because the increase in energy that you supply by pedaling increases the amount of current the generator produces. The faster you pedal, the faster the electromagnet spins. When more current is generated, the bulb is brighter.

## Check and Explain

1. Name two ways a magnet can induce current in a wire.

2. Describe two uses of electromagnetic induction.

3. **Compare and Contrast**  Describe how energy conversion in an electric motor differs from the energy conversion in a generator.

4. **Predict**  What would happen if the number of coils on both sides of a transformer were the same?

# Chapter 12 Review

## Concept Summary

### 12.1 Magnets and Magnetism

▶ A magnet has two magnetic poles and is surrounded by a magnetic field. Like poles repel and unlike poles attract.

▶ Metals contain magnetic regions called domains. When the poles of the domains line up in the same direction, the metal is magnetized.

▶ The earth has a magnetic field that resembles a giant bar magnet.

### 12.2 Electricity to Magnetism

▶ An electric current in a wire produces a magnetic field around the wire. The magnetic poles change when the direction of the current changes.

▶ An electric motor converts electric energy to mechanical energy. A spinning electromagnet turns a drive shaft that does work.

▶ In a galvanometer, an electromagnet works against springs to move a pointer along a numbered scale.

### 12.3 Magnetism to Electricity

▶ When a magnetic field moves through a wire coil, it induces an electric current.

▶ Electromagnetic induction is used to operate electric generators, transformers, and many other devices.

▶ A generator converts mechanical energy to electric energy. An outside energy source turns a drive shaft that rotates a coil in a magnetic field.

## Chapter Vocabulary

magnetic pole (12.1)

magnetic field (12.1)

magnetic domain (12.1)

permanent magnet (12.1)

compass (12.1)

electromagnet (12.2)

electromagnetic induction (12.3)

## Check Your Vocabulary

Use the vocabulary words above to complete the following sentences correctly.

1. A current-carrying wire wrapped around an iron core is (a)n ____ .

2. A magnetized steel needle that aligns with the magnetic field of the earth is a(n) ____ .

3. Every magnet has a north and a south ____ .

4. During the process of ____ , a magnetic field moves across a wire coil.

5. Every magnet is surrounded by a(n) ____ .

6. Iron atoms respond to a microscopic magnetic region called a(n) ____ .

7. Unlike a(n) ____ , an electromagnet can be turned on and off.

Pair each numbered word with a vocabulary term. Explain in a complete sentence how the words are related.

1. Alignment
2. Nickel
3. Pattern
4. Two
5. Direction
6. Coil
7. Generator
8. Aurora
9. Galvanometer

## Write Your Vocabulary

Write sentences using the vocabulary words above. Show that you know what each word means.

# Chapter 12 Review

## Check Your Knowledge

Answer the following in complete sentences.

1. What is magnetism?

2. What are the two kinds of magnets? Describe each type.

3. What is a magnetic field? Where is a magnetic field strongest?

4. How is the earth like a magnet?

5. Explain how a compass works.

6. Why can an electromagnet be turned on and off?

7. List the steps involved in the operation of an electric motor.

8. Describe how an electric generator produces electricity.

9. What does a transformer do?

10. Name five everyday devices that contain electromagnets.

Choose the answer that best completes each sentence.

11. A compass needle always points to the earth's (north geographic pole, south geographic pole, north magnetic pole, sun).

12. When you cut a magnet in half you get (a north pole and a south pole, one north pole, two magnets, one south pole).

13. The armature of a generator rotates because (like poles repel, unlike poles attract, current flows out, an outside force turns it).

## Check Your Understanding

Apply the concepts you have learned to answer each question.

1. How are magnetic poles like electric charges? How are they different?

2. Auroras are seen most often in the regions near the earth's north and south magnetic poles. Suggest a possible reason for this.

3. **Mystery Photo**  The photograph on page 286 is an artificially colored magnetic resonance image, or MRI, of a section of a human head. To create the image, the patient is placed inside a machine with a huge magnet. The magnetic field causes the nuclei of certain atoms within the body to line up. The machine then sends out a radio signal that causes the nuclei to change direction. These changes create weak radio signals that a computer shows as an image.

   a. What parts of the head can you identify?

   b. Why do you think that MRI is a useful tool for doctors?

4. **Critical Thinking**  How is an electric motor like a generator? How is it different?

5. **Application**  Many small, electric devices require low voltage and can't be plugged directly into a wall socket. A small box plugs into the wall socket. A wire connects the device to the box. Explain what is happening in the box.

## Develop Your Skills

Use the skills you have developed in this chapter to complete each activity.

1. **Make a Model**  Make a model of the magnetic field of a bar magnet.

2. **Interpret Data**  The drawing below shows four electromagnets. Each is made from a coil of current-carrying wire wrapped around a nail. Using what you have learned about electromagnets, answer the following questions.

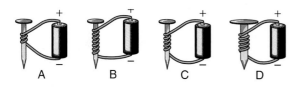

a. Which electromagnet produces a stronger magnetic field? *A* or *B*? Why?

b. Which electromagnet produces a stronger magnetic field? *C* or *D*? Why?

c. Which electromagnet produces a stronger magnetic field? *B* or *C*? Why?

3. **Data Bank**  The map on page 639 shows lines of magnetic declination in the continental United States.

a. Why are the lines closer together at the top of the map than at the bottom?

b. In what state does a compass point to true north?

c. If you read a compass in Maine, how many degrees and in what direction does your compass needle vary from true north?

d. In Los Angeles, is true north to the left or to the right of magnetic north?

## Make Connections

1. **Link the Concepts**  Below is a concept map showing how some of the main concepts in this chapter link together. Only part of the map is filled in. Finish the map, using words and ideas you find on the previous pages.

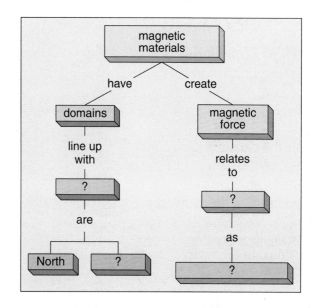

2. **Science and Social Studies**  Navigation has been an important task for people all over the world since ancient times. Research the methods used by different cultures for navigation. Compare and contrast methods that involve the earth's magnetic field with other methods of navigation.

3. **Science and Literature**  During the 1800s, different explorers led expeditions in an effort to be the first humans to reach the earth's north or south poles. The real-life adventure stories of these expeditions are available at the library. Locate a book about one of these expeditions and write a report on it.

# Chapter 13   Electronics

## Chapter Sections

**13.1** Electronic Devices

**13.2** Audio and Video Electronics

**13.3** Computers

## What do you see?

"The picture in question appears to be a close-up of a microchip used in computers and appliances. Computer chips are often used for calculating large and complicated problems and for processing and storing information. You would find them in computers and appliances such as televisions for changing colors and volume."

*Li Ping Chu*
*Sage Park Middle School*
*Windsor, Connecticut*

To find out more about the photograph, look on page 328. As you read this chapter, you will learn about electronic devices and how they work.

# 13.1 Electronic Devices

## Objectives

▶ **Relate** electric currents to signals.

▶ **Explain** how a vacuum-tube amplifier works.

▶ **Generalize** about the advantages of semiconductors over vacuum tubes.

▶ **Compare** and **contrast** various types of vacuum-tube and semiconductor devices.

How has the world changed over the past 50 years? Your grandparents would probably mention advances in electronics. A radio used to be so big you needed two strong arms to lift it. Today you can wear a radio on your head and forget it's even there! The electronic pen shown in Figure 13.1 was not commonly used until recent years. Computers once filled several rooms. Today, business people can carry computers in their briefcases.

## Types of Electronic Devices

The specialized field of **electronics** deals with the behavior and control of electric currents. You know that electric current is moving electrons. Electronics uses electric current to carry information in the form of a signal. Signals represent sounds, pictures, numbers, or other information. Electric current is controlled using electronic devices. Computers, radar scanners, or other kinds of electronic equipment may contain hundreds to millions of electronic devices.

Electronic devices can be divided into two main groups: those that use vacuum tubes and those that use semiconductors. Older electronic devices used vacuum tubes. Televisions still use a special type of vacuum tube to produce a picture. Most newer devices, use semiconductors. Radios, calculators, computers, and many other kinds of electronic equipment use semiconductors. An important function of vacuum tubes and semiconductors in electronic devices is to strengthen, or amplify, weak electric signals.

**Figure 13.1** ▲
This laser pen is really an electronic scanner. The laser reads information coded in a bar code, such as the item's name and price.

# Vacuum Tubes

The careful control of electrons began with the **vacuum tube**. The first vacuum tube was developed for commercial use in 1904. It had two terminals, or electrodes, and was called a **diode**. Electrons flow through a diode in only one direction. Diodes strongly resist the flow of electric current in the opposite direction. Look at Figure 13.2 to see how a simple vacuum-tube diode works.

**Figure 13.2    A Vacuum Tube** ▼

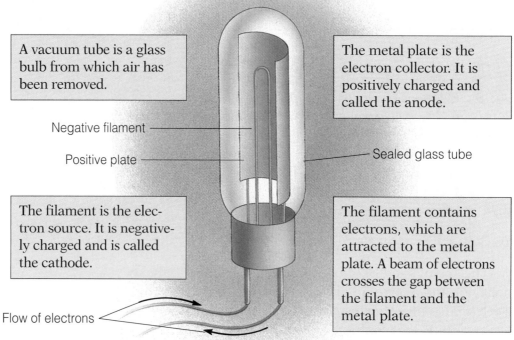

A vacuum tube is a glass bulb from which air has been removed.

The metal plate is the electron collector. It is positively charged and called the anode.

Negative filament

Positive plate

Sealed glass tube

The filament is the electron source. It is negatively charged and is called the cathode.

The filament contains electrons, which are attracted to the metal plate. A beam of electrons crosses the gap between the filament and the metal plate.

Flow of electrons

**Rectifiers**   Some vacuum-tube diodes are **rectifiers**. A rectifier changes alternating current into direct current. The electricity supplied to your home by an electric power company is alternating current. Recall that in each alternating current cycle the electrons move first in one direction and then in the other.

Alternating current passes easily through rectifiers in one direction, but not in the opposite direction. Current will only pass through the rectifier during half of each AC cycle. The resulting current is direct and pulses in only one direction. Some electronic equipment has parts that require direct current. This equipment contains rectifiers so that it can operate on the alternating current in your home. Televisions, computers, and microwave ovens are a few examples of electronic equipment that contain rectifiers.

**Amplifiers** Small, unsteady electric currents, or signals, carry information that is strengthened by amplifiers. For example, a signal is set up in your radio antenna as it receives a broadcast from your favorite radio station. Amplifiers in your radio strengthen the signal, and you hear the music. Amplifiers also increase the strength of weak signals produced by playing a phonograph record. As it makes contact with the grooves in a vinyl record, a phonograph needle creates signals. The amplifier makes the signal powerful enough to operate a loudspeaker. In modern electronic equipment, amplifiers have been replaced by semiconductors. Figure 13.3 shows how a vacuum-tube amplifier works with a loudspeaker.

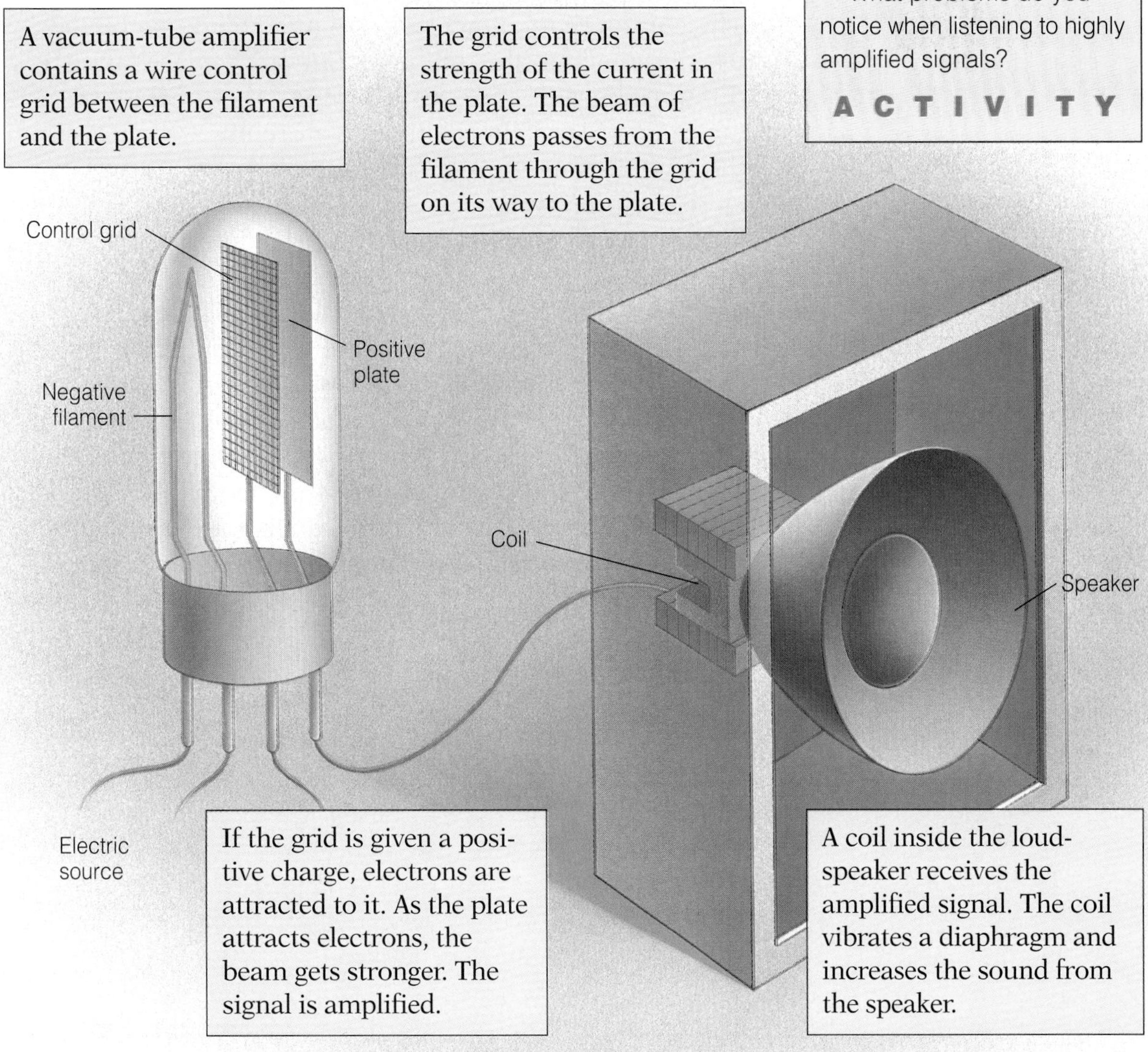

**Astronomy**

**L I N K**

Radio telescopes use amplifiers to increase the strength of incoming radio waves. You can investigate amplified signals. Obtain a microphone, speakers, and an amplifier.

**1.** Set up the system. Turn the volume up high.

**2.** Sitting quietly, listen to the amplified signals. Tap on the microphone and describe the result.

What problems do you notice when listening to highly amplified signals?

**A C T I V I T Y**

**Figure 13.3   A Vacuum-Tube Amplifier** ▼

A vacuum-tube amplifier contains a wire control grid between the filament and the plate.

The grid controls the strength of the current in the plate. The beam of electrons passes from the filament through the grid on its way to the plate.

Control grid

Positive plate

Negative filament

Coil

Speaker

Electric source

If the grid is given a positive charge, electrons are attracted to it. As the plate attracts electrons, the beam gets stronger. The signal is amplified.

A coil inside the loudspeaker receives the amplified signal. The coil vibrates a diaphragm and increases the sound from the speaker.

# ACTIVITY

### Dopey Devices

Research the development of semiconductors. When were they developed and how were they used?

**SKILLS WORKOUT**

## Semiconductors

Today most electronic devices use semiconducting materials to control electrons. A **semiconductor** is a substance that has a conductivity range between that of a conductor and that of an insulator. Like vacuum tubes, semiconductors are used to amplify currents. Semiconductors have several advantages over vacuum tubes. They are much smaller and give off less heat than vacuum tubes do. Semiconductors also last longer, cost less, use less electricity, and are very durable.

You know that the difference between a conductor and an insulator depends on how electrons move through them. The elements germanium and silicon have crystal structures that cause them to act like diodes. Current passes easily through these elements in one direction only. The conductivity of germanium and silicon increases when a small number of their atoms are replaced with a different kind of atom, called an impurity. Small amounts of these impurities add or remove electrons from the crystal structure of a substance.

Two different types of semiconductors being manufactured are shown in Figure 13.4. The difference between them is the type of impurity used. If the impurity is arsenic, which adds electrons, the semiconductor is called a negative-type, or n-type, semiconductor. If the impurity is gallium, which leaves a lack of electrons in the semiconductor, it becomes slightly positively charged. This is called a positive-type, or p-type, semiconductor. Thin layers of n-type and p-type semiconducting materials sandwiched together make up transistors. Transistors and integrated circuits use semiconducting material.

**Figure 13.4**

Adding impurities to semiconductors to increase their conductivity is called doping. ▼

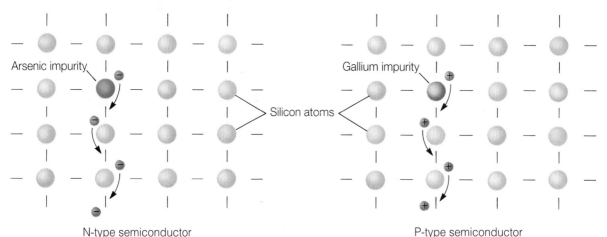

Arsenic impurity

Silicon atoms

Gallium impurity

N-type semiconductor

P-type semiconductor

**Transistors** A semiconducting device that contains layered n-type and p-type semiconducting materials is called a **transistor**. A transistor has three semiconducting sections. Each section is treated with a different impurity. Small wires attached to the layers conduct electricity in and out. The middle portion, called the base, is usually about 0.001 cm thick. The semiconductors on either side of the base are called the emitter and the collector. Weak signals pass through the transistor and are amplified. Today engineers can put more than 100,000 transistors on a silicon chip. A typical chip is about the size of a fingernail!

The commercial use of transistors began in the early 1950s. They were used as amplifiers in hearing aids and pocket radios. By the 1960s, diodes and semiconducting amplifiers had replaced vacuum tubes in many kinds of electronic equipment. In the 1990s, you have transistors in your radio, stereo, and pocket calculator. Some different kinds of transistors are shown in Figure 13.5.

**Integrated Circuits** A recent breakthrough in electronics is the development of miniaturized circuits. These tiny circuits are called **integrated circuits**. An integrated circuit consists of a tiny semiconductor crystal, or silicon chip, which is razor thin.

This single silicon chip contains extremely small amounts of impurities placed at specific locations. Transistors, diodes, resistors, and other circuit elements are constructed at these locations.

Connections between these circuit elements are made by painting "wires" on the chip. It is possible to create a complicated electronic network within a very small area. Wires also connect the integrated circuit to other devices. A small portion of an integrated circuit, or chip, is shown in Figure 13.6.

Integrated circuits have greatly reduced the size of electronic instruments and have revolutionized our way of life. Integrated circuits are much smaller and lighter than wired circuits and are often substituted for them. Home computers, digital watches, spacecraft, and calculators all use integrated circuits.

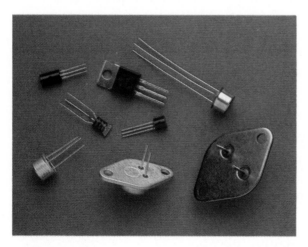

**Figure 13.5** ▲
Transistors come in a variety of shapes and sizes. How are these transistors alike? How are they different?

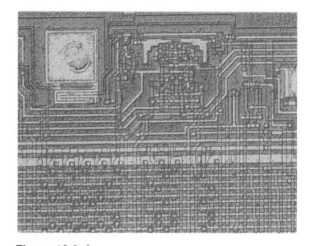

**Figure 13.6** ▲
This small portion of an integrated circuit contains 1,000 electronic devices. It is about the size of a baby's fingernail.

## Science and Society *Smart Cards*

An automatic teller machine, or ATM , card and credit cards make it convenient to get cash and to make large purchases. Some people carry a dozen or more plastic cards in their wallets. The cards are easy to carry, but it can be time consuming to deal with the monthly bills for each card. Wouldn't it be more convenient to have just one card? What if it could do more than all the other cards combined?

Credit cards would be more useful if they were "smarter." "Smart cards" look like traditional credit cards but are actually miniature computers. They are composed of tiny electronic circuits, chips, and digital memories sandwiched together.

Smart cards and ATM cards are similar. When inserted into card-reader terminals, a personal identification number, or PIN, is requested. Once the PIN is approved, you tell the terminal the type of transaction you want to make.

Instead of accessing information from a central source like the ATM card does, a smart card stores the information on its own chip. When a purchase is made with a smart card, a record of the transaction is stored in the card's chip. The amount of the purchase can be automatically deducted from the holder's bank account.

In Japan and in many European countries, smart cards are already being used. Banks, transportation systems, telephones, and pay TV use smart cards. In fact, within 15 years, you will probably use a smart card almost daily to make all sorts of transactions.

Microchip

**Figure 13.7** ▲

A smart card is like an ATM card and a credit card, but can do more.

---

## Check and Explain

1. How does electronics use electric current?

2. How does a vacuum-tube amplifier work?

3. **Generalize** What are the advantages semiconductors have over vacuum tubes?

4. **Compare and Contrast** Describe the similarities and differences between vacuum tubes and semiconducting devices.

# 13.2 Audio and Video Electronics

## Objectives

▶ **Describe** how a telephone works.

▶ **Distinguish** between analog and digital signals.

▶ **Communicate** how a TV works.

▶ **Compare** sound recording techniques.

Whenever you watch TV, talk on the telephone, or listen to compact disks (CDs) or tapes, you are using audio and video communication. You know that audio refers to sound and video refers to pictures. Often audio and video are used together to create a sound-and-sight combination. TV combines audio and video communication.

During the past 20 years, cable TV, video cassette recorders, or VCRs, cellular phones, and video games have become commonplace. Advances in audio and video electronics are being made so rapidly that it's difficult to know what kinds of electronics people will use 20 years from now. What kind of electronic equipment do you predict will become commonplace in the next 20 years?

## Audio

People have always found ways to communicate with each other over some distance. They have used drums, written letters, and even used mirrors to send messages. The development of electricity made communication rapid and reliable. In the United States, one of the first ways that people communicated over electric wires was with the telegraph. The telegraph was patented in 1844 by Samuel F. B. Morse.

Vacuum tubes improved early radios and made TV possible. Transistors made radios and TVs smaller and more powerful. Today one of the most important audio communication devices is still the telephone. People around the world are able to communicate instantly by telephone.

**Figure 13.8 ▲**
The telegraph was one of the first electronic ways of sending messages. What are two ways to send electronic messages today?

**Radio** When your favorite radio station broadcasts, it sends out radio waves from a transmitting antenna. The waves become a small, unsteady current, or signal, in the antenna of your radio. A receiver inside your radio picks up the signal. An amplifier in your radio strengthens the signal to separate it from the broadcasts sent by other radio stations. Another amplifier in the radio strengthens the separated signal so that it is strong enough to operate the loudspeakers in your radio.

**Telephone** The telephone in your home has a transmitter and a receiver. The transmitter changes sounds from your voice into a signal. The signal travels over wires to your friend's telephone. The receiver in your friend's telephone changes the signal back into sound. To see how your telephone works, look at Figure 13.9.

**Figure 13.9 The Telephone** ▼

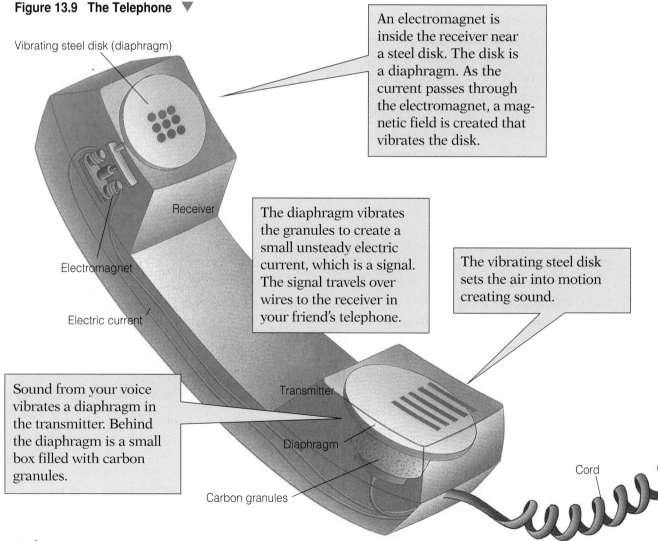

Vibrating steel disk (diaphragm)

An electromagnet is inside the receiver near a steel disk. The disk is a diaphragm. As the current passes through the electromagnet, a magnetic field is created that vibrates the disk.

Receiver

The diaphragm vibrates the granules to create a small unsteady electric current, which is a signal. The signal travels over wires to the receiver in your friend's telephone.

The vibrating steel disk sets the air into motion creating sound.

Electromagnet

Electric current

Sound from your voice vibrates a diaphragm in the transmitter. Behind the diaphragm is a small box filled with carbon granules.

Transmitter

Diaphragm

Cord

Carbon granules

**Sound Recording** Sound can be recorded in two ways, as analog or digital sound. Records and tapes are analog sound recordings. CDs are digital sound recordings.

Analog sound recording is a process of engraving a tape or record with waves that represent the structure of the sound. To make a record, the sound is first recorded on a stereo master tape. A metal stereo master disk is made from the tape. To make the master disk, electric signals representing sounds are sent from the tape to a sharp recording cutter. The cutter engraves a wavy groove in a plastic-coated metal disk. The pattern of the groove determines the sounds recorded on the record. Plastic copies are made from the master disk.

Digital sound recording is a process of etching microscopic pits on the underside of an aluminum and plastic disk. Pitted regions represent 0s. Regions without pits represent 1s. A laser beam scans the disk. The 0s and 1s form a digital signal. A resistor in the CD player converts the digital recording into an analog signal. The analog signal is amplified and played back through loudspeakers.

The quality of the music produced by digital sound recording is much better than the quality of music on records or cassette tapes. Unlike a record or tape that uses a needle or magnetic head to pick up signals, light is the only thing that touches the CD. Therefore, the

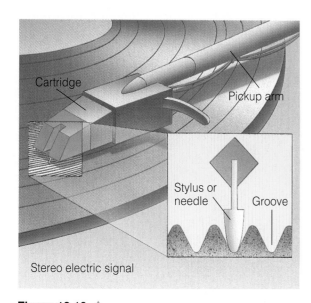

**Figure 13.10** ▲

When the stylus rides in the record's groove an analog signal is produced.

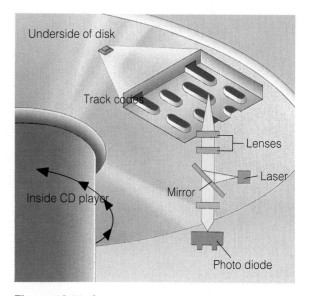

**Figure 13.11** ▲

When the laser scans the underside of the CD, a digital signal is produced.

## Meteorology
### L I N K

Weather conditions greatly affect how well audio and video signals can be received. To explore how weather affects transmitted signals, you need either a television that is hooked up to an antenna, or a radio.

**1.** On a clear, calm day see how many channels or stations your device receives. Describe the quality of each channel or station.

**2.** Repeat the above step on a stormy, rainy day.

Compare your observations on the two different days. Explain the effect of weather on transmitted signals.

### A C T I V I T Y

**Figure 13.12**

How does the CRT create a picture from an electric signal? ▼

surface of a CD doesn't scratch or wear down. The two-hundredth play of the CD is as good as the first play. The music played from a CD is free of the pops, crackles, and hisses you might hear on a record or tape.

CDs can be played in cars just like audio tapes. Automobile CD players have an extra track on each side of the main track. This extra track helps to keep the laser light focused when the car hits a bump.

## Video

Video communication technology began with the type of vacuum tube called the **c**athode-**r**ay **t**ube, or CRT. A CRT is a large vacuum tube that contains an electron source at one end and a fluorescent screen at the other end. The picture tube used in TVs, in computer display terminals, and in oscilloscopes is a CRT.

**Television** When you watch TV, you are looking at a CRT. The diagram in Figure 13.12 shows how a TV picture is created. A video signal is received from a TV antenna. The signal passes through a tuner and decoder and instructs three electron guns in the CRT to shoot electron beams at the screen. The beams sweep across the screen's inner surface the same way your eyes sweep across each line on this page.

The inside of the screen has tiny circles of fluorescent

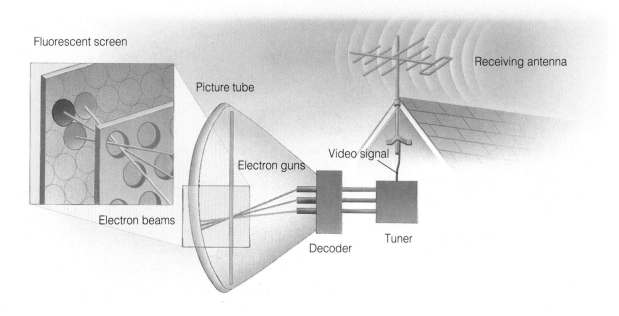

Fluorescent screen

Picture tube

Receiving antenna

Electron guns

Video signal

Electron beams

Decoder

Tuner

material that give off red, green, and blue lights. Three electron beams, one for each primary color, scan across the shadow mask behind the screen. The mask contains holes. The beams pass through the holes and strike the stripes of fluorescent material. Each beam strikes only circles of the correct color. The circles light up as each beam passes. The brightness of the circles depends on the strength of the beam. The information for controlling and directing the beams is coded within the color-picture signal.

**Video Recording**  VCRs can record TV programs on a video cassette so you can watch them at any time. Audio and video signals that represent the TV show are transferred to videotape. The audio and video signals from a TV station go to audio and video heads inside your VCR. The signals create changing magnetic fields in the heads. The video tape contains magnetic particles on its surface. As the video tape passes over the heads, the mag-

## Consider This

### Do Computer Networks Invade Your Privacy?

Computers offer you many advantages. They can store enormous amounts of information for you and about you. They will play an even larger role in your life in the future.

Computers from banks, stores, medical facilities, and insurance and government agencies store information about you. These computers are linked together. Computers that are linked together form computer networks. These networks make it easy to identify you in an emergency or when you use your credit card.

Computer networks also have disadvantages. The biggest concern is privacy. By storing your personal information on computer networks, many people have access to information that could be used against you. Advertisers, insurance agents, politicians, and many other groups of people would be interested in knowing what you buy, the state of your health, who you call on the telephone, and other information about you. How might personal information be used against you?

**Consider Some Issues**  Is the increased convenience provided by computer networks worth the risk of having your privacy invaded?

**Think About It**  An insurance company finds out through a computer network that you have a family history of heart disease. Should the company be allowed to deny you medical insurance even though you seem perfectly healthy?

**Write About It**  Pretend you are a U.S. senator. Write a report in which you: (a) Identify the issue of having personal information stored on computer networks. (b) Write a law that would minimize the problem.

netic fields change the patterns of the magnetic particles on the tape. The pattern of the magnetic particles recorded on the video tape corresponds to the TV signals. The audio and video signals are magnetically recorded in diagonal tracks on the videotape.

To replay the video tape, it is reversed through the heads of a VCR. The heads convert the magnetic recordings on the video tape to audio and video signals. These signals are sent to a TV and changed back into sounds and pictures.

## Science and Technology *CD-ROM*

Compact Disc-Read-Only Memory systems, or CD-ROM, is a technology that might change the way you learn and play. A CD-ROM system is a product that uses the visuals of a TV, the control of a computer, and the sound capability of a CD player. The system includes a disc, a player, and a computer or television.

CD-ROM is a multi-media technology. Each medium is digitized so a computer can understand and control it. A program can jump back and forth between video, film, CD-quality sound, graphics, animation, photos, and text.

Perhaps the most exciting thing about CD-ROM is that it is interactive. The user controls the action, or information. The interactive feature makes it an easy way to learn about or to do almost anything. By touching the screen with your finger, or moving a "mouse," you can interrupt the program, go instantly back to any previous spot, or explore a concept in more detail. You can manipulate the information in many ways to match your learning style. CD-ROM is already used in industry, entertainment, and education.

## Check and Explain

1. Describe how a telephone works.

2. How are analog and digital signals different?

3. **Communicate** How does a color television form a picture?

4. **Compare and Contrast** How do sound recording techniques differ for records and CDs?

# Activity 13 *How are dots used to make pictures?*

**Skills** Hypothesize; Infer; Observe; Compare and Contrast

## Task 1 Prelab Prep
Collect the following items: a large, simple color picture from a magazine, a piece of "tracing" graph paper, tape, and colored pencils or pens.

## Task 2 Data Record
Construct a table like Table 13.1.

**Table 13.1 Dot picture observation**

| Distance | Observation |
|----------|-------------|
| 1 m | |
| 3 m | |
| 5 m | |
| 7 m | |
| 9 m | |

## Task 3 Procedure
1. Discuss with a classmate how you think newspaper and television pictures are made. Give reasons why you think so.
2. Write down your hypothesis.
3. Tape a piece of graph paper over the magazine picture.

4. Color each small square on the graph paper entirely with the one color that best matches the color of the picture underneath the square.
5. Repeat this process until each square is colored.
6. You now have two 8 1/2″× 11″ pictures: the original magazine picture and your copy of it made with colored squares. Hang both pictures next to each other on a wall or bulletin board.
7. Compare the graph-paper picture to the original picture at the following distances. Briefly describe your observations in your table.
   a) 1 m
   b) 3 m
   c) 5 m
   d) 7 m
   e) 9 m

## Task 4 Analysis
1. At what distance do the two pictures look most similar? Why?
2. How would increasing or decreasing the size of the graph-paper squares affect the clarity of the graph-paper picture?

## Task 5 Conclusion
Explain how pictures are made from tiny dots or squares. Discuss how your distance from the dot picture and the size of the dots affect how clear the picture appears.

## Extension
Use a magnifying glass to look closely at a newspaper picture. If a TV is available in your classroom, use a magnifying glass to look at the screen. How are newspaper and TV pictures similar to your graph picture? How are they different? How do TV and newspaper pictures compare to the magazine picture?

# 13.3 Computers

*Long Multiplication*

Time how long it takes to multiply 4,562 by 9,483 without using a calculator. How long does it take to multiply the same numbers with a calculator? What are some advantages and disadvantages of calculators?

**SKILLS WARMUP**

## Objectives

▶ **Identify** the parts of a computer.

▶ **Compare** the advantages and disadvantages of computer networks.

▶ **Classify** parts of a computer as hardware or software.

M any business transactions involve computers. When you buy groceries or check a book out of your library, the transaction is recorded in a computer. Business, government, medicine, science, and most industries rely heavily on computers. Computers are used to diagnose diseases, guide spaceships, forecast weather, and make music. They make robots move and even design new computers. Recent advances in microelectronics allow smaller and more powerful computers to be built.

## Development of Computers

In the 1890s, American inventor Dr. Herman Hollerith developed the "census machine." This device was the first computer to use electricity. The 1890 U.S. census was completed in a record time of three years. In 1946 the United States Army built the Electronic Numerical Integrator and Computer, or ENIAC. Not much more than a gigantic calculator, ENIAC contained thousands of vacuum tubes and used punched tape or cards that carried information. In 1951, the stored-program computer called the Universal Automatic Computer, or UNIVAC, was completed. UNIVAC was the first computer to use magnetic tape instead of punched tape or cards for information input.

As technology developed, computers became smaller, more compact, more versatile, and less expensive. Today computers are made with **microprocessors**. A microprocessor is an integrated circuit that can hold all of a computer's problem-solving capabilities on one small silicon chip.

**Figure 13.13**

The ENIAC computer was made using vacuum tubes. What kind of material replaced vacuum tubes in modern computers? ▼

# Computer Hardware

Computer **hardware** is the equipment and components that make up the computer. Hardware, as shown in Figure 13.14, includes a central processing unit, main storage, input devices, and output devices.

**CPU** The actual computing is done in the central processing unit, or CPU. An important part of the CPU is a microprocessor. The microprocessor is a chip, which stores permanent and short-term memory.

**Main Storage** Main storage hardware holds the information that you input, and saves it for future use. Main storage includes both hard disks and floppy disks. Both hard and floppy disks store information magnetically.

The hard disk contains very large amounts of information and is permanently sealed inside the computer's casing. On the hard disk, information is stored magnetically.

Information can also be stored magnetically on a floppy disk, which is a smaller round tape encased in a small, plastic cassette. A floppy disk can be carried in a pocket and used in any compatible computer. A floppy disk stores less information than a hard disk.

**Input devices** Hardware that is used to load information into the computer is called an input device. The most common input device is the keyboard. A "mouse" is an input device that rolls over a pad. The mouse moves a cursor around the screen, open files, and chooses commands. You can input information into some computers with an electronic pen, also. Some computers even respond to a human voice.

**Output device** An output device receives information from the CPU. Examples include the computer screen and printer. A voice synthesizer and a robot that receives instructions from a computer are also output devices.

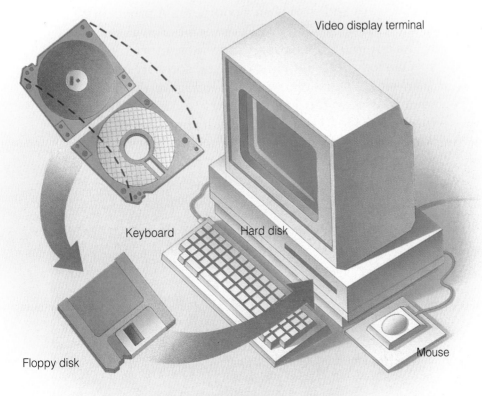

Video display terminal

Keyboard

Hard disk

Mouse

Floppy disk

◀ **Figure 13.14**
A hard disk is built into many personal computers. How is a hard disk different from a floppy disk?

```
100 REM THIS PROGRAM
    WILL GREET YOU BY
    NAME
110 REM N$ = YOUR NAME
120 PRINT "WHAT IS YOUR
    NAME?"
130 INPUT N$
140 PRINT "HELLO"; N$
150 END
```

**Figure 13.15** ▲

The simple numbered statements shown are a program for printing your name. How does this program relate to the flowchart on the next page?

# Computer Software

In order for a computer to operate, it needs a set of instructions that tells it exactly what to do. Programs that instruct the hardware during operation are called **software**. There are two different types of software: applications software and operating-system software. Neither one can function effectively without the other.

Applications software allows you to perform specific tasks without having to write the programs yourself. It is provided by the computer manufacturer or can be purchased from a computer store. Video games are an example of applications software.

Operating-system software is a set of instructions that command the electronic parts inside the computer. The instructions tell the computer to operate in a specific way and to accept instructions from the applications software. Working together, the two programs provide the specific results you desire when you operate the computer.

Thousands of applications-software programs are available for computers. You can create your own computer programs, or you can buy ready-made ones. Packaged programs available for computers include adventure games, spreadsheets, and word-processing programs. Word-processing programs allow you to write essays and stories on a computer. A program is usually saved on a hard disk or on a floppy disk.

As computer technology increases, more highly specialized computer hardware and software are being developed. Virtual reality shown in Figure 13.16, will soon be used in medicine, industry, and entertainment. Interactive video is another new technology that involves video, CD, and computer technologies.

**Figure 13.16** ▶

Virtual reality combines computer software and special hardware to create realistic images. This photo shows what you would see if you were looking through the virtual-reality hardware.

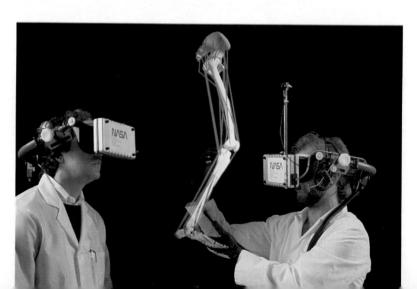

## Computer Networks

One of the fastest-growing areas in communication involves computers linked together so that people can communicate with each other. You can link two computers together by telephone. To do this, you need a hardware device called a "modem" and special communications software.

When a number of computers are linked together, they form a network. When the computers are linked together in the same room or building, a local-area network, or LAN, is formed. LANs connect computers with cables or wires.

In a LAN, one powerful central computer is connected to many smaller computers. Schools and businesses often use this type of network to save time and share data files and programs. Networks can be expanded into global networks that connect computer users by telephone lines and satellites. Global networks allow information to be sent from city to city, across the nation, and to other countries throughout the world.

## *SkillBuilder* *Making Models*

### *Flowcharting*

Software programs tell your computer what to do with the information you input. Computer programmers use flowcharts to plan their programs. A flowchart is a diagram of a program. The flowchart on the right shows a program to print your name. The table beside the flowchart explains the meaning of each shape that is used in a flowchart. In this *SkillBuilder*, you will practice writing a flowchart.

Draw a flowchart for a program that asks for a number and prints it on the screen. Follow the steps below.

**1.** Draw an oval with the word *Start* in it. Draw an arrow pointing downward from the oval to the next step.

**2.** Draw a parallelogram below the arrow. Write a statement in it that asks for a specific number. Draw an arrow pointing downward from the parallelogram.

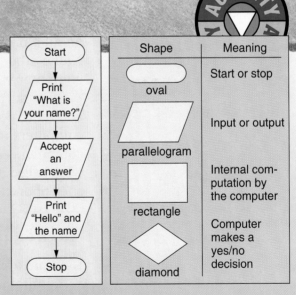

**3.** Draw another parallelogram that asks the computer to print the number on the screen. Draw an arrow downward to the next step.

**4.** Draw an oval with the word *Stop* in it. Look at your flowchart. It should look similar to the one above. Draw a flowchart that asks you to make a yes or no decision.

Computers are getting smaller and smarter! Imagine yourself in science class five years from now. Your teacher asks you to take out your textbook. Instead of a book, you place a small computer on your lap. The teacher asks you to read page 326. You type in *Science* and *page 326*. The text on page 326 instantly appears on the computer screen.

Next the teacher wants you to take some lecture notes. You press several keys, and a new page appears. The new page has the words *Science Notes* and the date on the top of the page. As your teacher delivers the lecture, you take notes on your computer. This kind of computer, called a laptop computer, is already being used worldwide by many business people and some students.

Laptops are personal computers that operate on rechargeable batteries. Because they can fit into a small briefcase, they are commonly used by traveling business people. Travelers can prepare and even print out reports while flying to a meeting. In their parked cars, sales representatives may use laptops to review information about a prospective client before making the sales call. Name other professions or situations where a laptop computer would be useful.

New advances in computer technology, such as smaller and more powerful microprocessing chips, make laptop computers more convenient and useful. Many laptop computers can print documents. Special built-in hardware called a modem allows laptops to send faxes from a telephone.

## ACTIVITY

### Collecting Data

*Prime Programs*

Locate the software ads in a newspaper or magazine. Make a list of the software programs in five ads. Which software programs are advertised the most? What is the prime function of most of the programs in the ads?

**SKILLS WORKOUT**

## Check and Explain

1. What are the main hardware components of a computer?

2. What are the two types of software? Give examples of each.

3. **Compare** What are the advantages and disadvantages of a computer network?

4. **Classify** Identify each of the following as hardware or software: word-processing program, keyboard, hard disk, printer, video game, modem.

# Chapter 13 Review

## Concept Summary

### 13.1 Electronic Devices
▶ Electronic devices use electric current to carry information as a signal.
▶ Electronic devices are made of vacuum tubes or semiconductors.
▶ Amplifiers increase the strength of a signal.
▶ Rectifiers change alternating current to direct current.
▶ Semiconductors act like diodes and contain impurities to increase their conductivity.

### 13.2 Audio and Video Electronics
▶ Sound and visual images are used in audio and video communication.

▶ Phonograph records, as well as audio and video tape recordings, use analog signals.
▶ To make sound, CDs use digital signals, which consist of many different combinations of 0s and 1s.

### 13.3 Computers
▶ Computer hardware is the equipment used in a computer system.
▶ A computer software program gives instructions to the computer hardware during operation.
▶ A network is formed when computers are linked together.

## Chapter Vocabulary

electronics (13.1)  rectifier (13.1)  integrated circuit (13.1)  hardware (13.3)

vacuum tube (13.1)  semiconductor (13.1)  microprocessor (13.3)  software (13.3)

diode (13.1)  transistor (13.1)

## Check Your Vocabulary

Use the vocabulary words above to complete the following sentences correctly.

1. A CPU, main storage, input devices, and output devices are all ____.

2. A device that contains thin layers of semiconducting materials sandwiched together is called a(n) ____.

3. Electronic devices first used ____, to control electrons.

4. A(n) ____ has a conductivity range between that of a conductor and an insulator.

5. Computer programs called ____ instruct hardware during operation.

6. An integrated circuit that holds all a computer's problem-solving capabilities on one silicon chip is called a(n) ____.

7. The specialized field of ____ deals with the behavior and control of electric currents.

8. The first vacuum tube developed for commercial use was the two-electrode tube called a(n) ____.

9. To convert alternating current to direct current, an appliance uses an electronic device called a(n) ____

10. A single silicon chip called a(n) ____ contains transistors, diodes, resistors, and other circuit elements.

## Write Your Vocabulary

Write sentences using each vocabulary word above. Show that you know what each word means.

# Chapter 13 Review

## Check Your Knowledge

Answer the following in complete sentences.

1. What is the function of a rectifier?

2. Identify the function of each part of a telephone.

3. How is an audio tape like a video tape? How is it different?

4. List three uses of computers.

5. How is a floppy disk similar to a hard disk? How is it different?

6. Name the two main types of computer software.

7. Identify three electronic devices in a computer.

8. Describe three advantages of semiconductors over vacuum tubes.

9. How does a vacuum-tube amplifier increase the strength of an electric current?

Determine whether each statement is true or false. Write *true* if it is true. If it is false, change the underlined word to make the statement true.

10. The process of engraving a tape or record with waves that represent sounds is called a <u>digital</u> sound recording.

11. Today most electronic devices use <u>semiconductors</u> to control electrons.

12. The cathode-ray tube inside a television set is a type of <u>vacuum tube</u>.

13. A <u>floppy disk</u> is permanently attached to the inside of the computer.

14. A keyboard is an example of an <u>input device</u>.

15. Electronics uses current as a <u>power source</u>.

## Check Your Understanding

Apply the concepts you have learned to answer each question.

1. **Application**  Describe how a computer network could be used in a business or at your school.

2. How many different kinds of amplifiers does a radio contain? Explain why each amplifier is important in a radio.

3. **Mystery Photo**  The photograph on page 308 shows two 16K integrated circuits, or chips. The photograph shows the chips magnified about 50 times. The green band is the division between the two chips.

   a. What do the circuit paths on each chip look like?

   b. Will electric current flow over the green areas on the chip? Explain your answer.

4. Explain why the quality of sound on a phonograph record is different from the sound quality of a compact disk.

5. **Infer**  Could information on any of the following formats be damaged by a strong magnetic field? Provide a reason for each answer.

   a. CD                  d. Phonograph record
   b. Video tape     e. Floppy disk
   c. Audio tape     f.  Hard disk

6. **Application**  What are the advantages of a floppy disk? What are the advantages of a hard disk? Why would you want your computer to have both?

7. **Critical Thinking**  Why do you think the cost of electronic components has decreased over the years?

## Develop Your Skills

Use the skills you have developed in this chapter to complete each activity.

1. **Interpret Data** Morse code is a system of signals that uses a code of dots and dashes to represent numbers, letters, and punctuation.

   a. Translate this message:

   | ■●● | ■■■ | ■●● | ■ | ■■● | ●● | ●●●■ | ● | ●●■ |
   | ●■■● | ●■●■● | | | | | | | |

   | A<br>●■ | B<br>■●●● | C<br>■●■● | D<br>■●● | E<br>● | F<br>●●■● |
   |---|---|---|---|---|---|
   | G<br>■■● | H<br>●●●● | I<br>●● | J<br>●■■■ | K<br>■●■ | L<br>●■●● |
   | M<br>■■ | N<br>■● | O<br>■■■ | P<br>●■■● | Q<br>■■●■ | R<br>●■● |
   | S<br>●●● | T<br>■ | U<br>●●■ | V<br>●●●■ | W<br>●■■ | X<br>■●●■ |
   | Y<br>■●■■ | Z<br>■■●● | 1<br>●■■■■ | 2<br>●●■■■ | 3<br>●●●■■ | 4<br>●●●●■ |
   | 5<br>●●●●● | 6<br>■●●●● | 7<br>■■●●● | 8<br>■■■●● | 9<br>■■■■● | 0<br>■■■■■ |
   | .<br>●■●■●■ | ,<br>■■●●■■ | ?<br>●●■■●● | S.O.S.<br>●●●■■■●●● | | Start<br>■●■ |
   | End of Message<br>●■●■● | | Understand<br>●■● | | Error<br>●●●●●●●● | |

   b. Write a message to a classmate. Exchange messages and translate the message you receive.

   c. Write a short reply in Morse code to the message you translated.

2. **Communicate** Make a flowchart that shows how you get ready for school in the morning.

3. **Data Bank** Use the information on page 636 to answer the following questions.

   a. Copy the time line onto a piece of paper; then add events you learned about in this chapter that are missing.

   b. Extend the time line to show how you think computers will change in the next 5 to 20 years. Illustrate your predictions.

## Make Connections

1. **Link the Concepts** Make a concept map to show how the following concepts from this chapter link together: electronic devices, vacuum tubes, semiconductors, diodes, CRTs, amplify, rectify, transistors, and integrated circuits.

2. **Science and Media** Science fiction often discusses the future and technology. Find a science fiction book at the library, or watch a science fiction show on TV. While you read or watch, keep a list of predictions that are made about advances in electronic technology. Write a brief report explaining why you think these predictions could or couldn't come true.

3. **Science and Social Studies** Some of the earliest computers were used in the national census. Research the current role of computers in the national census. How do computers make compiling and sorting information easier, faster, or better? What type of computers does the Census Bureau use? Is census information available to companies or the public on floppy disks?

4. **Science and Society** Choose one electronic device or piece of electronic equipment that has been invented or has become a common consumer item since you were born. Use the library to do research to provide the following information about the item you choose:

   a. Identify the device or equipment.

   b. How and when was it developed?

   c. What is it used for?

   d. How does it work?

   e. How has it changed society?

# Science and Literature Connection

It wasn't a bad birthday as birthdays go. After dinner Uncle Rocky took me aside and slipped a ten-dollar bill into my hand. "Buy something you really like," he whispered.

Just before they left, Aunt Jean cornered me in the kitchen and tucked a twenty-dollar bill into my skirt pocket.

"I meant to put it inside the lamp, but I forgot," she said.

And then, after they left, we all watched one of my favorite movies on the VCR: *A Night at the Opera*. The Marx Brothers always make me laugh, no matter how down I am.

I had one last piece of birthday cheesecake and went up to my room.

"Close your windows," my mother said. "It's just starting to rain.". . .

Suddenly there was a tremendous clap of thunder and a bolt of lightning so bright that I could see it even through my closed eyelids.

"YIKES!" I opened my eyes. It was completely dark in my room. I blinked a couple of times, trying to see.

"Jeannie?" my father called. "Are you okay?"

"It's dark in here!"

"The lights went out. That was a close one."

Another flash of lightning lit up my room for a moment. I noticed the teapot lamp on my night table.

"Hey!" I yelled. "If someone would bring me a match I could light this stupid lamp Aunt Jean gave me. I don't think it will do any good, but . . ."

## Genie With the Light Blue Hair

*The following excerpts are from the novel*
Genie With the Light Blue Hair
*by Ellen Conford*

"Coming right up." A flashlight beam shone on the stairway, and my mother came into my room. . . .

"Isn't it funny," she said, "that we have a storm the day Aunt Jean gives you the lamp?"

I shrugged. "Just a coincidence."

"But what about losing the electricity? You know how unusual that is."

"It's happened before," I said. "But it will be a good thing to say in a thank-you note."

I took the lid off and struck a match. I had to reach down into the lamp because the candle was so short and stubby. I nearly burned my fingertips before the wick caught the flame. . . .

I saw a little wisp of smoke rise up from the flame. The smoke seemed to be blue. Another puff of smoke followed. They floated toward the ceiling. The second puff joined the first one, and formed what looked like a chubby, upside-down exclamation point.

"There's a rational explanation for this," I told myself. "It must be air currents, or some unusual atmospheric disturbance."

There was nothing to be afraid of. I was on my way to bed anyway. I'd just blow out the candle. . . .

I took a step toward my bed.

The upside-down exclamation point

was growing. Larger. Larger. Until it was the size of an adult human. . . .

As I looked at it, I began to see a body.

I gasped. The body was blue. It had on long, billowy harem pants. And a blue vest. It was entirely blue, from the top of its turban to the tips of its pointy-slippered feet.

Now I began to see a face. It was blue also, except for a thick black moustache that looked as if it had been painted on with shoe polish, and bushy black eyebrows. It wore a pair of black-framed eyeglasses.

I could see arms. And hands, and fingers. It was holding a long, black cigar between its thumb and forefinger.

"Help," I squeaked. "Help."

But the words stuck in my throat. I was weak with fright.

The shadow tapped the cigar with its middle finger.

"Got a light?"

## Skills in Science

### Reading Skills in Science

1. **Find Causes** Identify the sequence of events leading from the storm to the appearance of the genie.

2. **Classify** Identify events or objects in the excerpt that require electricity.

### Writing Skills in Science

1. **Find Causes** Explain how lightning can cause a home to lose its electrical power.

2. **Predict** Imagine you are in the narrator's place at the end of the excerpt. Write a short story explaining what happens next.

3. **Observe** Using pictures of the Marx Brothers, give a written description of each of the four brothers.

### Activities

**Communicate** Research how electricity comes into a home. Make a diagram that illustrates what you learned.

**Collect Data** Choose a common device that uses electricity. Find out how the device works. Describe the role of electricity in its operation.

### Where to Read More

*More Power to You* by Vicki Cobb. Boston: Little, Brown and Company, 1986. This reader-friendly text uses experiments to explain the nature of electric power.

*Simple Electrical Devices* by Martin J. Gutnik. New York: Franklin Watts, 1986. The clear, concise directions in this text show you how to build simple electric devices.

# Unit 5

# Waves, Sound, and Light

## Chapters

14 Waves
15 Sound
16 Using Sound
17 Light
18 Using Light

# Data Bank

Use the information on pages 634 to 643 to answer the questions about topics explored in this unit.

## *Interpreting Data*

Does sound travel faster through gases or through liquids?

## *Calculating*

How much higher is the frequency of VHF waves than the frequency of short wave radio?

## *Predicting*

Why is the central circle in a color wheel black?

## *Generalizing*

What types of sounds are near the pain threshold? What types are barely audible?

The photograph to the left shows pots of different colors of paint. Name some colors you could make by blending the paints.

# Chapter 14 Waves

## Chapter Sections

**14.1** Nature of Waves

**14.2** Wave Properties

**14.3** Wave Interactions

## What do you see?

❝A drop of liquid falls into a calm pool of liquid. The impact of the drop forces it down into the pool and displaces some of the pool's liquid. Notice the rippling wave of liquid, showing the energy radiating in waves.❞

*Carmen León*
*Shattuck Junior High School*
*Neenah, Wisconsin*

To find out more about the photograph, look on page 356. As you read this chapter, you will learn about the properties and behavior of waves.

# 14.1 Nature of Waves

## Objectives

▶ **Relate** waves and the transfer of energy.

▶ **Distinguish** between transverse waves and longitudinal waves.

▶ **Predict** the motion of a medium as a wave of energy passes through it.

▶ **Infer** the energy content of a longitudinal wave.

When you think of waves, you probably think of waves on water. Actually, waves surround you all the time. Light waves make the world around you visible. Sound waves bring voices and music to your ears. Heat waves warm your skin on a summer day.

## Waves and Energy Transfer

Throw a pebble into a pond. Notice how it disturbs the surface of the water. A ripple moves outward from the place where the pebble enters the water.

When the pebble hits the water, kinetic energy transfers to nearby water molecules causing them to collide with other water molecules. Through a series of collisions between molecules, the energy is carried through the water. You see the energy from the pebble move as a small wave or ripple. A **wave** is a disturbance that transfers energy through matter or through space.

Some kinds of waves move through a medium, such as water or air. A medium is matter that is made of molecules and takes up space. A medium may be a solid, liquid, or gas. Other kinds of waves, such as light waves, can move through a vacuum. Light waves are unique in that they don't require a medium.

When energy waves move through a medium, the medium remains at the same location. You can see this occur if you throw a pebble near a leaf floating in water. As the wave of energy passes, the leaf bobs up and down. It doesn't move outward with the wave because the water molecules beneath it remain in the same location. The water molecules simply transfer energy.

▼ **ACTIVITY**

### Making a Model

*Do the Wave*

Demonstrate a human energy wave.

**1.** Line up in a straight line with eight or ten classmates.

**2.** Each student in line crouches and then stands up and stretches, in succession.

Describe how the energy wave moves through your line of students.

**SKILLS WARMUP**

**Oceanography**

**L I N K**

Ocean waves are formed as wind blows across the water's surface. Obtain a plate.

**1.** Place the plate on a level surface and fill it with water until it's almost full.

**2.** Gently blow across the surface of the water and observe the waves.

**3.** Repeat step 2, blowing slightly harder this time.

Describe the waves that formed. How did your blowing affect the waves?

**A C T I V I T Y**

## Types of Waves
All waves don't have the same effect on a medium. For example, the energy in heat waves and sound waves produces two different types of waves, called transverse waves and longitudinal waves. You can identify the type of wave passing through a medium by the way the medium is disturbed.

**Transverse Waves** You produce transverse waves when you shake dirt from a blanket or a rug. If you watch closely, you see that the motion of your hand, flipping the edge of the blanket up and down, produces waves in the blanket.

The **crest** is the highest point of a transverse wave. The **trough** is the lowest point of a transverse wave. The waves move through the blanket away from your hand. The threads in the blanket, however, don't move away from you. They only move up and down. Any wave in which the medium moves at right angles to the direction of the wave is a **transverse wave**.

You can see how a transverse wave moves through a rope in Figure 14.1. If you repeatedly move one end of the rope up and down, you produce transverse waves in the rope. The waves move through the rope horizontally from left to right. The fibers that make up the rope, however, only move up and down, or vertically. So, the direction of the moving wave and the direction of the movement of the rope are at right angles to each other.

**Figure 14.1**

Transverse waves move at right angles to the medium. What is the medium in this photo? ▼

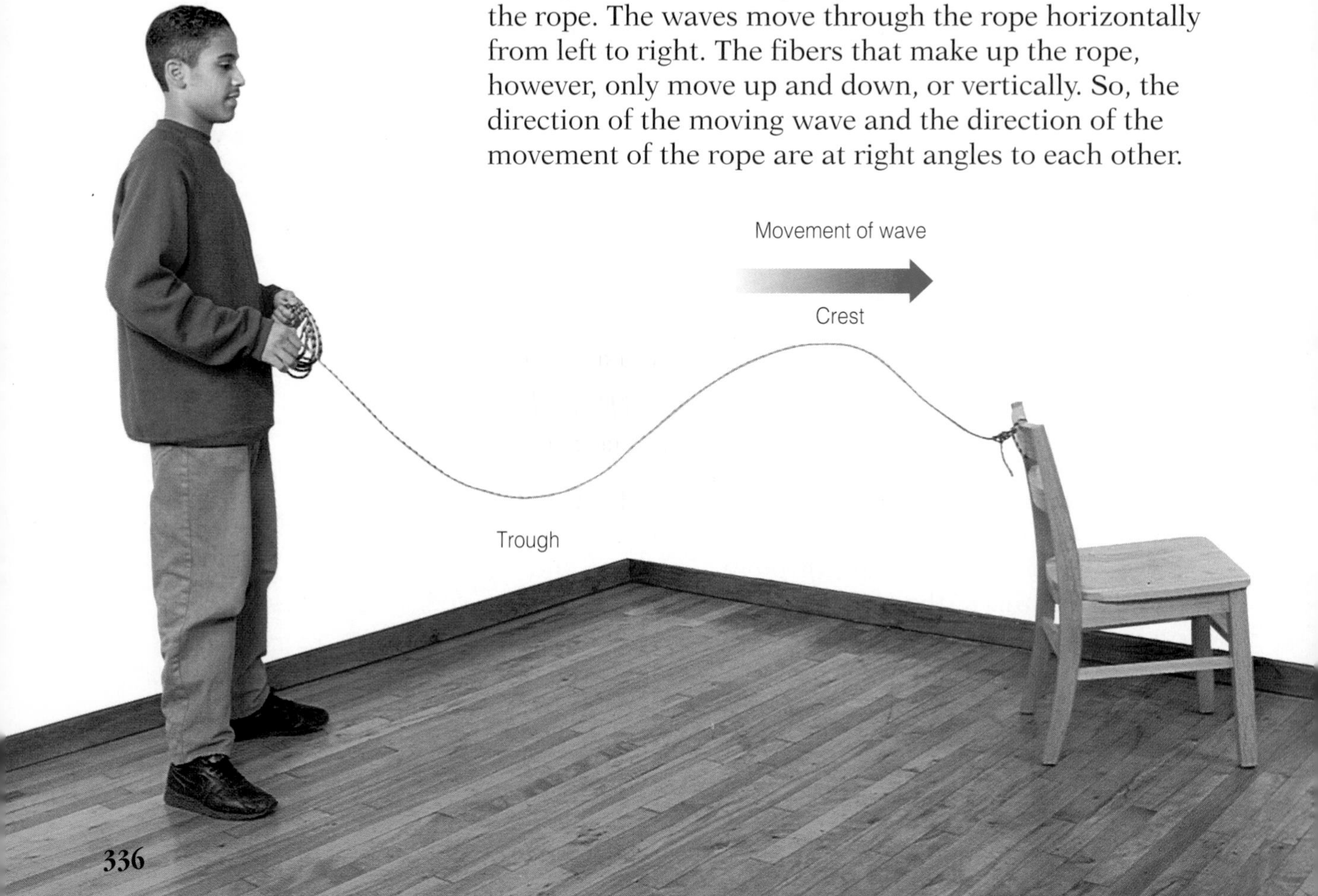

Movement of wave

Crest

Trough

**336**

You can see transverse waves in flags or patches of tall grass when the wind blows. Can you think of another example of a transverse wave? Does the wave you're thinking of move at a right angle to the movement of the medium?

**Longitudinal Waves**   Energy can also move in the same direction as the medium. You can see longitudinal (lahn juh TOOD uh nuhl) waves in a spring, like the one shown in Figure 14.2. Unlike a transverse wave, a **longitudinal wave** moves in the same direction as the medium.

The energy in the spring comes from compressing several coils to produce potential energy. When the compressed coils are released, the potential energy becomes kinetic energy, which moves through the spring like a wave. The wave motion is in the same direction as the motion of the spring, or medium.

The part of a longitudinal wave where the particles of matter are close together is called a **compression**. Compression means "pushed together." The coils in the spring that are pushed together create a compression.

If you look closely at Figure 14.2, you'll see the coils in the part of the spring following the compression are spread out. You can't compress coils in one part of a spring without causing coils to spread apart in another part of the spring. A **rarefaction** (RAIR uh FAK shuhn) is the part of a longitudinal wave where the particles spread apart. All longitudinal waves consist of alternating compressions and rarefactions. Energy transfers from one particle to another in the compressions that move through the medium.

▼ **ACTIVITY**

**Comparing**

*Spring Waves*

   Using a large spring, produce both a transverse wave and a longitudinal wave. Compare how each of the waves looks. How is the action you used to create each wave different?

**SKILLS WORKOUT**

**Figure 14.2**
Longitudinal waves move in the same direction as the disturbance in the medium.
▼

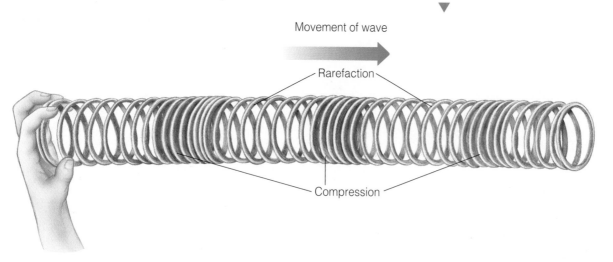

Movement of wave

Rarefaction

Compression

## Wave Motion

What do tiny wind ripples in a pond and huge ocean waves have in common? They are both examples of waves that move through the surface of a medium. These waves are called surface waves.

Ocean surface waves are created by the force of friction when the wind moves across the water's surface to make ripples. The ripples expose more surface area for the wind to act upon. The small waves gain energy from the wind and increase in size.

The individual water molecules in an ocean wave move in a circle as shown in Figure 14.3. The size of the circle becomes smaller as the depth of the water increases. The decrease in circle size is due to the decreasing energy of the wave.

Most ocean waves are less than 3 m high. Waves set up by storms may get over 20 m high! These waves travel several thousand kilometers over the open sea. As they move outside the storm area, the height of the wave decreases and the wavelength increases. These waves can do much damage to a shoreline with a sloping beach.

**Figure 14.3**
**Ocean Waves** ▼

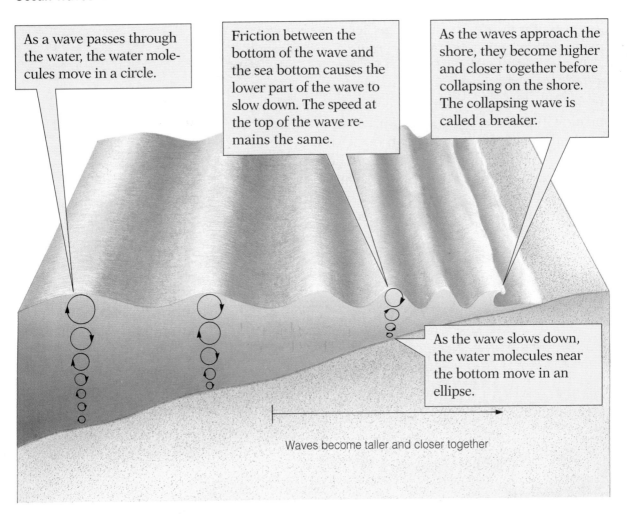

As a wave passes through the water, the water molecules move in a circle.

Friction between the bottom of the wave and the sea bottom causes the lower part of the wave to slow down. The speed at the top of the wave remains the same.

As the waves approach the shore, they become higher and closer together before collapsing on the shore. The collapsing wave is called a breaker.

As the wave slows down, the water molecules near the bottom move in an ellipse.

Waves become taller and closer together

## Science and Society  *Surfing*

Maybe you've enjoyed the thrill of being carried toward shore by the force of a rolling wave. For many people, this is just fun. For others, it is a sport called surfing.

Surfing, or surfboard riding, started in Hawaii. Surfing is a blend of two sports that were brought to the islands by the Polynesians. Surfing combines *paipai*, "riding waves while lying down on a flat board," with *paka*, "riding waves while standing up in a small canoe."

Modern surfers ride a wave while standing on a flat, tapered board called a surfboard. Most surfboards are made of lightweight plastic resins. They measure about 2 m long, 0.8 m wide, and 3 cm thick.

Successful surfing depends on a person's ability to stay balanced on the surfboard as it slides down the front, or face, of a wave. The surfer in Figure 14.4 started by lying on his board out in the ocean beyond the breakers. As a tall wave approached, the surfer paddled his board just ahead of the wave toward the shore. When the crest of the wave lifted his board, he quickly stood up. As the breaking wave carried him toward the shore, the surfer shifted his weight. He steered the board across the face of the wave, or the smooth water just under the crest. The surfer and the wave moved forward at the same speed.

**Figure 14.4** ▲
Surfing requires good balance, sense of timing, and coordination. Surfers can reach speeds of 55 km/h.

## Check and Explain

1. What causes the ripple in a pond when a pebble is thrown into the water?

2. Give five examples of waves moving through a medium. List whether each example is produced by a transverse or longitudinal wave. How can you tell?

3. **Predict** What will be the motion of a cork floating in a tub of water as waves pass by it? Give reasons for your prediction.

4. **Infer** In one spring, the compressions consist of four coils. The compressions in a second spring have ten coils. Which spring has more energy? Explain.

# Activity 14  How does the water surface move when waves pass?

## Task 1  Prelab Prep

1. Collect the following items: 20 cm of string, table-tennis ball, tape, 2 heavy metal washers, metric ruler, tub or basin about 12 cm deep, and water.
2. Tie the piece of string around a table-tennis ball. Use tape to secure it.
3. Tie 2 metal washers to the opposite end of the string. Leave about 10 cm of string between the washers and the table-tennis ball.
4. Place the washers and the attached table-tennis ball in the center of the tub. Fill the tub with water until the string is almost straight.

## Task 2  Data Record

1. On a separate sheet of paper, draw a data table, like the one shown.
2. Use the table to record all your observations about the motion of the table-tennis ball.

## Task 3  Procedure

1. When the water is perfectly still, insert the ruler into the water near the edge of the basin. Use the ruler to gently push the surface of the water back and forth in the direction of the table-tennis ball.
2. Observe the motion of the table-tennis ball as each wave passes. Record your observations in the table for trial 1. Allow the water to become perfectly still.

3. Repeat steps 1 and 2. For trial 2, use the same rhythm, but use more force when you move the ruler.
4. Repeat steps 1 and 2 again. For trial 3, use the same gentle force as in trial 1, but push the ruler back and forth more frequently.

## Task 4  Analysis

1. Describe the motion of the table tennis ball as the wave passes in trial 1.
2. How were the waves different when you pushed the ruler with more force?
3. How were the waves different when you pushed the ruler more frequently?

## Task 5  Conclusion

Explain how frequency and force affect the behavior of surface waves. Explain what gives some waves a larger amplitude than others.

## Extension

Hurricanes often cause waves that do a great deal of damage. Research a recent hurricane. Write an account of damage done by sea waves. Explain how wave height relates to wind energy.

## Everyday Application

Buoys are floating devices which are anchored to the ocean bottom. They mark channel depth and hazards for ships. Use what you learned in this activity to explain how a buoy is anchored and how it is affected by tides and storms.

**Table 14.1   Wave Movement**

| Trial | Motion of Ruler | Observations |
|-------|-----------------|--------------|
| 1 |  |  |
| 2 |  |  |
| 3 |  |  |

# 14.2 Wave Properties

## Objectives

▶ **Identify** the parts of transverse and longitudinal waves.

▶ **Calculate** the wave speed if given the frequency and the wavelength.

▶ **Predict** how energy affects the amplitude of a wave.

▶ **Compare** and **contrast** wave height and amplitude.

"Here comes a big wave," one surfer yells to another surfer bobbing in the ocean. "It'll be here in four or five seconds."

"The waves are too close together. We won't be able to stand up in time to catch the big wave. Three waves will pass by before we catch one," the second surfer responds.

These surfers are describing the four properties of waves. A "big wave" refers to the height, or amplitude, of the wave. "Four or five seconds" is the time it takes the wave to travel from its present location to the surfers. This is the wave speed. "The waves are too close together" is the distance between two consecutive crests, or two consecutive troughs. This is a wavelength. "Three waves will pass by before we catch one" identifies the frequency of the waves.

## Wave Behavior

Many of the characteristics of ocean waves change as they approach the shoreline. What do you notice about the waves shown in Figure 14.5? Are all the waves exactly the same? Actually, the size, speed, and shape of each wave are different.

Even though waves often differ, they all share common characteristics. Waves transfer energy. They have height, speed, length, and frequency. The exact height, speed, length, and frequency of waves, however, will vary from wave to wave. Similarly, all the students in your class have height. However, the height of each student is not the same.

**Figure 14.5** ▲
What wave properties are seen as the waves approach the beach?

# Characteristics of Waves

Just as your body has different identifiable parts, so does a wave. Some of the wave parts you should learn are shown in Figure 14.6. Look at the transverse wave shown on this page and the longitudinal wave shown on page 343.

Each kind of wave behaves differently in a medium. When a transverse wave passes through a medium, it looks like a moving snake. However, when a longitudinal wave passes through a medium, it looks more like a traveling earthworm.

By observing the behavior of a medium, you can see the different parts of transverse and longitudinal waves. Compare the different parts of the transverse and longitudinal waves shown in Figure 14.6. How does the behavior of each type of wave determine the way the different parts are identified?

**Figure 14.6**
**Parts of a Wave** ▼

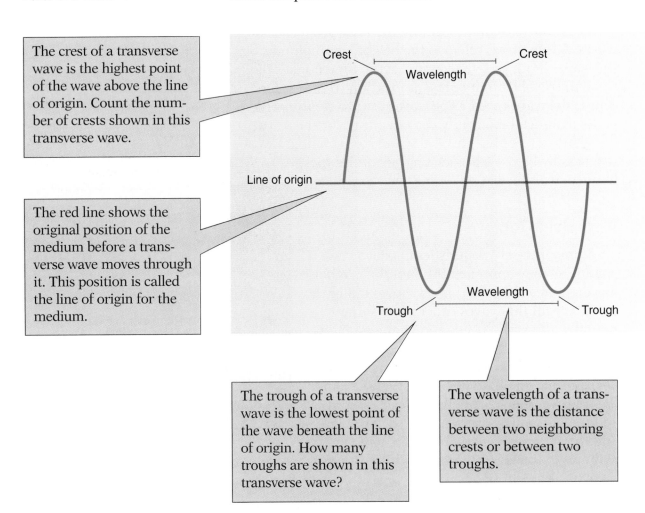

The crest of a transverse wave is the highest point of the wave above the line of origin. Count the number of crests shown in this transverse wave.

The red line shows the original position of the medium before a transverse wave moves through it. This position is called the line of origin for the medium.

The trough of a transverse wave is the lowest point of the wave beneath the line of origin. How many troughs are shown in this transverse wave?

The wavelength of a transverse wave is the distance between two neighboring crests or between two troughs.

Crest

Crest

Wavelength

Line of origin

Wavelength

Trough

Trough

As you compare the transverse and the longitudinal waves, notice that many parts on each wave are comparable. Longitudinal waves, for example, have compressions, while transverse waves do not. Instead, transverse waves have crests. Even though compressions are not the same as crests, they correspond to one another. Compressions and crests both indicate the amount of energy in the wave. Rarefactions and troughs also correspond to each other. They indicate the lowest energy.

**Wavelength** The parts of transverse and longitudinal waves are used to describe their characteristics. One characteristic, for example, is wavelength. On a transverse wave, **wavelength** is the distance between two consecutive crests, or two consecutive troughs. The wavelength of a longitudinal wave is the distance between two consecutive compressions, or two consecutive rarefactions.

### Life Science
### L I N K

An electrocardiogram (EKG) is a record of electrical changes occurring while your heart beats. A typical EKG has three recognizable deflection waves. Research what an electrocardiogram looks like for a healthy heart. Draw an EKG for a healthy heart. On your drawing, label the P wave, the QRS complex, and the T wave. How are these waves like the wave shown in Figure 14.6?

**A C T I V I T Y**

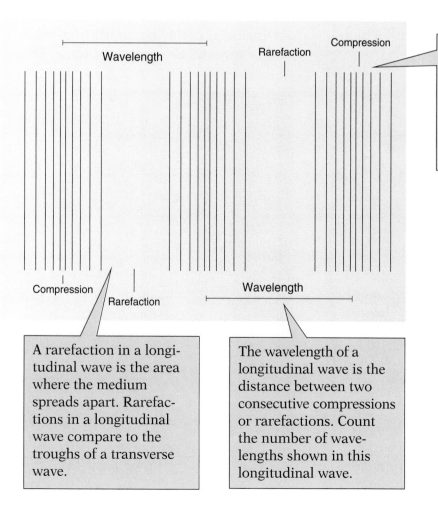

Wavelength

Rarefaction

Compression

Compression

Rarefaction

Wavelength

A compression in a longitudinal wave is the area where the medium is pushed together. Compressions in a longitudinal wave compare to the crests of a transverse wave.

A rarefaction in a longitudinal wave is the area where the medium spreads apart. Rarefactions in a longitudinal wave compare to the troughs of a transverse wave.

The wavelength of a longitudinal wave is the distance between two consecutive compressions or rarefactions. Count the number of wavelengths shown in this longitudinal wave.

**Wave Amplitude** If you're standing in the surf, you may be knocked over by a wave. Another wave barely nudges you. The two waves differ in some characteristic. What is it? The difference between the ocean waves is the **amplitude** (AM pluh tood) of the waves.

Look at Figure 14.7. The amplitude of a transverse wave is the vertical distance between the line of origin and each crest or trough. The amplitude is related to how much energy the wave transfers through in the medium. A wave with a high amplitude has more energy than a wave with a low amplitude.

The height of the ocean wave is a good indication of whether or not it has enough energy to knock you over. How would you avoid being knocked over? Your best move would be to run to the shore when you see a wave with a high amplitude.

**Wave Frequency** You're in the surf, and a wave knocks you down. No harm done. You get ready for the next wave to arrive. You expect it to arrive 15 or 20 seconds later. You may be caught off guard if the wave arrives in just 5 or 6 seconds. Waves that arrive every 5 or 6 seconds have a greater frequency (FREE kwuhn see) than those arriving every 15 or 20 seconds.

The **frequency** of a wave is the number of wavelengths that pass a point in a given amount of time, such as a second. The unit for frequency is hertz (Hz). One wave per second equals 1 Hz. Hertz was named after Heinrich Hertz, a German physicist who studied waves during the 1800s.

Look at Figure 14.8. The difference between a 1 Hz and 2 Hz wave in a rope is shown. How many complete waves are included in the line indicating 1 second in wave C? How many in wave D?

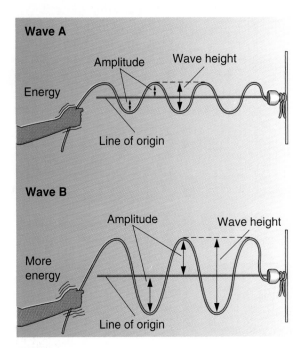

**Figure 14.7** ▲
The greater the amount of energy in a wave, the greater is its amplitude. Which rope has the most energy?

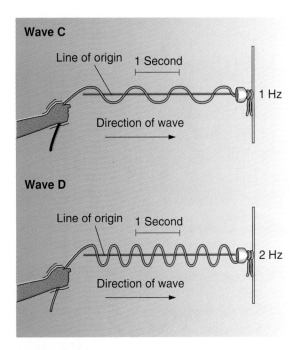

**Figure 14.8** ▲
How do you increase the frequency in a rope? How is amplitude affected by a change in frequency?

**Wave Speed**   Imagine you are at the beach, waist high in the water. A huge wave approaches. What are your first thoughts? You probably don't care about the wavelength or frequency of the wave. What concerns you is how fast the wave is moving toward you—or its speed.

The frequency and wavelength determine the speed of a wave. If you had time to get to the beach before the wave hit you, you could measure its wavelength and calculate its frequency. One thing you don't have to worry about is that the wave might change its speed. Waves don't change speed as they travel through a medium.

The speed of a wave is equal to the frequency times the wavelength. The speed of the wave is measured in meters per second. Frequency is waves per second, or Hz. Wavelength is measured in meters.

The relationship that exists between the speed, frequency, and wavelength of a wave is expressed in the equation:

$$\text{speed} = \text{frequency} \times \text{wavelength}$$

## SkillBuilder *Interpreting Data*

## The Center of an Earthquake

Earthquakes are caused by waves moving through the earth. An earthquake produces fast-moving P-waves, which are longitudinal waves, and slower-moving S-waves, which are transverse waves. The exact origin of an earthquake, or the epicenter, is determined by knowing the time difference between the arrival of P- and S-waves at three different locations.

P- and S-waves arrived at station A 3 s apart. From this information, it was determined that the epicenter was 15 km away. In a similar way, it was determined that the epicenter was 45 km from station B and 60 km from station C.

The next step involves a map. Copy the map shown onto a separate piece of paper. Draw a circle around each station on your map with a compass. The size of the circles is important. The radius of each circle is the distance from the station to the origin. Use the scale provided to change

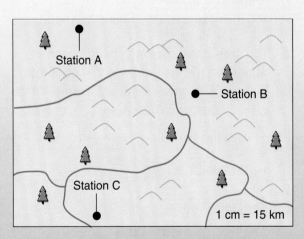

km to cm. The epicenter is the point where the three circles intersect. Mark the origin with an *X*.

1. This method is called *triangulation*. Why does the word tell you about the method being used?

2. Describe another situation, real or imaginary, where you could use triangulation.

# Sample Problems

**1.** The frequency of the waves produced by a passing motorboat is 2 Hz. The wavelength is 3 m. How fast are the waves moving toward the beach?

**Plan**  Use the equation for speed.

speed = frequency × wavelength

**Gather Data**  frequency = 2 Hz

wavelength = 3 m

**Solution**  Express frequency as the number of waves per second. Express the wavelength as the distance between two wave crests.

$$\text{frequency} = 2 \ \frac{\text{waves}}{\text{second}}$$

$$\text{wavelength} = 3 \ \frac{\text{meters}}{\text{wave}}$$

Solve for the speed.

$$\text{speed} = 2 \ \frac{\text{waves}}{\text{second}} \times 3 \ \frac{\text{meters}}{\text{waves}} = 6 \ \frac{\text{meters}}{\text{second}}$$

Wave speed is expressed in meters per second (m/s), which is the SI unit for speed.

**2.** The speed of the approaching ocean waves is 4 meters per second. The length between two wave crests is 2 meters. What is the frequency in waves/second, or Hz?

**Plan**  Use the formula

$$\text{frequency} = \frac{\text{speed}}{\text{wavelength}}$$

**Gather Data**  wavelength = 2 m

speed = 4 m/s

**Solution**  Divide speed by wavelength.

$$\text{frequency} = \frac{4 \text{ m/s}}{2 \text{ m}}$$

$$\text{frequency} = \frac{2 \text{ waves}}{\text{s}} = 2 \text{ Hz}$$

# Practice Problems

**1.** You are holding one end of a jump rope while your friend is flicking the other end up and down. The waves have a frequency of 3 Hz and a wavelength of 1.2 m. What is the speed of the waves in the rope?

**2.** A sound wave traveling toward you from a rock concert has a frequency of 680 Hz and a wavelength of 0.5 m in air. What is the speed of the sound wave?

**3.** The wake of a boat is moving at 3 m/s. The waves are 1.5 m apart. What is the frequency?

**4.** You are standing in the ocean 8 m from the beach. You see a big wave heading toward you. The wave is 200 m from the beach. Its frequency is 0.2 Hz, and its wavelength is 100 m. You can move an average of 2 m/s in water. How fast do you have to move to get out of the water before the wave hits you? Explain.

## Science and Society
### *Earthquake-Proof Buildings*

Earthquakes are caused by waves produced when the rocks deep within the earth move. The energy that is released travels through the earth. The amount of damage done by an earthquake depends on the strength of the waves and the design of the building.

People in ancient cultures who lived in earthquake areas built earthquake-resistant buildings. A Buddhist pagoda in Japan is shown in the bottom of Figure 14.9. The central shaft is sunk into the ground. Flexible joints attach the roof sections to the central shaft. The shaft sways during an earthquake, but the roof doesn't fall.

Chinese architects designed tentlike structures. Each building had a sloping, tiled roof. A central wooden beam supported the length of the roof. Each end of the beam had vertical shafts driven deep into rock. Lightweight bamboo walls hung from the roof, almost like curtains. The walls absorbed energy by swaying, since they were supported by the roof and not by the ground.

In the American Southwest and in Central America, adobe buildings remain standing after numerous earthquakes. Adobe walls are made of clay bricks with a crisscross network of twigs. This construction gives flexibility to each wall. The walls absorb the energy of earthquake waves to remain standing.

**Figure 14.9** ▲
Seismographs (top) measure speed, strength, and arrival time of an earthquake. A pagoda (bottom) is a Buddhist shrine.

## Check and Explain

1. Draw a transverse wave and a longitudinal wave. Label the parts of each wave.

2. An earthquake wave has a frequency of 20 Hz and a wavelength of 50 km. How fast is the wave?

3. **Predict** How does adding energy to a wave affect its amplitude?

4. **Compare** The height of a wave is the vertical distance between a crest and a trough. Compare wave height to amplitude for a transverse wave.

*Making Waves*

Obtain a jump rope.

**1.** Hold one end of the rope perfectly still.

**2.** Have a person at the other end make waves in the rope by moving it up and down.

**3.** Now move your end of the rope up and down in the opposite direction.

What happens to the waves in the rope?

**SKILLS WARMUP**

# 14.3 Wave Interactions

## Objectives

▶ **Describe** four kinds of wave interactions.

▶ **Explain** the relationship between the angle of incidence and the angle of reflection.

▶ **Compare** and **contrast** constructive and destructive interference.

▶ **Predict** how a wave will behave if it moves from air into water.

D id you ever watch the waves caused by a motorboat? You probably saw a series of waves rolling towards you. You might have noticed that many things change the direction or behavior of the waves. Waves change when they run into a sharp-edged rock jutting out of the water or when they meet a smooth sandbar arching above the water's surface. You might have wondered what happens if two different waves run into each other far out in the water. Perhaps a bigger wave forms, or maybe the collision will suddenly make the water flat.

## Interaction, Energy, and Change

You learned that a wave is energy moving through a medium. Recall that when an object with energy interacts with another object, energy is either lost or gained. When a wave interacts with an object or other waves, the amount of energy in the wave changes. The change in energy affects the wave's properties.

Look at Figure 14.10. How do the properties of the waves change when they reach the rocky shoreline? If some of the wave's energy is absorbed by another object, the amplitude, speed, or wavelength of the wave may change.

Sometimes the wave's behavior is altered. The direction of the moving wave may change. The wave may also break apart or pass the structure, and then re-form.

**Figure 14.10** ▲

Where is the energy from these waves being absorbed? How do you know?

# Reflection

The next time you see raindrops fall into a water fountain, observe the ripples. The ripples move outward, hit the fountain wall, and bounce off. The interaction between the ripples and the fountain wall is called **reflection**. Reflection occurs when a wave bounces off a surface. Look at Figure 14.11 to learn how waves reflect.

Reflected waves carry energy. The amount of energy depends on how much energy is absorbed by the surface that the wave hits. The energy not absorbed by the surface is carried by the reflected waves.

**Figure 14.11**
**Reflection of a Wave** ▼

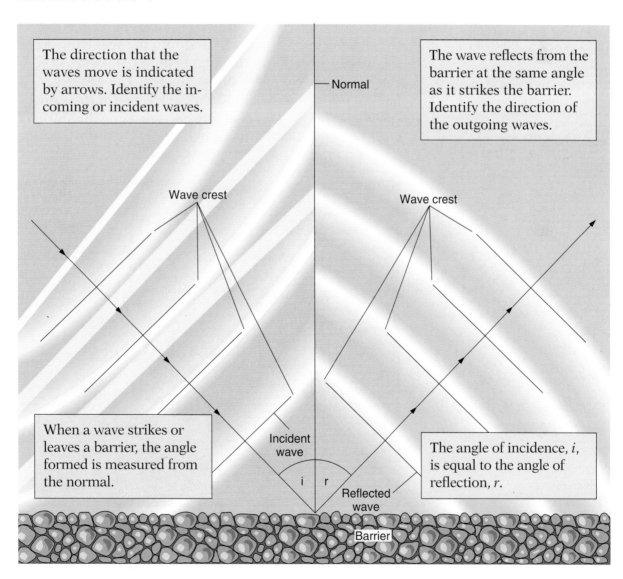

The direction that the waves move is indicated by arrows. Identify the incoming or incident waves.

The wave reflects from the barrier at the same angle as it strikes the barrier. Identify the direction of the outgoing waves.

Normal

Wave crest

Wave crest

When a wave strikes or leaves a barrier, the angle formed is measured from the normal.

Incident wave

The angle of incidence, $i$, is equal to the angle of reflection, $r$.

$i$   $r$

Reflected wave

Barrier

## Diffraction

When you stand in a shallow pool of water facing into the breeze, you can look down and see waves reflected by your shins. If you look behind you, you'll see that the waves have reformed. They appear to have gone right through your legs! How can that be?

If you look closely, you'll see that sections of the wave near the sides of your legs begin to bend as they pass by your legs. They bend so much that they come together a short distance behind your legs to re-form the wave. This bending makes it appear that the wave passes right through you. The bending of a wave as a result of the interaction between a wave and the edge of an object is called **diffraction**.

Look at Figure 14.12. The waves move at an angle toward the rock. You can see the waves bend around the sharp rock that juts farthest into the sea. How do the waves spread into the area behind the rock? As you can see, the wavelength didn't change. The waves before, next to, and behind the rock travel at the same speed and frequency. The only change is the direction of waves as they pass by the rock's edge.

**Figure 14.12** ▲
The waves bend around the angular rock, but the wavelength remains unchanged. Notice how the energy of waves erodes the shoreline.

## Refraction

Waves passing undisturbed through a single medium, such as water, don't change properties or direction. However, waves can change as they pass from one medium to another. A wave entering a new medium at an angle changes direction, as shown in Figure 14.13. In air, the light waves move in a straight line. When light waves enter the new medium, they bend. Bending occurs because the wave speed is different for each medium. The bending of a wave as a result of a change in speed is called **refraction**.

To better understand refraction, imagine mowing a lawn. The wheels of the lawn mower represent a wave. One wheel moves into grass while the other continues to roll on a sidewalk. The wheels move at different speeds because they are on different mediums.

Look at what happens to the lawn mower in Figure 14.14. When the mower enters the grass at an angle, only one of the wheels is on the grass. The wheel on the grass slows down. The wheel on the sidewalk does not. The mower turns. If both wheels enter the grass at the same time, each would be affected equally, and the mower wouldn't change direction.

**Figure 14.13** ▲
The beam of light bends when it moves from air into water. What causes the light waves to change direction?

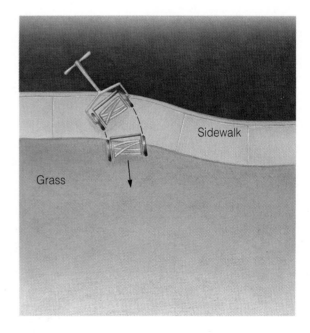

**Figure 14.14** ▲
When one wheel slows down before the other wheel does, the lawnmower changes direction. This is a model of refraction.

## Interference

Waves change when they interact with a surface, an edge, or a boundary. Waves also change when they interact with each other. The effect of two or more waves interacting is called **interference**. The interaction between two waves when they meet may produce a large single wave or no wave at all.

What happens as two wave crests meet? A single wave forms as the two crests begin to overlap. When two crests are at the same location at the same time, constructive interference takes place. A single wave with a crest of maximum amplitude is produced. The amplitude of the wave formed is the sum of the amplitudes of the interfering crests.

What happens when a crest of one wave meets a trough of another wave? The crest and trough subtract from each other to form a single wave, or possibly, no wave. Destructive interference takes place. As you can see in Figure 14.15, destructive interference produces water waves with a reduced amplitude. If the amplitudes of the crest and the trough were equal, the waves would cancel out one another.

**Figure 14.15**
When the water waves from the two boats meet, the amplitude of the resulting waves changes. Why is the amplitude of the waves reduced? ▼

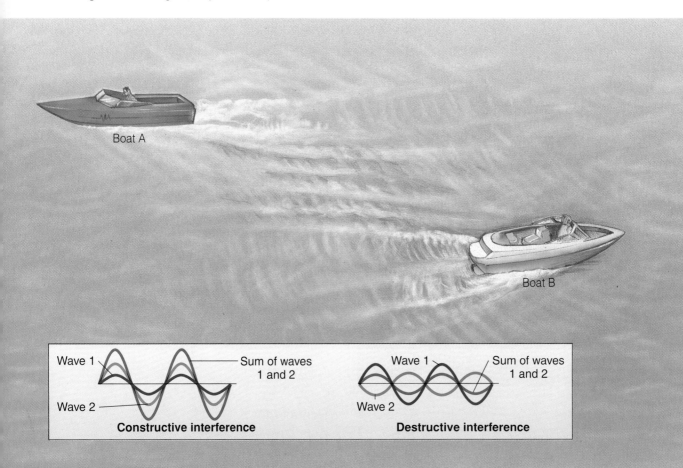

# Consider This

## Should Breakwaters and Wave Barriers Be Built?

Walk barefoot along the edge of the surf and you can feel the sand shifting constantly beneath your feet. The movement of the water causes the sand to move. Waves, tides, and water currents cause the natural formation and erosion of beaches.

Breakwaters and wave barriers are long walls built near harbors or along the shoreline. Breakwaters and wave barriers protect areas such as harbors, recreational areas, and private homes from erosion by forcing incoming waves to break farther from the shore. Breakwaters also prevent damage to the harbor during heavy storms.

**Consider Some Issues** By changing wave action and redirecting water currents, these barriers cause sand deposits and beach erosion elsewhere. These changes affect the ecology of the shoreline. Often the habitat of wildlife is destroyed.

Construction costs of breakwaters and wave barriers are high. Because of the force of the waves against them, they are also expensive to maintain.

**Think About It** What are the benefits of these structures?

Should nature be left to take its course or should people interfere with the natural processes?

**Write About It** Write a paper stating your position for or against building breakwaters and wave barriers. Include your reasons for choosing your position.

## Science and Technology
### *Computer Models of Waveforms*

A wind can create dangerous vibrations in a bridge spanning a river. Earthquake waves shake the surface of the earth. Overhead power lines release electromagnetic waves into the air. Heat waves spread away from the hot metal of a car exhaust. All these waves affect people's lives in some way. To better understand waves, scientists and engineers use computers to construct models of waves.

Computers produce complex waves by adding two or more simple waves. Computers also analyze the makeup of complex waves. Most complex waves that occur naturally are produced by the interference of many waves. To analyze complex waves, the computer generates a series of simple waves that make up the complex wave. By studying the simple waves produced by the computer, scientists are able to determine the behavior of complex waves. By understanding how complex waves interact,

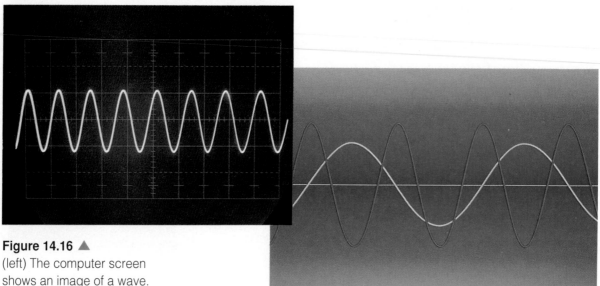

**Figure 14.16** ▲
(left) The computer screen shows an image of a wave. (right) Computers can separate complex waves into a series of simple waves.

engineers and designers can solve problems that arise during the design and construction of buildings and bridges.

The picture of a transverse wave on the left, in Figure 14.16, looks like rope. The curved line was actually produced on a computer screen. The computer calculated the position of each point on the curved line. The screen displayed each position to produce the curved line. This curved line is called a waveform. Some waveforms are very complex. Look at the waves shown on the right in Figure 14.16. This series of simple waves make up a complex wave.

## Check and Explain

1. Explain how the motion of a wave is affected by each of the following interactions.

   a. reflection      b. diffraction
   c. refraction      d. interference

2. In wave reflection, how does the angle of incidence compare to the angle of reflection?

3. **Compare and Contrast** How does constructive and destructive wave interference differ?

4. **Predict** How would a light wave be affected as it passes from air into water at an angle?

# Chapter 14 Review

## Concept Summary

### 14.1 Nature of Waves
▶ Waves are produced when energy is transferred through a medium.
▶ Only the energy carried by a wave moves forward through the medium.
▶ Waves are classified as either transverse or longitudinal, depending on how the medium is disturbed.

### 14.2 Wave Properties
▶ The parts of a transverse wave include crests and troughs.
▶ The parts of a longitudinal wave include compressions and rarefactions.
▶ Both transverse and longitudinal waves have wavelengths.

▶ A wave amplitude is the distance from the line of origin to the crest or trough. Amplitude is related to its energy.
▶ The speed of a wave is the product of frequency multiplied by wavelength.

### 14.3 Wave Interactions
▶ Reflection, diffraction, refraction, and interference occur when waves interact.
▶ During reflection, diffraction, and refraction, waves change direction.
▶ During refraction a wave changes speed and bends as it moves from one medium to another.
▶ Wave amplitude increases during constructive interference and decreases during destructive interference.

## Chapter Vocabulary

| | | | |
|---|---|---|---|
| wave (14.1) | longitudinal wave (14.1) | amplitude (14.2) | refraction (14.3) |
| crest (14.1) | compression (14.1) | frequency (14.2) | interference (14.3) |
| trough (14.1) | rarefaction (14.1) | reflection (14.3) | |
| transverse wave (14.1) | wavelength (14.2) | diffraction (14.3) | |

## Check Your Vocabulary

Use the vocabulary words above to complete the following sentences correctly.

1. The top of a transverse wave is called the _____ .
2. A light wave bending as it passes from air to water is called _____ .
3. Matter spreads out in the _____ of a longitudinal wave.
4. Energy moves through a medium as a(n) _____ .
5. The lowest point of a transverse wave is a(n) _____ .
6. The distance from the line of origin to a crest is the _____ of a transverse wave.
7. The number of waves per unit time is _____ .
8. Angle of incidence applies to _____ .
9. The medium moves at right angles to the wave direction in a(n) _____ .
10. Waves interact with each other to produce _____ .
11. A wave that moves in the same direction as the medium is a(n) _____ .
12. The bending of a wave is called _____ .
13. The distance between two consecutive crests is _____ .
14. Matter in a longitudinal wave is close together in a(n) _____ .

## Write Your Vocabulary

Write sentences using the vocabulary words above. Show that you know what each word means.

# Chapter 14 Review

## Check Your Knowledge

Answer the following in complete sentences.

1. Why does a pebble dropped into a pond produce waves?

2. What causes an ocean wave to curl or break?

3. How do parts of transverse waves correspond to parts of longitudinal waves?

4. When a wave reflects from a surface, what is the relationship between the angle of incidence and the angle of reflection?

5. Why does a beam of light change direction when it passes from air into water?

6. What happens when a crest and a trough of two waves of equal amplitude meet at the same place?

Choose the answer that best completes each sentence.

7. Longitudinal waves have (crests and compressions, troughs and rarefactions, crests and troughs, compressions and rarefactions).

8. The motion of ocean waves is started by friction between surface water and (the seafloor, wind, water, rocks).

9. The number of waves that pass a point in a given time is a measure of (wavelength, frequency, trough, amplitude).

10. If a wave's frequency is 2 Hz and its wavelength is 3 m, its speed is (5 m/s, 5 Hz/s, 6 m/s, 6 Hz/s).

11. If a wave's frequency increases but its speed stays the same, you can assume that its wavelength (stays the same, increases, decreases, is zero).

## Check Your Understanding

Apply the concepts you have learned to answer each question.

1. **Application**  If the crest of a wave whose amplitude is 4 m meets the trough of a wave whose amplitude is 3 m, what is the amplitude of the resulting wave?

2. Which of the following describes a transverse wave? Which describes a longitudinal wave?

   a. close together, spread out

   b. up and down

   c. wind blowing grass

3. You go to the beach on a calm day to find large waves pounding the shore. What can you infer from this observation?

4. You go to the beach and see waves breaking about 300 m from the shore. What can you infer about the slope of the sea bottom?

5. If the wavelength stays the same, but the speed of a wave slows, how will the frequency of the wave be affected?

6. When building a structure in an area where earthquakes occur frequently, what general principle of construction should be followed?

7. **Application**  You are fishing in the middle of a lake from an anchored rowboat. A motorboat 100 m away passes you at a high speed. Describe how the wake of the motorboat will affect the rowboat in which you are sitting.

8. **Mystery Photo**  The photograph on page 334 shows surface waves forming in water. Describe in scientific terms the cause of the ripples in the water.

## Develop Your Skills

Use the skills you have developed in this chapter to complete each activity.

1. **Interpret Data** The table below shows the relationship between the frequency and the wavelength of three sounds.

| Sound | Frequency (Hz) | Wavelength (m) |
|-------|----------------|----------------|
| 1 | 750 | 1.5 |
| 2 | 975 | 1.2 |
| 3 | 990 | 1.1 |

a. Which sound has the largest frequency? The smallest?

b. Which sound has the longest wavelength? The shortest?

c. How does the wavelength affect the frequency of each sound?

d. Calculate the speed of each sound.

2. **Data Bank** Use the information on page 638 to answer the following questions.

a. Which type of wave has the highest frequency? The lowest?

b. Which type of wave has the shortest wavelength? The longest?

c. What is the relationship between frequency and wavelength?

3. **Hypothesize** Recall how ocean waves are produced. Design a simple experiment to test the effect of wind speed on the amplitude of surface waves. Describe the problem, materials, procedure, expected observations, and conclusion.

## Make Connections

1. **Link the Concepts** Below is a concept map showing how some of the main concepts in this chapter link together. Only part of the map is filled in. Finish the map, using words and ideas you find on the previous pages.

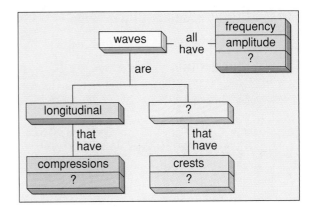

2. **Science and You** Surfing with a board or with just your body can be great fun, but it also can cause injury. Do research to find out how to ride the surf safely. Find out how competitive surfers train to reduce their chances of injury.

3. **Science and Society** The opinions of citizens affect how laws are written and whether they are passed. Design a survey addressing the use and protection of a local beach or other ecologically-sensitive area. Ask people in your community or school to fill in the survey sheets. Analyze the data. Based on your analysis, suggest regulations that reflect the views of the local citizens.

4. **Science and Art** Using clay, make a model of a wave as it approaches shore. Show how the shape of the wave changes as the water depth changes.

# Chapter **15**    Sound

## Chapter Sections

15.1   Wave Model of Sound

15.2   Properties of Sound

15.3   Sound-Wave Interactions

## What do you see?

**❝**I see strings that are tough and strong. This instrument works by plucking the strings with your fingers to make sounds. If you press on any of the shiny bars on which the strings lay, the sound will change. A person would use this wooden instrument by plucking and running her fingers across the strings while the other hand presses down on the parallel and shiny bars.**❞**

*Elizabeth Hayes*
*Santa Fe High School*
*Santa Fe, New Mexico*

To find out more about the photograph, look on page 382. As you read this chapter, you will learn about sound and how different sounds are made.

# 15.1 Wave Model of Sound

## Objectives

▶ **Describe** the characteristics of a sound wave.

▶ **Identify** two factors that affect the speed of sound.

▶ **Compare** and **contrast** the behavior of sound before and during a sonic boom.

▶ **Make a model** to show how the speed of sound differs in the three phases of matter.

What do the twang of a guitar and the boom of a bass drum have in common? They are sounds. All sounds have a source. In a guitar, the sound comes from a plucked string. In a drum, the sound comes from the vibration of the drumhead.

How does sound get from its source to your ears? Recall that sound is a form of energy, and it travels as a wave. While some forms of energy can move through a vacuum, sound waves only move through matter. Sound travels through solids, liquids, and gases.

## Sound Waves

When you strum guitar strings, they move rapidly back and forth. You cause the strings to vibrate. Often this back-and-forth motion is too fast for you to see. Each string blurs and looks like two or more strings. Look at the vibrating strings of the guitar in Figure 15.1.

Sound moves from its source through matter in the form of **sound waves**. A sound wave is produced in matter by a vibrating object. For example, you can make a sound by plucking a stretched rubber band. The rubber band pushes on the molecules in the surrounding air. This motion produces a series of compressions and rarefactions through the air.

Recall that a series of compressions and rarefactions forms a longitudinal wave. Molecules of matter are close together in a compression and spread apart in a rarefaction. Since the motion of the molecules is parallel to the direction of the wave, sound waves are longitudinal waves.

**Figure 15.1** ▲
Vibrating guitar strings are a source of sound.

# How Sound Waves Travel

The stretched spring in Figure 15.2 is a good model of how sound energy moves through matter. When the spring is stretched and then released, energy moves from coil to coil. Because each vibrating coil pushes and is pushed by neighboring coils, energy moves through the spring. As sound energy moves through matter, the particles of matter move back and forth in a similar manner.

The compressions and rarefactions of a longitudinal sound wave can be compared to the parts of a transverse wave. Look at Figure 15.2. Compressions correspond to crests. Rarefactions correspond to troughs. The size of a compression indicates how much energy the sound wave has and corresponds to the amplitude of a transverse wave. For example, a sound wave with a high amplitude will have large compressions. A sound wave with a low amplitude will have small compressions.

**Figure 15.2
Comparing Waves** ▼

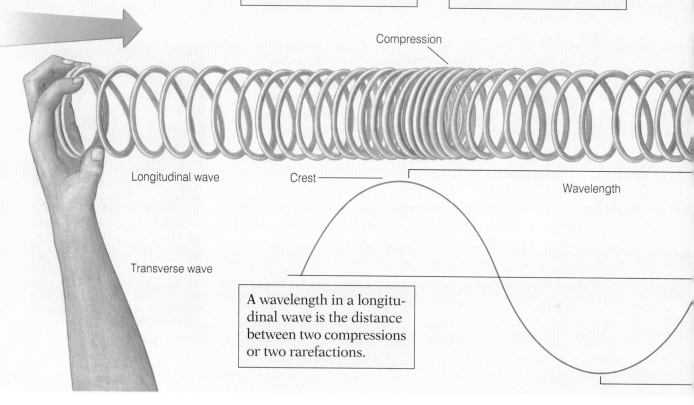

A sound wave travels in much the same way as a pulse of energy expands and contracts the coils of a spring.

The compression in a longitudinal wave corresponds to the crest in a transverse wave.

Compression

Longitudinal wave

Crest

Wavelength

Transverse wave

A wavelength in a longitudinal wave is the distance between two compressions or two rarefactions.

Did you ever notice that several seconds pass between the time you see lightning and you hear thunder. Actually, lightning and thunder occur at the same time. What's happening during this time lapse? Both light and sound are moving through the air toward you. However, light travels faster than sound does, so you see the lightning flash before you hear the thunder.

## Factors Affecting the Speed of Sound

Sound waves can only move through matter, either solids, liquids, or gases. If you put your ear to a solid door, you can hear a conversation on the other side. Dolphins and many other marine mammals communicate by sending sound waves through water. When your teacher speaks to the class, the sound waves travel through air. Since there's no matter in outer space, sound can't move through it.

The speed at which sound waves move depends on the matter, or medium, through which they move, and not on the source. Notice that when a band begins to play in a large stadium, the sounds of the tuba and the drums reach your ears at the same time. Sound from both instruments is moving through the same medium. Several factors influence the speed of sound through a medium—the temperature and the elasticity and density of the medium.

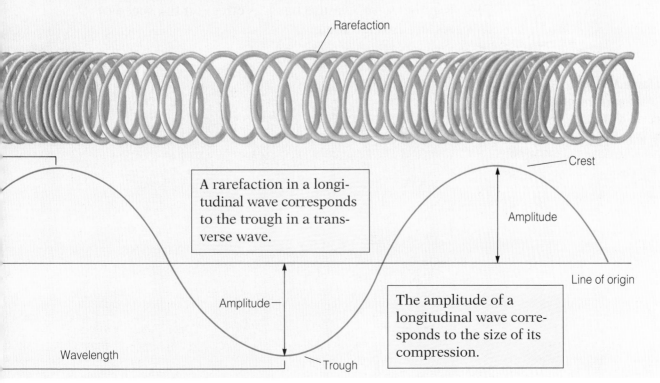

Rarefaction

Crest

A rarefaction in a longitudinal wave corresponds to the trough in a transverse wave.

Amplitude

Line of origin

Amplitude—

The amplitude of a longitudinal wave corresponds to the size of its compression.

Wavelength

Trough

**Elasticity and Density**   Sound waves move quickly through matter that is elastic. Matter is elastic if its molecules return quickly to their original position when disturbed. Some metals, like iron and nickel, are very elastic and transmit sound well. Most liquids aren't very elastic, so they don't transmit sound well. Gases are the least elastic and are poor transmitters of sound.

Sound moves well through a dense material, such as metal or wood, because the molecules are close together. Air density also affects the speed of sound. Because of the pressure of the air above it, air at sea level is denser than it is at high altitudes. At high altitudes, the air molecules are spread out and sound doesn't move as fast as it does through air at low altitudes.

**Temperature**   When the temperature of air increases, the speed of sound also increases. Sound moves 344 m/s through 20°C air. However, if the air temperature is 0°C, sound moves through it at a speed of 331 m/s. Why? A sound wave moves through air when vibrating particles come into contact with other particles. As the temperature of air increases, molecules of air collide more often because they're moving around faster. As a result, a sound wave moves through warm air faster than it moves through cool air. Since molecules in liquids and solids are close together, temperature has less effect on the speed of sound through them.

**Figure 15.3** ▶

The dots represent air molecules. Molecules are more active in warm air than in cold air. How does this fact affect the speed of sound?

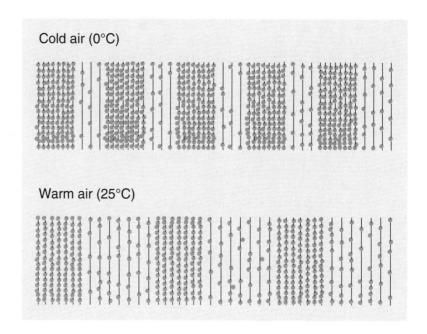

Cold air (0°C)

Warm air (25°C)

**Material** The speed of sound varies in different materials, or media. Look at the information in Table 15.1. The table lists the speed of sound through different kinds of material that are at the same temperature. Examine the table to locate at least one solid, liquid, and gas. Through which material does sound move fastest? The speed of sound in a fence rail made of oak at 20°C is 3,850 m/s. In an iron rail at the same temperature, the speed of sound soars to 5,130 m/s. Through which of these mediums does sound travel the slowest? What inferences can you make about how fast sound travels through different materials around you?

Listen, while a friend who is some distance away from where you are, hammers on an iron or wooden fence rail. Touch a portion of the rail with your hand. You might be surprised to discover that you can feel vibrations in the rail before you hear the sound. What accounts for this difference?

**Table 15.1**
**Speed of Sound**

| Medium | Speed of Sound at 20°C (m/s) |
|--------|------------------------------|
| Iron | 5,130 |
| Glass | 4,540 |
| Wood (oak) | 3,850 |
| Water | 1,500 |
| Alcohol | 1,240 |
| Cork | 500 |
| Air | 344 |

## *SkillBuilder* Inferring

### *Musical Bottles*

Sounds can be produced in many different ways. All of them involve vibrations moving through some medium. Musical instruments cause vibrations in the air.

When you blow across the mouth of a bottle that is partly filled with liquid, air vibrates and you can make a sound. By increasing or decreasing the amount of liquid in the bottle, you can change the pitch of the sound it produces. How does the sound change when there are different amounts of liquid in the bottle?

1. Locate four glass bottles of approximately the same size and type. The bottles should have narrow necks.

2. Fill each bottle with decreasing amounts of water at room-temperature.

3. Use masking tape and markers to label your

bottles A through D. Bottle A should have the most water in it. Bottle D should have the least amount of water in it.

4. Blow across each bottle to make a sound. Listen to the sound each one makes, and identify the pitch of each sound as high, medium, or low.

Answer the following questions.

1. Which bottle emits the lowest sound? Which emits the highest sound?

2. How does the pitch of each sound relate to the amount of water in the bottle?

3. Infer what would happen to the sound the bottles produced if you changed the temperature of the water in the bottles. Test your prediction.

# The Sound Barrier

The speed of sound in air probably seems fast to you. However, many jet planes, such as the one shown in Figure 15.4, cruise at even faster speeds. When a jet reaches a speed that is as fast or faster than sound, it produces a loud, thunderlike sound called a sonic boom.

By traveling faster than the speed of sound, a jet moves past the sound waves it creates in the air. A pattern of wave crests build up like those in Figure 15.5 (left). Where the wave crests overlap, constructive interference occurs and a conical shell results (right). The conical shell is the shock wave, or sonic boom, you hear when the jet passes.

Before the first jet plane broke the sound barrier, many engineers claimed it would be impossible to fly a plane faster than the speed of sound. They thought a plane going that fast would be destroyed. The first sonic boom produced by human beings "shattered" the air over California's Mojave (mo HAH vay) Desert on October 14, 1947. On that historic day, test pilot Chuck Yeager, flying in the experimental rocket plane called the X-1, reached the speed of sound. As the X-1 passed the speed of sound, observers could hear and feel the sound vibrations.

**Figure 15.4** ▶
The Concorde is a supersonic jet.

**Figure 15.5**

What happens when a jet plane like the Concorde flies faster than the speed of sound? ▼

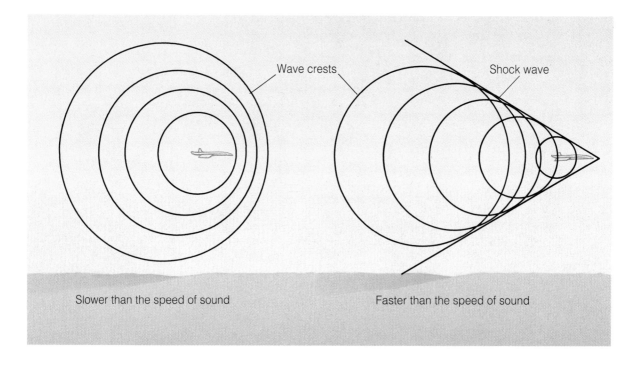

Wave crests    Shock wave

Slower than the speed of sound            Faster than the speed of sound

## Science and You
### *Listening Through Your Bones*

Crunch! Crunch! Chewing a crisp apple is a noisy activity. You probably think that most students in the cafeteria can hear you. Don't worry. Your chewing is much noisier to you than it is to those around you.

When you chew something crunchy, the sound of your chewing is carried directly to your inner ear through the bones of your skull. Sound energy conducted through your bones bypasses your eardrum. For others to hear you crunch the apple, the sound waves created by your chewing must move through the air to reach them. Some energy is lost when the sound waves move through the air, and when they vibrate the listener's eardrums.

By the time sound waves from your chewing reach the eardrums of those around you, they have lost energy. Sound waves that carry less energy vibrate your inner ear with less force. The sound you hear as you crunch the apple is louder than the sound others hear because your eardrum will vibrate more.

Most of the sounds you hear come into your ear from the air. For example, when someone is speaking to you, the sound energy moves through the air before it enters your outer ear and causes your eardrum to vibrate. The vibration is transferred to your inner ear. When you create sounds in your mouth by eating, however, the sound energy is conducted directly to your inner ear. You are listening through your bones.

 **ACTIVITY**

**Generalizing**

*Listening Outside*

Obtain a dinner fork.

**1.** Hit the prongs of the fork on a table without damaging the table.

**2.** Quickly place the fork's handle against a bone behind your ear.

**3.** Repeat several times, placing the fork on a different bone near your ear each time.

How can you explain your observations?

**SKILLS WORKOUT**

## Check and Explain

1. Describe the rarefactions and compressions of a sound wave.

2. Explain how temperature affects the speed of sound in air.

3. **Compare and Contrast**  How do sound waves during a sonic boom compare with sound waves traveling at a slower speed?

4. **Make a Model**  Use a drawing to illustrate how the compressions and rarefactions of a sound wave change when they travel through air, water, and solids.

# 15.2 Properties of Sound

## ACTIVITY

### Predicting

**Let It Rip**

Obtain two 5-cm by 30-cm pieces of paper.

**1.** Listen as you rip one piece of paper lengthwise.

**2.** Predict what will happen to the sound if you rip the second piece of paper faster. Test your prediction.

Try this with different kinds of paper.

**SKILLS WARMUP**

## Objectives

▶ **Identify** three properties of sound.

▶ **Estimate** the intensity of some familiar sounds.

▶ **Infer** how loudness, pitch, and timbre relate to the properties of sound waves.

▶ **Define operationally** how movement affects the pitch of sound.

Think of all the things you can do with your voice. You can shout, sing, talk, and whisper. You can even imitate the sounds of machines and nature. What makes the sound waves of a whisper different from those of a shout? Why is the sound of a singing voice different from that of a speaking voice?

If you think of how you made some of these sounds, you can understand how properties of sound waves can affect what you hear. The properties of sound waves include intensity, frequency, and quality. The effects of these three properties are loudness, pitch, and timbre.

## Intensity of Sound

You're reading your report to the class. Because you're a little nervous, you speak softly. When the teacher asks you to speak louder, you force more air from your lungs. Your voice becomes louder because you use more energy to speak. When a sound wave has more energy, the amplitude is greater. Recall that the amplitude of a longitudinal wave depends on its energy.

Two sound waves produced by the same tuning fork are shown in Figure 15.6. The tuning fork at the top has more energy because it was struck harder than the one at the bottom. Except for their amplitudes, the two sound waves are similar. Which tuning fork in Figure 15.6 makes the louder sound?

The sound wave from the tuning fork that was struck hard has a high amplitude. The sound is louder because the sound wave has more energy and does more work to vibrate your eardrum. Loudness depends on your sensitivity to sound and the amplitude of the sound wave.

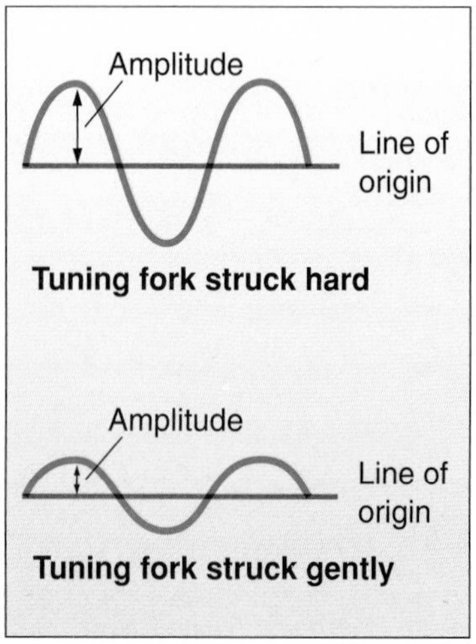

**Figure 15.6** ▲

Which sound wave has greater amplitude?

Think about making sound with a stretched rubber band. When you pull it, the work you do on it gives it energy. When you release the rubber band, its energy does work on the molecules of air in the form of a sound wave.

## Decibels

Everyone might not agree when music is too loud. However, loudness can be measured. The **decibel** (dB) is the unit used to measure sound intensity or loudness. The sound of a leaf falling on the ground has a loudness of about 10 dB. A rock concert can produce sounds of 100 dB or more. Look at Table 15.2 for the decibel level of different common sounds.

You might see a jackhammer operator or an airport worker wearing ear protectors. These protectors decrease the loudness, or energy, of the sounds the worker hears. Your ears need protection because very loud sounds can be harmful. Sounds greater than 120 dB can cause pain. They can also cause vibrations that are intense enough to rupture an eardrum. Constant or daily exposure to high decibel sound, such as very loud music, can cause permanent hearing loss. The delicate bones and nerves that carry sound through your ears to your brain can be damaged by the intense compressions caused by very loud sound.

**Table 15.2**
**Loudness of Common Sounds**

| Sound | Decibels (dB) |
|---|---|
| Jet engine | 170 |
| Rock concert | 100–125 |
| Thunderstorm | 90–110 |
| Vacuum cleaner | 75–80 |
| Conversation | 60–70 |
| Classroom | 35 |
| Whispering | 10–20 |
| Falling leaves | 10 |

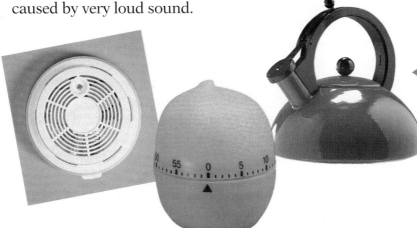

◀ **Figure 15.7**
How loud is the sound each of these objects makes?

## Frequency and Pitch

When you sing the "Happy Birthday" song, you change your voice to sing the tune. The loudness of your voice doesn't change. The **pitch** does. Pitch describes how high or low a sound is. When you sing the word *birthday*, you raise the pitch of your voice.

**Figure 15.8**

How is the frequency of a
high-pitch sound different from
that of a low-pitch sound? ▶

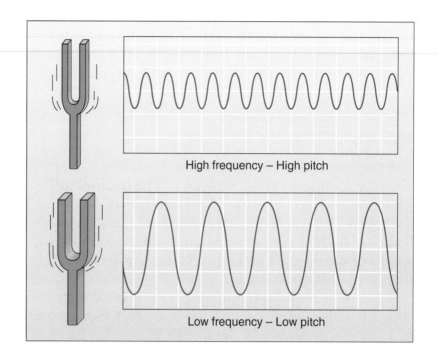

**Table 15.3**
**Frequency Range of**
**Some Sounds**

| Sound Source | Frequency Range (Hz) |
|---|---|
| Porpoise | 7,000–120,000 |
| Bat | 10,000–120,000 |
| Stereo system | 15–30,000 |
| Dog whistle | 20,000–24,000 |
| Frog | 50–8,000 |
| Piano | 30–4,100 |
| Dog | 450–1,800 |
| Human | 85–1,100 |
| Trumpet | 190–990 |

When you change the pitch of your voice, you're changing the frequency of the sound waves you produce. The pitch of a sound depends on its frequency. Sound frequency is the number of sound waves that pass a point in a certain amount of time, such as one second.

The faster the sound waves move, the greater the frequency and the higher the pitch. You hear high-pitch sounds, such as a bird's chirp, when high-frequency sound waves strike your eardrum. Low-frequency sound waves are heard as low-pitch sounds. One example of a low-pitch, low-frequency sound is a note played on a tuba. Give an example of a high-pitch sound.

The **hertz** is a unit used to measure frequency. Because a sound's pitch depends on the frequency of the sound waves, pitch is measured in hertz (Hz), also. The frequency of some common sounds are shown in Table 15.3.

If you have perfect hearing, you can hear sounds ranging from 20 to 20 000 Hz. You can hear a much wider range of frequencies than you can produce with your vocal cords. Many animals can hear sounds that are well beyond the range of human hearing.

Sound above the human range of hearing is called ultrasonic sound. Not only do many kinds of dolphins and bats hear ultrasonic sounds, they also produce them. Some of these animals produce ultrasonic sound to navigate and to find food.

## The Doppler Effect

The increasing loudness of a wailing siren acts as a warning that an emergency vehicle is approaching. If you listen closely to the siren of an ambulance, you'll notice that the pitch of its siren increases as the ambulance approaches. As the ambulance moves away, the pitch of the siren decreases. The noticeable difference in pitch is caused by the movement of the ambulance in relation to the listener.

A change in the frequency and pitch of a sound that is caused by either the movement of the source or the listener is known as the **Doppler effect**. Look at Figure 15.9. The Doppler effect explains the change in the frequency and pitch of the ambulance siren as it moves toward and then away from the listener.

You observe the Doppler effect often. Have you ever been on a train that was moving past a railroad crossing? The pitch of the warning bells increases as you approach them. It decreases as you go by. In Figure 15.9, the sound source is moving and the listener is stationary.

**Figure 15.9
The Doppler Effect** ▼

The sound waves ahead of the ambulance are close together. The frequency and pitch of the siren increases as it approaches the girl.

As the ambulance moves away, the sound waves are farther apart and reach the girl later. The frequency and pitch decrease.

## Sound Quality

The next time you're listening to a band or an orchestra, pay attention to the sounds of the individual instruments. Can you distinguish between them? If the instruments are playing the same note, you must use the *quality* of the sounds to make the distinction.

An instrument produces sound by vibrating air at a certain frequency. Musical instruments actually vibrate air at several different frequencies at the same time. Each frequency produces sound with a different pitch. The pitches produced by an instrument blend and give sound its quality, or timbre. The **timbre** (TIHM bur) of a sound is the blending of different-frequency sound waves that produce sound quality. If you listen carefully, you can hear that a sound produced by one instrument has a different quality than the same-pitch sound produced by another instrument.

The timbre of a sound can fool you about its source. For example, sound synthezisers can produce sounds electronically that have the same timbre as sounds produced by almost any sound source. A synthesizer can duplicate sounds that match the loudness, pitch, and timbre of every instrument in an orchestra. One synthesizer can sound like an entire orchestra.

**Figure 15.10** ▲ ▶

The wave patterns show what each instrument's sound would look like if you could see it. How are the wave patterns different?

## Science and Technology
*Sound-Effects Machines*

When you hear a scary groan in a play or booming thunder in a radio show, you're probably hearing a sound-effects machine that can imitate a certain sound. For example, a radio show can't depend on a thunderstorm to appear on cue, but a thunder machine can produce a similar sound and it is more reliable.

What kind of machine sounds like thunder? One way to create the sound of a distant rumble is to fill a cart with bricks and stones. The cart should have uneven wheels. When the cart is pushed across the floor, the uneven wheels cause the bricks and stones to shift in the cart. The resulting sound is a constant rumble, resembling an approaching storm.

Another kind of sound-effects machine can produce the sound of rainfall. The rain machine is made with a zigzag-shaped metal chute. Dried peas create the sound when poured through the top of the chute. As they make their way through the chute, the peas sound like rain falling on a roof.

An open-ended wooden barrel can create groans, creaks, and squeals. The barrel has a piece of rope fitted into the bottom. In order to produce sounds, the rope is held tightly, and a piece of leather is rubbed against the rope. The barrel acts to reinforce and prolong sounds. This machine can produce a variety of sounds, depending on how and where the leather is rubbed along the rope.

### ACTIVITY

**Making a Model**

*Sound Device*

Use every-day objects at home or in your classroom to create a simple device that makes a sound effect. Try it out on your classmates. See if they can guess what sound you're trying to simulate.

**SKILLS WORKOUT**

## Check and Explain

1. Identify and describe three properties of sound.

2. Estimate the sound intensity of a pencil falling on a tile floor, an accelerating motorcycle, a barking dog, and the siren on an ambulance. Use Table 15.2 as a reference.

3. **Infer** How do loudness, pitch, and timbre relate to a sound's intensity, frequency, and quality?

4. **Define Operationally** Someone in a parked car is honking the horn. As you drive by, you notice that the pitch of the horn becomes lower. How might you account for your observation?

### Inferring

*Sound Cup*

Listen to the sounds in your classroom. Now cup your hands and place them behind each of your ears. How are sounds different? What do you think is happening to the sound waves?

**SKILLS WARMUP**

# 15.3 Sound-Wave Interactions

## Objectives

▶ **Identify** five types of sound-wave interaction.

▶ **Define** resonance.

▶ **Generalize** about the behavior of echoes.

▶ **Infer** how sound waves interact to affect sound.

How do movie sound directors make a hallway seem long and empty? They add sound effects, such as the distant echo of footsteps. Sound directors know how a sound changes in different surroundings. They can change the sound of the footsteps so that they seem to be on a wooden floor or on concrete stairs.

## Reflection of Sound

You've probably noticed that a shout sounds different in a vacant gym than it does in a cluttered classroom. When you shout, the sound of your voice moves away from your mouth. But what happens if the sound waves strike a hard, flat surface, such as a wall? As you can see in Figure 15.11, the sound waves of the singer's voice bounce back into the auditorium when they reflect off of the back wall.

**Figure 15.11**
Think of where you were the last time you heard an echo. How was that place like the auditorium shown here? ▼

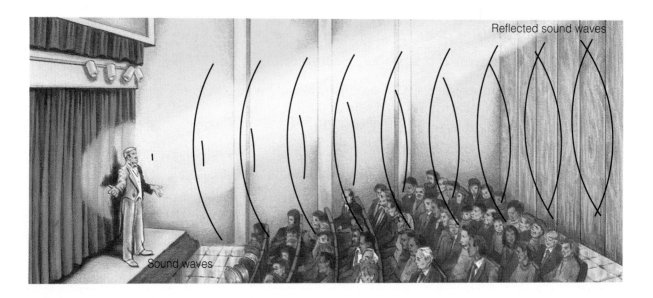

Reflected sound waves

Sound waves

Some energy from the sound wave passes through or is absorbed by the wall, but most of the sound is reflected. If you're sitting in the audience, the first sound you hear comes directly from its source, the speaker. A fraction of a second later, you hear the reflected sound wave. The reflected sound is an echo.

Why would you hear an echo in some auditoriums and not in others? The properties of the reflecting surface and the distance of the reflecting surface from the sound source affect echoes. Look at Figure 15.12. Notice that a curtain hangs from the back wall of the auditorium. Also notice that sound waves are not reflected off of the curtained wall as they are off of the hard, flat wall shown in Figure 15.11. Because the curtains at the back of the auditorium absorb most of the sound waves, very little sound is reflected into the auditorium. By changing a surface that reflects sound easily, echoes can be reduced or eliminated.

The distance of the reflecting surface from the sound source also determines if echoes are present. You can hear an echo if it comes at least 0.1 second after the original sound. For example, to hear an echo of your own voice, the reflected sound waves must reach your ears at least 0.1 second after you shout. During that time, sound waves travel about 34 m in air. To hear an echo of your voice, you must be at least 17 m from the reflecting surface. An echo can only occur naturally in an uncluttered space, such as a gymnasium. How would the amount of clutter affect sound waves?

**Figure 15.12**
Think of an auditorium with curtains on the back wall. What will happen to the sound waves when they reach the back wall? ▼

Sound waves are absorbed

Sound waves

## Diffraction of Sound

Suppose you're standing in the hallway of your school. Can you hear a conversation around the corner? Of course you can. Sound waves diffract, or bend, around barriers like walls.

As waves move through an opening in a barrier, they fan out into the area beyond the barrier. Sound waves moving through an open hallway fan out similarly into the bend in the hallway. Because of the diffraction of sound waves, you can hear the sounds coming from places you can't see. You can see how sound waves diffract through an open door in Figure 15.13.

Wave diffraction is greatest when the wavelength of a wave is about the same as the width of the opening in the barrier. Most windows and doorways are about 0.75 to 1 m wide. In air, sounds that have a pitch between 350 to 400 Hz have a wavelength close to these values.

Lower-frequency sound waves diffract more than higher-frequency sound waves do. You're able to hear mostly low-pitch sounds, such as rumbling traffic, through an open window. High-pitch sounds, such as voices, are less noticeable.

**Figure 15.13**

Why can the students next to the door hear the people in the hallway? ▼

## Refraction of Sound

Everyone knows that it's more difficult to see at night than during the day. But the reverse is true when it comes to the sounds you hear. Why is this so?

To answer this question, you first have to explore how waves behave when they travel from one medium to another. When the wave enters a new medium, its speed changes. If the wave enters the new medium at an angle, the change in its speed causes a change in its direction. The change in the direction of a wave moving from one material into another is called refraction. What does this have to do with hearing better at night?

The speed of sound waves in air increases as air temperature increases. If sound waves move through air at different temperatures, the sound waves bend or refract. The direction of sound waves traveling in air that is warmed by the ground, as it is during the day, is shown in Figure 15.14 on the right. The left side shows sound waves moving through air that is cooler near the ground. The air is cooler near the ground during the evening.

Study the art carefully to see how the direction of the sound waves differs when air temperature is different. When the air near the ground is cold, sound waves are directed toward the ground rather than away from it. Since you're on the ground, the sound waves get directed toward you rather than away from you. At night, the air is usually colder near the ground. So, you can usually hear sounds better at night than during the day.

**Figure 15.14**

Why are the children not aware of the passing car during the day? ▼

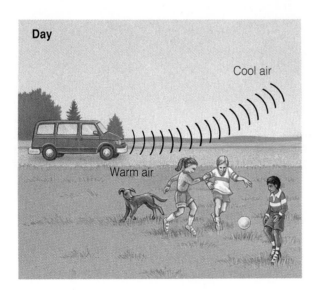

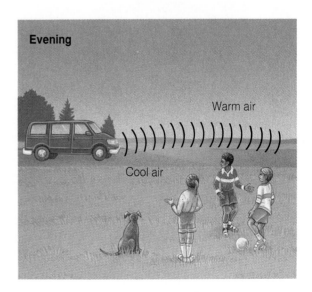

## Sound Interference

Sometimes it's harder to hear in some sections of an auditorium than in others. You wouldn't want to be sitting in these sections for a rock concert. You want to be in a seat where you can see *and* hear everything.

Why are sounds easier to hear in some locations than in others? The answer has to do with the interference of the sound waves. Sound waves can interfere in two ways. Look at Figure 15.15. The spacing of the dots represents compressions and rarefactions, or the amplitude, of the sound waves. On the left, the waves that combine result in **destructive interference**. On the right, the waves that combine result in **constructive interference**.

**Figure 15.15**
**Destructive and Constructive Interference** ▼

When the high amplitude of one sound wave is subtracted from the low amplitude of the other, the sound will be less than either of the two sounds that produced it.

When the high amplitudes of two sound waves add to each other, the sound will be louder than either of the two sounds that produced it.

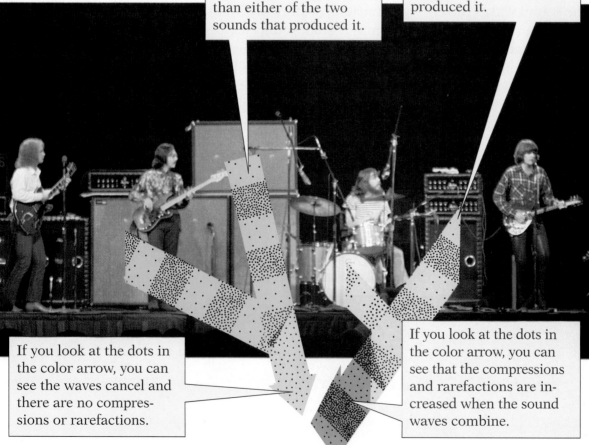

If you look at the dots in the color arrow, you can see the waves cancel and there are no compressions or rarefactions.

If you look at the dots in the color arrow, you can see that the compressions and rarefactions are increased when the sound waves combine.

The difference between constructive and destructive interference depends on when sound waves arrive at the same point. If they arrive at the same time, the waves are in phase, and the interference is *constructive*. The intensity of the sound is increased. If they arrive at intervals, then the waves are out of phase and the interference is *destructive*. The sound intensity is reduced.

In most auditoriums and arenas, sounds are amplified electronically. Sounds come from loud speakers placed in different locations. Interference occurs wherever sound waves from one speaker meet the reflected sound waves from other speakers. Interference happens at many locations in the auditorium. If you change your seat, you can move from an area of destructive interference to one of constructive interference.

## Resonance

A struck bell, a plucked guitar string, and a dropped table knife will vibrate and make sounds. Each object vibrates at a particular frequency, known as its natural frequency. The frequency of a sound wave results in a particular pitch. The natural frequency of a small bell is higher than that of a large bell. When struck, the smaller bell will ring at a higher pitch.

A tuning fork is shown in Figure 15.16. When the tuning fork is struck, it makes a sound in a particular pitch.

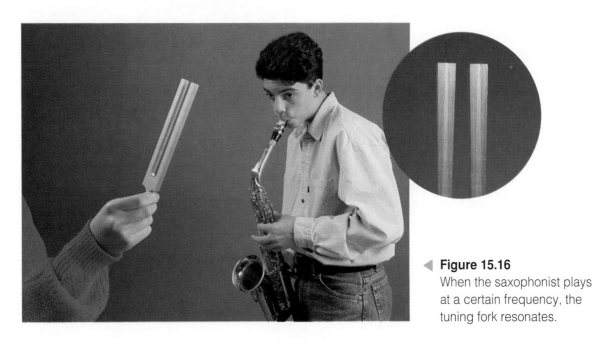

◀ **Figure 15.16**
When the saxophonist plays at a certain frequency, the tuning fork resonates.

Tuning forks are used to tune musical instruments. The musician plays a note on his instrument and compares its pitch to the pitch made by the tuning fork. He adjusts his instrument so the pitch of each note matches the pitch made by the tuning fork for that note.

When the saxophone player in Figure 15.16 plays at the natural frequency of the tuning fork, the vibrations create resonance (REHZ uh nuhnts) in the tuning fork. The vibration of an object at its natural frequency is called **resonance**. You can experiment with an instrument to find the natural frequency of an unlabeled tuning fork by playing different notes and seeing which one causes the tuning fork to resonate.

Finding the natural frequency of a tuning fork is just one example of resonance. Many objects have a natural frequency that is easily matched by other vibrating objects. The windows in your home rattle when the sound given off by a passing truck matches their natural frequency.

## *Historical Notebook*

### *Incident at Tacoma Narrows Bridge*

A marching band can create rhythmic vibrations even when it isn't playing music. Sometimes you can feel the ground vibrate from marching feet. Do you know why bands and military units don't march in step across suspension bridges?

The rhythm of the marching can cause the bridge to vibrate. If the frequency of the vibration caused by the marching matches the natural frequency of the bridge, resonance can occur. Resonance can cause the bridge to move up and down until its structure weakens and collapses.

English cavalry troops marching across a footbridge in 1831 caused the bridge to collapse when they marched in rhythm with the natural frequency of the bridge. Winds can also cause vibrations in suspension bridges. On November 7, 1940, vibrations caused by a mild gale produced resonance in the Tacoma Narrows Bridge in the state of Washington. In a few hours, the flexible

suspension bridge was torn apart and collapsed. Engineers now design suspension bridges with heavier, less-flexible roadbeds that aren't affected by wind.

1. Why is the flexibility of a suspension bridge important for developing resonance?

2. Explain how the wind or the rhythm of marching feet can cause a bridge to vibrate at its natural frequency.

## Science and Technology
### *Acoustics—Sound Control*

You might go to your school auditorium to hear a speaker, watch a play, or listen to a concert by the school chorus or band. If you can hear most of the sound from the stage in any location, the auditorium has good acoustics (uh KOO stihks). The concert hall in Figure 15.17 has a special design. Acoustics engineers design concert halls, theaters, and recording studios to control sound waves.

Reflected sound waves can add richness to sounds. Reflected sound waves in a room make sounds lively by making them last a little longer. To be heard, speech sounds should be reflected about a second in a small auditorium. The sound of music should be reflected one to two seconds in a concert hall. If sounds last too long, they can become garbled.

Reflected sound waves can interfere with the acoustics of a room by creating loud spots and dead spots. If a room is large enough, reflected sound waves cause echoes. Acoustics engineers know how to control reflected sounds. They use hard surfaces to direct reflected sounds to the audience or in the direction of a recording microphone. Reflected sounds are controlled by covering hard surfaces with materials, such as fabric or cork, that absorb sound waves. Good acoustics are the result of the effective use of knowledge about sound.

**Figure 15.17** ▲
How do you think the roof over the stage affects sound?

## Check and Explain

1. Identify five types of sound-wave interactions.

2. What is resonance?

3. **Generalize** Why must a reflecting surface be at least 17 m away for you to hear an echo of your shout?

4. **Infer** On two consecutive nights, you attend concerts in an outdoor stadium. Each night you listen to the same entertainer sing the same songs. On the second night, you sit in a different seat. You can't hear the singer's voice as well as you did on the first night. What might cause the change?

# Activity 15  How do sound waves reflect?

*Skills* Observe; Model; Predict; Infer

## Task 1  Prelab Prep
Collect the following items: paper, pencil, 4 identical cardboard tubes, tape, 26 × 40 cm sheet of cardboard, a protractor, and a ticking clock or watch.

## Task 2  Data Record
1. At the top of a sheet of paper, write *Observations*.
2. Copy Table 15.4. Include 5 empty rows to record your data.
3. Notice in the figure shown that tube *A* and tube *B* form an angle. You will adjust this angle for each of the five trials of the experiment. To record the position of the tubes in each trial, draw the angle they form in the appropriate row in the table, using two straight lines.
4. Record the loudness you observe in each trial, using a scale from 1–10. Use 1 for a very faint sound and 10 for a very loud sound.

## Task 3  Procedure
1. Make two long tubes by taping two of the short tubes together. Label the tubes *A* and *B*.
2. Have a classmate hold the sheet of cardboard perpendicular to a table top. Arrange the ticking clock and the two tubes in the positions shown in the figure.

## Table 15.4  Loudness of Ticking

| Position of Tubes | Loudness (1-10) | Prediction |
|---|---|---|
|  |  |  |
|  |  |  |
|  |  |  |
|  |  |  |

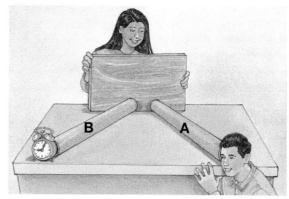

3. Cover one ear with your hand. Place your other ear near the opening of tube *A* and listen. Record the position of the tube and the loudness of the ticking sound.
4. Move tube *B* and the clock to a new position. Don't move tube *A*. Predict the position of tube *B* where the ticking will be loudest. Record your prediction. Repeat step 3.
5. Repeat steps 3 and 4 four more times.

## Task 4  Analysis
1. Identify the angle of tubes *A* and *B* when the ticking of the clock was loudest.
2. Identify the angle of tubes *A* and *B* when the ticking of the clock was faintest.
3. How did your predictions compare to the actual result in each trial?

## Task 5  Conclusion
How did the position of tube *B* influence the volume of the sound? Explain why the angle of the tube influences the amount of sound energy reflected. On what did you base your prediction about the position of the tube?

## Application
Observe reflected sound in and around your home or school. Make a list of places where you can create echoes with your voice. Make a list of places where your voice won't echo. Describe the best surfaces for reflecting sound.

# Chapter 15 Review

## Concept Summary

### 15.1 Wave Model of Sound
▶ Sound waves are produced by a vibrating object.
▶ A sound wave is a longitudinal wave composed of compressions and rarefactions that move through matter in the direction of the sound.
▶ The speed of sound depends on the elasticity, density, and temperature of the material through which sound waves travel.
▶ A sonic boom occurs when an object moves faster than the speed of sound.

### 15.2 Properties of Sound
▶ The unit for loudness, or intensity, is the decibel. The unit for pitch, or frequency, is called the hertz.
▶ Some animals can hear sound beyond the range of human hearing.
▶ The amplitude of a sound wave is a measure of its loudness, or intensity.
▶ The frequency of a sound wave is a measure of its pitch.
▶ The timbre of a sound is the sound quality produced by a mixture of different frequency sound waves.

### 15.3 Sound-Wave Interactions
▶ Sound waves interact to produce sound reflection, diffraction, refraction, interference, and resonance.
▶ Resonance occurs when the vibration of an object at its natural frequency is caused by another object vibrating at the same frequency.
▶ Echoes are produced when sound waves reflect from a surface.

## Chapter Vocabulary

| | | |
|---|---|---|
| sound wave (15.1) | hertz (15.2) | destructive interference (15.3) |
| decibel (15.2) | Doppler effect (15.2) | constructive interference (15.3) |
| pitch (15.2) | timbre (15.2) | resonance (15.3) |

## Check Your Vocabulary

Use the vocabulary words above to complete the following sentences correctly.

1. The unit used to measure sound frequency is the ____.

2. When two sound waves interact in ____, one amplitude is subtracted from the other.

3. Sound travels through matter as a(n) ____.

4. The unit used to measure the loudness of sound is the ____.

5. An increase in frequency will cause an increase in the ____ of the sound.

6. The change in pitch of an approaching siren is due to the ____.

7. When the amplitudes of two sound waves add to each other, the result is ____.

8. Sound quality, or ____, is the blending of different-frequency sound waves.

9. An object vibrating at its natural frequency is also known as ____.

## Write Your Vocabulary

Write sentences using the vocabulary words above. Show that you know what each word means.

# Chapter 15 Review

## Check Your Knowledge

Answer the following in complete sentences.

1. What are the characteristics of a sound wave?

2. How are sound waves produced?

3. Why doesn't sound travel through a vacuum?

4. What kind of sound waves produce a high pitch?

5. What is the Doppler effect? When does it occur?

6. What happens to a sound wave when it is refracted?

7. What causes two sound waves to combine and produce no sound?

Determine whether each statement is true or false. Write *true* if it is true. If it is false, change the underlined term(s) to make the statement true.

8. The <u>compression</u> in a sound wave compares to the trough in a transverse wave.

9. Planes that fly <u>faster</u> than the speed of sound can create a sonic boom.

10. If the frequency of a sound wave increases, its pitch becomes <u>lower</u>.

11. Drapes, furniture, and carpeting <u>reflect</u> most sound waves.

12. When sounds in a large room are garbled, the cause is probably caused by the <u>constructive interference</u> of sound waves.

13. You can hear better at night because of a sound-wave interaction called <u>destructive interference</u>.

14. The loudness of a sound depends on the <u>amplitude</u> of its sound wave.

## Check Your Understanding

Apply the concepts you have learned to answer each question.

1. **Application** Describe two situations where a person might suffer hearing loss. What could a person do to avoid damage to their hearing in these situations?

2. If you are 700 m from a batter when you see her hit a ball, how long will you wait to hear the sound of the bat hitting the ball? The temperature of the air is 20°C.

3. Draw sound waves which compare and contrast the concepts of loudness and pitch.

4. Classify each of the following as having a high pitch or a low pitch.

   a. siren
   b. human infant voice
   c. bass fiddle
   d. flute
   e. whistle
   f. thunder

5. What variables might affect the measurement of the speed of sound at any particular location? Describe a location and its variables.

6. **Mystery Photo** The photograph on page 358 shows a Chinese stringed instrument called a liuyen ch'in. Different pitches are possible because the strings are of different thicknesses. The wavelength of a particular string can be shortened by pressing it against a fret, or ridge, located on the neck of the instrument. The sound is amplified in the hollow body of the instrument.

   a. If a player shortened the length of a string, how would that influence the sound when the string is plucked?

   b. How does the shape of its hollow body affect the sound of the instrument?

## Develop Your Skills

Use the skills you have developed in this chapter to complete each activity.

1. **Interpret Data** Study the illustrations shown below.

   a. Which represents the loudest sound?

   b. Which represents the next-loudest sound?

   c. Which represents the least-loud sound?

   d. Which characteristic of a sound wave is associated with loudness?

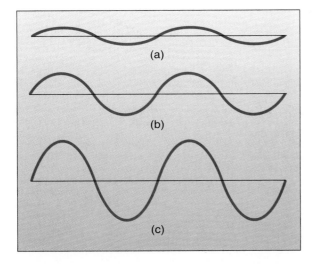

2. **Make a Model** Gather bits of paper or coins. These items will represent molecules. Make models of the molecules in a gas, a liquid, and a solid. Demonstrate how the speed of sound varies in each of these states of matter.

3. **Data Bank** Examine the table on page 640. Based on the data, answer the following question: What relationship exists between the density of a substance and the speed at which sound travels through it?

## Make Connections

1. **Link the Concepts** Below is a concept map showing how some of the main concepts in this chapter link together. Only part of the map is filled in. Finish the map, using words and ideas you find on the previous pages.

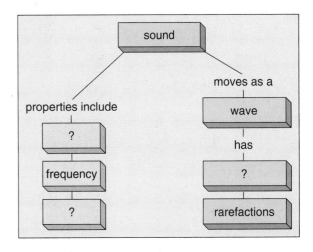

2. **Science and Literature** Many writers have used the word *sound* to create poetic images or to communicate ideas and emotions. Below is a reference to sound from William Shakespeare's play *Henry V*. In your own words state what you think Shakespeare wished to communicate.

   "But the saying is true, 'The empty vessel makes the greatest sound.'"

3. **Science and Technology** Hearing impairment is neither new nor uncommon. New technology has developed devices that improve the impaired hearing of many people. Research the history of hearing aids and other audio devices. Write a report on the development of the hearing aid used inside the ear. Include current research for new and better devices and techniques.

# Chapter 16 Using Sound

## Chapter Sections

16.1 How You Hear

16.2 Sounds You Hear

16.3 Sound Technology

## What do you see?

"It looks like the ear canal of a human. It is located near the brain on each side of the head. It is part of the human sense of hearing. When sound goes through the ear, it causes the ear bones to vibrate, and nerves send messages to the brain registering the sound. That is why you can hear."

*Jason Ko*
*Durham Academy*
*Durham, North Carolina*

To find out more about the photograph, look on page 406. As you read this chapter, you will learn about how you use sound.

# 16.1 How You Hear

## Objectives

▶ **Describe** the structure and functions of the ear.

▶ **Trace** the path of a sound wave through the ear.

▶ **Infer** how hearing can be damaged by exposure to sound.

▶ **Make a model** of the ear.

▼ **ACTIVITY**

**Observing**

*Hear! Hear!*

**1.** Use one hand to cover one ear. Close your eyes.

**2.** Have someone clap or whistle from a location about 5 m away.

**3.** Try to guess the location of the sound. Record your response. Repeat two more times.

**4.** Uncover your ear and repeat the procedure.

Are two ears better than one?

**SKILLS WARMUP**

What you probably enjoy most at a fireworks display are the spectacular bursts of color. You also hear whistling and booming sounds as the fireworks explode high in the sky. The sounds you hear heighten your awareness of the world around you.

Sounds you hear also give you information. What would movies and TV shows be like without sound? You'd have to guess what the actors were saying. There wouldn't be any music, sound effects, or applause.

## Hearing and Balance

Sound surrounds you all the time, but you can't hear every sound. Your ears aren't sensitive enough to hear sounds outside a certain range. However, your ears can detect the tiny vibrations a pin makes when it falls to the floor. Your ears also detect large vibrations, such as the crash of thunder or a pounding bass drum. Look at Figure 16.1. What sound would your ears detect if you were standing nearby?

You can hear your friend's voice as you carry on a conversation in a noisy crowd. You can detect that sound although other sounds interfere. You hear all the many different sounds your friend's voice makes when forming words. When you listen to music, you hear the different sounds of the various instruments.

In addition to detecting sounds, your ears have another function. Part of your ear controls your sense of balance. The semicircular canals in your ears are filled with liquid. They also contain hair cells. The hair cells respond to changes in the position of your head. You are able to detect which direction is up and which is down, and to maintain your balance.

**Figure 16.1** ▲
What is the vibrating sound source? What sound does it make?

# The Human Ear

The human ear is divided into three sections—the outer, middle, and inner ear. As you read about the parts of the human ear, find each one in Figure 16.2. The part of your ear that you can see and the ear canal make up your **outer ear**. The ear canal ends with a tightly stretched membrane called the eardrum.

Behind the eardrum is the **middle ear**. The middle ear contains the three smallest bones in the human body—the hammer, the anvil, and the stirrup. Find these bones in Figure 16.2. The stirrup presses against another membrane called the oval window.

The oval window separates your middle ear from your **inner ear**. The semicircular canals and the cochlea (KOHK-lee-uh) are part of the inner ear. Find the cochlea. It is the coiled organ in the inner ear.

You can't see inside the cochlea in Figure 16.2, but if you could, you would see tiny hair cells lining it. The cochlea is filled with liquid. Motion of the cochlea causes the liquid to move and stimulate the hair cells. The hair cells send signals to the auditory nerve. The auditory nerve relays the signals to your brain. Your brain interprets the signals as sound.

How does your ear detect sound? Sound must travel to reach your ear. Sound travels in waves caused by a series of compressions and rarefactions in the air. When sound waves reach your ears, a series of events occurs allowing you to hear a sound. Study these events in Figure 16.2.

**Figure 16.2
How You Hear** ▼

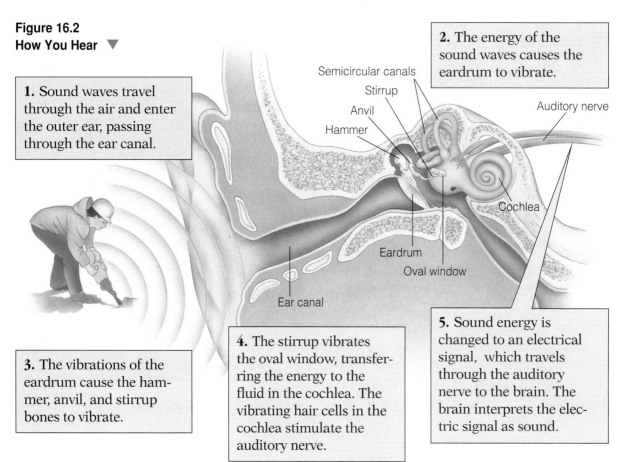

**1.** Sound waves travel through the air and enter the outer ear, passing through the ear canal.

Semicircular canals
Stirrup
Anvil
Hammer
Auditory nerve
Cochlea
Eardrum
Oval window
Ear canal

**2.** The energy of the sound waves causes the eardrum to vibrate.

**3.** The vibrations of the eardrum cause the hammer, anvil, and stirrup bones to vibrate.

**4.** The stirrup vibrates the oval window, transferring the energy to the fluid in the cochlea. The vibrating hair cells in the cochlea stimulate the auditory nerve.

**5.** Sound energy is changed to an electrical signal, which travels through the auditory nerve to the brain. The brain interprets the electric signal as sound.

# Hearing Range

How well you hear a sound depends on its frequency and intensity. Recall that frequency is the number of waves that passes a certain point every second. Frequency determines the pitch of sound. High-frequency sound waves have a high pitch. Low-frequency sounds have a low pitch. You hear a range of sounds from frequencies as low as 20 cycles per second, or 20 Hz, up to 20,000 cycles per second, or 20,000 Hz. Sounds with frequencies below 20 Hz or above 20,000 Hz are beyond the range of human hearing. Study Table 16.1. How does the range of human hearing compare to that of other animals?

Your hearing is also sensitive to the loudness, or intensity, of sound. Recall that the unit used to measure sound intensity is the decibel (dB). A sound of 0 dB is the least sound humans can hear. Sounds above 120 dB, such as the sound of a jet plane at takeoff, can actually rupture your eardrums and cause permanent hearing loss.

The substance through which a sound travels can also affect what you hear. For example, you may not hear sound waves coming through the air from your neighbor's stereo. However, you may hear sound traveling through a solid wall. Look at Figure 16.3. Will the sound travel farther through water or through air? How is the speed of a sound related to the phase of the medium through which it travels?

**Table 16.1**
**Ranges of Hearing**

| Organism | Frequency (in Hz) |
|----------|-------------------|
| Dolphin | 150–150,000 |
| Bat | 1,000–120,000 |
| Cat | 60–70,000 |
| Dog | 15–50,000 |
| Human | 20–20,000 |

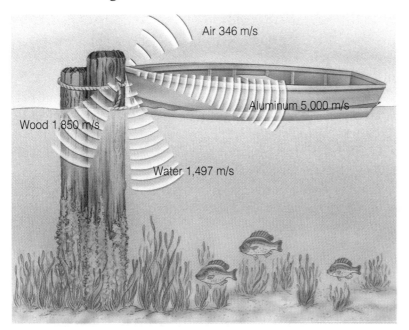

Air 346 m/s

Aluminum 5,000 m/s

Wood 1,850 m/s

Water 1,497 m/s

◀ **Figure 16.3**
Sound moves at different speeds and distances through water, air, aluminum, and wood. As a sound wave travels faster, its energy can travel farther.

# Consider This

## Should There Be More Regulation of Noise Pollution?

In 1972, Congress enacted the Noise Control Act to protect people from "noise that jeopardizes their health and welfare." The Environmental Protection Agency, or EPA, estimated that 34 million people experience noise levels that cause hearing loss in locations other than the workplace.

### Consider Some Issues

Even noise that isn't loud enough to damage hearing can be harmful to health. Noise is linked to headaches, ulcers, stress, and high blood pressure. It can upset sleep patterns and the ability to learn for some people.

Some people believe that any restriction on noise interferes with their rights. Some feel that music must be loud to be fully appreciated. Representatives of industry claim that noisy machinery is unavoidable.

**Think About It** Is your ability to concentrate affected by loud noise? Do loudness levels affect you? Do you enjoy the sound of loud music? Should you be prevented from turning up the volume of your radio or stereo?

**Write About It** Write a paper stating your position for or against laws that control noise. Explain your reasons for your opinion.

## Science and You *Hearing Protectors*

Exposure to loud sounds can damage your hearing. You can avoid damage by using devices called hearing protectors. Hearing protectors can prevent both temporary and permanent hearing loss.

In many workplaces, noise levels are carefully monitored. If the sound is too loud, it can rupture a worker's eardrums. If the sound level isn't very loud, but continues over a long period of time, hearing loss can result. The hearing loss occurs because the hair cells inside the cochlea become damaged by overuse. Constant noise levels at lower volumes can also affect a worker's health by causing stress.

Two basic kinds of hearing protectors are available. One kind is earplugs, made of a material that absorbs sound-wave energy. To protect yourself from loud sounds, you insert the earplugs directly into the ear canal. Earplugs are custom fit to your ear canal to

block the most sound possible. Many different kinds of earplugs are available in drug stores at low cost.

Another kind of hearing protector looks like a pair of earmuffs. When you put on the earmuffs, they completely enclose your outer ears. The earmuffs are filled with a foamlike material that absorbs sound-wave energy. The earmuffs usually block sound better than earplugs do.

Look at Figure 16.4. Airport employees working near jet aircraft wear hearing protectors to block the roar of a jet engine. The sound from a jet engine can measure 170 dB. Human hearing can be damaged easily by sound this intense. In what other situations might it be important to use hearing protectors?

## Check and Explain

1. List the parts of the ear that play a role in hearing. Identify whether each part is located in the outer, middle, or inner ear.

2. Describe the path a sound wave travels before you hear a whistle being blown.

3. **Infer** How could sound damage your hearing? Give examples of dangerous sounds.

4. **Make a Model** Use paper and pencil, or materials of your choice, to make a model of the ear.

*Musical Listing*

Make a list of all the musical instruments you can think of. Study your list and devise a way to classify the instruments. What characteristics did you use to classify the instruments?

**SKILLS WARMUP**

# 16.2 Sounds You Hear

## Objectives

▶ **Explain** how musical instruments make sound.

▶ **Distinguish** between stringed, wind, and percussion instruments.

▶ **Compare** and **contrast** musical sounds with noise.

▶ **Make a model** of a musical instrument.

Y ou recognize many different kinds of sound. On the radio or TV, you hear many kinds of music. You may hear rock or country bands that perform with electric guitars or other kinds of instruments.

For thousands of years, people all over the world have invented their own instruments and musical styles. Look at the instruments in Figure 16.5. In Australia, people play a long instrument called a *didjeridoo*, made from a tree trunk. It produces a raspy, low, twangy sound. In China, people invented many stringed instruments. One instrument, the *ch'in*, looks like a long, narrow Greek lyre and sounds like a mandolin. In West Africa, people developed the *cora*. The cora looks like a banjo, but it sounds like a harp. All musical instruments produce and amplify vibrations. These vibrations produce sound waves that people recognize as music.

**Figure 16.5**
**Musical Instruments from Around the World** ▼

Cora

Didjeridoo

Ch'in

## Music

People like music because it has an interesting beat and it produces pleasing sounds. The characteristics of musical sounds are pitch, intensity, rhythm, melody, harmony, and quality. A sound played at a specific frequency is called a note.

Pitch is the highness or lowness of the note, or the tone. Intensity is the loudness of the note. Because notes last different lengths of time, music also has rhythm. Rhythm is a repeating pattern of beats, or accents. The repeating pattern makes it possible for you to keep time to the music.

Each piece of music has a different melody, or series of pitches. Look at Figure 16.6. The melody of a song is easy to remember. You can hum or sing it. Most musical pieces also have harmony. Harmony occurs when three or more notes are played together to produce a pleasing sound. The note combinations selected for harmonies vary for different cultures and styles of music.

Music usually has several pitches that blend together. For example, a violin string vibrates at a certain frequency to produce its main tone. If parts of the string also vibrate at a different rate, you hear higher tones, or **overtones**.

Each musical instrument produces a different combination of overtones. The combination of overtones help to give each instrument a distinctive sound. For example, a flute and a clarinet can play a note with the same pitch. However, the sound of the note will be different for each instrument due to the overtones.

### ▼ ACTIVITY

**Observing**

*Sound Instruments*

Using a sound recording, listen to sounds made by the three different kinds of instruments. How do the sounds relate to the size of each instrument? Do your observations apply to other kinds of instruments? Explain.

**SKILLS WORKOUT**

**Figure 16.6**
The notes on the top staff indicate the melody. The notes on the bottom staff are a harmony that fits with the melody. ▼

# Musical Instruments

Musical instruments look very different. They are classified into three main groups: string, wind, and percussion. String instruments, such as the guitar, violin, and piano, produce a tone when their strings vibrate. Long, thick strings make low-pitch sounds. Short, thin strings have a higher pitch. When the strings vibrate more, the volume of sound increases. String instruments usually have a wooden sound box that amplifies the sounds of the vibrating strings.

Wind instruments, such as the flute, trumpet, and saxophone, contain a column of air that vibrates when you blow into the instrument. Varying the length of the air column changes the pitch. A long air column

### Koto

A koto is an example of a stringed instrument from a different culture. In Japan, people play the koto in traditional orchestras. The 2 m-long wooden sound box rests on the floor. The player uses three ivory picks worn on her fingers to pluck the waxed silk strings. The 13 strings are tuned to different pitches. ▼

### Violin ▲

A violin has four strings. Different notes are played by pressing a finger on the strings to change their lengths. If the string is shortened, a higher pitch is produced. The violinist draws a bow across the strings to make them vibrate. The bow is made of tightly stretched horsehair attached to a flexible stick.

### Keyboard Instruments ▲

Keyboard instruments differ in how they produce sound. Each key of a piano causes a string or a set of strings to vibrate and make a tone. Strings of different length and thickness produce different pitches. Each key of a pipe organ opens a pipe with a column of air. Each different-size pipe produces a different pitch. Each key of a synthesizer keyboard triggers a different internal-tone generator.

produces a low note, while a shorter air column produces a high note. If you blow harder into the instrument, the volume of sound increases.

You can play a percussion instrument, such as a drum or cymbal, by striking it. You control the sound intensity by how hard you strike. The covering can be tightened or loosened so that it vibrates at different frequencies. The tension on the drum covering affects pitch.

Look at the different instruments on these pages. Read about how each instrument works. What other string, wind, or percussion instruments can you name?

## Physical Science

### L I N K

Make your own instrument. Obtain five straws and tape.

**1.** Tape the straws together, side-by-side.

**2.** Cut off each straw so it is shorter than the next one.

**3.** Blow across the top.

What is vibrating and producing the sound?

### A C T I V I T Y

**Drums**

A drummer striking the drumhead, or skin, of a drum causes vibrations. The body of the drum amplifies these vibrations. Drums of different sizes and materials produce different sounds. Also, the placement of the drumstick on the head and the force of the drumstick striking the head changes the sounds produced. ▼

**Saxophone** ▲

A saxophonist blows across a reed in the mouthpiece. The vibrating reed vibrates the air inside the instrument to produce sound. The saxophone also has holes along the side that can be opened and closed to produce different notes. Opening and closing the holes changes the length of the vibrating air column. Sound frequency depends on the length of the air column.

**Trumpet** ▲

A trumpet player blows a stream of air into the trumpet mouthpiece. The column of air inside the trumpet vibrates and produces a tone. To change the pitch, the player opens and closes valves that change the length of the air column.

## Noise

Imagine being stuck in a big-city traffic jam. The city streets are clogged with stalled traffic. The motors of the cars, buses, and trucks make a constant rumbling sound. Drivers begin to lean on their horns. Some drivers shout from their car windows. Other drivers try to block out the sounds by turning up the volume on their car radios. The streets are filled with annoying, unwanted sounds—noise.

Noise has been a concern to people for a long time. For example, the Roman ruler Julius Caesar was so upset by the street noise in Rome that he banned chariots from the city. In general, any sound that disturbs or threatens your mental or physical health is noise. However, people don't always agree on what noise is.

Everyone agrees that sounds loud enough to burst a person's eardrums are noise. However, not everyone agrees on when a sound is too loud. Loud music from a

## Historical Notebook

### History of Musical Instruments

People have played music and danced since prehistoric times. The first musical instruments probably involved tapping the ground, special rocks, hollow logs, or the human body itself. By 10,000 B.C., people were making flutes from hollow bones. Perhaps stringed instruments began when a hunter picked up a bow and began to play notes. A 5,000-year-old image of a harp has been found in Sumer, near Iraq and Iran. Stringed instruments existed even earlier in Africa.

Flutes and musical pipes were used in Egypt more than 6,000 years ago. In many parts of the world, people made flutelike instruments by drilling holes in cow horns. Such flutes later became a part of the bagpipe. Slender pipes made of wood or cane were played by the Etruscans long before the Romans ruled Italy. In North and South America, people made a variety of flutes long before the arrival of the Europeans.

In ancient China, people understood that sound is made by vibrations and that it is carried through the air to the ear. They tuned drums and bells to make different sounds. In ancient Rome, people played metal trumpets during ceremonies and parades. Early Muslim leaders, called Caliphs, had vast military bands that played trumpets, drums, and cymbals.

1. Study this short history of musical instruments. What ideas most surprised you? Explain why.

2. Musical instruments from different parts of the world show many similarities. How do you explain this?

3. Do library research on the history of a musical instrument. Make an illustrated timeline showing the development of the instrument.

radio may be pleasing to some people, but it may be noise to others. You might even classify soft music or conversation that disturbs your sleep as noise.

Most sounds that people classify as noise lack pleasing sound quality, definite pitch, rhythm, and pattern. Look at Figure 16.7a and 16.7b. Compare the sound waves produced by music to the sound waves produced by noise. Notice that the music waves have a regular pattern. In contrast, the waves produced by noise are random and irregular.

Some modern composers deliberately blur the distinction between noise and music. They blend sounds of machines or other noisy objects into their compositions. For example, the sound of helicopters could be used to introduce a song and later fade into the music. Although the sound of helicopters is considered noise, the effect would be dramatic, and it might serve to make the words and feelings of the song more meaningful. Musicians can use electronic keyboards to record noises, such as a door slamming or glass breaking. Electronic keyboards can reproduce these noises in a variety of pitches. What music can you name that uses sound this way?

## ▼ ACTIVITY

### Classifying

*Noise*

List all the sounds you hear in three different places, such as a school hall, the inside of a bus, your dinner table, or a street corner. Identify the sounds you would classify as noise. Explain your choices.

**SKILLS WORKOUT**

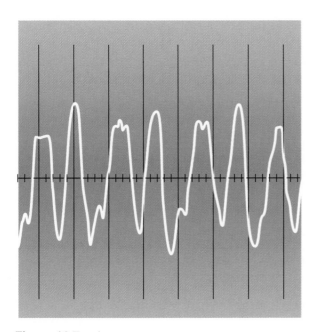

**Figure 16.7a** ▲
Study the pattern of sound waves made by a clarinet. Compare them to the pattern of sound waves in Figure 16.7b.

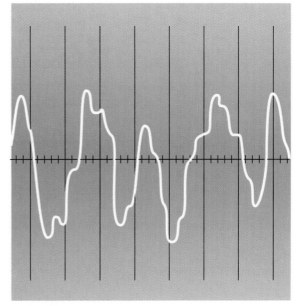

**Figure 16.7b** ▲
These sound waves are random and irregular. Sounds classified as noise often make sound waves like these.

**Table 16.2**
**Noise Exposure Limits**

| Sound Level (decibels) | Maximum Duration Per Day (in hours) |
| --- | --- |
| 90 | 8 |
| 92 | 6 |
| 95 | 4 |
| 97 | 3 |
| 100 | 2 |
| 102 | 1 1/4 |
| 105 | 1 |
| 110 | 1/2 |
| 115 | 1/4 |

## Science and Society *Noise Pollution*

Loud sounds that harm your hearing, interfere with your ability to concentrate, or make you feel stressed are examples of noise pollution. Noise can prevent you from carrying on a conversation or keep you from sleeping. Studies show that constant noise can cause high blood pressure. In addition, it may cause headaches, digestive problems, ulcers, and asthma. Because of these problems, people are taking steps to control noise pollution.

You can do something about noise pollution by controlling the noise you make and by encouraging others to do the same. When you have to do a noisy job, you can warn people nearby. Most people can accept some noise if they know it won't last too long. You can also choose a time to do your work that will be less disturbing to other people. Encourage your family to choose quiet models of machines, such as vacuum cleaners, blow dryers, or power saws. Also, you can encourage your peers to consider others when adjusting the stereo or TV volume.

U.S. government agencies set limits for exposure to loud noises for all federal employees. These limits are shown in Table 16.2. The sound of an auto horn is 110 dB. According to federal regulations, no worker should endure sounds that loud for more than one-half hour at a time. What is the maximum duration a worker should be exposed to a 115 dB sound? Find out about local laws concerning noise. Does your community have a process for reporting sources of disturbing noise?

## Check and Explain

1. How does a violinist make different sounds? How does a trumpeter make sounds?

2. How do string, wind, and percussion instruments differ from one another?

3. **Compare and Contrast** How are music and noise different? How are they similar?

4. **Make a Model** Using materials of your choice, make a model of a musical instrument. Explain how it makes sound.

# Activity 16  *What musical instruments can be made from common materials?*

***Skills***  Model; Observe; Compare; Infer; Interpret Data

## Task 1  Prelab Prep

1. Collect the following items: shoe box, index card, 6 rubber bands, 12 paper fasteners, 0.5 meter piece of rubber hose, funnel, 5 drinking straws, masking tape, scissors, small metal can with a lid, a handful of seeds or beads, 6 metal bottle tops, 2 paper plates, 5 bells, safety pins, tongue depressor, 12 smooth round stones, 0.5 meter piece of heavy cord, metal fork, metal tray, sock, wooden broom handle, 5 walnut shells, 5 coat buttons, and a ball of yarn.
2. Study the list of instruments in the table. Use reference sources, if needed, to find out what each instrument looks like.

## Task 2  Data Record

1. On a separate sheet of paper, draw the data table shown.
2. Record all your observations about the sounds the instruments make.

### Table 16.1  Homemade Instruments

| Instrument | Observations |
|------------|-------------|
| Castanets |  |
| Guitar |  |
| Kettledrum |  |
| Panpipe |  |
| Shaker |  |
| Stone bells |  |
| Tambourine |  |
| Trumpet |  |

## Task 3  Procedure

1. Decide which materials you can use to make each of the instruments listed in the data table.
2. Work to make each instrument play as many clear tones as possible. If the instrument is used simply to produce a rhythm, it may not have a tone.
3. After completing an instrument, try to play a tune. Record your observations about the sound the instrument makes.

## Task 4  Analysis

1. Identify the variables in this activity.
2. How does the tone quality of each instrument vary?
3. How did you change the pitch of your instruments?
4. How are your homemade instruments different from the actual instruments? How are they alike?
5. Explain how you might improve your homemade instruments.

## Task 5  Conclusion

Explain how common materials are used to make a musical instrument. Identify the type of sounds you made with your instrument and explain how the sound was made and changed.

### *Everyday Application*

Test ordinary objects in your home to see if they have a musical tone. Make a list and describe the tone they make.

### *Extension*

Visit a museum that has a section on musical instruments. Observe the materials used to make different instruments. Write a report comparing the musical instruments of various cultures.

# 16.3 Sound Technology

*Silent Noise?*

Some people use a "silent" dog whistle to call their dog. Why is the dog whistle silent to people but not to dogs?

**SKILLS WARMUP**

## Objectives

▶ **Identify** the medical and industrial uses of ultrasound.

▶ **Explain** how sonar works.

▶ **Compare** animal echolocation with sonar.

▶ **Make an analogy** between using sonar to find the depth of the ocean and making other distance measurements.

A ship slowly plows through the ocean far from shore. Below deck, a group of scientists and technicians huddles around a screen like the one shown in Figure 16.8. The ship is a floating laboratory. The people on board are on a voyage of discovery. Their goal is to map the ocean floor that is thousands of meters below the ship. Their tools are sound waves. They send the sound waves where they can't go themselves. The sound waves enable the scientists to "see" the ocean bottom.

Scientists aren't the only people to use this kind of sound technology. Prospectors use sound waves to hunt for oil. Dentists use sound waves to drill and clean teeth. Sound has many uses that you probably never thought about!

**Figure 16.8** ▲
The images on this sonar screen are made by reflected sound waves or echoes.

## Ultrasound

Some sounds are too high pitched for people to hear. Most people can't hear frequencies greater than 20,000 Hz. Sounds above the range of human hearing are called **ultrasound**. Even though you can't hear ultrasound, it has many important medical and commercial uses. You may have experienced ultrasound without being aware of it.

Scientists produce ultrasound by changing electric or magnetic energy into mechanical energy. They use a device called an ultrasonic transducer. The transducer has a quartz or ceramic disk that can be charged with electricity. When charged, the disk vibrates very rapidly. The high-frequency vibration produces ultrasonic waves.

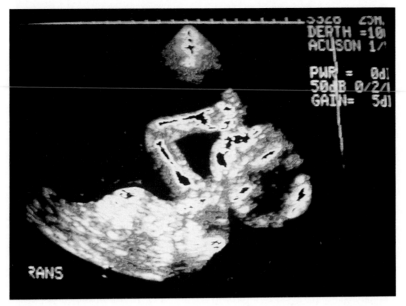

**◄ Figure 16.9**
This sonogram of a developing fetus shows the imaging power of ultrasound.

**Medical Uses** Doctors use ultrasound to observe soft tissues in the human body. Soft tissues, such as those that make up the liver, are almost invisible on an X-ray picture. However, ultrasonic waves reflect off soft tissues. A computer transforms the reflected waves into a picture on a computer screen. The picture is called a *sonogram*. Using a sonogram, a surgeon can detect a tumor or examine valves in the heart. Pregnant women routinely have sonograms to determine the development of the fetus. How is ultrasound being used in Figure 16.9?

Other medical professionals also use ultrasonic devices. Physicians use ultrasonic vibrations to get rid of stones that form in the kidney and gall bladder. The ultrasonic vibrations break the stones into very small pieces so they can pass out of the body naturally. Dental hygienists use high-frequency vibrations to loosen plaque deposits on teeth. Physical therapists use ultrasound to produce a deep-heating effect for muscle spasms and sprains.

**Commercial Uses** Ultrasound is used to clean small, intricate metal items, such as jewelry and small machine parts. The item to be cleaned is placed in a liquid bath. Ultrasonic vibrations travel through the liquid bath to loosen and remove dirt and corrosion. Ultrasound makes it easy to clean cracks and crevices that can't be reached by hand-polishing methods.

# Sonar

Ultrasound is used to locate underwater objects. Ultrasonic waves travel for many kilometers underwater. When the ultrasonic waves strike an obstacle, the waves are reflected. The technique of using sound waves to locate underwater objects is called **sonar**. The word *sonar* comes from "**so**und **na**vigation and **r**anging."

Sonar helps oceanographers and ship captains determine the depth of the ocean. Look at Figure 16.10. A ship sends ultrasonic waves downward. When the sound waves reach the ocean floor, they are reflected back to the ship. The time it takes for the signals to

**Figure 16.10
Uses of Sonar** ▼

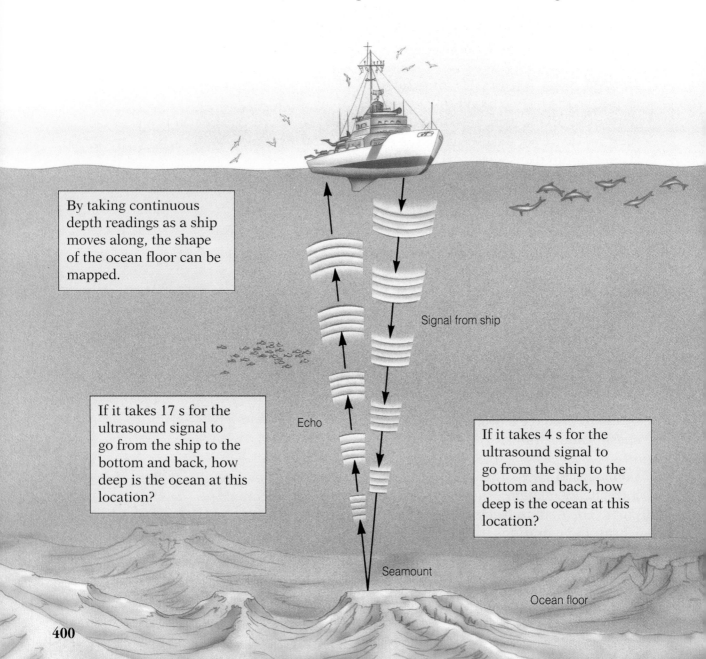

By taking continuous depth readings as a ship moves along, the shape of the ocean floor can be mapped.

Signal from ship

Echo

If it takes 17 s for the ultrasound signal to go from the ship to the bottom and back, how deep is the ocean at this location?

If it takes 4 s for the ultrasound signal to go from the ship to the bottom and back, how deep is the ocean at this location?

Seamount

Ocean floor

return is used to calculate the depth of the water below the ship. Since sound travels at about 1,500 m/s in ocean water, the depth of the ocean can be calculated using this formula:

$$\frac{\text{round trip time (s)}}{2} \times \frac{\text{1,500 m}}{\text{s}} = \text{distance to ocean bottom}$$

The French scientist Paul Langevin invented sonar in 1915 to help ships detect icebergs. In 1925, scientists discovered the Mid-Atlantic Ridge with the aid of an echo sounder. The Mid-Atlantic Ridge is an undersea mountain range that runs down the middle of the Atlantic Ocean. Its discovery helped to explain how the continents move.

Commercial fishers use sonar to detect schools of fish.

The undersea research vessel *Alvin* uses sonar to help navigate underwater. Echo sounders tell the pilot how far the craft is from the seafloor, the surface, and approaching objects.

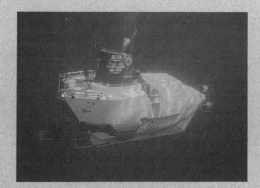

Sonar was used to determine the height and shape of the mountains in the Mid-Atlantic Ridge.

# Animal Echolocation

Many animals live in environments where their sense of vision is of little use. Some live in dark caves or deep within the sea where there is no sunlight. Others are active only at night. Some of these animals use high-frequency sound waves to guide them in the dark. They use a system that is similar to sonar, called **echolocation** (EHK oh loh KAY shuhn). Echolocation involves sending out sounds to judge the location, size, and motion of objects from the returning echoes. Look at the dolphins below to find out how they use echolocation.

▲ Dolphins use both a high- and low-frequency sound for echolocation. Since low-frequency sound travels farthest, a dolphin uses low frequencies first to detect an object. The dolphin then switches to a high-frequency sound, which gives a more accurate picture of the object. Dolphins have a hearing range between 150 Hz and 150,000 Hz.

▲ Often dolphins use their echolocation system for communication with other dolphins. They have a complex pattern of calls for navigation, distress, and recognition. You are able to hear some of the sounds made by dolphins.

Echolocation allows dolphins to detect small differences in the shape, size, and thickness of objects. ▶

Dolphins also use echolocation for navigation and to locate prey and avoid predators. Dolphins have a very advanced echolocation system. Many of their sounds have frequencies between 120,000 to 150,000 Hz, which are well beyond the range of human hearing.

Using echolocation, bats can fly in total darkness through caves with many obstacles without running into anything. They emit high-pitch clicks and listen for the returning echoes. Moths use high-pitch sounds for defense and for communication. Look at the bat and the moths below to find out how they use high-frequency sound.

◀ Bats emit high frequencies that range between 10,000 and 120,000 Hz. Each species of bat emits its own distinctive sounds. The echoes from these sounds help bats to navigate and to locate their prey.

▲ In addition to using echolocation for defense, some moths communicate with each other by emitting ultrasounds. What kinds of information do you think moths communicate?

Some moths, a favorite food animal of bats, have the ability to produce high-pitch clicks like those of bats. These sounds seem to interfere with the bats' echolocation system. Thus, the moths can sometimes evade a bat on the hunt for a meal. ▶

Recall how sound waves move through your ear. What would happen if the movement of the stirrup bone were limited? It wouldn't transmit much sound energy to the fluid in the inner ear. Hair cells in the cochlea wouldn't move very much. The nerve impulses to the brain would be weaker. The person's hearing would be impaired. As long as the person's inner ear is healthy, problems with the stirrup bone can be corrected with a hearing aid.

A hearing aid is a device that increases the loudness, or intensity, of incoming sound waves. A hearing aid has three main parts, as shown in Figure 16.11.

▶ A microphone picks up sounds and changes the sound waves into electric signals.

▶ An amplifier makes the electric signal stronger.

▶ An earphone, or speaker, changes the electric signal back into sound waves.

A hearing aid is similar to a telephone because it changes sound energy into electric energy and then back into sound energy. At low frequencies, the performance of a hearing aid is limited by the quality of the microphone. At high frequencies, the earphone is the limiting factor.

Small hearing aids can be worn behind the ear, in eyeglass frames, or completely inside the outer ear. Larger hearing aids that can be attached to clothing are more effective but not as convenient to use.

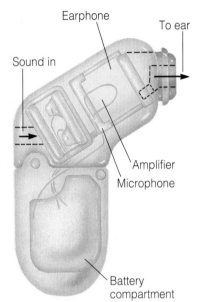

**Figure 16.11** ▲
A hearing aid can be designed to amplify all incoming sounds or to boost certain frequencies.

---

## Check and Explain

1. Give three examples of medical and other uses of ultrasound.

2. How does sonar work?

3. **Compare and Contrast**  How does echolocation in animals compare with sonar?

4. **Make an Analogy**  How does using sonar to determine the depth of the ocean compare to using the sound of thunder to determine the distance of a lightning flash?

# Chapter 16 Review

## Concept Summary

### 16.1 How You Hear
▶ The ear consists of three major regions: the outer ear, the middle ear, and the inner ear.
▶ The energy of sound waves is transferred from the eardrum in the outer ear, then to the three bones of the middle ear, and finally to the cochlea and auditory nerve of the inner ear.
▶ Sounds with an intensity over 120 dB can damage structures in the ear and impair hearing.

### 16.2 Sounds You Hear
▶ Musical instruments produce sounds that have pitch, intensity, rhythm, harmony, quality, and overtones.
▶ Musical instruments are classified as string, wind, or percussion.

▶ Noise is unwanted, annoying, or sometimes unhealthy sound. Noise often has irregular sound-wave patterns.

### 16.3 Sound Technology
▶ Ultrasound waves have frequencies above 20,000 Hz. These frequencies are beyond the range that humans can hear.
▶ Ultrasound waves are used to produce images of organs and tissues inside the body. These images are called sonograms.
▶ Sonar is a device that reflects sound waves off undersea objects. Sonar was used to map the ocean floor.
▶ Echolocation is used by animals such as dolphins, bats, and moths for communication, defense, and to locate objects underwater or in darkness.

---

### Chapter Vocabulary

| | | |
|---|---|---|
| outer ear (16.1) | overtone (16.2) | sonar (16.3) |
| middle ear (16.1) | ultrasound (16.3) | echolocation (16.3) |
| inner ear (16.1) | | |

---

## Check Your Vocabulary

Use the vocabulary words above to complete the following sentences correctly.

1. Ships use ____ to map the ocean floor.

2. Sound waves with a frequency exceeding 20,000 Hz are called ____ .

3. The ear canal is part of the ____ .

4. A second frequency sound produced by a violin string is called a(n) ____ .

5. The anvil bone is located in the ____ .

6. Bats avoid obstacles in total darkness by using ____ .

7. The semicircular canals are located in the ____ .

Pair each numbered word with a vocabulary term. Explain in a complete sentence how the words relate.

8. hammer

9. high frequency

10. semicircular canals

11. oval window

12. irregular

13. Mid-Atlantic Ridge

## Write Your Vocabulary

Write sentences using the vocabulary words above. Show that you know what each word means.

# Chapter 16 Review

## Check Your Knowledge

Answer the following in complete sentences.

1. How do incoming sound waves reach the inner ear?

2. What is the role of hair cells during the process of hearing?

3. How do sounds that measure more than 120 dB affect hearing?

4. What are the six characteristics of musical sounds?

5. How would you describe noise?

6. In medical technology, when are ultrasonic waves used instead of X-rays?

7. What properties of ultrasonic waves make them useful in sonar?

Check the answer that best completes each sentence.

8. The bone nearest the oval window is the (hammer, anvil, stirrup, cochlea).

9. The auditory nerve leads from the ear to the (eardrum, cochlea, hair cells, brain).

10. The range of human hearing is (10 to 20,000 Hz, 20 to 20,000 Hz, 20 to 30,000 Hz, 0 to120 dB).

11. The loudness of a musical note is the same as its (pitch, intensity, melody, quality).

12. A piano is a (wind, string, percussion, plucked) instrument.

13. Sonar stands for (sound arrival and reflection, sound notes and reflection, sound navigation and ranging, sound navy and ranging).

14. Echolocation is used by (people and bats, dolphins and bats, dogs and dolphins, moths and people).

## Check Your Understanding

Apply the concepts you have learned to answer each question.

1. How do music sound waves differ from noise sound waves? Explain the differences in terms of sound waves.

2. Compare echolocation to sonar.

3. Why are there laws limiting noise exposure in the workplace?

4. **Critical Thinking** You observe a bat chasing two different kinds of moths. The bat always catches one kind of moth but has difficulty catching the second kind. Explain why the bat has trouble catching the one kind of moth.

5. **Mystery Photo** The photograph on page 384 shows a human inner ear.

   a. What is the spiral structure?

   b. How does the spiral structure function in hearing?

   c. What other structures can you identify? Give the function of each.

6. Based on what you know about the structure of the ear, give a possible explanation of why people can't hear sounds with frequencies higher than 20,000 Hz.

7. **Application** You hear the sound from two wind instruments. One instrument tends to produce higher pitch sounds than the other. What might you conclude about the length of the air column in each instrument?

8. **Application** Many people listen to music with headphones. Sometimes the volume is so loud that people around them can hear it. What can happen to their inner ear if people do this regularly?

## Develop Your Skills

Use the skills you have developed in this chapter to complete each activity.

1. **Interpret Data** The screens below show wave patterns representing four different sounds.

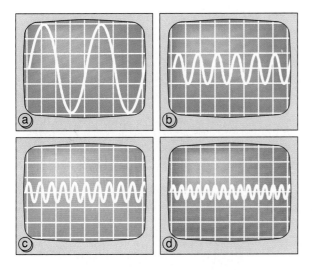

a. Which screen shows the loudest sound? The softest sound?

b. Which image shows the highest pitch? The lowest pitch?

2. **Infer** You are using sonar to locate a school of fish. Your first set of sonar waves returns in 2.4 seconds. The second set takes 2.6 seconds. What does this tell you about the fish?

3. **Predict** If bats were active during the day, would echolocation be as useful for catching prey? Explain.

4. **Data Bank** The graph on page 639 shows the frequency and intensity of different sounds.

a. Which sound has the greatest intensity?

b. Which sound has the widest range of frequencies? The narrowest range?

## Make Connections

1. **Link the Concepts** Below is a concept map showing how some of the main concepts in this chapter link together. Only part of the map is filled in. Finish the map, using words and ideas you find on the previous pages.

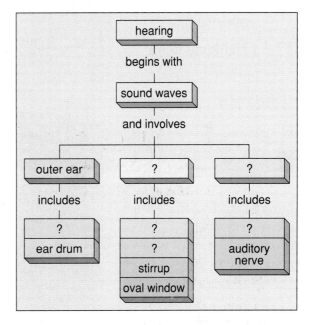

2. **Science and You** Close your eyes and spin around for several minutes. Record how you feel when you stop spinning. Why does this occur?

3. **Science and Society** Design a TV or newspaper ad that convinces people to use hearing protectors.

4. **Science and Social Studies** People in different cultures use many kinds of musical styles and harmonies. Do library research on the musical scales and harmonies used in different styles of music. Listen to examples from library record and tape collections. Find out about the cultures from which the music comes. Prepare a class presentation.

# Chapter 17 Light

## Chapter Sections

17.1   The Nature of Light

17.2   The Electromagnetic Spectrum

17.3   Light and Color

## What do you see?

66 I think this photograph is just color, nothing in particular. The reason for the different colors is that different light waves are reflected off of the paint. Certain light waves are absorbed by it, and some are reflected. For example, all colors are absorbed except the primaries, that is what we see as red, blue, and yellow. 99

*Aashish Mewada*
*Carman Ainsworth Junior*
*High School*
*Flint, Michigan*

To find out more about the photograph, look on page 430.
As you read this chapter, you will learn about light and color.

**408**

# 17.1 Nature of Light

## Objectives

▶ **Identify** three sources of light.

▶ **Describe** how light is produced.

▶ **Compare** the wave model and particle model of light.

▶ **Calculate** time and distance using the speed of light.

▼ **ACTIVITY**

**Generalizing**

*Thin Light*

**1.** Hold two fingers close together to form a slit.

**2.** Look at a light bulb through the slit. Describe the pattern of light you see.

**3.** Vary the size of the slit. How does the size of the slit affect what you see?

**SKILLS WARMUP**

H ave you ever walked into a darkened room late at night? If so, you probably walked slowly and carefully to keep from bumping into things. When you found the light and switched it on, everything changed. Things you couldn't see were suddenly visible. Light was reflected off of objects to make them visible. You could see form, shape, and color.

Light affects your life in many ways. You need light to read this book. When you look at a clear sky at night, you can see the light from distant stars. By making things visible, light links you to objects that are close by or far away!

## Light Energy

Light is a form of energy that your eyes can detect. Where does light come from, and how does it reach your eyes? Objects that produce light are sources of light. The sun, a light bulb, and flames all produce light. Most objects don't produce their own light, they reflect light from some source. You can't see the furniture in a dark room until you switch on the lights. Only when light is reflected by the furniture can you see it.

Light is produced when electrons change energy levels in an atom. The electrons moving around the nucleus of an atom have different amounts of energy. The energy of an electron depends on its distance from the nucleus. Look at Figure 17.1. If an electron absorbs extra energy, it jumps to a higher energy level away from the nucleus. When the electron falls back to a lower energy level, it gives off the added energy as a packet of light. A packet of light energy is called a **photon** (FOH tahn).

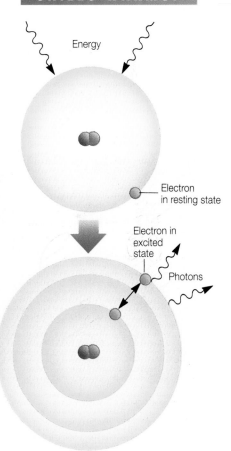

Energy

Electron in resting state

Electron in excited state

Photons

**Figure 17.1** ▲
The electron absorbs energy added to the atom (top). The electron moves to a higher energy level. As the electron falls back to its original position, photons are released (bottom).

# Models of Light

In the late 1600s, Isaac Newton reasoned that because light travels in straight lines and casts sharp shadows, it must behave like a tiny stream of particles. Other scientists disagreed. They argued that light traveled in waves, because it bends slightly around objects and two light beams can pass through one another. This could only happen if light traveled in waves.

The controversy ended when it was demonstrated that light displayed an interference pattern. Since only waves exhibit interference patterns, light must be waves. A hundred years later, Albert Einstein challenged this theory after studying the behavior of light striking metal objects. Einstein stated that light was tiny energy packages, or photons.

Is light composed of waves or particles? Scientists have concluded that light has the properties of both waves and particles. When it travels, light acts like a wave. When it is given off or absorbed by objects, light acts like a particle.

**Figure 17.2** ▲
Light waves projected through this diffraction grating produce an interference pattern. What colors are between the bands of interference?

**Light as a Wave** Interference patterns that prove light is a wave can be shown with a diffraction grating like the one in Figure 17.2. A diffraction grating is a glass plate that has thousands of tiny grooves in it. When light passes through the spaces between the grooves, it spreads out. The images from each groove interfere with each other to produce bands of light.

Recall that there are two kinds of waves, longitudinal waves and transverse waves. Light behaves as a transverse wave. Transverse waves, such as those of sunlight, vibrate in all directions.

Light waves can be aligned so they all vibrate in the same direction by passing the light through a special filter. The filter works by only allowing light waves that vibrate in a single direction to pass through the filter. The rest of the light waves are blocked. After passing through the filter, the light waves are all parallel and vibrate in the same direction. These waves are said to be **polarized**. Some sunglasses contain polarizing filters for reducing glare.

## Polarized Sunglasses

The lenses in some sunglasses contain polarized filters. Compare the difference in light when viewing an object without a polarized lens, with a polarized lens, and with two polarized lenses. Record what you see in all three observations.

1. Observe a light-colored object in full sunlight or under the light from a 100-watt light bulb. **CAUTION! Never look directly at the sun.**

2. Put on a pair of polarized glasses. Observe the object under the same light.

3. Position a second pair of polarized glasses so one lens is perpendicular to a lens of the first pair of glasses. Observe the object under the same light.

Complete the following questions.

1. Use the diagrams to explain what happened to the light waves when you held two polarized lenses perpendicular to each other.

2. Why might you choose to wear polarized sunglasses?

3. Identify the control in the experiment?

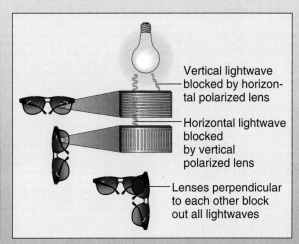

Vertical lightwave blocked by horizontal polarized lens

Horizontal lightwave blocked by vertical polarized lens

Lenses perpendicular to each other block out all lightwaves

**Light as a Particle**   Evidence also supports the idea that light acts like a particle. When a beam of high-energy light strikes a metal plate, electrons are released from the metal atoms. Enough electrons are released to produce an electric current that can be measured. The release of electrons when high-energy light strikes a metal is called the **photoelectric effect**.

In 1905, Albert Einstein offered an explanation of the photoelectric effect. He suggested that light is a stream of tiny packets of energy, or photons. When a photon strikes an atom in a metal plate, an electron in the atom absorbs energy from the photon. If the photon carries enough energy, an electron can escape from the metal plate.

Metals that release electrons are said to be photosensitive, that is, they are sensitive to light. Only high-frequency light, such as violet light, will supply enough energy to release electrons from metals. Low frequency light, such as red light, does not have enough energy to release electrons when it strikes a photoelectric metal.

*Light*

Make two models. One to represent the particle model of light and the other to represent the wave model of light. You should be able to explain the photoelectric effect using your particle model.

**SKILLS WORKOUT**

An illustration of how light behaves like a particle is shown in Figure 17.3. Imagine that the cue ball, which is the white ball on a pool table, is a photon. You aim the cue ball at a triangle of tightly packed numbered balls, which represent electrons in a metal. If the cue ball hits with enough force, its energy will knock one or more numbered balls out of the triangle. According to scientists, the particle theory of light is the only concept that accounts for the photoelectric effect.

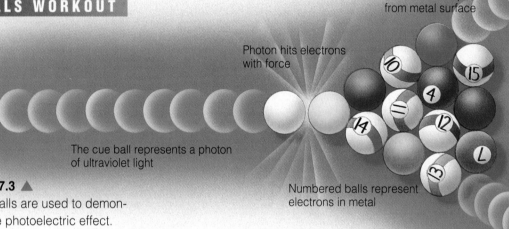

Electrons escape from metal surface

Photon hits electrons with force

The cue ball represents a photon of ultraviolet light

Numbered balls represent electrons in metal

**Figure 17.3** ▲
Billiard balls are used to demonstrate the photoelectric effect. The photoelectric effect provides evidence for the particle theory of light.

## Light Intensity

As you walk toward a light in the distance, the light source becomes brighter as you get closer. The particle nature of light explains why the brightness, or intensity, of light varies with distance. Particles of light travel in a straight line from the light source. At the source, all of the light particles are very close together. This makes the light bright. As the distance from the source increases, the light spreads out. The light seems dim because the distance between the straight line paths increases as well.

A change in light intensity is similar to using paint from a spray can. If you were to spray the paint when the nozzle is very close to a piece of paper, a small dense painted area would result. As you increase your distance from the paper, the paint on the paper spreads over a large area. Like the paint on the paper, the intensity of light decreases with distance. However, the amount of light released from the source remains the same.

# Speed of Light

During ancient times, people thought the speed of light was infinite. Actually, the instruments and measuring techniques couldn't measure such a high speed. In 1926, physicist Albert Michelson performed an experiment in California to measure the speed of light.

Michelson measured the distance between a location on Mount Wilson and a second location on Mount San Antonio. The distance was 35.4 km. A beam of light was sent from a special mirror on Mount Wilson to a mirror on Mount San Antonio, as shown in Figure 17.4.

Michelson used very accurate timing devices to measure the amount of time the light took to travel the 35.4 km distance. He divided the distance, by the time, to get a speed of 299 798 km/s. Today, using modern instruments, scientists determined that Michelson's measurement was very close to the actual speed of light.

The speed of light varies, depending on the medium it passes through. In space, which is a vacuum, light travels at about 299 793 km/s. In air, light moves at about 99 percent of its speed in space. In water, light slows to about 223 000 km/s. Through glass, light slows down to about 200 000 km/s. The time it takes light to travel between various locations is shown in Table 17.1.

## Table 17.1   Travel Time of Light

| Location 1 | Location 2 | Distance (km) | Travel Time Between Locations |
|------------|------------|--------------:|-------------------------------|
| Mountain 1 | Mountain 2 | 35.4 | 0.0001180795 s |
| Los Angeles | New York | 4 025 | 0.0135 s |
| Moon | Earth | 384 365 | 1 min 20 s |
| Sun | Earth | 149 596 000 | 8 min 20 s |
| Pluto | Earth | 5 750 098 000 | 5 h 20 s |

**Figure 17.4**

Timing a light beam as it traveled between two mountains was the first accurate measurement of the speed of light. ▼

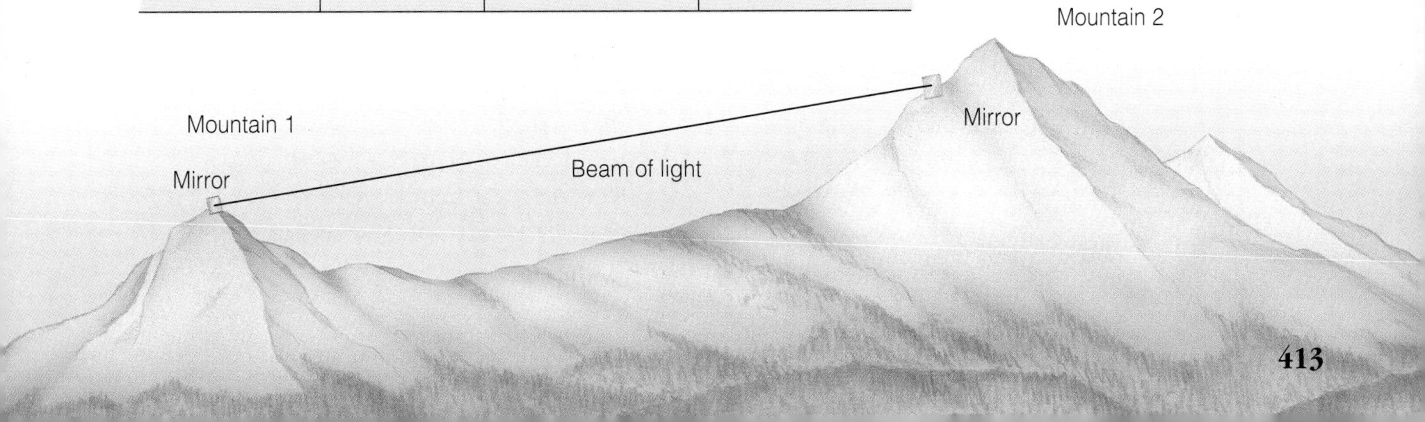

Mountain 2

Mountain 1

Mirror

Mirror

Beam of light

*Traveling Light*

   The nearest star is
39 707 876 380 000 km away.
How long would it take a
message traveling at light-
speed to reach there?

Since distances beyond the solar system are so large, kilometer measurements are not practical. For example, the distance between the earth and its nearest star beyond the solar system is 39 707 876 380 000 km. Instead of kilometers, astronomers measure large distances in light-years. A light-year is the distance light travels through space in one year. This distance is 9.46 trillion km ($9.46 \times 10^{12}$ km).

## Science and Society  *Light Cures SADness*

Do you know someone who feels depressed as the days grow shorter? A condition called Seasonal Affective Disorder, or SAD, is a change in a person's emotional state caused by a change in seasons. People with SAD sleep more and can become severely depressed. They may also overeat and gain weight.

Why does light affect a person's mood? Light triggers the release of chemicals that the body needs to function. During the seasonal change from summer to autumn and winter, the amount of daylight decreases. A winter day has fewer hours of daylight than a summer day. Most people aren't greatly affected by the chemical changes that occur in their bodies during the winter months. However, those with SAD don't adjust easily. Explain why you think the symptoms of SAD are better or worse for people with this condition living far away from the equator?

Luckily for SAD sufferers, strong artificial lighting can bring relief. The brightness of the light must be similar to the light in the sky 40 minutes after sunrise. After an hour or so of exposure to such light, SAD victims find that their depression disappears.

## Check and Explain

1. Identify three sources of light that you use everyday.

2. Describe how light is produced in an atom.

3. **Compare and Contrast**  Discuss how light behaves both as a wave and as a particle.

4. **Calculate**  How many minutes does it take light reflected from Venus to reach Earth? From Mars? Venus is 40 200 000 km from Earth. Mars is 78 390 000 km away. (Hint: Divide the distance by the speed of light.)

# *Activity 17*   *Does light travel in a straight line?*

***Skills***   Observe; Infer

## Task 1   Prelab Prep

1.  Collect a sheet of white shelf paper 30 cm long, pencil, four index cards, metric ruler, hole punch, 4 rubber stoppers slit in the center, small flashlight or penlight.
2.  Use the ruler to draw a line lengthwise down the center of the paper. Start at one end of the line and mark a point at 6 cm, 12 cm, 18 cm, and 24 cm.
3.  On one of the index cards, mark a point 3.2 cm from the bottom and 2 cm from the left side. Put the marked card on top of 2 cards and punch a hole over the mark through all 3 cards.
4.  Place a card in the slit of each stopper.

## Task 2   Data Record

1.  On a separate piece of paper, copy the data table shown below.
2.  Record all of your observations for each index card.

### Table 17.2   Behavior of Light Beam

| Index card | Observation |
|------------|-------------|
| 6 cm       |             |
| 12 cm      |             |
| 18 cm      |             |
| 24 cm      |             |

## Task 3   Procedure

1.  Place a card without a hole at the 24 cm mark and the others at the 6 cm, 12 cm, and 18 cm marks.
2.  Line up the holes as shown.
3.  Darken the room and shine the beam of the flashlight directly through the hole on the first card.

4.  Observe the path of light and the size of the beam on each card. Record your observations.
5.  Move the light at a 45° angle and shine it through the hole of the first card. Observe the path of the light. Record your observations.

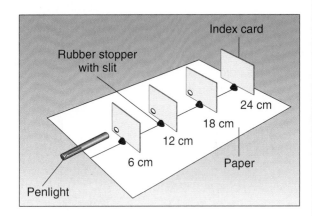

## Task 4   Analysis

1.  How is the size of the light beam different on each card?
2.  What happened when you changed the angle of the light?
3.  What evidence shows that light travels in a straight line?

## Task 5   Conclusion

Explain how you showed that light travels in a straight line.

## *Everyday Application*

Go into a dark room at night and leave the door slightly ajar. Describe the light pattern on the floor. How is the light pattern similar or different from the light on the cards? Explain.

## *Extension*

Try setting the cards in different positions so that the light beam will still pass through all three holes. Did you show that light does not travel in a straight line by doing this? Explain.

*Light Through Glass*

Obtain a drinking glass and a pad of white paper.

**1.** Fill the glass to the top with water.

**2.** Place the glass in a sunny window or outside in the sun.

**3.** Place the pad of paper so that the sun shines through the glass onto the paper.

What colors do you see on the paper? List the colors in the correct order.

**SKILLS WARMUP**

# 17.2 The Electromagnetic Spectrum

## Objectives

▶ **Identify** six kinds of invisible electromagnetic waves.

▶ **Relate** wavelength to the colors of visible light.

▶ **Compare** and **contrast** visible and invisible electromagnetic waves.

▶ **Infer** how different colors of light combine to produce new colors.

When you hear the word *light*, you probably think about sunlight that keeps you warm or the lights you use in your classroom. Actually, you use many kinds of light energy. The kind of light energy is determined by the amount of energy in photons.

You can't see some kinds of light. You don't see radio waves, which are made of low-energy photons. A picture of your bones is taken with invisible X-rays, which are high-energy photons. Photons in light you can see have a moderate amount of energy.

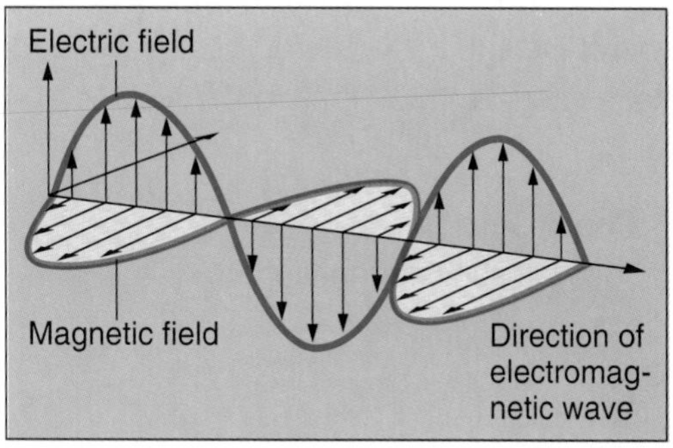

**Figure 17.5** ▲
In an electromagnetic wave, the electric field and the magnetic field are at 90° angles.

## Electromagnetic Waves

Like other forms of energy, light energy moves in waves. All light waves are transverse waves. Light waves produce both an electric field and a magnetic field and are called electromagnetic waves. Electromagnetic waves are different from other kinds of energy waves.

Electromagnetic waves can travel through a vacuum. Unlike sound waves and heat waves, electromagnetic waves don't require a medium. For example, light waves travel from the sun through outer space, which is empty of matter.

In an electromagnetic wave, both the electric field and the magnetic field are at a right angle to the direction of the wave and perpendicular to each other. Recall that for transverse waves, the medium moves at a right angle to the direction of the wave. You can see in Figure 17.5 how the electric field and the magnetic field move in relation to each other and to the direction of the wave.

All electromagnetic waves are not the same. Recall that the energy in the photons varies for different kinds of electromagnetic waves. The wavelength and frequency of electromagnetic waves also varies.

**Wavelength** Wavelength varies for different kinds of electromagnetic waves. Very long electromagnetic wavelengths, called radio frequencies, reach 300 km. The shortest gamma rays are $3.0 \times 10^{-14}$ km, or 0.0000003 nanometers ($3.0 \times 10^{-7}$) nm. One nanometer is equal to one trillionth of a kilometer.

**Frequency** Recall that the wave frequency is the number of waves that pass a point in one second. When the wavelength is short, the frequency is high because more waves pass a point in one second. The relationship between frequency and the wavelength is shown in Figure 17.6. The unit for the frequency of electromagnetic waves is hertz (Hz). The frequencies for electromagnetic waves range from $1 \times 10^2$ to $1 \times 10^{24}$ hertz.

## Electromagnetic Spectrum

Electromagnetic waves arranged in order of their wavelength and frequency, is called the **electromagnetic spectrum**. Radio waves with a frequency of $1 \times 10^6$ hertz are low on the electromagnetic spectrum. X-rays with a frequency of $1 \times 10^{19}$ hertz are high on the electromagnetic spectrum. Electromagnetic waves that can be seen by the human eye are a small band called the visible spectrum, which is near the center. Light bent by the prism in Figure 17.7 shows the colors of light in the visible spectrum.

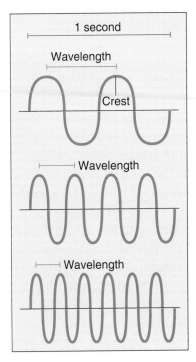

**Figure 17.6** ▲
The greater the number of wavelengths that pass a point in one second, the greater is the frequency.

◀ **Figure 17.7**
The prism bends white light to show the visible colors in part of the electromagnetic spectrum. What colors of light do you see?

## Visible Spectrum

Each color in the visible spectrum—red orange, yellow, green, blue, indigo, and violet—has a different frequency. For example, the frequency of the shortest wave length is 750 trillion hertz ($7.5 \times 10^{14}$ Hz) and produces violet light. The frequency of the longest wavelength is 430 trillion hertz ($4.3 \times 10^{14}$ Hz) and produces red light.

When all the colors of light are combined, you see white light. Sunlight is one example of white light. Use Figure 17.8 to locate the colors in the visible spectrum.

Red, green, and blue are called the primary colors of light. These colors combine in different amounts to produce other colors of light. For example, red and blue light mixed in equal amounts produces the color magenta. Green and blue light combine to make a color called cyan. Any two colors of light that mix to form white light are called complementary colors. For example, cyan and red light mix to produce white light.

Not all animals see the same colors you do. For example, bees can see blue, yellow, and ultraviolet light. Ultraviolet light is high-energy electromagnetic waves that your eyes can't see. Some animals see only black and white. Monkeys and apes see the same colors you do. Since birds have brightly colored feathers that attract a mate, they probably also see color.

**Figure 17.8**
**The Electromagnetic Spectrum** ▼

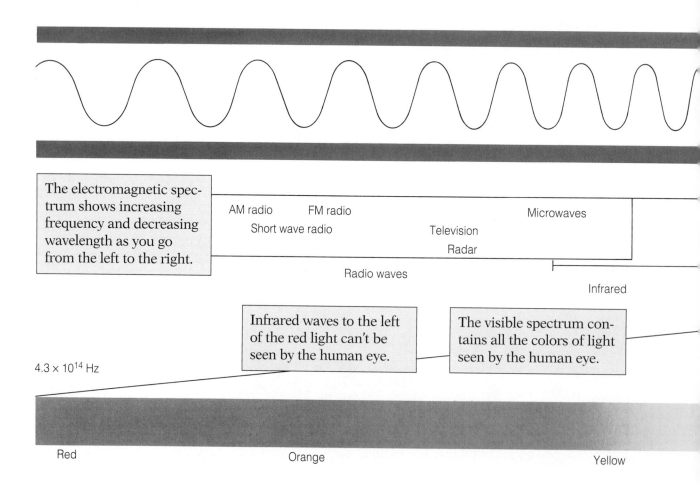

The electromagnetic spectrum shows increasing frequency and decreasing wavelength as you go from the left to the right.

AM radio　FM radio

Short wave radio

Microwaves

Television

Radar

Radio waves

Infrared

Infrared waves to the left of the red light can't be seen by the human eye.

The visible spectrum contains all the colors of light seen by the human eye.

$4.3 \times 10^{14}$ Hz

Red

Orange

Yellow

## Invisible Spectrum

The waves on both sides of the visible spectrum make up the invisible spectrum. You can't see wavelengths shorter than 430 nm or longer than 750 nm. Locate the invisible spectrum in Figure 17.8.

**Radio Waves**  Radio waves sent through the air from radio stations carry the music you hear on the radio. To pick up a signal, you must tune your radio to the same wave frequency as the waves from the radio station. Radio stations transmit radio waves by amplitude modulation (AM) or by frequency modulation (FM). AM radio waves have a pattern of amplitude changes. FM changes the pattern of radio wave frequency.

FM waves carry the picture portion of most television shows. The sound portion of most television shows is on AM waves. AM waves are longer than FM waves, so AM waves can bend around objects more easily. This explains why sometimes you receive the sound but not the picture for a TV program.

**Microwaves**  High energy radio waves are called microwaves. They have wavelengths between 100 mm and 30 cm. Like other radio waves, microwaves are used in communications. Since microwaves reflect off certain substances, such as metal or wood, radar uses microwaves to locate objects and to determine their speed. Because some substances absorb microwaves, they are also used for cooking.

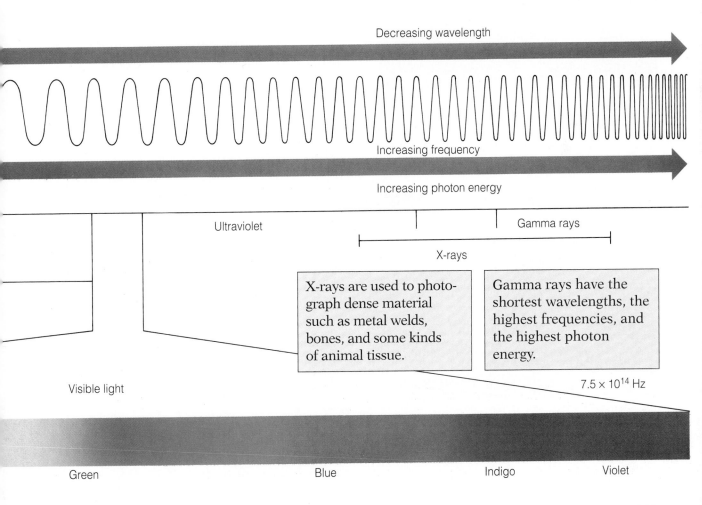

Decreasing wavelength

Increasing frequency

Increasing photon energy

Ultraviolet

Gamma rays

X-rays

X-rays are used to photograph dense material such as metal welds, bones, and some kinds of animal tissue.

Gamma rays have the shortest wavelengths, the highest frequencies, and the highest photon energy.

$7.5 \times 10^{14}$ Hz

Visible light

Green          Blue          Indigo          Violet

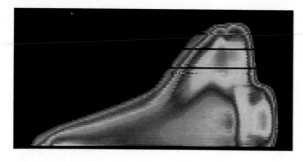

**Figure 17.9** ▲

The red area in the film indicates the location of the highest temperature. Which areas are the coolest?

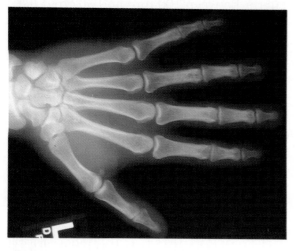

**Figure 17.10** ▲

What areas of the bones shown in the X-ray of the person's hand contain the most calcium? How do you know?

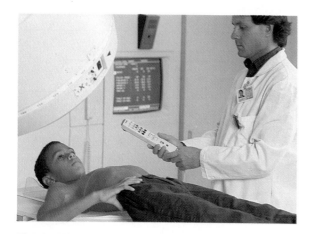

**Figure 17.11** ▲

The technician avoids destroying healthy cells by controlling the amount of gamma rays and by targeting only cancer cells.

**Infrared Rays**   Electromagnetic waves with wavelengths between 750 nm and 30 000 nm are **infrared** rays. They are called "infrared" because their wavelengths are slightly longer than those of visible red light. You detect infrared rays with your skin when you feel heat. Infrared radiation causes the molecules in an object to vibrate more rapidly. The vibrations produce heat and cause the temperature of the object to rise. Certain camera film can take a picture like the one in Figure 17.9 that only shows the heat given off by objects. Such films are sensitive to infrared rays but not to visible light.

**X-rays**   High energy waves with lengths from 0.001 nm to 10 nm are **X-rays**. X-rays can travel through matter. Look at the X-ray of a hand in Figure 17.10. The calcium in the bones of the hand absorbs X-rays better than muscle or skin do. That's why the bones show up as light areas on an X-ray photograph.

**Ultraviolet Rays**   Waves between 10 nm and 430 nm in length are called **ultraviolet** rays. The main source of ultraviolet rays is sunlight. Ultraviolet rays destroy bacteria and viruses. They also stimulate your body to produce vitamin D, which you need for healthy bones. However, overexposure to ultraviolet rays can burn your skin and is one cause of skin cancer. Sunscreen reduces absorption of ultraviolet rays.

**Gamma Rays**   The waves with the shortest wavelengths are **gamma rays**. Their wavelengths range from 0.0000003 nm ($3.0 \times 10^{-7}$) to 0.003 nm ($3.0 \times 10^{-3}$). Radioactive materials and nuclear reactions give off gamma rays. Gamma rays can harm living cells. They are used in cancer treatment to destroy cancer cells.

# Science and Technology
## *Using A Microwave Oven*

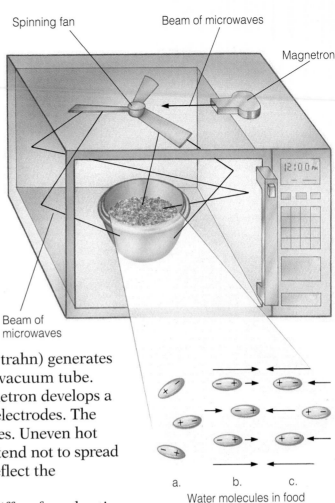

Spinning fan    Beam of microwaves

Magnetron

Beam of microwaves

a.    b.    c.
Water molecules in food

**Figure 17.12** ▲

The poles of water molecules in food are not aligned (a). Microwaves cause the poles to line up (b) and reverse direction rapidly (c), producing heat.

Suppose there's leftover pizza in the refrigerator. You're in a hurry, and you don't have time to wait for your conventional oven to heat the pizza. What can you do? With a microwave oven, you have hot pizza in two minutes!

A microwave oven heats food quickly by using high-energy microwaves. All foods, including your pizza, contain water molecules. Microwaves excite the water molecules so that they move very quickly. This rapid movement produces heat.

Notice in Figure 17.12 that a device called a magnetron (MAG nuh trahn) generates microwaves. A magnetron is a special vacuum tube. When the oven switches on, the magnetron develops a large potential difference between its electrodes. The negative electrode sends out microwaves. Uneven hot spots may occur because microwaves tend not to spread out evenly. A fan in the oven helps to deflect the microwaves to all parts of the food.

Heating food in a microwave oven differs from heating food in a regular oven. In a regular oven, heat radiates from inside the oven to the food. In a microwave oven, the heat is produced right inside the food when its water molecules begin to vibrate.

## Check and Explain

1. List the electromagnetic waves in the invisible spectrum and give one use for each kind of wave.

2. Explain how colors are related to wavelength.

3. **Compare and Contrast**  Why are some parts of the electromagnetic spectrum visible and others are not?

4. **Infer**  To light the stage for a school play, you need yellow, cyan, and magenta beams of light. Unfortunately, you have only one spotlight and three sheets of glass. The glass sheets are cyan, magenta, and yellow. What can you do?

### Up Close

Look at the color picture in Figure 17.13 through a hand lens. Describe what each color looks like. Notice which colors seem to be combinations of more than one color. Why do some colors seem darker or lighter?

**Figure 17.13**

What color must be seen by the bee in order for it to be aware of the flower? ▼

# 17.3 Light and Color

## Objectives

▶ **Identify** three surfaces that interact with light.

▶ **Explain** why the daytime sky appears blue.

▶ **Infer** how dark and light objects reflect light.

▶ **Predict** the colors that will be produced when pigments of various colors are mixed.

I magine a world of black, white, and gray. It would not be as interesting or as beautiful as the world that surrounds you every day. Did you know that colors can also affect your mood and behavior? Bright colors tend to make you feel happy. Gray or drab colors tend to make a scene somber and sad.

Colors are important in nature. The color of flowering plants attracts insects and other animals, which helps the flowering plants to reproduce. For example, pollen from a flower will stick to a bee as it gathers nectar. The bee will carry the pollen to another flower, which uses the pollen to reproduce. At every visit, the bee picks up pollen from one flower and drops off pollen from other flowers.

Plant colors help some animals identify food. The bright color of the flower helps the bee locate nectar. Animals, such as deer, use color to blend into their surroundings. The deer is not easily seen by its predators. Color helps some animals to find and select mates. In many species of birds, the female chooses the male bird with the brightest feathers.

## Light from a Surface

Imagine you are at a picnic. You notice how sunlight reacts with nearby objects. Depending upon the material the object is made of, the light may be transmitted, absorbed, or scattered. When light is transmitted through clear plastic bags, it passes through the material it strikes. A black object, such as charcoal, absorbs all the light that strikes it. Wax paper scatters light. Scattered light makes food look fuzzy through the wax paper.

Objects can be classified as transparent, opaque, or translucent, depending on how the material reacts with light. Objects that transmit almost all the light that strikes them are **transparent**. Transparent materials reflect some light from their surface. Otherwise, you wouldn't see them at all. Have you ever accidentally bumped into a sliding glass door that reflected so little light that you didn't see it?

Materials that transmit light and scatter it are **translucent** (tranz LOOS uhnt). An image is difficult to see through a translucent material. The image is unclear and lacks detail. Wax paper and shower doors are translucent materials.

Materials that block the transmission of light are **opaque** (oh PAYK). An opaque object absorbs most of the light that strikes it. You can't see through opaque objects. Look around the room. What objects do you see that are opaque?

## Life Science LINK

Obtain blue paper, green paper, scissors, small containers, and sugar water.
**1.** Cut flower shapes (about 5 cm in diameter) from blue and green paper.
**2.** Arrange the flowers outside in small containers with sugar water at the centers.
What happened? Does color affect whether bees are attracted to a flower?

**ACTIVITY**

**Transparent** ▲
Light passes through clear glass and water in straight lines. These materials are transparent. Notice that the outline of the glass and the water line are visible. Even transparent materials reflect some light.

**Translucent**
Light reflects off the strawberries at the bottom of the bowl. The reflected light does not pass through the translucent glass in straight lines. As the light passes through the bowl, it scatters and looks fuzzy. How much detail can you see through the bowl? ▼

**Opaque** ▲
The vacuum bottle is opaque because the light that strikes it is either absorbed or reflected. Because light is reflected from its surface, the cap of the bottle looks shiny.

# Interactions of Light

Light waves interact with the surface of an object or with a medium. Light waves are reflected when they bounce off an object. Because light reflected from an uneven surface scatters, it is called a diffuse reflection. Light reflected off the moon's surface is a diffuse reflection.

Refraction occurs as light waves pass from one medium to another. The light wave slows down and is bent, or refracted. When they strike a barrier, light waves spread out, or diffract. As light diffracts around the edge of an object, it forms a shadow that appears fuzzy.

Interference occurs when two waves arrive at the same point at the same time. Interference in light waves produces bands of bright light and bands of no light. The bands of color seen on a compact disc are due to the interference of light waves.

## Reflection

Light waves bounce off the girl's face into the mirror. A clear image is reflected from the mirror because it has a very smooth surface. The smooth surface does not scatter light. ▼

## Diffraction ▶

When light waves move past a barrier, they bend or diffract. Why will the area directly behind the barrier be dark?

## Refraction ▲

The speed of light depends on the medium. Light slows down in water, so the part of the pencil in water looks bent, or refracted.

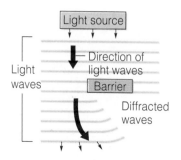

## Interference

Constructive interference results in a larger wave. Destructive interference cancels out the light waves. So, interference produces bands of light. ▼

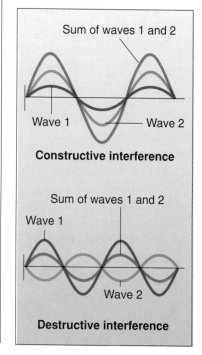

## Color of the Sky

On a bright sunny day the sky appears blue. A blue sky is caused by the interaction of lightwaves with particles in the atmosphere. These particles include molecules of gases and water, and tiny specks of dust. When light strikes a particle in the atmosphere, it is reflected.

Remember that sunlight contains the wavelength of every color in the visible spectrum. When light of a particular wavelength strikes an atmospheric particle, the wavelength is scattered in all directions. The particles in the atmosphere scatter the short wavelengths more than the long wavelengths. Since blue and violet have short wavelengths, more blue and violet light reaches your eyes from all directions in the atmosphere. To you the sky appears blue.

The sky in Figure 17.14 doesn't appear blue. Instead, it is various shades of red and orange. This color change occurs only at sunrise and sunset when the sun is low on the horizon. Light rays must travel a greater distance through the atmosphere before reaching your eye. At this greater distance, the particles in the air scatter the blue, yellow, and green wavelengths. By the time the light reaches your eyes, the only wavelengths left for you to see are the red and orange ones.

**Figure 17.14**

What does the sky at sunset tell you about the wavelengths of light you see? ▼

## Color Vision

Unlike humans, many animals do not see color. Your eyes have special cells called cones that enable you to see a red apple or the green grass. To see color, light enters your eye through an opening called the pupil. Light focuses on the retina at the back of your eye. The retina is made of two kinds of cells called rods and cones. Rods are very sensitive but cannot detect color. The cones, however, are sensitive to color.

Chemicals in the cones are sensitive to red, green, or blue light. Each cone is sensitive to a particular primary color. When a mixture of different colored light enters your eye, you see the mixture as a single color.

You see a plum as purple when reflected red and blue light enters your eyes. Each color stimulates an electric signal in the cones. These signals travel to the brain through the optic nerve. The brain unscrambles the signals. Instead of interpreting each color separately, the signals for red light and blue light combine to form purple. Most of the colors you see are combined signals.

## Color of Objects

Look at the object in Figure 17.15. What color do you see? You see the color red because all of the colors in white light are absorbed except red. The red surface reflects only red light.

Look at the same object shown in Figure 17.16. What color is it? If you shine a blue light on the same object, it appears purple. The object absorbs some wavelengths of the blue light, but reflects purple light. Black is the absence of all color.

A white shirt reflects all the wavelengths of light. That's why it looks white. You feel cooler when you wear a white shirt than when you wear a black shirt. The white shirt reflects sunlight. However, a black shirt absorbs sunlight. The light energy from the sun's rays changes to heat energy and you feel warm.

Look out the window. You can see colored objects through the window because the clear glass transmits all wavelengths of the visible spectrum. However, tinted glass is not transparent to all wavelengths. For example, glass tinted green absorbs all the colors of white light except green. Green glass transmits green light.

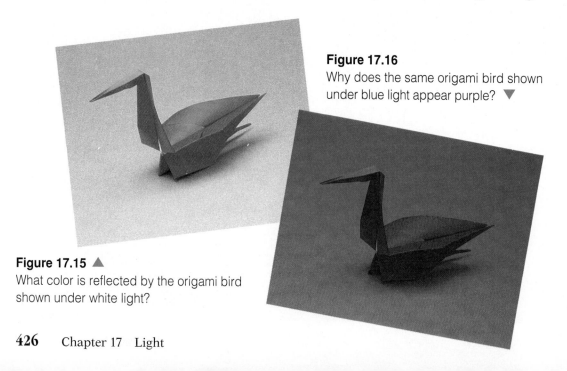

**Figure 17.16**
Why does the same origami bird shown under blue light appear purple? ▼

**Figure 17.15** ▲
What color is reflected by the origami bird shown under white light?

## Paint and Pigments

Paint is made of coloring particles, called pigments, mixed in a liquid. Each pigment absorbs and reflects different colors of light. The colors you see depend on which colors the pigments absorb and which colors they reflect.

The primary colors of light are red, green, and blue. Similarly, there are three primary pigments. The three primary pigments are magenta, yellow, and cyan. Recall that when primary colors combine, they produce white light. The primary pigments behave differently than the primary colors of light. Mixing equal amounts of the three primary pigments produces black. Combinations of the primary pigments produce different colors. Figure 17.17 illustrates what color results when you mix two primary pigments. When you mix yellow and cyan, you get green. Mixing magenta and cyan produces purple. How does this compare to combining red and blue light?

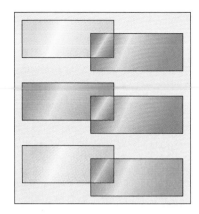

**Figure 17.17** ▲
Combining pigments forms new colors. What color is formed from the combination of cyan and yellow pigments?

# Historical Notebook

## Color and Impressionism

Imagine you are visiting an art museum. You see many different paintings. There are paintings of people, nature, and objects. Then you come to another painting and see nothing but dots of colors. You step back and a beautiful picture emerges on the canvas. In the late 19th century, a group of innovative painters developed this creative use of color.

The painting by Georges Seurat illustrates how these painters used color in a unique way. They built up their painting with many colored points instead of using brush strokes. When viewed from a distance, the points of color blend to form images.

This technique, known as pointillism, set these artists apart from other painters. They did not try to tell a story with their painting. Instead, they tried to capture a moment in the lives of ordinary people.

1. How was the use of color by pointillists different from the way other painters employed color?

2. Do library research to locate works of other pointillist painters. Which painter's use of color do you think is most effective?

## Science and Technology
*Four-Color Printing*

This book has colored pictures on many pages. To print a photograph like the one shown in Figure 17.18 requires several steps. The printer first separates the colors in the photograph. To do this, four pictures of the original photograph are taken. For each shot, the photographer puts a different color filter over the camera lens.

In addition, the photographer takes each picture through a screen that causes the colors to appear as tiny dots. The position of the screen is changed slightly for each different color. One filter blocks out all colors except yellow. This produces a photographic negative with only a yellow color. The process is repeated using different filters to produce three more negatives—a magenta, a cyan, and a black negative. Recall that magenta, cyan, and yellow are all primary pigments.

Next, the four dot negatives are used to make separate pictures on metal plates coated with photographic chemicals. The plates are then treated with an acid to make the dots higher than the rest of the plate. During the printing process, each plate distributes ink of a matching color on paper. As the paper moves from one plate to the next, it picks up each color. The final product is a full-color picture. The combinations of primary colored dot patterns give an illusion of different colors. Notice the magnified dot pattern of the four-color picture shown in Figure 17.18.

**Figure 17.18** ▲
Locate four different colors used to print this photograph.

---

## Check and Explain

1. How does a light wave react when it strikes an opaque surface? A translucent surface? A transparent surface?

2. Why does the daytime sky look blue?

3. **Infer** Explain why is it wise for people walking along a road at night to wear white clothing.

4. **Predict** What colors are produced by mixing the following pigments: one part magenta and three parts yellow; one part cyan and three parts magenta? You may wish to test your predictions.

# Chapter 17 Review

## Concept Summary

### 17.1 The Nature of Light
▶ Objects are visible because they either produce light or reflect light.
▶ Light has the properties of both waves and particles.
▶ Light is produced when electrons change energy levels in an atom.
▶ The speed of light is 299 793 km/s.

### 17.2 The Electromagnetic Spectrum
▶ The electromagnetic spectrum contains radio waves, microwaves, infrared rays, visible light waves, ultraviolet rays, X-rays, and gamma rays.
▶ The color of visible light is determined by its wavelength. White light is composed of all the colors in the visible spectrum.

▶ Electromagnetic waves can travel through a vacuum.

### 17.3 Light and Color
▶ Surfaces can be opaque, translucent, or transparent.
▶ When light waves strike a material, they change direction by reflection, refraction, diffraction, or interference.
▶ When light strikes a surface, the color you see is the color reflected by the surface.
▶ The primary colors of light are red, green, and blue.
▶ Primary colors combine to produce white. Primary pigments combine to produce black.

## Chapter Vocabulary

photon (17.1)
polarized (17.1)
photoelectric effect (17.1)
electromagnetic spectrum (17.2)

infrared (17.2)
X-ray (17.2)
ultraviolet (17.2)
gamma ray (17.2)

transparent (17.3)
translucent (17.3)
opaque (17.3)

## Check Your Vocabulary

Use the vocabulary words above to complete the following sentences correctly.

1. A packet of light energy is called a(n) _____ .

2. Objects look fuzzy when viewed through _____ materials, such as wax paper or frosted glass.

3. Heat can be felt when your skin is exposed to _____ rays.

4. Some sunglasses have _____ lenses that reduce glare.

5. Doctors use a(n) _____ to take a picture of bones.

6. The glass in the window of an automobile is _____ .

7. In the invisible electromagnetic spectrum, a(n) _____ has the shortest wavelength.

8. A(n) _____ object blocks the passage of all light.

9. Visible and invisible wavelengths combine to make up the _____ .

10. The _____ supports the idea that light behaves like a particle.

11. Sunburn and skin cancer are caused by _____ waves.

## Write Your Vocabulary

Write sentences using the vocabulary words above. Show that you know what each word means.

# Chapter 17 Review

## Check Your Knowledge

Answer the following in complete sentences.

1. What evidence did scientists give to support that light is a wave?

2. During the photoelectric effect, what happens when a photon strikes a metal plate?

3. How do electromagnetic waves differ from one another?

4. How do microwaves increase the temperature of food?

5. How are ultraviolet rays both good and bad for you?

6. What accounts for the difference between one color and another?

7. Why does the sky appear to be blue?

Determine whether each statement is true or false. Write *true* if it is true. If it is false, change the underlined term to make the statement true.

8. Light is a form of <u>matter</u>.

9. When light is <u>refracted</u>, it changes direction.

10. The photoelectric effect is caused by <u>infrared</u> waves.

11. A light-year is a measure of <u>time</u>.

12. All electromagnetic waves are <u>longitudinal</u>.

13. The <u>shortest</u> waves possess the greatest energy.

14. When the primary pigments are mixed in equal amounts, they produce <u>white</u>.

15. Materials that are <u>transparent</u> transmit light but scatter it so that clear images can't be seen.

16. A prism separates <u>white</u> light into colors.

## Check Your Understanding

Apply the concepts you have learned to answer each question.

1. Identify which of the following are visible parts of the electromagnetic spectrum and which aren't: violet light, infrared rays, radio waves, microwaves, ultraviolet rays, and gamma rays.

2. How do the sources of the primary colors of light and the primary pigments differ?

3. What characteristics do all parts of the electromagnetic spectrum share?

4. Why does light passing through a pinhole project a circle that is a larger circle than the pinhole itself?

5. Why did ancient people assume that the speed of light was infinite?

6. **Critical Thinking** What evidence supports the conclusion that the condition called Seasonal Affective Disorder is caused by a reduction in daylight?

7. **Mystery Photo** The photograph on page 408 shows paints containing different pigments. Explain why you see various colors.

8. **Application** Sometimes you see a rainbow after a rainstorm. List the colors of a rainbow in order of their appearance. Explain how the moisture in the air forms a rainbow. How could you form a rainbow in your own backyard?

9. **Extension** Draw a rainbow, then extend it to show where each wavelength of the invisible spectrum would be placed. Show each wavelength of the invisible spectrum.

10. Rank the photon energy of the following parts of the electromagnetic spectrum from highest to lowest: ultraviolet waves, visible light waves, X-rays, radio waves, gamma rays, microwaves.

## Develop Your Skills

Use the skills you have developed to complete each activity.

1. **Interpreting Data** Study the table and answer the following questions.

   a. Which source has the longest waves?

   b. Which has the shortest?

   c. What is the relationship between wavelength and wave frequency?

| Energy Source | Wavelength | Wave Frequency (Hz) |
|---|---|---|
| Radio waves | 1 m – 30 km | $10^4 - 10^8$ |
| Microwaves | 1 mm – 30 cm | $10^9 - 10^{12}$ |
| Infrared rays | 750 nm – 30 000 nm | $10^{12} - 4.3 \times 10^{14}$ |
| Visible light | 430 nm – 750 nm | $4.3 \times 10^{14} - 7.5 \times 10^{14}$ |
| Ultraviolet rays | 10 nm – 430 nm | $7.6 \times 10^{14} - 4.0 \times 10^{17}$ |
| X-rays | 0.001 nm – 10 nm | $4.0 \times 10^{17} - 10^{19}$ |
| Gamma rays | 0.0000003 – 0.003 nm | $10^{19} - 10^{24}$ |

2. **Hypothesize** Suggest an explanation for the fact that radio waves, microwaves, and infrared waves don't produce a photoelectric effect, but ultraviolet waves, X-rays, and gamma rays do.

3. **Data Bank** Use the informaton on page 640 to answer the following question. What is the complementary color of each primary color?

## Make Connections

1. **Link the Concepts** Below is a concept map showing how some of the main concepts in this chapter link together. Only part of the map is filled in. Finish the map, using words and ideas you find on the previous pages.

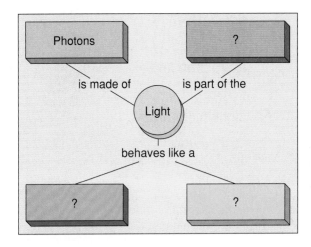

2. **Science and Math** Below are the names of some stars and their distances from the earth in light-years. Calculate the distance of each in kilometers. Use 300 000 km/s for the speed of light. Express your results in scientific notation.

   a. Sirius          8.6 light-years

   b. Alpha Centauri    4.3 light-years

   c. Vega          26 light-years

3. **Science and You** The containers of all sunscreen products have a large number written on them. This number stands for the **s**un **p**rotection **f**actor, or SPF. Do research to find out the practical meaning of this number. Also find out what variables affect a person's reaction to exposure to sunlight. Based on this data, determine what SPF is best for you.

# Chapter 18 Using Light

## Chapter Sections

18.1 Light Sources
18.2 Vision
18.3 Reflection and Mirrors
18.4 Refraction and Lenses
18.5 Light Technology

## What do you see?

66 This looks like many glass cylinders. Instead of having smooth tops, they are cut unevenly. Perhaps light is shined through them in a certain way that is useful. 99

*Tahsha Scott*
*Milton High School*
*Milton, Massachusetts*

To find out more about the photograph, look on page 460. As you read this chapter, you will learn about the many ways, such as seeing, that you use light.

# 18.1 Light Sources

## Objectives

▶ **Name** and **describe** three types of artificial light.

▶ **Distinguish** between lighted and luminous objects.

▶ **Compare** the efficiency of fluorescent and incandescent lights.

▶ **Infer** why one kind of artificial light may be more useful than another.

Light comes from a variety of sources and has a variety of uses. You come in contact with many sources of light each day. In fact, the beginning of each day is marked by the rise of the sun—the earth's main source of light.

You use light to see things, but light also has other uses. For example, light is used during the filming of a movie, both to brighten the movie set and to help set the mood of a scene. Light is also used to communicate, as in neon signs and traffic signals.

People aren't the only living things that use light. You may have seen a firefly's light at night. Fireflies use light to attract and identify a mate.

## Lighted Objects

Although all light is a form of energy, it doesn't come from the same source. The sun, neon lights, candles, and fireflies are all sources of light. Any object that produces its own light is referred to as **luminous** (LOO muh nuhs). Recall that an object produces light when the electrons in its atoms give off energy.

You've probably looked at stars and the moon in the nighttime sky. Each star, like the sun, is a luminous object—it produces its own light. The moon, however, isn't a luminous object. Look at the moon in Figure 18.1. Although the moon appears to be luminous, the light from the moon is actually light from the sun that is reflected by the moon. The moon is an example of an *illuminated* object. An illuminated object reflects light.

**Figure 18.1** ▲
The moon is illuminated by light from the sun. Why does the moon sometimes appear fully illuminated and sometimes only partially illuminated?

# Light from Luminous Objects

You use several types of artificial light. For example, the light in your classroom is probably fluorescent light. Fluorescent light is produced in glass tubes that contain gases. How do fluorescent lights compare to the kinds of lights you have in your home? Although you may have some fluorescent lights in your home, most of the light is probably produced from ordinary incandescent

## Fluorescent Light

Electrons collide with gas molecules contained at low pressure to produce **fluorescent** light. The phosphor-coated glass tube contains mercury and argon gas. When excited, the gas molecules give off photons of ultraviolet light.

When the UV light strikes the phosphor coating, it changes to visible light. Fluorescent bulbs are cool. They are more energy efficient than incandescent bulbs. ▼

## Incandescent Light

◀ Light that is produced by heating an object until it glows is **incandescent** light. An incandescent light bulb gives off light when a thin piece of tungsten wire inside the bulb, called the filament, is heated until it glows by a flow of electricity.

A vacuum inside the bulb helps to keep the filament from burning in two, which would cause the bulb to burn out. Incandescent lights are not efficient. Most of their energy is given off as heat.

## Animal Light ▶

A firefly gives off cool light when chemicals in its abdomen react. The ability of living things to give off light is called *bioluminescence* (BY oh LOO muh NES uhns). Some kinds of fish, some protists, and some fungi can also produce light. How do you think these organisms use bioluminescence?

light bulbs. The kind of light produced from these bulbs is called incandescent light.

Another kind of light that may be familiar to you is neon light. Neon light is often seen in brightly colored lighted signs and storefronts. It is produced by passing electrons through neon gas inside a thin, glass tube. Neon light is bright and colorful. Study the different types of artificial light shown. How is each type of light produced?

**Tungsten-Halogen Light** ▲

A *tungsten-halogen* bulb has a tungsten filament and is filled with a halogen gas, such as iodine, bromine, or fluorine. The gas reduces wear on the filament. A tungsten-halogen bulb doesn't "burn out" for a long time. Tungsten-halogen bulbs give off very bright incandescent light. They also produce a large amount of heat.

**Neon Light** ▲

The color of the light given off depends on the gas in the tube. Neon gives off bright red light. Mercury vapor gives off a greenish-blue light. Krypton produces purple light, and helium gives off yellow light.

**Sodium-Vapor Light** ▲

When electrons are passed through a sodium-vapor lamp, the lamp gives off a yellow-orange light. Sodium-vapor lamps are energy efficient and give off very bright light with little glare. These characteristics make sodium-vapor lights especially useful as streetlights.

## Science and Society
### *Energy-Saving Light Bulbs*

Scientists and engineers are developing new kinds of lights that use less energy than the incandescent light bulbs used in most homes. One of these new developments is the compact fluorescent light bulb. Unlike ordinary fluorescent bulbs, the compact fluorescent bulb can be used in place of ordinary incandescent light bulbs. These bulbs are also useful for growing plants because they give off UV light.

Compact fluorescent bulbs cost more to buy than incandescent bulbs, but they cost less to use. For example, an 18-watt compact fluorescent bulb gives off as much light as a 75-watt incandescent bulb. The cost of electricity to use an 18-watt compact fluorescent bulb three hours each day for a year is about $2.00. The cost of electricity for using a 75-watt incandescent bulb is about $8.50 per year. The fluorescent bulb also lasts 5 to 13 times longer than an incandescent bulb does.

Tungsten-halogen bulbs are also new. Because of their brightness, tungsten-halogen bulbs are common in automobiles, stadiums, and parking areas, as well as in the home. These bulbs have several advantages over ordinary incandescent light bulbs. They are small, use less electricity, and give off more light. One disadvantage to tungsten-halogen bulbs is the large amount of heat they give off. Fixtures that use these bulbs require thick, glass heat shields. The heat shields prevent objects from touching the bulb and catching fire.

▼ **ACTIVITY**

**Collecting Data**

*Tracking Lighting*

During the day, count the different kinds of light sources you see. Keep track of how many of each kind you see. What kind did you see the most? What kinds didn't you see?

**SKILLS WORKOUT**

## Check and Explain

1. Identify the kind of light produced by each of the following: the red, purple, and yellow lights of an advertising sign, the lights in your classroom, a tungsten-halogen light bulb, and a plant light.

2. How does an illuminated object differ from a luminous object? Give two examples for each.

3. **Compare**  Which is more energy efficient, fluorescent light or incandescent light? Explain.

4. **Infer**  Why would fluorescent light be the best artificial light for a terrarium?

# 18.2 Vision

## Objectives

▶ **Identify** each part of the eye and explain its function.

▶ **Trace** the path of light through the eye.

▶ **Compare** where light rays focus for normal, nearsighted, and farsighted vision.

▶ **Make a model** to show how each part of the eye helps to focus light on the retina.

Living things can see because of the structure of their eyes. The field of vision for living things depends on the location of their eyes. Your eyes are located at the front of your head at a distance of about 3 to 7 cm apart. Because of the position of your eyes, you see nearly the same image with each eye. Seeing the same image with both eyes helps you to judge distances, but it also gives you a relatively narrow field of vision.

You've probably noticed that a bird's eyes are located at the sides of its head. Because its eyes are so far apart, a bird's field of vision is much wider than yours. A bird sees a different image with each of its eyes, as shown in Figure 18.2. Only a small portion of the bird's field of vision is covered by both eyes.

## Parts of the Eye

If you look at your eyes or the eyes of someone else, you can easily observe three different parts. At the center of your eye is a black circle, called the *pupil*. The pupil is actually an opening through which light enters your eye. Surrounding the pupil is a colored disk called the *iris*. The iris is surrounded by the white part of the eye, called the *sclera*. The pupil, iris, and sclera aren't the only parts of the eye. It has other parts that aren't easily observed. All the parts of your eye work together with your brain to allow you to see.

Your eyes are covered by eyelids. The eyelids keep dirt and harmful substances from entering your eyes. Eyelids also spread tears over the eyes when you blink.

 One eye     Both eyes

**Figure 18.2** ▲
Identify the area the bird sees with its right eye, its left eye, and with both eyes. In what way is this field of vision useful to the bird?

**Iris and Pupil** The iris adjusts the size of the pupil to control the amount of light that enters your eye. Locate the iris and the pupil in Figure 18.3. When light is bright, the muscles of the iris contract to make the pupil smaller. Less light enters the eye. In the dim light, the muscles of the iris relax and let in more light. Why is it important for the eye to control the amount of light that enters your eye?

**Cornea and Lens** A transparent structure, called the *cornea*, covers and protects the pupil and the iris. The cornea lets light into your eye. Look carefully at Figure 18.3. You will see that the cornea is part of the sclera.

Another transparent structure, called the lens, is located behind the pupil. Your eye's lens bends light rays to focus an image on your retina. The shape of the lens changes in order to focus the image. Find the cornea and the lens in Figure 18.3.

**Retina** The *retina* is the inner layer of the back of your eye. Look at Figure 18.3. Light passing through the lens forms an image on the retina.

The retina contains light-sensitive cells, called rods and cones. Rods allow you to see black and white. The rods can function in dim light. Cones allow you to see colors. The cones require bright light. Three kinds of cones are needed to see each of the primary colors of light. Some people are color deficient. They don't have all three kinds of cones, so they don't see all colors.

**Optic Nerve** Nerve fibers connected to the rods and cones of the retina form the *optic nerve*. When the rod and cone cells in the retina absorb light rays, the energy in the light changes to electric signals. The optic nerve carries the electric signals formed in the retina to your brain. Your brain interprets these signals as vision.

**Figure 18.3** ▶
This cross section of the eye shows its main parts. Trace the path of light through the eye.

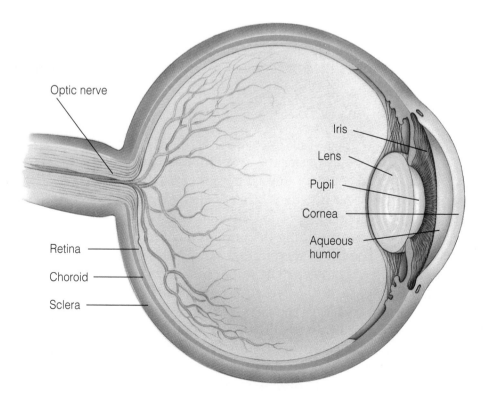

Optic nerve

Iris

Lens

Pupil

Cornea

Aqueous humor

Retina

Choroid

Sclera

## The Path of Light

For perfect vision, light travels through the cornea, the pupil, and the lens, and focuses directly on the retina. Not everyone has eyes that function perfectly. However, most vision disorders can be corrected.

Like a camera, your eye can adjust in order to focus on things near or far. Unlike a camera lens, your eye's lens has muscles around it that change its shape to adjust to different distances. When the lens is unable to adjust to make an image focus directly on the retina, a person is either nearsighted or farsighted.

Look at Figure 18.4 to see how an image can focus in the eye. A nearsighted person sees nearby objects clearly, but far-off objects appear blurred. Light rays from distant objects focus in front of the retina, as shown in the center.

For a farsighted person, light rays from distant objects focus correctly on the retina. However, close-up objects appear blurred. Light rays from nearby objects focus behind the retina, as shown at the bottom.

If the cornea of the eye isn't correctly shaped, light entering the eye may bend more in one direction than in another. This problem is called *astigmatism*. People with astigmatism can't focus light rays on the retina—all images appear blurred.

Perfect vision

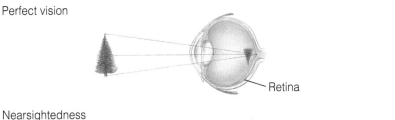

Retina

**Figure 18.4
Correcting Vision Problems**
▼

Nearsightedness

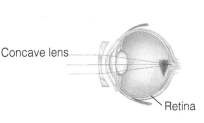

Concave lens — Retina

Retina

To correct nearsighted vision, a concave lens in front of the eye bends light rays so that light focuses on the retina.

Farsightedness

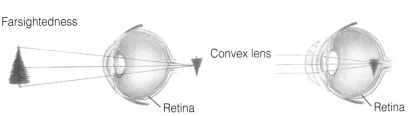

Convex lens — Retina

Retina

To correct farsighted vision, a convex lens in front of the eye bends light rays so that light focuses on the retina.

How would your life be different if you couldn't see light? For millions of people, living in darkness is part of their daily life. These people were either born unable to see or lost their sight as a result of illness or injury.

Imagine trying to get to class or to the store without using your eyes. Sight-impaired people face such challenges every day. Some use canes or trained dogs to help them get around. They also memorize the number of steps between objects in familiar places.

In the early 1800s, a 15-year-old French boy named Louis Braille created an alphabet blind people could use. The braille system uses patterns of raised dots to represent numbers and letters. People who have lost their sight can enjoy books written in braille that are available at many libraries. Machines called braille writers also allow people to communicate in braille. Many elevators and ATMs now have instructions in braille.

Some disorders that cause sight loss are diabetes, cataracts, and glaucoma. Diabetics can help to prevent sight loss with medication and special diets. Cataracts are a condition that clouds the eye's lens. Cataracts can be corrected surgically by replacing the clouded lens with an artificial one. Glaucoma is caused by pressure within the eyeball. It is treated with drugs or surgery.

Eye injuries can occur if chemicals or objects enter the eyes. Such injuries are prevented with safety goggles. Athletes at risk for eye injury can wear helmets or protective eye wear. Protecting your eyes can be as simple as wearing sunglasses.

**Figure 18.5** ▲
Name some ways the seeing-eye dog helps the woman find her way around.

## Check and Explain

1.  Describe the functions of the following parts of the eye: pupil, iris, cornea, lens, retina, and optic nerve.

2.  Explain how vision occurs: begin with light entering the eye and end with the role of the brain.

3.  **Compare** Compare how light rays focus on the retina for normal, nearsighted, and farsighted vision.

4.  **Make a Model** Draw a diagram showing light focusing on the retina. Show all the parts of the eye and include two light rays reflected from an object.

# 18.3 Reflection and Mirrors

## Objectives

▶ **Explain** how light interacts with three types of mirrors.

▶ **Identify** two uses for a plane, a concave, and a convex mirror.

▶ **Compare** and **contrast** the image formed by each of the three types of mirrors.

▶ **Measure** the areas reflected by a concave mirror and a convex mirror.

**H**ave you ever looked at yourself in a pool of water? When the surface of the water is calm, light bounces off your body to form your image on the water. You see a reflection of yourself. When there are ripples on the water, you don't see your reflection. You only see the surface of the water.

Look at the water in Figure 18.6. Notice that the surface of the water acts like a mirror to create a perfect image of the surroundings. Why does the surface of a body of water reflect an image when the water is perfectly still?

## Reflection

A reflection occurs when light rays from some light source directed at an object bounce off the object. The light rays that approach an object are called *incident rays*. Light rays that bounce off and are directed away from a surface are called *reflected rays*. Because a perfectly calm lake, or a mirror, reflects most of the incident rays and doesn't scatter the reflected rays, it produces a clear, sharp image.

Any object you can see is reflecting light rays to your eyes. Cars, walls, windows, and even people reflect some amount of light rays. Otherwise, you would not be able to see them. Smooth, shiny surfaces, such as metals, glass, polished wood, and the surface of liquids reflect light easily. In what other kinds of surfaces can you see your reflection?

**Figure 18.6** ▲
How does the detail in the reflection differ from the actual scene? Try looking at the photo upside down.

# Mirrors

A common mirror is a flat or curved piece of glass. It has been painted on the back with a thin coating of metal. The metal gives the glass a shiny surface that reflects most of the light rays that strike it.

Images in a mirror appear to be reversed left to right. Light rays from the right side of an image reflect off the mirror and strike the left side of your eye. The way a mirror reflects light depends on the shape of its surface. Mirrors are classified as plane, concave, or convex.

**Plane Mirrors**  A mirror with a flat surface is a plane mirror. The image appears to be behind a plane mirror. Also, the image appears to be the same size and distance behind the mirror as the object is in front of it.

The image that you see in a plane mirror is called a **virtual** image. A virtual image is not where it appears to be and is seen only in a mirror. A virtual image can be compared to another type of image, called a real image, which is formed by converging light rays. A real image can be projected onto a surface. A virtual image, however, can't be projected onto a surface.

**Figure 18.7**
**A Light Beam Reflected Off a Plane Mirror** ▼

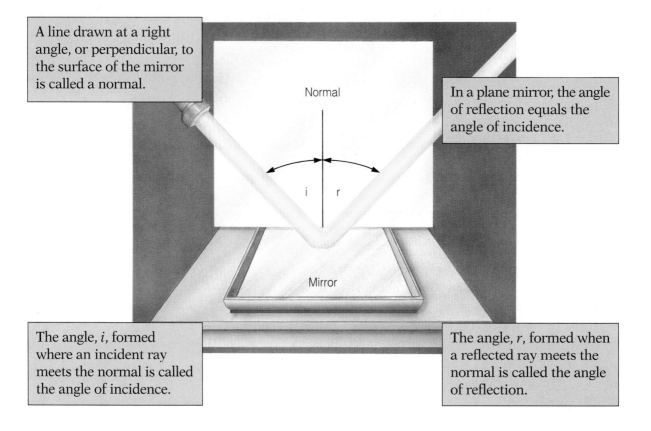

A line drawn at a right angle, or perpendicular, to the surface of the mirror is called a normal.

Normal

In a plane mirror, the angle of reflection equals the angle of incidence.

i    r

Mirror

The angle, *i*, formed where an incident ray meets the normal is called the angle of incidence.

The angle, *r*, formed when a reflected ray meets the normal is called the angle of reflection.

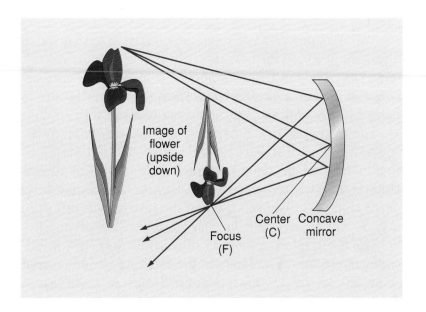

**Concave Mirrors**  A mirror that curves inward, like the bowl of the spoon in Figure 18.8, is a **concave** mirror. Unlike the image produced by a plane mirror, a concave mirror produces a real image. A real image forms when light rays pass through it and can be projected onto a surface.

The distance between an object and a concave mirror determines the kind of image that forms. If an object is close to the concave surface of the mirror, the reflected image appears larger than the object. People sometimes use these mirrors when applying cosmetics or shaving. If the object is farther away from the mirror than the place where the reflected rays meet, or converge, the image is upside down and smaller than the object. This kind of image is seen in Figure 18.8.

**Convex Mirrors**  A mirror that curves outward, like the back side of the spoon, shown in Figure 18.9, is a **convex** mirror. Light rays reflected from a convex mirror spread out. Thus, the reflected image also spreads out. A convex mirror forms a virtual image that appears to be behind the mirror. The image is always upright and is smaller than the object being reflected.

Convex mirrors provide a very wide angle of view, so a large area can be seen. They are often used in stores to prevent shoplifting. The side-view mirrors on some cars are often convex mirrors. Where have you used a convex mirror?

**Figure 18.8** ▲
The diagram shows how the concave bowl of the spoon reflects the image of the flowers. What kind of an image appears in the spoon?

**Figure 18.9** ▲
Explain how the image of the flowers on the back of the spoon differs from the image on the bowl of the spoon.

## Science and Technology *Super Telescopes*

Astronomers are using new super telescopes that allow them to see far beyond the range of any previous telescope. The main component of a super telescope is a concave mirror. The slightest imperfection on the surface of a super telescope's mirror badly distorts the image.

The mirror of one new telescope was designed to be so smooth that if it were as wide as the United States, there would be no rise on its surface higher than 10 cm. Unfortunately, after six years of construction, a major imperfection was discovered when the mirror was put into use. So, the telescope is far less effective than planned.

The Keck telescope is one of this new generation of super telescopes. The heart of the Keck telescope is what scientists are calling an ingenious design of 36 hexagonal mirrors. These adjustable mirrors join to form the telescope's concave mirror. The Keck telescope's mirror measures almost 10 m in diameter and is the largest ever built.

With the completion of the construction of the Keck telescope, scientists will be able to study eight times more of the universe than is visible with other telescopes. A super telescope, such as the Keck, can identify the light of a candle 800,000 km away. The Keck telescope will also provide a look back in time as well as across space. The light it will see was given off billions of years ago, traveling across space for all this time.

### ▼ ACTIVITY

**Predicting**

*Learning the Angles*

Obtain a ball.

**1.** Predict at which angle the ball will bounce back if you throw it against a wall from a certain angle.

**2.** Use a different angle each time you throw the ball.

How well did you predict the angle at which the ball bounces back? What did you learn about the angle at which the ball bounces back?

**SKILLS WORKOUT**

### Check and Explain

1. What kind of image does each of the three types of mirrors form?

2. Describe two uses each for plane mirrors, concave mirrors, and convex mirrors.

3. **Compare and Contrast** How does the image formed by a plane mirror differ from that formed by concave and convex mirrors?

4. **Measure** Look at a concave mirror, observe the reflected area. Measure the reflected area with a measuring tape. Repeat the procedure with a convex mirror of the same size. How do the sizes of the reflected areas compare?

# 18.4 Refraction and Lenses

## Objectives

▶ **Explain** how convex and concave lenses affect light rays.

▶ **Identify** two uses for convex and concave lenses.

▶ **Infer** why lenses refract light.

▶ **Make a model** that shows how focal length affects an object being observed through a convex lens.

I f you've ever tried to use a net to catch a fish in an aquarium, you've probably found that the fish was harder to catch than you expected. Light rays bend when they enter water. So, the fish appears to be in a location where it isn't.

You can see this same effect in Figure 18.10. Water bends the light from the straws. As a result, the straws appear to be broken at the place where they meet the surface of the water.

## Refraction

You know that the straws in Figure 18.10 aren't really bent. The straws appear to be bent because light rays bend as they enter the water. The bending of light rays is called *refraction*.

Light usually travels in straight lines and at a constant speed. However, when light passes from one medium to one with a different density, the speed and the direction of light change. Use Figure 18.10 to see what happens when light passes from air to water. The light slows down and bends, or refracts. The light changes direction again when it passes from the water to the air. As a result, the straw appears to be in different positions above and below the water's surface. How else is the appearance of the straws different?

If you wear eyeglasses, you're probably familiar with refraction. The density of the glass is greater than the density of air. Eyeglasses bend the light entering your eye. The light from an object refracts and focuses correctly on your retina. How do you think a hand lens affects light?

**Figure 18.10** ▲
Light rays bend when they pass from air into water. Bending light rays make these straws appear to be bent.

# Lenses

**Figure 18.11** ▲
How is the drop of water on the leaf similar to the convex lens in the diagram?

An optical **lens** is a transparent material that refracts light passing through it. Lenses may have one or more curved surfaces. Most lenses are made of glass or plastic. Eyeglasses, cameras, microscopes, and telescopes all use lenses.

Recall that mirrors reflect light rays. Lenses differ from mirrors because they transmit light. Lenses allow light to pass through rather than reflecting it. There are two types of lenses: convex and concave. Each type of lens refracts light differently.

**Convex Lenses**   A convex lens is thicker in the center than at the edges. As parallel light rays pass through a convex lens, the rays bend toward the thickest part, or center, of the lens. The point at which the light rays come together, or converge, is called the point of focus. The distance from a lens to its point of focus is called *focal length*. The diagram in Figure 18.12 shows an image that is one focal length from the object.

The image a convex lens forms is determined by distance of the object from the lens. An object that is between one and two focal lengths from the lens forms a real image. The image is enlarged and upside-down as shown in Figure 18.12. The convex lens in a microscope or slide projector forms this type of image.

An object more than two focal lengths from a convex lens also forms a real image. It is an upside-down image that is smaller than the object. The lens of a camera and the lens in your eye form this kind of image.

**Figure 18.12** ▶
Why do the flowers in the diagram appear upside down and larger in this ray diagram?

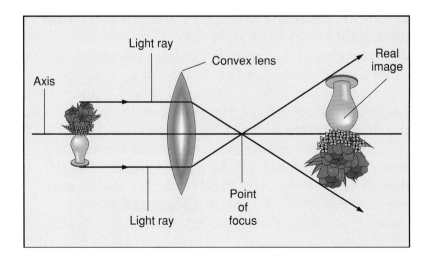

A convex lens forms a virtual image if an object is placed between the lens and its focal point. The virtual image is right-side up and enlarged. The image you see in a magnifying glass is a virtual image.

**Concave Lenses**  A lens that is thinner at the center than it is at the edges is a concave lens. Parallel light rays passing through a concave lens bend toward the thickest part of the lens. Instead of coming together at a point of focus, light rays passing through a concave lens spread apart, or diverge. The point of focus is behind the image. Find the point of focus in the diagram in Figure 18.14.

Notice what happens to the light rays as they pass through a concave lens in the diagram. The light rays spread out, or diverge, behind the lens. How is this different from the light rays passing through a convex lens?

Concave lenses form images that are right side up and smaller than the object. An image observed through a concave lens is virtual. Explain why a concave lens forms a virtual image.

Recall that for a nearsighted person, light rays from distant objects converge in front of the retina instead of on it. A concave lens in front of the eye makes the light rays diverge. The natural lens of the eye, which is convex, can then converge the light rays correctly on the retina.

Concave lenses are used in some kinds of optical equipment. Together with convex lenses, concave lenses are used to focus telescopes. Concave lenses are also used in optical targets.

**Figure 18.13** ▲
Is more or less area of the stamp visible in the concave lense? Explain

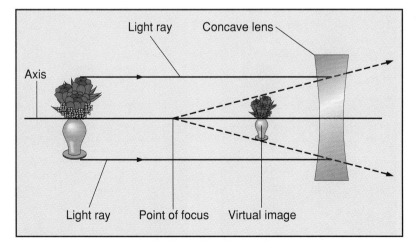

◀ **Figure 18.14**
Which image of the flowers would you see if you were looking through the concave lens from the right?

## Astronomy
### L I N K

Obtain a kaleidoscope.

**1.** Ask a classmate who wears glasses to remove her glasses, look through the kaleidoscope, and tell what she sees.

**2.** Now ask the student to replace her glasses and look through the kaleidoscope. What are the differences?

The repairs made to the Hubble Telescope included the placement of corrective lenses. Research this topic and write a paragraph comparing glasses with the lenses placed on the Hubble.

### A C T I V I T Y

## Science and Technology
### *Correcting Your Vision*

About 50% of the population of the United States wears corrective lenses. Advances in technology have made it possible for corrective lenses to correct many different vision problems. Prescription eyeglasses or contact lenses correct common vision problems, such as near-sightedness, farsightedness, and astigmatism.

A bifocal lens has one corrective lens on the top half and another on the bottom half. The top half corrects distance vision and the bottom half corrects close vision. Before bifocals were developed, to a farsighted person wearing a pair of glasses to see close-up objects, distant objects were blurred.

With bifocals, a person doesn't need to switch eyeglasses to see both far and near. Scientists have also developed trifocal lenses. With three different lenses, a person can see distant, middle-range, and close-up objects clearly without switching glasses.

Contact lenses replaced eyeglasses for many people. Hard contact lenses, made of glass or plastic, float on a thin layer of tears on the cornea. They were developed in the 1950s.

Soft contact lenses were developed in the 1970s. Soft contacts are more comfortable to wear because they absorb moisture and contain water. Because they are more likely to cause infection, most soft contacts must be cleaned and sterilized daily.

**Figure 18.15**

Use what you learned to identify the type of lens in each photo. ▼

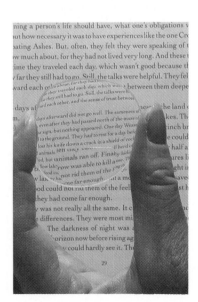

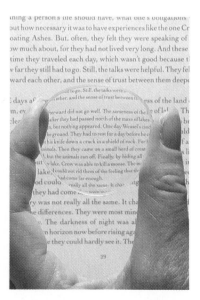

# Career Corner Optician

## Who Makes and Fits Your Glasses?

Suppose you have a prescription for new eyeglasses or contact lenses. You can purchase your new glasses or contact lenses from an optician. An optician makes the glasses or contact lenses you need according to your eyeglass prescription.

The optician will also measure and record the distance between the center of one pupil to the center of the other pupil. This distance is important to make sure your new lenses form a sharp, clear image. She can help you to select eyeglass frames that fit you well and look good on you.

The optician will order lenses that match your prescription. She cuts the lenses to fit your frames. Once your eyeglasses are made, the optician adjusts them to make sure your glasses fit properly.

To work as an optician requires good math skills and the ability to make accurate measurements. You should have an interest in both physical and life sciences. You should also enjoy working with people.

In some states, high-school graduates may receive on-the-

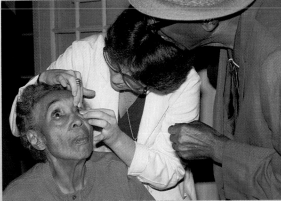

job training as opticians. Others receive formal training in a trade school. Many states require candidates to take a state board exam to obtain a medical assurance certificate before they can practice as an optician.

Extended-wear lenses and disposable contacts are special soft contacts that can be worn for a week without cleaning. A person can wear disposable contacts for a week, throw them away, and replace them with another pair. Some special soft contact lenses change the color of the wearer's iris. Another type can treat diseases by slowly releasing medicine into the eye.

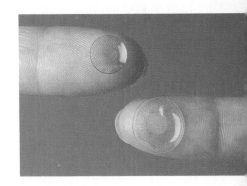

**Figure 18.16** ▲
The contact lens at the top is a hard lens. The contact lens at the bottom is a soft lens. Describe how they are different.

## Check and Explain

1. How do convex and concave lenses affect incoming parallel light rays?

2. Describe two uses for convex and concave lenses.

3. **Infer** Why does light refract when it passes through a lens?

4. **Make a Model** Draw ray diagrams that show how an image formed by a convex lens changes as focal length changes.

# Activity 18 *Is a convex hand lens like an eye?*

***Skills*** Observe; Predict; Measure

## Task 1  Prelab Prep
Collect the following items: paper, hand lens, and a metric ruler.

## Task 2  Data Record
1. Prepare a ray diagram similar to the one below to record your observations. Look through the window. Choose one object, such as a tree, on which to focus your lens.
2. Draw a side view of a convex lens in the center of a sheet of paper. To the right of the lens, draw a horizontal line to the center of the lens. Choose a spot along the line that represents the focus, and write an *F* at that spot.
3. To the left of the diagram, at a distance greater from the lens than the focus is on the right, draw the object on which you have chosen to focus the lens.

## Task 3  Procedure
1. On a bright or sunny day, darken all the windows in a room except for one.
2. Hold the hand lens about 1.5 m from the window at the same level as the object outside.
3. Hold up the piece of paper on the opposite side of the lens from the window. Line the paper up with the object. Predict where a focused image of the object will appear on the paper and what the image will look like.
4. Move the paper back and forth until an image of the object appears on the paper. Measure the distance between the lens and the paper.
5. Complete your ray diagram by drawing the image you observed in the proper place.

## Task 4  Analysis
1. How far from the lens did the image appear? How close was your prediction?
2. Describe the image that formed on the paper. Explain why it appeared as it did.

## Task 5  Conclusion
Explain how the image you formed with the convex lens is like an image formed on the retina of the eye.

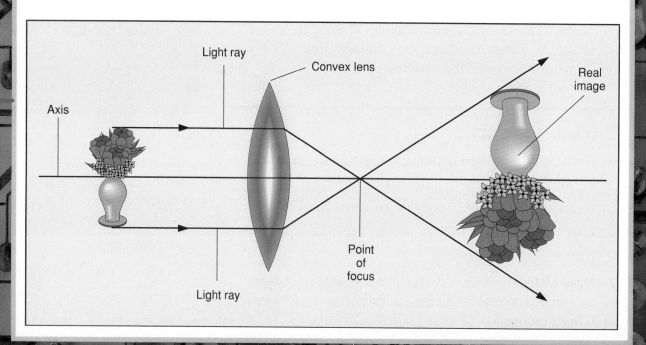

# 18.5 Light Technology

## Objectives

▶ **Explain** how cameras, telescopes, and microscopes work.

▶ **Compare** the technology in lasers, holography, and fiber optics.

▶ **Infer** about new ways to use lasers.

▶ **Make a model** to explain how a camera forms an image on film.

You know that light allows you to see. Did you know that light can also help you to hear? It sounds unbelievable, but the voices you hear on the telephone actually travel as light.

New technology makes it possible to change the sound energy of a human voice into light signals. These light signals are carried through glass fibers over very long distances to all parts of the country. The light signals are changed back into sound before they reach your telephone. As a result, you are able to pick up the telephone and talk to people anywhere. This amazing technology is part of the science of fiber optics.

## Using Mirrors and Lenses

You know that mirrors reflect and that lenses refract, or bend, light. The ability of mirrors and lenses to focus light and form images makes them very useful. For example, people use mirrors to check their appearance, put on makeup, shave, or to check traffic when driving a car. Lenses are used in eyeglasses and optical instruments.

Cameras, telescopes, and microscopes are optical instruments that have many uses. Each of these instruments uses mirrors or lenses, or both. Surgeons can now use light instead of a scalpel to perform delicate surgeries. Artists use light to create three-dimensional images on a two-dimensional surface. As technology develops, scientists and engineers continue to find new and better ways to make light work for you. More powerful cameras, telescopes, and microscopes are being developed.

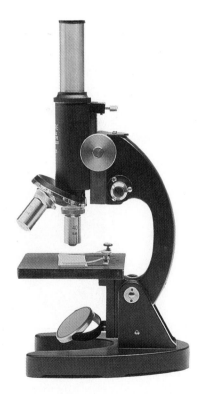

**Figure 18.17** ▲
The microscope's mirror reflects light through the object being viewed. The lenses magnify the object.

**Cameras** You know that a camera uses light and lenses to record images on film. In many ways, a camera is like your eye. Both have structures that control the amount of light that enters. They each have a convex lens that produces a real and upside-down image.

Look at Figure 18.18. Notice how a camera and an eye are different. Instead of forming an image on the retina, a camera records an image on film that is sensitive to light. The image on the film is then reproduced on paper as a photograph. What are some other ways a camera and an eye are different?

**Figure 18.18**
**How a Camera Works** ▼

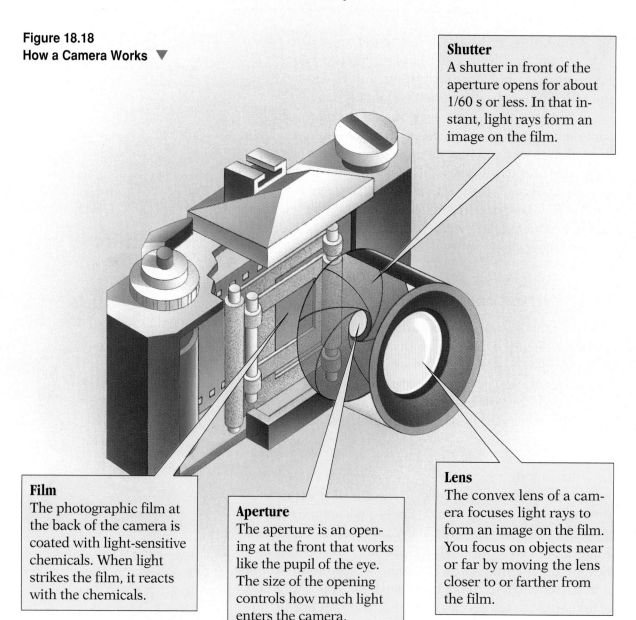

**Shutter**
A shutter in front of the aperture opens for about 1/60 s or less. In that instant, light rays form an image on the film.

**Film**
The photographic film at the back of the camera is coated with light-sensitive chemicals. When light strikes the film, it reacts with the chemicals.

**Aperture**
The aperture is an opening at the front that works like the pupil of the eye. The size of the opening controls how much light enters the camera.

**Lens**
The convex lens of a camera focuses light rays to form an image on the film. You focus on objects near or far by moving the lens closer to or farther from the film.

**Telescopes**  If you have ever looked at the stars away from city lights, you probably noticed that the stars were much brighter. Even under ideal conditions, objects in outer space are too far away to study in detail without using a telescope. Two kinds of telescopes are used to see distant objects, a refracting telescope and a reflecting telescope.

A simple refracting telescope is shown on the left in Figure 18.19. It is used to see objects on land. It has two lenses: an objective lens and an eyepiece lens. An image from the objective lens is focused and enlarged by the eyepiece lens. The eyepiece lens is positioned within one focal length of the image made by the objective lens. What kind of image is formed by the eyepiece lens?

A reflecting telescope, which is used mostly by astronomers, is shown on the right in Figure 18.19. Light rays entering the telescope are reflected onto mirrors. The mirrors form a real image within one focal length of the eyepiece lens. The eyepiece lens forms the virtual image you see when you look into a telescope. Why do you think astronomers use a reflecting telescope?

**Figure 18.19**
**Refracting and Reflecting Telescopes** ▼

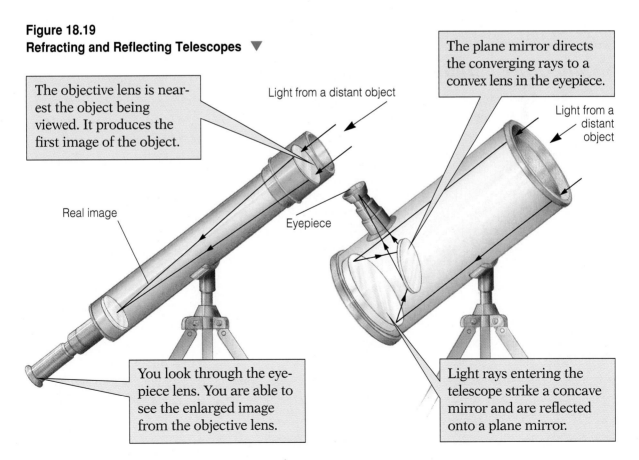

The objective lens is nearest the object being viewed. It produces the first image of the object.

Light from a distant object

The plane mirror directs the converging rays to a convex lens in the eyepiece.

Light from a distant object

Real image

Eyepiece

You look through the eyepiece lens. You are able to see the enlarged image from the objective lens.

Light rays entering the telescope strike a concave mirror and are reflected onto a plane mirror.

**Light Microscopes**  Have you used a microscope to study a very small object? Actually, a hand lens is a microscope. It is a simple microscope because it has only one lens. A microscope with two or more lenses is called a compound microscope. It is called a light microscope because light is needed to view very small objects.

Light enters a compound microscope from a light source, which may be an electric light bulb. Some microscopes have mirrors that reflect light from a window. Light travels from its source, through the object being viewed, and into the objective lens. The objective lens is a convex lens which forms an enlarged, real image.

The eyepiece lens of a microscope is also a convex lens. The eyepiece lens further magnifies the image formed by the objective lens. The eyepiece lens forms the virtual image you see when you look into the microscope. The total magnification of the virtual image is the product of the magnification of the objective and the eyepiece.

## *Consider This*

## *Should Office Buildings Leave Lights On at Night?*

To conserve electricity, most people turn off unneeded lights in their homes. However, this is not done in many stores and office buildings. It is more common to keep lights on 24 hours a day.

**Consider Some Issues**  One reason people who manage stores and offices leave the lights on at night is security. Lights inside a building make it possible to see into the building from the outside. This practice helps to prevent crime. The lights also reduce the risk of injury for anyone working at night in the building.

Leaving lights on can save money. Light bulbs undergo less wear and last longer when they are not turned on and off frequently. The cost of the electricity needed to keep the bulbs on at night is less than the cost of replacing burned-out bulbs.

Buildings that use large amounts of electricity pay for electricity at a lower rate than individuals do. The electricity to keep lights on in a large building is cheaper than replacing the bulbs more often. The additional electricity used to keep the lights on at night increases the use of fossil fuels, which can't be replaced.

Greater usage of electricity also increases the amount of pollution caused by burning fossil fuels.

**Think About It**  Are there greater benefits or drawbacks to keeping lights on in large buildings day and night? Which is more important, security and saving money now or preserving resources for the future?

**Write About It**  Write a paper stating your position on leaving office lights on all day and night. Include your reasons for choosing your position.

## Lasers

You know that white light spreads out equally in all directions as it travels. A beam of light that doesn't spread out as it travels can be produced by a **laser**. The word *laser* is an acronym for **l**ight **a**mplification by **s**timulated **e**missions of **r**adiation.

Laser light is unique. In addition to traveling in one direction, it is generally of one wavelength, and it is coherent. Light is coherent when all its waves move in the same direction and the crests and troughs of the light waves match up.

A laser is made of a flashtube, mirrors, and a rod that is usually made of ruby crystals. The rod is closed off at each end with a mirror. Look at Figure 18.20 to see how a laser works.

Light from the coiled tube focuses on the rod to excite the electrons in it. The electrons give off photons. These photons travel in the same direction and have the same wavelength. The photons reflect off the mirrors at each end of the rod. They strike other atoms and set off a chain reaction that releases more photons. The laser increases, or amplifies, the strength of the light waves. Some amplified light leaves the laser as a beam of laser light.

Surveyors use lasers to measure land distances. In industry, lasers are used to cut through metals. Surgeons use the cutting power of lasers to replace the scalpel.

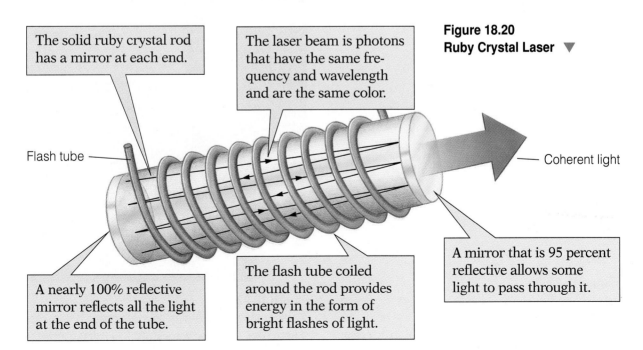

The solid ruby crystal rod has a mirror at each end.

The laser beam is photons that have the same frequency and wavelength and are the same color.

**Figure 18.20
Ruby Crystal Laser** ▼

Flash tube

Coherent light

A nearly 100% reflective mirror reflects all the light at the end of the tube.

The flash tube coiled around the rod provides energy in the form of bright flashes of light.

A mirror that is 95 percent reflective allows some light to pass through it.

# Holography

Have you ever seen an exhibit or a movie in which a three-dimensional figure seemed to appear from nowhere? The effect may seem like magic, but it is more likely that the image is a product of holography. Holography is a technology that uses lasers to make the three-dimensional image called a **hologram**.

**Hologram Uses** Holograms have many applications. They are now used as special effects in movies and plays. Holograms may someday be used to produce three-dimensional television.

Because they are difficult to duplicate, holograms are used as security devices. For example, some credit-card companies now put holograms on their credit cards. The holograms help to prevent the forgery of credit cards.

Holograms can also be used as educational tools. For example, holograms can be used to display a three-dimensional image of internal body organs. Medical students can use the images as a model to study the human body.

**Hologram Technology** Now that you know about lasers, you can learn how a hologram is formed. Refer to Figure 18.21 as you read about the process for making a hologram.

1. A laser beam is split into two beams. One beam, called the reference beam, is focused on a photographic plate. The other beam is focused on an object and is reflected onto the photographic plate. An interference pattern forms where the reference beam and the reflected light meet.

2. The photographic plate is developed, but it doesn't appear any different from the way it did before developing. However, chemicals in the developing fluid have etched a pattern on the plate.

3. A laser beam aimed at the developed plate produces a three-dimensional image of the object. The image produced is a hologram, like the ones in Figure 18.22.

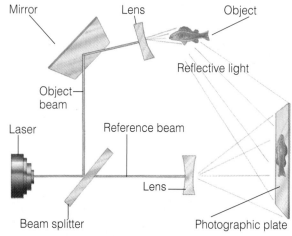

**Figure 18.21** ▲
An interference pattern is formed where the reference beam meets light reflected from the fish. A holographic image is etched on the photographic plate.

**Figure 18.22** ▲
A hologram is a three-dimensional version of a photograph. What are some ways you could use holograms?

# Fiber Optics

Through the technology of fiber optics, a doctor can now look at organs inside your body without performing surgery. Fiber optics involves the transmission of light signals through thin, flexible, transparent fibers made of glass or plastic. Each fiber is called an **optical fiber**.

**Internal Reflection**   How do optical fibers work? Look at Figure 18.23. Think of an optical fiber as a "light pipe." Imagine that you aimed a flashlight into one end of a straight piece of pipe. What would happen to the light? It would pass through the pipe and come out the other end.

What do you think would happen to the light if the pipe were bent instead of straight? If the inside of the pipe is highly reflective, the light reflects off the inner walls of the pipe. The reflection of light within the pipe is called *internal reflection*.

Because of internal reflection, light can be piped from one location to another within glass or plastic fibers. Light is aimed inside one end of the fiber. When the light reaches a bend in the transparent fiber, it doesn't pass through the fiber. Instead it bounces off the walls of the fiber, as shown in Figure 18.23. The light travels through the fiber, reflecting off the walls within the fiber, until it reaches the end.

**Uses of Fiber Optics**   When two sets of optical fibers are placed side by side, light signals sent through one set can be returned along the other set. This idea is used in a fiberscope. Doctors use fiberscopes to view organs inside the body. Mechanics can also use fiberscopes to look at the inside of a machine.

In some places, optical fibers are used for telephone communication instead of wires. The fibers are more efficient because a single fiber can carry as much information as a large bundle of wires.

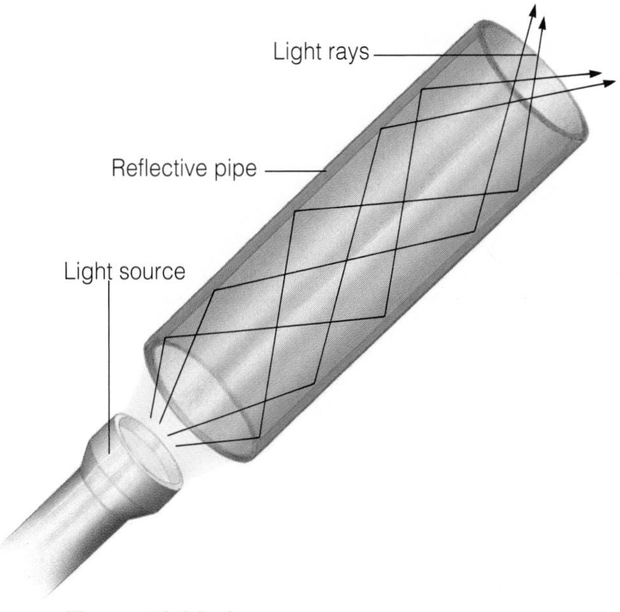

**Figure 18.23** ▲
Light rays travel in the confined space of an optical fiber in much the same way as light waves travel through a pipe.

*Light rays*

*Reflective pipe*

*Light source*

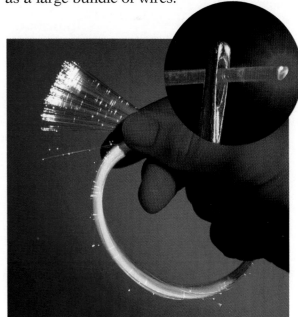

**Figure 18.24** ▲
Each of the thin optical fibers is small enough to fit through the eye of a needle. Why is the size of the fiber important?

Optical fibers are changing the way people communicate. Optical fibers are replacing old telephone wires worldwide. Light sent through the fibers does the same job as electric signals sent through wires. However, optical fibers do the job more efficiently.

Today optical fibers make it possible for people to use their computers for shopping and banking. People can use their phone to "visit" libraries across the country. When they find information they want, they can have the information sent over fiber-optic phone lines to their home computer. They then use their computer to print out the information.

In the future, other kinds of communication will be carried through optical fibers. For example, optical fibers will be used to deliver television signals to your home. Programs from around the world will be available to you.

Scientists are also developing a fiber-optics communication system that combines video and computer technologies. Using this technology, a person working at a computer can speak with a person in another city on the telephone about information appearing on both computer screens. At the same time, these people can see each other's faces in a window on their computers. This device, called a videophone, is shown in Figure 18.25. Some day this same kind of conferencing could allow people in three or four different places to have a "face to face" conversation by videophone.

**Figure 18.25** ▲
The woman is able to see and be seen by the person she's talking to. What kinds of businesses would benefit from videophones?

## Check and Explain

1. Describe the role of the lenses used in cameras, telescopes, and microscopes.

2. How is the technology used in lasers, holography, and fiber optics similar?

3. **Infer** Why are lasers useful as surgical instruments?

4. **Make a Model** Using the figure on page 452 as a guide, create a flowchart that traces the path of light through a camera to form an image on film.

# Chapter 18 Review

## Concept Summary

### 18.1 Light Sources
▶ A luminous object makes its own light.
▶ An illuminated object reflects light.
▶ Three types of artificial light are fluorescent, incandescent, and neon light.

### 18.2 Vision
▶ Light enters your eye through the cornea and the pupil, and is focused by the lens on the retina. The optic nerve carries signals from the retina to the brain.
▶ Nearsightedness and farsightedness result when the lens doesn't focus light rays on the retina.

### 18.3 Reflection and Mirrors
▶ Light is reflected when it bounces off a surface.
▶ A flat, or plane, mirror forms a virtual image that is right side up and reversed.
▶ A concave mirror bends inward at the center and forms a real image.

▶ A convex mirror curves outward at the center and forms a virtual image.

### 18.4 Refraction and Lenses
▶ Refraction is the bending of light.
▶ The image formed by a convex lens depends on the object's distance from the lens.
▶ A concave lens forms a virtual, upright image that is smaller than the object.

### 18.5 Light Technology
▶ Cameras, telescopes, and microscopes are optical instruments that use mirrors, lenses, or both.
▶ A laser produces a beam of coherent light of only one wavelength.
▶ A hologram is a three-dimensional image made with a laser.
▶ Fiber optics are glass or plastic rods that are used to transmit information in the form of light.

## Chapter Vocabulary

| | | | |
|---|---|---|---|
| luminous (18.1) | virtual image (18.3) | lens (18.4) | optical fiber (18.5) |
| fluorescent (18.1) | concave (18.3) | laser (18.5) | |
| incandescent (18.1) | convex (18.3) | hologram (18.5) | |

## Check Your Vocabulary

Use the vocabulary words above to complete the following sentences correctly.

1. A three-dimensional image produced with laser technology is a(n) _____ .

2. Light produced by heating an object until it glows is _____ .

3. Close-up objects are magnified by a(n) _____ mirror.

4. The kind of mirror that provides a wide angle of view is a(n) _____ mirror.

5. An object producing its own light is _____ .

6. A device that produces an intense beam of coherent light is a(n) _____ .

7. A concave lens produces a(n) _____ .

8. A fiber that transmits light is a(n) _____ .

9. Passing electrons through a phosphor-coated tube produces _____ light.

10. A curved piece of glass is a(n) _____ .

## Write Your Vocabulary

Write sentences using the vocabulary words above. Show that you know what each word means.

# Chapter 18 Review

## Check Your Knowledge

Choose the answer that best completes each sentence.

1. A reflecting telescope makes use of (mirrors, lasers, lenses, mirrors and lenses).

2. The technology that uses lasers to produce a three-dimensional image is (fiber optics, holography, biolumines-cence, refraction).

3. A tungsten-halogen light bulb produces (incandescent, neon, coherent, fluorescent) light.

4. Of the following, all are luminous objects except (the sun, a campfire, a mirror, a flashlight).

Determine whether each statement is true or false. Write *true* if it is true. If it is false, change the underlined word(s) to make the statement true.

5. Most of the energy from an incandescent light is given off as <u>light</u>.

6. The film in a camera works like the <u>cornea</u> of the eye.

7. Light is <u>coherent</u> when the crests and troughs of the light waves match up and move in the same direction.

8. In a compound telescope or microscope, the lens nearest the object being viewed is the <u>objective</u> lens.

9. Light rays don't actually pass where a <u>virtual</u> image appears to be.

10. Rays that pass through a <u>concave</u> lens spread outward.

11. The part of the eye that focuses light on the retina is the <u>pupil</u>.

## Check Your Understanding

Apply the concepts you have learned to answer each question.

1. Which of the following are luminous objects?

   a. stars
   b. plane mirrors
   c. fireflies
   d. sodium-vapor lights
   e. convex mirrors
   f. lenses
   g. neon lights
   h. some fishes

2. How does the way a convex lens bends light differ from the way a concave lens bends light?

3. When using a concave mirror, what is the position of the object in relation to the focal point when:

   a. a real, upside-down image is produced?

   b. a virtual image that is right-side up is produced?

4. What might you infer about the efficiency of the lights described? A neon light produces little heat and uses a small amount of electricity. A tungsten-halogen light uses more electricity than a neon light and produces a large amount of heat.

5. **Mystery Photo** The photograph on page 432 shows a bundle of optical fibers. Describe how fiber optics makes use of internal reflection. What would happen if light rays in an optical fiber weren't reflected internally?

6. **Application** You find a pair of eyeglasses that have convex lenses. Based on the shape of the lenses, what kind of vision does the owner of the glasses have?

# Develop Your Skills

Use the skills you have developed to complete each activity.

1. **Interpret Data**  Design your own neon sign. Use the information in the table below to indicate which gases you would use to produce the colors you want.

| Gas | Color of Light |
|-----|----------------|
| Helium | Yellow |
| Krypton | Purple |
| Mercury vapor | Greenish-blue |
| Neon | Red |

2. **Data Bank**  Use the information on page 642 to answer the following questions.

   a. How much light (in lumens) do two 100-watt incandescent light bulbs produce?

   b. Which fluorescent bulb produces about the same amount of light as two 100-watt bulbs?

   c. Compare other incandescent and fluorescent bulbs that have about the same amount of watts. Which type is the most energy-efficient?

   d. Which type of light bulb will last the longest?

3. **Application**  An incident ray strikes a plane mirror at a 35-degree angle. What is the angle of reflection? Why?

4. **Observe**  Examine any single letter on this page both with and without a hand lens. Make careful drawings of your observations both with and without the lens. Describe any differences you may have observed. How can you explain these differences?

# Make Connections

1. **Link the Concepts**  Draw a concept map showing how the concepts below link together. Add terms to link, or connect, the concepts.

   | | |
   |---|---|
   | light | lenses |
   | mirrors | convex |
   | concave | plane |
   | telescopes | microscopes |

2. **Science and Math**  How large would objects of the following sizes appear under a microscope at a magnification of 250 times?

   a. 0.015 mm  c. 0.08 mm
   b. 0.036 mm  d. 0.007 mm

3. **Science and Social Studies**  Describe the impact one of the following had on society. Use the library for your research.

   Nicholas Copernicus
   Thomas Edison
   Anton van Leeuwenhoek
   Kitt Peak Observatory
   Palomar Observatory

4. **Science and You**  Imagine videophones were available at the price of a regular telephone. Would you want to replace your family's phones with videophones? How would using the phone change if all telephones were videophones?

5. **Science and Society**  Form a team of four students to find out about services available for sight-deficient people in your community. Make a list of the services available and the organization offering each service. Discuss your list as a group. Which services would you find most important if you were sight deficient? Identify any additional services you think should be available.

# Science and Literature Connection

The doors opened to the public and the seats began to fill. The lights dimmed shortly. Joyce watched everything from behind the makeshift wing, awaiting her cue.

Magic began. A kalimba tinkled an introduction and was accompanied by an elder, whose rich contralto linked the spiritual and the cries of the Congo. From the wings children appeared in number, doing a jumping dance. They formed a circle around the elder, answering her cries with a sweet, lyrical chant.

As the children disappeared, the sounds of gourd instruments and birdcalls were woven into the music. Maidens entered in three rows with baskets of fruit perched on their heads, all held high. Tamu led the magnificent spectrum of multicolored maidens, from the flawless ebonies and earthy cafés to the clay reds and creamy yellows. The bells around their ankles sang joyously as they stamped their feet into the ground.

They exited in threes, all bowing stage right where the men were to enter. The tinkling of the kalimba was overtaken by four drummers in dreadlocks. A thunder rolled off the congas while the warriors paraded

## Blue Tights

*The following excerpts are taken from the novel* Blue Tights *by Rita Williams-Garcia*

their oiled bodies in loincloths. They came at the audience, hurling powerful kicks and firm fists. Scott broke away from the male chorus to solo.

Joyce became so engrossed in the stage magic that Hassan had to eject her from the wings onto the floor when the time came. She jumped in like a wriggling salmon with the drumbeat as her mighty stream. She immediately felt at ease on the stage. It was finally her turn to dance.

The heavy percussion soothed into a slow samba as the nuptial couple neared center stage. The audience responded enthusiastically to their courtship ritual, consisting of subtle hip movements, winding torsos, and floating arms.

Her people had to be out in the crowd. All she heard was "Get it, Joyce!" and "Joyceeeee!" And that was music enough. She could burst from the sheer joy of it. . . .

In an effortless sweep, the groom perched his bride onto his shoulder. They focused longingly into each other's gaze in a moment of created stage ardor, and he whisked her off into the wings. A low sigh resounded from the audience.

Then the ensemble sprang onto the stage. The nuptial couple returned. The

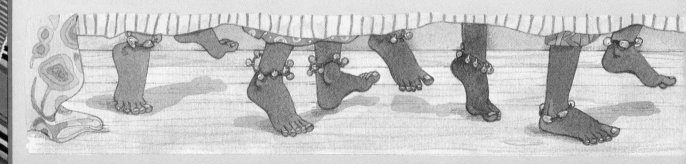

elder showered them with blessings of children, harvest, and old age. To consecrate the earth, the dancers began a vigorous funga. One hundred feet striking the stage sent a tremor throughout the stands.

Without warning, Clarke spun Joyce out into the center of the stage.

And that's when they took her hands and said "come, daughter. Come, child." The women in her back root, with warm and strong hands, broad hips, and loving bosoms. The Ibo and the Mali women, watching down at the Child dancing. Joyce heard the drum within her and stirred a mighty passion of feet and hips and head. And oh! the Child couldn't stop dancing, beyond music, beyond limit. "Leave her be! She touched by the dance!" they mused, spinning her, turning her, smiling down at the Child, who was touched by their spirit.

She whirled and whirled to the sound of some three-hundred-odd home folks and others shouting her name. As the drums halted, the audience roared. The dancers bowed in turn, then in unison.

---

## Skills in Science

### Reading Skills in Science

1. **Use Context Clues** What kind of performance takes place in this passage? Where does it take place?

2. **Accurate Observations** List five sources of sound in this selection. Describe how each one makes sound.

### Writing Skills in Science

1. **Compare and Contrast** Compare the sound waves of "the tinkling of the kalimba" and the "thunder" from the congas. Which has longer wavelength? Which has a greater amplitude?

2. **Find Causes** The passage describes "a spectrum of multicolored maidens." Describe how light reflects off the dancers to cause their skin tones to look different.

### Activities

**Collect Data** Research two kinds of African drums. Describe the sound each drum produces. Explain how the drums are used, and the groups that use them.

**Communicate** Find out about the role of dance in the Ibo or the Mali culture. Describe the ceremonies in which dance is important.

### Where to Read More

*The Voyage of the Frog* by Gary Paulsen. New York: Orchard Books, 1989. A teenager encounters a life-threatening storm when he sails to scatter his uncle's ashes.

*A Boat to Nowhere* by Maureen Wartski. New York: DAL-Dutton, 1981. Mai and her family leave Vietnam in search of a better life.

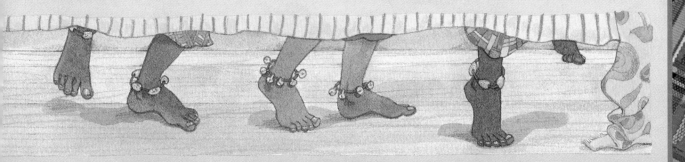

# Unit 6
# Interactions of Matter

## Chapters

**19**  Chemical Bonding

**20**  Chemical Reactions

**21**  Solution Chemistry

**22**  Carbon Compounds and the Chemistry of Life

**23**  Nuclear Chemistry

# Data Bank

Use the information on pages 634 to 643 to answer the questions about topics explored in this unit.

## Inferring

What kind of an ingredient is added to distilled water to make soda water?

## Graphing

Make a graph showing the average yearly dosage of five sources of radiation.

## Predicting

How would the energy per gram of fats, proteins, and carbohydrates influence the diet of a very active, thin person?

## Interpreting Data

Which atom in periods 2 and 3 has the smallest radius? How does the radius of the ion of that element compare to the radius of the atom?

The photograph to the left shows how copper pennies change color as they age. What kind of a change affects the color of the pennies?

# Chapter **19** Chemical Bonding

## Chapter Sections

**19.1** Atoms and Bonding

**19.2** Ionic Bonds

**19.3** Covalent Bonds

## What do you see?

"I think that these are magnified salt or sugar crystals with some type of coloring. They are composed of little particles that formed together. Chemical bonding holds the crystallized salt or sugar together."

*Greg Sarbacher*
*Einstein Middle School*
*Sacramento, California*

To find out more about the photograph, look on page 486. As you read this chapter, you will learn about chemical bonding.

# 19.1 Atoms and Bonding

## Objectives

▶ **Describe** the role of electrons in chemical bonding.

▶ **Explain** why atoms form chemical bonds.

▶ **Infer** the relationship between chemical bonds and chemical changes.

What is water? You might answer that water is a compound, which is correct. You might also answer that water is made up of the elements oxygen and hydrogen. This answer is correct, too. But did you know that there is another compound made up of hydrogen and oxygen? Look at Figure 19.1. This compound, which is used as an antiseptic, is hydrogen peroxide. Hydrogen peroxide's properties differ from those of water.

Why can hydrogen and oxygen combine chemically to form two different compounds? The reason is that an oxygen atom can combine with more than one other atom. It can form a compound with either two hydrogen atoms, or two hydrogen atoms and another oxygen atom with its own hydrogen atom.

Atoms of different elements can combine with each other in many different ways. How an atom combines chemically with other atoms is its most important property. What happens to atoms when they combine? How are they held together?

## Chemical Bonds

When atoms combine chemically, they create a **chemical bond**. A chemical bond is an attractive force that holds atoms or ions together. Chemical bonds exist between particles in most of the matter surrounding you and in most of the matter that makes up your body.

**Electrons and Bonding** To understand chemical bonding, recall what you have learned about atomic structure. An atom is made up of a small, positively charged nucleus surrounded by a cloud of negatively charged electrons. It is the electrons that are involved in bonding.

**Figure 19.1** ▲
The oxygen and hydrogen atoms in water ($H_2O$) and hydrogen peroxide ($H_2O_2$) are bonded together in different ways.

Electrons in an atom occupy different energy levels. Think of each level as a layer, or shell, like those shown in Figure 19.2 below. Each level holds a specific number of electrons. The first energy level can hold two electrons, and the second has room for eight. As the elements increase in atomic number, electrons fill the energy levels in an orderly way. Lower energy levels are always filled with electrons before higher levels are filled. A carbon atom, for example, has its first energy level filled with two electrons, leaving just four in the second level.

The number of electrons in an atom's highest, or outer, energy level determines how it will bond with other atoms. All the elements with *unfilled* outer energy levels can form chemical bonds. The noble gases do not readily form bonds because their highest energy levels are filled with electrons.

**Figure 19.2
Electron Shell Diagram
of an Atom**

▼

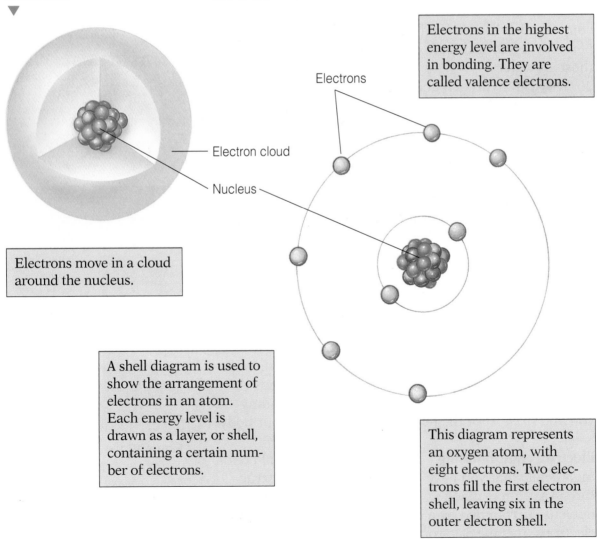

Electrons in the highest energy level are involved in bonding. They are called valence electrons.

Electrons

Electron cloud

Nucleus

Electrons move in a cloud around the nucleus.

A shell diagram is used to show the arrangement of electrons in an atom. Each energy level is drawn as a layer, or shell, containing a certain number of electrons.

This diagram represents an oxygen atom, with eight electrons. Two electrons fill the first electron shell, leaving six in the outer electron shell.

**Chemical Bonds and Stability**   Why do atoms form bonds? Recall that all matter tends to exist in its lowest possible energy state. Matter in its lowest energy state is more *stable* than it is in a higher energy state. The more stable matter is, the less likely it is to undergo a change. Having a partially filled outer energy level is a higher energy state than having a full one. Therefore, an atom with a full outer energy level is more stable than an atom with an unfilled outer level.

An atom with an unfilled outer energy level can become more stable if the right number of electrons are added to fill the level. Where can these electrons come from? They come from other atoms! Atoms interact in ways that give them the electrons they "need" to have full outer energy levels. These interactions cause chemical bonds to form.

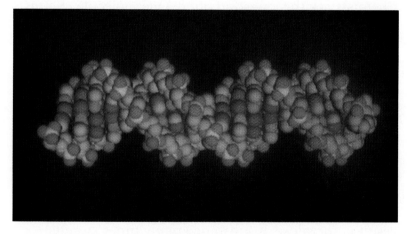

◀ **Figure 19.3**
Scientists often make models of chemical compounds, showing how the atoms that make them up are bonded. This model was made on a computer.

Picture two atoms of hydrogen as an example. Each hydrogen atom has only one electron, and each needs one more electron to fill its only energy level. If the atoms come near enough for their electron clouds to overlap, they can share their two electrons. The fast-moving electrons will spend time around both atoms. Each atom will have a full outer energy level. They will form a chemical bond because when bonded together, they are more stable than if they remained separate.

As you will see, there are three different kinds of chemical bonds: ionic (eye AHN ihk), covalent (KOH vay lehnt), and metallic. In ionic bonds, electrons are transferred from atom to atom. In covalent bonds, electrons are shared. Metallic bonds involve the sharing of electrons among many atoms.

# Science and Technology
## *Designer Molecules*

**Table 19.1**
**Sweetness and Sweeteners**

| Sweetener | Relative Sweetness* |
|---|---|
| Sucrose (cane sugar) | 1 |
| Cyclamate | 30–80 |
| Aspartame | 100–200 |
| Saccharine | 500-700 |
| Sucralose | 650 |

*Relative sweetness depends on the taste tester. For example, some people find aspartame 200 times sweeter than sugar, others do not.

Imagine that you have a big pile of plastic foam balls, all different colors and sizes, and a box of toothpicks. What would you do? You might start building some kind of object with the balls, sticking them together with the toothpicks.

Building a spaceship or a funny giraffe with plastic foam balls and toothpicks is similar to what some chemists do in their laboratories. The chemists, however, work with atoms and molecules instead of foam balls. They assemble custom-made molecules that have some desirable set of properties. They put together the pieces of these molecules not with toothpicks but by breaking and forming chemical bonds.

What kind of molecule would you want to design? Chemists ask this question often. One molecule chemists have wanted to create is a sweet-tasting substance with fewer calories than sugar. Several sugar substitutes, such as saccharin and cyclamate, have been known for many years. Even though they have different structures from the sugar molecule sucrose, they taste sweet. Most sugar substitutes, however, have drawbacks ranging from a bitter aftertaste to possible health risks.

Recently, some chemists turned to the sucrose molecule itself as a model for a better artificial sweetener. They started with sucrose and simply changed some of the atoms bonded to the main part of the molecule. The result is sucralose, a substance many times sweeter than sucrose itself.

## Check and Explain

1. How are electrons involved in chemical bonding?

2. Why do atoms form chemical bonds?

3. **Predict** Will an oxygen atom, with eight total electrons, form a bond with other atoms? Make a model on paper to explain your answer.

4. **Infer** You combine two compounds, and a chemical change occurs, producing a new substance. Infer what happened to the chemical bonds between the atoms in the original compounds.

# 19.2 Ionic Bonds

## Objectives

▶ **Explain** how an ionic bond forms.

▶ **Describe** the structure of solid ionic compounds.

▶ **Make a model** that explains ionic bonding.

I t's a hot summer day and you want to go swimming with a friend. But you find out that your friend has no bathing suit. Then you remember that you have several bathing suits and so you give one to your friend. You both go swimming and have fun cooling off. By giving up your extra suit, both of you benefit.

## Transfer of Electrons

In ionic bonding, atoms of two different elements make an exchange similar to the one between you and your friend. One atom gives up one or more electrons, and another accepts them. Why does this transfer of electrons happen?

Remember that an atom is more stable with a full outer energy level, or electron shell. If an atom has just one or two electrons in its outer shell, it can release these electrons. The original outer shell disappears, making the shell next to it the new outer shell. This new outer shell is full. The opposite also happens. An atom needing just one or two electrons to fill its outer shell can get these electrons from another atom.

When an atom with "extra" electrons interacts with an atom "needing" electrons, one or more electrons may be transferred. The atom that released electrons becomes a positive ion. The atom that accepted the electrons becomes a negative ion. The two ions are attracted because they have opposite charges. They form an **ionic bond**. An ionic bond is an electrostatic attraction between oppositely charged ions.

Ionic compounds are made up of ions bonded together with ionic bonds. You may recall that sodium chloride, which is common table salt, is an ionic compound. Many other common and useful substances are ionic compounds.

**Figure 19.4** ▲
The particles making up concrete are held together by ionic bonds.

# Forming an Ionic Bond

Look at the sodium and chlorine atoms in Figure 19.5. Sodium has only one electron in its outer electron shell. If it empties this outer shell by releasing the electron, it will become more stable. Chlorine needs only one electron to fill its outer shell. If it gains an electron, it will become more stable. Notice that before any transfer of electrons takes place, each of the two atoms is electrically neutral. The positive charge of the nucleus cancels out the negative charge of the electrons.

Now look on the next page. The sodium atom has transferred its outer electron to the chlorine atom. The sodium atom has become a sodium ion. It has a charge of 1+. Look at the calculation below to check that this is true. A sodium ion has the symbol $Na^+$.

**Figure 19.5**
**Ionic Bonding in Sodium Chloride** ▼

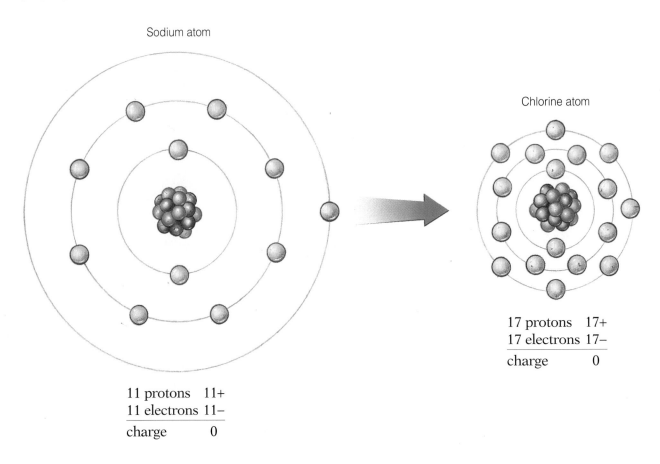

Sodium atom

11 protons    11+
11 electrons  11−
charge         0

Chlorine atom

17 protons    17+
17 electrons  17−
charge         0

Sodium has only one electron in its highest energy level. If this electron is given up, a full outer electron shell will remain.

The outer shell of chlorine has seven electrons. An additional electron from the sodium atom will fill the outer shell.

Having gained an electron, the chlorine atom has become a chlor*ide* ion. It has a charge of 1-, as you can see in the calculation below. The symbol for the chloride ion is Cl⁻. Both ions now have eight electrons in their outer electron shells. Both are stable because their outer shells are full.

Notice that the sodium ion is smaller than the sodium atom. Notice also that the chloride ion is larger than the chlorine atom. Why do you think ions and atoms of the same element differ in size?

The chloride ion and the sodium ion have opposite charges and so are attracted to each other. They are partners in an ionic bond. The positive charge of the sodium ion and the negative charge of the chloride ion cancel each other out. Together, they are electrically neutral. What is the name of the ionic compound they have formed? What is its chemical formula?

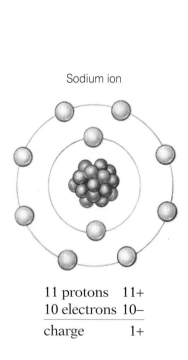

Sodium ion

| 11 protons | 11+ |
|---|---|
| 10 electrons | 10– |
| charge | 1+ |

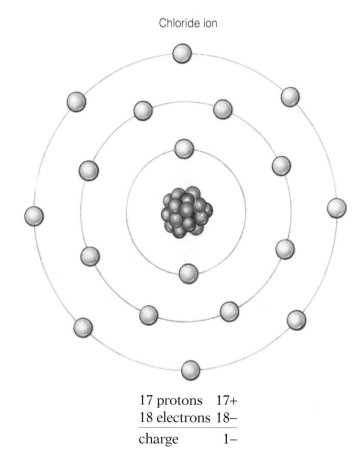

Chloride ion

| 17 protons | 17+ |
|---|---|
| 18 electrons | 18– |
| charge | 1– |

After the sodium atom loses its outer electron, it becomes a more stable sodium ion with a charge of 1+.

After the chlorine atom gains the electron from the sodium atom, its outer shell is filled. It is now a chloride ion with a charge of 1-.

# The Crystal Lattice

A grain of salt contains many millions of ions. How are these ions arranged? Each ion is bonded not with just one other oppositely charged ion, but with several others. Look at Figure 19.6. Notice how chloride and sodium ions alternate with each other. In a grain of salt, six sodium ions surround each chloride ion, and six chloride ions surround each sodium ion.

The ions in table salt and in other ionic solids are arranged in an orderly three-dimensional pattern that repeats itself over and over again. This structure is called a *crystal lattice*. Each ion is bonded with all the oppositely charged ions that directly surround it.

Look at Figure 19.6. The salt particles have a cube shape. The shape of these visible particles is the same cube shape formed by four sodium ions and four chloride ions in the crystal lattice.

**Crystal Shapes** The cube shape of the sodium chloride crystal is just one of seven crystal shapes taken on by ionic solids. In a cubic crystal, all the sides meet at right angles. Other crystal shapes have corners in which one or more of the angles are not right angles.

You can find many beautiful examples of crystals in nature. Epsom salt, a compound of magnesium, sulfur, oxygen, and hydrogen, forms long needle-shaped crystals. Crystals of calcite, a mineral found in limestone, look like parallelograms. In each case, the shape of the crystal you can see is determined by how the ions are arranged in the crystal lattice.

**Crystal Formation** Crystals form in two ways. One way they form is when a solution containing a dissolved ionic compound is allowed to evaporate. As the water vaporizes, the ions fall into their lattice structure. A second way crystals form is when an ionic solid is heated until it melts and the liquid is allowed to cool. The crystals in igneous rocks are formed in this way.

A crystal grows by regularly adding ions to all of its sides. This means that under the right conditions a crystal will keep the same shape no matter how large it becomes. How do crystals grow differently than you do?

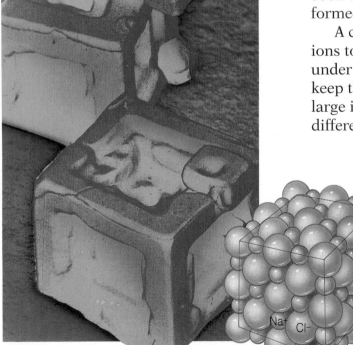

Na⁺  Cl⁻

◀ **Figure 19.6**
Crystals of table salt appear as cubes under a hand lens (far left). The sodium and chloride ions in table salt are arranged in a crystal lattice. What is the shape of this lattice structure?

## Ions

Look at the periodic table on pages 186 to 187 and find the metals. These elements have few electrons in their highest energy levels. Metals tend to lose electrons and become positive ions. Now find the nonmetals. Most of these elements have nearly full outer energy levels. Nonmetals tend to gain electrons and become negative ions. As you may infer, ionic bonds form between metallic elements and nonmetallic elements.

Within a group in the periodic table, all the elements form ions with the same charge. The halogens, for example, all form ions with a 1- charge. The alkali metals all form ions with a 1+ charge. The alkaline earth metals all form 2+ ions.

### Size of Ions

Recall that when an atom becomes an ion, it changes in size. Look at the magnesium atom in Figure 19.7 below. Notice that when it loses the two electrons in its outer shell, it becomes much smaller. Positive ions are always smaller than the atoms from which they are formed, because the nucleus holds the remaining electrons more tightly. Negative ions, in contrast, are larger than their corresponding atoms, because the nucleus cannot hold a larger number of electrons as tightly. The chloride ion, for example, has nearly twice the radius of the chlorine atom!

**Astronomy**

**L I N K**

The ionosphere is a layer of air in the atmosphere where the electrons have been stripped off the atoms to form ions. Because of the charge in the ionosphere, radio waves bounce off it.

Obtain a radio. On a clear night, tune the radio in-between two local stations. Take the radio outside, and see what stations you pick up.

How many and what kinds of stations did you pick up?

**A C T I V I T Y**

**Figure 19.7**
The nitrogen ion is much larger than the nitrogen atom. Why is the magnesium ion smaller than the magnesium atom? ▼

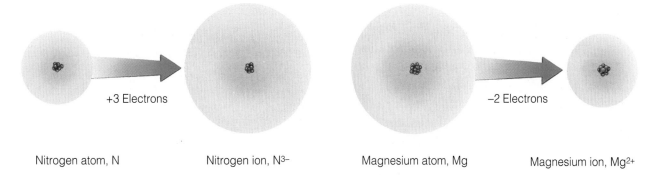

Nitrogen atom, N          +3 Electrons          Nitrogen ion, $N^{3-}$          Magnesium atom, Mg          −2 Electrons          Magnesium ion, $Mg^{2+}$

The size of ions varies with atomic number. The size of ions decreases from left to right across the metallic elements in a period. The size of ions also decreases from left to right across the nonmetallic elements in a period. This decrease in size occurs because of the increase in the positive charge of the nucleus and its pull on the electrons.

**Dissolved Ions** What happens when you put table salt in water? The table salt, like many ionic compounds, will dissolve in water. When an ionic compound dissolves, each ion is surrounded by molecules of water. The crystal lattice structure of the solid breaks down.

Dissolved ions are very important to all living things. Plants take up the ions dissolved in water and use them as nutrients. Ions help your nerve cells to communicate with each other. Your blood contains many different kinds of dissolved ions. All your body cells contain many dissolved ions.

**Ions in Plasma** Plasma, the fourth state of matter, is a mixture of electrons and positively charged ions. Except in lightning bolts, natural plasmas do not exist on the earth. They exist only in stars, where the temperature is high enough to strip the electrons off atoms and prevent them from rejoining.

## *SkillBuilder* *Observing*

## *Properties of Ionic Solids*

Many products in your home are ionic compounds or mixtures of ionic compounds. You can learn about some of the properties of ionic compounds by observing some familiar examples. Copy the table shown here on a separate sheet of paper. Using a hand lens, observe the color, size, and shape of particles of sodium chloride (table salt), potassium chloride (salt substitute), sodium bicarbonate (baking soda), and magnesium sulfate (Epsom salt). Record your observations in the table.

Make a solution of each ionic compound by adding about a spoonful to about 50mL of water. Label each solution. Then answer the following questions.

1. What happened to each compound when placed in water? Record this information in the table. What does the behavior of these compounds in water tell you about them?

2. What properties do all four ionic compounds have in common? In what ways are they different?

3. How could you learn more about each compound? Suggest an experiment that might provide data about an additional property of these elements.

| Common Ionic Compounds | | |
|---|---|---|
| **Name** | **Description of Particles** | **Behavior in Water** |
| Sodium chloride | | |
| Potassium chloride | | |
| Sodium bicarbonate | | |
| Magnesium sulfate | | |

## Science and You  *Trading in Ions*

Our drinking water naturally contains a variety of dissolved ions, both positive and negative. Water containing calcium and magnesium ions is called hard water. Soap lathers poorly in hard water and is less effective at cleaning. For these reasons, people have developed ways of softening water.

In one early method of water softening, a compound known as washing soda was added, along with soap, to the water used for washing clothes. Washing soda reacts with hard-water ions, forming compounds that do not dissolve in water. The rinse water carried away these insoluble compounds.

Today, many homes have devices that soften water by an ion-exchange process. In this process, water filters through mineral substances called zeolites, or through ion-exchange resins. Both zeolites and ion-exchange resins contain sodium ions.

As hard water flows through the ion exchange resin, sodium ions from the resin dissolve in the water. Calcium and magnesium ions from the hard water replace the sodium ions and become caught in the exchanger. When the exchanger can hold no more calcium and magnesium ions, a concentrated solution of sodium chloride can be pumped through it to reverse the ion-exchange process. Sodium ions again fill the ion exchanger. The hard-water ions are removed with the waste water.

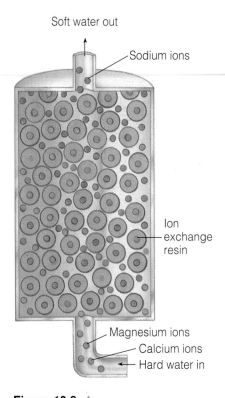

**Figure 19.8** ▲
A home water softener removes calcium and magnesium ions from water, replacing them with sodium ions.

## Check and Explain

1. How does an ionic bond form?

2. How are the ions arranged in a solid ionic compound? Give an example.

3. **Predict**  Find potassium (K) and iodine (I) in the periodic table. When an atom of potassium reacts with an atom of iodine, which atom will give up electrons? How many electrons will be transferred?

4. **Make a Model**  Draw shell diagrams to show ionic bonding between magnesium and oxygen. Refer to the periodic table to determine the number of electrons in the outer electron shells of these elements.

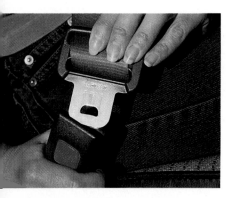

## ACTIVITY

### Contrasting

*Like Salt?*

Water, vegetable oil, sugar, cornstarch, rubbing alcohol, plastic wrap, and rubber are all made up of atoms held together by covalent bonds. For each substance, describe at least one way in which it differs from the ionic compound table salt.

**SKILLS WARMUP**

# 19.3 Covalent Bonds

## Objectives

▶ **Describe** a covalent bond.

▶ **Identify** three covalently-bonded substances.

▶ **Relate** metallic bonding to properties of metals.

▶ **Make a model** that explains covalent bonding.

What would you do if you and a friend were caught in the rain with only one umbrella? You would probably share it. The umbrella would keep both of you reasonably dry. Sharing is a good way to solve many problems because it can help more than one person at the same time.

## Shared Electron Bonding

You have just learned that atoms may transfer electrons from one to another, becoming ions joined by an ionic bond. This bonding occurs when one atom has extra electrons and the other needs electrons. But what happens between two atoms that both "need" a small number of electrons to have full outer electron shells? Like two people with one umbrella, they share.

Look at the chlorine atom on page 472. Its outer electron shell is one electron short of being full. If two chlorine atoms come together, they can share a pair of electrons. Each atom gives up one electron to the pair. The two electrons in the pair give both atoms a full outer shell. The shared pair of electrons makes up a **covalent bond**, the second major type of chemical bond.

Recall that ionic bonds form between the metals and nonmetals. Covalent bonds, in contrast, form between the atoms of nonmetallic elements. These are elements with outer electron shells that are at least half full. Covalent bonds can form not only between different nonmetals, but also between atoms of the same nonmetal. A covalent bond, for example, holds together two oxygen atoms in $O_2$, the oxygen molecule in the air we breathe.

Atoms joined with covalent bonds form molecules. Molecules are very different from the rigid network of

**Figure 19.9** ▲

Two seat belt ends, when joined, become useful. In a similar way, unpaired electrons from two atoms come together to form a covalent bond.

ions in an ionic compound. The definite size of a molecule contrasts with the unlimited size of an ionic solid. Molecules may exist as liquids, gases, or solids depending on their size. Ionic compounds, in contrast, are nearly always solids.

Covalent bonding among atoms can be shown with electron dot diagrams. These diagrams are similar to shell diagrams, except that only the valence electrons are shown. Look at the electron dot diagrams below. Because covalent bonds are *pairs* of shared electrons, the electrons in an atom's outer shell are shown as paired and unpaired dots. Each unpaired electron around an atom can join with another atom's unpaired electron to form a covalent bond. Atoms bond covalently to achieve the stable arrangement of electrons found in a noble gas atom.

**Figure 19.10**
**Forming Covalent Bonds**
▼

The noble gas, argon, has a full outer electron ▶ shell. All eight electrons are paired, so argon can't form a covalent bond.

▲ Hydrogen's single electron is shown as an unpaired dot. Six of chlorine's seven outer electrons are paired, leaving one unpaired.

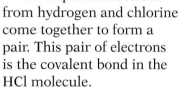
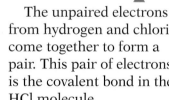

The unpaired electrons from hydrogen and chlorine come together to form a pair. This pair of electrons is the covalent bond in the HCl molecule.

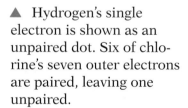

▲ Four of oxygen's six outer electrons are paired, leaving two unpaired electrons. Each unpaired electron can form a bond.

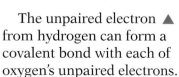
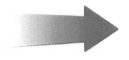

The unpaired electron ▲ from hydrogen can form a covalent bond with each of oxygen's unpaired electrons.

Compounds formed from covalently bonded atoms are far more common than ionic compounds. For example, the millions of carbon compounds found in living things are held together with covalent bonds. The major nutrients in your food, including carbohydrates, proteins, fats, and vitamins, are also covalent compounds. Even the oxygen molecules you breathe in and the carbon dioxide you breathe out are covalently bonded.

**Network Solids** Atoms joined by covalent bonds usually form molecules, but certain substances held together by covalent bonds are not molecules. These substances have a structure like that of an ionic solid. They are called network solids because all of their atoms are connected in a network by covalent bonds.

Diamond is a good example of a network solid. It is made up of carbon atoms, each bonded covalently to four neighboring carbon atoms. Quartz, sapphire, emerald, and ruby are also network solids. Network solids are generally hard but not malleable. They melt only at very high temperatures.

**Covalently Bonded Ions** Certain molecules held together by covalent bonds tend to gain or lose electrons as a unit. The whole group of atoms becomes an ion with a positive or negative charge. These groups of covalently bonded atoms are called **polyatomic ions**. Polyatomic ions form ionic bonds with other ions just like single ions do. One example of a polyatomic ion is the carbonate ion, $CO_3^{2-}$. It bonds with a calcium ion to form calcium carbonate, which makes up limestone. Other examples of polyatomic ions are shown in Figure 19.11 below. Polyatomic ions are contained in many common substances, such as baking soda and Epsom salts.

**Figure 19.11**
Some polyatomic ions have a negative charge, and others have a positive charge. How are the atoms that make up each ion held together? ▼

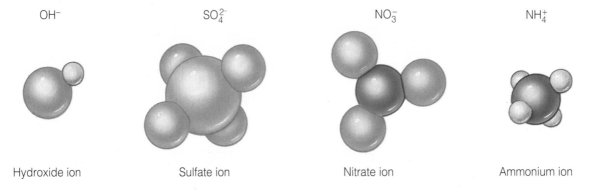

| $OH^-$ | $SO_4^{2-}$ | $NO_3^-$ | $NH_4^+$ |

Hydroxide ion  Sulfate ion  Nitrate ion  Ammonium ion

## Metallic Bonds

Metallic bonds, as you have probably guessed, occur in metals. Like covalent bonds, they involve the sharing of electrons. In a covalent bond, two atoms share a pair of electrons. However, in a **metallic bond**, many atoms share many electrons.

In a sample of a pure metal, such as silver or copper, the valence electrons make up a "sea" of electrons that can flow freely through the piece of metal. Because the valence electrons do not belong to individual atoms, the atoms actually exist as positive ions. The positive charges of all the ions in a sample of metal are canceled out by the negative charges of all the electrons.

Look at Figure 19.12. You can see that the positive silver ions are arranged in a lattice structure and surrounded by loose electrons. Because they are attracted to all the metal ions, the moving electrons serve as the bond that holds the metal lattice together.

This model of bonding in a metal helps explain many of the properties of metals. Most metals have a high density. The high density is caused by the lattice structure of a metal. Actually, there is very little empty space between the positive ions. Metals are also malleable. In a malleable substance, the electrons are free to move and keep the ions bonded to each other when a stress changes the positions of the ions. The malleability of metals contrasts with the brittleness of other crystalline solids. The freely-moving electrons also account for the ability of metals to conduct electricity.

**Figure 19.12**
Metallic bonding allows metal ions to change position without breaking apart from each other. The spoon is made of malleable metal.

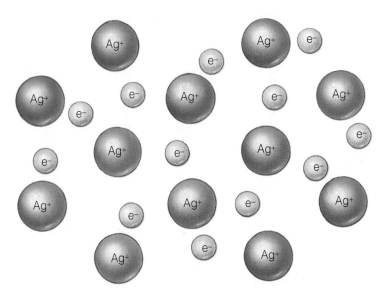

## Science and You *A Sticky Problem*

How many times in the past week have you made two things stick together? Maybe you pasted together some cardboard or sealed an envelope. Or possibly you stuck a sticker somewhere or fixed something with glue. Substances that make things stick, called adhesives, are important in our daily lives. But did you know that things tend to stick together even without adhesives?

Most substances are slightly sticky because the molecules that make them up are attracted to other molecules. This attraction occurs in part because the electrons in many molecules are not evenly distributed throughout the molecule. Certain atoms hold shared electrons more tightly than the atoms to which they are bonded. As a result, parts of the molecules are *slightly* positive, and parts are *slightly* negative. The negative parts of one molecule attract the positive parts of other

# Consider This

## Stricter Regulations for Food Additives?

Look on the label of a packaged food, and you'll probably see some ingredients with strange names such as BHA, sodium benzoate, and diglyceride. These are food additives. Substances are added to foods to improve nutrition, flavor, or consistency, or as preservatives.

About 3,000 different food additives are commonly used today. Many additives are synthetic compounds. People manufacture them by breaking chemical bonds in raw materials and reforming new bonds. The use of all food additives is regulated by the Food and Drug Administration, or FDA.

**Consider Some Issues** Food additives make food taste better and keep it from spoiling, but are they safe? Even though the FDA must test and approve all new additives, many additives in use before 1958 have never been tested for approval.

In addition, some people are concerned that many approved food additives may still be dangerous. Tests may not be able to determine all possible health risks over a lifetime of eating the additive.

Food companies claim all their products are safe. They believe the FDA's current rules are more than strict enough to

ensure consumer safety. They don't feel there is enough evidence to prove that food additives are harmful.

**Think About It** When foods contain certain additives, warning labels are required. Should more additives be treated in this way? Should food labels give the *amounts* of all food additives? Should the FDA test all the additives now used in foods?

**Write About It** Write a short paper describing how the FDA should regulate food additives, giving reasons for your position.

**Figure 19.13** ▲
Adhesives are found in nature as well as in tubes of glue. Barnacles (above) secrete an adhesive that permanently attaches them to a surface. A sticky substance in the spider web helps to trap the moth.

molecules, and the positive parts attract other molecules' negative parts. Each attraction is relatively weak, but they combine to create a stickiness.

Usually you don't notice this stickiness, called intermolecular attraction, because most surfaces aren't really flat or clean at a microscopic level. When two surfaces touch, air molecules, dirt, and surface roughness prevent most molecules in the two surfaces from coming close enough to be attracted. That's why an adhesive, such as glue, comes in handy.

Glue can flow into the microscopic valleys of a surface, coming in contact with all the surface molecules. The molecules in the glue are attracted to the surface molecules, causing them to stick together. The same thing occurs when another surface is pressed onto the glue. As long as the glue holds itself together, the two surfaces will stick together.

## Check and Explain

1. What is a covalent bond?

2. Describe the covalent bond in three molecules identified in this chapter.

3. **Relate** Explain how metallic bonding accounts for two properties of metals.

4. **Make a Model** Draw an electron dot diagram to show covalent bonding between one nitrogen atom and three hydrogen atoms in an $NH_3$ molecule.

# *Activity 19*  *How do ionic and covalent compounds differ?*

*Skills*  Measure; Observe; Infer; Interpret Data

## Task 1  Prelab Prep

1.  Collect the following items: table salt, sugar, distilled water, 2 test tubes, 2 measuring cups, stirring rod, test-tube holder, 4 small labels, Bunsen burner, low-voltage dry cell, small light bulb and socket, 3 connecting wires, timer, safety goggles. Make sure the wires can be attached to both the light bulb socket and the terminals of the dry cell.
2.  Label a test tube and a measuring cup *Salt*. Label the other test tube and measuring cup *Sugar*.

## Task 2  Data Record

1.  Copy Table 19.2 on a sheet of paper.
2.  Record all your observations about the properties of salt and sugar in the table.

### Table 19.2  Properties of Salt and Sugar

| Substance | Melting Time | Conduction of Electricity |
|-----------|--------------|---------------------------|
| Salt      |              |                           |
| Sugar     |              |                           |

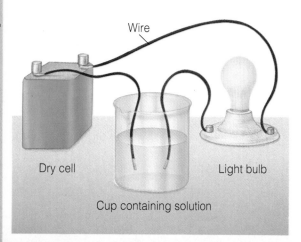

Wire

Dry cell

Light bulb

Cup containing solution

## Task 3  Procedure

1.  Put a small amount of salt in the test tube labeled *Salt*. Put an equal amount of sugar in the second test tube.
2.  Using the test-tube holder, heat the test tube of salt over the Bunsen burner. **CAUTION: Wear goggles and point the test tube away from you and others.** Note the time. Observe whether the salt melts within two minutes. If it melts, record the time it takes.
3.  Repeat step 2, using sugar instead of salt.
4.  Pour 50 mL of distilled water into the measuring cup labeled *Salt*. Add salt and stir until it is dissolved. Repeat the procedure using the same amount of sugar.
5.  Set up a circuit as shown, using the measuring cup of salt water. Observe whether the solution will conduct electricity and record the results. Repeat the procedure using the sugar solution.

## Task 4  Analysis

1.  Which compound took longer to melt? From your data, what can you infer about the melting point of the compounds?
2.  Which compound is a better conductor of electricity? How could you tell?
3.  Which compound is ionic and which is covalently bonded? How do you know?

## Task 5  Conclusion

Write a short paragraph explaining how the properties you observed relate to the type of bonding in each compound.

## *Extension*

Develop a hypothesis that explains why you used distilled water to make the salt and sugar solutions. How would you test your hypothesis?

## Concept Summary

### 19.1 Atoms and Bonding

▶ A chemical bond is an attractive force that holds the atoms of a compound together.

▶ Atoms of elements with unfilled outer energy levels can form bonds.

▶ When atoms form chemical bonds they fill their outer energy levels with electrons and become more stable.

▶ There are three main types of chemical bonds: ionic, covalent, and metallic.

### 19.2 Ionic Bonds

▶ An ionic bond forms when electrons are transferred from one atom to another.

▶ An ionic bond is an electrostatic attraction between ions that have opposite charges.

▶ Ionic bonds form between the atoms of metallic and nonmetallic elements.

▶ The ions that make up ionic solids are arranged in a three-dimensional structure called a crystal lattice.

### 19.3 Covalent Bonds

▶ A shared pair of electrons makes up a covalent bond between two atoms.

▶ Covalently bonded atoms form either molecules or network solids.

▶ Polyatomic ions, such as ammonium and sulfate ions, are groups of covalently bonded atoms with an overall charge.

▶ Metallic bonds occur in metals, where a sea of shared electrons surrounds positive metal ions arranged in a lattice structure.

## Chapter Vocabulary

| | | |
|---|---|---|
| chemical bond (19.1) | covalent bond (19.3) | metallic bond (19.3) |
| ionic bond (19.2) | polyatomic ion (19.3) | |

## Check Your Vocabulary

Use the vocabulary words above to complete the following sentences correctly.

1. An attachment between atoms that involves the sharing of electrons is called a(n) _____ .

2. A charged particle such as $NH_4^+$ is called a(n) _____ .

3. A(n) _____ is the result of an electrostatic attraction that forms between oppositely charged ions.

4. Many atoms share many electrons in a(n) _____ .

5. A general term that is used to describe the force that holds together the atoms or ions in a molecule is a(n) _____ .

Pair each numbered word or words with a vocabulary term. Explain in a complete sentence how the words are related.

6. Nonmetallic elements

7. $NO_3^-$

8. Sodium chloride

9. Transfer

10. Network solid

11. Lattice

12. Electron dot diagram

## Write Your Vocabulary

Write sentences using the vocabulary words above. Show that you know what each word means.

# Chapter 19 Review

## Check Your Knowledge

Answer the following in complete sentences.

1. What is a network solid?

2. Why do noble gases not form compounds under ordinary circumstances?

3. Which electrons in an atom are involved in chemical bonding?

4. How does an atom become an ion?

5. Which is generally larger, an atom or its negative ion?

6. What is a crystal lattice? What kinds of substances have a crystal lattice?

7. Which energy levels are the first to fill with electrons.

Determine whether each statement is true or false. Write *true* if it is true. If it is false, change the underlined word or words to make the statement true.

8. Elements in the same group of the periodic table have similar properties because they have the same number of neutrons.

9. An atom losing two electrons becomes a molecule with a 2- charge.

10. During ionic bonding, electrons are transferred from atom to atom.

11. Covalent bonds usually form between the atoms of metals.

12. In an electron dot diagram of an atom, only the valence electrons are shown.

13. Diamond and quartz are examples of ionic solids.

14. In covalent compounds, atoms are held together by a sea of electrons.

## Check Your Understanding

Apply the concepts you have learned to answer each question.

1. Draw electron dot diagrams for each of the following atoms: magnesium, aluminum, silicon, phosphorus, and sulfur. Refer to the periodic table on pages 186 to 187 for the information you need.

2. **Generalize** Copy and complete this table describing the kind of bonding that occurs between elements.

| Substance | Metal | Nonmetal |
|-----------|-------|----------|
| Metal | ? | ? |
| Nonmetal | Ionic | ? |

3. **Interpret Data** Use the periodic table to determine which noble gas has the same number of electrons as each of the following ions.

   a. $N^{3-}$   b. $I^-$   c. $S^{2-}$   d. $K^+$

4. **Mystery Photo** The photograph on page 466 shows crystals of table salt, sodium chloride (NaCl). Explain why sodium chloride crystals have this appearance.

5. **Infer** A substance is found to be flexible and to conduct heat and electricity well. What can you infer about the chemical bonds that hold it together?

6. **Compare and Contrast** How do polyatomic ions compare with ordinary ions? How do they compare with covalently bonded molecules?

## Develop Your Skills

Use the skills you have developed in this chapter to complete each activity.

1. **Interpret Data** The graph below shows how the radius of different ions varies with their atomic number.

   a. What trend do you see among the sizes of the four positive ions shown?

   b. What happens to ionic radii as atomic number increases from 14 to 15? Why does this occur?

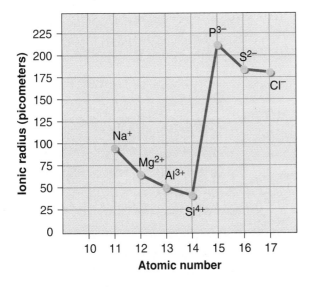

2. **Make a Model** Use plastic foam balls and toothpicks to make models of water ($H_2O$), diamond, and potassium chloride (KCl). Use a different color ball for each element.

3. **Data Bank** Use the information on page 637 to answer the following questions.

   a. What is the radius of a beryllium ion?

   b. How much smaller is a beryllium ion than a beryllium atom?

   c. Name an element with atoms that are the same size as the fluoride ion.

## Make Connections

1. **Link the Concepts** Below is a concept map that shows connections between some of the main concepts in this chapter. Only part of the map has been filled in. Copy the map and complete it, using words and ideas from the chapter.

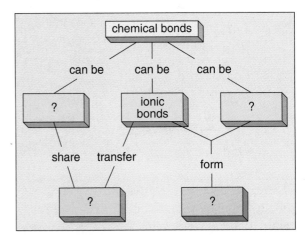

2. **Science and Art** Cut disks out of heavy paper to represent the outer electron shells of hydrogen, magnesium, oxygen, and chlorine atoms. Make the disks different sizes to account for the different numbers of electron shells in the elements. Draw inner circles to represent inner shells. Then, place pennies on the disks to represent the electrons in each atom. Decide which atoms will form an ionic bond and use the pennies to show how the bond forms. Do the same for atoms that will form covalent bonds.

3. **Science and You** Find out what dissolved ions your drinking water contains. The utility company or government agency that supplies your water will have this information. Determine if your water is hard, and if any of the ions are present in unusually high amounts.

# Chapter 20 Chemical Reactions

## Chapter Sections

20.1 Characteristics of Chemical Reactions

20.2 Chemical Equations

20.3 Types of Chemical Reactions

20.4 Energy and Reaction Rate

## What do you see?

"I see what looks like small sheets of metal overlapping to form one large piece of metal with ridges. The metal is covered with an orangish-brown substance. I think the orangish-brown substance is rust, and it formed by the metal being exposed to oxygen. Rust is composed of iron and oxygen."

*Bridget Dunne*
*Swanson Middle School*
*Arlington, Virginia*

To find out more about the photograph, look on page 512. As you read this chapter, you will learn about chemical reactions.

# 20.1 Characteristics of Chemical Reactions

## Objectives

▶ **Identify** everyday chemical reactions.

▶ **Describe** four kinds of evidence for chemical reactions.

▶ **Distinguish** between exothermic and endothermic chemical reactions.

▶ **Make a model** that shows bonding changes in a chemical reaction.

**W**hat ingredients do you need to bake a cake? Include flour, eggs, sugar, water—and don't forget the baking powder! The person who baked the cake in the top of Figure 20.1 forgot to add baking powder, and look what happened. The cake didn't rise. What is it about baking powder that makes a cake rise?

Baking powder contains substances that begin to undergo a chemical change when they are mixed with water. The substances combine to produce bubbles of carbon dioxide gas. When these gas bubbles are trapped in the cake batter, they cause a cake to rise.

## Chemical Changes and Chemical Reactions

If you think about it, chemical changes similar to what happens to baking powder occur all the time. Recall that a chemical change in matter results in a new substance being formed. New substances are produced when you fry an egg, eat a piece of pizza, operate a power mower, snap a photograph, or light a candle. Even as you read these words, the cells in your body are creating new substances that you need to survive.

What is actually happening to atoms and molecules when a chemical change occurs? Every chemical change involves a **chemical reaction**. When a chemical reaction occurs, chemical bonds between atoms or ions break, and new bonds form between different atoms or ions. A chemical reaction creates one or more new substances. The new substance has properties that are different from the properties of the original substances.

**Figure 20.1** ▲
Which of these cakes was baked without baking powder?

# Evidence for Chemical Reactions

You can't see chemical bonds breaking or forming. So how do you know when a chemical change is happening? If you have a window in your oven, you can watch a cake bake and see little bubbles break the surface. These bubbles are evidence that a chemical reaction is taking place in the cake batter. Most chemical reactions give you very good clues that a new substance is being produced. Here are four of the most important kinds of clues.

## Precipitate

A white substance forms when household ammonia is added to a solution of alum. The white substance is called a *precipitate* (pree SIHP uh TAYT). The appearance of a precipitate is a sign of a chemical reaction. ▼

## Color Change ▲

The colorful substance is a clue that a chemical reaction occurred. Here a colorless solution is added to another colorless solution to form a bright yellow product.

## Release of Energy

Many chemical reactions give off some form of energy. Here you can see light energy given off by burning magnesium. Other reactions release heat energy alone. ▼

## Gas Formation

◀ The release of gas indicates that a chemical reaction is taking place. Hydrogen gas bubbles form as zinc reacts with hydrochloric acid.

# Mechanics of Chemical Reactions

During a chemical reaction, at least one new substance with different properties is produced. Look at Figure 20.2 below. It shows a chemical reaction. The original substances are on the left. What are they? What elements make them up? How are the atoms bonded? The new substance produced in the reaction is on the right. What has changed during the reaction? How did these changes occur?

Notice that in the original substances on the left, chemical bonds join atoms of the same element. When the two different molecules come together with enough energy, the bonds that hold the atoms together begin to break. At the same time, new bonds form. Take a look at Figure 20.2. Each chlorine atom begins to form a bond with a hydrogen atom. New hydrogen chloride molecules are produced when the old bonds break. Now the chemical bonds are between atoms of different elements. Hydrogen chloride molecules have been formed. All this takes place in a very short, almost immeasurable, period of time.

As you will see, there are many kinds of chemical reactions. Compounds can break down into elements, and elements can join to form compounds. Compounds can react with elements or other compounds to form one, two, or more new substances. The substances involved in a chemical reaction can be pure metals, ionic solids, or covalently bonded molecules. They can be solids, liquids, or gases.

In all chemical reactions, however, old bonds break and new bonds form. The same elements present in the original substances are also present in the new substances. The atoms or ions are simply rearranged during the reaction. Why do you think the atoms remain as either an element or in a compound?

**Figure 20.2**

In a chemical reaction, bonds between atoms break and re-form between different atoms.

▼

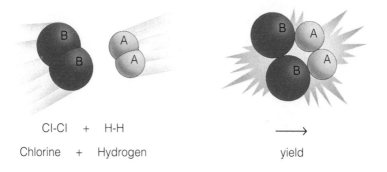

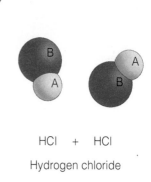

| Cl-Cl | + | H-H | | | HCl | + | HCl |
| Chlorine | + | Hydrogen | yield | | Hydrogen chloride | | |

# Energy and Chemical Reactions

Energy changes occur whenever chemical bonds break or form. Some chemical reactions release energy; others absorb energy. The law of conservation of mass and energy, however, applies to chemical reactions.

In other words, chemical reactions do not create or destroy energy. Any energy released in a reaction was present in the chemical bonds of the original substances. Any energy absorbed in a reaction becomes part of the chemical bonds of the new substances.

**Exothermic Reactions** You probably can think of several chemical reactions that release energy. Such reactions heat your home, cook your food, and run your family's car. The explosion in Figure 20.3 is a chemical reaction that released a large amount of energy.

A reaction that releases energy is called an **exothermic** (EHK soh THER mihk) **reaction**. All exothermic reactions fit this chemical description.

$$\text{original substances} \longrightarrow \text{new substances} + \text{energy}$$

Exothermic reactions most often produce energy in the form of heat, light, or electricity.

**Endothermic Reactions** Chemical reactions that absorb energy, called **endothermic** (EHN doh THER mihk) **reactions**, are probably less familiar to you. Here is the chemical description for an endothermic reaction.

$$\text{original substances} + \text{energy} \longrightarrow \text{new substances}$$

Look at Figure 20.4. If you could feel the glass, you would notice the water becomes colder as the antacid tablet disappears. The chemical reaction that is taking place absorbs heat energy from the water.

Some reactions absorb energy in the form of light or electricity. For example, when you take a photograph, light energy enters the camera. The light energy is absorbed by the film and molecules in the film undergo a chemical change. When electric energy is added to water, the water molecules absorb the electricity. The water molecules undergo a chemical change, breaking apart into hydrogen and oxygen.

**Figure 20.3** ▲

An explosion is a very exothermic chemical reaction.

**Figure 20.4** ▲

What kind of energy is absorbed in this endothermic reaction?

## Science and You
### *Chemistry Celebration: The Fourth of July*

You probably see fireworks every Fourth of July. Have you ever wondered how the dazzling colors and thunderous sounds of fireworks are made? They are carefully controlled exothermic reactions. Safety is a major concern in making fireworks.

Modern fireworks are shells launched from tubes on the ground. A fast-burning fuse ignites a charge of black powder that propels the shell skyward. When the shell is high in the air, a slower-burning fuse ignites other compartments filled with flash powder. Pellets inside these charges produce colors. Usually, another charge explodes in a final big bang.

Making fireworks is both a science and an art. It requires a great deal of knowledge of chemistry. Each color, for example, is the result of a certain mixture of elements or compounds in the pellets. Green stars come from barium compounds, red from strontium, and blue from copper. Because the color-producing compounds aren't very stable, they must be created during the explosion of the charge. Making the right chemical reactions occur in the correct way is one of the biggest challenges of building fireworks.

Each pattern you see when a fireworks shell explodes is the result of a different arrangement of the color-producing pellets inside the flash-powder charges. A fireworks company carefully guards its secret "recipes" for packing its fireworks shells.

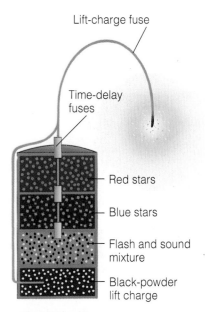

**Figure 20.5** ▲

Which of the compartments in a fireworks shell ignites first?

## Check and Explain

1. Describe three everyday chemical reactions.

2. What kinds of evidence can tell you that a chemical reaction is taking place in a beaker?

3. **Compare and Contrast** What is the difference between exothermic and endothermic reactions? How can you identify a reaction as one or the other?

4. **Make a Model** On paper, draw a model that shows how you think the chemical bonds change when an atom of sulfur (S) and a molecule of oxygen ($O_2$) react to form a molecule of sulfur dioxide ($SO_2$).

*Secret Code*

Write two or three messages to a friend using different pictures as symbols for words.

**SKILLS WARMUP**

# 20.2 Chemical Equations

## Objectives

▶ **Identify** the reactants and products of a chemical reaction.

▶ **Distinguish** between subscripts and coefficients.

▶ **Communicate** what happens during a chemical change by writing a balanced chemical equation.

---

**H**ave you ever written a message in a secret code? In one example of a simple number code, 1 represents *A*, 2 represents *B*, and so on. The words *secret code* are written in this code as 19-5-3-18-5-20 3-15-4-5. Pictures can also represent words. What does the picture message ☏ ♥ **U** mean?

Numbers and pictures are symbols. You use symbols every day because they are very useful. In math, for example, you substitute symbols for words when you solve word problems. What other kinds of symbols do you use regularly?

Chemists use symbols to show what happens during a chemical reaction. Many of these symbols you already know. As you will see, describing a chemical reaction with symbols is much like writing a word puzzle.

## Equations in Chemistry

Suppose you want to describe the chemical reaction that occurs when baking soda and vinegar are mixed together. You could say, "Sodium bicarbonate reacts with a solution of acetic acid to produce carbon dioxide gas, sodium acetate, and water." This statement says exactly what you mean, but it takes up a lot of space.

You need a short, precise way to state what happens in a chemical reaction. The way to do this is to write a **chemical equation**. A chemical equation is an expression that uses symbols to describe a chemical reaction. Because the same chemical symbols are used worldwide, a chemical equation can be understood in any country in the world.

An equation is like a sentence in chemical terms. The sentence begins at the left with the formulas for the starting materials, called **reactants** (ree AK tuhnts).

**Reactants**

Compounds or elements on the left side of the equation are the starting materials, or reactants. When more than one reactant is present, a plus sign separates them.

**Yield Sign**

As its name implies, the yield sign means "yield" or "produce." It is similar to the equal sign in a mathematical equation.

**Products**

New substances formed in a reaction are its products. They are placed to the right of the yield sign. A plus sign separates different products when there is more than one.

**Figure 20.6** ▲
**Parts of a Chemical Equation**

The reactants are the substances that undergo a chemical change. When combined, the reactants begin the chemical equation. Look at the chemical equation shown in Figure 20.6. In this equation, the reactants are sodium hydroxide (NaOH) and hydrochloric acid (HCl).

An arrow, called a yield sign, connects the two sides of the equation. The yield sign acts like the verb of the sentence. When you read the chemical equation you read the arrow as "yield." The yield sign also shows the direction of the reaction. The sentence ends with the formulas for the new substances formed by the reaction. The substances formed are called the **products**. As Figure 20.6 shows, the products of this reaction are sodium chloride (NaCl) and water ($H_2O$).

To show whether a reaction is exothermic or endothermic, the word *energy* is sometimes added to the appropriate side of an equation. Energy, however, is neither a reactant nor a product. Can you explain why?

Chemical equations are always written to represent one set of reactants and one set of products. Thus, one equation describes equally well what happens to two molecules or to a beaker full of those molecules. But, as you will see, equations must sometimes be written to include more than one molecule or unit of the same substance.

▼ **ACTIVITY**

**Communicating**

*The Right Equation*

Write a chemical equation for the following reaction: Silicon (Si) reacts with oxygen ($O_2$) to form silicon dioxide ($SiO_2$).

**SKILLS WORKOUT**

### Life Science LINK

Photosynthesis is the process by which plants use the energy of the sun to make food. A chemical equation shows how this works:

$$CO_2 + H_2O + light \rightarrow C_6H_{12}O_6 + O_2$$

Rewrite the photosynthesis equation and balance it.

**A C T I V I T Y**

Look again at Figure 20.6. How many atoms of sodium are on the left side of the equation? How many are on the right side? Also, count the numbers of hydrogen, oxygen, and chlorine atoms. You should come up with an equal number of atoms for each element on each side of the equation. Why?

The law of conservation of mass and energy states that mass can't be lost or gained in a chemical reaction. The atoms present in the reactants must also be present in the products. Chemical equations, therefore, are often written so that the numbers of each kind of atom on one side equal the numbers of each kind of atom on the other side. A chemical equation written in this way is called a *balanced* chemical equation.

The equation in Figure 20.6 is already balanced. You will come across many chemical equations, however, in which you know the *kinds* of substances involved but not *how many* molecules or atoms of each are present. These equations must be balanced.

When you balance an equation, you write numbers in front of the formulas where they are needed. These numbers, called **coefficients** (KOH eh FIHSH uhnts),

**Figure 20.7** ▼
**Balancing a Chemical Equation**

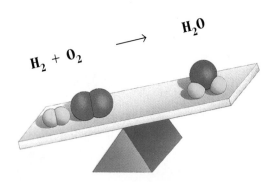

**Unbalanced Chemical Equation** ▲

Why is this equation unbalanced? Count the number of hydrogen atoms. You'll find there are two on each side. The number of oxygen atoms, however, are not equal on each side. There are two oxygen atoms on the left and only one on the right.

**Balanced Chemical Equation**

The equation is balanced when the coefficient 2 is placed in front of the formula for water on the right and the formula for hydrogen on the left. You can see that there are now two oxygen atoms on the left and two on the right. There are four hydrogen atoms on the left and four on the right. ▼

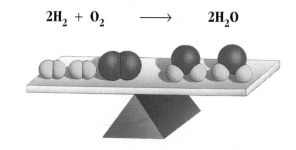

indicate how many atoms or molecules of a substance are involved in a reaction. For example, $2H_2O$ means there are two molecules of water. Be careful not to confuse coefficients and subscripts. A subscript, which shows how many *atoms* of an element are present in a molecule, can't be changed to balance an equation. Only the coefficient can be changed.

Look at Figure 20.7. The equation on the left needs balancing. Count the number of atoms of hydrogen and oxygen on each side of the equation. As you can see, the hydrogens balance, but the oxygens don't.

How can you make the number of oxygen atoms on the right side equal the number on the left side while keeping the hydrogens balanced? You can put a 2 in front of the formula for hydrogen and a 2 in front of the formula for water. With these coefficients, the equation says that two molecules of hydrogen and one molecule of oxygen react to form two molecules of water.

## *SkillBuilder* *Calculating*

### *Writing Chemical Equations*

Writing chemical equations is an important skill that you learn through practice. Write chemical equations for the word equations that follow. Each problem includes the formulas you need to write the equation.

1. Calcium and hydrochloric acid yield calcium chloride and hydrogen.

   hydrochloric acid: HCl
   calcium chloride: $CaCl_2$     hydrogen: $H_2$

2. Magnesium and oxygen yield magnesium oxide.

   oxygen: $O_2$
   magnesium oxide: MgO

3. Sodium and water yield sodium hydroxide and hydrogen.

   sodium hydroxide: NaOH

Remember that an equation is not finished until it is balanced. Go back and balance each of the equations you've just written by following these steps.

   a. Count the number of atoms of each element on each side of the equation.
   b. Use coefficients to balance the numbers of atoms.
   c. Check your work by repeating step a.

Are you getting better at balancing equations? Sharpen your skill even more by balancing the equations below.

4. $Br_2 + KI \longrightarrow KBr + I_2$

5. $Zn + HCl \longrightarrow ZnCl_2 + H_2$

6. $Fe + Cl_2 \longrightarrow FeCl_3$

7. $HCl + CaCO_3 \longrightarrow CaCl_2 + CO_2 + H_2O$

# Science and Society
## *Chain Reactions in the Ozone Layer*

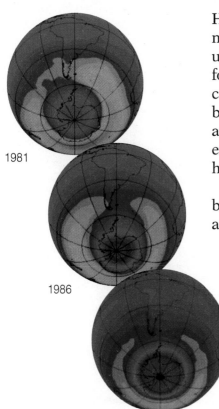

1981

1986

1990

**Figure 20.8** ▲

In these computer images, yellow shows areas where the ozone layer is thick. Blue and purple areas have a very thin layer of ozone.

High above the earth's surface, a thin layer of ozone molecules protects all life on earth from the sun's harmful ultraviolet radiation. Ozone is a form of oxygen with the formula $O_3$. In 1974, scientists discovered that substances called chlorofluorocarbons (CLOR oh FLOR oh KAR buhns), or CFCs, were destroying the ozone layer. CFCs are synthetic gases used in some spray cans and in refrigerators and air conditioners. Look at Figure 20.8 to see how the ozone layer over the South Pole has thinned.

As CFCs rise in the atmosphere, ultraviolet radiation breaks the bonds between their carbon and chlorine atoms.

$$2CF_2Cl_2 \longrightarrow 2CF_2Cl + Cl_2$$

The chlorine molecules produced in this reaction are split apart by ultraviolet radiation to form chlorine atoms.

$$Cl_2 \longrightarrow 2Cl$$

The chlorine atoms then attack ozone molecules.

$$Cl + O_3 \longrightarrow ClO + O_2$$

The ordinary oxygen molecules that result from this chain of reactions don't prevent ultraviolet radiation from reaching the earth's surface. Many people are worried because too much ultraviolet radiation can cause skin cancer and damage food crops. In 1990, 93 nations agreed to stop using CFCs by the year 2000. This action, however, may not be enough to stop the gradual destruction of ozone.

## Check and Explain

1. Identify the reactants and the products in this equation: $Ca + 2HCl \longrightarrow CaCl_2 + H_2$.

2. Balance this equation: $NaCl + H_2SO_4 \longrightarrow Na_2SO_4 + HCl$.

3. **Compare and Contrast** How are coefficients and subscripts alike? How are they different?

4. **Communicate** Write a balanced equation for this reaction: iron + oxygen yields iron oxide. The formula for iron oxide is $Fe_2O_3$.

# 20.3 Types of Chemical Reactions

## Objectives

▶ **Name** four types of chemical reactions.

▶ **Describe** each type of chemical reaction and give an example of each.

▶ **Classify** chemical equations by reaction type.

▶ **Make a model** that describes the generalized form of each type of chemical reaction.

As you probably realized when you wrote and balanced chemical equations, there are a great variety of chemical reactions. The reactants and products both vary in number. The substances involved in reactions can be elements or compounds, atoms or molecules. And in different reactions, atoms rearrange themselves in different ways.

## Patterns in Chemistry

Scientists have observed and described millions of different chemical reactions. Although each one is unique, there are similarities between reactions. For example, did you notice in the equations you just studied that in several reactions two atoms traded places? The atoms that moved were different each time, but the process of chemical reaction was the same. The closer you look, the more similarities you see. Long ago, scientists realized that when substances react, they follow some basic patterns.

Most chemical reactions can be divided into four main types, depending on the pattern they follow. These reaction types are synthesis reactions, decomposition reactions, single-replacement reactions, and double-replacement reactions. By carefully examining the equation for a reaction, you can determine which of the four types it is. Classifying reactions by type is useful because it helps make sense of the huge variety of chemical reactions in nature.

**Figure 20.9** ▲
Chlorine gas reacts with the iron in steel wool to form a single substance.

## Synthesis Reactions

When two simple substances combine to form a third, more complex substance, a **synthesis reaction** has occurred. The word *synthesize* means "to put together or combine." Synthesis reactions are also called combination, or composition, reactions.

An example of a synthesis reaction is shown in Figure 20.10. Nitrogen combines with oxygen to form nitric oxide. Many other synthesis reactions involve two elements that combine to form a compound. When you heat a mixture of iron (Fe) and sulfur (S), for example, these elements combine to form iron sulfide (FeS).

$$Fe + S \longrightarrow FeS$$

Two compounds can also combine in a synthesis reaction to form a single product. For example, calcium oxide combines with water to form calcium hydroxide.

$$CaO + H_2O \longrightarrow Ca(OH)_2$$

Many synthesis reactions, such as the burning of coal, are exothermic.

$$C + O_2 \longrightarrow CO_2 + heat + light$$

## Decomposition Reactions

When a leaf decomposes, it breaks down into simpler substances. The word *decomposition* is used in a similar way in chemistry. In a **decomposition reaction**, a single reactant breaks down into elements or simpler compounds.

Look at the equation in Figure 20.11. It shows the decomposition of water into hydrogen and oxygen. Like many decomposition reactions, the decomposition of water is endothermic. Electric energy must be added to make the reaction happen.

The decomposition of many compounds is triggered by heat. For example, mercury oxide (HgO) decomposes when heated in a test tube. Oxygen gas and silvery beads of mercury are formed.

$$2HgO + heat \longrightarrow 2Hg + O_2$$

If you reverse the arrow of a decomposition reaction, it becomes a synthesis reaction. So, synthesis and decomposition reactions are opposites. Notice that if you reverse the equation for the decomposition of water in Figure 20.11, it becomes the equation for the synthesis of water shown in Figure 20.7.

**Figure 20.10** ▶
**Synthesis Reaction**

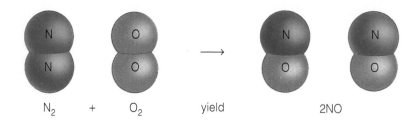

$$N_2 \quad + \quad O_2 \quad \text{yield} \quad 2NO$$

**Figure 20.11** ▶
**Decomposition Reaction**

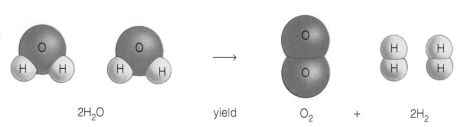

$$2H_2O \quad \text{yield} \quad O_2 \quad + \quad 2H_2$$

## Single-Replacement Reactions

Look at the equation in Figure 20.12. It shows the reaction between iron and copper sulfate. The reactants are an element and a compound. The products are a different element and a different compound. If you look closely at the equation, you can see that iron has replaced the copper in copper sulfate. This kind of chemical reaction, in which atoms of one element replace atoms of another element in a compound, is called a **single-replacement reaction**.

Three kinds of single-replacement reactions are possible. In the first, a nonmetal replaces another nonmetal. In the second, a metal atom replaces a hydrogen atom. In the third and most common, a metal replaces another metal.

You can predict if one metal will replace another by comparing their reactivity. Iron replaces copper in the above reaction because iron is more reactive than copper. Gold doesn't react with copper sulfate because gold is less reactive than copper. A list of metals arranged by reactivity is called an activity series of metals.

## Double-Replacement Reactions

The reaction in Figure 20.13 shows what happens when silver nitrate and potassium chloride react. These two compounds react to form two new compounds, silver chloride and potassium nitrate. This is an example of a **double-replacement reaction**, in which two positive ions trade places between different ionic compounds.

One common product of a double-replacement reaction is a precipitate. Remember that a precipitate is an insoluble solid that forms in a solution. In the reaction in Figure 20.13, for example, the product silver chloride is a precipitate. The other product, potassium nitrate, stays dissolved in solution. In another reaction, iron chloride combines with ammonium hydroxide to form the precipitate iron hydroxide.

$$FeCl_3 + 3NH_4OH \longrightarrow Fe(OH)_3 + 3NH_4Cl$$

Another common product of a double-replacement reaction is a gas. Sodium chloride combined with sulfuric acid forms sodium hydrogen sulfate and hydrogen chloride gas.

$$NaCl + H_2SO_4 \longrightarrow NaHSO_4 + HCl$$

**Figure 20.12** ▼
**Single-Replacement Reaction**

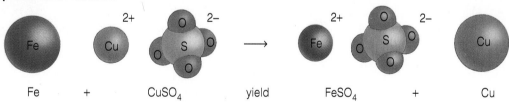

Fe + CuSO$_4$    yield    FeSO$_4$ + Cu

**Figure 20.13** ▼
**Double-Replacement Reaction**

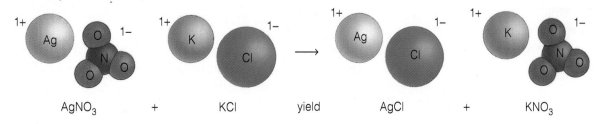

AgNO$_3$ + KCl    yield    AgCl + KNO$_3$

# ▼ ACTIVITY

## Classifying

### Reaction Type

The equation to the right shows the reaction between an acid and a base. What type of reaction is it? How do you know?

**SKILLS WORKOUT**

## Science and You
### *How Antacids Work*

Have you ever had a burning sensation in your chest? It's probably caused by stomach acid backing up into your esophagus, the tube between your throat and stomach. You take an antacid tablet. Soon, you're better. What's the chemistry of your relief?

An antacid contains a base. Bases combine with and neutralize acids. For example, when sodium hydroxide, which is a base, combines with hydrochloric acid, the following reaction occurs:

$$NaOH + HCl \longrightarrow NaCl + H_2O$$

The products, sodium chloride and water, are neither acidic nor basic. Both reactants are poisonous. However, the products form a harmless solution of salt water.

Of the many bases that can neutralize acids, only a few weak bases are safe enough to be used in antacids. The labels on over-the-counter antacids tell you which weak base they contain. Common weak bases in antacids include calcium carbonate and magnesium hydroxide. Each compound differs in the amount of acid it can neutralize and the rate at which it acts.

## Check and Explain

1. List the four types of chemical reactions. Give an example of each.

2. Write a balanced equation that describes each type of chemical reaction.

3. **Classify** Classify each of the following reactions as one of the four types of chemical reactions:

    a. $3KOH + AlCl_3 \longrightarrow Al(OH)_3 + 3KCl$

    b. $2Na + Cl_2 \longrightarrow 2NaCl$

    c. $2Na + 2H_2O \longrightarrow 2NaOH + H_2$

    d. $NH_4NO_2 \longrightarrow N_2 + 2H_2O$

4. **Make a Model** You could describe all synthesis reactions with a general equation like $A + B \longrightarrow AB$. Use your own set of symbols to create similar general equations for each of the four types of reactions.

# 20.4 Energy and Reaction Rate

## Objectives

▶ **Define** activation energy and explain its role in getting a reaction started.

▶ **Identify** three factors that affect the rate of a chemical reaction.

▶ **Describe** how enzymes contribute to body processes.

▶ **Make** a graph showing how a catalyst lowers the activation energy of a chemical reaction.

**Y**ou may wish it weren't true, but your homework won't get done if you just put your book, paper, and a pencil together on your desk. Nor will your room get clean unless you put some energy into it. Just like any activity, chemical reactions also need energy to happen. Breaking and forming chemical bonds requires energy.

## Getting a Reaction Started

Some reactions, as you have seen, occur at room temperature when the reactants are mixed. For example, if you put a piece of sodium in water, the sodium will leap around the water as it reacts violently. It produces a sizzle of hydrogen bubbles, sodium hydroxide, and heat. Other reactions, however, do not occur unless some condition is changed. Heat must be added or pressure must increase.

You may be tempted to think that exothermic reactions always happen by themselves; they don't need any added energy. This inference is logical, but incorrect.

Many familiar reactions, in fact, are exothermic but need added energy before they will happen. The burning of paper, for example, is exothermic. But paper doesn't burst into flame when exposed to air. To get the reaction started, you need to add the heat energy from a lighted match. More than just the energy change of a reaction is needed to explain whether a reaction will start under a certain set of conditions. The key factor for any chemical reaction is how much energy is needed to drive its first step: the breaking of chemical bonds in the reactants.

**Figure 20.14 ▲**
What is needed to start this reaction between paper and oxygen?

## Activation Energy

The flame of a match provides the energy needed to get the reactants in paper and air to begin to combine. This start-up energy is called **activation energy**. All chemical reactions need some amount of activation energy.

Look at the graph in Figure 20.15. It is an energy graph, a way of showing the energy changes that occur as a reaction goes from reactants to products. The "hill" in the graph shows the activation energy for the reaction.

$$2H_2 + O_2 \longrightarrow 2H_2O$$

The energy it takes to get the reactants over the activation-energy hill can be compared to the energy it would take to push a boulder up a real hill.

The height of the "energy hill" determines the amount of energy needed to get a reaction started. Reactions that happen by themselves at room temperature have a low activation energy.

The energy needed to start the reaction is contained in the energy of the reactants themselves, as measured by their temperature.

Once a reaction has started, the energy level of its products compared to its reactants determines whether it needs a continuous supply of added energy to keep going. An endothermic reaction needs a constant supply of added energy, even if it has a low activation energy.

An exothermic reaction, in contrast, will keep going on its own. The burning of paper is a good example. The energy released as some molecules react provides the activation energy other molecules need to start reacting.

**Figure 20.15**
**An Energy Graph** ▼

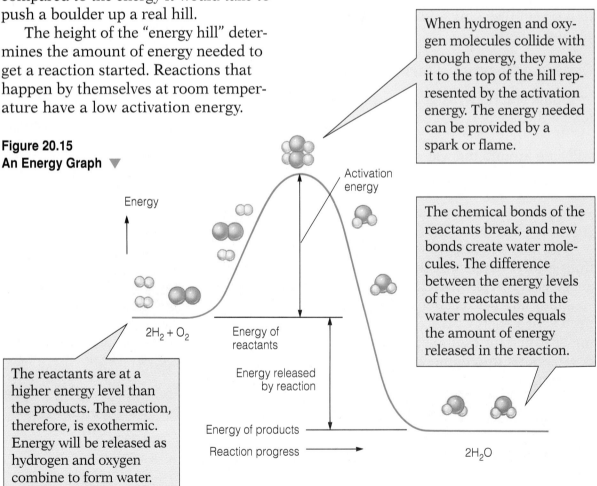

When hydrogen and oxygen molecules collide with enough energy, they make it to the top of the hill represented by the activation energy. The energy needed can be provided by a spark or flame.

The chemical bonds of the reactants break, and new bonds create water molecules. The difference between the energy levels of the reactants and the water molecules equals the amount of energy released in the reaction.

The reactants are at a higher energy level than the products. The reaction, therefore, is exothermic. Energy will be released as hydrogen and oxygen combine to form water.

Energy

Activation energy

$2H_2 + O_2$

Energy of reactants

Energy released by reaction

Energy of products

Reaction progress

$2H_2O$

# Reaction Rate

A chemical reaction occurs when reactant particles collide with enough energy to break and form chemical bonds. The more reactant particles there are, the more collisions there will be. With more reactant particles, the speed, or rate, of a reaction increases. The reaction rate also increases when the force of the collisions between reacting particles increases. You can control the rate of a reaction, therefore, by changing factors that affect the collisions between reacting particles.

## Surface Area

◀ Have you ever made a fire in a fireplace? Several small pieces of wood ignite faster than one big piece. Why? The total surface area of several small objects is much greater than that of one object with the same volume. Greater surface area means more reactant particles come in contact with each other, causing an increase in the rate of reaction. Solids, for example, react much faster as powders because powders have a very large surface area.

## Temperature

An increase in temperature makes particles absorb energy and move faster. They collide more often and with more energy. As a result, more particles react. You can see that the reaction causing a light stick to glow happens faster at a higher temperature. ▼

## Concentration ▲

A candle burns much faster in pure oxygen than it does in air. The difference is in the number of oxygen molecules available to react with the candle wax. When more particles are packed into a certain space, the number of collisions increases. Therefore, an increase in the concentration of one or more reactants increases the reaction rate.

# Catalysts

Many chemical reactions can be made to go much more rapidly without raising the temperature, and without increasing the surface area or concentration of the reactants. All that's necessary is to add a small amount of a substance that speeds up a reaction without being used up in the process, a **catalyst** (CAT uh lihst).

The effect of a catalyst is often very dramatic. If you pour a solution of the common disinfectant, hydrogen peroxide, into a beaker, it will take months for a small amount to decompose quietly into water and oxygen. Add a pinch of the catalyst manganese dioxide ($MnO_2$), however, and the hydrogen peroxide will decompose so rapidly that oxygen gas fizzes out. How does a catalyst produce such results?

Recall that for a chemical reaction to proceed, it needs a certain amount of activation energy. A catalyst lowers the amount of activation energy needed for a reaction to take place. A catalyst does this by providing the necessary energy.

Look at Figure 20.16. It compares a chemical reaction to driving over a hill. Both actions require energy.

**Figure 20.16**
**Effect of a Catalyst** ▼

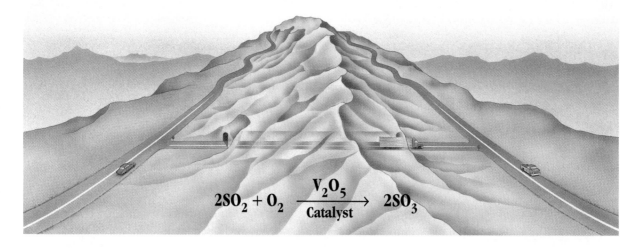

$$2SO_2 + O_2 \xrightarrow[\text{Catalyst}]{V_2O_5} 2SO_3$$

Colliding oxygen and sulfur dioxide molecules must overcome a large activation energy to react and form sulfur trioxide. It is as if they must climb a steep mountain.

The addition of the catalyst $V_2O_5$ lowers the activation energy of the reaction. It's like using a tunnel through a mountain. Colliding reactants don't need as much energy to react.

With the catalyst, the reaction proceeds rapidly. Large amounts of the product, sulfur trioxide, can be produced because more reactants have the energy needed to react.

Once energy has been used to get up the hill, going downhill is easy. A catalyst is compared to a shortcut through the mountain tunnel. It reduces the energy required and allows the reaction to take place.

A catalyst is neither a reactant nor a product in a chemical reaction. When the reaction is over, all the added catalyst can be recovered. When you write an equation for a reaction that uses a catalyst, the catalyst is written above the yield sign. Look at Figure 20.16 to see how this is done.

Catalysts are vital in the manufacturing of many products. Using a catalyst saves energy and reduces costs. A small amount of catalyst can be used over and over. Catalysts are especially useful when changing the factors of temperature, surface area, or concentration is impractical or expensive. Some of the common products that require the aid of catalysts are ammonia, polyester, margarine, and gasoline.

## Life Science LINK

There are many catalysts that speed up reactions in the human body. One of these is salivary amylase, which is produced in the mouth. Salivary amylase breaks down starches into sugars called glucose and maltose.

Obtain some saltine crackers. Put one in your mouth and chew it until it tastes sweet.

Write a word equation for the break down of starch in your mouth.

**ACTIVITY**

# *Career Corner*  *Quality-Control Chemist*

## *Who Checks the Quality of Products?*

When you wash your hair, how do you know the shampoo won't damage it? Most chemical products used by people are tested for harmful side effects before they are put on the market. Thus, you can be fairly confident that the products won't hurt you.

What if something goes wrong, however, in the manufacturing process? Could a bad batch of a product harm you? Not if the quality-control chemists do their jobs.

Quality-control chemists work in laboratories where they test samples of the different products that people buy.

These chemists make sure that the products contain just the right kinds and amounts of chemicals they are supposed to contain.

If you want to be a quality-control chemist, you need to be good at math. You should also like to work with electronic instruments. A quality-control chemist needs to pay careful attention to a great number of details. A single wrong calculation or missed reading of a number on a computer screen could endanger the health of many consumers.

To get a job as a quality-control chemist, you need a

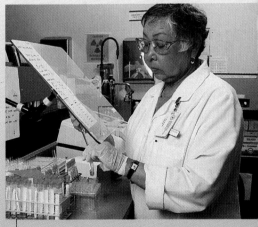

bachelor's degree in chemistry. In high school, you should take classes in biology, chemistry, physics, algebra, and geometry. English composition and computer classes are also good preparation for this career.

## Enzymes: Biological Catalysts

If you chew a potato for a few minutes, you will begin to taste something sweet. Since there is no sugar in the potato, where does the sweet taste come from? The salivary glands in your mouth produce a catalyst that helps split starch molecules in the potato into sugar molecules.

Organisms produce many such catalysts. These biological catalysts are called **enzymes**. Enzymes are protein molecules that control the rate of chemical reactions that occur in living things. Each enzyme affects a specific reaction. These reactions occur thousands or even millions of times faster with enzymes than they would without them.

Some enzymes, such as the one that converts starch to sugar, play a role in the digestion of foods. Other enzymes help in the conduction of nerve impulses, the clotting of blood, the contraction of muscle tissue, and the everyday functioning of cells, tissues, and organs.

Of the more than 2,000 enzymes known to be produced by various living things, about 150 have commercial uses. Cheese, for example, is made with the aid of an enzyme called rennin. Candy makers use an enzyme called invertase to create liquid-centered candies, such as chocolate-covered cherries.

**Figure 20.17** ▶
A cheesemaker checks the consistency of milk that has been curdled by rennin.

# Science and Technology
## *Catalytic Converters and Smog Reduction*

Explosive chemical reactions inside a car's engine are what make the crankshaft turn and the wheels go around. Gasoline reacts with oxygen in the air to form water, carbon dioxide, and energy. In the high temperatures that exist in an engine cylinder, other reactions also occur. Nitrogen in the air reacts with the gasoline to form various oxides of nitrogen. Some of the gasoline doesn't burn completely, producing carbon monoxide (CO) and other substances that are known to be harmful to people.

Over the past 20 years, efforts have been made to reduce the amount of harmful gases in automobile exhaust. One of the most important anti-smog devices is the catalytic converter introduced in 1975. A catalytic converter is a mufflerlike reaction chamber installed in a vehicle's exhaust system. It contains several catalysts, usually finely divided metals, such as platinum, palladium, and rhodium.

Look at the diagram of a catalytic converter in Figure 20.18. When a mixture of exhaust gases from the engine and outside air passes over the catalysts, several chemical reactions occur. These reactions change harmful gases into compounds that are safe for both people and the environment.

Gases safe for the environment

Catalysts

Harmful gases

**Figure 20.18** ▲
What is the purpose of an automobile's catalytic converter?

---

## Check and Explain

1.  What is activation energy? Draw an energy graph and identify the activation energy.

2.  Name three ways to increase the rate of a reaction. Explain how each works.

3.  **Reason and Conclude**   Use an everyday example to explain why the surface area, temperature, and concentration of reactants affect the rate of a reaction.

4.  **Make a Graph**   A catalyst lowers the activation energy of a certain exothermic reaction by 50 percent. Draw an energy graph showing both the catalyzed and uncatalyzed reactions. Label all of the parts of your graph.

# Activity 20  *How do some everyday substances react chemically?*

**Skills** Observe; Infer; Interpret Data

## Task 1  Prelab Prep
Collect the following items: iron nail, beaker or glass jar, test tube, copper sulfate solution, sugar, test-tube holder, Bunsen burner.

## Task 2  Data Record
On a separate sheet of paper, copy the data table shown. Use the table to record your observations of the chemical reactions.

## Task 3  Procedure
1. Put the iron nail in the beaker or jar.
2. Add enough copper sulfate solution to the beaker to cover the nail. Set the beaker aside while you do the next two steps.
3. Place about 1 cm of sugar into the test tube. Light the Bunsen burner. Using the test-tube holder, hold the test tube over the tip of the Bunsen burner flame. Move the test tube around in the flame in order to heat the sugar evenly. **CAUTION! Wear your goggles. Be careful around the open flame. When heating a test tube, hold the open end away from you.**
4. Record in your data table what happens as the sugar is heated.
5. Observe the nail in the copper sulfate solution. Has any change occurred? If not, wait 5 minutes or more.
6. Record in your data table the changes you observe in the nail and the copper sulfate solution.

## Task 4  Analysis
1. What changes occurred when you heated the sugar?
2. The formula for sugar is $C_{12}H_{22}O_{11}$. Based on this information and your observations, how many new substances do you think were formed when the sugar was heated? Give reasons for your answer.
3. What type of chemical reaction do you think took place in the sugar?
4. What changes did you observe in the nail or copper sulfate?
5. The formula for copper sulfate is $CuSO_4$. Iron (Fe) replaces the copper in copper sulfate. Knowing this, what do you think makes up the coating you observed on the nail?
6. What type of chemical reaction occurred between the nail and the copper sulfate? How do you know?

## Task 5  Conclusion
Describe the two chemical reactions. Explain how they differ.

## *Everyday Application*
What happens when food is heated too hot or for too long? What chemical change occurs? How do you prevent this from happening when you cook your food?

## *Extension*
Write balanced equations for both reactions in this activity.

| Reactants | Evidence of Chemical Reaction |
|---|---|
| Heated sugar | |
| Copper sulfate and iron | |

# Chapter 20 Review

## Concept Summary

### 20.1 Characteristics of Chemical Reactions
▶ Evidence of a chemical reaction is formation of a gas or precipitate, energy release, or color change.
▶ During a chemical reaction, bonds among reactants break and new bonds form.
▶ Exothermic reactions release energy; endothermic reactions absorb energy.

### 20.2 Chemical Equations
▶ In a chemical equation, reactants are on the left and products on the right.
▶ The number of atoms on each side of a chemical equation must be equal.
▶ Coefficients balance an equation.

### 20.3 Types of Chemical Reactions
▶ In a synthesis reaction, two substances combine to form a third substance. In a decomposition reaction, one substance breaks down to form two or more substances.
▶ In a single-replacement reaction, one element replaces another in a compound; in a double-replacement reaction, the metal elements of two ionic compounds change places.

### 20.4 Energy and Reaction Rate
▶ All chemical reactions require energy.
▶ A catalyst speeds up a reaction.
▶ Enzymes are catalysts.

## Chapter Vocabulary

chemical reaction (20.1)
exothermic reaction (20.1)
endothermic reaction (20.1)
chemical equation (20.2)
reactant (20.2)

product (20.2)
coefficient (20.2)
synthesis reaction (20.3)
decomposition reaction (20.3)
single-replacement reaction (20.3)

double-replacement
   reaction (20.3)
activation energy (20.4)
catalyst (20.4)
enzyme (20.4)

## Check Your Vocabulary

Use the vocabulary words above to complete the following sentences correctly.

1. Biological catalysts are called ____ .

2. In a(n) ____ , two elements exchange places in two compounds.

3. In general, a process that causes a chemical change is called a(n) ____ .

4. In a(n) ____ , a metal atom replaces another metal atom.

5. In a(n) ____ , symbols are used to represent a reaction.

6. Reactions that absorb energy are ____ .

7. The left side of a chemical equation contains the ____ .

8. To speed up certain reactions, a(n) ____ can be used.

9. In a(n) ____ , a substance breaks down to form two new substances.

10. Reactions that release energy are ____ .

11. Colliding reactant particles must overcome the ____ to react.

12. The opposite of a decomposition reaction is a(n) ____ .

13. Balanced equations may have ____ .

14. A reaction produces ____ .

## Write Your Vocabulary

Write sentences using the vocabulary words above. Show that you know what each word means.

## Check Your Knowledge

Answer the following in complete sentences.

1. What observations might lead you to conclude that a chemical reaction has occurred?

2. In what way does a balanced chemical equation relate to the law of conservation of mass and energy?

3. Describe how reactants are related to products.

4. What is the difference between a subscript and a coefficient?

5. Compare synthesis and decomposition reactions.

6. How are single- and double-replacement reactions similar and how are they different?

7. Why is activation energy like rolling a ball to the top of a hill?

8. What must occur if two reactant particles are to react?

Choose the answer that best completes each sentence.

9. The production of a (catalyst, enzyme, precipitate, coefficient) is evidence of a chemical reaction.

10. During a chemical reaction, energy may be (created, absorbed, destroyed, changed into matter).

11. To balance a chemical equation, you add (coefficients, subscripts, formulas, atoms).

12. An exothermic reaction (releases energy, creates a radioactive substance, creates matter, absorbs energy).

13. A catalyst (slows down, stops, speeds up, reverses) a chemical reaction.

## Check Your Understanding

Apply the concepts you have learned to answer each question.

1. **Classify**   Identify each of the following reactions as exothermic or endothermic.

   a. $2H_2O + electricity \rightarrow 2H_2 + 2O$
   b. $2Na + 2H_2O \rightarrow 2NaOH + H_2 + heat$
   c. $2H_2 + 2O \rightarrow 2H_2O + heat, light, and sound$

2. **Predict**   In each pair of reactions, which will go faster?

   a. Zinc in concentrated hydrochloric acid or zinc in dilute hydrochloric acid?
   b. Zinc in sulfuric acid at 15°C or zinc in sulfuric acid at 20°C?

3. **Mystery Photo**   The photograph on page 488 shows iron siding that was protected with a thin layer of zinc to prevent rusting. In places where the zinc is gone, rust has formed. Hypothesize why zinc prevents iron from rusting.

4. Classify each reaction below as synthesis, decomposition, single replacement, or double replacement.

   a. $Zn + S \rightarrow ZnS$
   b. $MgBr_2 + 2K \rightarrow Mg + 2KBr$
   c. $C_{12}H_{22}O_{11} \rightarrow 12C + 11H_2O$
   d. $BaCl_2 + H_2SO_4 \rightarrow BaSO_4 + 2HCl$

5. Balance the following equations.

   a. $BaCl_2 + Na_2SO_4 \rightarrow BaSO_4 + NaCl$
   b. $PbO_2 \rightarrow PbO + O_2$

6. **Find Causes**   Why do you think chemical processes slow down in hibernating animals?

## Develop Your Skills

Use the skills you have developed in this chapter to complete each activity.

1. **Interpret Data**  The energy graph below shows the energy level of the reactants and products of a certain chemical reaction.

   a. Does this graph represent an exothermic or an endothermic reaction? How do you know?

   b. Which has the greater amount of energy, the reactants or the products?

   c. What does *A* represent? What does *B* represent?

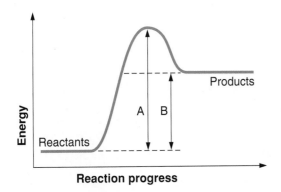

2. **Data Bank**  Use the information on page 638 to answer the following questions.

   a. Which is more reactive, sodium or magnesium?

   b. Zinc replaces copper in a certain single-replacement reaction because zinc is more reactive than copper. Will aluminum replace iron in $Fe_2O_3$? Explain.

   c. Will copper replace magnesium in $MgBr_2$? Explain.

## Make Connections

1. **Link the Concepts**  Below is a concept map showing how some of the main concepts in this chapter link together. Only parts of the map are filled in. Copy the map. Using words and ideas from the chapter, complete the map.

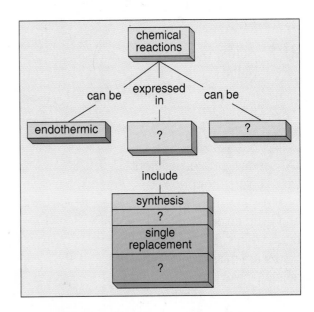

2. **Science and Literature**  Write a short story using the title "The Catalyst." The story should be about a relationship among three people and how one "catalyzes" a change in the other two. Try to explain the human interaction so that it is similar in some way to chemical reactions.

3. **Science and Society**  Do research to find out how the uses and production of CFCs are being regulated to protect the ozone layer. Suggest additional laws or regulations you think would be effective. Find out what substances are being developed to replace CFCs.

# Chapter 21 Solution Chemistry

## Chapter Sections

21.1 Solutions

21.2 Suspensions and Colloids

21.3 Acids, Bases, and Salts

## What do you see?

❝I see two or three different water colors dropped in a beaker of water. The water is changing colors as the colors dissolve in it. Some of the colors are mixing with each other. It looks like a mixture of water and a solute. So they make a solution.❞

*Eric Jacobs*
*South High School*
*Minneapolis, Minnesota*

To find out more about the photograph, look on page 534. As you read this chapter, you will learn about solution chemistry.

# 21.1 Solutions

## Objectives

▶ **List** the nine types of solutions and give an example of each.

▶ **Identify** the factors that affect solution rate and solubility.

▶ **Compare** and **contrast** the difference between saturated, unsaturated, and supersaturated solutions.

▶ **Calculate** the concentration of a solution.

**ACTIVITY**

**Defining Operationally**

*Solutions*

Based on your own observations and experiences, explain what a solution is. Give examples.

**SKILLS WARMUP**

W hat happens when you put a spoonful of table salt into a glass of water? The solid crystals disappear. They seem to be swallowed up by the liquid. But even though you can't see it, you know the salt is still there because you can taste it.

Salt water is an example of a **solution**. A solution is the same as a homogeneous mixture. Remember that in a homogeneous mixture, two or more different substances are mixed evenly together.

## Types of Solutions

The two substances that make up a solution have different chemical roles. One role is that of the **solvent**. A solvent is the substance that takes in, or dissolves, the other substance or substances. Usually the solvent is present in the greater amount. The other role is that of the **solute**. A solute is what gets taken in, or dissolved by, the solvent. A solution is usually described as something *dissolved* in something else. In salt water, salt is dissolved in water.

You are most familiar with solutions, such as salt water, in which the solvent is a liquid. However, according to the definition above, a solution doesn't have to be a liquid. The air you breathe, for example, is a solution made up of gases dissolved in a gas. Metal alloys are solutions of a solid dissolved in a solid. A liquid dissolved in a solid, a liquid dissolved in a gas, and a gas dissolved in a solid are other possible kinds of solutions. In fact, the three phases of matter can be paired together in nine different ways to make solutions. Thus, there are a total of nine different kinds of solutions.

**Figure 21.1** ▲
The salt in these piles was once part of a solution—the salty ocean water of a lagoon. How do you think the salt was separated from the water?

**Figure 21.2** ▲
What is the solvent in a carbonated drink? What are the solutes?

The nine different types of solutions are shown in Table 21.1. As you can see, each type of solution is a different combination of two of the three phases of matter. Some types are more common than others. A gas dissolved in a liquid is one common type of solution. You can find such a solution in a can of soda, for example. Solutions of one liquid dissolved in another liquid are also common. A familiar example is automobile antifreeze, a mixture of ethylene glycol and water. Give an example of a solid dissolved in a liquid. Give an example of a solid dissolved in a solid.

In a solution, solvent particles surround each particle of solute. Attractions between solute particles and solvent particles keep this arrangement stable, even though the particles move. This stable relationship between solvent and solute particles is what makes a solution a homogeneous mixture.

For solvent particles to surround solute particles in a solution, the solute particles must be extremely small. Solute particles are so small that they can't be separated from a solution by filtering. The molecules or ions of the solute simply pass through even the tiniest pores in a filter. For example, tea is a solution in which the solvent particles can't be filtered out. All liquid solutions share this property of being nonfilterable.

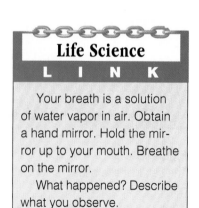

**Life Science**
**L I N K**

Your breath is a solution of water vapor in air. Obtain a hand mirror. Hold the mirror up to your mouth. Breathe on the mirror.

What happened? Describe what you observe.

**A C T I V I T Y**

**Table 21.1   Types of Solutions**

| Solute | Solvent | Example |
|--------|---------|---------|
| Gas | Gas | Air (oxygen in nitrogen) |
| Gas | Liquid | Carbonated beverages ($CO_2$ in water) |
| Gas | Solid | Hydrogen fuel storage (hydrogen in metal hydrides) |
| Liquid | Gas | Humid air (water in air) |
| Liquid | Liquid | Vinegar (acetic acid in water) |
| Liquid | Solid | Dental fillings (mercury in silver) |
| Solid | Gas | Air surrounding mothballs (naphthalene in air) |
| Solid | Liquid | Salt water |
| Solid | Solid | Stainless steel (carbon in iron) |

## Water as a Solvent

Of all the different substances that can be solvents, water is the most important. Water carries dissolved nutrients in the body fluids of living things. Many of the liquids you use every day are water solutions.

Water can dissolve so many different substances that it is often called the *universal solvent*. What makes water so special? Look at Figure 21.3. The oxygen atom of a water molecule holds electrons more strongly than the hydrogen atoms. The shared electrons in the two covalent bonds, therefore, are drawn closer to the oxygen. As a result, the oxygen takes on a slightly negative charge and the hydrogens a slightly positive charge. Because of the molecule's shape, one end is positive and the other end negative.

Water molecules can act as little magnets. As you can see in Figure 21.3, the positive ends of water molecules are attracted to solute particles that have a negative charge. The negative ends of water molecules are attracted to positively-charged solute particles.

Water dissolves most ionic solids because its molecules pull apart the ions that make up the solid. Water can also form a solution with molecules that have slightly negative and slightly positive parts. However, because molecules of fats and oils have their electrical charges evenly distributed, they repel water molecules instead of attracting them.

▼ **ACTIVITY**

**Observing**

*Water's Properties*

Based on your experience with water, make a list of its properties and uses. Then use each item on your list to compare water with other common substances. What unique properties does water have?

**SKILLS WORKOUT**

**Figure 21.3**
Water dissolves many substances because of the structure of water molecules. Water molecules are slightly positive at one end and slightly negative at the other. ▼

Slightly negative

Slightly positive

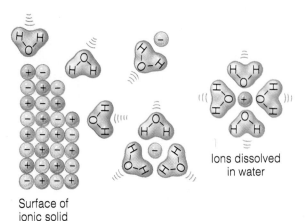

Surface of ionic solid

Ions dissolved in water

# Factors Affecting Solution Rate

Dissolving a solid in a liquid is an everyday experience for many people. You create this kind of solution, for example, when you make up a powdered drink mix. Scientists also commonly dissolve solids in liquids to make solutions. How does this dissolving process take place?

Think of what happens when you dissolve a powdered drink mix in water. The solid doesn't disappear instantly in the liquid. The process of dissolving takes a certain amount of time. The particles making up the solute must be pulled apart by the solvent particles. Such action can only occur at the surface of the solid, where it contacts the solvent. The rate at which a solid dissolves in a liquid can be increased in three different ways. You have probably used all three methods yourself.

### Particle Size
Which will dissolve faster, the large salt crystals or the same mass of salt in powdered form? Since the process of dissolving takes place at the surface of a solid, the larger the surface, the more rapidly it will dissolve. The surface area of an object increases greatly when it is broken down into smaller and smaller bits. ▼

### Movement ▲
When ions are pulled off the surface of an ionic solid, they stay nearby. They fill the available spaces between the closest water molecules, and the dissolving process slows down. If you stirred this solution, however, water molecules that still had empty spaces around them could contact the surface of the solid, and the dissolving process would speed up.

### Temperature ▲
You probably know that hot water will dissolve a solid faster than cold water. When you make tea, for example, you always use hot water. Molecules of hot water have more kinetic energy than those of cold water. They move around faster and come in contact more frequently with the substance to be dissolved.

## Factors Affecting Solubility

No matter how fast you can make something dissolve, there is a limit to *how much* of it you can dissolve in a certain amount of liquid. What happens when you add sugar, a spoonful at a time, to a glass of water? At some point, the sugar no longer dissolves. Some of it remains on the bottom of the glass no matter how long you stir. The ability of one substance to dissolve in another is called its **solubility**.

The solubility of different substances in water varies greatly. In fact, many substances aren't soluble at all. Solubility is usually expressed as the grams (g) of solute that will dissolve in 100 g of water at a certain temperature. At room temperature, the solubility of sugar is about 200 g per 100 g of water; and the solubility of table salt is only about 36 g per 100 g of water.

Solubility varies with temperature. It is important that a measurement of solubility always includes a temperature. For most solids, an increase in temperature causes an increase in solubility.

Gases, however, behave differently. The solubility of a gas in water *decreases* as the temperature increases. For example, more than twice as much oxygen will dissolve in water at 23°C, than will dissolve in water at 60°C.

In addition to temperature, the solubility of a gas depends on its pressure. When you reduce the pressure in a bottle of soda by removing the cap, bubbles of carbon dioxide fizz to the top. The lower pressure forces carbon dioxide out of the solution. In general, increasing the pressure of a gas increases the amount that will dissolve in a liquid. The particle model of matter helps to explain why pressure affects the solubility of a gas.

Particles of a gas dissolved in a liquid are constantly being pushed out of the liquid by movement of the liquid particles. At the same time, particles of the gas above the liquid are constantly being pushed into the liquid. This exchange of particles is balanced at a particular pressure. An increase in the pressure of the gas, however, squeezes gas particles closer together, and more of them are pushed into the liquid.

◄ **Figure 21.4**
The fish in this aquarium depend on oxygen dissolved in the water. If the aquarium water is heated above room temperature, how will the oxygen content in the water change?

Pools of water near the ocean usually contain salt. As the water in the pools evaporates, the concentration of the salt solution changes and salt beds or deposits are left. Collect the following items: 2-L glass bowl, 1-cup measure, tablespoon, and salt.

**1.** Mix 1 c of water and 4 T of salt in the bowl.

**2.** Leave the solution untouched until the water evaporates. (about 3 weeks)

Write a paragraph describing what you observed.

**A C T I V I T Y**

## Concentration of Solutions

If you add too much water when you make up a can of frozen juice, it tastes weak. In other words, there aren't enough solute particles for the amount of solvent to provide a pleasing taste. Whenever you express a relationship between the amount of solute and the amount of solvent, you are identifying **concentration**. Concentration is the amount of solute per given volume of solvent.

To compare the concentration of different solutions, you can use the words *concentrated* and *dilute*. A dilute solution contains very little solute. A concentrated solution contains a large amount of solute. These terms are not precise, since they can refer to a wide range of actual concentrations.

You can also classify solutions as **saturated**, **unsaturated**, or **supersaturated**. When you add salt to water until no more will dissolve, the solution is saturated.

## *SkillBuilder* *Interpreting Data*

### Soluble or Insoluble?

Scientists often want to know how soluble a substance is and how its solubility changes with temperature. Even more basic is knowing whether a substance is soluble at all. The solubility table to the right describes various ionic compounds as either soluble or insoluble in water.

Positive ions appear in the column down the left side and negative ions in the row across the top. To find the solubility of aluminum oxide, look at the aluminum row and the oxide column, then find where they meet. Use the table to answer the questions.

1.  Is aluminum oxide soluble or insoluble? How about copper bromide?

2.  Name an insoluble compound of magnesium.

3.  Name a soluble hydroxide compound.

4.  Which negative ion listed in the table forms only soluble compounds?

In a short paragraph, make generalizations about the solubility patterns you see in the table.

| Solubilities of Compounds | | | | | |
|---|:---:|:---:|:---:|:---:|:---:|
| | **bromide** | **carbonate** | **hydroxide** | **nitrate** | **oxide** |
| **aluminum** | S | — | I | S | I |
| **ammonium** | S | S | S | S | — |
| **copper** | S | — | I | S | I |
| **magnesium** | S | I | I | S | I |
| **silver** | I | I | — | S | I |
| **sodium** | S | S | S | S | S |

**Key:**  S = Soluble   I = Insoluble   — = No such compound

A saturated solution contains all the solute a solvent will dissolve at a certain temperature and pressure. A solution that contains less solute than this amount is called unsaturated. An unsaturated solution can range from dilute to concentrated.

In some cases, you can create a supersaturated solution—one that goes beyond the point of saturation. You make a saturated solution at a high temperature and then cool it very slowly. If the solution isn't disturbed, all the solute will stay dissolved. At room temperature, it will contain more solute than could normally dissolve at that temperature.

### Science and You *Kitchen Solutions*

You don't have to look beyond your kitchen to find all sorts of different solutions. Vanilla extract, vinegar, and maple syrup are just a few of the many solutions that are probably sitting on your kitchen shelves.

Vanilla extract is made by dissolving oil from the vanilla bean in alcohol. This solution is then dissolved in water. Vanilla extract flavors many of the foods you eat.

Vinegar is one of the most versatile kitchen solutions. It is a dilute solution of acetic acid. Vinegar flavors and preserves many foods, such as pickles. Maple syrup is a concentrated solution of sugars from maple-tree sap. The sap is heated to boil away most of the water, leaving it thick and syrupy.

**Figure 21.5** ▲
Maple tree sap is a solution of sugars in water. How is it turned into maple syrup?

---

## Check and Explain

1. Give examples of three types of solutions and tell the phase of matter of each solute and solvent.

2. What three things could you do if you wanted to increase the rate at which sugar dissolves in water?

3. **Compare and Contrast**  Is a dilute solution always unsaturated? Is an unsaturated solution always dilute? Explain.

4. **Calculate**  The solubility of $AgNO_3$ is 222.0 g per 100 g of water at 20°C. What kind of solution will you create if you add 110.99 g of $AgNO_3$ to 50 g of water at 20°C? What kind of solution will it become if you add 10 g more of $AgNO_3$?

# 21.2 Suspensions and Colloids

## Objectives

▶ **Describe** what a suspension is and give common examples.

▶ **Compare** and **contrast** colloids, solutions, and suspensions.

▶ **Classify** five kinds of colloids.

Is milk a solution? What about a fruit jelly? Muddy water? Shaving cream? To tell if these mixtures are solutions, you have to be a kind of microscopic detective. The size of their particles makes some substances mixtures, but not solutions.

Imagine you have been shrunk to the size of a molecule. If you are placed in a mixture in which the particles are your size or smaller, you're in a solution. If you find yourself in a mixture with particles much larger than you, you're not in a solution. Mixtures with large particles can't be completely homogeneous mixtures. So, they can't be solutions. These mixtures have their own special names and properties.

## Suspensions

What happens when you shake a mixture of soil and water in a jar and then let it stand? The soil particles slowly settle at the bottom of the jar. A mixture in which some of the particles will settle out is called a **suspension**.

The particles in a suspension are relatively large and are usually visible. They settle out because they aren't closely tied to water molecules. Over time, the force of gravity makes them sink to the bottom. Unlike the particles of solute in a solution, the particles in a suspension are large enough to be filtered out.

What common mixtures do you think are suspensions? A medicine or food product labeled "shake well" probably contains a suspension. You must shake it to distribute its contents evenly. After it sits for a while, the particles settle to the bottom. In a solution, the particles are always evenly distributed and don't settle out.

Rapidly moving rivers and streams often carry a load of suspended particles called *silt*. The larger particles gradually settle out as the water slows down along its

**Figure 21.6** ▲
What happens to the particles of soil carried in muddy river water?

course. You may have seen silt built up on the banks of a river. Air also often contains suspended particles. City air usually contains soot, which are tiny carbon particles that form when fuels burn. These particles settle out of the air, leaving a black coating on buildings.

## Colloids

Solutions and suspensions are very different kinds of mixtures. Solutions are homogeneous mixtures with very small particles. Suspensions are heterogeneous mixtures with large particles. As you may have guessed, there are also mixtures that are halfway between solutions and suspensions. These mixtures, called **colloids** (KAHL oydz), have particles that are larger than the particles in solutions and smaller than those in a suspension. A colloid isn't completely homogeneous, nor is it as heterogeneous as a suspension.

A colloid can be clear, just like a liquid solution. So, how do you tell the difference between a colloid and a solution? The simple test shown in Figure 21.7 provides the answer. Although colloidal particles are too small to be seen by the unaided eye, they are large enough to reflect light off their surfaces. When you pass a beam of light through a colloid, the beam becomes visible, just as it does in a suspension. A beam of light isn't visible as it passes through a solution. Why is it possible to see a beam of sunlight between a cloud and the ground?

**Figure 21.7**
Why is the beam of light visible in the colloid and suspension but not in the solution? ▼

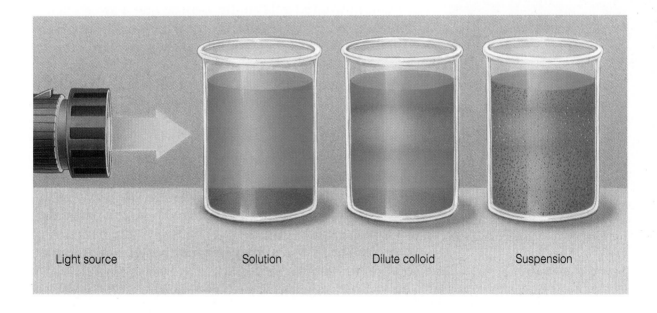

Light source      Solution      Dilute colloid      Suspension

It's easy to tell the difference between a colloid and a suspension. Even though a colloid may be cloudy like a suspension, the particles in a colloid don't settle out on standing. In addition, colloidal particles are small enough to pass through a filter.

There are many types of colloids. The particles in a colloid may be grains of solid, droplets of liquid, or bubbles of gas. The material in which the particles are spread out, or dispersed, may also be a solid, liquid, or a gas. Five common types of colloids are sols, gels, aerosols, foams, and emulsions.

**Sols** A colloid composed of a solid dispersed in either a solid or a liquid is called a sol (SAHLZ). Many paints and inks are liquid sols. They contain tiny particles of pigment dispersed in a liquid. Putty, potter's clay, milk of magnesia, and toothpaste all belong to this group of colloids. Red glass is an example of a solid sol. The red color comes from tiny bits of gold dispersed in the glass. Pearls and the gemstones called opals are also solid sols. Because they are sols, opals do not have a crystal structure like other gemstones.

**Gels** A gel is a jellylike colloid in which long particles form a branching structure that traps a liquid inside. Gels behave like flexible solids. In many gels, the branching structure is made of gelatin, a protein obtained from the skin and bones of animals. Gelatin dessert mixes contain powdered gelatin, flavorings, and a sweetener. Jams and jellies are other familiar gels. They are made with pectin, a substance found in the skins and cores of fruit. Pectin causes the fruit juice to "jell." Campers sometimes ignite a can of a jellylike substance to use for cooking. This gel is a mixture of alcohol and calcium acetate.

**Aerosols** Smoke, clouds, fog, and mist are natural colloids called aerosols (AIR oh SAHLZ). They are made up of solid or liquid particles dispersed in air. The particles in smoke are solids. In clouds, fog, and mist, the particles are water droplets. Some spray cans contain artificial aerosols. The fine mist they produce consists of liquid or solid particles dispersed in a gas. Name some different kinds of aerosols you use.

**Figure 21.8** ▲

What type of colloid is fog?

**Foams** Foam is a colloid of gas bubbles dispersed in liquid. Chemical foams are used to put out fires. Whipped cream, marshmallows, and shaving cream are some common examples of foam.

**Emulsions** A colloid made up of tiny droplets of a liquid dispersed in another liquid is an emulsion (ee MUHL shuhn). Because the particles in an emulsion cling to each other, individual particles don't settle out. Many of the foods you eat are emulsions. Homogenized milk, butter, and margarine are all emulsions of oil in water. Most of the creams and ointments used in cosmetics and medicine are also emulsions.

**Table 21.2  Properties of Solutions, Colloids, and Suspensions**

|  | **Solution** | **Suspension** | **Colloid** |
|---|---|---|---|
| **Size of particles** | Molecules or ions | Large enough to be seen | Between that of solutions and suspensions |
| **Type of mixture** | Homogeneous | Heterogeneous | Borderline |
| Do particles settle out? | No | Yes | No |
| Can particles be separated by filtering? | No | Yes | No |
| Do particles scatter light? | No | Yes | Yes |

You know what happens when you try to mix oil and water: The two liquids quickly separate into layers. If you add a few drops of egg yolk to the mixture before shaking, however, the liquids separate more slowly. The egg yolk breaks up the oil into tiny droplets that mix more easily with water.

Egg yolk is a natural *emulsifier* (ee MUHL suh FY er), a substance that helps disperse tiny particles of one liquid in another. Emulsifiers improve the uniformity, consistency, stability, and texture of food products. Recipes for homemade mayonnaise always include egg yolks, because an emulsifier is needed to keep the oil and water in mayonnaise from separating.

Peanut butter is a common food that usually contains an emulsifier. To get an idea of its effect, examine a jar of "natural" peanut butter, which contains only peanuts and salt. A layer of oil will probably be on the top. In peanut butter with an added emulsifier, the oil doesn't separate.

Emulsifiers are found in many other foods. When solid chocolate undergoes a temperature change, its surface tends to change color because the cocoa butter separates from the rest of the chocolate. An emulsifier keeps the cocoa butter in a more stable emulsion within the chocolate. Most ice creams and many other frozen desserts owe much of their smoothness and consistency to added emulsifiers. Look at the labels of different food products. Which foods contain emulsifiers?

## ACTIVITY

### Observing

*Heavy on the Mayo*

Find a recipe for mayonnaise and make some. Observe what happens during the process.

What kind of tool do you need to make mayonnaise? What does this tool do to the oil and egg yolk ingredients?

**SKILLS WORKOUT**

## Check and Explain

1. Describe a suspension from the point of view of one of its particles.

2. What are the five types of colloids you learned about in this chapter? Give one example of each.

3. **Compare and Contrast** How are solutions, suspensions, and colloids alike? How are they different?

4. **Classify** Draw a table to classify sols, gels, emulsions, foams, and aerosols. Identify the states of matter involved in each and give an example.

# 21.3 Acids, Bases, and Salts

## Objectives

▶ **Compare** the properties of acids, bases, and salts.

▶ **Interpret** measurements on the pH scale.

▶ **Predict** what salt will be formed by a neutralization reaction.

**▼ ACTIVITY**

### Comparing

*Lemons and Vinegar*

What properties do lemon juice and vinegar share? How are they different from other substances?

**SKILLS WARMUP**

**W**hat do you think of when you hear the word *acid*? Many people think all acids are harsh liquids that burn your skin and eat away at metal and stone. However, this is true of only a few acids in their concentrated forms. In fact, you put acids into your body whenever you eat pickles or sauerkraut, or drink orange juice.

In chemical terms, an **acid** is a substance that gives up hydrogen ions ($H^+$) in a water solution. This characteristic makes acids chemically active. The chemical activity of acids is shared by another group of substances, **bases**. A base is a substance that gives up or creates hydroxide ($OH^-$) ions in a water solution. Both acids and bases are important in the manufacture of many products, in food making, and in the life processes of organisms.

## Properties of Acids

What do vinegar and lemon juice have in common? They both taste sour because they both contain acids. In addition to a sour taste, acids have a number of other common properties. Acids turn blue litmus paper red, for example. They react with bases in a process called *neutralization*. The process is termed neutralization because its products are neither acids nor bases. Acids also react with metals, to form hydrogen gas, and with baking soda and limestone, to form carbon dioxide gas.

Acids are classified as strong or weak. Only strong acids, such as sulfuric acid, nitric acid, and hydrochloric acid, have the properties many people associate with acids. These acids can burn your skin and make holes in your clothes. You must handle them very carefully. Weak acids are common in many foods and plants. Citrus fruits and tomatoes contain citric acid, for example.

**Figure 21.11 ▲**
The acid in lemon juice can keep apples from turning brown.

**Figure 21.12** ▲
What does this change in the color of the litmus paper indicate?

**Table 21.3   Common Acids and Their Uses**

| Name of Acid | Formula | Uses |
|---|---|---|
| Acetic acid (vinegar) | $CH_3COOH$ | Seasons and preserves foods; cleans and deodorizes |
| Hydrochloric acid | $HCl$ | Produced by stomach and aids digestion; used in toilet-bowl cleaners and for cleaning metal surfaces |
| Sulfuric acid | $H_2SO_4$ | Used in automobile batteries and in making fertilizers, dyes, and plastics |
| Nitric acid | $HNO_3$ | Used in making explosives and fertilizers |
| Phosphoric acid | $H_3PO_4$ | Removes hard-water deposits; used in making fertilizer |
| Carbonic acid | $H_2CO_3$ | Formed in carbonated drinks |
| Acetylsalicylic acid (aspirin) | $C_9H_8O_4$ | Reduces pain and inflammation |

Look at the formulas for the acids listed in Table 21.3. All of these acids contain a hydrogen atom that can be lost when the acid is in a water solution. The presence of hydrogen ions in acid solutions is responsible for most of the properties of acids.

## Properties of Bases

In some ways, bases are just the opposite of acids. Bases turn red litmus paper blue, and they neutralize acids. Bases taste bitter. They feel slippery because they react with oils in your skin to form soap. A solution containing a base is said to be *basic*.

Look at the formulas for the bases listed in Table 21.4. Except for baking soda, they all contain hydroxide ions that are given off when they are dissolved in water. The presence of these ions in water is responsible for most of the properties of bases.

Sodium hydroxide and potassium hydroxide are strong bases. Like strong acids, they are very dangerous and must be handled with care. Products such as oven and drain cleaners contain these bases because they can break down greases that make ovens grimy and clog drains.

## Table 21.4  Common Bases and Their Uses

| Name of Base | Formula | Uses |
|---|---|---|
| Sodium hydroxide | NaOH | Used in making soaps, detergents, drain and oven cleaners |
| Calcium hydroxide | Ca(OH)$_2$ | Softens water; neutralizes acid in soil; used in making mortar, plaster, and cement |
| Magnesium hydroxide | Mg(OH)$_2$ | Used in antacids |
| Ammonium hydroxide | NH$_4$OH | Used in cleaning solutions |
| Sodium bicarbonate (baking soda) | NaHCO$_3$ | Used in baking and cleaning |

**Figure 21.13** ▲
The litmus paper shows that this solution is basic.

## Forming a Salt

When an acid and a base react, the hydrogen ion from the acid and the hydroxide ion from the base combine to form water. What happens, then, to the rest of the acid and the rest of the base? They combine to form a **salt**. A salt is an ionic compound made up of a metal and a nonmetal. The metal part of the salt comes from the base and the nonmetal part comes from the acid.

The equation below shows a typical neutralization reaction.

$$\underset{\text{(acid)}}{\text{HNO}_3} + \underset{\text{(base)}}{\text{KOH}} \longrightarrow \underset{\text{(salt)}}{\text{KNO}_3} + \underset{\text{(water)}}{\text{HOH}}$$

The salt formed in this reaction, potassium nitrate, (KNO$_3$) contains the K$^+$ ion from the base and the NO$_3^-$ ion from the acid. By writing the water molecule as HOH, it's easier to see that the H and the OH come from different substances. You can make a wide variety of salts by mixing different acids and bases.

## The pH Scale

You know that both acids and bases vary in strength. These differences in strength can be measured very precisely. A measurement called **pH** tells how acidic or basic a solution is.

When measuring pH, the same scale of numbers is used for both acids and bases. Look at the pH scale in

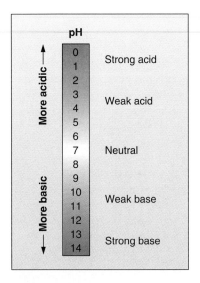

**Figure 21.14** ▲
The pH scale is used to describe the strength of acids and bases.

Figure 21.14. Notice the numbers on the scale range from 0 to 14. The midpoint, 7, represents the pH of a neutral solution. Solutions with a pH below 7 are acidic; the smaller the number, the stronger the acid. Solutions with a pH above 7 are basic. The larger the number is, the stronger the base is.

You can measure the pH of a solution with a substance called an indicator. An indicator changes color depending on a solution's pH. Each color corresponds to a pH number shown on a color chart for that indicator. Some indicators are solutions, such as phenolphthalein (FEE nohl THAL een). Other indicators are added to strips of paper. These strips, called pH papers, are then used for testing substances.

The indicator in pH paper, for example, turns a bright pink in a strong acid, such as hydrochloric acid. In sodium hydroxide, pH paper turns a dark blue. In a neutral solution, the paper turns greenish yellow.

## Consider This

### Should the pH of lakes be adjusted?

When fossil fuels are burned, sulfur oxides and nitrogen oxides are released into the atmosphere. These gases combine with water in the atmosphere to form sulfuric and nitric acids. Their presence reduces the pH of rain. When its pH falls below 5.6, rain is called *acid* rain.

Acid rain can concentrate in lakes and decrease the pH. When a lake's pH drops below 6, many of the plants and animals living in it begin to die. If enough plants and animals die, the entire body of water can become polluted. This is a problem in many of the lakes in the northeast region of the United States.

It is possible, however, to artificially raise the pH of a lake that has become too acidic. The base calcium carbonate is added to the lake in the form of powdered limestone. The calcium carbonate reacts with and neutralizes the acids in the lake. This process is called liming.

**Consider Some Issues**  Many people who enjoy fishing, boating, and the beauty of lakes believe lakes damaged by acid rain should be limed to keep them healthy. Others say the procedure is too expensive. It only treats the effects of the acid rain problem. It does not eliminate the causes. They also point out that poorly controlled liming can make a lake too basic.

**Think About It**  How important to you is saving fish and other living things in lakes? Is it worth the cost of liming? Should the acid rain problem be solved in another way?

**Write About It**  Write a paper stating your position for or against liming lakes. Include your reasons for choosing your position.

## Science and You *The pH of Your Blood*

Right now, something quite amazing is happening inside you. All sorts of adjustments are taking place automatically and continuously. One thing your body adjusts is the pH of your blood. Your body keeps the pH of your blood and other body fluids between 7.35 and 7.45.

The chemical reactions that occur in your body don't work very well in solutions with a pH below 7.35 or above 7.45. Your daily activities, however, can begin to push the pH of your blood out of this narrow range of safety. Eating certain foods, exercising, and becoming ill can change your blood pH.

The concentration of carbon dioxide in your blood is the main factor that determines the blood's pH. Carbon dioxide is carried in your blood as waste from cell respiration. It reacts with water in the blood to form carbonic acid. The greater the amount of carbon dioxide in the blood, the lower is the pH. Usually, the amount of carbon dioxide that enters the bloodstream is balanced by the amount removed through the lungs.

Whenever the amount of carbon dioxide in the blood changes, your body makes adjustments to bring it back in line. When your blood pH falls too low, you automatically exhale larger amounts of carbon dioxide. The concentration of carbonic acid in your blood goes down, and the pH goes up. When the pH of your blood gets too high, the opposite action brings the pH back down.

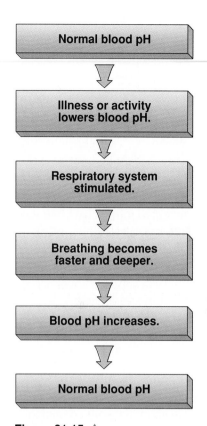

**Figure 21.15** ▲
What does your body do when the pH of your blood gets too high?

---

## Check and Explain

1. List two properties of acids and two properties of bases.

2. Describe two different ways you can tell whether a solution is acidic or basic.

3. **Classify** You test eight solutions and get the following pH measurements: 2.0, 6.5, 7.7, 8.0, 11.1, 1.7, 12.3, and 5.5. Classify these measurements into four groups.

4. **Predict** What salt forms when sodium hydroxide (NaOH) reacts with nitric acid ($HNO_3$)? What salt forms when potassium hydroxide (KOH) reacts with hydrochloric acid (HCl)?

# Activity 21   *What's an acid and what's a base?*

***Skills***   Observe; Infer; Interpret Data

## Task 1   Prelab Prep

Collect the following items: distilled water, 4 small glass containers, baking soda, colorless vinegar, red and blue litmus paper, phenolphthalein solution, and samples of at least four substances to be tested for pH. **CAUTION: Handle glassware carefully. Keep all chemicals away from your face.**

## Task 2   Data Record

1. On a separate sheet of paper, copy Table 21.5. Add an extra line for each sample.
2. Record all your observations.

## Task 3   Procedure

1. Put 5 mL of distilled water into three of the containers. Add a small amount of baking soda to the first container and stir. Label it *Baking Soda.* Add a small amount of vinegar to the second container and stir. Label it *Vinegar.* Don't add anything to the third container. Label it *Distilled Water.*
2. Test the liquids in the three containers with red and blue litmus paper. Record your observations. Then add 2 drops of phenolphthalein to the liquid in each container. Record your observations.
3. Put a small amount of the first sample to be tested in the fourth container. Test the sample with the litmus papers first and then with phenolphthalein. You may want to compare the test colors with those of the vinegar and baking soda solutions. Record your observations.
4. Test each of the remaining samples by repeating step 3.

## Task 4   Analysis

1. How does baking soda affect litmus paper and phenolphthalein? How does vinegar affect these indicators? What can you conclude from your observations?
2. What kind of substance is distilled water? Why might a water inspector test a sample of drinking water with an indicator?
3. Which substances affected the indicators in the same way as baking soda? Are these substances acids or bases?
4. Which substances tested the same as vinegar? Are these substances acids or bases?
5. Which substances tested the same as distilled water? Classify these substances.

## Task 5   Conclusion

Write a paragraph summarizing your findings. Which test method gave the clearer results? Can you use your data to determine the strength of each acid and base?

## *Everyday Application*

What generalizations can you make about the pH of foods? Of cleaning products?

## Table 21.5   pH Tests

| Substance | Red Litmus-Paper Test | Blue Litmus-Paper Test | Phenolphthalein Test |
|---|---|---|---|
| Baking soda | | | |
| Vinegar | | | |
| Distilled water | | | |

# Chapter 21 Review

## Concept Summary

### 21.1 Solutions
▶ A solution is a homogeneous mixture of two or more evenly mixed substances.
▶ The rate at which a solid dissolves in a liquid is affected by movement, temperature, and particle size.
▶ The solubility of one substance in another varies with temperature and, in the case of gases, pressure.
▶ A saturated solution contains as much solute as will dissolve at a certain temperature and pressure.

### 21.2 Suspensions and Colloids
▶ A suspension contains large particles that settle out on standing.

▶ A colloid contains particles smaller than those in a suspension but larger than those in a solution. The particles in a colloid don't settle out.

### 21.3 Acids, Bases, and Salts
▶ Acids are sour and turn blue litmus paper red.
▶ Bases are bitter, slippery, and turn red litmus paper blue.
▶ A salt forms when an acid and base neutralize each other.
▶ The pH of a solution indicates if it is an acid, a base, or neutral. A pH of 7 indicates a neutral solution.

## Chapter Vocabulary

| | | | |
|---|---|---|---|
| solution (21.1) | concentration (21.2) | suspension (21.2) | salt (21.3) |
| solvent (21.1) | saturated (21.1) | colloid (21.2) | pH (21.3) |
| solute (21.1) | unsaturated (21.1) | acid (21.3) | |
| solubility (21.1) | supersaturated (21.1) | base (21.3) | |

## Check Your Vocabulary

Use the vocabulary words above to complete the following sentences correctly.

1. A(n) ____ solution holds more solute than usual at a certain temperature.
2. A pH of 5.0 indicates a(n) ____ solution.
3. Particles settle out of a(n) ____.
4. Water is a(n) ____.
5. A solution that feels soapy is a(n) ____.
6. When an acid reacts with a base, water and a(n) ____ are formed.
7. The particles in a(n) ____ scatter light but don't settle out.
8. A substance that dissolves in a solvent becomes a(n) ____.
9. You can compare the strength of acids and bases by measuring their ____.

10. When more solute is added to a(n) ____ solution, the additional solute won't dissolve.
11. If a large amount of a substance will dissolve in water, it has a high ____.
12. You can dissolve more solute in a(n) ____ solution.
13. The amount of solute in a certain volume of solvent is called the solute's ____.
14. Another name for a homogeneous mixture is a(n) ____.

## Write Your Vocabulary
Write sentences using the vocabulary words above. Show that you know what each word means.

# Chapter 21 Review

## Check Your Knowledge

Answer the following in complete sentences.

1. How do particles behave in a solution?

2. Why can water dissolve so many different substances?

3. Why do stirring, heating, and smaller particle size increase solution rate?

4. How does a colloid differ from a suspension?

5. Why does a beam of light become visible in a colloid but not in a solution?

6. What is the major difference between the molecules of acids and bases?

7. How would you describe a salt?

8. How does a solution's pH number relate to how acidic or basic it is?

Determine whether each statement is true or false. Write *true* if it is true. If it is false, change the underlined term to make the statement true.

9. A solution that holds 2 g of NaCl in 100 mL of water is <u>more</u> dilute than a solution that holds 1 g of NaCl in 100 mL of water.

10. If you add a crystal of solute to a supersaturated solution, the crystal <u>will</u> dissolve in the solution.

11. If you were to shine a beam of light through dusty air, the beam would be <u>invisible</u>.

12. Silt deposited by a river tells you that river water is a <u>colloid</u>.

13. A solution with a pH of 3.5 is an <u>acid</u>.

14. A neutralization reaction produces water and a <u>base</u>.

## Check Your Understanding

Apply the concepts you have learned to answer each question.

1. In each of the following, what phases of matter make up the solute and the solvent?

   a. Ocean water

   b. Sweetened tea

   c. Gold jewelry

   d. Oxygen in an aquarium

   e. Poison gas sticking to charcoal

   f. Air

2. In a solution of 25 mL of water and 75 mL of alcohol, which substance is the solute and which is the solvent?

3. Colloids include many different mixtures of phases of matter but not gases dispersed in gases. Why?

4. Temperature affects both the rate at which a substance will dissolve and its solubility. Explain.

5. In what ways are solutions, suspensions, and colloids similar?

6. **Mystery Photo**  The photograph on page 514 shows a dye in water. If you stirred the mixture and took another photo a few minutes later, what would it look like?

7. **Application**  If you mix 100 mL of water and 100 mL of alcohol, the resulting solution has a volume of less than 200 mL! Explain this fact based on what you know about solutions and the particle model of matter.

8. Which is more concentrated? A solution of 10 g of KBr in 25 g of water or a solution of 25 g of KBr in 50 g of water?

## Develop Your Skills

Use the skills you have developed in this chapter to complete each activity.

1. **Model** Obtain blocks of clay and small objects of different colors and sizes, such as BBs, peas, or marbles. Embed the objects on the surface of the three blocks of clay to represent a solution, a suspension, and a colloid.

2. **Interpret Data** The graph below compares the amounts of three different substances that can dissolve in 100 g of water at temperatures between 0°C and 100°C.

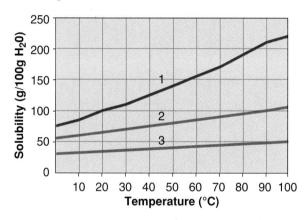

a. What is the difference in the solubility of chemical 2 at 20°C and at 100°C? How many more grams of chemical 2 can be dissolved in water at 100°C than at 20°C?

b. Is chemical 3 more soluble at 100°C than chemical 2 is at 0°C?

3. **Data Bank** Use the information on page 643 to answer the following questions.

a. What is the pH of toothpaste?

b. Which substance produced by the body is more acidic? Blood or digestive juices in the stomach?

c. What color does universal indicator become when added to a solution of sodium hydroxide?

## Make Connections

1. **Link the Concepts** Below is a concept map showing how some of the main concepts in this chapter link together. Only parts of the map are filled in. Copy the map. Using words and ideas from the chapter, complete the map.

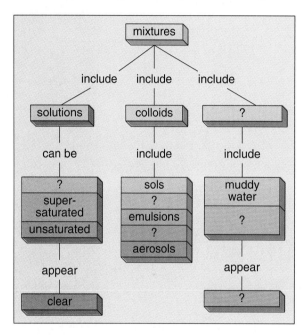

2. **Science and Literature** Expressing his feelings about the death of a friend, Daniel Defoe, author of *Robinson Crusoe*, wrote these lines:

> The best of men cannot suspend their fate
>
> The good die early, and the bad die late.

Compare Defoe's use of the word *suspend* with what you have learned about suspensions.

3. **Science and Technology** Find out what is being done to lower the emissions of nitrogen and sulfur oxides from power plants in order to reduce acid rain. What methods have been developed?

## Chapter 22

# Carbon Compounds and the Chemistry of Life

## Chapter Sections

**22.1** A World of Carbon

**22.2** Food Chemistry

**22.3** Energy in Living Things

## What do you see?

❝I see a tangle of lines. It looks like it could be inside of a cell. It could also be ropes tied together. It could be used to make a net or web of some kind, like a net hanging on a basketball rim.❞

*Steven Duke*
*Washington High School*
*Fremont, California*

To find out more about the photograph, look on page 558. As you read this chapter, you will learn about carbon compounds in living things.

# 22.1 A World of Carbon

## Objectives

▶ **Explain** why carbon can form many different compounds.

▶ **Distinguish** between saturated and unsaturated hydrocarbon molecules.

▶ **Describe** and give examples of isomers.

▶ **Make models** of simple hydrocarbons.

### ACTIVITY

**Comparing**

*Substance of Life*

List ten substances that you think came from, or were produced by, a living thing. Then write down similarities that any of these substances have.

**SKILLS WARMUP**

**W**hat has four arms and is found in hamburgers, clothing, oil, blood, trees, and plastics? The answer to this chemical riddle is in the title of this chapter—carbon. An atom of carbon doesn't really have four arms, but four is the number of bonds it can form with other atoms. This special characteristic makes carbon one of the most important elements. It is also the reason you can find carbon in things as different as hamburgers and trees.

## Carbon and Living Things

Carbon compounds are the chemicals of life. Every organism, dead or alive, and almost any substance produced by an organism, contain large numbers of carbon atoms. To carry on their life processes, organisms manufacture large carbon-containing molecules out of smaller molecules containing carbon. The main purpose of eating, in fact, is to provide your body with a source of carbon. Every cell in the giraffe's body, in Figure 22.1, is made of carbon compounds. The giraffe is consuming carbon as well.

The early scientists found carbon compounds only in organisms. They thought that organisms alone had the ability to produce carbon compounds. Today, carbon compounds are made daily in laboratories and in factories.

The direct connection between carbon and the living, or organic, world has survived in the scientific name originally given to carbon compounds. Nearly all compounds that contain carbon are still classified as **organic compounds**. Many organic compounds are not produced directly by organisms.

**Figure 22.1** ▲
All organisms need carbon compounds. How is the giraffe's eating leaves like your eating a salad?

## Structure of Organic Compounds

Carbon is essential to living things because its atoms can form the "backbone" of large molecules. Reach around and feel your backbone. It is made up of units called vertebrae (VUR tuh bree). In your upper back, each vertebra is attached to two other vertebrae and two ribs. The vertebrae thus form the core of your skeleton—the framework that holds your body together. Carbon atoms function very much like vertebrae when they form a molecule's "backbone."

A carbon atom has four electrons in its outer electron shell. These electrons can be shared in four covalent bonds with other atoms. For example, since a carbon atom can form four chemical bonds, it can bond with two other carbon atoms and still have two bonds left over to bond with other atoms.

**Figure 22.2** ▲

Carbon compounds make up many common items. This girl, the apple she's eating, and even her clothes are made up of carbon compounds.

**Carbon Backbone Shapes**  The basic backbone shape formed by carbon atoms is a straight chain. Like a string of beads, a molecule with a chain of carbon atoms can be any length. Many common organic compounds have chains dozens of carbon atoms long.

$$-\overset{|}{\underset{|}{C}}-\overset{|}{\underset{|}{C}}-\overset{|}{\underset{|}{C}}-\overset{|}{\underset{|}{C}}-\overset{|}{\underset{|}{C}}- \quad \text{Straight chain}$$

A second kind of carbon backbone is a branched chain. A different shape of molecules occurs when a carbon atom is bonded to three or four other carbons instead of only two. What other branched-chain shapes can you imagine?

$$-\overset{|}{\underset{|}{C}}-\overset{|}{\underset{|}{C}}-\overset{|}{\underset{|}{C}}-\overset{|}{\underset{|}{C}}- \quad \text{Branched chain}$$

In a third kind of arrangement, the ends of a carbon chain can be joined to form a circle, or ring. You can see a model of a carbon ring below.

Ring

**Carbon-Carbon Bonds** A carbon atom can share four pairs of electrons with other atoms. But, it doesn't have to share these electron pairs in four separate bonds. Two or even three pairs of electrons can be shared in bonding between two carbons.

When two atoms share two pairs of electrons, they form a *double covalent bond*. When they share three pairs, they form a *triple covalent bond*. The way to represent these types of carbon-carbon bonds on paper is shown in the figure below. Double and triple bonds can occur almost anywhere in a carbon chain, branched chain, or ring.

Single bond          Double bond          Triple bond

Double bonds in a chain

Double bond in a ring

Double and triple bond in a chain

## Hydrocarbons

Many materials you use contain only hydrogen and carbon atoms. Compounds with only hydrogen and carbon atoms are **hydrocarbons** (HY droh KAR buhnz). Hydrocarbons are made up of straight chains, branched chains, or rings of carbon atoms with hydrogen atoms attached.

Bonds that aren't carbon-carbon bonds in a hydrocarbon are carbon-hydrogen bonds. Hydrocarbons, such as oil and natural gas, are a major source of energy for heating buildings and running machines. Gasoline is made up of several different hydrocarbons. Other hydrocarbons are the raw materials used for making plastics, medicines, and synthetic materials, such as nylon and acrylic fibers.

**Environmental Science**
**L I N K**

To identify the hydrocarbons that make up recyclable plastics, a plastic container code system has been developed. Collect several different kinds of plastic containers. Look for a number in a triangle and some capital letters on each container. Make a list of the capital letter combinations. These letters are abbreviations of the hydrocarbon name. Match the ones you found with the name below.
- PETE (polyethylene-terephthalate)
- HDPE (high-density polyethylene)
- V (vinyl or polyvinyl chloride)
- PP (polypropylene)
- PS (polystyrene)

Which recyclable hydrocarbon was used most often at your house?

**A C T I V I T Y**

The simplest hydrocarbon is the compound methane (MEHTH ayn). You can see in Figure 22.3 that a methane molecule has only a single carbon atom. How do you write the formula for methane?

A hydrocarbon with two carbon atoms is ethane. The two carbon atoms in ethane share one bond with each other. That leaves each carbon atom with three bonds left to share with hydrogen atoms. The formula for ethane is $C_2H_6$. How would a space-filling model for ethane differ from the methane molecule shown?

Some hydrocarbons contain double or triple bonds between carbon atoms. The simplest hydrocarbon with a double bond is ethene (EHTH een). Find ethene's formula and structure in Table 22.1. How is ethene different from ethane? A special property of a double bond, such as the one in ethene, is that it prevents the two carbon atoms that share it from rotating around one another. What would a space-filling model of an ethene molecule look like?

**Figure 22.3  Methane** ▼

Methane is one carbon atom bonded with four hydrogen atoms. Each shared pair of electrons making up a bond is shown as a single line.

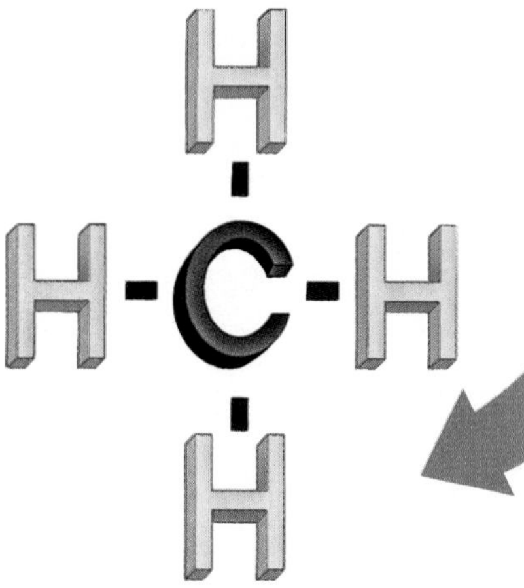

A space-filling model of a methane molecule shows how it looks in three dimensions.

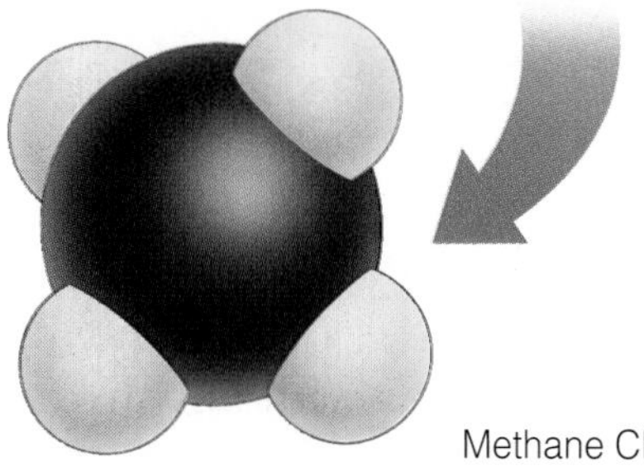

Methane $CH_4$

**Table 22.1  Common Hydrocarbons**

| Name, Formula, and Structure | | | | |
|---|---|---|---|---|
| **Methane** $CH_4$ | **Ethane** $C_2H_6$ | **Propane** $C_3H_8$ | **Butane** $C_4H_{10}$ | **Ethene** $C_2H_4$ |
| H<br>&#124;<br>H&minus;C&minus;H<br>&#124;<br>H | H  H<br>&#124; &#124;<br>H&minus;C&minus;C&minus;H<br>&#124; &#124;<br>H  H | H  H  H<br>&#124; &#124; &#124;<br>H&minus;C&minus;C&minus;C&minus;H<br>&#124; &#124; &#124;<br>H  H  H | H  H  H  H<br>&#124; &#124; &#124; &#124;<br>H&minus;C&minus;C&minus;C&minus;C&minus;H<br>&#124; &#124; &#124; &#124;<br>H  H  H  H | H    H<br>\  /<br>C=C<br>/  \<br>H    H |

## Unsaturated Hydrocarbons

Hydrocarbons in which all the carbon atoms are joined to one another by single covalent bonds are called **saturated hydrocarbons**. A saturated hydrocarbon has hydrogen or other atoms bonded to its carbon atoms.

In contrast, hydrocarbons that contain carbon-carbon double or triple bonds are called **unsaturated hydrocarbons**. All their carbon atoms aren't "saturated" with other atoms. Each double or triple carbon-carbon bond can be turned into a single carbon bond, making it possible to add additional atoms to the molecule.

## Polymers

Plastics are made up of very long carbon-containing molecules. They are created by joining together large numbers of much smaller hydrocarbon molecules. Any similar type of molecule, formed from the covalent bonding of smaller repeated units, is called a **polymer** (PAHL uh muhr). The molecules from which a polymer is made are called *monomers*.

## Isomers

What's the structure of the hydrocarbon with the formula $C_4H_{10}$? If you think it is a molecule with four carbons in a row, you're right. But, that isn't the only correct answer!

Actually, two different compounds have the formula $C_4H_{10}$. You can see what they look like in Figure 22.4. When more than one structure exists for one chemical formula, each structure is called an **isomer** (EYE soh mur) of the other. Isomers have different properties because their atoms are arranged differently. The greater the number of carbon atoms in a molecule, the more isomers it's likely to have. How many isomers can you draw for $C_5H_{12}$?

Look at Figure 22.5. It shows another kind of isomer, a geometric isomer. Geometric isomers have the same atoms and bonds in the same order. However, they have a different arrangement of atoms around a double bond. Remember that the carbons sharing a double bond can't rotate. Therefore, the two molecules in Figure 22.5 can't become the same.

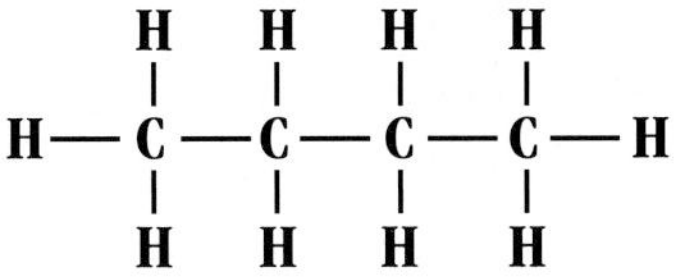

Butane ($C_4H_{10}$)

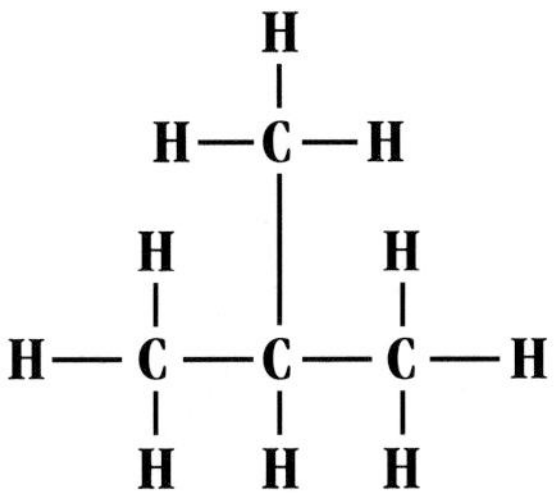

Methylpropane ($C_4H_{10}$)

**Figure 22.4** ▲
How do the structures of these isomers differ?

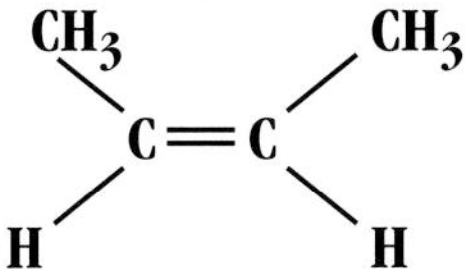

*Cis*-2-butene ($C_4H_8$)

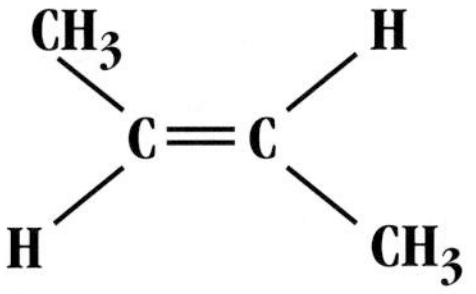

*Trans*-2-butene ($C_4H_8$)

**Figure 22.5** ▲
What is the difference between these two geometric isomers?

# Substituted Hydrocarbons

**Figure 22.6** ▲

Many different esters combine to produce the aromas that you recognize as banana, pineapple, or grape.

What happens when you remove one of the hydrogen atoms of a hydrocarbon and replace it with another kind of atom or group of atoms? You create a **substituted hydrocarbon**. The atom or group of atoms substituted for hydrogen is called a *functional group*. Common functional groups are single atoms of a halogen, and other groups such as hydroxyls (-OH) and amines ($-NH_2$). Each functional group brings a certain set of chemical properties to its molecule.

Among the substituted hydrocarbons are alcohols. In alcohols, an -OH group has been substituted for a hydrogen atom. The simplest alcohol is methanol. Look at Table 22.2 to see the formula and structure of methanol.

The carboxylic (KAR bahk SIHL ihk) acids are another group of substituted hydrocarbons. They contain the functional group -COOH, the structure of which is shown in Table 22.2. The acid in vinegar, acetic acid, is a carboxylic acid.

When a carboxylic acid and an alcohol react, they form an ester (EHS tur). Most esters have a pleasant smell and taste. Esters produce the aromas of pineapples, apples, oranges, bananas, and apricots.

When a halogen atom, such as a chlorine or a bromine, substitutes for a hydrogen atom in a hydrocarbon, a halocarbon (HAL uh KAR buhn) forms. Very few halocarbons are found in nature. They are manufactured and used for many different purposes. Examples of halocarbons include chloroform ($CHCl_3$), which is used as a general anesthetic, and carbon tetrachloride, ($CCl_4$), which is used in dry cleaning.

**Table 22.2   Common Substituted Hydrocarbons**

| Name, Type, Formula, and Structure | | | |
|---|---|---|---|
| **Methanol** | **Acetic acid** | **Ethyl acetate** | **Methyl chloride** |
| Alcohol $CH_3OH$ | Carboxylic acid $CH_3COOH$ | Ester $CH_3COOHC_2H_5$ | Halocarbon $CH_3Cl$ |
| 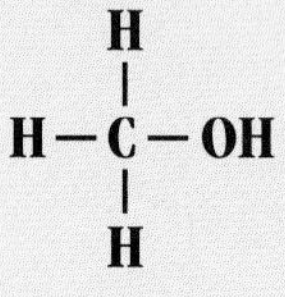 $H$ <br> $\vert$ <br> $H-C-OH$ <br> $\vert$ <br> $H$ | 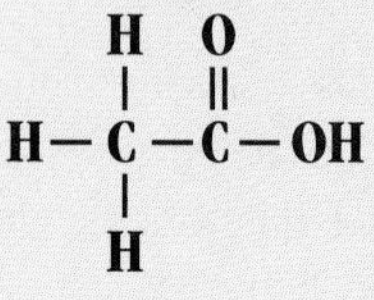 $H\quad O$ <br> $\vert\quad\parallel$ <br> $H-C-C-OH$ <br> $\vert$ <br> $H$ | 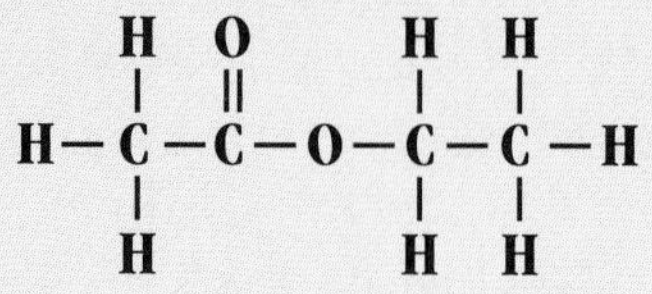 $H\quad O\quad\quad H\quad H$ <br> $\vert\quad\parallel\quad\quad\vert\quad\vert$ <br> $H-C-C-O-C-C-H$ <br> $\vert\quad\quad\quad\vert\quad\vert$ <br> $H\quad\quad\quad H\quad H$ | 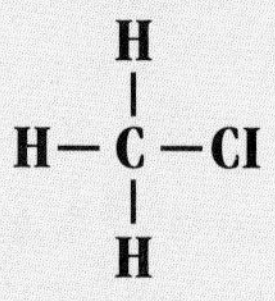 $H$ <br> $\vert$ <br> $H-C-Cl$ <br> $\vert$ <br> $H$ |

## Science and Technology   *Presto! Plastics!*

A student in the laboratory holds a large beaker. It contains two liquids, one is clear and one is translucent. The liquids are layered in the beaker, one above the other. The student explains that the two liquids have been heated but don't mix. The student dips tweezers to where the two solutions meet. She pulls the tweezers up, and to everyone's astonishment, a solid fiber clings to them. The fiber is nylon, a synthetic polymer.

The two liquids in the beaker are solutions of different organic compounds. Each compound has a certain functional group on each end. The functional groups of the two compounds react with each other at the boundary between the two solutions. Monomers link together in long strings to form nylon. The long strings of monomers make up the nylon polymer.

Synthetic polymers such as nylon have many useful features. They are strong, light, and very durable. When researchers tested materials to use for artificial body parts, such as knee joints and heart valves, they chose synthetic polymers.

Synthetic polymers are used in many other products. For example, automobiles are becoming lighter and more fuel efficient because polymers are quickly replacing heavy metal parts. Polymers also turn up in such various items as telephones, toothbrushes, pop bottles, and tennis rackets. Name other items you use daily that are made from polymers.

**▼ ACTIVITY**

**Applying**

*Plastic*

List all the plastic objects that you used or came across today. For each object, give a reason why it is made from plastic and not another material.

**SKILLS WORKOUT**

## Check and Explain

1. Why can carbon form more compounds than other elements?

2. What is the difference between a saturated hydrocarbon and an unsaturated hydrocarbon?

3. **Predict** How many isomers exist for the formula $C_6H_{14}$?

4. **Make a Model** Make three-dimensional models of simple hydrocarbons. Use polystyrene balls of two different sizes to represent carbon and hydrogen atoms. Use toothpicks to represent the bonds. Base your models on structural diagrams in this chapter.

# Activity 22  How can you capture a scent?

**Skills**  Measure; Observe; Infer

## Task 1  Prelab Prep
1. Collect the following items: 2 labels, pen, 2 small jars with lids, 30 whole cloves, water, and rubbing alcohol. **CAUTION: Keep rubbing alcohol away from your mouth. It is a poison.**
2. On one label write *Water* and on the other write *Rubbing Alcohol*.
3. Attach a label to each jar.

## Task 2  Data Record
1. On a separate sheet of paper, draw a data table like the one shown.
2. Record all your observations about the solutions in the data table like the one at the bottom of the page.

## Task 3  Procedure
1. Place 15 whole cloves in each jar.
2. Fill one jar half full with water. Fill the other jar half full with rubbing alcohol.
3. Close both jars and screw the lids on tightly. Don't open the jars for one full week.
4. When the week is over, put a few drops of the liquid from the water jar on your left wrist. Put a few drops of the alcohol solution on your right wrist. When the liquids evaporate, smell each wrist.

## Task 4  Analysis
1. Which liquid had the strongest scent?
2. Why are water and alcohol called solvents in this activity?

3. In the jar with the strongest scent, what substance do you think dissolved from the cloves? If you removed the cloves from the liquid, would the liquid still have the same scent a week from now? Give reasons for your answer.

## Task 5  Conclusion
In a short paragraph explain how the scent from the cloves formed in the liquids. Hint: think of how this relates to the scent of fruits like pineapples and bananas.

## Everyday Application
Many food colorings are made from the leaves of plants. Orange and vanilla and other liquid flavorings are made from other plant parts, such as peels and beans. Read the labels on bottles of such products. Based on what you read, what can you conclude about the solvents used to make food colorings and liquid flavors?

## Extension
Experiment with various spices, herbs, and flower petals to make your own perfumes. Select both dry and fresh spices, herbs, and flower petals. Experiment by using the items whole and ground up. Identify any difference between fresh and dried materials. How does grinding or crushing affect the strength of the perfumes? Which solvent from this experiment is better to use for perfumes? Why?

## Table 22.3  Clove Perfumes

| Solvent | Observations |
|---------|--------------|
| Water   |              |
| Alcohol |              |

# 22.2 Food Chemistry

## Objectives

▶ **Give examples** of foods that are rich in carbohydrates, lipids, and proteins.

▶ **Describe** the general chemical structure of each group of nutrients.

▶ **Contrast** saturated and unsaturated lipids.

▶ **Make a table** comparing the roles of carbohydrates, lipids, and proteins in human nutrition.

**A**re you getting hungry for some good, tasty organic compounds? When you eat your next meal, you will probably take into your body hundreds of different organic compounds. Your body will break down most of these compounds into simpler substances during the process of digestion. The products of digestion will then be used for energy and as building blocks for new substances you need to live and grow.

Organic compounds in foods are classified in three main groups: carbohydrates, lipids, and proteins. These organic compounds are called nutrients. Each group of nutrients plays a different role in the body.

## Carbohydrates

The runners in Figure 22.7 are competing in a marathon. Since a marathon can take more than two hours to complete, a lot of energy will be needed. Much of the energy used during the race will be released from organic compounds stored in each athlete's body. These energy-providing compounds are called **carbohydrates** (KAR boh HY drayts). Carbohydrates are organic compounds that contain hydrogen and oxygen atoms in a ratio of two to one.

About three days before a marathon, a runner begins "carbohydrate loading." The runner eats large amounts of breads, pasta, grains, and potatoes, which are all rich in carbohydrates. Carbohydrate loading provides the marathon runner with a supply of stored carbohydrates large enough to last the race.

**Figure 22.7**
These runners prepared to run this race by eating extra carbohydrates beforehand. ▼

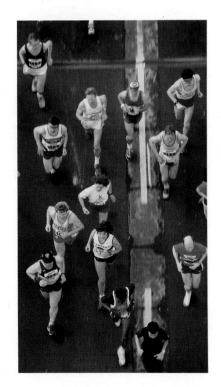

Carbohydrates aren't just for athletes. Everyone relies on them as a basic source of energy for life processes. For most people, carbohydrates make up the largest part of their diet.

Most of the carbohydrates you eat are in the form of starch. A starch is a polymer made up of simpler carbohydrates called sugars. Your body breaks down starches into sugars because sugars are the carbohydrates your cells use for energy.

An important simple sugar is *glucose* (GLOO kohs). It has the formula $C_6H_{12}O_6$. Look at Figure 22.8 to see the structure of glucose. How is it different from other organic compounds you studied? Glucose is one of the main products of digestion of starches. Glucose is sent through your blood to all the cells in your body. Your cells break the chemical bonds in glucose to release the energy stored in them.

Although sugars are your cells' actual energy source, your body works best when it takes in starches and converts them to sugars. Nutritionists recommend that about 55 to 60 percent of the Calories you take in daily should be from starchy carbohydrates like those in Figure 22.8. What other foods do you think are high in starch?

**Figure 22.8**

Carbohydrates provide energy for your body the way wood fuels a fire. ▼

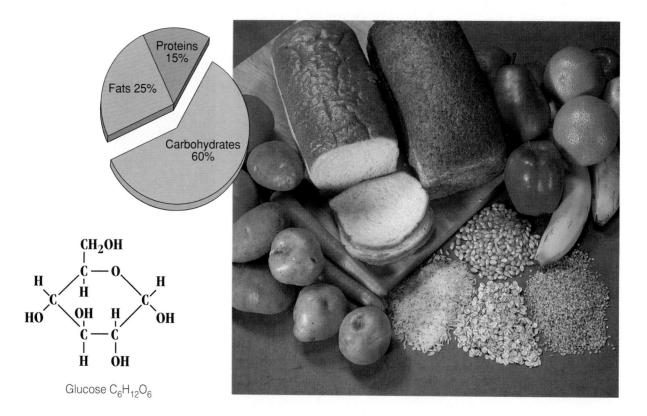

Glucose $C_6H_{12}O_6$

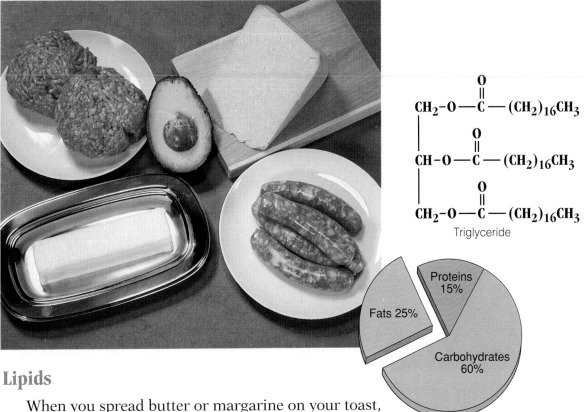

$$CH_2-O-\overset{\displaystyle O}{\overset{\|}{C}}-(CH_2)_{16}CH_3$$

$$CH-O-\overset{\displaystyle O}{\overset{\|}{C}}-(CH_2)_{16}CH_3$$

$$CH_2-O-\overset{\displaystyle O}{\overset{\|}{C}}-(CH_2)_{16}CH_3$$

Triglyceride

Proteins 15%

Fats 25%

Carbohydrates 60%

**Figure 22.9** ▲

Fats and oils help to insulate your body from cold the way a blanket does.

## Lipids

When you spread butter or margarine on your toast, you are adding organic compounds that belong to a second group of nutrients. These nutrients, which include fats and oils, are called **lipids** (LIHP ihdz). Lipids are organic compounds that have long hydrocarbon chains and don't dissolve in water.

Your body uses lipids to produce substances that protect nerves, insulate you from the cold, and transmit messages among organs. Lipids, like carbohydrates, can also be used as an energy source. Gram for gram, however, lipids contain more energy than carbohydrates. Thus, when you take in a large amount of lipids, not all of them can be used. Excess lipids get stored as body fat. For this reason, less than 25 percent of the Calories you take in should come from fats and oils.

You should also be concerned about what kinds of lipids you eat. Lipids that contain only single bonds are called saturated lipids. These are found mostly in animal foods, such as meats, poultry, and dairy products. Eating large amounts of saturated lipids may be a major cause of heart disease. Unsaturated lipids, which have double bonds in their structures, are better for your body. Olive oil, peanut oil, canola oil, and other oils from plants all contain mostly unsaturated lipids.

## Proteins

What do dried beans, nuts, eggs, dairy products, and meats have in common? They are all rich in a third group of nutrients called **proteins** (PROH teenz). Proteins are large, complex molecules made up of 20 different building blocks called amino (uh MEE noh) acids. Amino acids are organic molecules that contain both a carboxyl group (-COOH) and an amine group ($-NH_2$). The structure of one of the amino acids is shown in Figure 22.10.

When you eat a protein, it is broken down into the amino acids that make it up. The cells in your body use these amino acids to build your body's own proteins. To make a protein, a cell links together different amino acids in a certain order, like beads on a string. Each protein has its own unique order of amino acids.

The proteins made by your cells serve many functions. They are the chief materials that make up new cells. They help transport oxygen throughout the body. As catalysts, or enzymes, they help digest food and make thousands of other vital chemical reactions possible.

Your body produces some, but not all, of the amino acids it needs. To obtain the amino acids your body doesn't make, you must eat foods that contain them. Eggs, dairy products, and meats contain all the amino acids your body needs. You can also get these amino acids by eating a combination of dried beans and grains.

**Figure 22.10**

Proteins are the materials that your body uses to build new cells, just as construction workers build a house out of wood or brick. ▼

Proteins 15%

Fats 25%

Carbohydrates 60%

$$H_2N - \overset{\overset{\displaystyle H}{|}}{\underset{\underset{\displaystyle H}{|}}{C}} - CO_2H$$

Glycine

You've probably seen row upon row of bottles of vitamin pills in the store. If you read the label of a multiple-vitamin product, you'll see it contains vitamins A, C, D, E, K, and several different B vitamins. What are vitamins and why are they essential?

Vitamins are special nutrients not classified as carbohydrates, lipids, or proteins. Their structures vary, but all vitamins are organic compounds necessary for your body to function properly. Most vitamins work together with enzymes to make possible the chemical reactions that occur in your body.

By eating a well-balanced diet, you can get all the vitamins you need. Meats, eggs, and dairy products contain B vitamins and vitamins A, D, and K. Citrus fruits and tomatoes are rich sources of vitamin C. Green, leafy vegetables have large amounts of vitamins A, E, and K. Dried beans and grains provide you with B vitamins.

## *Career Corner* Food Scientist

### Who Develops New Food Products?

Almost every month a new food product comes to your market. Nonfat ice cream, sugarless cakes, and salt-free cereals are some examples. Who is responsible for these new foods? Researchers known as food scientists create them.

Food scientists often work to produce foods that are healthier for people to eat. They may find ways to make foods taste good, even though the foods have less fat, sugar, or salt.

Some food scientists may work with other scientists to test special diets on animals, or even on people, to see how diet might prevent or cure certain diseases. Food scientists also search for ways to keep foods fresh longer so they won't spoil on supermarket shelves or soon after you bring them home.

Food scientists may also test foods to make sure they are safe. Safety standards for food are set by government agencies such as the Food and Drug Administration, or FDA. Some food scientists work for the FDA to monitor the quality of manufactured foods, such as meats, vegetables, fruits, and seafood.

A person with a bachelor's degree in biology or nutrition may work as a food scientist. But, food-science jobs related to creating new foods may require advanced degrees.

## ▼ ACTIVITY

### Making a Table

*Vitamins*

List in a table the vitamins mentioned on this page. Next to each vitamin, write down the foods you ate today with that vitamin in it. Which vitamins are missing from your diet?

**SKILLS WORKOUT**

Your body doesn't need any of the essential vitamins in large amounts. However, some amount of each vitamin is important to your health. Many people in the world have diets that lack a sufficient amount of one or more vitamins. These people often suffer from what is called a deficiency disease.

Look at Table 22.4. It lists some essential vitamins, their function, and the deficiency disease caused by a lack of the vitamin. Some people take vitamin supplements to be sure they get enough vitamins. However, excessive amounts of some vitamins can be harmful.

**Table 22.4  Vitamins**

| Vitamin | Function | Deficiency Disease |
|---|---|---|
| A | Maintains healthy skin, eyes, and bones | Night blindness; permanent blindness |
| B (complex) | Needed to break down carbohydrates, fats, and proteins, and to manufacture proteins | Beriberi; loss of appetite; skin disorders; anemia |
| C | Helps in the formation of bones | Scurvy; slow healing; gum disease |
| D | Promotes bone growth; helps the body use calcium | Rickets |
| E | Prevents damage to cell membranes | Breakdown of red blood cells; anemia |
| K | Helps blood to clot | Uncontrolled bleeding |

## Check and Explain

1. What are two foods that are a good source of carbohydrates? Of fats? Of protein?

2. What is the difference between a saturated and an unsaturated fat?

3. **Compare and Contrast**  How are the chemical structures of carbohydrates, lipids, and proteins similar? How are they different?

4. **Make a Table**  Compare the roles of carbohydrates, fats, and proteins in human nutrition.

# 22.3 Energy in Living Things

## Objectives

▶ **Describe** the flow of energy from the sun through plants and animals.

▶ **Summarize** the process of photosynthesis.

▶ **Explain** what occurs during cell respiration.

▶ **Make a model** that shows how respiration is the reverse of photosynthesis.

Powered by contracting muscles, your feet, legs, arms, and torso move to the rhythm of the music at your school's dance. You're using energy stored in your body, energy that not only keeps you dancing but keeps you alive. Where does this all-important energy come from?

If you say your energy comes from food, you are right. But what is the source of the energy in food? The leaves, fruits, seeds, milk, meat, and eggs that you eat are made up of organic compounds. These compounds all contain energy in their chemical bonds.

Look at Figure 22.11. You can see that the original source of all the energy in the organic compounds you eat is the sun. Plants are an important link in this flow of energy. Plants are used as food by many animals. You use both plants and animals as food. Plants can capture the sun's energy and store it in the bonds of organic compounds. How are plants able to do this?

◀ **Figure 22.11**
The energy in a hamburger you eat originated from the sun.

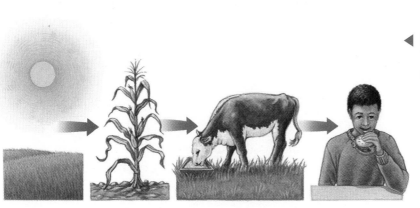

Energy from the sun

Corn receives sun's energy

Cattle eat corn

People eat beef

**Figure 22.12**
**Photosynthesis** ▼

# Photosynthesis: Storing Solar Energy

You know the sun beams energy to the earth. You can feel the energy as heat. You can see the energy as light. The energy from the sun feels good and lets you see everything around you. But, since you aren't a plant, you can't use the sun's energy directly to power your muscles or carry on all the other life processes in your body.

Plants capture the energy of the sun in a chemical process called **photosynthesis** (FOHT oh SIHN thuh sihs). During photosynthesis, water and carbon dioxide are combined to make glucose and oxygen. The glucose molecule produced in photosynthesis contains in its chemical bonds the energy absorbed from sunlight.

Sun

Energy

The sun radiates light energy to the earth. Plants absorb this light energy and convert it into stored chemical energy in the process of photosynthesis.

Plants grow toward the sun. Their leaves expose a large surface area to sunlight.

The roots of plants reach down into the soil where they absorb water and nutrients.

Water

Plant cells

Leaves not only take in the sun's energy but also absorb carbon dioxide, which is needed for photosynthesis. Water is carried to the leaf through the stem.

Oxygen

Carbon dioxide

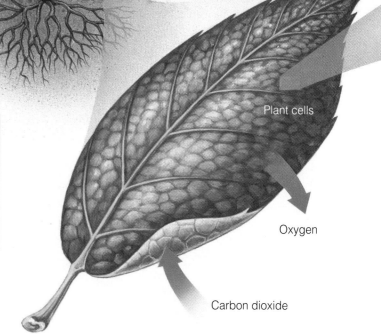

Plants carry on photosynthesis in the cells of their leaves. Each of these cells contains a kind of glucose factory, a chloroplast (KLOR uh PLAST). Chloroplasts have inside them all the compounds and structures needed to carry out the reactions needed for photosynthesis to take place.

Plants use the glucose they produce to make the larger organic compounds they need to live and grow. These organic compounds include carbohydrates, lipids, and proteins. Like glucose, the chemical bonds of these compounds store energy that originally came from the sun.

Cells near the top surface of the leaf are specialized for photosynthesis.

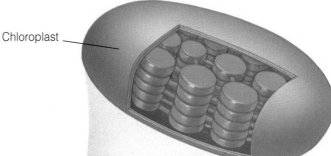

Chloroplast

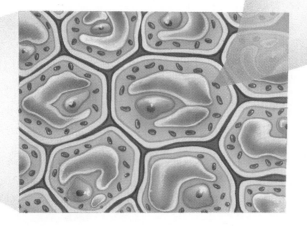

The chemical reactions of photosynthesis occur inside the cell's chloroplast. These cell structures contain chlorophyll, the green pigment that captures light energy from the sun.

$$6CO_2 \ + \ 6H_2O \ + \ \text{Light Energy} \longrightarrow C_6H_{12}O_6 \ + \ 6O_2$$

During photosynthesis, carbon dioxide, $CO_2$, from the air combines with water, $H_2O$, from the soil. Light energy from the sun creates chemical bonds.

Glucose, $C_6H_{12}O_6$, is the sugar the plant uses as food. The plant stores food as starch.

Oxygen, $O_2$, produced during photosynthesis is released into the atmosphere. Animals use oxygen to live.

# Cell Respiration: Using Energy

How does your body get energy from food? The first step in the process is digestion. Chewing and stomach contractions help break the food you eat into small pieces. Acids and enzymes in the stomach work to break down the small pieces. Eventually, the food breaks down into the molecules it's made of. Some of those molecules are glucose molecules. After digestion, your bloodstream carries the glucose from your digestive system to all the cells of your body.

To harvest the energy in the chemical bonds of glucose, your cells need oxygen. This oxygen comes from the air you breathe. It is picked up from the lungs by red blood cells and then carried to your body cells.

With a supply of both oxygen and glucose, your cells carry out the process called **respiration**. During respiration, oxygen reacts with glucose, breaking the bonds in glucose and releasing their energy.

## *SkillBuilder*  *Interpreting Data*

### *The Best Light for Photosynthesis*

You know that sunlight is actually made up of light of many different wavelengths. Each wavelength corresponds to a different color of light. Scientists have observed that plants can absorb light of certain wavelengths better than others. This infers that plants use only certain colors of light to manufacture glucose during photosynthesis.

The graph to the right shows how the rate of photosynthesis in a plant varies according to the wavelength of light that strikes it. Study the graph and answer the following questions.

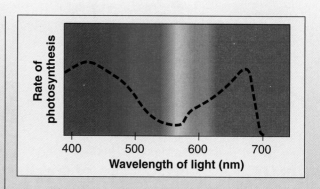

1. What colors of light produce the highest rate of photosynthesis? What are the approximate wavelengths of these colors?

2. What colors of light produce the lowest rate of photosynthesis?

3. What color of light has the sharpest drop rate?

4. If the only light a plant receives has wavelengths of between 500 and 600 nanometers (nm), what will happen to the growth rate of the plant? Why?

Write a paragraph describing how light of different wavelengths affects the growth of plants. Include an explanation of why the leaves of many plants appear green.

The equation below summarizes the respiration process.

$$C_6H_{12}O_6 + 6O_2 \longrightarrow 6CO_2 + 6H_2O + \text{energy}$$

The equation probably looks familiar to you. Actually, you've seen it before—in reverse. Respiration is, in many ways, the opposite of photosynthesis, as you can see in Table 22.5.

**Table 22.5 Photosynthesis versus Respiration**

| Photosynthesis | Respiration |
| --- | --- |
| Uses water | Gives off water |
| Uses carbon dioxide | Gives off carbon dioxide |
| Makes glucose | Breaks down glucose |
| Gives off oxygen | Uses oxygen |
| Takes in energy (sunlight) | Releases energy |
| Occurs only in cells of plants and some bacteria and protists | Occurs in cells of all organisms |

A major difference between photosynthesis and respiration is that respiration takes place constantly and photosynthesis doesn't. Study the formulas again. Notice that respiration gives off energy. Light energy is not needed for respiration to take place. However, for photosynthesis to take place, light energy must be present. Photosynthesis can't take place in the dark!

Much of the energy released during respiration is in the form of heat. The rest of the energy, however, is stored in the chemical bonds of a compound called adenosine triphosphate (ATP). Unlike glucose, a molecule of ATP easily gives up the energy stored in it. Molecules of ATP can move around the cell and power any chemical reaction. When you dance, for example, the energy of ATP molecules in your muscle cells is converted into kinetic energy.

Respiration, or some related process, occurs in all known organisms. Even plants, the makers of glucose, must respire to harness the energy they capture from the sun. Respiration and photosynthesis fit together to form the energy cycle of life on earth.

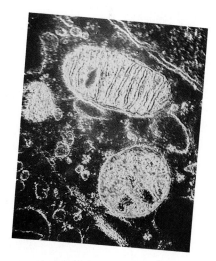

**Figure 22.13** ▲
Mitochondria, like those shown here, are often called the powerhouses of a cell. ATP is produced in mitochondria by respiration.

## Science and You
### *Your Body's Energy Budget*

The amount of energy in the food you eat is usually in balance with the amount of energy your body uses. As you may know, the amount of energy you use varies with your level of activity. When you are resting, you use only 60 to 70 Calories per hour. During heavy exercise, you may use over 2,000 Calories per hour. To stay in balance, then, you should eat more if you're active and less if you're not.

If you take in more Calories than you use, excess Calories are stored as fat, and you gain weight. If you take in fewer Calories than you use, your body uses stored fat for energy, and you lose weight. However, each person extracts energy from food at a different rate. This rate is called your metabolic rate. Two people may eat and exercise exactly the same, but only one of them gains weight because their metabolic rates differ.

If you have a weight problem, a doctor may want to measure your metabolic rate. If your metabolic rate is fast, it might account for your being underweight. If your metabolic rate is slow, it may explain why you're overweight.

One way to determine metabolic rate is to measure the amount of oxygen used by your body in a given period of time. You breathe into a respirometer (REHS pur AH muh tur) like the one in Figure 22.14. Soda lime in the respirometer reacts with the carbon dioxide you exhale and removes it. Every molecule of oxygen used in respiration produces one molecule of carbon dioxide. By measuring the amount of carbon dioxide, your doctor can tell how much oxygen your body uses.

**Figure 22.14** ▲
A device called a respirometer measures how much oxygen your body uses. How does the amount of oxygen used relate to your metabolic rate?

## Check and Explain

1. Summarize the process of photosynthesis by writing a word equation.

2. What happens during cell respiration?

3. **Infer**  What might happen if many of the plants on the earth died?

4. **Make a Model**  Draw a diagram or other model that shows respiration is the reverse of photosynthesis.

# Chapter 22  Review

## Concept Summary

### 22.1  A World of Carbon
▶ Carbon is part of many different compounds because a carbon atom can form bonds with four other atoms.
▶ Carbon atoms form straight chains, branched chains, and rings.
▶ A saturated hydrocarbon has single bonds between all carbon atoms; an unsaturated hydrocarbon has at least one double or triple bond.
▶ When more than one structure exists for a formula, each structure is called an isomer.

### 22.2  Food Chemistry
▶ Carbohydrates serve as the body's main energy source.

▶ Lipids are used by the body to make substances that are necessary for its functioning. Some lipids are saturated, others are unsaturated.
▶ Proteins provide the body with the amino acids it needs to make other proteins.

### 22.3  Energy in Living Things
▶ Through photosynthesis, plants convert sunlight into chemical energy stored in the chemical bonds of glucose.
▶ Living things constantly release the energy stored in glucose through the process of respiration.
▶ Together, photosynthesis and respiration make it possible for organisms to use the sun's energy.

---

## Chapter Vocabulary

organic compound (22.1)      polymer (22.1)      lipids (22.2)
hydrocarbon (22.1)      isomer (22.1)      protein (22.2)
saturated hydrocarbon (22.1)      substituted hydrocarbon (22.1)      photosynthesis (22.3)
unsaturated hydrocarbon (22.1)      carbohydrate (22.2)      respiration (22.3)

---

## Check Your Vocabulary

Use the vocabulary words above to complete the following sentences correctly.

1. By replacing a hydrogen atom in a hydrocarbon with another kind of atom, you make a(n) _____ .

2. Only green plants can undergo _____ .

3. Nearly all compounds that contain carbon atoms are called _____ .

4. A(n) _____ is formed from the linking of many monomers.

5. A(n) _____ is made up of many amino acids.

6. Fats and oils are classified as _____ .

7. Glucose and starch are _____ .

8. A(n) _____ contains only carbon and hydrogen atoms.

9. Compounds with identical formulas but different structures are called _____ .

10. A(n) _____ contains only single bonds between carbon atoms.

11. Living things release the energy stored in glucose through the process of _____ .

12. An organic compound with a double or triple carbon bond is called a(n) _____ .

## Write Your Vocabulary

Write sentences using the vocabulary words above. Show that you know what each word means.

# Chapter 22 Review

## Check Your Knowledge

Answer the following in complete sentences.

1. Why is carbon considered to be one of the most important elements on the earth?

2. How does a hydrocarbon differ from a substituted hydrocarbon?

3. What is the main identifying characteristic of a carbohydrate molecule?

4. Why should you limit your intake of saturated lipids?

5. What are the compounds that make up proteins? What functional groups do they contain?

6. Why are vitamins important nutrients?

7. Explain the relationship between photosynthesis and respiration.

Choose the answer that best completes each sentence.

8. A carbon atom can form (one, two, three, four) bonds.

9. The simplest hydrocarbon is (methane, ethane, propane, butane).

10. Proteins are the only nutrients that contain (oxygen, nitrogen, hydrogen, carbon).

11. The ratio of hydrogen to oxygen atoms in a carbohydrate is (1:1, 2:1, 3:1, 4:1).

12. During photosynthesis, energy is stored in the chemical bonds of (glucose, carbon dioxide, oxygen, water).

13. The products of respiration include carbon dioxide and (glucose, methane, oxygen, water).

14. A saturated hydrocarbon contains only (single, double, triple, protein) bonds.

## Check Your Understanding

Apply the concepts you have learned to answer each question.

1. **Classify** Which of the following are organic compounds?

   a. $CCl_4$      d. $HCl$
   b. $C_6H_6$     e. $CH_4$
   c. $NaCl$     f. $C_2H_5OH$

2. **Infer** If you discovered that a particular hydrocarbon had two carbon atoms and two hydrogen atoms, would you conclude that it was saturated or unsaturated? Why?

3. **Compare and Contrast** How are methane and chloroform similar? How are they different?

4. **Infer** If you were given a mystery organic compound and found that it contained atoms of nitrogen, what might you infer?

5. **Hypothesize** If you were a doctor and a patient came to you complaining of difficulty seeing at night, what would you suspect to be the cause of the problem? What questions would you ask the patient?

6. **Compare and Contrast** How are starches and sugars similar? How do they differ?

7. **Mystery Photo** The photograph on page 536 shows collagen fibers magnified approximately 50,000 times. Collagen is a protein that provides a weblike structure for connective tissues, such as your skin. Using a metric ruler and a calculator, determine the approximate width of a real collagen fiber.

## Develop Your Skills

Use the skills you have developed to complete each activity.

1. **Model** Draw models of the following molecules: $CH_4$, $CHCl_3$, $C_2H_6$, $C_2H_4$, $C_2H_2$.

2. **Interpret Data** The table below shows the boiling point of hydrocarbons.

| Compound | Formula | Boiling Point (°C) |
|----------|---------|--------------------|
| Methane | $CH_4$ | -161.0 |
| Ethane | $C_2H_6$ | -88.5 |
| Propane | $C_3H_8$ | -42.0 |
| Butane | $C_4H_{10}$ | 0.5 |
| Pentane | $C_5H_{12}$ | 36.0 |
| Hexane | $C_6H_{14}$ | 68.7 |

a. What is the boiling point of butane?

b. Which of the compounds are liquid at room temperature (25°C)?

c. Describe the pattern that you observe in the relationship between the boiling point and number of carbon atoms.

3. **Data Bank** Use the information on page 637 to answer the following questions.

a. How many Calories of energy can your body release from 1 g of carbohydrates?

b. Which provides more energy per gram, proteins or carbohydrates?

c. How many grams of carbohydrates does it take to equal the energy contained in 1 g of fat?

## Make Connections

1. **Link the Concepts** Below is a concept map showing how some of the main concepts in this chapter link together. Only parts of the map are filled in. Copy the map. Using words and ideas from the chapter, complete the map.

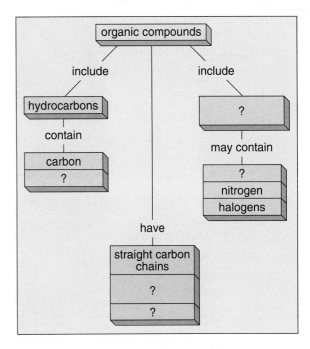

2. **Science and Physical Education** Your basketball team has lost all its substitutes because of injuries. You and four other players will have to go the distance in the upcoming championship game. Based on what you've learned in this chapter, how can you best prepare your body for the big game?

3. **Science and Technology** One problem of using synthetic polymers for packaging is that they are *too* durable. They fill up garbage dumps, pollute the environment, create litter, and harm living things. Find out what scientists are doing to develop biodegradable plastics—synthetic polymers that break down in the environment.

# Chapter 23 Nuclear Chemistry

## Chapter Sections

**23.1** Radioactivity

**23.2** Radioactive Decay

**23.3** Energy from the Nucleus

## What do you see?

❝This picture of subatomic particles looks sort of like a star chart made in 100 B.C. The tracks of the subatomic particles look like comets and falling stars making patterns in the sky. I know this picture was made in a bubble chamber, but it looks like it was painted. Scientists can use this to study the nature and interaction of subatomic particles.❞

*Bobby Way*
*Iroquois Middle School*
*Grand Rapids, Michigan*

To find out more about the photograph, look on page 576. As you read this chapter, you will learn about radioactivity and nuclear chemistry.

# 23.1 Radioactivity

## Objectives

▶ **Describe** how radioactivity was discovered.

▶ **Identify** the source of radioactivity.

▶ **Compare** and **contrast** stable and unstable nuclei.

▶ **Make a model** representing different isotopes.

"**P**ress your chest against the metal plate. Turn your shoulders in. Hold it." Click! You don't feel a thing. Yet energy has passed through your body and created an image on film. When the film is developed, dense tissues, such as those in bones, will show up as white shadows. The energy that has allowed your doctor to see inside you is X-ray, a kind of radiation.

You've probably heard the word *radiation* many times. It can be used to describe many forms of energy, including heat and light. These common kinds of radiation carry relatively small amounts of energy. Other kinds of radiation are much more energetic. They come from the nuclei of atoms.

## Discovery of Radioactivity

On March 1, 1896, French chemist Antoine Becquerel opened a desk drawer and removed a photographic plate he had been storing along with a sample of uranium ore. When he developed the film, he was amazed to see an image on it, even though it had never been exposed to light. The image was the shape of a key that had been lying on top of the film.

Becquerel hypothesized that the ore had given off invisible energy rays that had clouded the film except where the key had blocked them. Two of Becquerel's students, Marie and Pierre Curie, began studying this invisible energy. They found that the uranium atoms in the ore emitted the rays. They also discovered other elements with the same property. Marie Curie called this ability of certain elements to give off invisible energy **radioactivity**.

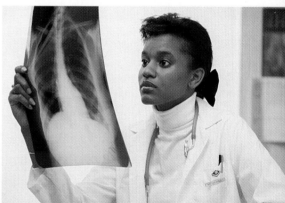

**Figure 23.1** ▲
Doctors read X-rays by holding them up to the light. The dense tissues inside your body appear as white areas on the X-ray.

## ▼ ACTIVITY

### Stable and Unstable Nuclei

**Interpreting Data**

*Stable Nuclei*

Copy the graph in Figure 23.2 on a sheet of paper. Using the periodic table on pages 634 to 635, find out which element is represented by each stable nucleus shown on the graph. On your graph, label each stable nucleus with its symbol.

**SKILLS WORKOUT**

What is the source of the radiation in a radioactive element? It is the nuclei of the element's atoms. Radioactivity results from the release of energy or matter from nuclei. Only some atoms, such as those of the elements discovered by the Curies, are radioactive. Most atoms in nature aren't radioactive. What is the reason for the difference?

As you know, the nucleus of an atom is packed with two kinds of particles, protons and neutrons. These particles are held together by a strong force. The energy of the strong force is called **binding energy**. The attractive force of binding energy makes up for the repulsive forces between all the protons in a nucleus. In most atoms, the binding energy is great enough to hold together permanently the particles that make up the nucleus. These nuclei are stable.

Nuclei without enough binding energy to hold them together permanently are unstable. Unstable nuclei are radioactive. They release energy or matter spontaneously, that is, without any force acting on them from the outside.

Why do some nuclei have enough binding energy to be stable and others don't? The repulsive forces in the nucleus begin to overwhelm the binding energy when there is an imbalance in the number of protons and neutrons. Most radioactive nuclei have too many neutrons compared to the number of protons. In addition, all nuclei with more than 83 protons are radioactive.

**Figure 23.2**
**Stable and Unstable Nuclei** ▼

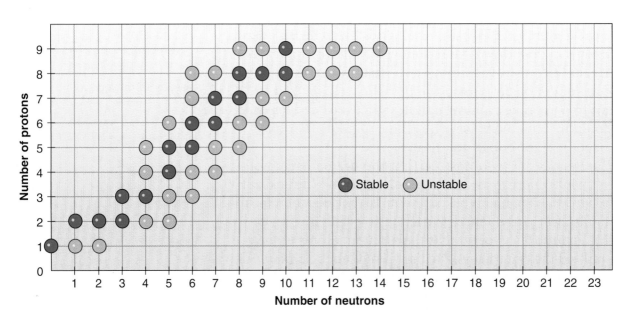

## Radioactive Isotopes

The Curies discovered that in samples of some elements, all the atoms were radioactive. What they didn't know was that most elements have at least some radioactive atoms. Recall that atoms of the same element can differ in their number of neutrons. These different atoms of the same element are *isotopes*. If an isotope has too few or too many neutrons compared with its number of protons, it is unstable and radioactive.

Radioactive isotopes have many uses in industry and medicine. For example, radioactive iodine-131 is used to determine the health of the thyroid gland. The thyroid needs iodine to make a hormone. A healthy thyroid picks up as much iodine as it needs from the bloodstream. To test how much iodine a person's thyroid is picking up, the patient is given radioactive iodine. Special machines that detect radiation can measure how much radioactive iodine goes into the thyroid.

**Table 23.1**
**Common Radioactive Isotopes**

| Stable Isotope | Radioactive Isotope |
|---|---|
| Hydrogen-1 | Hydrogen-2 |
| Carbon-12 | Carbon-14 |
| Sodium-23 | Sodium-24 |
| Iron-56 | Iron-59 |
| Cobalt-59 | Cobalt-60 |
| Iodine-127 | Iodine-131 |

## *SkillBuilder* *Estimating*

ACTIVITY ACTIVITY

## *Your Annual Radiation Dose*

You are exposed to nuclear radiation every day. Exposure to radiation, or radiation dosage, is measured in millirems (mrem). The National Council on Radiation Protection recommends that your total annual radiation dose not exceed 500 mrem. What is your annual dose of radiation? Use the table on page 643 of the Data Bank to estimate your radiation exposure from each possible source. Copy the table to the right, fill in your estimates, and add them up. Answer the following questions.

1. The average annual exposure per person in the United States is 230 mrem. How does your total compare with this number?

2. Why might your average radiation dose differ from year to year?

3. What source of radiation contributed the most to your annual exposure?

| Source of Radiation | Annual Dose (mrem) |
|---|---|
| Radiation from space | |
| TV and computer screens | |
| Living in a brick or stone house | |
| Dental X-ray (whole mouth) | |
| Air travel | |
| Air, water, food | |
| Rocks and soil | |
| Smoke detectors, luminous watch dials | |
| Total | |

*Click ... click ... click.* This is the sound of a Geiger counter, a tool that detects and measures radiation. The number of clicks per second indicates the strength of radiation. Natural, or background, radiation causes a slow, random clicking. Background radiation is normal, but greater levels of radiation can be dangerous.

Radiation damages body cells by ionizing the atoms that make them up. Ionized atoms have different chemical properties than normal atoms and can cause harmful changes in a cell. Cancer is one possible result of exposure to radiation. Because radiation is so dangerous, it is important to monitor levels of radioactivity for people who may be exposed to more than background radiation.

Geiger counters test radiation levels at work sites where radiation levels may be high, such as nuclear power plants and radiation laboratories. Radiation enters a gas-filled tube in the counter and ionizes the gas by removing the electrons. The electrons are attracted to a positive wire and create a high-voltage discharge. The discharge produces a current that makes a click in the speaker.

Another instrument for monitoring radiation exposure is a film badge. People who work near sources of radiation wear the badges clipped to their clothes. The film is protected from exposure to normal light. High levels of radiation go through the protective cover and change the color of the film. A color change, therefore, alerts workers to possible radiation exposure.

**Figure 23.3** ▲

A worker who is exposed to radiation may be scanned with a Geiger counter. A film badge (right) may also be worn to monitor radiation on the job.

## Check and Explain

1. How was radioactivity discovered?

2. What is the cause of radioactivity?

3. **Compare**  Describe how the stability of a nucleus is related to the number of neutrons and protons it contains.

4. **Make a Model**  Make models of the nuclei of helium-4 and helium-6, both of which have an atomic number of 2. Which of these helium isotopes is radioactive?

# 23.2 Radioactive Decay

## Objectives

▶ **Identify** the three types of radioactive decay.

▶ **Describe** the role of radioactive decay in the transmutation of elements.

▶ **Compare** and **contrast** the three different types of radioactive decay.

▶ **Graph** the decay rate of a carbon-14 sample.

Imagine turning lead into gold! Centuries ago, alchemists tried to find ways to turn one element into another through chemical reactions. As you might guess, the alchemists didn't succeed in reaching this goal.

One element can't be turned into another by chemical means. However, elements do change into other elements in nature. In addition, scientists can now turn one element into another, and even create elements that never existed before. What the alchemists didn't know is that the process of one element turning into another isn't chemical. The change occurs in the nucleus of the atom itself.

## Changes in the Nucleus

The release of radioactivity from an unstable atomic nucleus changes the nucleus. The result is a different kind of nucleus. It may have a different atomic mass than the original nucleus. The new nucleus may have a different atomic number than the original nucleus. The process by which this nuclear change occurs is called **radioactive decay**. Radioactive decay is the spontaneous breakdown of an unstable nucleus.

Unstable nuclei decay in three different ways. In two kinds of decay, the nucleus releases particles. In the third kind of radioactive decay, the nucleus gives off energy. Each kind of decay produces a different type of radiation with a different level of energy. All three kinds of radiation, however, can be harmful to you and to other living things.

**Figure 23.4** ▲
The alchemists were some of the first chemists. However, they worked on the wrong kinds of reactions to try to turn lead into gold.

**Alpha Decay**   Some nuclei decay by releasing a package of particles made up of two protons and two neutrons. This package, called an alpha particle, is represented by the Greek letter alpha, α. You might recognize the alpha particle as being the positively charged nucleus of a helium atom. The release of an alpha particle is called **alpha decay**.

Alpha particles aren't very energetic. A few sheets of paper or light clothing will stop them. Alpha particles usually aren't very dangerous to living things. A source of alpha radiation, however, can be very harmful if taken into the body.

**Beta Decay**   Other nuclei decay by giving off a negatively charged subatomic particle called a beta particle. A beta particle is represented by the Greek letter beta, β. Beta particles come from neutrons. When a neutron emits a beta particle, the neutron becomes a proton. This process is called **beta decay**. Beta particles have more energy than alpha particles, but they travel less than 1 m in air. Beta radiation can be stopped by metal foil.

**Gamma Decay**   Both alpha and beta decay involve the release of particles. The third kind of decay, **gamma decay**, is the release of energy alone. This energy is called gamma radiation or gamma rays. Gamma radiation is represented by the Greek letter gamma, γ. Gamma decay usually occurs along with alpha and beta decay.

Gamma rays are very energetic and can be blocked only by thick sheets of high-density materials, such as lead. These sheets must be several centimeters thick to block gamma rays. Gamma rays can penetrate deep into your body and damage vital cell materials. A high dose of gamma rays can cause radiation sickness, a life-threatening disease.

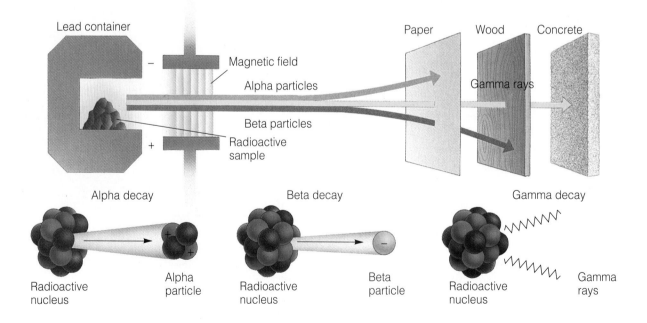

**Figure 23.5** ▲
Why does the magnetic field affect the types of radiation differently? (above)
How is the nucleus affected when it gives off radiation? (below)

## Transmutation of Elements

Both alpha decay and beta decay change the number of protons in a nucleus. Both forms of decay, therefore, change one element into another. The process of an element changing into a different element is called **transmutation** (TRANZ myoo TAY shuhn).

Look at Figure 23.6 below. It shows the series of transmutations that a nucleus of uranium-238 (U-238) goes through. The final product of these many steps is a stable nucleus of lead.

Find U-238 on the chart. This isotope undergoes alpha decay, losing two protons and two neutrons. Its atomic number, therefore, changes from 92 to 90. Its atomic mass drops by four, from 238 to 234. The element that results is thorium-234 (Th-234).

A transmutation can be shown as an equation by using special symbols. The atomic number of a nucleus is shown as a subscript to the left of its symbol: $_{92}$U. Its atomic mass is shown as a superscript: $_{92}^{238}$U. These numbers help you keep track of the protons and neutrons in a transmutation equation such as the one below.

$$_{92}^{238}\text{U} \rightarrow {}_{90}^{234}\text{Th} + {}_{2}^{4}\text{He}$$

What does $_{2}^{4}$He represent in this equation?

Look again at Figure 23.6. What kind of decay does $_{90}^{234}$Th undergo? Why does its atomic number increase by one? A beta particle can be written as $_{-1}^{0}$e. Can you write an equation for this transmutation?

With huge devices called particle accelerators, scientists can produce transmutations that don't occur in nature. In a particle accelerator, high-speed protons and neutrons are smashed into atomic nuclei. Some of the nuclei absorb one or more of these particles, creating a new element. All elements with an atomic number of 93 or higher were made in this way.

**Figure 23.6    Radioactive Decay of Uranium-238** ▼

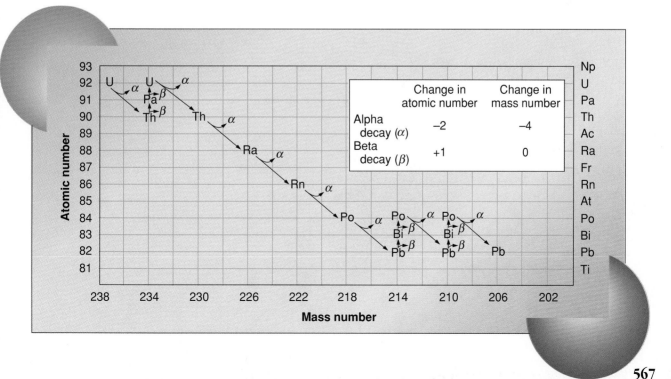

## Decay Rate

The chances that a single atom of uranium-238 will decay during a one-minute period are very low. In contrast, the chances that an atom of polonium-214 will decay in this same time period are very high. This difference in decay rate means that polonium-214 will decay at a much faster rate than uranium-238.

Each radioactive isotope has its own rate of decay. This rate is measured as a **half-life**. An isotope's half-life is the amount of time it takes for half of the atoms in a sample of the element to decay. Half-lives vary greatly, from milliseconds to billions of years.

The half-life of lead-214, for example, is 27 minutes. Every 27 minutes, half the nuclei in a sample of pure lead-214 will undergo beta decay to become bismuth-214. After the first 27-minute period, a 10-g sample of pure lead-214 will contain 5 g of lead-214 and 5 g of bismuth-214.

## Carbon-14 Dating

All living things are made up mainly of carbon compounds. A tiny amount of the carbon in these compounds is carbon-14. Carbon-14 is a radioactive isotope of carbon with a half-life of 5,730 years. The stable isotope carbon-12 makes up the rest of the carbon in organisms.

The amount of carbon-14 in an organism's tissues stays the same while the organism is alive. When an organism dies, the carbon-14 within its tissues decays to nitrogen-14. With each passing half-life of 5,730 years, the organism's remains have half as much carbon-14. However, the amount of carbon-12 does not change.

The decay of carbon-14 acts like a clock. By determining the ratio of carbon-12 to carbon-14 in its remains, a scientist can estimate when an organism died. This process, called carbon-14 dating, is used to estimate the age of organisms that lived on the earth thousands of years ago.

**Figure 23.7**

What happens to the atoms of the carbon-14 isotope when an organism dies? ▼

The plant takes in $CO_2$ from the atmosphere. Some of this $CO_2$ contains radioactive carbon-14. Atoms of carbon-14 become part of the plant.

As a result of the animal eating the plant, carbon-14 becomes part of the animal.

The carbon-14 left in the remains of the animal decays at a constant rate.

## Science and Technology *Nuclear Medicine*

Radiation, as you know, can be very harmful to organisms. Health professionals, however, use radiation and radioactive isotopes to help save lives. Nuclear medicine has become important in diagnosing and treating medical problems.

For diagnosing cancers and circulatory problems, health workers often use radioactive isotopes with short half-lives, called tracers. Patients are injected with or drink the tracer. Inside the body, tracers behave like atoms of the same element found naturally in the body.

Doctors can follow the movement of the tracers with radiation detectors. For example, to monitor the flow of blood in a patient, the radioactive isotope sodium-24 is injected into the bloodstream. Normal blood is about 1 percent sodium chloride. The tracer, sodium-24, flows through the blood just as normal sodium would. Its location is picked up on X-ray film like the one shown on top in Figure 23.8. Places where there is a narrowing or blockage in the circulatory system show up on the X-ray.

Radiation is also a common treatment for cancerous tumors. A beam of radiation directed at a tumor destroys the cancer cells. Like all serious medical procedures, however, radiation therapy carries risks. Radiation damages healthy tissue as well as cancerous tumors. Often it produces side effects, such as hair loss and nausea. Another problem is that all forms of nuclear medicine produce hazardous radioactive waste. This waste is difficult to dispose of safely.

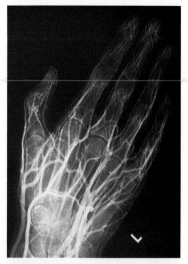
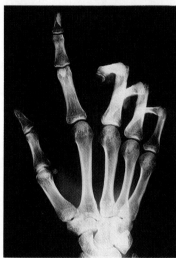

**Figure 23.8** ▲
Look carefully at the X-rays. Which one gives more information about the patient? How do you know?

## Check and Explain

1. What are three types of radioactive decay?

2. What is transmutation? Describe a transmutation in words and with an equation.

3. **Compare and Contrast** How are the three different types of radioactive decay similar? How are they different?

4. **Graph** Make a bar graph that illustrates the mass of carbon-14 that remains in a 24-g sample at the end of each of its first five half-lives.

# Activity 23    *How can you make a model of radioactive decay?*

*Skills*  Observe; Interpret Data; Infer;
          Graph; Predict

## Task 1  Prelab Prep
Collect the following items: pencil, paper, 100 coins, and a bag made of durable material.

## Task 2  Data Record
1.  On a separate sheet of paper, draw the data table shown.
2.  Record the results of each round in the data table.

**Table 23.2   "Radioactive Decay" of Coin Sample**

| Round | Coins Removed | Coins Remaining |
|-------|---------------|-----------------|
| 0     | 0             | 100             |
| 1     |               |                 |
| 2     |               |                 |
| 3     |               |                 |
| 4     |               |                 |
| 5     |               |                 |
| 6     |               |                 |
| 7     |               |                 |
| 8     |               |                 |
| 9     |               |                 |

## Task 3  Procedure
1.  Clear the top of a desk or other smooth surface. Put the coins in the bag. Close the bag and shake it hard.
2.  Carefully spill the coins out onto the desktop, making sure none fall onto the floor.
3.  Collect all the coins that are showing heads. Count these coins and put them aside. Record this number of coins in the table under the *Coins Removed* column. Calculate the number to put in the *Coins Remaining* column.
4.  Put the coins that are showing tails back into the bag. Close the bag and shake it hard.
5.  Repeat steps 2, 3, and 4 until there are no coins left to put back into the bag.
6.  Use the data you have recorded in your table to draw a bar graph showing the change in the size of the coin sample over time.

## Task 4  Analysis
1.  In this activity, what does each coin represent?
2.  How many rounds did it take for all the coins to "decay"?
3.  What happened to the size of the coin sample during this activity? Describe the pattern you observed. How does the bar graph show this pattern?
4.  If each round were equal to one year, what would be the "half-life" of your coin sample? How many half-lives does it take for your coin sample to "decay" completely?
5.  If you repeated this activity, how do you think your results would vary?

## Task 5  Conclusion
Write a short paragraph explaining why this activity is a model of radioactive decay. How is it similar to the actual decay of a radioactive substance? How is it different?

## *Extension*
Repeat this activity to test the predictions you made in question 5 above. How do you account for the differences in the two trials? Do you think similar differences would occur in the decay of two identical samples of a radioactive substance? Explain.

# 23.3 Energy from the Nucleus

## Objectives

▶ **Summarize** the events of nuclear fission.

▶ **Describe** a nuclear chain reaction and the process of nuclear fusion.

▶ **Compare** and **contrast** fission and fusion reactors.

▶ **Communicate** the meaning of a nuclear equation.

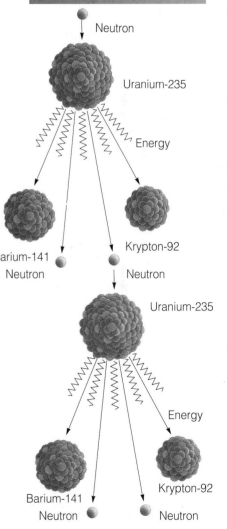

**Figure 23.9** ▲
The neutrons released when one nucleus is split during fission may cause other nuclei to undergo fission as well.

If you could measure the mass of an unstable nucleus and the mass of its decay products, would the two masses be equal? If you remember that matter can't be created or destroyed, a logical answer is that the two masses will be the same. After radioactive decay, however, the mass of the products is less than the mass of the original nucleus! How can this be? Where did the missing matter go? The answer is that the "missing" matter was converted into energy.

## Nuclear Fission

Radioactive decay is a natural process in which very small amounts of matter are converted into energy. Scientists, however, have learned how to create an artificial kind of radioactive decay. They split the nucleus of a heavy element into two smaller nuclei. This process converts some matter from the original nucleus into a large amount of energy. The process is called **nuclear fission**.

How is fission made to occur? Look at Figure 23.9. A neutron is smashed into a nucleus of uranium-235. The nucleus splits into two smaller nuclei of similar size. As it splits, the uranium-235 nucleus releases more neutrons and a great deal of energy. This process is fission.

If other uranium-235 nuclei are nearby, some of them are struck by neutrons from the first nucleus. These nuclei, in turn, undergo fission. The result is a *chain reaction*. If the chain reaction is controlled, the energy released can be used to do work. If the chain reaction isn't controlled, huge amounts of energy are released all at once. The explosion that takes place in an atomic bomb is an uncontrolled chain reaction.

# Fission Reactors

The energy produced by fission is harnessed in a device called a fission reactor. Look at the diagram of a typical fission reactor in Figure 23.10. Rods made of uranium-235 are positioned inside the reactor between movable rods made of cadmium. Because the cadmium rods absorb neutrons, they can control the rate that uranium-235 nuclei undergo fission. The rods are moved in or out to keep the fission rate constant. Heat energy given off by the reactor turns water into steam, which drives a turbine that generates electricity.

Fission reactors are built with many safeguards. These safeguards are designed to prevent the nuclear reaction from going out of control and to keep radiation from being released into the environment. Even so, serious nuclear accidents have occurred.

The most serious nuclear accident occurred on April 28, 1986, at a nuclear power plant in Chernobyl, Ukraine. The nuclear reactions went out of control, melting part of the inside of the reactor and releasing radioactivity. People died from radiation poisoning, and about 40,000 were evacuated from the area. The wind carried radioactive clouds caused by this accident over the entire world.

**Figure 23.10**
**Nuclear Fission Reactor ▼**

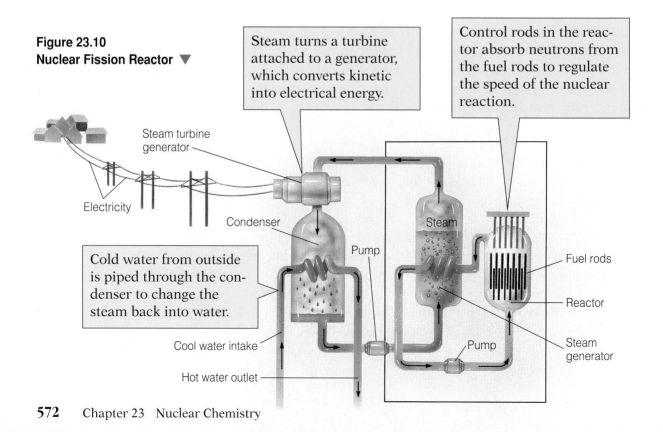

Steam turns a turbine attached to a generator, which converts kinetic into electrical energy.

Control rods in the reactor absorb neutrons from the fuel rods to regulate the speed of the nuclear reaction.

Steam turbine generator

Electricity

Condenser

Steam

Pump

Cold water from outside is piped through the condenser to change the steam back into water.

Cool water intake

Hot water outlet

Fuel rods

Reactor

Pump

Steam generator

## Nuclear Fusion

Within the sun, a different, more powerful type of nuclear reaction occurs. This reaction is called **nuclear fusion**. During nuclear fusion, two or more nuclei are joined or "fused" together. As the particles form a single nucleus, some mass is converted into energy.

Most of the sun's nuclear fuel is hydrogen. Hydrogen nuclei fuse to form helium in the extremely high temperatures of the sun. Nuclei of these light elements also combine to form heavier elements. Great amounts of heat are given off during fusion. Fusion in the sun is the source of the solar radiation reaching earth.

Unlike fission, fusion doesn't happen spontaneously. It occurs only at extremely high temperatures. For this reason, scientists haven't yet found a practical way of harnessing fusion energy on the earth. They have discovered, however, how to cause an uncontrolled fusion reaction to take place.

## Consider This

### Should New Nuclear Power Plants Be Built?

When the first nuclear power plants were built, experts said nuclear power would become our most important energy source. Since then, however, many questions have come up concerning the safety and cost of nuclear power. At present, nuclear energy supplies 16 percent of the power in the United States.

**Consider Some Issues**
Supporters of nuclear power feel it has many advantages over other sources of energy. Nuclear-fuel supplies will last up to 1,000 years, much longer than fossil fuels. In addition, nuclear reactors don't normally produce air pollution.

However, critics point out that nuclear power is very dangerous. Although safety regulations for nuclear power plants have been tightened, accidents can still happen. A major accident could cause deaths, illnesses, and environmental damage. Another big problem is that the waste from nuclear reactors is highly radioactive for a long time.

Overall the costs of adding safeguards and disposing of waste make nuclear power much more expensive than anyone originally thought.

**Think About It** Can nuclear power plants be made safe enough? Is it worth the risks to build more of them? Are there other sources of energy that should be developed instead?

**Write About It** Write a paper stating your position for or against building new nuclear power plants. Include your reasons for choosing your position.

## Fusion-Reactor Projects

For many years, scientists have tried to build a fusion reactor. The main problem they face is that no material can withstand the extremely high temperatures of a fusion reaction. In some experimental fusion reactors, called tokamaks, a powerful magnetic field confines the hot hydrogen nuclei in the center of the reactor. Unfortunately, these reactors and others like them use more energy than they produce. If these problems can be solved, fusion may one day be an important energy source. It is relatively clean, and the hydrogen used as fuel is plentiful.

## Science and Society  *Nuclear Waste*

Nuclear power plants, nuclear weapons plants, and uranium mines all produce tons of nuclear waste every year. Nuclear waste is very dangerous. It causes serious health problems, such as cancer and birth defects. In some cases, the waste will remain dangerous for as long as 200,000 years. How can nuclear waste be disposed of safely?

A truly safe method of disposal may never be found. Scientists are still considering which of several options is the safest. Possibilities include burying the waste under the seafloor, disposing of it in the Antarctic ice cap, shooting it into space, and burying it under mountains.

Burying the waste is favored by many because it is easiest and the least costly. However, if the nuclear waste were to leak into the ground water, it could poison the environment for many generations. Most nuclear waste is now stored in radiation-proof containers at temporary storage sites.

**Figure 23.11**
This drum of nuclear waste must be stored in a place where it won't pollute water or land. ▼

## Check and Explain

1.  What causes a nucleus of U-235 to undergo fission?

2.  What is nuclear fusion?

3.  **Compare and Contrast**  How are fission and fusion reactors similar? How are they different?

4.  **Communicate**  In your own words, explain the following equation.

$$^{235}_{92}U + ^{1}_{0}n \rightarrow ^{141}_{56}Ba + ^{92}_{36}Kr + 3^{1}_{0}n$$

# Chapter 23 Review

## Concept Summary

### 23.1 Radioactivity
▶ The source of radioactivity is the unstable nuclei of some atoms.
▶ The stability of a nucleus is determined by the number of protons and neutrons it contains.
▶ Most elements have isotopes that are radioactive.
▶ Unstable nuclei are radioactive. All nuclei with more than 83 protons are radioactive.

### 23.2 Radioactive Decay
▶ There are three kinds of radioactive decay. Alpha decay is the release of a helium nucleus. Beta decay is the release of a negatively charged particle with almost no mass. Gamma decay is the release of energy.

▶ Alpha and beta decay change one element into another.
▶ A half-life is the period of time required for half of the mass of a radioactive material to decay. The decay rate depends on the radioactive element or isotope.
▶ Carbon-14 decay can be used to estimate the age of the remains of organisms.

### 23.3 Energy from the Nucleus
▶ During nuclear fission, matter is converted into energy.
▶ Fission reactors control nuclear reactions and produce energy.
▶ During nuclear fusion, two light nuclei combine to form one heavier nucleus, releasing large amounts of energy.
▶ Fusion occurs only at extremely high temperatures.

## Chapter Vocabulary

radioactivity (23.1)     alpha decay (23.2)     transmutation (23.2)     nuclear fusion (23.3)
binding energy (23.1)     beta decay (23.2)     half-life (23.2)
radioactive decay (23.2)     gamma decay (23.2)     nuclear fission (23.3)

## Check Your Vocabulary

Use the vocabulary words above to complete the following sentences correctly.

1. During _____ , a helium nucleus is released from an unstable nucleus.
2. Protons and neutrons are held together by _____ in a nucleus.
3. An element with unstable nuclei produces _____ .
4. The change of one element into another element is called _____ .
5. During _____ , hydrogen nuclei come together to form a helium nucleus.
6. A neutron changes into a proton during _____ decay.

7. The release of alpha particles is one kind of _____ .
8. The most energetic type of radioactive decay is _____ .
9. The _____ of a radioactive substance is a measure of its rate of decay.
10. When a nucleus of uranium-235 undergoes _____ , two smaller nuclei result.

## Write Your Vocabulary

Write sentences using the vocabulary words above. Show that you know what each word means.

# Chapter 23 Review

## Check Your Knowledge

Answer the following in complete sentences.

1. In a stable nucleus, how does the number of protons compare to the number of neutrons?

2. What happens to an unstable nucleus?

3. When are isotopes radioactive?

4. What happens during radioactive decay?

5. Why is gamma radiation dangerous to living things?

6. What happens to an element during transmutation?

7. What is the main problem in developing a fusion reactor?

Determine whether each statement is true or false. Write *true* if it is true. If it is false, change the underlined term to make the statement true.

8. The source of radioactivity is the <u>nuclei</u> of atoms.

9. Protons and neutrons are held together in a nucleus by <u>electrons</u>.

10. Carbon-12 and carbon-14 are <u>isotopes</u>.

11. Alpha decay produces an <u>electron</u>.

12. A sheet of aluminum will protect you from <u>gamma radiation</u>.

13. Alpha and beta decay cause <u>transmutations</u>.

14. During nuclear <u>fission</u>, hydrogen nuclei join to produce helium nuclei.

15. Experimental fusion reactors produce <u>more</u> energy than they use.

## Check Your Understanding

Apply the concepts you have learned to answer each question.

1. **Classify** Which of the following nuclear changes is a transmutation?

   a. C-14 to C-12

   b. C-14 to N-14

   c. $_1^3H$ to $_1^2H$

   d. U-238 to Th-234

   e. $_{84}^{210}Po \rightarrow _{82}^{206}Pb + _2^4He$

   f. Ra-226 to Rn-222

2. As elements increase in atomic number, the number of isotopes they have increases. Explain why this is true.

3. **Generalize** What are the characteristics of radioactive substances?

4. **Infer** A nuclear reaction produces particles with less total mass than the starting material. It also produces energy. What can you infer?

5. **Find Causes** What kind of decay would cause each of the following nuclear changes?

   a. $_{88}^{226}Ra$ to $_{86}^{222}Rn$

   b. $_{82}^{214}Pb$ to $_{83}^{214}Bi$

6. **Predict** What might happen if technicians couldn't move control rods into a nuclear reactor?

7. **Infer** What is happening to the amount of helium in the sun?

8. **Mystery Photo** The photograph on page 560 shows the paths made by subatomic particles inside a bubble chamber. The particles come from nuclei bombarded with high-speed neutrons or protons produced by a particle accelerator. Why do you think some of the paths are curved and some are straight?

## Develop Your Skills

Use the skills you have developed to complete each activity.

1. **Calculate** After 12 years, 0.4 g of a 16-g sample of a radioactive substance remains. What is its half-life?

2. **Interpret Data** The graph below shows the decay of carbon-14 over time.

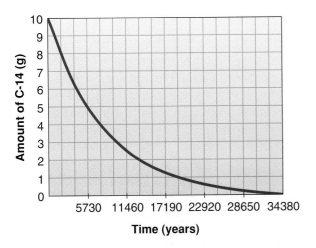

a. How much carbon-14 did the sample begin with?

b. How many half-lives pass before the amount of carbon-14 nears zero?

c. Estimate the age of the sample when it contains 4 g of carbon-14.

d. Do you think the age of an object older than 1 million years can be determined by carbon-14 dating? Explain.

3. **Data Bank** Use the information on page 643 to answer the following questions.

a. How much radiation does the average person receive every year from air, water, and food?

b. How much radiation do you receive on a 10-hr plane flight?

c. For most people, which is the greatest source of radiation exposure, television or outer space?

## Make Connections

1. **Link the Concepts** Construct a concept map that shows how the following concepts in this chapter link together: alpha particles, stable nuclei, transmutation, beta particles, unstable nuclei, radioactive decay, gamma rays.

2. **Science and Health** Radon, a radioactive gas, is thought to cause some lung cancers. It is sometimes found in the basements of houses. Find the answers to the following questions about radon: Where does radon come from? Why might it cause lung cancer? How can people find out whether radon is present in their basements? What can people do to protect themselves from exposure to radon?

3. **Science and Society** Electricity is the main source of energy used in homes, factories, and businesses. Most of the electricity used in the United States comes from burning fossil fuels, such as oil and coal. The world's supply of these fuels is limited, and the power plants that burn them produce air pollution. How do each of the following sources of energy compare with the energy in fossil fuels? Radioactive elements, wind, flowing water, tides, heat from inside the earth, and solar radiation. Choose one and write a report about its advantages and disadvantages as an energy source.

4. **Science and Technology** What are the latest advances in nuclear fusion research? Are scientists any closer to creating a fusion reaction that generates more energy than it uses? Do library research to discover what fusion research is being done.

# Science and Literature Connection

There was nothing funny about Yollie needing a new outfit for the eighth-grade fall dance. They couldn't afford one. . . . The best Mrs. Moreno could do was buy Yollie a pair of black shoes with velvet bows and fabric dye to color her white summer dress black.

"We can color your dress so it will look brand-new," her mother said brightly, shaking the bottle of dye as she ran hot water into a plastic dish tub. She poured the black liquid into the tub and stirred it with a pencil. Then, slowly and carefully, she lowered the dress into the tub.

Yollie couldn't stand to watch. She knew it wouldn't work. . . .

To Yollie's surprise, the dress came out shiny black. It looked brand-new and sophisticated, like what the people in New York wear. She beamed at her mother, who hugged Yollie and said, "See, what did I tell you?"

The dance was important to Yollie because she was in love with Ernie Castillo, the third-best speller in the class. She bathed, dressed, did her hair and nails, and primped until her mother yelled, "All right already." Yollie sprayed her neck and wrists with Mrs. Moreno's Avon perfume and bounced into the car.

Mrs. Moreno let Yollie out in front of the school. She waved and told her to have a good time but behave herself, then

## Mother and Daughter

*The following excerpts are from the short story* "Mother and Daughter" *by Gary Soto*

roared off, blue smoke trailing from the tail pipe of the old Nova . . .

The evening was warm but thick with clouds. Gusts of wind picked up the paper lanterns hanging in the trees and swung them, blurring the night with reds and yellows. The lanterns made the evening seem romantic, like a scene from a movie. Everyone danced, sipped punch, and stood in knots of threes and fours, talking. . . .

Yollie, who kept smoothing her dress down when the wind picked up, had her eye on Ernie. It turned out that Ernie had his mind on Yollie, too. He ate a handful of cookies nervously, then asked her for a dance.

"Sure," she said, nearly throwing herself into his arms.

They danced two fast ones before they got a slow one. As they circled under the lanterns, rain began falling, lightly at first. Yollie loved the sound of the raindrops ticking against the leaves. She leaned her head on Ernie's shoulder, though his sweater was scratchy. He felt warm and tender. Yollie could tell that he was in love, and with her, of course. The dance continued successfully, romantically, until it began to pour. . . .

The girls and boys raced into the cafeteria. Inside, the girls, drenched to the bone, hurried to the restrooms to brush their hair and dry themselves. One girl cried because her velvet dress was ruined.

Yollie felt sorry for her and helped her dry the dress off with paper towels, but it was no use. The dress was ruined.

Yollie went to a mirror. She looked a little gray now that some of her mother's makeup had washed away but not as bad as some of the other girls. She combed her damp hair, careful not to pull too hard. She couldn't wait to get back to Ernie.

Yollie bent over to pick up a bobby pin, and shame spread across her face. A black puddle was forming at her feet. Drip, black drip. Drip, black drip. The dye was falling from her dress like black tears. Yollie stood up. Her dress was now the color of ash. She looked around the room. The other girls, unaware of Yollie's problem, were busy grooming themselves. What could she do? Everyone would laugh. They would know she dyed an old dress because she couldn't afford a new one. She hurried from the restroom with her head down, across the cafeteria floor and out the door. She raced through the storm, crying as the rain mixed with her tears and ran into twig-choked gutters.

## Skills in Science

### Reading Skills in Science

1.  **Find the Main Idea** What caused the dye to come out of Yollie's dress?

2.  **Classify** Identify the solvent and the solute in the dye solution used to change the color of the dress.

### Writing Skills in Science

1.  **Find Causes** After Mrs. Moreno dropped Yollie off, "there was blue smoke trailing from the tail pipe of the old Nova." What chemical reaction is producing this smoke?

2.  **Compare and Contrast** How did Yollie's reaction to the girl's velvet dress ruined by the rain compare to the reaction of the others to Yollie's ruined dress?

3.  **Finding Causes** What was Yollie's biggest concern when the dye washed off her dress? Do you think her reaction was reasonable. Explain.

4.  **If . . . Then Arguments** If you were Yollie, would you have left the dance? Write an ending to the story describing what you would have done.

### Activities

**Gather Information** Natural dyes have been used to dye fabrics and other materials for over 5,000 years. Use reference tools to learn about plants that provide natural dyes. Make a chart that shows five different plants and how each is used for dyeing.

**Model** Place a raw egg and a handful of yellow onion skins in a pan of cold water. Boil the egg and the onion skins together for five minutes. Describe what happens to the egg shell?

### Where to Read More

*Adventures with Atoms and Molecules Book 3* by Robert C. Mebane and Thomas R. Rybolt. Hillside, New Jersey: Enslow Publishers, Inc., 1991. Thirty experiments demonstrate the properties and behavior of atoms and molecules.

*Chemically Active!* by Vicki Cobb. New York: J.B. Lippincott, 1985. Interesting experiments illustrate chemistry basics using common materials.

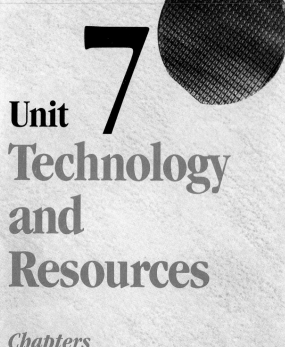

# Unit 7

# Technology and Resources

*Chapters*

**24**  Energy Use and Technology

**25**  Chemical Technology

# Data Bank

Use the information on pages 634 to 643 to answer the questions about topics explored in this unit.

## *Inferring*

If motor vehicles used electricity instead of gasoline, how would the usage of crude oil change?

## *Interpreting Data*

Approximately what portion of the products made from crude oil is directly related to transportation?

## *Classifying*

List the three largest individual consumers of industrial energy.

The photograph to the left shows how individual chips are placed on a wafer. What kinds of electronic devices might use a microchip wafer?

# Chapter 24 Energy Use and Technology

## Chapter Sections

24.1 Generating and Using Electric Power

24.2 Alternative Energy Technologies

24.3 Energy Conservation Decisions

## What do you see?

"I think it is a solar energy collector. It absorbs energy from the sun. It is shiny because the light is reflecting off it. This technology is important because it helps save our natural resources. With it we use the energy from the sun instead of energy from the earth."

*Elisa Shzu*
*Parkhill Junior High School*
*Dallas, Texas*

To find out more about the photograph, look on page 602. As you read this chapter, you will learn about energy sources and how electric power is generated.

# 24.1 Generating and Using Electric Power

## Objectives

▶ **Identify** how the sun's energy changes to form an energy pathway.

▶ **Describe** four ways of producing electricity.

▶ **Explain** how electricity from a power plant is delivered to the home.

▶ **Compare** and **contrast** the advantages and disadvantages of conventional energy sources.

### ▼ ACTIVITY

**Inferring**

*Energy Sources*

List all the things you did yesterday that required the use of some form of energy. Identify the energy sources you used.

**SKILLS WARMUP**

Imagine that you lived 100 years ago. People had no telephones, washing machines, air conditioners, or sewing machines. They cooked over an open fire or on a wood-burning stove like the one shown in Figure 24.1. They scrubbed their clothes on stones in a river or on a washboard, and hung them in the open air to dry.

Today electric power makes your life easier and more comfortable. Furnaces, air conditioners, and fans keep you warm in winter and cool in summer. Appliances, such as washers and dryers, help you to do work. Radios, TVs, and CD players provide you with entertainment. What are the sources of the electric power that make all these things work?

## Energy Pathways

Changes of the sun's energy from one form to another are called pathways of energy. For example, by heating the earth and its atmosphere, the sun creates the winds that circulate over the earth. A windmill may change the wind energy into mechanical energy that operates a water pump.

In some energy pathways, the sun's energy is stored for a very long time. For example, coal, oil, and natural gas are the remains of plants or organisms that lived hundreds of millions of years ago. The energy stored in the plants and organisms that created these fuels originally came from the sun.

**Figure 24.1**
Wood burned inside this stove not only cooked food, it also was the main heat source for the entire room. ▼

# Electric Power

Most electricity is manufactured from some form of energy. The electricity you use comes from a power plant. All power plants do the same thing. They convert mechanical energy into electric energy.

Electricity is made from many different energy sources. Some power plants use moving water as a source of mechanical energy. Others burn coal or oil to make steam. Steam pressure is used to turn a generator coil, which produces electricity.

**Figure 24.2
Electricity Production and
Distribution** ▼

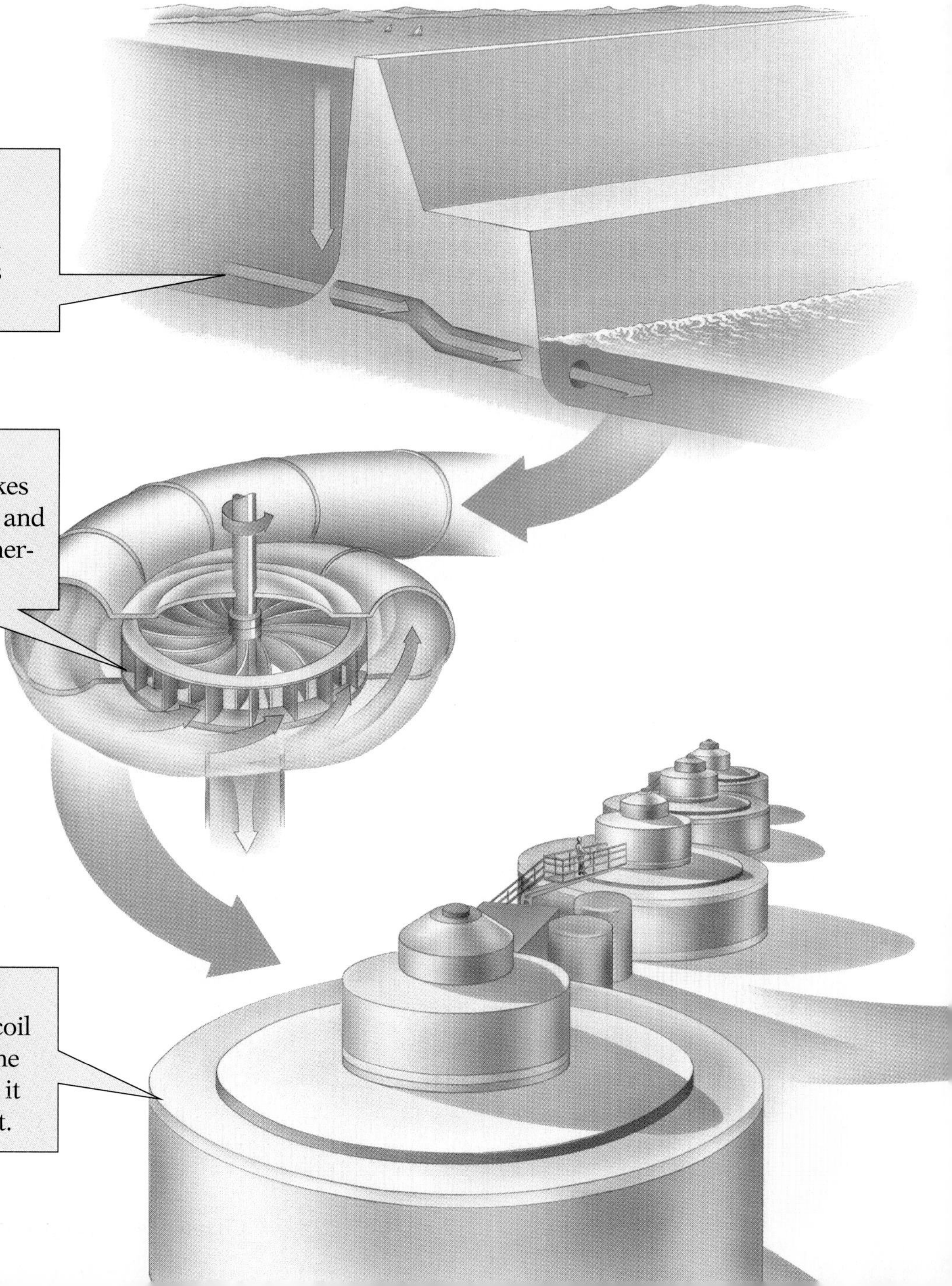

**Energy Source**
Mechanical energy is released as water from behind the dam moves through the pipes.

**Turbine**
The moving water strikes the blades of a turbine and turns the shaft of a generator connected to it.

**Generator**
Inside this housing, a coil connected to the turbine generates electricity as it rotates inside a magnet.

Electric power plants normally serve large areas. Study Figure 24.2 to learn how electricity is produced and supplied to homes and industry. Some of the electric energy must be transported great distances. Electricity travels quickly and efficiently through high-voltage wires called transmission lines. Like a network of roads, power lines carry electricity to farms, homes, and businesses in your community.

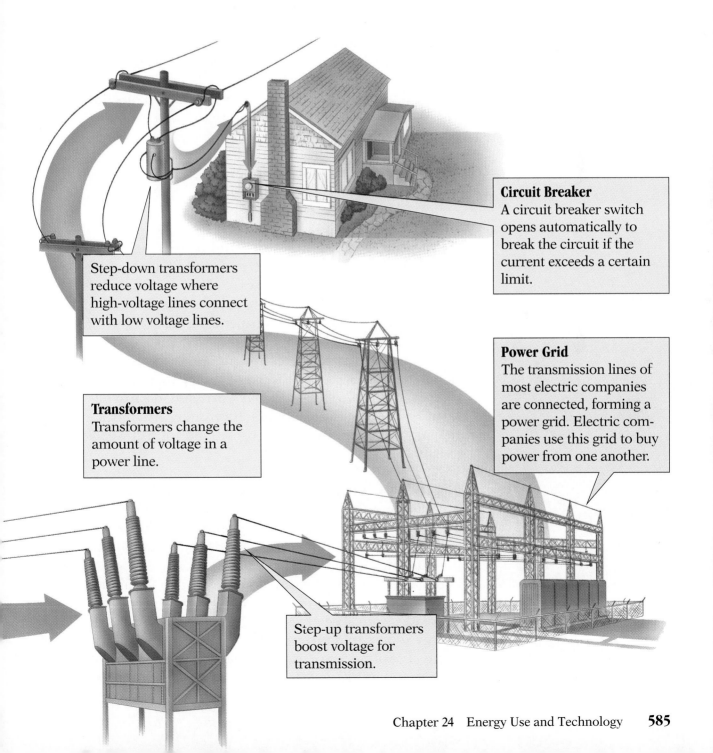

**Circuit Breaker**
A circuit breaker switch opens automatically to break the circuit if the current exceeds a certain limit.

Step-down transformers reduce voltage where high-voltage lines connect with low voltage lines.

**Power Grid**
The transmission lines of most electric companies are connected, forming a power grid. Electric companies use this grid to buy power from one another.

**Transformers**
Transformers change the amount of voltage in a power line.

Step-up transformers boost voltage for transmission.

# Sources of Electric Power

**Sources of Energy**

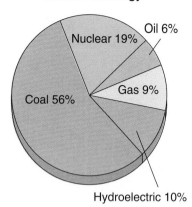

**Figure 24.3** ▲

What percent of the total fuel sources are water power and nuclear power?

**Figure 24.4** ▲

After being buried and put under heat and pressure, plants like these became the coal we use today.

In the United States, utility companies use five energy sources to make most electricity—water, coal, oil, natural gas, and nuclear. The percentage contributed by each energy source is shown in Figure 24.3. Notice that coal, oil, and gas account for more than 70 percent of the total energy.

**Hydroelectric Power**   Electricity generated by moving water from dams is called **hydroelectric power**. The sun provides heat energy that evaporates surface water from oceans, lakes, and streams. The water returns to the earth as rain or snow. Reservoirs behind dams built across river valleys collect and store the water.

The mechanical energy of the moving water as it leaves the dam is converted to electricity. The amount of kinetic energy in the falling water depends on the speed and the volume of the water available to turn the generators. About 10 percent of the electricity used in the United States is produced by hydroelectric power.

Generating electricity with water power is efficient and clean. Little energy is lost, and no pollutants are produced. Another advantage of hydroelectric power is its low cost. Although dams are expensive to build, hydroelectric plants have low operating costs.

The lakes, or reservoirs, behind the dams also provide water storage for irrigation and serve as recreational areas. However, building a dam changes a river forever. It floods low-lying areas upstream, destroying farmland and wildlife habitats. Dams may also block the migration and survival of some kinds of fish, such as salmon.

**Fossil Fuels**   Fuels formed from the remains of ancient organisms are called **fossil fuels**. These plants and animals were buried under layers of mud and silt. Heat and pressure gradually transformed their organic compounds into concentrated chemical energy. Coal, oil, and natural gas are the three most common fossil fuels.

Fossil fuels are burned to heat water under pressure to create steam. The pressurized steam is the mechanical energy source that turns a turbine and generates electricity. Fossil fuels are used all over the world because they are relatively easy to get and are easy to transport.

Coal is the cheapest and most abundant energy source in the United States. However, coal is a dirty fuel. The smoke from burning coal contains large amounts of sulfur and carbon dioxide. Surface mining destroys the land environment. Drainage from surface mining pollutes water.

Oil is the major source of gasoline and other liquid fuels used for transportation and heat. The United States must import 40 to 45 percent of its oil supply. Burning oil also adds pollutants to the atmosphere, such as carbon dioxide, sulfur dioxide, and other gases. The production and transportation of oil can also pollute the environment, especially if an oil spill occurs.

Natural gas is the cleanest-burning fossil fuel. It generates fewer air pollutants and less carbon dioxide than other fossil fuels do. Gas is an efficient fuel and is used a great deal in industry, transportation, and power generation.

**Nuclear Power**   Some electricity in the United States is produced by nuclear fission. In principle, a nuclear power plant is similar to a fossil-fuel plant—both produce heat that boils water to make steam. The fuel is very different, however. In a nuclear plant, an unstable isotope of uranium or plutonium produces the heat.

Nuclear power plants have two main advantages over fossil-fuel plants. The energy stored in a small amount of nuclear fuel is enormous. For example, 1 kg of nuclear fuel contains nearly three million times the energy that is in 1 kg of coal. In addition, nuclear plants don't give off air pollutants.

Nuclear power plants have two major disadvantages. One disadvantage is the danger of nuclear accidents. Because nuclear power plants use radioactive material, accidents can release radioactive material into the environment that are extremely dangerous to living things. Accidents have occurred at nuclear reactors. The nuclear power industry has responded by developing safer reactor designs.

The disposal of nuclear wastes is another disadvantage and a serious problem facing the industry. Nuclear waste materials remain dangerously radioactive for thousands of years. Because the United States has no permanent storage facilities for these wastes, they are stored at the reactor sites.

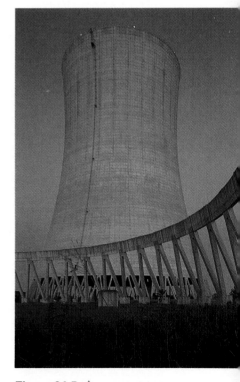

**Figure 24.5** ▲
The stack of a nuclear power plant is a cooling tower that releases hot steam into the atmosphere.

The next time you eat your lunch, think of the cost of the energy needed to make it. The food you eat is at the end of a long chain of energy-consuming processes. These processes use far more energy than the food itself contains.

Take bread, for example. It takes 20 megajoules of energy to produce a 1-kg loaf of bread. Twenty percent of the energy is used to grow the wheat. Milling the wheat into flour uses about 15 percent, and baking uses about 65 percent. The same amount of energy is needed to drive a car a distance of 5 km.

Part of the energy consumed in growing food is used to operate farm machinery and for irrigation. The rest goes into the production of agricultural chemicals, animal feeds, and other farm supplies.

Processing and distributing food also uses large amounts of energy. For example, it takes energy to peel, mash, and strain grapes for grape juice. The packaging itself consumes a large amount of energy. To produce one aluminum pop-top can, almost 7 megajoules of energy are needed.

At the end of the chain, energy is used to light and heat the supermarket, and to keep food fresh. You use energy to take your food home, to cool it in your refrigerator, and to prepare it. The next time you eat lunch, think of all the ways energy was used to grow, package, and transport the food to you.

▼ **ACTIVITY**

**Calculating**

*Cost of Food Processing*

Find out how much energy is used daily by a food processing company. What is the energy cost per item of several kinds of food the company produces?

**SKILLS WORKOUT**

## Check and Explain

1. Identify an energy pathway from the sun to electric power.

2. Name four sources of electric power and describe how each produces electricity.

3. **Define Operationally** Explain the process of making electricity and moving it from a power plant to the homes and buildings in your city.

4. **Compare and Contrast** In a table, list two advantages and two disadvantages of the five energy sources described in this section.

# 24.2 Alternative Energy Technologies

## Objectives

▶ **Infer** ways to use solar energy in a home.

▶ **Relate** wind, geothermal, and tidal processes to the production of electricity.

▶ **Compare** and **contrast** the benefits of biomass and synthetic fuels.

▶ **Communicate** the role of the sun's energy in three alternative energy sources.

Until the eighteenth century, wind, water, and wood were the primary sources of energy. Dependence on fossil fuels began with the Industrial Revolution and the increased use of coal. Discoveries of oil and large pools of gas from the mid-1800s to the early 1900s made these convenient, inexpensive fossil fuels popular.

In 1973, a shortage of gasoline created long gas lines like the one in Figure 24.6. Periodic shortages of gasoline and other oil products since then made people aware of their dependence on oil. The need to supplement and eventually replace fossil fuels became a reality. Increased awareness of environmental problems also intensified the search for safer, more dependable alternate energy sources.

## Alternative Energy Sources

Opinions vary on how long the present supply of fossil fuels will last. However, most experts admit that sooner or later the supply will run out. As fossil-fuel reserves are used up, the need for energy continues to grow. The modern lifestyle of many countries requires large amounts of energy.

Unfortunately, the world can't wait to run out of fossil fuels before finding other energy resources. What will those resources be? Some energy sources are more promising over the long term than others are.

**Figure 24.6** ▲
People waiting in long lines like these were often limited in the amount of gas they could buy. How much gas do your parents buy each week?

**Solar Power** Solar energy is heat and light energy from the sun. For a long time, people have dreamed about harnessing this free, limitless, and non-polluting source of energy. Today the technology exists to convert solar energy into both heat and electricity.

A **solar cell** is a device containing a semiconductor that converts sunlight directly into electricity. When sunlight strikes solar cells, like those shown in Figure 24.7, electrons flow from one part of the cell to another. This action produces electricity.

Solar energy is converted into heat by using an active solar heating system, such as the one used to heat houses in Figure 24.8. Flat-plate solar collectors trap heat from the sun's rays. Pipes filled with water heated by the solar collector carry the heat to other places in the house where it is used or stored for future use.

**Figure 24.8** ▲
Solar collectors on a south-facing roof will absorb a maximum amount of energy from the sun.

The major disadvantage of using solar power for commercial use is cost. Harnessing solar energy is difficult. Sunlight isn't a concentrated form of energy. To collect this widely scattered energy, solar power plants need vast amounts of land and equipment. Also, exposure to sunlight varies with latitude, season, time of day, and weather conditions. Power plants need costly equipment to store solar energy for use when sunlight isn't available.

Advances in materials and design are making solar cells less expensive and more competitive with conventional energy sources. One breakthrough is "thin-film" solar technology. Perhaps you have a watch or a calculator that uses this inexpensive source of solar power. Thin-film modules don't convert solar energy very efficiently. However, their low cost makes it reasonable to use large numbers of them.

**Figure 24.7** ▲
Large numbers of solar cells on panels are needed to heat a home.

**Wind Generators** Wind energy is used to generate electricity. Wind is caused by differences in temperature and atmospheric pressure at the earth's surface. Because the earth and its atmosphere are heated by the sun, wind energy is an indirect form of solar power.

Wind generators often feature two or three large turbine blades on top of a tall tower. Height is important because wind speed is greater and more constant high above the earth's surface.

Wind generators don't produce any air or water pollution. They can, however, be noisy. Large numbers of them can interfere with TV and microwave transmission.

A major disadvantage of wind power is its variable nature. To produce electricity efficiently, a steady wind speed of 19 to 24 km per hour is needed. These conditions don't always exist where wind power is needed. In the United States, the right conditions occur mainly in the mountains, along certain coastal areas, and on the Great Plains.

**Figure 24.10** ▲
Biomass from waste materials is dried and compressed to form these pellets. The pellets are used as fuel source.

**Figure 24.9** ▲
The shaft of the windmill connects the turbine blades to a coil in the generator. When wind turns the turbine, the generator produces electricity.

**Biomass** Organic matter that can be used as fuel is called **biomass**. Plant material in any form and organic wastes, such as garbage and manure, are also biomass.

When burned, most biomass releases at least half the energy of high-grade coal. Nearly any kind of dry biomass is easy to burn. Materials, such as sawdust, corncobs, and walnut shells make good fuels.

Biomass can also be converted into liquids and gases that burn. The action of bacteria on a mixture of sewage and water produces methane gas. Methane can be liquefied and used as a fuel.

An important advantage of biomass is that it is easily replenished. The main disadvantage is that it requires large areas of farmland. Land used to produce biomass won't be available for food crops.

**Synthetic Fuels** Synthetic fuels are liquids and gases made from energy sources other than fossil fuels. Ethanol and methanol are both alcohols made from biomass. Gasohol is gasoline blended with ethanol.

Ethanol is made by fermenting corn or sugar cane. Methanol is made from wood. These synthetic fuels burn cleaner and produce less carbon dioxide than gasoline does.

Kerogen and bitumen are organic substances that can be converted into synthetic oil or gas. Kerogen is found in an oil-bearing shale. Bitumen is a thick, black substance in tar sands. Oil shale and tar sands are plentiful energy sources. However, to extract them requires large amounts of energy and water and produces mountains of waste rock.

**Figure 24.12** ▲
This power station in Iceland uses geothermal steam to generate electricity.

**Figure 24.11** ▲
The cornstalk is used as biomass that is burned. The corn is used to make ethanol, which is a fuel used in car engines.

**Geothermal Energy** Heat produced beneath the earth's surface is **geothermal** energy. Hot magma or molten rock in the earth's crust is the source of geothermal energy. Magma near the earth's surface heats the surrounding rock. The rocks heat underground water to form geothermal reservoirs.

Geothermal wells in the reservoirs bring a mixture of steam and hot water to the surface. After the water and impurities are removed from the steam, the steam is piped into turbine generators to produce electricity. Most of the hot water is used for heating buildings.

Geothermal energy is an almost limitless source of power, but it's practical only where the source of heat is close to the earth's surface. Environmentally, geothermal power appears to be less harmful than nuclear or fossil fuel plants. Also, geothermal plants require smaller areas of land than other electricity plants. Minerals dissolved in the hot water corrode turbines. The wastewater can damage soil.

**Tidal Power** Recall that tides are the rise and fall of the ocean's surface caused by the gravitational pull on the water by the sun and the moon. The back and forth flow of ocean water near the shore can provide a source of energy that doesn't pollute and never runs out.

Tidal power is harnessed in much the same way as hydroelectric power is. A dam is used to control the flow of water, which turns a turbine. Tidal-power electric plants are practical only in narrow bays or estuaries. The difference between the level of the sea water and the water in the channel must be at least 5 m.

Building and maintaining a tidal power plant is very expensive. Also, the amount of electricity generated by a tidal power plant varies during the day, and from day to day and month to month. As a result, tidal power plants don't always generate electricity when it's most needed. One successful tidal power plant is in northern France on the Rance River estuary.

## *Career*  *Electrical Engineer*

### *Who Designs the Circuits in a Computer?*

Electrical engineering is a broad field. Electrical engineers design and develop electric motors and other kinds of electric machinery. Some electrical engineers design power equipment and distribution systems that provide you with electricity.

Electrical engineers working in electronics develop, produce, and test electronic equipment, such as radios, TVs, telephone networks, and computers. Software engineers design automation systems for factories and controls for airplanes, spaceships, and other systems.

To be an electrical engineer requires good math skills and a knowledge of physics, chemistry, and electricity. You should be curious about mechanical operations and enjoy finding new ways of doing things. An interest in computers, model-building, and math games is useful. You also need to be able to analyze problems and to communicate your ideas, both in writing and in diagrams.

Electrical engineers must complete a bachelor's degree at a college or university. Some schools have cooperative education programs.

These programs allow you to alternate between taking classes and working as an engineering trainee.

In high school, you should take mathematics, chemistry, physics, and English.

## Science and Technology
### *The Hydrogen Stove*

In the late 1970s, an energy experiment turned an ordinary house in Provo, Utah, into a "hydrogen homestead." Hydrogen gas operated the stove, oven, water heater, gas furnace, and outdoor barbecue. It also fueled a car and a lawn tractor.

In many ways, hydrogen is an ideal fuel. It can be made from ordinary water. You can burn hydrogen in a stove, a power plant, or an internal-combustion engine. When it burns, hydrogen produces no pollution. The only products are heat and water.

What prevents the widespread use of this ideal fuel? The biggest problem is cost. Breaking the strong chemical bonds between the hydrogen and oxygen atoms in water takes a great deal of energy. Making hydrogen from water uses more energy than the gas gives up when it recombines with oxygen. Recent advances in solar-cell technology might solve this problem. Thin-film solar cells are a cheap energy source.

Storing hydrogen safely is another problem. Hydrogen gas is very explosive. It reacts violently in air when ignited. The system used in the "hydrogen homestead" is probably the safest method available. The storage tank holds fine particles of a metal alloy that absorbs hydrogen like a sponge, forming a compound known as a metal hydride. Heating the tank releases the hydrogen gas slowly and safely.

▼ **ACTIVITY**

**Hypothesizing**

*Hydrogen as Fuel*

Use the library to find out more about the "hydrogen homestead." Write a hypothesis about why hydrogen was a success or failure as a cost-efficient fuel.

**SKILLS WORKOUT**

## Check and Explain

1. Describe three ways to use solar energy in a conventional home.

2. Explain how technology uses wind, geothermal, and tidal processes to produce electricity.

3. **Compare and Contrast**  List the advantages and disadvantages of using biomass and synthetic fuels. Which has the most advantages? Which has the most disadvantages?

4. **Communicate**  Draw a flowchart that shows the role of the sun's energy in three alternative energy sources.

# Activity 24  *How do you make a solar hot-dog cooker?*

*Skills* Observe; Infer

### Task 1  Prelab Prep
Collect the following items: shoe box, aluminum foil, scissors, long wooden skewer, and a hot dog.

### Task 2  Data Record
Draw a table like the one shown. Record all of your observations in your table.

**Table 24.1  Data Record**

| Time (Minutes) | Observations |
| --- | --- |
| 10 | |
| 20 | |
| 30 | |
| 40 | |
| 50 | |
| 60 | |

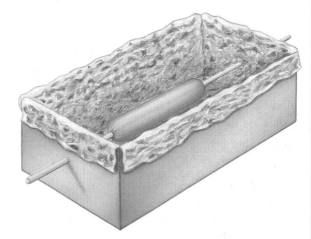

### Task 3  Procedure
1. Completely line the inside of the shoe box with aluminum foil with the shiny side out. The foil should extend a few centimeters above the top of the box. Fold the foil down over the edge of the box.
2. Make a small hole in the center of each end of the shoe box with the point of a pair of scissors. From the outside of the box, push the skewer through one of the holes.
3. Push the skewer through the length of the hot dog. Be sure the hot dog is centered on the skewer.
4. Push the skewer through the hole in the other end of the shoe box. The skewer should be firmly in place.
5. Put the shoe-box solar cooker in a sunny place. It needs to be in full sunlight for at least one hour.
6. Feel the hot dog every ten minutes and record your observations in your table.

### Task 4  Analysis
1. What change did you observe in the temperature of the hot dog?
2. What was the source of the energy that caused this change?
3. What was the purpose of lining the box with aluminum foil?
4. What is the effect of the foil lining on the time required to cook the hot dog?

### Task 5  Conclusion
Explain how your solar hot-dog cooker works. Identify the most important parts of the solar cooker.

### *Everyday Application*
What factors affect how long it takes to cook a hot dog in a solar cooker? Suggest one or more ways to speed up the process.

### *Extension*
Try cooking other kinds of food in your solar cooker. Identify foods that cook slower or faster than a hot dog. What do foods that cook at the same rate have in common?

*Energy Map*

Draw a diagram of your classroom. Label the places where energy is used. List some ways you or your school could save energy in that room. Share your list with the class.

# 24.3 Energy Conservation Decisions

## Objectives

▶ **Identify** three nonrenewable and three renewable sources of energy.

▶ **Analyze** the risks and benefits of four energy sources.

▶ **Infer** how conserving energy can affect natural resources.

▶ **Collect data** on personal energy conservation.

The United States has enough coal to last for several hundred years. What will happen to future generations when the coal supply runs out? Should the United States continue to rely on coal as a source of energy?

Someday you may be involved in making long-range energy decisions. There are several things you can do right now to conserve energy. You can save energy by turning off lights when they aren't needed or by taking a quick shower instead of a bath. Conserving energy is the cleanest, cheapest, and quickest way to stretch precious energy resources.

## Nonrenewable and Renewable Energy

Energy sources not replaced by natural processes within the span of a person's lifetime are classified as **nonrenewable resources**. People are using fossil fuels at a rate that is thousands of times faster than the rate at which fossil fuels form. Although no one can predict exactly how long it will take, the world supply of coal, oil, and natural gas will eventually run out.

Natural resources replaced by ecological cycles or by natural chemical or physical processes are **renewable resources**. Look at Table 24.2. Solar energy is a renewable resource. It comes from nuclear fusion reactions in the sun's interior that will continue for billions of years. Hydroelectric power is also renewable. The energy of moving water is supplied by the natural water cycle that provides rain or snow. Which of the renewable energy sources listed are practical in your area?

**Table 24.2  Energy Sources**

| Renewable | Nonrenewable |
|---|---|
| Hydroelectric | Coal |
| Wind | Natural gas |
| Tides | Oil |
| Geothermal* | Uranium |
| Biomass | Oil shale |
| Ethanol/ methanol† | Tar sands |
| Sunlight | |

\* Individual fields may run out
† Renewable when made from biomass

## Technology Risks and Benefits

Every energy technology or project has both risks and benefits. For example, oil companies wanted to build a gas pipeline from Alaska to the United States. Two benefits of the project were new jobs, and the availability of fuel where it was needed.

The project also carried risks. Drilling for oil in Alaska would upset the ecology of wilderness areas and displace wildlife. To pay for the project, oil companies were authorized to increase charges to their customers—before the pipeline was built. The cost of development is one kind of risk. A change in the environment is another kind of risk.

Risk-benefit analysis is used to evaluate the risks and benefits of a new technology. If a project carries more risks than benefits, it shouldn't be done. A technology is acceptable if the benefits outweigh the risks, and if consumers are willing to accept the risks.

*SkillBuilder* *Analyzing*

### A Risk-Benefit Analysis

Imagine that you are in charge of an environmental-assessment group. Your group must decide whether or not a utility company should build a large dam and hydroelectric power plant on the Great Whale River in Quebec, Canada.

The plant is part of a $12.7 billion project that will generate 3,168 megawatts of electricity— enough to serve a city of 700,000 people. The project will create many needed jobs. The government says the project is essential to the economic growth of Quebec.

The project will reduce the flow of the Great Whale River by 85 percent. About 17,500 Native-Canadians who live in the wilderness area where the dam will be built will be affected. The supply of river fish, which is their main food source, will be greatly reduced. Also, the dam will flood their ancestral hunting grounds and destroy thousands of sacred sites.

1. List the benefits of building the hydroelectric power plant. Consider the benefits to people, the economy, and the environment. Rate each benefit as unimportant, important, or very important.

2. Use the same method to list and rate the risks to the people and the environment involved in building the power plant.

3. Compare your two lists. Do the benefits outweigh the risks? If not, are the people who will be affected the most by this project willing to accept the risks?

4. Use your risk-benefit analysis to make your decision.

Write a short report stating your decision about the power project. Be sure to include your reasons for making that decision.

# Energy Conservation

Energy consumption in the United States can be divided among three main users—home, transportation, and industry. All three areas must be involved in reducing energy consumption.

Conservation is using less energy in order to preserve natural resources. It's important to use existing energy sources wisely while new sources and new technology are being developed. Using less fuel also protects other natural resources by reducing pollution.

**Home** Many energy conservation measures require only a change in personal or family habits. Look at Figure 24.13. What are some ways you can save energy at home?

**Figure 24.13
Energy Conservation
at Home** ▼

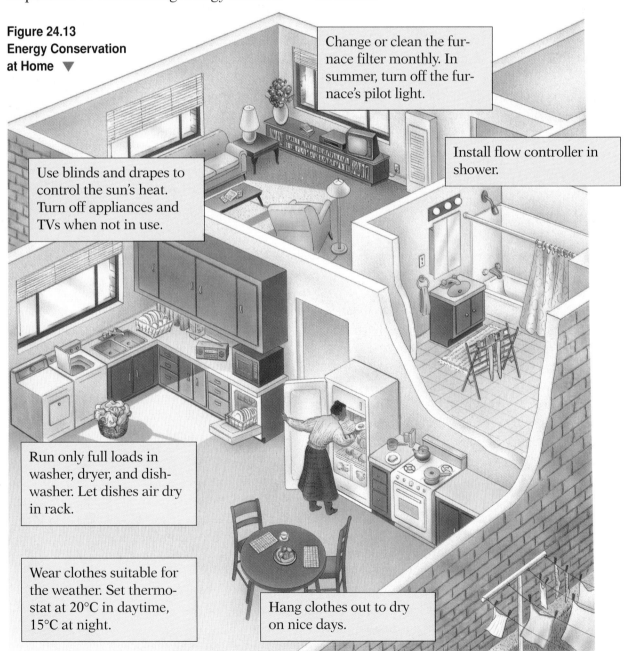

Change or clean the furnace filter monthly. In summer, turn off the furnace's pilot light.

Install flow controller in shower.

Use blinds and drapes to control the sun's heat. Turn off appliances and TVs when not in use.

Run only full loads in washer, dryer, and dishwasher. Let dishes air dry in rack.

Wear clothes suitable for the weather. Set thermostat at 20°C in daytime, 15°C at night.

Hang clothes out to dry on nice days.

**Transportation** Motor vehicles use 40 percent of the oil consumed in the United States. You can save some of this energy by riding a bicycle or walking whenever possible. Sharing rides with friends or using public transportation also saves energy. Automobile usage can be reduced by planning shopping trips in advance to combine errands. Eliminate automobile trips whenever possible.

Encourage your family to drive a small car that conserves fuel. Keep vehicles operating at peak efficiency with proper maintenance. Regular car tune-ups can improve mileage up to 10 percent. Clean engine filters, frequent oil changes, and proper tire pressure also increase gasoline efficiency.

Driving skills affect the fuel economy of a vehicle. Driving at moderate speeds saves energy. Most cars get about 20 percent more kilometers per liter at 88 km per hour than they do at 112 km per hour. Driving at a steady speed also saves energy. Sudden starts and stops and racing an engine waste gasoline.

**Industry** Industry is the biggest energy user. It also has the greatest potential for energy savings. Industries can save energy by doing many of the same things your family can do at home. For example, industries can add insulation and turn off lights.

The biggest energy savings in industry come from streamlining manufacturing processes and installing more efficient equipment. These changes are expensive to make. However, the investment can pay off in lower manufacturing costs.

Some industries are saving energy by burning wastes as fuel. Others recover waste heat from machinery and use it for space heating or other purposes. Industries can also conserve by a process called *cogeneration*. This process involves producing heat and electricity from the same fuel source. For example, power plants heat water as they operate. Instead of dumping the hot water, some power plants use it to heat their offices.

Many utilities are promoting energy conservation among their customers. Some utility companies will pay part of the bill when a business or a family makes improvements to save energy. By reducing demand for electric power, utility companies can save the cost of building and maintaining new power plants.

**Figure 24.14** ▲
How does using public transportation save energy?

▼ **ACTIVITY**

**Graphing**

*Energy Distribution*

Make a circle graph to show the distribution of energy use for each of the following: Industry and business, 52%; Transportation, 26%; Homes, 22%. Label all the parts of your graph.

**SKILLS WORKOUT**

## Science and Society
### *Saving Energy by Recycling*

An average family in the United States produces about 45 kg of trash every week! By recycling some of these materials instead of throwing them away, you can save energy and natural resources. Recycling also reduces pollution and the need for landfill space.

Recycling is any activity that keeps matter in use. One way to recycle is to find another use for a product. You can use discarded envelopes for phone messages or grocery lists, for example. Using products more than once for the same purpose is another form of recycling. Instead of throwing away old clothes, books, toys, or furniture, give them to someone who can use them.

One of the best ways to save energy is to take part in local recycling programs. Many communities have curbside pickup for items that can be recycled, such as aluminum cans, glass bottles, newspapers, and some plastics. In other places, you must take items to a collection center.

Each aluminum can you recycle saves the amount of energy in about 2 liters of gasoline. The energy you save by recycling a single glass bottle could light a 100-watt light bulb for four hours. Recycling paper saves about half the energy it takes to make paper from new materials. The results of saving paper are shown in Figure 24.15. What are some other ways you could recycle items instead of throwing them away?

**Figure 24.15** ▲
Each stack of newspapers represents a pine tree ten times its height. Explain why recycling is important.

## Check and Explain

1.  Explain the difference between nonrenewable and renewable resources. Identify three of each resource.

2.  Make a table that compares the risks and benefits of developing one of the energy sources in this chapter. Which alternative is the most promising? Explain.

3.  **Infer**  List three ways you can conserve energy. How do these methods affect natural resources?

4.  **Collect Data**  Keep a record by listing all of the ways you conserve energy for one week. Organize your data into a table or chart.

## Concept Summary

### 24.1 Generating and Using Electric Power
▶ Energy sources used to produce electricity are coal, oil, natural gas, moving water, and nuclear reactions.
▶ Electric power plants use mechanical energy to generate electric energy.
▶ High-voltage transmission lines carry electricity from a power plant over long distances to homes and industry.

### 24.2 Alternative Energy Technologies
▶ Solar power can be used to produce heat and electricity.
▶ Wind, geothermal steam, and the motion of the tides are alternative energy sources used to generate electricity.
▶ Dried organic material can be burned as biomass fuel. Biomass fuels can be grown as crops or made from garbage.
▶ Synthetic fuels can be used in industry and automobiles instead of gasoline and other fuels made from oil.

### 24.3 Energy Conservation Decisions
▶ Nonrenewable resources aren't naturally replaced or regenerated in a person's lifetime. Renewable resources are easily replaced.
▶ Efforts to conserve energy can be made in business, industry, transportation, and at home.
▶ Risk-benefit analysis helps people to make better decisions about energy use by comparing the risks and benefits of an action.

## Chapter Vocabulary

hydroelectric power (24.1)    biomass (24.2)    nonrenewable resources (24.3)
fossil fuel (24.1)    geothermal (24.2)    renewable resources (24.3)
solar cell (24.2)

## Check Your Vocabulary

Use the vocabulary words above to complete the following sentences correctly.

1. Solar power can produce an electric current in a device called a(n) _____ .
2. Heat energy from hot magma beneath the earth's surface is _____ energy.
3. An energy source that is the remains of plants and animals that lived long ago and that changed over millions of years is a(n) _____ .
4. At a(n) _____ plant, water released through a dam turns a turbine that operates a generator.
5. Hydroelectric power, wind power, and solar power are examples of _____ energy sources.

6. Plant material and other organic matter used as fuel is called _____ .
7. Energy sources not replenished by natural biological, chemical, and physical processes are _____ energy sources.

Explain the differences between the words in each pair.

8. renewable, nonrenewable
9. geothermal, hydroelectric
10. fossil fuel, biomass

## Write Your Vocabulary

Write sentences using the vocabulary words above. Show that you know what each word means.

# Chapter 24 Review

## Check Your Knowledge

Answer the following in complete sentences.

1. How is electricity produced?

2. What are fossil fuels? How are they formed?

3. What is hydroelectric power? How is it produced?

4. Trace the path of electricity from a power station to your home.

5. What are the advantages and disadvantages of nuclear power?

6. What is geothermal power? How is it produced?

7. How does a tidal power plant differ from a hydroelectric power plant? How are they similar?

8. Why is it important to develop alternative energy sources now?

9. What are two advantages to using biomass as an energy source? What are two possible disadvantages?

Choose the answer that best completes each sentence.

10. Some electric power plants use moving water or steam to turn a (power grid, turbine, circuit breaker, transformer).

11. Supplies of fossil fuels, such as coal and oil, are (unlimited, increasing, limited, widely available).

12. A solar cell (collects heat, changes sunlight to electricity, contains a generator, burns biomass).

13. Materials such as corncobs, sawdust, sewage, and manure are all forms of (fossil fuel, hydrogen, biomass, nuclear power).

## Check Your Understanding

Apply the concepts you have learned to answer each question.

1. **Application** Identify three items in your home that could be used as biomass.

2. Explain the advantages of "thin-film" solar technology.

3. How does recycling save energy? Give two examples.

4. **Mystery Photo** The photograph on page 582 shows solar reflectors used to concentrate light from the sun. The energy from the concentrated sunlight is eventually converted into electric energy.

   a. Why is concentrating the sunlight important?

   b. How does the design of the reflectors work to concentrate light from the sun?

   c. What is one way the energy from the concentrated sunlight could be converted to electricity?

5. **Application** Imagine that you are an architect designing a vacation home. The home is to be built in a mountain area where there aren't any electric power lines. Describe how you would supply the home with heat, hot water, and electricity.

6. Prepare a risk-benefit analysis for converting your home or school to a solar-heating system from its present heating system.

7. Design a poster that motivates and shows people how they can save energy at home.

## Develop Your Skills

1. **Interpret Data** The table below contains data about nonindustrial energy use in the United States.

**Nonindustrial Energy Use**

| Transportation | | Home Use | |
|---|---|---|---|
| Autos | 29% | Heating and air conditioning | 29% |
| Trucks | 13% | Water heating | 6% |
| Air conditioning | 4% | Appliances | 6% |
| Other | 9% | Lighting | 4% |

   a. What are the biggest nonindustrial energy users?

   b. Based on the table, what actions could the average person take that would result in the greatest energy savings?

2. **Infer** Which do you think requires more energy to produce: 10 kg of corn on the cob or 10 kg of corn chips? Explain.

3. **Data Bank** Use the information on page 642 to answer the following questions.

   a. What is the largest overall energy user in the United States?

   b. What industrial process uses the most energy? What could be done to reduce the amount of energy used for this purpose?

   c. About what percentage of the total energy could be saved if people drove their cars only half as much?

## Make Connections

1. **Link the Concepts** Below is a concept map showing how some of the main concepts in this chapter link together. Only part of the map is filled in. Finish the map, using words and ideas from the chapter.

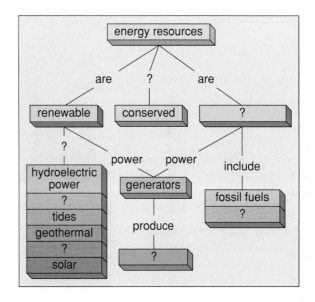

2. **Science and Social Studies** Research the energy crisis of the 1970s. Use articles from magazines and newspapers to find out why the energy crisis took place and how people felt about it. Report your findings to the class.

3. **Science and Literature** Many novels and short stories describe life in the United States before electric power. Read such a novel or story, and write a report about it. Discuss how the people in the story met their energy needs for heat, light, transportation, and other uses.

4. **Science and You** Develop an energy-savings plan for your home. Try the plan for one week, and write a report about your experiences.

# Chapter **25** Chemical Technology

## Chapter Sections

**25.1** Petroleum Fuels

**25.2** Petrochemical Products

**25.3** Materials Science

**25.4** Technology and the Environment

## What do you see?

"This is a picture of a ceramic bowl and plate on a table. The plate and bowl were probably shaped by hand out of wet clay and then glazed, baked, and painted. The pattern was carefully designed and painted onto the bowl and dish. These are no doubt ancient artifacts of some old civilization."

*Katie Sherwin*
*Bethlehem Central*
*Middle School*
*Delmar, New York*

To find out more about the photograph, look on page 630. As you read this chapter, you will learn about chemical technology.

# 25.1 Petroleum Fuels

## Objectives

▶ **Identify** the source of petroleum.

▶ **Explain** how petroleum is refined.

▶ **Compare** and **contrast** the properties of various petroleum hydrocarbons.

▶ **Interpret** a diagram on the activity in a fractionating tower.

Imagine filling the gas tank of a car with prehistoric sunlight! The gasoline that flows into a car's tank doesn't look like sunlight. However, gasoline contains energy that once was light. The light energy came from nuclear fusion reactions that occurred in the sun.

Light energy was absorbed by plants, algae, and microscopic animals. Through the process of photosynthesis, some living things converted light energy into stored chemical energy. When microscopic ocean organisms died, their buried remains still contained chemical energy. Over millions of years, some of the dead organisms were changed into crude oil.

**Figure 25.1**
These microscopic organisms, called diatoms, float freely in the ocean. They get energy from sunlight by the process of photosynthesis. ▼

## Oil and Gas Formation

Crude oil and natural gas formed from the bodies of microscopic ocean organisms. These organisms had skeletons made of silica and soft parts made up of organic compounds. When ancient ocean organisms died, their remains often settled on the ocean floor. Similar organisms can be seen in Figure 25.1.

Clay and mud sediments also settled on the ocean floor. These sediments buried and compacted the remains of the organisms. Over time, the weight of many layers of sediment produced pressure and heat that changed the organic material into crude oil, or **petroleum**. Petroleum, a greenish-black oily liquid, is a mixture of hydrocarbons. Petroleum is usually found along with natural gas. Natural gas, a mixture of flammable gases, is mostly methane ($CH_4$).

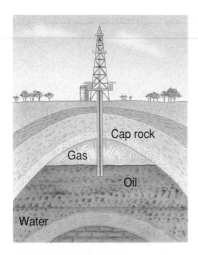

**Figure 25.2** ▲

The amount of natural gas in a trap varies. Small amounts of natural gas are usually burned off as waste.

## Petroleum Deposits

Recall that hydrocarbons are organic molecules that contain only hydrogen and carbon. The carbon atoms are attached to hydrogen atoms to form long or short chains. Petroleum is a mixture of long-chain and short-chain hydrocarbons. Some hydrocarbons in petroleum include gasoline, kerosene, wax, and lubricating oil.

Petroleum deposits often form in "traps," like the one shown in Figure 25.2. A trap is a geologic structure of porous and nonporous rock. A nonporous rock, such as shale, is called a cap rock because it lies on top of the trap. Because the petroleum can't flow through the cap rock, it collects in the lower layers of porous rock.

By drilling a hole through the cap rock, the petroleum can be removed from the trap. A well-pipe is inserted through the hole into the oil-saturated rock. Pressure caused by underground water pushes the petroleum toward the surface through the well pipe. If there isn't enough water pressure, pumps draw the petroleum up to the surface.

Some natural gas is dissolved in the liquid petroleum. Often the natural gas collects in a pocket above the petroleum deposit. The map in Figure 25.3 shows the locations of known petroleum and natural gas deposits in the United States.

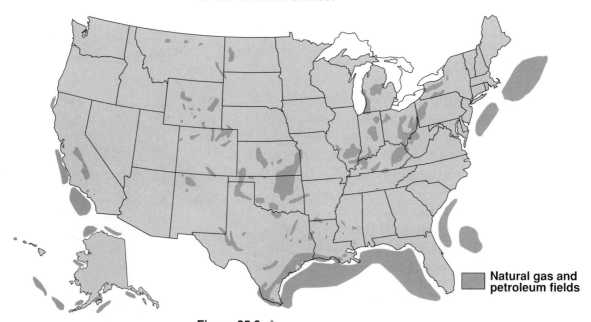

**Natural gas and petroleum fields**

**Figure 25.3** ▲

What kind of land surfaces have oil deposits? Use an atlas to help you find the answer.

# Petroleum Refining

Petroleum contains many different kinds of hydrocarbons. A process called *fractional distillation* separates hydrocarbons with similar properties into groups. Each group of petroleum hydrocarbons is called a fraction.

Pumps transport petroleum into the bottom of a fractionating tower. At the bottom, which is the hottest part of the tower, most of the hydrocarbons vaporize and begin to rise. As the vapor rises, it starts to cool. Each fraction condenses, or cools to a liquid, within a certain temperature range. The temperature ranges are shown in Figure 25.4. As a result, each fraction condenses at a different height in the tower. As each fraction becomes liquid, pipes carry it from the tower to holding tanks.

**Figure 25.4**
A fractionating tower refines crude oil. Which fractions do you use everyday? ▼

**Below 0°C**
Methane and other gaseous fractions are piped from the tower. The fractions are cooled to liquids and used as fuel or in the chemical industry.

**260°C to 370°C**
This gas-oil fraction is processed into heating oil and diesel fuel. Some of these hydrocarbons are also processed into gasoline.

**0°C to 200°C**
This fraction of petroleum contains hydrocarbons that are processed into gasoline. Gasoline accounts for nearly half of all petroleum products.

**330°C to 460°C**
This fraction includes lubricating oils and greases that are used to decrease friction in the moving parts of machinery.

**180°C to 270°C**
Kerosene and solvents form this fraction. Kerosene is mixed with gasoline to make jet fuel. Solvents are used in industry.

**Over 460°C**
Asphalt and other heavy residues remain as liquids and are drained off. Asphalt is used in roofing materials and to pave roads.

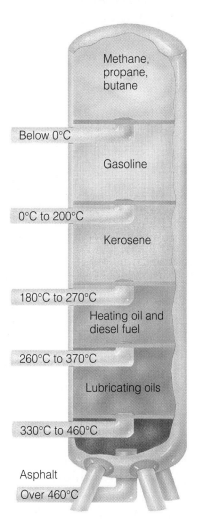

**Fractionating Tower**

Methane, propane, butane

Below 0°C

Gasoline

0°C to 200°C

Kerosene

180°C to 270°C

Heating oil and diesel fuel

260°C to 370°C

Lubricating oils

330°C to 460°C

Asphalt
Over 460°C

## Science and Society *Petroleum Reserves*

How can you tell if a car is low on gas? The gas gauge indicates how much fuel is in the gas tank. When the needle points to "F," the fuel tank holds its maximum amount of fuel. As the engine uses fuel, the needle moves toward "E." Soon it's time to refill the tank.

Suppose you were to use a gauge to show how much petroleum the earth has in reserve. What would the gauge show? To construct such a gauge, you need to know two things: how much petroleum was in the earth when its tank was "full" and how much of this petroleum has been used.

An optimistic estimate of the earth's total petroleum reserve suggests that at one time there were about 2,000 billion barrels. Of this amount, only half has been discovered. About 500 billion barrels of petroleum are already used up. Observable geologic structures suggest that 1,000 billion barrels of petroleum still remain undiscovered. Environmental protection laws prohibit tapping some of the remaining reserves. Some undiscovered reserves may be located on protected land or water. Some reserves are too deep in the earth, near expensive real estate, or not large enough to be profitable.

If you include both the known and the possible petroleum reserves, "F" on your gauge would equal about 2,000 billion barrels of petroleum. If you subtract the 500 billion barrels that have been used, the needle would point to about "3/4" full. About 20 billion barrels of petroleum are extracted from the ground each year. At this rate, the needle on your gauge will point to a little over "1/2" by the year 2010. Where will the needle point to in 2060?

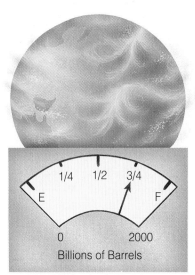

**Earth's Fuel Gauge**

**Figure 25.5** ▲

Read the gauge showing the amount of petroleum remaining on the earth. What happens when it registers "Empty"?

## Check and Explain

1. How is petroleum formed?

2. Why is heat important for refining petroleum?

3. **Compare and Contrast** How do the uses of asphalt differ from those of heating oil or lubricating oil?

4. **Interpret Data** Look at the fractionating tower on page 607. Which substances condense at the highest temperatures? The lowest temperatures?

# 25.2 Petrochemical Products

## Objectives

▶ **List** examples of products made from petrochemicals.

▶ **Identify** the characteristics of a polymer.

▶ **Compare** and **contrast** the properties of plastics and synthetic fibers.

▶ **Make a model** of the arrangement of molecules in a synthetic fiber.

What does the sole of your sneaker have in common with a plastic chair, nylon fabric, antifreeze, paint, and the ink on this page? Like the items in Figure 25.6, all of these materials are made from petroleum! Recall that petroleum is made up of groups, or fractions, that contain different hydrocarbons. Some fractions, such as fuel oil and gasoline, can be used without being broken down further. Other fractions are combined with various chemical substances to produce synthetic materials. Synthetic materials and chemical substances produced from petroleum are called **petrochemicals.**

## Properties of Petrochemicals

Recall that hydrocarbon molecules can be broken apart and rejoined to form petrochemicals with different properties. Dyes, plastics, synthetic fibers, and rubber substitutes are petrochemicals with complex structures. They are formed only by controlled chemical reactions.

Plastics and synthetic fibers are made of chains of many small molecules. Each small molecule is called a *monomer*. A chain of linked monomers forms a large molecule called a **polymer**. Each polymer may contain hundreds or thousands of monomers.

The properties of each petrochemical are due to its molecular structure and composition. For example, hard plastics contain a rigid framework of polymers. Plastics that stretch contain "bunched up" polymers that lengthen when pulled. Fibers contain polymers that run in the same direction and can slide past each other.

**Figure 25.6**
The nylon fibers of the fanny pack and the paint in the bucket are made from petroleum. What other things that you use are made from petroleum? ▼

What types of plastic are used in the packaging of your lunch? A number code identifies the type of plastic used in a container.

**1.** List the number codes you found. Find out what plastics the codes stand for.

**2.** Why are these codes used?

**A C T I V I T Y**

## Plastics

Dozens of objects in your home and school are made from plastic. Some items contain many different plastics. For example, a telephone has a base and receiver made from a hard, shock-resistant plastic. The coiled wires that connect the receiver and base are covered with a flexible plastic that can uncoil and then return to its coiled shape. A third kind of plastic covers the wires that connect the base to the wall jack.

Air injected into plastic makes a soft and pliable foam. Artificial sponges are made of plastic foam with an open-cell structure that can hold water. Plastics with a closed-cell structure are stiff and hold very little water.

### Polymers

All plastics are made from polymers. In a polymer, monomer units are connected in a chain. What represents the monomers in this model of a polymer? Plastics like those in the sandal are classified by the kind of polymer from which they are made. ▼

### PVC Plastics ▲

Acetylene and chlorine gas combine to form a monomer called vinyl chloride. Vinyl chloride monomers join together to form the polymer called polyvinyl chloride, or PVC. PVC is a strong, rigid, heat-resistant plastic used to make many useful products. Cups, dishes, pipes, rain gutters, and rainwear are PVC products.

### Polystyrene Plastics

Acetylene and benzene combine to form the monomer called styrene. When styrene monomers join together, they form polystyrene, a lightweight, low-density plastic. Water absorbed by a diver's wet suit, which is made of polystyrene, is kept warm by the diver's body. The diver is kept warm by the suit.

▼

## Synthetic Fibers

The polymers that make up synthetic fibers, such as nylon, rayon, and polyester, are long, straight chains of monomers. The chains line up next to each other in a side-by-side arrangement. Bonding forces between neighboring chains keep the polymers close together. However, the polymers can slide past each other. This sliding action produces a long, thin arrangement of molecules called a strand or fiber.

You can see the strands that make up nylon in Figure 25.7. The strands can be produced in different thicknesses and woven together in various ways to produce many kinds of nylon fabric. For example, nylon is used to make a stretchable fabric for stockings. Thin strands of nylon can be tightly woven to make fabrics that are wind-resistant and water-repellent. Unlike natural fibers, synthetic fibers like nylon don't break down easily.

**Figure 25.7**

The petrochemical liquids in the beaker combine to make a polymer that forms a nylon fiber. Which items owe their brilliant color to petrochemical dyes?

▼

## Dyes

Some petrochemicals add color to clothing, cosmetics, and other products. These colorful chemicals are called dyes. Until the 1850s, most dyes came from plants or animals. The blue dye called indigo was made from plants. The dye called royal purple came from shellfish. Today most dyes are made from petrochemicals.

Petrochemical dyes offer several advantages over natural dyes. Petrochemical dyes have a consistent color and are cheap to produce. In addition, petrochemical dyes have a wider range of color, and work on a wider variety of materials than natural dyes do.

## Pharmaceuticals

In industrial nations like the United States, many drugs, or pharmaceuticals, are made from petrochemicals. For example, the active ingredient in aspirin was once extracted from the bark of willow trees. Today this active ingredient is manufactured from coal tar.

## Solvents

Have you ever tried to clean out a brush that contained enamel paint, or fingernail polish? If so, you know that these substances don't wash out with soap and water. To remove materials that won't dissolve in water, such as oil paint or lacquer, you need to use a petrochemical solvent. When you write with a felt-tip marker, the odor you smell is that of the petrochemical solvent used to thin the ink. Some kinds of petrochemical solvents are paint thinner, ammonia, acetone, and benzene.

Petrochemical solvents are used in the manufacture of pharmaceuticals, cosmetics, textiles, and computer chips. Some petrochemical solvents are used in the dry-cleaning process. Cleaning solvents easily dissolve body oils, oily food, and ink stains from cloth. Petrochemical solvents give off fumes that can be hazardous to health. All solvents should be used in a well-ventilated room, and disposed of properly.

## *Consider This*

### Are Biodegradable Plastics Good for the Environment?

Most solid wastes, including plastics, end up buried in landfills. They remain in the landfill without ever being recycled into the environment. By mixing plastic polymers with substances that break down easily, a material called biodegradable plastic is produced.

**Consider Some Issues**
Supporters of biodegradable plastic think that it should be used for making disposable items. They say that unlike regular plastic, the biodegradable plastics will decompose more readily into recyclable materials.

Opponents of biodegradable plastic feel that this product is more of a hazard than a help. They claim that very little of this material will break down in a landfill. They also think that marketing biodegradable plastics interferes with efforts to recycle other plastics. Consumers may choose to buy disposable containers instead of those designed to be recycled.

**Think About It** Which strategy would use less of the world's petroleum reserve—using biodegradable plastic or recyclable plastic?

**Write About It** Write a paper stating your position for or against the use of biodegradable plastics. Include your reasons for choosing your position. Share your position with the class.

## Science and You *Plastic Recycling*

What do the letters *PET* and *HDPE* mean to you? If you sort and recycle plastics, you may already know the answer! These letters identify two of the most commonly recycled plastics. The clear plastic PET, which stands for polyethylene terephthalate, is used to make carbonated-beverage containers. The translucent plastic HDPE, or high-density polyethylene, is used in milk and juice containers.

To help identify recyclable plastics, the containers are marked with a code. The code is either printed on the package label or molded into the plastic itself. Look at Figure 25.8. The code appears as a number within a triangle that is formed by three arrows. The number 1 identifies a PET container. The number 2 identifies an HDPE container.

A recycling plant sorts the containers it accepts. Unwanted materials, such as metal caps, are removed from the plastic. Machines cut the plastic containers into small, confetti-like flakes. The plastic flakes are washed and sorted again to remove contaminants. After drying, the plastic flakes are packaged and transported to manufacturers that use recycled plastics.

Recycled plastic flakes have many uses. For example, after they've been processed, flakes can be used as an insulating material in articles such as sleeping bags. Plastic flakes can also be bonded together to form a material that can be substituted for lumber. This wood substitute doesn't rot or break down easily. Manufacturers hope that plastic lumber will someday replace the wood used to build things like decks, picnic tables, and piers.

**Figure 25.8** ▲

The number 1 in a triangle is the code for a recyclable, clear plastic called polyethylene terephthalate, or PET. Where can you see this code?

## Check and Explain

1. List five examples of products made from petrochemicals.

2. What is a polymer?

3. **Compare and Contrast**  How are the properties of plastics and synthetic fibers similar? How do they differ?

4. **Make a Model**  Design a model of the arrangement of the polymers in a synthetic fiber.

## ACTIVITY

**Classifying**

*Building Materials*

Make a list of 12 materials you would need to build a house. Classify each building material as a plant or animal product, metal, ceramic, plastic, or substance of unknown origin. Some items may fall into more than one group.

**SKILLS WARMUP**

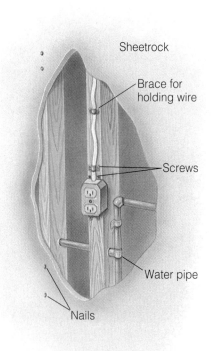

Sheetrock

Brace for holding wire

Screws

Water pipe

Nails

**Figure 25.9** ▲

What metal items can you identify in this drawing of the inside of the wall of a building?

# 25.3 Materials Science

## Objectives

▶ **Describe** metallurgy and explain its importance.

▶ **Describe** how steel is made.

▶ **Compare** and **contrast** the processes for making ceramics and glass.

▶ **Infer** the properties of a composite material.

How many objects do you use every day that are made from metal? You have many metal objects inside your home, such as kitchen utensils, appliances, and light fixtures. Your home also has many hidden metal parts.

If you could look behind the walls, as in Figure 25.9, you'd find steel nails, brackets, and screws that hold the frame of your home together. You'd also find pipes and electric wires made of copper. You might even observe a metal-foil backing on fiberglass wall insulation.

## Metallurgy

The complete process of taking metals from the earth and making them into useful products is called **metallurgy** (MEHT uh LUR jee). Many familiar metals, such as iron, silver, and copper, look very different when they come out of the earth as an ore. A metal ore is a naturally occurring compound or mixture from which a metal is removed. For example, iron ore contains iron, oxygen, sulfur, and sand.

After an ore deposit is found, the ore is mined and brought to the surface. The metal is separated from the ore. Once the metal is refined, it can be mixed with other materials or shaped into usable forms.

Metallurgy is so important to human society that periods of history have been named for metals. For example, the Bronze Age began approximately 3500 B.C. with the discovery of bronze. Bronze is an alloy of copper and tin and is very strong. It can be easily shaped into tools. The Iron Age began approximately 1000 B.C., when iron tools and weapons were developed.

# From Iron Ore to Steel

Steel-making is a step-by-step process that begins with the location of iron-ore deposits. After the ore is mined, the refining process begins. Follow the steps of the steel-making process in Figure 25.10.

**Figure 25.10**
**The Steel-making Process** ▼

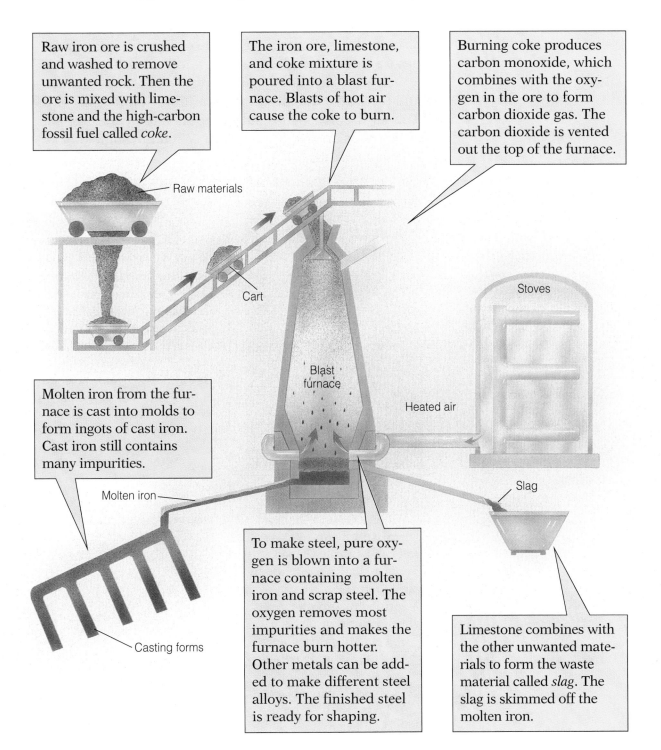

Raw iron ore is crushed and washed to remove unwanted rock. Then the ore is mixed with limestone and the high-carbon fossil fuel called *coke*.

The iron ore, limestone, and coke mixture is poured into a blast furnace. Blasts of hot air cause the coke to burn.

Burning coke produces carbon monoxide, which combines with the oxygen in the ore to form carbon dioxide gas. The carbon dioxide is vented out the top of the furnace.

Raw materials

Cart

Stoves

Blast furnace

Heated air

Molten iron from the furnace is cast into molds to form ingots of cast iron. Cast iron still contains many impurities.

Molten iron

Slag

Casting forms

To make steel, pure oxygen is blown into a furnace containing molten iron and scrap steel. The oxygen removes most impurities and makes the furnace burn hotter. Other metals can be added to make different steel alloys. The finished steel is ready for shaping.

Limestone combines with the other unwanted materials to form the waste material called *slag*. The slag is skimmed off the molten iron.

# Ceramics

Clay and other earth materials that are shaped and fired at high temperatures form materials called **ceramics** [seh RAM ihks]. You are probably familiar with many different kinds of ceramics. The earthenware in flower pots is a ceramic. Earthenware is made of a coarse red clay. Fine china and porcelain statues are also ceramics. Porcelain is made of very fine clay and has a smooth and glassy appearance.

Ceramics are good insulators, are resistant to water, and can withstand high temperatures. Spark plugs have a ceramic collar that is subject to high temperatures and also acts as an electric insulator. What are some other uses for ceramics?

## Ceramic Clay

Silicate minerals and clays used in ceramics are mined from the earth. These materials are crushed into a fine powder. Different kinds and amounts of clay and mineral powders determine what kind of object will be made. Bowls, plates, and vases are just a few examples of objects made from ceramic clay. ▼

## Clay Shapes ▲

Water added to the powder mixture forms a clay that can be easily shaped. Ceramic shapes are made by hand, poured into a mold, or formed on a potter's wheel. Round or circular objects are easily shaped on the spinning potter's wheel. After shaping, the wet clay objects dry in the air and harden.

## Firing

After the dry object is painted, it is fired in a kiln. Firing is a method of high-temperature heating. During firing, the intense heat in the kiln burns off impurities and causes physical and chemical reactions to take place. Firing hardens the clay and brings out the color of the paint. The clay changes to ceramic. After firing, the object can be glazed.▼

## Glass

What happens if you drop a porcelain cup or dish? It shatters just like glass! Porcelain and glass have many similar properties. They are both brittle, heat resistant, and poor conductors of electricity.

The raw materials used in glass are sand, limestone, and a sodium compound called soda. These materials are ground into a powder and blended together. The amount of each ingredient detemines if the glass is heat-resistant, shatterproof, or common plate glass.

To make glass, the powdered materials are heated and melted into a thick liquid. The liquid is continually stirred to allow waste products to bubble off. After several days, the hot liquid glass is removed from the furnace and shaped. Plate glass is made by squeezing molten glass between rollers to form sheets. Dishes are pressed in a mold. Bottles and similar containers are blown or injected into molds to give them their hollow shape.

## Historical Notebook

### Ceramic Pottery

Thousands of years ago, people on different continents learned to make ceramic pottery. Some of this ancient pottery still exists. The characteristics of the pottery give clues to the techniques and materials that were used to make it.

In ancient Africa, people made two-color ceramic pots. They buried part of the pot in the ashes of a fire. The clay that was buried in the ashes produced a black ceramic, while the part exposed to the air turned red.

In ancient America, people also made two-colored ceramic vessels and figurines. The ancient Americans, however, colored their ceramics with paint. The paints were made using pigments from local mineral deposits.

About 2,000 years ago in China, people discovered how to make the smooth, glassy ceramic known as porcelain. They used a local white clay called kaolin. Objects made from this very fine clay were fired at very high temperatures. The shiny porcelain surface is a glass that forms from the melted mineral crystals in kaolin clay.

1. How could the area in which people lived affect the kinds of ceramics they made?

2. Why do you think pottery might be important in studying about ancient cultures?

3. Choose a geographic area and do library research on the kinds of ceramics made there in ancient or modern times. Write a one-page report.

## ACTIVITY

## Composites

Special materials, called **composites**, were developed and manufactured for their properties. Composites are made up of fibers that are embedded in a layer of material called a **matrix**. The matrix material determines such properties as density, resistance to heat, and ability to conduct electricity. The fibers determine such properties as the strength and flexibility of the composite.

The choice of the matrix material and of the fiber depends on how the composite will be used. If the composite must be heat resistant, ceramics are the best choice for the matrix. Carbon-based fibers are strong and can withstand temperature extremes. Composites made with carbon-based fibers are used to construct some parts for aircraft and space vehicles. Plastics are strong, lightweight, and resist corrosion. However, plastics can't withstand extreme heat. Plastics are used as a matrix in composites like fiberglass.

Fiberglass is a strong and lightweight composite. It is a good material for building and repairing boat hulls and automobile bodies. The fibers are thin strands of glass. Glass fibers are inexpensive, strong, and easy to handle. Plastic polymers, such as polyester, are used as the matrix.

Fiberglass is commonly used as an insulating material. There are air spaces between the glass fibers. Air gets trapped between the fibers. Also, glass is a poor conductor of heat, so the heat does not escape. Look closely at the fiberglass in Figure 25.11. It looks like fabric covered with a transparent coating. Actually, the fabric is made from glass fibers that have been woven and matted together. The matrix is hardened plastic. What are some other uses of fiberglass?

**Figure 25.11**

The body of this automobile is made of fiberglass similar to the sample. Can you identify the fibers and the matrix in the fiberglass sample? ▼

## Science and Technology *Ceramic Engines*

As petroleum use increases, people are more concerned about the supply of fossil fuel. Automakers are looking for ways to make more energy-efficient, nonpolluting vehicles. New developments in ceramic technology may help automakers to build better cars.

The internal-combustion engine used in most cars isn't very fuel efficient. Only about one third of the energy from the burning gasoline is used to move the car. The remaining two thirds of the energy is carried away as waste heat.

By replacing some of the metal parts with parts made of ceramics or ceramic composites, the car's fuel efficiency could be improved. A car with ceramic parts would be lighter than a car with metal parts. A lighter car would use less energy. Also, ceramic engine parts could withstand higher temperatures. As a result, cars with ceramic parts wouldn't need a cooling system. The extra heat could be used to produce more engine power.

Ceramics developed for space vehicles may be used to design a more energy-efficient automobile engine. Ceramics, such as silicon carbide and silicon nitride, developed for the space shuttle shown in Figure 25.12, could be used in gas-turbine engines. As the cost for producing space-age ceramics decreases, ceramics are more likely to be molded into the car engines of the future.

**Figure 25.12** ▲
The space shuttle uses high-tech ceramic materials to withstand extreme temperature changes that are caused by friction as the shuttle re-enters the earth's atmosphere.

## Check and Explain

1. What is metallurgy? Why is it important?

2. Describe how steel is made from iron ore. Explain the purpose of each step in the process.

3. **Compare and Contrast** How are the processes used for making ceramics and glass similar? How are they different?

4. **Infer** Imagine that you're an engineer designing a composite material for the space shuttle. You need a strong, lightweight, and heat-resistant composite. What kind of materials would you use for the fiber? What would you use for the matrix? Explain.

# Activity 25  *How can the properties of a polymer be changed?*

## Task 1  Prelab Prep

Collect the following items: safety goggles, 2 identical small-size jars, 15 mL of 50 percent white-glue solution, 5 mL of 4 percent borax solution, 1 thick, plastic self-lock bag.

## Task 2  Data Record

Draw a data table like the one below.

## Task 3  Procedure

1. Pour 15 mL of the white-glue solution into one of the small jars. Observe the solution and record your observations in the data table. Include the solution's color, odor, and texture. To observe texture, gently swirl the jar without touching the solution. You can smell the solution by gently fanning air from the top of the jar toward your nose. **CAUTION! Handle glass jar carefully to avoid breakage.**

2. Fill the other jar with 5 mL of the borax solution. **CAUTION! Do not touch the borax solution.** Record your observations of the borax solution in the data table. Include the solution's color, odor, and texture. To observe texture, gently swirl the jar without touching the solution. You can smell the solution by gently fanning air from the top of the jar toward your nose.

3. Pour the white-glue solution from the jar into the bag.

4. Pour the borax solution from the other jar into the bag. Seal the bag.

5. Knead the solutions through the bag until they are evenly mixed. No excess liquid should remain.

6. Remove the product from the bag and knead it with your hands. After you've finished, wash your hands.

7. Record your observations of the product in the data table. Include the product's color, odor, and texture.

## Task 4  Analysis

1. How are the properties of the solutions and the product similar? How are they different?

2. Describe what happens to the molecules when two substances that are mixed together form a product with properties that are different than both substances.

## Task 5  Conclusion

The 50 percent white-glue solution contains many individual molecules of the polymer polyvinyl acetate. Write a paragraph explaining what you think happened to the polymer molecules after they were mixed with borax solution to produce the changes you observed. What role did the borax play? Make *before* and *after* drawings to illustrate your ideas.

## *Everyday Application*

You probably use white glue to stick things together. In terms of a polymer and what you learned from this activity, explain how glue sticks things together.

**Table 25.1**

| Substance | Color | Odor | Texture |
|---|---|---|---|
| Glue solution | | | |
| Borax solution | | | |
| Product | | | |

# 25.4 Technology and the Environment

## Objectives

▶ **Identify** two causes of air, water, and land pollution.

▶ **Explain** how waste disposal affects the environment.

▶ **Communicate** how technology creates and solves water pollution problems.

▶ **Infer** how air pollution affects water quality and land quality.

### ▼ ACTIVITY

#### Classifying

*Separating Refuse*

List 15 items that you used today. Classify each item as either recyclable or degradable. What items did you list that don't fall into either group?

**SKILLS WARMUP**

Look around your classroom. The desks, walls, books, and even your clothes are all manufactured by some industrial process. Industrial processes use natural resources and energy. Both the school bus you ride on and the street are made of petroleum products. The quality of the air, water, and land is affected by human activity. It is also affected by natural processes.

The next time you smell car exhaust, watch oily water run off the street, or see dirt erode from a hill, think about where these substances are headed. The earth is a closed system. It recycles its natural resources.

## Air Quality

The air you breathe is a mixture of nitrogen, oxygen, carbon dioxide, and trace amounts of helium, neon, and several other gases. Air also contains water vapor. Pure air contains only the gases and water vapor needed for the earth's environment to be healthy.

Too often air contains pollutants. Pollutants are substances, or even energy, that harm living things. Some pollutants in the atmosphere can change the earth's overall temperature and affect climate.

A high concentration of pollutants in the air is called **air pollution**. Some air pollution comes from natural sources, such as the dust and smoke from volcanic eruptions and forest fires. However, most air pollution is caused by human activity. For example, automobile exhaust and industrial smoke release chemical pollutants.

**Figure 25.13** ▲
The quality of the air in the earth's atmosphere depends on human activity.

**Temperature Inversion**  Normally, the temperature of the air is warmer near the ground than it is at high altitudes. However, sometimes a blanket of cold air is trapped beneath a thick layer of warm air. This reversed layering of air is called a *temperature inversion*.

During a temperature inversion, air near the ground doesn't circulate. Pollutants released by cars and industry build up in the cold air at the surface. The air quality becomes unhealthy. Temperature inversions may last for several weeks.

**Greenhouse Effect**  Why does the air temperature inside a car increase when the windows are closed on a sunny day? As sunlight passes through the windows, the car's interior absorbs and radiates heat energy. Air inside the closed car is warmed by the heat energy. Trapping heat energy from sunlight is called the **greenhouse effect**.

The greenhouse effect also happens globally. Look at Figure 25.13. Gases, such as carbon dioxide, methane, and nitrous oxide, build up in the atmosphere. These gases, called greenhouse gases, trap energy in the lowest layer of the earth's atmosphere.

Many scientists are concerned about a global greenhouse effect increasing temperatures worldwide. The increase of the earth's atmospheric temperature due to the greenhouse effect is called **global warming**. If average global temperatures increase even a few degrees, worldwide climate changes might occur. Rainfall patterns could change and cause the types and amount of plant life in many areas to change.

**Figure 25.13 The Greenhouse Effect** ▼

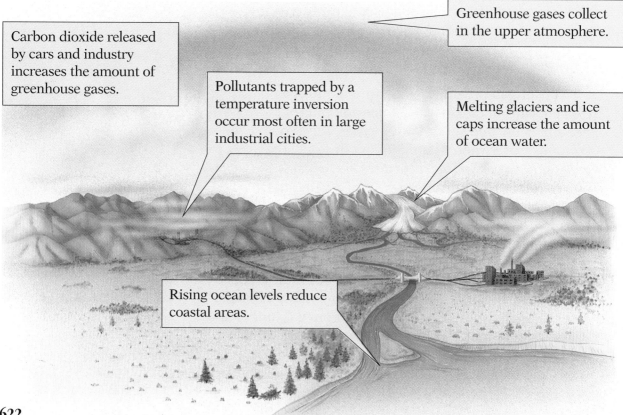

Carbon dioxide released by cars and industry increases the amount of greenhouse gases.

Pollutants trapped by a temperature inversion occur most often in large industrial cities.

Greenhouse gases collect in the upper atmosphere.

Melting glaciers and ice caps increase the amount of ocean water.

Rising ocean levels reduce coastal areas.

622

**Smog**   When you hear the words *air pollution*, you probably think *smog*. Smog is a mixture of smoke and fog. Two kinds of smog are photochemical smog and industrial smog. Photochemical smog contains formaldehyde (for MAL duh HYD), ozone, and other pollutants from cars and power plants. Industrial smog contains sulfur oxide and solid particles that are released when fossil fuels are burned. Air pollutant levels set by the Environmental Protection Agency (EPA) protect human health and control pollution.

**Table 25.2**
**U.S. Air Quality Standards**

| Air Pollutant | Concentration (ppm) |
| --- | --- |
| Sulfur oxides | 0.14 |
| Carbon monoxide | 35.00 |
| Ozone | 0.12 |
| Hydro-carbons | 0.24 |

**Industrial Smog** ▲

When factories burn coal or oil, they release pollutants that combine with moisture in the air to form industrial smog. Industrial smog appears as a grayish haze and usually forms over heavily industrialized cities.

**Photochemical Smog** ▶

The action of sunlight on nitrogen oxide and hydrocarbons combines them to form the chemical compounds in photochemical smog. Photochemical smog appears as a brownish-orange haze in the air, and usually occurs over large cities.

**Scrubbers**

To meet EPA standards, scrubbers are attached to smokestacks to remove pollutants from smoke before it is released. Solid particles and gases are trapped as they pass through a fine water mist in the scrubber. The pollutant-laden waste water is processed into sludge, which is used in bricks.
◀

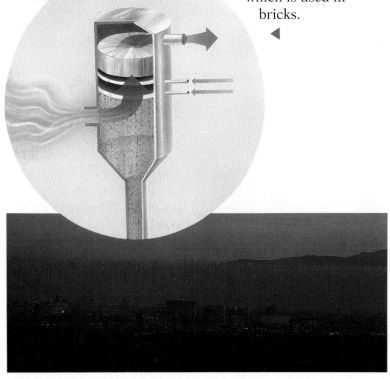

# Water Quality

Do you know where the water you use comes from? Fresh water is stored in the ice caps, in glaciers, lakes, rivers, and ponds, or underground in the spaces between rocks. Actually the earth's total freshwater supply is limited. Water is constantly being recycled from surface water that evaporates, then condenses in the atmosphere, and returns to the earth as precipitation. This cycle of evaporation, condensation, and precipitation is called the water cycle.

## Oil Spills ▲

Ocean oil spills come from ruptured oil tankers, oil rig drilling accidents, and oil dumped into rivers. Oil spills damage beaches and kill fish, birds, and marine mammals. It takes many years for an unhealthy river or ocean environment to rebuild. ▼

## Acid Rain ▲

When sulfur dioxide and nitrogen oxide are released by burning fossil fuels, they combine with water in the atmosphere to form sulfuric and nitric acids. If enough of these acids are present to lower the pH of pure rainwater to below 5.7, **acid rain** forms. Leaves of trees and plants are damaged by acid rain. Photosynthesis can't take place, and many plants die.

## Effects of Acid Rain

Acid rain dissolves the marble and limestone in buildings and statues. Many historic buildings and monuments have been damaged by acid rain. Acid rain also weakens the exposed metal in bridges and automobiles. ▼

The quality of fresh water depends on the chemicals and waste material, or pollutants, dumped into surface waters and onto the ground. Water pollution is any physical or chemical change in water that harms organisms. Water pollutants often spread throughout an entire river system. Sometimes pollutants can become concentrated in small lakes and ponds.

## Thermal Pollution ▲

An increase in water temperature that harms living organisms is called **thermal pollution**. Thermal pollution is a physical change that occurs when large amounts of hot waste water from power plants and refineries are dumped into surface water. Fish and microscopic organisms that live in the water die from lack of oxygen that results from the higher temperatures.

## Chemical Pollution ▶

Chemicals that make water unsafe for drinking cause water pollution. Water runoff from streets contains asbestos and oil from cars, and salt used on icy roads. Mercury from processing plastics and nitrates from sewage plants are also water pollutants.

### Table 25.3
### EPA Water Quality Standards

| Toxic Chemical | Concentration (ppm) |
|---|---|
| arsenic | 50 |
| lead | 50 |
| mercury | 2 |
| nitrate | 10,000 |
| selenium | 10 |
| 2,4-D fertilizer | 100 |

## Water Standards ▲

EPA standards were set in the 1970s to control water safety. Industries were no longer allowed to dump unprocessed waste water into rivers and lakes. Farms were required to control water contaminated with animal waste and fertilizers.

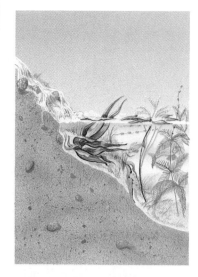

## Pollution from Runoff

Many lakes become clogged by plants that feed on sewage, industrial waste, and fertilizer runoff from cities and farms. An overgrowth of plant life reduces the oxygen supply in the water. Fish and other organisms die from lack of oxygen. The lakes become polluted. ▼

## Land Quality

How much garbage did you produce today? Does your home have wood doors? Perhaps your classroom is heated by oil or coal. Everything you use affects the quality of the land. When you throw away an empty carton or an apple core, you add to the garbage pile. Whenever lumber is cut from a forest, or oil and coal are brought to the surface, land quality is affected in some way.

### Litter ▲

The garbage, or litter, your city dumps each day adds up to a staggering amount each year. Dumping and burying garbage often limit future use of the dump site. Some kinds of litter, such as plastics, take years to break down into safe, usable substances. Chemicals make the soil unsuitable for agriculture.

### Strip Mining ▲

A process called strip mining removes coal and ores that are close to the earth's surface. The top layers of rock and dirt are stripped away and pushed aside. Nutrient-rich topsoil erodes into streams and rivers. Harmful chemicals concentrate in the soil. Plants and animals are unable to survive.

### Oil Transport

◀ Oil from Alaska is transported through pipelines that are above the ground. Because the frozen tundra in Alaska is a fragile land environment, it is easily damaged by oil spilled during transport and drilling.

**Hazardous Wastes** Waste materials that are poisonous, or toxic, to people and animals are called hazardous wastes. Wastes are created when the products you use are manufactured. Your standard of living depends on these products.

Proper disposal of hazardous wastes is vital to all living things. Some toxic wastes are made harmless, or detoxified, by treating them so they are no longer poisonous. Other toxic wastes are collected and stored in places where they can't get into the environment.

One process for disposing of toxic waste chemicals is called deep-well injection, shown in Figure 25.16. Toxic waste is pumped into the ground where it is trapped between two layers of impermeable rock that it can't penetrate. Wastes remain in deep-wells for many years.

**Nuclear Waste** Radioactive waste from nuclear reactors and mining sites presents a special disposal problem. Radioactive isotopes have a long half-life and are dangerous for thousands of years. Permanent disposal is needed for hun-

**Figure 25.15** ▲
Nuclear waste is transported long distances to a disposal site.

dreds of metric tons of nuclear waste being kept in temporary disposal sites.

One disposal method is to mix the radioactive wastes with molten glass. The waste hardens and is sealed in containers like the one shown in Figure 25.15. Some containers are buried in hardened rock deposits located in remote areas. Transporting nuclear waste is a major concern for many communities.

**Figure 25.16    Deep-well Injection** ▼
Waste chemicals injected into the ground can move slowly to other underground areas.

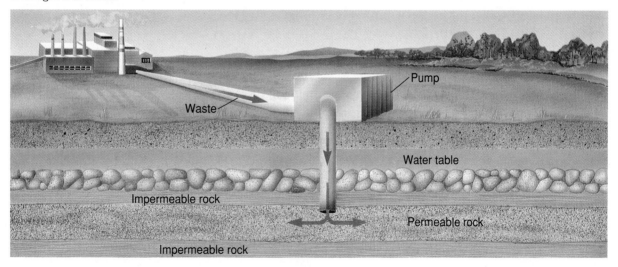

How can a river burn? In 1969, near the city of Cleveland, Ohio, that's actually what happened. The water at the mouth of the Cuyahoga River, which flows into Lake Erie, caught fire and burned! At the time of the fire, Lake Erie was so polluted that fish and other organisms were dying by the thousands.

At 64 meters deep, Lake Erie is the shallowest of the Great Lakes. Lake Erie could not contain all the waste dumped into it. Fertilizers and phosphates from detergents caused a thick growth of algae and other plants. The excess plant material caused the growth of bacteria that used up the lake's oxygen. Fish and other organisms died from lack of oxygen.

The fire so horrified the people and the governments in the Lake Erie area that steps were immediately taken to clean up the lake. New laws were passed to keep industries from dumping hazardous wastes into the lake. New sewage treatment plants were built that cleaned up 90 percent of the organic wastes. Detergents that contained phosphates were banned. Farmers were encouraged to reduce their use of fertilizers. People were educated about pollution and how to reduce it in their own homes.

The amount of new pollutants entering the lake was drastically reduced. Lake Erie was able to clean itself through biological and chemical processes that occur naturally in a lake. People can swim and fish in Lake Erie once again.

**Figure 25.17** ▲
The inset photo shows the algae growth that clogged Lake Erie. What kinds of pollutants do you think caused the lake to catch fire?

## Check and Explain

1. What causes smog to form?

2. How does hazardous waste disposal harm the quality of land and water?

3. **Communicate** Research the source of your community's water supply. Explain how the quality of the water is controlled.

4. **Infer** How are water quality and land quality directly affected by air pollution? Explain.

# Chapter 25 Review

## Concept Summary

### 25.1 Petroleum Fuels
▶ Petroleum is formed from the remains of microscopic ocean organisms.
▶ Fractional distillation is used to separate crude oil into usable products.

### 25.2 Petrochemical Products
▶ Products containing plastics, synthetic fibers, dyes, and solvents are made from petrochemicals.
▶ Petrochemicals are composed of molecules of hydrocarbon called monomers that combine to form chainlike molecules called polymers.

### 25.3 Materials Science
▶ Metallurgy is taking metals from the earth and making them into products.

▶ To make steel, iron ore is combined with limestone and coke in a blast furnace and treated with pure oxygen.
▶ Ceramic and glass are made from earth materials that are heated to high temperatures.
▶ Composites are fibers that are embedded in a matrix.

### 25.4 Technology and the Environment
▶ The quality of air, water, and land is reduced by pollution.
▶ Pollutants are substances or energy that harm living things.
▶ Methods of disposing of hazardous waste materials, trash, and nuclear waste affect land quality.

## Chapter Vocabulary

| | | |
|---|---|---|
| petroleum (25.1) | ceramic (25.3) | greenhouse effect (25.4) |
| petrochemical (25.2) | composite (25.3) | global warming (25.4) |
| polymer (25.2) | matrix (25.3) | acid rain (25.4) |
| metallurgy (25.3) | air pollution (25.4) | thermal pollution (25.4) |

## Check Your Vocabulary

Use the vocabulary words above to complete the following sentences correctly.

1. Fiberglass contains glass fibers embedded in a plastic _____ .

2. The remains of microscopic ocean organisms were changed into _____ .

3. A high concentration of pollutants in the air is called _____ .

4. Monomers can form a larger molecule called a(n) _____ .

5. A chemical substance made from petroleum is called a(n) _____ .

6. Mining and processing metal-containing ore rocks is part of _____ .

7. A hard, glasslike substance made from earth materials is a(n) _____ .

8. Hot water released by nuclear power plants causes _____ .

9. A material made of fibers embedded in a solid matrix is a(n) _____ .

10. Trapping heat energy from sunlight is called the _____ .

11. Water in the atmosphere combines with pollutants to form _____ .

12. An increase in the earth's average temperature could cause _____ .

## Write Your Vocabulary

Write sentences using the vocabulary words above. Show that you know what each word means.

# Chapter 25 Review

## Check Your Knowledge

Answer the following in complete sentences.

1. Explain what petroleum is and how it forms.

2. Describe how acid rain is harmful to the environment.

3. Explain what a fractionating tower does and how it works.

4. Give four examples of petrochemicals and describe how each is used.

5. Describe the structure of a polymer.

6. Explain how nuclear power plants can pollute the water around them.

7. Name five kinds of land pollution. Identify the source of each one.

8. Explain how pure metals are obtained from ore.

9. How is oil removed from a trap?

Determine whether each statement is true or false. Write *true* if it is true. If it is false, change the underlined term to make the statement true.

10. Petroleum forms from the remains of land plants.

11. Petroleum contains a mixture of hydrocarbons.

12. When hazardous wastes are toxic, they are no longer poisonous.

13. PVC plastics are made from chemicals that come from petroleum.

14. Composites are made up of fibers embedded in a matrix.

15. Petroleum collects in the nonporous rock layers below a cap rock.

## Check Your Understanding

Apply the concepts you have learned to answer each question.

1. What is the role of heat in a fractionating tower?

2. Why can so many different products be made from petrochemicals?

3. **Critical Thinking** How can a substance combine with a polymer to form a product, such as a fiber, that isn't like the substance or the polymer?

4. **Mystery Photo** The photograph on page 604 shows North African pottery from the 1800s. The pottery is made from clay and other earth materials fired at a very high temperature. The heat turns the clay into a hard, glassy substance by a process called vitrification. Vitrification can be total or partial depending on the temperature.

   a. Do you think this pottery has undergone total or partial vitrification? Explain.

   b. Do you think the color designs on the pottery surface were added before or after firing? Explain.

5. **Application** Volcanic ash was released from Mt. Penatubo in 1990. What effect might this have on global warming?

6. **Critical Thinking** Advances in technology are responsible for smog, acid rain, thermal pollution, and water pollution. What are some kinds of technology being applied to solve these problems?

7. **Application** Ceramics are used to make such items as fireplace tiles and baking sheets. What properties of ceramics make them useful for these purposes?

## Develop Your Skills

Use the skills you have developed in this chapter to complete each activity.

1. **Interpret Data** The graph shows data about world petroleum production.

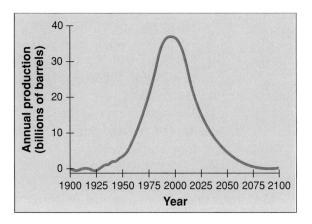

a. In what year is the world's petroleum production expected to peak?

b. When you are thirty, will there be more or less petroleum per person than when you were born? Explain.

2. **Infer** Injecting toxic wastes in deep wells, and burying nuclear waste deep in the ground are current disposal methods. How might these practices harm the environment?

3. **Data Bank** Use the information on page 636 to answer the following questions.

a. What percentage of a barrel of crude oil will be used for lubricants? Fuel oil? Petrochemicals?

b. Estimate the percentage of a barrel of crude oil that would be saved if everybody reduced their driving by 10 percent.

## Make Connections

1. **Link the Concepts** Make your own concept map to show how some of the main concepts in this chapter link together. Use words and ideas you find in the chapter.

2. **Science and Social Studies** The largest petroleum deposits are located in just a few countries of the world. Do library research to find out where these petroleum deposits are located and investigate their impact on politics and the global economy. Write a report or prepare a class presentation to share what you learn.

3. **Science and Art** Ancient civilizations from all over the world used metallurgy to create distinctive art and jewelry. Do library research on the metallurgy of an ancient culture, such as the Egyptians or the Incas. How did they get metal, and what techniques did they use to make the objects? Write a paper or prepare a poster report for the class.

4. **Science and You** Investigate plastic recycling in your community. Make a poster to tell people how they can recycle plastic items instead of throwing them away. Include information about the economic and environmental benefits of recycling.

5. **Science and Society** Many household products contain toxic or hazardous substances. When you throw these items in the trash, they may end up in a landfill that isn't prepared to contain hazardous waste. Research the efforts your community is making to separate these items from household trash. Give an oral report

# Science and Literature Connection

Two years ago bulldozers had come to make a cut at the top of Sarah's Mountain. They began uprooting trees and pushing subsoil in a huge pile to get at the coal. As the pile grew enormous, so had M.C.'s fear of it. He had nightmares in which the heap came tumbling down. Over and over again, it buried his family on the side of the mountain.

But his dreams hadn't come true. The spoil heap didn't fall. Slowly his nightmares had ceased and his fear faded within. But then something would remind him, like the chance to get off the mountainside with the dude's coming . . .

To the north and east had been ranges of hills with farmhouses nestled in draws and lower valleys. But now the hills looked as if some gray-brown snake had curled itself along their ridges. The snake loops were mining cuts just like the one across Sarah's Mountain, only they were a continuous gash. They went on and on, following fifty miles of a coal seam. As far as M.C.'s eyes could see, the summits of hills had been shredded away into rock and ruin which spilled down into cropland at the base of the hills.

## M.C. Higgins the Great

*The following excerpts are from the novel* M.C. Higgins the Great *by Virginia Hamilton*

Glad I don't have to see it, M.C. thought. He turned away riverward, where the hills in front of Sarah's rolled and folded, green and perfect.

"Now that's beauty-*ful*, I'll tell you," the dude said, gazing after M.C. He breathed in deeply, as if he would swallow the sight of the rich river land. "It's like a picture-painting but ever so much better because it's so real. Hills, untouched. Not a thing like it where I come from."

M.C. felt suddenly better, proud of his hills. . . .

"Now you lead and I'll follow."

At once M.C. struck out along the top of Sarah's until he came to where a road began, twisting down into the mining cut. The walk along the road was not hard and soon they were standing in the cut, with seventy feet of a sheer wall to their backs…

"Was all this wall a coal seam at one time?" Lewis asked him.

M.C. sighed inwardly. He didn't want to talk about it. He wanted to get down to home. But he found himself answering, his hands moving, scratching his neck and arms: "Only about ten feet at the bottom of it was ever coal. The rest was just trees and rocks and soils."

"Lordy," the dude said, shaking his head. "Sixty feet of mountain gone for ten foot of coal. I tell you, there ought-a be a law."

"They take most of the dirt and rocks away in trucks," M.C. said. "But a big pile they just push over the edge of the road with the trees. Then they blasted that coal."

"They didn't!" the dude said.

"Yessir," M.C. said. "We were just playing down around the house when there was a bursting noise. Some rock and coal hit the back of the house real hard. It fell around my sister on her tricycle. Knock holes in her spokes, too. It fell all around her and she never was touched."

"That surely was a blessing," the dude said.

"Yessir," M.C. said.

## Skills in Science

### Reading Skills in Science

1. **Detect the Writer's Mood** How do you think the author of this selection feels about the mining of Sarah's Mountain? Support your answer with evidence from the selection.

2. **Predict** How do you think the mining on and near Sarah's Mountain affected the farms along the base of the hills?

### Writing Skills in Science

1. **Reason and Conclude** Imagine you are M.C. Higgins. Write a letter to your elected officials expressing your opinion regarding the mining of Sarah's Mountain. Give reasons for your opinion and for any action that you think should be taken.

2. **Predict** Suppose M.C.'s nightmares came true and the spoil heap suddenly fell down upon his home. Write a short story describing what happens.

### Activities

**Collect Data** In a library, research various methods of mining coal and the laws regulating the environmental aspects of coal-mining in the United States. How do the laws apply to the mining described in the selection?

**Communicate** Use photos from magazines to make a collage that illustrates the activity in the selection. Give an oral report on your collage.

### Where to Read More

*Save the Earth* by Betty Miles. New York: Alfred Knopf, Inc., 1991. This handbook provides an overview of environmental problems and offers suggestions on how students can help protect the earth.

*Restoring Our Earth* by Lawrence Pringle. Hillside, N.J.: Enslow Publishing, 1987. This text examines the ecological restoration of prairies, marshes, forests, rivers, and other ecosystems damaged by humans.

## Periodic Table of Elements

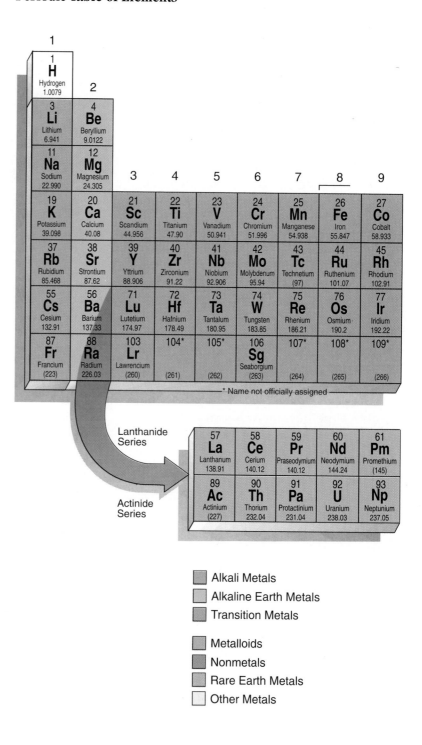

Alkali Metals
Alkaline Earth Metals
Transition Metals

Metalloids
Nonmetals
Rare Earth Metals
Other Metals

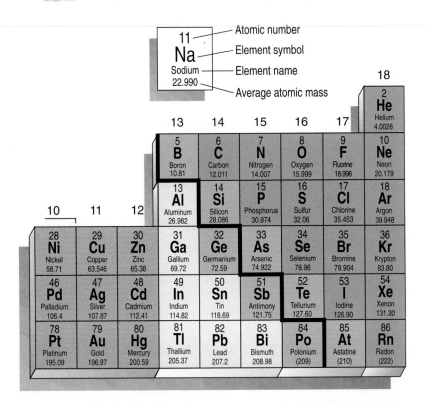

| | 11 | | Atomic number |
| | Na | | Element symbol |
| | Sodium | | Element name |
| | 22.990 | | Average atomic mass |

| | | | | | | | 18 |
|---|---|---|---|---|---|---|---|
| | | | | | | | 2 He Helium 4.0026 |

| | | | 13 | 14 | 15 | 16 | 17 | |
|---|---|---|---|---|---|---|---|---|
| | | | 5 B Boron 10.81 | 6 C Carbon 12.011 | 7 N Nitrogen 14.007 | 8 O Oxygen 15.999 | 9 F Fluorine 18.998 | 10 Ne Neon 20.179 |

| 10 | 11 | 12 | 13 Al Aluminum 26.982 | 14 Si Silicon 28.086 | 15 P Phosphorus 30.974 | 16 S Sulfur 32.06 | 17 Cl Chlorine 35.453 | 18 Ar Argon 39.948 |
|---|---|---|---|---|---|---|---|---|
| 28 Ni Nickel 58.71 | 29 Cu Copper 63.546 | 30 Zn Zinc 65.38 | 31 Ga Gallium 69.72 | 32 Ge Germanium 72.59 | 33 As Arsenic 74.922 | 34 Se Selenium 78.96 | 35 Br Bromine 79.904 | 36 Kr Krypton 83.80 |
| 46 Pd Palladium 106.4 | 47 Ag Silver 107.87 | 48 Cd Cadmium 112.41 | 49 In Indium 114.82 | 50 Sn Tin 118.69 | 51 Sb Antimony 121.75 | 52 Te Tellurium 127.60 | 53 I Iodine 126.90 | 54 Xe Xenon 131.30 |
| 78 Pt Platinum 195.09 | 79 Au Gold 196.97 | 80 Hg Mercury 200.59 | 81 Tl Thallium 205.37 | 82 Pb Lead 207.2 | 83 Bi Bismuth 208.98 | 84 Po Polonium (209) | 85 At Astatine (210) | 86 Rn Radon (222) |

| 62 Sm Samarium 150.4 | 63 Eu Europium 151.96 | 64 Gd Gadolinium 157.25 | 65 Tb Terbium 158.93 | 66 Dy Dysprosium 162.50 | 67 Ho Holmium 164.93 | 68 Er Erbium 167.26 | 69 Tm Thulium 168.93 | 70 Yb Ytterbium 173.04 |
|---|---|---|---|---|---|---|---|---|
| 94 Pu Plutonium (244) | 95 Am Americium (243) | 96 Cm Curium (247) | 97 Bk Berkelium (247) | 98 Cf Californium (247) | 99 Es Einsteinium (254) | 100 Fm Fermium (257) | 101 Md Mendelevium (258) | 102 No Nobelium (259) |

## Surface Gravity of Bodies in the Solar System

| Body | Surface Gravity |
|------|-----------------|
| Sun | 27.90 |
| Jupiter | 2.54 |
| Saturn | 1.06 |
| Neptune | 1.20 |
| Uranus | 0.92 |
| Earth | 1.00 |
| Venus | 0.92 |
| Mars | 0.38 |
| Pluto | 0.07 |
| Mercury | 0.38 |

*The surface gravity of each body is based on the surface gravity of Earth, which is expressed as 1.00.

## Products from One Barrel of Crude Oil

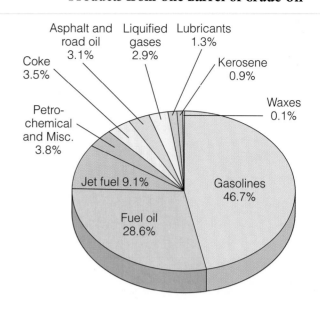

Asphalt and road oil 3.1%
Liquified gases 2.9%
Lubricants 1.3%
Coke 3.5%
Kerosene 0.9%
Petro-chemical and Misc. 3.8%
Waxes 0.1%
Jet fuel 9.1%
Gasolines 46.7%
Fuel oil 28.6%

## Development of the Computer

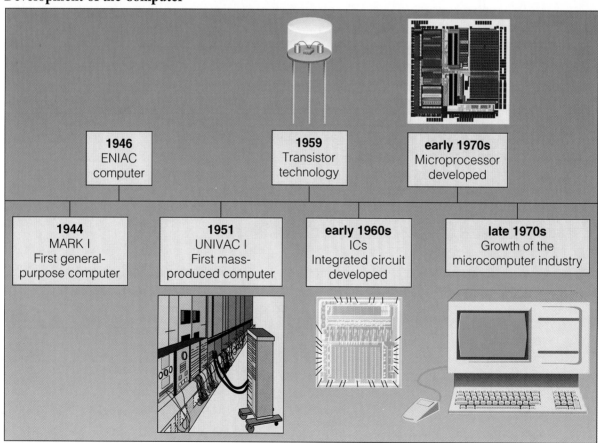

**1946** ENIAC computer

**1959** Transistor technology

**early 1970s** Microprocessor developed

**1944** MARK I First general-purpose computer

**1951** UNIVAC I First mass-produced computer

**early 1960s** ICs Integrated circuit developed

**late 1970s** Growth of the microcomputer industry

## Size of Atoms and Ions of Elements in Periods 2 and 3

| Atomic Number | Element | Radius of Atom (nanometers) | Ion | Radius of Ion (nanometers) |
|:---:|:---|:---:|:---:|:---:|
| 3 | Lithium | 0.123 | Li$^+$ | 0.060 |
| 4 | Beryllium | 0.089 | Be$^{2+}$ | 0.031 |
| 5 | Boron | 0.080 | B$^{3+}$ | 0.020 |
| 6 | Carbon | 0.077 | C$^{4+}$ | 0.015 |
| 7 | Nitrogen | 0.070 | N$^{3-}$ | 0.171 |
| 8 | Oxygen | 0.066 | O$^{2-}$ | 0.140 |
| 9 | Flourine | 0.064 | F$^-$ | 0.136 |
| 11 | Sodium | 0.157 | Na$^+$ | 0.095 |
| 12 | Magnesium | 0.136 | Mg$^{2+}$ | 0.065 |
| 13 | Aluminum | 0.125 | Al$^{3+}$ | 0.050 |
| 14 | Silicon | 0.117 | Si$^{4+}$ | 0.041 |
| 15 | Phosphorus | 0.110 | P$^{3-}$ | 0.212 |
| 16 | Sulfur | 0.104 | S$^{2-}$ | 0.184 |
| 17 | Chlorine | 0.099 | Cl$^-$ | 0.181 |

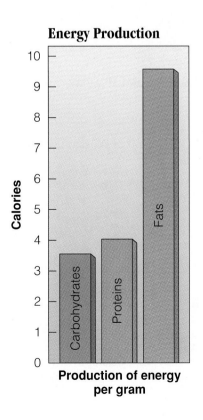

### Energy Production

Calories

Carbohydrates
Proteins
Fats

**Production of energy per gram**

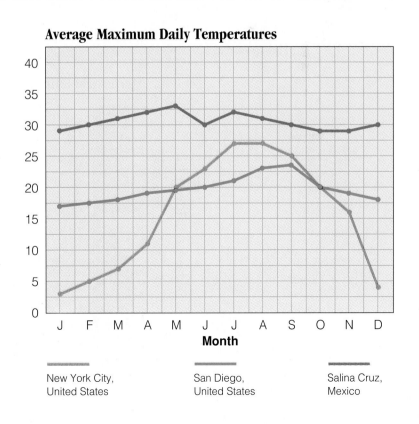

### Average Maximum Daily Temperatures

Month

New York City, United States

San Diego, United States

Salina Cruz, Mexico

Data Bank

## Top Speed of Some Animals in Air

| Animal | Speed (km/hr) |
|---|---|
| Spine-tailed swift | 170 |
| Pigeon | 96 |
| Hawk moth | 53 |
| Monarch butterfly | 32 |
| Honeybee | 18 |

## Top Speed of Some Animals on Land

| Animal | Speed (km/hr) |
|---|---|
| Cheetah | 112 |
| Prong-horned antelope | 96 |
| Jackrabbit | 72 |
| Ostrich | 48 |
| Human | 43 |

## Top Speed of Some Animals in Water

| Animal | Speed (km/hr) |
|---|---|
| Sailfish | 96 |
| Flying fish | 64 |
| Dolphin | 59 |
| Trout | 24 |
| Human | 8 |

## Activity Series of Metals

**Most Active**

Lithium

Potassium

Barium

Calcium

Sodium

Magnesium

Aluminum

Zinc

Iron

Nickel

Tin

Lead

Copper

Mercury

Silver

Gold

**Least Active**

## Radio-Band Frequencies

| Type | Wave | Frequency |
|---|---|---|
| Short wave (AM) | | 2,300–26,100 kHz |
| Medium wave (AM) | | 525–1,700 kHz |
| Long wave (AM) | | 150–300 kHz |
| VHF (FM) | | 87–108 kHz |

## Mechanical Efficiency of Machines and Humans

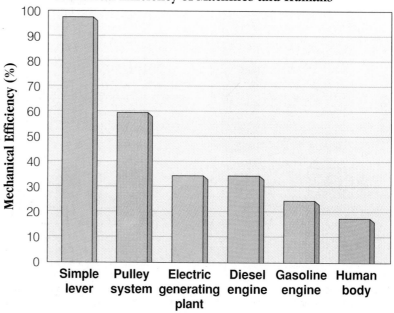

(Bar graph of Mechanical Efficiency (%) for: Simple lever, Pulley system, Electric generating plant, Diesel engine, Gasoline engine, Human body)

## Sound Spectrum

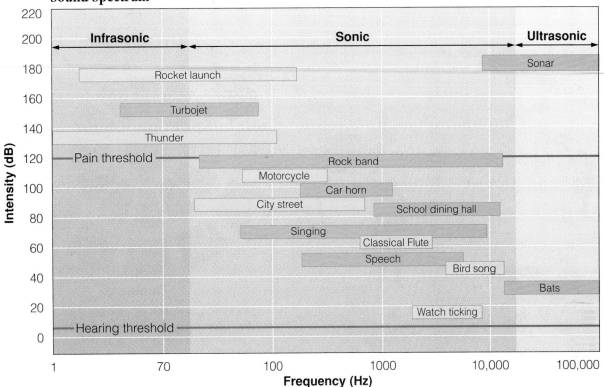

## Electric Conductivity of Metals at 20° C

| Material | % IACS* |
|----------|---------|
| Aluminum | 65 |
| Arsenic | 5 |
| Copper | 100 |
| Gold | 77 |
| Iron | 18 |
| Lead | 8 |
| Magnesium | 39 |
| Nickel | 25 |
| Platinum | 16 |
| Silver | 108 |
| Zinc | 29 |

*International Annealed Copper Standard
A value of 100% is given to copper when it is at a specific conductive state.

## Magnetic Declination in the United States

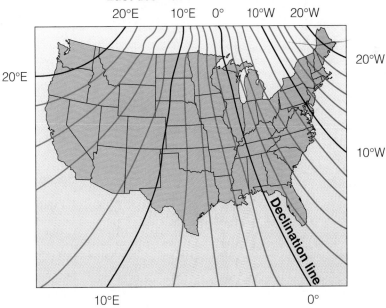

Each of the lines on this magnetic map shows the number of degrees a magnetic compass varies from true or geographic north. East declination means the compass needle is pulled to the east of true north. West declination means the compass needle is pulled to the west of true north.

# Normal Body Temperatures of Some Animals

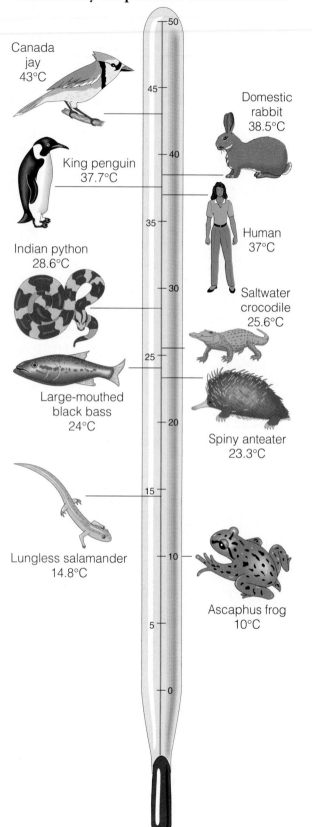

Canada jay
43°C

King penguin
37.7°C

Indian python
28.6°C

Large-mouthed black bass
24°C

Lungless salamander
14.8°C

Domestic rabbit
38.5°C

Human
37°C

Saltwater crocodile
25.6°C

Spiny anteater
23.3°C

Ascaphus frog
10°C

# Color Wheel

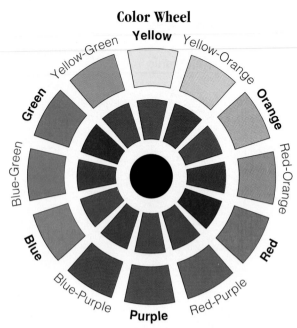

Yellow
Yellow-Green
Green
Yellow-Orange
Orange
Blue-Green
Red-Orange
Blue
Red
Blue-Purple
Purple
Red-Purple

The colors shown in the inner circle are obtained when the colors opposite each other in the outer circle are mixed together.

## Air Pollutant Sources from Combustion

| Pollutant | Major Source |
|---|---|
| Carbon monoxide | Transportation (68.4%) |
| Sulfur oxides | Power Plants/Heating (73.4.%) |
| Hydrocarbons | Transportation (60%) |
| Nitrogen oxides | Transportation (49.1%) |
| Particulates | Power Plants/Heating (42%) |

## Speed of Sound

| Material | Speed of Sound (m/s) |
|---|---|
| Air (0°C) | 331 |
| Helium (0°C) | 965 |
| Ethyl alcohol (25°C) | 1207 |
| Water (25°C) | 1498 |
| Copper | 3800 |
| Tempered glass | 5170 |

## Properties of Common Elements

| Element | Symbol | Atomic Number | Atomic Mass | Melting Point (°C) | Boiling Point (°C) | Density (g/cm³) | Specific Heat (J/kg°C) |
|---|---|---|---|---|---|---|---|
| Aluminum | Al | 13 | 26.982 | 660 | 2467 | 2.7 | 899 |
| Arsenic | As | 33 | 74.922 | 817 | 613 | 5.7 | 330 |
| Bromine | Br | 35 | 79.904 | −7 | 59 | 3.1 | 472 |
| Calcium | Ca | 20 | 40.08 | 839 | 1484 | 1.6 | 652 |
| Carbon | C | 6 | 12.011 | 3550 | 4827 | 2.3 | 711 |
| Chlorine | Cl | 17 | 35.453 | −101 | −35 | 0.0032 | 477 |
| Chromium | Cr | 24 | 51.996 | 1857 | 2672 | 7.2 | 447 |
| Copper | Cu | 29 | 63.546 | 1083 | 2567 | 8.96 | 385 |
| *Einsteinium | Es | 99 | (252) | — | — | — | 823 |
| Fluorine | F | 9 | 18.998 | −220 | −189 | 0.00179 | 823 |
| Gold | Au | 79 | 196.966 | 1064 | 3080 | 19.3 | 130 |
| Helium | He | 2 | 4.003 | −272 | −269 | 0.00018 | 5,183 |
| Hydrogen | H | 1 | 1.008 | −259 | −253 | 0.00009 | 14,253 |
| Iodine | I | 53 | 126.904 | 114 | 184 | 4.93 | 426 |
| Iron | Fe | 26 | 55.847 | 1535 | 2750 | 7.87 | 443 |
| Lead | Pb | 82 | 207.2 | 328 | 1740 | 11.35 | 159 |
| Lithium | Li | 3 | 6.941 | 181 | 1342 | 0.53 | 3,553 |
| Magnesium | Mg | 12 | 24.305 | 649 | 1090 | 1.74 | 1,016 |
| Mercury | Hg | 80 | 200.59 | −39 | 357 | 13.55 | 138 |
| Neon | Ne | 10 | 20.179 | −249 | −246 | 0.0009 | 1,028 |
| Nickel | Ni | 28 | 58.71 | 1453 | 2732 | 8.9 | 443 |
| Nitrogen | N | 7 | 14.007 | −210 | −196 | 0.0013 | 1,041 |
| Oxygen | O | 8 | 15.999 | −218 | −183 | 0.00143 | 915 |
| Phosphorus | P | 15 | 30.974 | 44 | 280 | 1.82 | 757 |
| Platinum | Pt | 78 | 195.09 | 1772 | 3827 | 21.45 | 133 |
| Potassium | K | 19 | 39.098 | 63 | 760 | 0.862 | 752 |
| Silicon | Si | 14 | 28.086 | 1410 | 2355 | 2.3 | 702 |
| Sodium | Na | 11 | 22.990 | 98 | 883 | 0.97 | 1,225 |
| Sulfur | S | 16 | 32.06 | 113 | 445 | 2.07 | 732 |
| Tin | Sn | 50 | 118.69 | 232 | 2270 | 7.31 | 213 |
| Uranium | U | 92 | 238.029 | 1132 | 3818 | 19.0 | 117 |
| Zinc | Zn | 30 | 65.38 | 420 | 907 | 7.133 | 389 |

*Some data is unavailable (—).

## Comparison of Fluorescent and Incandescent Light Bulbs

| Fluorescent | | | Incandescent | | |
|---|---|---|---|---|---|
| Fluorescent Lamp Type and Wattage | Light Output (lumens)* | Lamp Life (hrs) | Incandescent Bulbs Type and Wattage All 130 Volt | Light Output (lumens)* | Lamp Life (hrs) |
| 6 watt | 230 | 11,000 | 25 watt | 172 | 6,250 |
| 8 watt | 310 | 11,000 | 60 watt | 650 | 2,500 |
| 14 watt | 600 | 11,000 | 150 watt | 2080 | 1,875 |
| 20 watt | 1110 | 13,000 | 200 watt | 2847 | 1,875 |
| 8 watt | 263 | 9,000 | 40 watt | 350 | 3,750 |
| 14 watt | 521 | 9,000 | 64 watt | 504 | 7,500 |
| 18 watt | 740 | 9,000 | 75 watt | 730 | 7,500 |
| 40 watt | 2480 | 17,500 | 2/100 watt | 2496 | 1,875 |
| 19 watt | 610 | 17,500 | 60 watt | 650 | 2,500 |
| 22 watt | 740 | 17,500 | 75 watt | 730 | 6,250 |
| 32 watt | 1495 | 17,500 | 100 watt | 1248 | 1,875 |
| 7 watt | 400 | 10,500 | 40 watt | 350 | 2,750 |
| 9 watt | 600 | 10,500 | 60 watt | 650 | 2,500 |
| 13 watt | 900 | 10,500 | 75 watt | 730 | 6,250 |

*Approximate lumens at 40% of lamp life.

## Breakdown of Energy Consumption in the United States

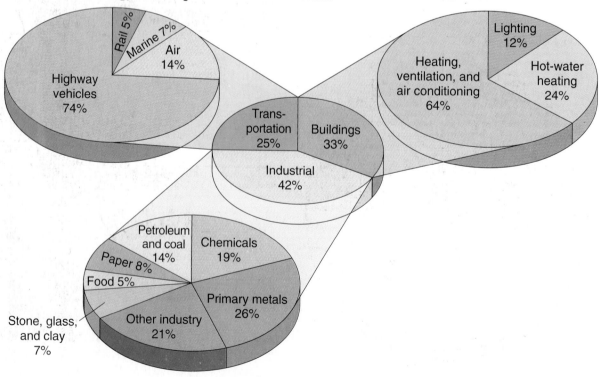

642

## Radiation Exposure in the United States

| Source of radiation | Average dose |
|---|---|
| Cosmic radiation (from space) | 40 mrem/year |
| TV and computer screens | 4 mrem/year (2 hours of viewing per day) |
| Living in a brick or stone house | 40 mrem/year |
| Dental X-ray (whole mouth) | 910 mrem |
| Air travel | 2 mrem per 2-hour flight |
| Air, water, food | 25 mrem/year |
| Rocks and soil | 55 mrem/year |
| Smoke detectors, luminous watch dials | 2 mrem/year |

*The unit for radiation is the *rem*. A millirem, or *mrem*, is $\frac{1}{1,000}$ of a rem. The U.S. Council on Radiation Protection recommends limiting radiation from all sources to 500 *mrem* per year.

## Elements in the Earth's Crust (in percent)

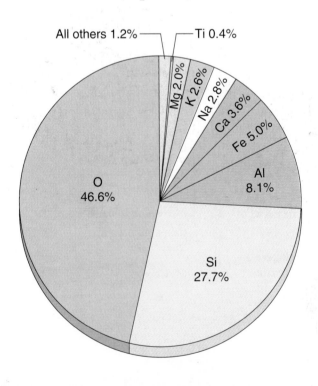

All others 1.2% — Ti 0.4%
Mg 2.0%
K 2.6%
Na 2.8%
Ca 3.6%
Fe 5.0%
Al 8.1%
O 46.6%
Si 27.7%

## The pH Scale

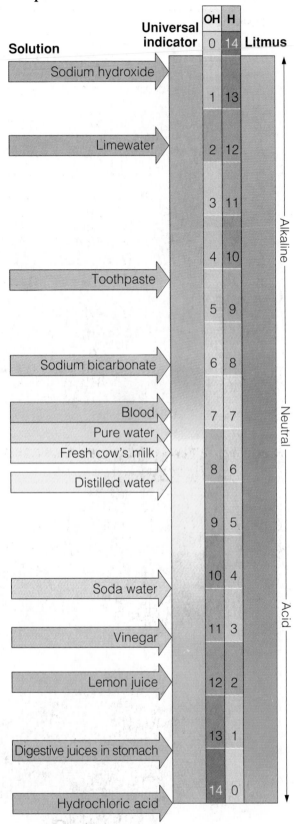

| Solution | Universal indicator | OH | H | Litmus |

Sodium hydroxide
Limewater
Toothpaste
Sodium bicarbonate
Blood
Pure water
Fresh cow's milk
Distilled water
Soda water
Vinegar
Lemon juice
Digestive juices in stomach
Hydrochloric acid

Alkaline — Neutral — Acid

# Math Appendix

## Symbols

| | | |
|---|---|---|
| $\alpha$ = alpha particle | $f$ = frequency | M.A. = mechanical advantage |
| $\beta$ = beta particle | G = universal gravity | N = newton |
| $\gamma$ = gamma ray | G.P.E. = gravitational potential energy | P = power |
| $\lambda$ = wavelength | $g$ = acceleration due to gravity (9.8 m/s$^2$) | P.E. = potential energy |
| $\Omega$ = ohm | | p = pressure |
| *a* = acceleration | h = height | R = resistance |
| A = amps | Hz = hertz | $r$ = angle of reflection |
| A = area | $I$ = electric current | T = temperature |
| c = speed of light | $i$ = angle of incidence | t = time |
| °C = degree Celsius | J = joule | $v$ = velocity |
| $d$ = density | K.E. = kinetic energy | V = volt |
| d = distance | kWh = kilowatt hour | v = volume |
| E = effort | l = length | W = watt |
| °F = degree Fahrenheit | $m$ = mass | w = weight |
| *F* = force | m = meter | $W$ = work |

## Formulas

**Chapter 1**

density

$$\text{density} = \frac{\text{mass}}{\text{volume}}$$

$$d = \frac{m}{v}$$

**Chapter 2**

acceleration

$$\text{acc.} = \frac{\text{final velocity} - \text{initial velocity}}{\text{time}}$$

$$a = \frac{v_f - v_i}{t}$$

velocity

$$\text{velocity} = \frac{\text{distance}}{\text{time}}$$

$$v = \frac{d}{t}$$

kinetic energy

$$\text{kinetic energy} = \frac{1}{2} \times \text{mass} \times \text{velocity}^2$$

$$\text{K.E.} = \frac{1}{2}mv^2$$

joule

joule = 1 newton-meter
= newton × meter

J = 1 N·m

gravitational potential energy

gravitational potential energy
= mass × gravity × height

$$\text{G.P.E.} = mgh$$

weight

weight = mass × gravity

$$w = mg$$

**Chapter 3**

newton

$$\text{newton} = 1 \text{ kilogram} \times \frac{\text{meter}}{\text{second}^2}$$

$$N = 1 \text{ kg} \cdot \frac{m}{s^2}$$

force

force = mass × acceleration

$$F = ma$$

momentum

momentum = mass × velocity

$$\text{momentum} = mv$$

**Chapter 4**

pressure

$$\text{pressure} = \frac{\text{force}}{\text{area}}$$

$$p = \frac{F}{A}$$

## Chapter 5

work        work = force x distance

$$W = \boldsymbol{F} \times d$$

power        $power = \dfrac{work}{time}$

$$P = \dfrac{W}{t}$$

mechanical advantage        mechanical advantage

$$= \dfrac{resistance\ force}{effort\ force}$$

$$M.A. = \dfrac{R}{E}$$

mechanical efficiency        mechanical efficiency

$$= \dfrac{work\ output}{work\ input} \times 100\%$$

$$efficiency = \dfrac{W_{out}}{W_{in}} \times 100\%$$

## Chapter 6

Charles' Law        As pressure (p) increases, volume (v) decreases.

Boyle's Law        As temperature (T) increases, volume (v) increases.

## Chapter 9

temperature conversions        $°F = \dfrac{9}{5}°C + 32$

$$°C = \dfrac{5}{9}(°F - 32)$$

heat        heat = mass × specific heat × temperature change

heat = $m$ × specific heat × $(T_2 - T_1)$

## Chapter 11

current        $current = \dfrac{voltage}{resistance}$

$$I = \dfrac{V}{R}$$

electric power        electric power = volt × current

$$P = VI$$

volt        volt = current × resistance

$$V = IR$$

energy        energy = power × time

energy = Pt

## Chapter 14

wave speed        speed = frequency × wavelength

speed = $f\lambda$

wave reflection        angle of incidence = angle of reflection

$$i = r$$

---

## *Practice Problems*

### Chapter 1

1. You are given the following information: mass = 48 g; volume = 24 cm³. What is the density of this substance?

2. What is the density of a rock if its mass is 36 g and its volume is 12 cm³?

3. If a block of wood has a density of 0.6 g/cm³ and a mass of 120 g, what is its volume?

4. Calculate the mass of a substance which has a volume of 35 cm³ and a density of 0.5 g/cm³.

5. If you have a gold brick that is 2 cm by 3 cm by 4 cm and has a density of 19.3 g/cm³, what is its mass?

6. What is the density of an object that has a mass of 25 g and a volume of 10 cm³?

### Chapter 2

1. A car is stopped at a red light. When the light turns green, it accelerates to 30 m/s in 15 s. What is the car's acceleration?

2. You took a car trip with your family to visit relatives who live 750 km away. The trip took 8 h. What was your average speed in km/h?

3. If you travel 50 km due east in 2 h, what is your velocity ?

4. A train goes from 20 m/s to 40 m/s in 5 min. What is the train's acceleration in m/s²?

5. A train takes 10 min to slow down to 10 m/s from 40 m/s. What is its acceleration?

6. The traffic on the highway you are traveling moves at 90 km/h. At this rate, how long will it take you to travel 450 km?

7. If a runner maintains a speed of 2.5 m/s, how far can he run in 15 s? In an hour?

8. You pedal your 20 kg bicycle at 3 m/s. What is the kinetic energy of your bicycle?

9. You are pedaling your bicycle at 3 m/s. If you add your mass in kg to the 20 kg bicycle, what is the kinetic energy of both you and the bicycle?

10. While ice skating, a 50 kg student has a kinetic energy of 2025 J. What is the student's velocity?

11. A baseball thrown at a velocity of 40 m/s has a kinetic energy of 64 joules, what is its mass?

12. A ball has a potential energy of 150 kg m and a mass of 0.25 kg. How high is the ball from the ground?

13. What is the gravitational potential energy of a 60 kg skier at the top of a hill that is 20 m high?

14. A rock has a mass of 63 kg. What is its weight on the earth?

15. Suppose you took a rock with a mass of 63 kg to the moon where the gravitational force is 1/6 that of the earth. What would the rock weigh on the moon?

## Chapter 3

1. What is a person's weight in newtons if she has a mass of 70 kg?

2. If a person weighs 588 N, what is his mass?

3. Imagine that you throw a baseball that weighs 0.1 kg with a force of 100 N, what is the acceleration of the baseball?

4. An arrow leaves the bow with a force of 500 N. The mass of the arrow is 250 g. What is its acceleration?

5. A 5,000 kg car is moving with a velocity of 30 m/s, what is its momentum?

6. What is the momentum of a 2,500 kg boulder rolling down a hill at a velocity of 20 m/s?

7. A rolling ball has a velocity of 5 m/s and a momentum of 250 kg·m/s. What is the mass of the ball?

8. A train has a momentum of 400 000 kg·m/s and a mass of 10,000 kg. What is its velocity?

## Chapter 4

1. If a pressure of 15 N/m$^2$ is applied over an area of 5 m$^2$, what is the force?

2. You are given the following information: Force = 20 N; Area = 5 m$^2$. Find pressure.

3. Find the cross-section area of a concrete piling if the force required to drive it into the ground is 10 N with a pressure of 25 N/m$^2$.

4. A person weighing 350 N is standing up. The area of the bottom of her feet is 0.04 m$^2$. What pressure is being exerted onto the ground, in N/m$^2$?

5. A bullet hits a target with a force of 500 N. The hole it leaves has an area of 0.002 m$^2$. What pressure did the bullet apply to the target?

## Chapter 5

1. If Maria uses 4 N of force to lift a box onto a shelf 0.5 m high, how much work did she do?

2. Joanne did 2 J of work in 5 s. How much power did she use?

3. How much work is required to push a 300 N box 10 m across the floor?

4. Suppose you weigh 300 N and you carry your books, which weigh 20 N, to your class on the fourth floor. Each flight of stairs is 5 m high. How much work did you do?

5. If a person does 200 J of work by lifting a box 2 m off the floor, how much does the box weigh?

6. A 450-N person ran up a flight of stairs which was 10 m high. How much work did the person do? If it took 30 s, what was the person's power?

7. What is the power of a motorboat that can do 5000 J of work in 25 s?

8. What is the mechanical advantage of a lever if the effort force is 15 N and the resistance force is 45 N?

9. A lever has a mechanical advantage of 7. If John applies 40 N of effort force, how much resistance force can he overcome?

10. If a machine has a mechanical advantage of 3, how much effort force is required to overcome a resistance force of 240 N?

11. If you need to put 12 N of work into a machine to get 8 N of work out, what is the mechanical efficiency of this machine?

12. A machine has an efficiency of 80%. If you need to get a work output of 400 N, how much work must you put in?

13. A machine can lift 1,500 kg to a height of 4 m, but it uses 8,000 J to do so. What is the work output of the machine? What is its mechanical efficiency?

## Chapter 6

1. You are given the following information: initial pressure) × (initial volume) = (final pressure) × (final volume); initial pressure = 3.0 N/m$^2$; initial volume = 12 mL; final pressure = 4.0 N/m$^2$. Calculate the final volume.

2. If a sample of gas has an initial volume of 30 mL at a pressure of 1.2 N/m$^2$, what is the final volume if the pressure is increased to 2.0 N/m$^2$, assuming no change in the temperature?

3. If you double the pressure on a specific amount of gas, what happens to its volume, assuming there is no temperature change?

4. If the volume of a 50 mL sample of gas at 2.1 N/m$^2$ of pressure is reduced to 30 mL, what is the final pressure?

5. Suppose you use all of the air from a filled balloon to blow up a toy that is only one half the size of the balloon. How will the pressure inside that toy compare to the original pressure in the balloon?

## Chapter 9

1. If today's air temperature is 41°F, what is the air temperature in °C.

2. What is the approximate temperature in °F of 20°C?

3. You take your temperature with a thermometer that measures in degrees Celsius. Your temperature is 40°C. Are you sick? What is your temperature in °F?

4. A radiator with a mass of 50 kg has an initial temperature of 95 °C and a final temperature of 50°C. Its specific heat is 448 J/kg°C. How much heat energy did it give off?

5. How much heat is required to raise the temperature of 0.5 kg of water from 20°C to 30°C ? The specific heat of water is 4,190 J/kg°C.

6. How much heat is needed to raise the temperature of 2 kg of copper by 5°C (specific heat of copper = 387 J/kg °C)

7. A 10 kg mass of an unknown substance gives off 180 200 J/kg°C of heat when it cools 20° C. What is its specific heat?

8. How much heat is needed to raise the temperature of 0.05 kg of iron from 20°C to 35°C? (specific heat of iron = 448 J/kg °C)

## Chapter 11

1. What is the current used by a toaster that has a resistance of 12 ohms and uses 120 volts?

2. What is the resistance of a light bulb if it uses 0.5 amps of current and 110 volts?

3. What is the voltage of a battery that can create a 1.5 amp current through a 8 ohm resistor?

4. What is the voltage in a circuit that uses 5 amps of current across a 10 ohm resistor?

5. If a 4 amp circuit has a resistance of 3 ohms, what is the voltage?

6. If a stereo draws 0.5 amps of current when plugged into a 120-volt outlet, how much power does it use?

7. How much power does a 1.5-volt battery have if it can produce a 0.05-amp current?

8. A 100-W light bulb was left on in your room while you were at school for 8 h. How much energy was wasted?

9. Suppose the electric company in your area charges $.08 per kWh, how much did it cost to use 8,000 W?

## Chapter 14

1. You are at the beach watching the waves roll in. You time them and determine that they hit the beach every 5 s and that the crests are 15 m apart. What is the speed of these waves?

2. The speed of sound in air is 340 m/s. If the frequency of the middle C note is 256 Hz, what is its wavelength?

3. What is the frequency of a sound wave that has a wavelength of 0.017 m?

4. What is the wavelength of a sound wave with a frequency of 20 Hz?

5. The speed of light is 3.00 x 10$^8$ m/s. Calculate the frequency of a wavelength that is 30 m.

6. A photographer wants to light up an object using light bounced off a blank wall. If the object is at a 45° angle to the wall, at what angle should she direct the spotlight towards the wall?

# *Glossary*

A simple, phonetic spelling is given for words in this book that may be unfamiliar or hard to pronounce.

Stressed syllables are printed in capital letters. Sometimes a word has two stressed syllables. The syllable with the primary stress is printed in FULL capitals. The syllable with the secondary stress is printed in SMALL capitals.

Most of the time, the phonetic spelling can be interpreted without referring to the key. The key below gives the pronunciations for letters that are commonly used for more than one sound.

***Example:*** *Bioluminescence* is pronounced BY oh LOO muh NES uhns.

## *Pronunciation Key*

| | | | |
|---|---|---|---|
| a | c**a**t | ih | p**i**n |
| ah | h**o**t | oh | gr**ow** |
| ai | c**a**re | oo | r**u**le, m**u**sic |
| aw | **a**ll | ow | n**ow** |
| ay | s**ay**, **a**ge | oy | v**oi**ce |
| ee | m**ee**t | u | p**u**t |
| eh | l**e**t | uh | s**u**n, **a**bout |
| eye | **i**ce or b**y** | ur | t**er**m |

**A**

**absolute zero**   The temperature at which molecules do not move; the lowest temperature matter can have. Abbreviated: 0 K. (p. 211)

**acceleration**   A change in velocity, or the rate at which this change occurs. (p. 39)

**acid**   A chemically active substance low on the pH scale that gives up hydrogen ions (H+) in a water solution. (p. 527)

**acid rain**   Rainwater polluted with sulfuric acid, nitric acid, or both. (p. 624)

**activation energy**   Energy required to start a chemical reaction. (p. 504)

**air pollution**   A high concentration of harmful gases and solids in the air. (p. 621)

**airfoil**   An object, such as a plane's wing, with one flat and one curved surface that causes a pressure difference and a reaction force when moving through air. (p. 98)

**alpha decay**   Radioactive decay in which alpha particles are released from the nucleus of an atom. (p. 566)

**ampere**   (AM peer) SI unit of electric current. Abbreviated: A, or amps. (p. 270)

**amplitude**   (AM pluh tood) The distance in a transverse wave between the line of origin and each crest or trough. (p. 344)

**applied science**   The use of science or technical knowledge to achieve a practical purpose; technology. (p. 21)

**astigmatism**   A vision disorder in which an imperfectly shaped cornea unevenly bends light entering the eye. (p. 439)

**atom**   The smallest particle of an element with all the properties of the element that can combine with other atoms to form a molecule. (p. 157)

**B**

**base**   A chemically active substance high on the pH scale that gives up hydroxide ions (OH-) in a water solution. (p. 527)

**basic**   Having the characteristics of a base or containing a base. (p. 528)

**beta decay**   Radioactive decay in which beta particles are released from the nucleus of an atom. (p. 566)

**binding energy**   Energy of the force that holds protons and neutrons together. (p. 562)

**bioluminescence**   (BY oh LOO muh NES uhns) The emission of light by living things. (p. 434)

**biomass**   Organic matter that can be used as fuel. (p. 591)

**boiling point**   The temperature at which a substance changes from a liquid to a gas. (p. 223)

**Boyle's Law**   The principle stating that the pressure of gas in a confined space increases when the volume of the gas is reduced, if its temperature is kept constant. (p. 143)

**buoyant force**   The upward force acting on an object in a fluid. Buoyant force equals the weight of the fluid displaced by the object. (p. 91)

**C**

**calorie**   The amount of heat needed to raise the temperature of 1g of water 1° C. (p. 217)

**carbohydrate**   (kar boh HY drayt) An organic compound of carbon, hydrogen, and oxygen, such as a starch or sugar, with a ratio of hydrogen and oxygen atoms that is two to one. (p. 545)

**catalyst** (CAT uh lihst)   A substance that initiates or speeds up a chemical reaction without being used up in the process. (p. 506)

**central heating system**   A network of wires, pipes, ducts, and vents that transfers heat throughout a building from a central location. (p. 231)

**centripetal acceleration**   (sehn TRIP uh tuhl) Acceleration caused by movement in a circle. (p. 43)

**centripetal force**   The force necessary to keep an object moving in a circle and that is directed inward toward the center. (p. 68)

**ceramic**   Material made by firing clay or other substance at a high temperature. (p. 616)

**charge**   Electric force of a proton, electron, or an object having an unequal number of protons and electrons. (p. 257)

**Charles' Law**   The principle stating that the volume of a gas increases as its temperature is increased, if its pressure remains constant. (p. 144)

**chemical bond**   The attractive force that holds atoms or ions together. (p. 467)

**chemical change**   Change in the chemical identity of a substance. (p. 149)

**chemical equation**   A combination of chemical symbols and formulas that represent a chemical reaction. (p. 494)

**chemical reaction**   Interaction between substances in which existing chemical bonds break and new bonds form, creating one or more new substances. (p. 489)

**circuit**   A closed, continuous path through which electric current flows. (p. 267)

**cochlea**   (KOHK lee uh) The coil-shaped organ in the inner ear that is lined with hair cells that detect motion, sound waves, and send a nerve impulse to the brain. (p. 386)

**coefficient**   (KOH uh FIHSH uhnt) The number in a chemical equation that shows how many atoms or molecules of a substance are involved in a reaction. (p. 496)

**cogeneration**   An energy-saving process in which heat and electricity are produced and utilized from the same fuel source. (p. 599)

**colloid**   (KAHL oyd) A mixture with particles larger than those in a solution and smaller than those in a suspension. Colloids are not completely homogeneous, but are less heterogeneous than suspensions. (p. 523)

**combustion**   Any type of chemical reaction with oxygen that gives off heat or light. (p. 244)

**compass**   An instrument for determining direction with a magnetized needle that aligns itself with the earth's magnetic field. (p. 290)

**composite**   Material made of fibers that are embedded in a matrix. (p. 618)

**compound machine**   A system of two or more simple machines. (p. 120)

**compound**   A substance made of two or more chemically combined elements. (p. 168)

**compression**   Part of a longitudinal wave where the particles of matter through which the energy wave is moving are pressed together. (p. 337)

**concave**   A surface that is curved or rounded inward, like the inside surface of a bowl. (p. 443)

**concentration**   The amount of solute relative to the amount of solvent. (p. 520)

**conduction**   The transfer of heat energy or electrons between objects in direct contact. (pp. 213, 262)

**conductor**   A substance through which electric charges or heat can move easily. (p. 263)

**constant**   The factor that is kept the same in a controlled experiment. (p. 7)

**constructive interference**   The interaction of energy waves in which the same parts of two waves match up so that the amplitudes of the waves add to each other. (pp. 376–377)

**controlled experiment**   An experiment with two test groups: an experimental group and a control group. (p. 7)

**convection**   The transfer of heat energy by the movement of a fluid. (p. 214)

**convex**   A surface that is curved or rounded outward like the surface of a ball. (p. 443)

**cornea**   The transparent structure that covers the pupil and the iris of the eye. (p. 438)

**covalent bond**   (koh VAY lent) A type of chemical bond formed between nonmetals in which atoms share one or more electrons. (pp. 469, 478)

**crest**   The highest point of a transverse wave. Indicates the amount of energy in the wave. (p. 336)

**crystal lattice**   The structure of an ionic solid in which an orderly three- dimensional pattern of atoms is repeated over and over. (p. 474)

**cubic meter**   The basic SI unit of volume; space occupied by a cube 1 m x 1 m x 1 m. Abbreviated: $m^3$. (p. 12)

 **data**   Information from which analyses and conclusions can be made. (p. 3)

**deceleration**   A decrease in velocity over a period of time. (p. 40)

**decibel**   The unit used to measure sound intensity. Abbreviated: dB. (p. 367)

**decomposition reaction**   A chemical reaction in which a single reactant breaks down into simpler parts, such as elements. (p. 500)

**density**   The measure of how much mass exists in a given volume; density = mass/volume. (p. 13)

**destructive interference**   The interaction of waves in which the same parts of each wave do not match. The amplitudes of the waves subtract from each other. (p. 376)

**diffraction**   Bending of a wave as a result of the interaction between the wave and the edge of an object. (p. 350)

**diode**   A vacuum tube through which electrons flow in only one direction. (p. 310)

**Doppler effect**   A change in wave frequency, and therefore the pitch of a sound, caused by movement of either the source or the receiver. (p. 369)

**double-replacement reaction**   A chemical reaction in which two different ions trade places between different ionic compounds, forming two new compounds. (p. 501)

**drag**   The force that opposes the movement of an object through a fluid. (p. 99)

*E*   **echolocation**   (EK oh loh KAY shuhn) The method used by animals to locate objects by sending and receiving high-frequency sound waves . (p. 402)

**electric current**   Flow of electric charge. Abbreviated: $I$. (p. 267)

**electromagnet**   A magnet made of a soft-iron core surrounded by a coil of wire through which an electric current is passed. (p. 294)

**electromagnetic induction**   The process of producing an electric current by moving a magnetic field through a wire coil without touching it. (p. 300)

**electromagnetic spectrum**   The entire range of visible and invisible electromagnetic waves. (p. 428)

**electron**   A subatomic particle with a negative charge located outside of an atom's nucleus. (p. 158)

**electronics**   The specialized field of physics dealing with behavior and control of electrons. (p. 309)

**element**   Matter that cannot be changed into a simpler form by any ordinary physical or chemical process. (p. 157)

**emulsifier**   (ee MUHL sih FY er) A substance that helps to disperse tiny particles of liquid throughout another substance. (p. 526)

**endothermic reaction**   (EN duh THER mihk) Any chemical reaction that absorbs energy. (p. 492)

**energy**   The ability to cause change or do work. (pp. 45– 46)

**enzyme**   A biological catalyst that controls the rate of a specific chemical reaction in a living thing. (p. 508)

**exothermic reaction**   (EK suh THER mihk) A chemical reaction that releases energy. (p. 492)

*F*   **fluid**   Any substance that tends to flow or to conform to the outline of its container, such as a liquid or a gas. (p. 85)

**fluorescent**   Referring to light produced by electrons colliding with gas particles in a tube coated with phosphor. (p. 434)

**focal length**   The distance from a lens to the point where light rays that pass through the lens are focused. (p. 446)

**force**   The push or pull on an object that causes motion or change. (p. 55)

**fossil fuel**   Fuel, such as oil, formed naturally from the remains of ancient organisms over millions of years. (p. 586)

**frame of reference**   A place or object that is assumed to be fixed and by which the movement of other objects is determined. (p. 31)

**frequency**   (FREE kwuhn see) The number of wavelengths that pass a point in a given time. (p. 344)

**friction**   The force of resistance that occurs when movement takes place between any two objects or substances that make contact. (p. 57)

**fulcrum**   The fixed point of a lever. (p. 117)

*G*   **gamma decay**   Radioactive decay in which no matter is released, but which releases energy called gamma radiation, or gamma rays. (p. 566)

**gamma ray**   The electromagnetic wave with the shortest wavelength that is emitted by radioactive materials during a nuclear reaction. (p. 420)

**gas**   Matter having no definite shape and no definite volume. (p. 142)

**geothermal**   Relating to the heat produced beneath the earth's surface. (p. 592)

**global warming**   The increase of the earth's atmospheric temperature as a result of the greenhouse effect. (p. 622)

**greenhouse effect**  A process that traps energy from the sun by allowing radiant energy to enter a given space, but prevents heat energy from escaping. (p. 622)

**H** **half-life**  The amount of time it takes for half the atoms of a quantity of a radioactive isotope to decay. (p. 568)

**halogen**  Any one of the five elements in Group 17 of the periodic table (fluorine, chlorine, bromine, iodine, and astatine) that can combine with a metal to form a salt. (p. 197)

**hardware**  The equipment and components that make up a computer, such as a central processing unit, main storage, input devices, and output devices. (p. 323)

**heat energy**  A form of energy produced by vibration of molecules that can be absorbed, given up, or transferred between substances. (p. 209)

**hertz**  The unit used to measure the frequency of waves. Abbreviated: Hz. (p. 368)

**heterogeneous mixture**  A mixture in which the components are not evenly mixed so that different parts of the mixture have different compositions. (p. 176)

**hologram**  A three-dimensional picture formed on photographic film by the interference pattern of a split beam of laser light. (p. 456)

**homogeneous mixture**  A mixture in which the components are evenly mixed so that every part of the mixture is the same as any other. Same as *solution*. (p. 176)

**hydrocarbon**  (hy druh KAR buhn) An organic compound that contains only hydrogen and carbon atoms. (p. 539)

**hydroelectric power**  Electricity generated by the power of moving water. (p. 586)

**I** **illuminated**  An object or substance that is visible because it is reflecting light. (p. 433)

**incandescent**  Light produced by a heated object that glows. (p. 434)

**inclined plane**  A slanted-surface, simple machine that is used to raise or lower an object. (p. 116)

**induction**  The transfer of electrons between objects that are not in direct contact. (p. 262)

**inertia**  The tendency of an object to remain at rest or in motion until acted upon by an external force. (p. 61)

**infrared**  Invisible electromagnetic waves with wavelengths slightly longer than red light. Infrared waves have a penetrating heating effect. (p. 420)

**inner ear**  The part of a human ear that contains the cochlea and the semicircular canals. (p. 386)

**insulation**  (ihn suh LAY shuhn) A substance that slows the transfer of heat. (p. 236)

**insulator**  A substance through which electric charges or heat can't move readily. (p. 263)

**integrated circuit**  A tiny electric circuit that contains transistors, diodes, and resistors usually located on a small piece of silicon. (p. 313)

**interference**  The effect of two or more waves interacting. (p. 352)

**internal energy**  The total amount of energy a substance contains. (p. 209)

**internal reflection**  The reflection of light off the inner surface of an object, as in a tube or optical fiber. (p. 457)

**ion**  An atom or group of atoms having an electric charge as a result of losing or gaining one or more electrons. (p. 170)

**ionic bond**  (eye AHN ihk) A chemical bond between a metal and a nonmetal in which electrons are transferred from one atom to another. (pp. 469, 471)

**iris**  The colored portion of the eye that surrounds the pupil. (p. 437)

**isomer**  (EYE suh mur) An organic compound that has the same chemical formula for which more than one structure is possible. (p. 541)

**isotope**  (EYE soh tohp) Atoms of the same element that have different numbers of neutrons, and therefore different atomic masses. (p. 161)

**J** **joule**  (JOOL) The metric unit that measures work or energy. Abbreviated: J. (p. 108)

**K** **Kelvin**  The SI temperature scale using units equivalent to Celsius degrees and beginning at absolute zero. (p. 211)

**kilogram**  The basic SI unit of mass. Abbreviated: kg. (p. 13)

**kinetic energy**  (KUH neht ihk) The energy of motion. Abbreviated: K.E. (p. 47)

**L** **laser**  A device that produces coherent light of one wavelength that does not spread out as it travels. An acronym for **L**ight **A**mplification by **S**timulated **E**missions of **R**adiation. (p. 455)

**Law of Conservation of Mass and Energy**   The principle that the amount of matter and energy in the universe cannot be created or destroyed. (p. 124)

**lens**   A curved transparent object that forms an image by refracting light passing through it. (p. 446)

**lever**   A simple machine that does work by moving around a fixed point. (p. 117)

**lift**   Upward force acting on an airfoil moving through air. (p. 98)

**lipid**   (LIH pihd) An organic compound, such as fat or oil, that has long hydrocarbon chains and does not dissolve in water. (p. 547)

**liquid**   Matter having definite volume but not definite shape. A fluid. (p. 141)

**liter**   A metric unit of volume. Abbreviated: L. (p. 12)

**longitudinal wave**   (lahn juh TOOD uh nuhl) An energy wave consisting of a series of compressions and rarefactions that moves through a medium in the same direction the wave is travelling. (p. 337)

**luminous**   (LOO muh nuhs) Referring to an object that produces light. (p. 433)

**luster**   A property of metal that enables it to reflect light from the surface. (p. 189)

**M** **machine**   A device that makes work easier by changing the direction or distance an object moves, or by reducing the amount of force needed to do work. (p. 112)

**magnetic domain**   Magnetic regions in which the poles of individual atoms line up and group together. (p. 289)

**magnetic field**   The area of magnetic force surrounding a magnet. (p. 288)

**magnetic pole**   One of the two ends of a magnet where magnetic force is strongest. (p. 288)

**malleability**   (MAL ee uh BIL uh tee) The ability to be flattened, bent, and shaped without breaking; a property of metals. (p. 189)

**mass**   The scientific measurement of the amount of matter that an object contains. Abbreviation: $m$. (p. 13)

**matrix**   Material in which another material or substance is embedded in a composite. (p. 618)

**matter**   Any object or substance that has mass and takes up space. (p. 135)

**mechanical advantage**   The advantage gained by using a machine to transmit force. Mechanical advantage = resistance force/effort force. Abbreviated: M.A. (p. 113)

**mechanical efficiency**   The measurement that compares a machine's work output with its work input. Mechanical efficiency = work output/work input x 100% (p. 114)

**melting point**   The temperature at which a substance changes from a solid to a liquid. (p. 224)

**metalloid**   An element that has the properties of both a metal and a nonmetal. (p. 187)

**metallurgy**   (MEHT uh LUR jee) The process and science of taking metals from the earth and making them into useful products. (p. 614)

**meter**   The basic SI unit of length. Abbreviated: m. (p. 12)

**microprocessor**   An integrated circuit that can hold all of a computer's problem-solving capabilities on one small silicon chip. (p. 322)

**middle ear**   The part of the human ear between the eardrum and the oval window containing the hammer, anvil, and stirrup. (p. 386)

**molecule**   Two or more chemically bonded atoms; the smallest part of a compound having all the properties of the compound. (p. 170)

**momentum**   The product of the mass and velocity of an object. Momentum = mass x velocity. (p. 67)

**N** **neutralization**   A process in which bases and acids react to form products that are neither acids nor bases. (p. 527)

**neutron**   (NOO trahn) A subatomic particle located in an atom's nucleus that has no electric charge and that has a mass similar to that of a proton. (p. 160)

**newton**   The basic SI unit of force. Abbreviated: N. (p. 56)

**noise**   An unwanted sound that may disturb or threaten mental or physical health. (p. 394)

**nonrenewable resource**   A natural resource, such as oil or natural gas, that can't be replaced by natural cycles or processes within a human lifetime. (p. 596)

**nuclear fission**   Splitting of an atom's nucleus into two smaller nuclei, releasing a large amount of energy. (p. 571)

**nuclear force**   The force within the nucleus of the atom that holds the parts of the nucleus together. (p. 78)

**nuclear fusion**   Joining of two or more atoms' nuclei, which releases an enormous amount of energy. (p. 573)

**nucleus**   The central region of an atom where neutrons and protons are located. (p. 159)

**ohm** (OHM) The SI unit of resistance force. Abbreviated: Ω. (p. 271)

**opaque** (oh PAYK) Referring to a material that absorbs most light that strikes it. (p. 423)

**optic nerve** Nerve fibers connecting the rods and cones of the retina to the brain. (p. 438)

**optical fiber** A thin, flexible, glass or plastic fiber that transmits light throughout its length by internal reflection. (p. 457)

**ore** A mineral containing a relatively large amount of a metal compound. (p. 192)

**organic compound** A carbon compound that occurs naturally in all living things. (p. 537)

**outer ear** The part of the human ear that is visible from the exterior, and includes the ear canal and the eardrum. (p. 386)

**overtone** One of the higher pitched tones produced when a note is sounded and that contributes to the timbre of the sound. (p. 391)

**P** **particle model** The idea stating that all matter is made of tiny particles which are in constant motion. (p. 135)

**periodic** Describing a regular, repeating pattern, such as the periodic table of the elements or the periodic phases of the moon. (p. 183)

**permanent magnet** A magnet that retains its magnetism after the magnetizing force is removed. (p. 289)

**petrochemicals** (peh troh KEHM ih cuhls) Synthetic materials and chemical substances produced from petroleum. (p. 609)

**petroleum** A dark, oily, liquid mixture of hydrocarbons formed from organic material over millions of years; crude oil. (p. 605)

**pH** A measurement that shows how acidic or basic a solution is. (p. 529)

**photoelectric effect** The release of electrons by certain substances, such as metals, when struck by high-energy light. (p. 411)

**photon** (FOH tahn) The packet of light energy given off by an atom. (p. 409)

**photosynthesis** (FOH toh SIHN theh suhs) A chemical process by which plants use water, carbon dioxide, and energy from the sun to make oxygen and glucose for energy. (p. 552)

**physical change** A change in a substance's physical properties but not in its chemical identity. (p. 147)

**pitch** The property of sound determined by the frequency of the sound waves producing it; highness or lowness of sound. (pp. 367–368)

**plasma** (PLAZ muh) The fourth phase of matter having unique properties and formed at very high temperatures. (p. 145)

**polarized** Referring to light waves that are parallel, usually as a result of passing through a special filter. (p. 410)

**polyatomic ion** A group of covalently bonded atoms that has an electric charge due to losing or gaining one or more electrons. (p. 480)

**polymer** (PAHL ih mur) A large molecule made of a chain of many smaller units connected by covalent bonds. (pp. 541, 609)

**potential energy** Energy due to the position of an object or the chemical bonds in a substance. Abbreviated: P.E. (p. 46)

**power** The rate at which work is done, measured in watts. Power = work/time. (p. 109)

**pressure** The force exerted on a surface. Pressure = force/area. (p. 85)

**product** A substance produced by a chemical reaction. (p. 495)

**protein** (PROH teen) An organic compound existing as a large, complex molecule made of amino acids. (p. 548)

**proton** A subatomic particle with a positive charge located in the nucleus of an atom. (p. 159)

**pulley** A simple machine made of a rope wrapped around a grooved wheel. (p. 119)

**pupil** The opening through which light enters the eye. (p. 437)

**R-value** The measurement of a material's ability to stop the flow of heat. (p. 236)

**radiation** The transfer of energy by infrared rays. (p. 215)

**radioactive decay** The process by which an unstable nucleus of a radioactive element breaks down spontaneously. (p. 565)

**radioactivity** The release of particles and energy from the nucleus of an atom. (p. 561)

**rarefaction** (RAIR uh FAK shun) Part of a longitudinal wave where the particles of matter through which the wave is moving are spread apart. (p. 337)

**reactant**   (ree AK tuhnt) The raw material in a chemical reaction; shown on the left side of a chemical equation. (pp. 494–495)

**real image**   An image formed by converging light rays. (p. 442)

**rectifier**   A vacuum tube diode that changes alternating current into direct current. (p. 310)

**reflection**   The action of a wave when it bounces off a surface. Also, the image formed by light rays reflected off a surface. (pp. 349, 441)

**refraction**   Bending of a wave caused by the change of speed that occurs when the wave moves from one medium to another. (pp. 351, 445)

**refrigerant**   A chemical that evaporates at a low temperature and removes heat as it changes from a liquid to a gas; used in cooling systems. (p. 241)

**renewable resource**   A natural resource that is replaced continuously by natural cycles or processes. (p. 596)

**resistance**   The force opposing the flow of electric current. Abbreviated: R. (p. 271)

**resonance**   (REZ uh nehnts) The vibration of an object at its natural frequency. (p. 378)

**respiration**   The chemical process in living organisms during which oxygen reacts with glucose to produce carbon dioxide, water, and energy in the form of ATP. (pp. 554–555)

**retina**   The inner layer of the back of the eye where light-sensitive cells are located. (p. 438)

**salt**   An ionic compound made of a metal and a nonmetal and formed when an acid and a base react. (p. 529)

**saturated hydrocarbon**   Hydrocarbon in which all carbon atoms are joined by single covalent bonds. (p. 541)

**saturated**   Referring to a solution that contains as much of the solute as can be dissolved at a given temperature and pressure. (pp. 520–521)

**scientific notation**   The method of expressing a very large or very small number by multiplying a number between 1 and 10 by some power of 10. (p. 14)

**sclera**   The visible white part of the eye surrounding the iris. (p. 437)

**semiconductor**   Material whose electric conductivity is between that of a conductor and that of an insulator. (p. 312)

**silt**   Very fine particles of earth material. (p. 522)

**simple machine**   A machine that does work in one movement. (p. 116)

**single-replacement reaction**   A chemical reaction in which atoms of one element replace atoms of another element in a compound, producing a different element and a different compound. (p. 501)

**smog**   A type of air pollution consisting primarily of smoke and fog. (p. 623)

**software**   Programs that instruct computer hardware to perform certain tasks. (p. 324)

**solar cell**   A device containing a semiconductor that converts sunlight into electricity. (p. 590)

**solid**   Matter having definite shape and a definite volume. (p. 141)

**solubility**   The ability of a substance to dissolve in another substance. (p. 519)

**solute**   The component of a solution that is dissolved in the solvent. (p. 515)

**solution**   A mixture in which the components are evenly mixed so that every part of the mixture is the same as any other. Same as *homogeneous mixture*. (p. 515)

**solvent**   A component of a solution in which the solute is dissolved. (p. 515)

**sonar**   The technique of using ultrasonic waves to locate underwater objects. Acronym for **so**und **n**avigation **a**nd **r**anging. (p. 400)

**sonogram**   The image created by ultrasonic waves reflected off the soft tissue of living organism. (p. 399)

**sound wave**   The longitudinal wave in matter that can be heard, produced by a vibrating object. (p. 359)

**specific heat**   The amount of heat necessary to raise the temperature of 1 g of a substance 1°C. (p. 216)

**speed**   The distance travelled in a given amount of time. (p. 34)

**strong force**   A nuclear force that holds protons and neutrons together by holding their quarks together. (p. 78)

**substituted hydrocarbon**   A hydrocarbon in which at least one hydrogen atom is replaced by another functional group. (p. 542)

**supersaturated**   Referring to a solution that contains more solute than could normally be dissolved at a given temperature and pressure. (pp. 520-521)

**suspension**   Mixture in which some particles are relatively large and will settle out when the mixture is not moving. (p. 522)

**synthesis reaction**   A chemical reaction in which two substances combine to form a third, more complex substance. Also called combination or composition reaction. (p. 500)

*T*   **technology**   The use of scientific or technical knowledge to solve a problem or to achieve a practical purpose; applied science. (p. 21)

**temperature**   The amount of heat energy in a substance, determined by the average kinetic energy of the molecules in the substance. (p. 209)

**terminal velocity**   The maximum velocity of a falling object, occurring when the force of friction equals the force of gravity. (pp. 57–58)

**thermal expansion**   An increase in the volume of a substance due to an increase in heat energy. (p. 225)

**thermal pollution**   An increase in water temperature that harms living things. (p. 625)

**thrust**   Force that moves an object forward. (pp. 98–99)

**timbre**   (TIM bur) The quality of a sound determined by the combination of different frequencies of the sound waves that make up the sound. (p. 370)

**transistor**   A semiconducting device that contains layered n-type and p-type semiconducting materials. (p. 313)

**translucent**   (tranz LOOS uhnt) Referring to a material that transmits some light but scatters it so that a sharp image is not seen. (p. 423)

**transmutation**   (trans myoo TAY shun) The process in which an element changes into a different element, such as by radioactive decay. (p. 567)

**transparent**   Describing a material that transmits almost all the light rays that strike it. (p. 423)

**transverse wave**   Wave in which matter moves at a right angle to the direction of the wave. (p. 336)

**trough**   The lowest point of a transverse wave. (p. 336)

**turbine**   A set of curved blades mounted on a long shaft that is turned by the flow of a fluid, such as steam. Used to generate electricity. (p. 247)

*U*   **ultrasound**   A sound with a wave frequency greater than those within the range of human hearing. (p. 398)

**ultraviolet**   Relating to invisible electromagnetic waves with wavelengths shorter than visible violet light and longer than X-rays. (p. 420)

**universal force**   One of the four forces common throughout the universe: gravitational, nuclear, electric, or magnetic. (p. 73)

**universal solvent**   Water, so called because of its ability to dissolve many substances. (p. 517)

**unsaturated**   Referring to a solution that contains less solute than can be dissolved at a given temperature and pressure. (pp. 520-521)

**unsaturated hydrocarbon**   A hydrocarbon that contains at least one double or triple covalent bond in its chain of carbon atoms. (p. 541)

*V*   **vacuum tube**   An early electronic device that consists of a glass vacuum bulb, a filament, and a plate. Used to control electrons. (p. 310)

**variable**   The factor that is changed in a controlled experiment. (p. 7)

**velocity**   (veh LAHS uh tee) The speed and direction of movement. (p. 34)

**virtual image**   An image, such as one seen in a plane mirror, formed by light rays that do not actually pass where the image appears. (p. 442)

**volt**   The SI unit of voltage. Abbreviated: V. (p. 270)

**voltage**   The amount of electric energy available to move a charge. (p. 270)

**volume**   The amount of space occupied by an object or substance. (p. 12)

*W*   **watt**   The basic SI unit of power; one watt equals one joule per second. Abbreviated: W. (p. 109)

**wave**   Disturbance that transfers energy through matter or space. (p. 335)

**wavelength**   The distance between two like parts of a wave, such as crests. (p. 343)

**weak force**   The nuclear force that holds together the particles within protons and neutrons. (p. 78)

**work**   Force acting upon an object in the direction the object moves. Work = force x distance. (p. 107)

**work input**   The amount of work put into a machine. (p. 114)

**work output**   The amount of work produced by a machine. (p. 114)

*X*   **X-ray**   A high energy electromagnetic wave that can travel through matter and has a wavelength of .001 nm to 10 nm. (p. 420)

# Index

**Note:** Boldfaced page numbers refer to definitions. Italicized page numbers refer to figures.

## A

Absolute zero, **211**
AC (alternating current), 269, 295, 298, 302, 310
Accelerated motion, 64-66, *65, 67*
Acceleration
  centripetal, *43,* 43
  change in direction and, *41,* 41
  definition of, **39**
  force and, 64, 65, 66
  graph of, *65,* 65-66
  mass and, 65-66
  measuring, *40,* 40, 66
  negative, *40,* 40-41
  positive, 40
  racer's, 41
Accelerator, 163
Acetic acid, *542,* 542
Acid rain, 530, **625**
Acids
  bases and, 502
  common, *528*
  definition of, **527**
  identifying, 532
  properties of, 527-528
  in stomach, 554
  strong, 527
  weak, 527
Acoustics, *379,* 379
Actinium, 192
Activation energy, **504**
Active solar heating system, *235,* 235, 590
Activity series of metals, 501
Additives, food, 482
Adenosine triphosphate (ATP), 555
Adhesives, *483,* 483
Adobe buildings, 347
Aerosols, 243, 498, **524**
Air
  elements of, 174
  in forced-air heating system, *232,* 232
  gases in, *17,* 17
  heat pumps and, *234,* 234
  in hot-water heating system, *232,* 232
  pollution, 248, **621,** 623
  pressure, *85,* 85-87, *86-87, 98,* 98
  quality of, *621,* 621-623, *622, 623*
  in radiant heating system, *233,* 233
  as solution, 515
  sound waves and, *387,* 387
  in steam heating system, *233,* 233

Air bags, 67
Airfoil, **98,** *98,* 100
Air navigation, 38
Airplane design, 99
Alcohols, 542
Algae, *628,* 628
Alkali metals, *186,* **191,** *191,* 475
Alkaline earth metals, *186,* **191,** *191,* 475
Alloys, **176,** *176, 193,* 193, 515
Alpha decay, **566,** *566*
Alternating current (AC), 269, 295, 298, 302, 310
Altitude, *86-87*
Aluminum (Al), 193, *195,* 195
Aluminum nails, 175
Americium, 188
Amines, 542, 548
Amino acids, 548
Ammeter, **270,** *270,* 297
Amorphous solids, 141
Ampere (amp or A), 270
Amplifiers, **311,** *311,* 316
Amplitude, *344,* 344, *352*
Analyzing, **5**
Animal echolocation, 402-403
Animal light, 434
Anodes, *310*
Antacids, 502
Antifreeze, 516
Antimony (Sb), *196,* 196
Aperture, *452*
Apothecary, 172-173
Applications-software programs, 324
Applied science, **21**
Archimedes' principle, 92
Argon (Ar), *164, 197,* 197, *479*
Aristotle, 37
Armature, 296, *302,* 302
Arsenic (As), *196,* 196, 312
Artifacts, *25,* 25, *78,* 78
Asphalt, *607*
Astatine (At), *197,* 197
Astigmatism, **439**
Astrophysics, **21**
ATM cards, 314
Atmospheric pressure, *86-87,* 86-87
Atomic mass
  atoms and, 162-163
  of copper, 163
  definition of, **162**
  graph of, 198
  of hydrogen, 162
  Mendeleev's work with, 184-185
  transmutation of elements and, 567
Atomic mass unit (amu), **162**
Atomic number, **161,** 185, 188, 198, 567

Atoms
  atomic mass and, 162-163
  atomic number and, 161
  chemical bonds and, 123, 467
  chemical reactions and, *491,* 491
  compounds and, 170
  definition of, **157**
  electromagnetic energy and, 123
  elements and, *157,* 157, 161
  isotopes and, *161,* 161
  mass number and, 162
  matter and, 157
  metals and, 190
  models of, 157-160, 162
  nuclear energy and, 123
  nucleus of, 159, 160
  subscript and, 171
ATP (adenosine triphosphate), 555
Attraction, force of, *258,* 258, 260
Audio electronic equipment, *315,* 315-318, *316, 317*
Aurora australis (southern lights), 291
Aurora borealis (northern lights), *291,* 291
Automobiles. *See* Cars
Average speed, 35
Axle, wheel and, **118**

## B

Baking soda, 137, 528
Balance, 385
Balanced chemical equations, *496,* 496-497
Balanced force, *71,* 71
Ball bearings, *63,* 63
Balloon rocket, 50
Bar graphs, **18,** *18*
Barnacles, *483*
Bases
  acids and, 502
  in antacids, 502
  common, *529*
  definition of, **527**
  identifying, 532
  properties of, 528, *529*
  strong, 528
Bats, 403
Battery, car, *268,* 268
Becquerel, Antoine, 561
Bernoulli, Daniel, 97
Bernoulli's principle, 97, 98
Beta decay, **566,** *566*
Bicycles, *121,* 121, *304,* 304
Bifocals, 448
Bikes, *121,* 121, *304,* 304
Billiard balls, *412,* 412
Binding energy, **562**
Biochemistry, **21**

Biodegradable plastics, 612
Biological catalysts, 508
Biology, 24
Bioluminescence, **434**
Biomass, **591**, *591, 592*
Bird flight, *100*, 100-101, *101*
Bismuth-214, 568
Bitumen, 592
Blood, pH in, *531*, 531
Boat design, Polynesian, 94
Body. *See* Human body
Bohr, Niels, 159
Bohr's model of atoms, 159
Boiling point of water, *211*, 211, **223**, *223*
Bones, 365
Borax, 195
Boron (B), *195*, 195
Boron group of nonmetals, *195*, 195
Boyle, Robert, *143*, 401
Boyle's Law, *143*, 143
Braille, Louis, 440
Brakes, car, *90*, 90
Breakwaters, *353*, 353
Bridges, 378
Bromine (Br), *197*, 197
Bronze Age, 614
Bronze tools, 614
Bubble chamber, *163*, 163
Buoyancy
 Archimedes' principle and, 92
 control of, 96
 definition of, **91**
 density and, 13, *93*, 93-94, *94*
 force and, *91*, 91-92
 Polynesian boat design and, 94
 ships and, *95*, 95
 volume and, *92*, 92
Buoys, 340

*C* Calcium (Ca), 166, *191*, 191, 477
Calcium carbonate ($CaCO_3$), 169, 171, 502
Calcium hydroxide, 500
Calcium oxide, 500
Calculating, 15-16, 41, 497. *See also* Measuring
Calendar, *183*, 183
Caloric theory of heat, 210
Calories, **217**, *220*, 220, 546, 556
Calorimeter, *217*, 217
Cameras, *452*, 452
Cancer, 564, 569
Candy makers, 508
Canning, 226
"Carbohydrate loading," 545
Carbohydrates, **545**-546, *545, 546*
Carbon (C), 171, 193, *195*, 195, 538
Carbon-12, *161*, 162, 568
Carbon-14, *161*, 162, 568
Carbon-14 dating, **568**, *568*

Carbon-based fibers, 618
Carbon-carbon bonds, 539
Carbon compounds
 carbon-carbon bonds and, 539
 hydrocarbons and, 539-541, *540, 542*, 542
 isomers and, *541*, 541
 isotopes of, *161*
 living things and, *537*, 537, *538*
 polymers and, 541
 structure of, 538
Carbon dioxide ($CO_2$), 169, *170*, 171, 519, 531
Carbon group of nonmetals, *195*, 195
Carbon monoxide, 169
Carboxylic acids, 542, 548
Cars
 batteries of, *268*, 268
 brakes of, *90*, 90
 catalytic converters of, *509*, 509
 chemical reactions in engines of, 509
 cooling systems of, *212*, 212
 electric, 273, *288*, 298
 radiators of, *212*, 212
 solar-powered engines and, *24*, 247
 velocity of, determining, *44*, 44
Catalysts, **506**-507, *506*, 508, 548
Catalytic converters, *509*, 509
Cataracts, 440
Cathode-ray tube (CRT), *318*, 318
Cathodes, *310*
CD-ROM (Compact Disc, Read-Only Memory), 320
CDs (compact discs), 315, *317*, 317, 320
Cell respiration, 554-555, *555*
Celsius (C), *11*, *14*, 14, *18*, 18, *211*, 211
Celsius, Anders, 211
Centimeter (cm), **12**
Central heating systems
 air pollution and, 248
 definition of, **231**
 forced-air heating, *232*, 232
 heat pumps, *234*, 234
 hot-water heating, *232*, 232
 radiant heating, *233*, 233
 steam heating, *233*, 233
 workings of, 231
Central processing unit (CPU), **323**
Centripetal acceleration, *43*, 43
Centripetal force, **68**, *68*
Ceramic clay, 616
Ceramic engines, 619
Ceramics, **616**, 617, 619
Cesium (Cs), *191*, 191
CFCs (chlorofluorocarbons), *243*, 243, 498
Chadwick, James, 160
Chain reactions, 498
Charge, **257**, *257. See also* Electric charge

Charles, Jacques, 144
Charles' Law, *144*, 144
Cheese, 508
Chefs, 150
Chemical bonds. *See also* Covalent bonds; Ionic bonds
 atoms and, 123, 467
 definition of, **467**
 designer molecules and, 470
 electrons and, 467-468, *468*
 of glucose, 554
 hydrogen and, *467*, 467
 metallic bonds, 469, *481*, 481
 stability of, *469*, 469
 types of, 469
Chemical changes in matter, **149**-150, *151*, 151, 152, 489
Chemical energy, *123*, 123, 125
Chemical engineering, 21
Chemical equations
 balanced, *496*, 496-497
 chain reactions and, 498
 definition of, **494**
 energy and, use of word in, 495
 parts of, 494-495, *495*
 unbalanced, *496*, 496
 writing, 497
Chemical pollution, **625**
Chemical reactions
 activation energy and, 504
 atoms and, *491*, 491
 in car's engine, 509
 catalysts and, *506*, 506-507, 508
 chemical changes and, 489
 combustion, 244
 definition of, **489**
 energy and, *492*, 492, *503*, 503
 of everyday substances, 510
 evidence for, *490*, 490
 fireworks and, *493*, 493
 mechanics of, *491*, 491
 of photosynthesis, *552-553*, 552-553
 reaction rate and, 505
 types of, *499*, 499-502, *500*
Chemical symbols of elements, *166*, 166
Chemistry, **21**, 24, 186, 499. *See also* Food chemistry
Chernobyl (Ukraine), 572
Ch'in, *390*, 390
China, 616
Chlorine (Cl)
 in chlorofluorocarbons, 243, 498
 electrons in, *472-473*, 472-473
 as halogen, *197*, 197
 hydrogen and, *491*, 491
Chlorofluorocarbons (CFCs), *243*, 243, 498
Chloroform ($CHCl_3$), 542
Chloroplast, 553
Chocolate milk, 175
Chromium (Cr), 167
Circle graphs, **17**, *17*

Circuit, **267.** *See also* Electric circuits
Circuit breakers, *281,* 281, *585*
Circuit diagrams, *274,* 274
Circuit protectors, *281,* 281
Circular motion, *43,* 43, *68,* 68
Classifying, **5,** *5*
Clay pottery, 137, 524, 616
Climate, *218-219,* 218-219
Coal, 500, 584, 586, 587
Cobalt (Co), 167
Cochlea, *386,* 386
Coefficient, **497**
Cogeneration, **599**
Coke, 615
Colloids, **523**-525, *523, 525*
Color
  as evidence of chemical reaction,
    490
  Impressionism and, *427,* 427
  light and, 425
  in nature, 422
  of objects, *426,* 426
  of paint and pigments, *427,* 427
  printing and, *428,* 428
  as property of elements, 165
  as property of matter, 136
  of sky, 425
  in visible electromagnetic spectrum,
    *417,* 417-418, *418*
  vision and, 426
Combustion, **244**
Combustion waste, 248
Communications, modern, *458,* 458
Commutator, 296
Compact Disc, Read-Only Memory
  (CD-ROM), 320
Compact discs (CDs), 315, *317,* 317,
  320
Compass, **290,** *292,* 292, *294,* 294
Composites, **618,** *618*
Compound machines, **120,** *120,* 121
Compounds
  atoms and, 170
  covalent, 484
  definition of, **168**
  elements and, *168,* 169
  formulas of, *171,* 171
  ionic, 170, *171,* 474, 476, 484
  mixtures and, 174
  organic, 537, 538-539
  properties of, 169
  of same formula, *541,* 541
  solubility of, 520
  in synthesis reactions, 500
  types of, *170,* 170
  water as, 169
Compression, **337,** *337, 360,* 360
Computers
  advances in technology of, 326
  CD-ROM and, 320
  development of, 322
  electrical engineers and, 593

hardware, *323,* 323
integrated circuits and, 313
laptop, 326
privacy and, 319
software, *324,* 324, 325
as tool of physical science, *22,* 22
use of, 322
waveform models and, *353,* 353-354
Concave lenses, **447,** *447*
Concave mirrors, **443,** *443*
Concentration, 505, **520**-521
Concorde, *364,* 364
Condensation, 141
Condenser, 234
Conduction
  definition of, **213, 262**
  heat energy and, *213,* 213, 215
  materials for, 213
  static electricity and, *262,* 262
Conductors
  copper as, 137
  definition of, **263**
  of electricity, 137, 192, 194, 282
  electrons and, 263
  metals as, 192, 263
  plastics as, 273
  static electricity and, *263,* 263
  transition metals as, 192
  water as, 263, 282
Cones, 426, 438
Conservation, 47, 67, 124. *See also*
  Energy conservation
Constant, **7**
Constant speed, 35, 37
Constructive interference, *352,* 352,
  *376,* 376-377
Contact lenses, 448
Continental shelf, *88*
Control group, 7
Controlled experiments, *7,* 7
Convection, **214,** *214,* 215
Conversion, 15, 124, 125
Convex hand lens, 450
Convex lenses, **446**-447, *446,* 452,
  454
Convex mirrors, **443,** *443*
Cooling systems
  of cars, *212,* 212
  chlorofluorocarbons in, *243,* 243
  of human body, *240,* 240
  principles of, 239
  refrigerants and, 241, 242, 243
  workings of, *242,* 242
Copper
  alloys and, 193
  atomic mass of, 163
  boiling point of, 223
  as conductor, 137
  in human body, 167
  use of, 165
Copper sulfate, *170,* 170, *501,* 501
Cora, *390,* 390

Cornea, **438,** *438*
Cornstalks, *592,* 592
Cost per unit volume, 146
Covalent bonds
  definition of, **478**
  electrons in, 469, 478-480, *479*
  hydrogen and, *479*
  ions in, 480
  molecules and, 478-479
  network solids and, 480
  oxygen and, *479*
Covalent compounds, 484
CPU (central processing unit), **323**
Credit cards, 314
Crest, **336,** *336,* 352
CRT (cathode-ray tube), *318,* 318
Crystal lattice, **474,** *474,* 476
Crystals, 141, *474,* 474
Cubic meter (m$^3$), *11,* **12**
Curie, Marie, 561
Curie, Pierre, 561
Current (I), 270, 271, 279
Current meters, *297,* 297
Curve, 19
Curve ball, 59
Cuyahoga River (United States), 628
Cyclamates, *470,* 470
Cylinders, 244

**D**  Dalton, John, 158, 161
     Dalton's model of atoms, 158
Dams, 586, 593
Data, **3**
DC (direct current), 269, 296, 298
Deceleration, *40,* 40-41
Decibel (dB), **367,** *367,* 387, *396,* 396
Decision making, 8, *9*
Decomposition reactions, 499, **500,**
  *500*
Deep-well injection, *627,* 627
Density
  buoyancy and, 13, *93,* 93-94, *94*
  definition of, **13**
  differences in, *93,* 93, 95
  of helium, 198
  measuring, *11, 13,* 13
  as property of matter, 136, 165
  speed of sound waves and, 362
Designer molecules, *470,* 470
Destructive interference, *352,* 352,
  *376,* 376-377
Diabetes, 440
Diamond, *138,* 138, 480
Didjerido, *390,* 390
Die, 189
Diesel engines, *246,* 246
Diffraction, **350,** *350, 374,* 374, 424
Digestion, 125, 508, 545
Digital sound recordings, 317
Dilution, 520
Dimensional analysis, **15**
Diodes, **310,** 313

Direct current (DC), 269, 296, 298
Directional changes, 41, *269*
Displacement, 92
Disposable contact lenses, 449
Distance-time graphs, *35*, 35, *40*, 40
Dolphins, *402*, 402-403
Doping, *312*
Doppler effect, **369**, *369*
Double covalent bond, 539
Double-replacement reactions, 499,
　**501**, *501*
Drag, **99**
Drag factor, *44*, 44
Drugs, making, 172-173, *173*
Drums, 393
Dry cells, 267, *268*, 268, 275
Ductile, **189**
Dyes, 611

**E** Ear, 86, *386*, 386.
　　　*See also* Hearing
Earmuffs, *389*, 389
Earplugs, 388-389
Ear protectors, 367, 388-389, *389*
Earth. *See also* Environment
　elements in atmosphere of, *164*
　frames of reference on, *32*, 32
　magnetic field of, *290*, 290
　magnetism of, *290*, 290-291
　moon and, *76*, 76
　petroleum reserves of, *608*, 608
　rotation of, *38*, 38
Earthenware, 616
Earthquake-resistant buildings, *347*,
　347
Earthquakes, 345, 347
Echoes, *372*, 372-373, *373*, 402-403
Echolocation, **402**-403
Effort force, *119*, 119
Egg yolk, 526
Einstein, Albert, 124, 188, 410, 411
Einsteinium (Es), 188
EKG (electrocardiogram), *79*, 79
Elasticity, 362
Electrical engineering, 21, 593
Electrical engineers, 593
Electric cars, 273, *298*, 298
Electric charge. *See also* Static elec-
　tricity
　build-up of, 261
　electric field and, 259
　in human body, 259
　negative, 257-258, *258*, 259, 266
　neutral, 257, *258*, 258
　occurrence of, *257*, 257
　positive, 257-258, *258*, 259, 266
Electric circuits. *See also* Electricity
　energy efficiency and, 278
　overloading, 281
　parts of, *274*, 274
　path of, *275*, 275
　resistors and, 274, *275*

shorting, 281
　types of, *276*, 276-277, *277*
Electric current. *See also* Electricity
　definition of, **267**
　electricians and, 272
　induction of, 300
　measuring, 269-271, *270*, *271*
　in radiant heating system, *233*, 233
　sources of, 267-268, *268*
　types of, 269
Electric field, **259**
Electric force, *77*, 77, 160
Electricians, 272
Electricity. *See also* Electric circuits;
　　Electric current; Electromagnetism
　bill for, 111
　circuit protectors and, *281*, 281
　conductors of, 137, 192, 194, 282
　conservation of, 436, 454
　directional changes and, *269*
　electric meters and, 280
　energy and, 261, 279, 492
　energy pathways and, 583
　magnetism and, 293, 300
　power of, 279, 280
　production and distribution of, *584-
　　585*, 584-585
　safety, *6*, *281*, 281-282
　sources of, *586*, 586-587, *587*
Electric meters, 280
Electric motors, *296*, 296
Electric power. *See* Electricity
Electrocardiogram (EKG), *79*, 79
Electrochemical cells, 267-268, 492
Electrodes, 268
Electrolytes, *268*, 268
Electromagnetic energy, *123*, 123
Electromagnetic induction
　definition of, **300**
　electromagnetism and, 300
　process of, *301*, 301
　uses of, *302*, 302-304, *303*, *304*
Electromagnetic spectrum
　definition of, **417**, *418-419*
　electromagnetic waves and, *416*,
　　416-417, *417*
　invisible, 419-420, *420*
　visible, *417*, 417-418, *418*
Electromagnetic waves, **416**-417, *416*,
　*417*
Electromagnetism. *See also* Electricity
　definition of, **293**
　discovery of, *293*, 293
　electromagnetic induction and, 300
　electromagnets and, *294*, 294-295
　uses for, 296-298
Electromagnets, **294**-295, *294*, 296
Electron cloud model of atoms, 160
Electronic devices
　semiconductors, *312*, 312-313, *313*
　types of, 309
　vacuum tubes, *310*, 310-311, *311*
Electronic equipment

audio, *315*, 315-318, *316*, *317*
　radios, 316
　smart cards and, *314*, 314
　sound recordings, *317*, 317-318
　telegraphs, *315*, 315
　telephones, *316*, 316
　video recordings, *318*, 318-320
Electronic Numerical Integrator and
　Computer (ENIAC), *322*, 322
Electronics, **309**, *309*. *See also*
　Electronic devices
Electrons
　in alkali metals, 191
　atomic number and, 161
　in Bohr's model of atoms, 159
　chemical bonds and, 467-468, *468*
　in chlorine, *472-473*, 472-473
　conductors and, 263
　in covalent bonds, 469, 478-480,
　　*479*
　definition of, **158**
　electrodes and, 268
　in electron cloud model of atoms,
　　160
　force of attraction and, 258
　force of repulsion and, 258
　in ionic bonds, 469, 471
　light and, *409*, 409
　in metal atoms, 190
　in metallic bonds, 469
　in plastics, 273
　resistance and, 271
　in Rutherford's model of atoms, 159
　in sodium, 472
　static discharge and, 264
　in Thomson's model of atoms, 158
　transfer of, 471
　valence, *468*
Electrophoresis gel, *23*, 23
Electroscopes, *261*, 261, *262*
Elements. *See also* Periodic table
　in air, 174
　in atmosphere of earth, *164*
　atoms and, *157*, 157, 161
　chemical symbols of, *166*, 166
　compounds and, *168*, 169
　definition of, **157**
　gases as, 165
　in kitchen, 200
　liquids as, 165
　matter and, 164
　properties of, 165
　radioactive, *562*, 562
　solids as, 165
　in synthesis reactions, 500
　synthetic, 188
　trace, 167
　transmutation of, 567
ELF (extremely low frequency) mag-
　netic field, 295
Emulsifiers, 526
Emulsions, **525**

Endothermic reactions, **492,** *492,* 495, 500, 504

Energy. *See also* Energy conservation; *specific types of energy*
 activation, 504
 binding, 562
 cell respiration and, 554-555
 change and, *46,* 46
 chemical, *123,* 123, 125
 chemical equations and, use of word in, 495
 chemical reactions and, *492,* 492, *503,* 503
 conversion, 124, 125
 definition of, **46**
 electricity and, 261, 279, 492
 electromagnetic, *123,* 123
 exothermic reactions and, 503, 504
 of falling water, *49,* 49
 food chemistry and, 556
 in food processing, 588
 geothermal, *592,* 592
 graph, *504,* 504
 gravity and, *48,* 48
 hydrocarbons and, 539
 internal, 209
 kinetic, *47,* 47, 123, 209, 211
 light, *409,* 409, 436, 454, 492
 mass and, 124
 measuring, 108, 279
 mechanical, *122,* 122, 125, *584*
 of motion, *45,* 45-49
 for movement of mass, 69
 nonrenewable sources of, *596,* 596
 nuclear, 123
 pathways of, 583
 potential, 46, 47, 48
 release of, 490
 renewable sources of, *596,* 596
 solar, *552-553,* 552-553
 sound, 365
 waves and, *348,* 348
 work and, 122, 126

Energy conservation
 electricity, 436, 454
 energy users and, 598
 heat, 237
 at home, *598,* 598
 in industry, 599
 law of, 47
 light, 436, 454
 need for, 589
 nonrenewable resources and, *596,* 596
 recycling and, *600,* 600
 renewable resources and, *596,* 596
 technology risks and, benefits of, 597
 transportation and, *599,* 599

Energy efficiency, *115,* 115, 278

Energy level, 159, 468

Engineering, 21, 114

Engines. *See* Heat engines

ENIAC (Electronic Numerical Integrator Computer), *322,* 322

Environment
 air quality and, *621,* 621-623, *622, 623*
 biodegradable plastics and, 612
 land quality and, 626-627, *627*
 water quality and, 624-625, *625*

Environmental Protection Agency (EPA), 388, *623,* 623, 625

Enzymes, **508,** 554

EPA. *See* Environmental Protection Agency

Equal force, 70-71, *71*

Equations in chemistry. *See* Chemical equations

Erosion, *148,* 148

Esters, *542,* 542

Estimating, **4,** *4*

Ethane ($C_2H_6$), *540,* 540

Ethanol, 592

Ethene ($C_2H_4$), *540,* 540

Evaporation, 125, 141, *240,* 240

Exercise, *220,* 220

Exothermic reactions, *492,* 492, 500, 503, 504

Experimental group, 7

Experiments, *7,* 7, *8*

Exponent, **14**

Extended-wear lenses, 449

External-combustion engines, *246,* 246-247

Extremely low frequency (ELF) magnetic field, 295

Eye, 426, *437,* 437-438, *438,* 440. *See also* Vision

Eyeglasses, 445, 448, 449

Eye injuries, 440

Eyelids, 437

Fabric softeners, 266

Fact, **9**

Fahrenheit (F), 14

Falling objects, *57,* 57-58, *59,* 80

Faraday, Michael, 300

Farsightedness, *439,* 439, 448

Ferris wheel, 55

Fiberglass, *236,* 236, *618,* 618

Fiber optics, *457,* 457, 458

Film, *452,* 452

Film badge, 564

Fireworks, *72,* 72, *493,* 493

Firing, in ceramics, 616

First class levers, 117

Fission reactors, *572,* 572

Fixed magnets, 288

Fixed pulley, *119,* 119

Flaps, 99

Flight
 airplane design and, 99
 bird, *100,* 100-101, *101*
 pressure and, *98,* 98-99

Floppy disks, 323

Flowcharting, 325

Flow rate, 270

Fluid friction, *62,* 62

Fluid pressure
 atmosphere and, *86-87,* 86-87
 brakes of car and, *90,* 90
 ear and, 86
 ocean and, *88-89,* 88-89

Fluids, **85,** *97,* 97. *See also* Fluid pressure; Liquids

Fluorescent light, **434,** 436

Fluoride, 172

Fluorine (F), 167, *197,* 197, 223

Fluorocarbons, 241

Focal length, **446**

Food
 additives, 482
 calories and, 220
 chemical changes in, 150
 digestion of, 125, 508, 545
 emulsifiers in, 526
 energy used to produce, 588
 food scientists and, 549
 frozen, 226, 241
 heat energy and, 125
 new products of, 549
 preserving, 226
 processing and distribution, 588

Food chemistry. *See also* Photosynthesis
 carbohydrates and, *545,* 545-456, *546*
 cell respiration and, 554-555, *555*
 digestion and, 545
 energy and, 556
 lipids and, *547,* 547
 proteins and, *548,* 548
 vitamins and, 549-550, *550*

Food scientists, 549

Force. *See also* Universal forces
 acceleration and, 64, 65, 66
 applying, *55,* 55
 of attraction, *258,* 258, 260
 balanced, *71,* 71
 buoyancy and, *91,* 91-92
 centripetal, *68,* 68
 charge and, 257
 curve ball and, 59
 definition of, **55**
 effort, *119,* 119
 equal, 70-71, *71*
 friction and, *57,* 57
 gravity and, *56,* 56
 magnetic, *77,* 77, 287, 299, 300
 of magnetism, *287,* 287
 measuring, 56, 57, 85
 mechanical advantage and, 113
 opposite, 70-71, *71*

projectile motion and, *58, 58*
of repulsion, *258,* 258
resistance, *117,* 117-118, *118, 119,* 119
strong, 160
terminal velocity and, 57-58
unbalanced, *71,* 71
work and, 107, 108
Forced-air heating, *232,* 232
Formaldehyde, 623
Fossil fuels, **586**-587, *586,* 589
Four-color printing, *428,* 428
Fractional distillation, **607**
Frames of reference
  definition of, **31**
  on earth, *32,* 32
  motion and, *31-32,* 31-33, 37
  in space, *33,* 33
Freezing point of water, *211,* 211, 224
Frequency
  of electromagnetic waves, *417,* 417
  pitch and, 367-368, *368*
  of radio waves, 419
  of sound waves, *368,* 368, *387,* 387
  of waves, *344,* 344
Friction
  from brushing hair, *258,* 266
  control of, *63,* 63
  force and, *57,* 57
  gravity and, *57,* 57
  in machine parts, *63,* 63
  motion and, 61-62
  ocean waves and, *338,* 338
  static electricity and, *258,* 262
  types of, *62,* 62
Frozen food, 226, 241
Fuels. *See specific types of fuels*
Fulcrum, *117,* 117-118, *118*
Functional group, 542
Fusion-reactor projects, 574

**G** Galileo, 37
  Gallium (Ga), 189, *195,* 195, 312
Galvanometer, *297,* 297
Gamma decay, **566,** *566*
Gamma rays, **420,** *420*
Garment sizes, *16,* 16
Gas, 490, 605, *607*
Gas chromatograph, *23,* 23
Gases
  in air, *17,* 17
  Boyle's Law and, *143,* 143
  Charles' Law and, *144,* 144
  definition of, **142**
  elasticity of, 362
  as elements, 165
  expansion of, 225
  heat energy and, 144
  molecular compound and, 170
  noble, *197,* 197, 198
  nonmetals and, 194

as phase of matter, *140, 142,* 142-144
  release of, 490
  solubility of, 519
  in turbines, 248
Gas laws, 142-144, *143, 144*
Gas mileage, 69
Gasohol, 592
Gasoline engines, *245,* 245-246
Gas shortages, *589,* 589
Gas-turbine engines, 619
Gas turbines, 248
Geiger counter, *564,* 564
Gelatin dessert mixes, 524
Gels, **524**
Gemstone, *139,* 139
Generators
  for bikes, *304,* 304
  in electricity production and distribution, *584*
  uses of electromagnetic induction and, *302,* 302
  wind, *591,* 591
Geometric isomers, *541,* 541
Geophysics, **21**
Geothermal energy, **592,** *592*
Germanium (Ge), *195,* 195, 312
Glass, 617
Glaucoma, 440
Global warming, **622**
Glucose, 546, 554
Glue, 483
Goiter, 167
Gold (Au), 166, 189, 193, 501
G.P.E. (gravitational potential energy), 47
Grams (g), 519
Grams of matter per cubic centimeter (g/cm³), 13
Graphite, *138,* 138, 195
Graphs
  of acceleration, *65,* 65-66
  of atomic mass and number, 198
  bar, *18,* 18
  circle, *17,* 17
  definition of, **17**
  distance-time, *35,* 35, *40,* 40
  energy, *504,* 504
  line, *19,* 19
  making, 18, 198
  for organizing and recording, 5
  science and, 20
  studying, 20
  use of, 17
Gravitational force, 73-74, *74-75, 76,* 76
Gravitational potential energy (G.P.E.), 47
Gravity
  energy and, *48,* 48
  force and, *56,* 56
  friction and, *57,* 57
Greenhouse, *235,* 235

Greenhouse effect, **622,** *622*
Ground-fault interrupter, 281
Group, **186,** *186-187*
Group number, **186,** *186-187*
Gulls, *101,* 101

**H** Hair conditioners, 266
  Hairstyles, 151
Half-life, **568,** 627
Halocarbon, *542,* 542
Halogens, **197,** *197,* 475, 542
Hanging magnets, 288
Hard contact lenses, 448
Hard disks, *323,* 323
Hardware, computer, **323,** *323*
Hard water, 177, 477
Hawks, *100,* 100
Hazardous wastes, 627. *See also* Nuclear waste disposal
HDPE, 613
Hearing
  aids, *404,* 404
  balance and, 385
  ear and, *386,* 386
  process of, *386*
  protectors, 386, 388-389, *389*
  range, *387,* 387
  sound and, 365, *385,* 385-388
Heartbeat, *79,* 79
Heat
  in atmosphere, 219
  caloric theory of, 210
  in everyday life, 209
  insulators, 238
  matter and, *222,* 222-225
  measuring, 209
  phase changes and, *222,* 222-224, *223, 224*
  specific, *216,* 216
  understanding, history of, 210
Heat energy. *See also* Heat transfer
  calories and, 217
  conduction and, *213,* 213, 215
  conservation of, 237
  convection and, *214,* 214, 215
  definition of, **123, 209**
  food and, 125
  in forced-air heating system, *232,* 232
  gases and, 144
  heat pumps and, *234,* 234
  in hot-water heating system, *232,* 232
  in radiant heating system, *233,* 233
  in steam heating system, *233,* 233
  thermal expansion and, 225
  transfer of, 213-217
  understanding, history of, 210
Heat engines
  ceramic, 619
  diesel, *246,* 246

external-combustion, *246,* 246-247
gasoline, *245,* 245-246
gas-turbine, 619
internal-combustion, *245,* 245-246, 619
solar-powered, 247
turbines, 247-248, 584, 591
workings of, 244
Heating systems
central, 231-234, *232, 233, 234,* 248
insulation, *236,* 236, 237, 238
solar, 234-235, *235*
Heat pumps, *234,* 234
Heat transfer
climate and, *218-219,* 218-219
conduction and, *213,* 213, 215
convection and, *214,* 214, 215
measuring, 216-217
methods of, *213,* 213
radiation and, *215,* 215
Helium (He)
density of, 198
hydrogen and, 197, 573
light of, 435
oxygen and, 199
properties of, 165, *197*
uses of, 198-199
Helium-3, 162
Henry, Joseph, 300
Hertz (Hz), 344, 368, 387, 398, 418
Hertz, Heinrich, 344
Heterogeneous mixtures, **176,** *176*
Hologram, **456,** *456*
Holography, *456,* 456
Homogeneous mixtures, **176,** *176,* 515, 516, 522
Homogenized milk, 525
Horsepower (hp), 109
Hot-water heating, *232,* 232
Human body. *See also* Hearing; Vision
acids in stomach of, 554
bones of, 365
cooling system of, *240,* 240
copper in, 167
digestion and, 125, 508, 545
ear, 86, *386,* 386
electric activity in, *79,* 79
electric charge in, 259
electricity safety and, 282
energy conversion in, 125
eye, 426, *437,* 437-438, *438,* 440
iron in, 167
metabolic rate and, 556
pH of blood in, *531,* 531
radiation on, 569
sound energy and, 365
temperature of, 125
trace elements in, 167
water in, 125
Hummingbirds, *101,* 101
Hydrocarbons, **539**-541, *540, 542,* 542

Hydrochloric acid, 502, 530
Hydroelectric power, **586**
Hydrogen (H)
atomic mass of, 162
atom of, 469
in bubble chamber, 163
chemical bonds and, *467,* 467
chlorine and, *491,* 491
covalent bonds and, *479*
helium and, 197, 573
nonmetals and, 197, 198
as nuclear fuel, 573
oxygen and, 169, *171,* 171
properties of, *197,* 197
stove, 594
in water, *467,* 467
Hydrogen chloride (HCl), *479, 491,* 491, 501
Hydrogen peroxide, 151, *467,* 467
Hydrogen stove, 594
Hydroxyls, 542
Hypothesis, **5**

*I* Illuminated objects, *433,* 433
Images, 442, 446, 447, 454
Impressionism, *427,* 427
Impurities, 312
Incandescent light, **434**-435, 436
Incident rays, **441**
Inclined plane, **116,** *116*
Indicator, 530
Indium (In), *195,* 195
Induction, **262,** *262*
Industrial smog, 623
Inertia, 60-**61**
Inferring, **4,** *4*
Infrared rays, **420,** *420*
Inner ear, **386**
Input devices, computer, *323,* 323
Insolubility, 520-521
Insulation, **236,** *236,* 237, 238
Insulators
ceramics as, 616
electric, 137
fiberglass as, 618
heat, 238
materials for, 221
plastics as, 137, 263
static electricity and, *263,* 263
Integrated circuits, **313,** *313*
Intensity, *366,* 366, 412
Interference
constructive, *352,* 352, *376,* 376-377
deconstructive, *352,* 352, *376,* 376-377
definition of, **352**
of light waves, 424
of sound waves, *376,* 376-377
of waves, *352,* 352
Internal-combustion engines, *245,* 245-246, 619

Internal energy, **209**
Internal reflection, **457**
Intertidal zone, *88*
Invertase, 508
Invisible electromagnetic spectrum, 419-420, *420*
Iodine (I), *166,* 167, *197,* 197
Iodine-131, 563
Iodized table salt, 175, 191, 529
Ion-exchange process, 477
Ion-exchange resins, 477
Ionic bonds
crystal lattice and, *474,* 474
definition of, **471**
electrons in, 469, 471
electron transfer and, 471
formation of, *472-473,* 472-473
ions in, *475,* 475-476, 477
sodium chloride and, *472-473,* 472-473
Ionic compounds, **170,** *170,* 474, 476, 484
Ionic solids, 474, 476
Ions
in alkali metals, 191, 475
chlorine, *472-473,* 472-473
in covalent bonds, 480
definition of, **170**
dissolved, 476
in halogens, 475
in ionic bonds, *475,* 475-476, 477
in ionic compounds, *170,* 170
magnesium, *475,* 475, 477
nitrogen, *475,* 475
nonmetals and, 194
in plasma, 476
polyatomic, *480,* 480
in rare-earth metals, 475
size of, 475
sodium, *472-473,* 472-473
Iris, **437,** *438,* 438, 449
Iron (Fe)
carbon in, 193
copper sulfate and, *501,* 501
in human body, 167
ore, *615,* 615
properties of, 165
sulfur and, 500
tools, 614
Iron Age, 614
Iron nails, 175
Iron sulfide (FeS), 500
Isomers, **541,** *541*
Isotopes
atoms and, *161,* 161
of carbon compounds, *161*
definition of, **161,** *163*
radioactive, 161, **563,** *563,* 569

*J* Joule, **108,** 209, 279
Joule, James Prescott, 210
Joules per second (J/s), 279

**K**

Keck telescope, 444
Kelvin (K), *211,* 211
Kelvin, Lord, 211
Kerogen, 592
Kerosene, *607*
Keyboard, computer, *323,* 323
Keyboard instruments, 392
Kiln, 616
Kilogram (kg), **13**
Kilometer measurements, *413,* 413-
414
Kilowatt-hour (KWh), 279, 280
Kinetic energy, **47,** *47,* 123, 209, 211
Kitchen solutions, 521
Kite flying, *102,* 102
Koto, 392
Krypton (Kr), *197,* 197, *199,* 199, 435

**L**

Laboratory safety, *6,* 6
Lake Erie (United States),
*628,* 628
Lakes, pH of, 530
Land quality, 626-627, *627*
Langevin, Paul, 401
LAN (local-area network), 325
Lanthanides, 192
Laptop computers, 326
Lasers, *455,* 455, 456
Lawn mower, *351,* 351
Laws
energy, conservation of, 47
mass and energy, conservation of,
124
momentum, conservation of, 67
motion, 60, 64, 66, 69, 70, *71,* 71
Ohm's, 271
in science, 9
universal gravitation, 76
Lead (Pb), *195,* 195
Lead-214, 568
Lemon juice, 527
Length, *11, 12,* 12
Lens, **438,** *438*
Lenses
cameras and, *452,* 452
concave, *447,* 447
convex, *446,* 446-447, 452, 454
convex hand, 450
definition of, **446**
microscopes and, 454
telescopes and, *453,* 453
in vision correction, *448,* 448-449,
*449*
Levers, **117**-118
Lift, **98**
Light. *See also* Light technology; Light
waves
animal, 434
bioluminescence and, 434
color and, 425

electrons and, *409,* 409
energy, *409,* 409, 436, 454, 492
fluorescent, 434, 436
of helium, 435
illuminated objects and, *433,* 433
incandescent, 434-435, 436
intensity of, 412
luminous objects and, *433,* 433-435
models of, 410
neon, 435
particles, 411-413, *412*
path of, 415, 439
photoelectric effect and, 411-412,
*412*
for photosynthesis, 554
polarized sunglasses and, *411,* 411
Seasonal Affective Disorder and,
414
sodium-vapor, 435
sources of, 433
from surface, 422-423
Tungsten-halogen lights and, 435,
436
ultraviolet rays and, 436
waves, *410,* 410
Light bulbs, 436
Light microscopes, 454
Lightning, 261, *264-265,* 264-265, 361
Light technology
cameras, *452,* 452
fiber optics, *457,* 457, 458
holography, *456,* 456
lasers, *455,* 455, 456
microscopes, *451,* 451
telescopes, *453,* 453
Light waves
diffraction of, 424
interaction of, 424
interference of, 424
reflection of, 424, *441,* 441
refraction of, 424, *445,* 445
speed of, 37, 300, 361, *413,* 413-
414
wavelength of, 425
Light-years, **413**
Line graphs, **19,** *19*
Lipids, **547,** *547*
Liquid fuel, 72
Liquids. *See also* Solutions
definition of, **141**
elasticity of, 362
elements as, 165
expansion of, 225
as molecular compounds, 170
packaging, *146,* 146
as phase of matter, 140, *141,* 141
Liter (L), *11,* **12**
Litmus paper, 527, *529*
Litter, 626
Local-area network (LAN), 325
Longitudinal waves, **337,** *337,* 342-
343, *343*

Luminous objects, *433,* 433-435
Luster, 136, 165, **189,** 194

**M**

Machines
compound, *120,* 120, 121
definition of, **112**
designing, 114, 190
energy efficiency and, 115
friction in parts of, *63,* 63
machinists and, 190
mechanical advantage and, *113,*
113
mechanical efficiency and, 114, 115
simple, *116,* 116-119, *119*
sound-effects, 371
Machinists, 190
Magma, 592
Magnesium (Mg)
as alkaline earth metal, *191,* 191
ions, *475,* 475, 477
source of, *166*
uses of, *166*
Magnesium hydroxide, 191, 502, 524
Magnetic declination, 290
Magnetic domains, **289,** *289*
Magnetic field
definition of, **288,** *288*
of earth, *290,* 290
extremely low frequency, 295
magnetism and, 288, 295
matter and, 137
Magnetic field lines, *288,* 288
Magnetic force, *77, 77,* 287, 299, 300.
*See also* Magnetism
Magnetic materials, *289,* 289
Magnetic north, *290,* 290
Magnetic poles, **288,** *288*
Magnetic storms, 291
Magnetism. *See also*
Electromagnetism; Magnetic force;
Magnets
in ancient times, 289
of earth, *290,* 290-291
effects of, *291,* 291
electricity and, 293, 300
force of, *287,* 287
magnetic field and, 288, 295
magnetic materials and, *289,* 289
magnetic poles and, *288,* 288
Magnetite, 291
Magnetron, **421,** *421*
Magnets. *See also* Magnetism
fixed, 288
hanging, 288
in motors, *77,* 77
permanent, 289, 302
properties of, 287-288
Main storage, computer, 323
Malleability, 137, **189,** *481,* 481
M.A. (mechanical advantage), **113,**
*113,* 118, *119,* 119

Maple tree sap, *521,* 521
Mass
  acceleration and, 65-66
  definition of, **13**
  energy and, 124
  energy for moving, 69
  kinetic energy and, 47
  measuring, *11, 13,* 13
  as property of matter, 136
Mass number, **162**
Materials science
  ceramics, 616, 617, 619
  composites, *618,* 618
  glass, 617
  metallurgy, *614,* 614
  steelmaking, *615,* 615
Matrix, **618**
Matter. *See also* Phases of matter
  atoms and, 157
  Boyle's Law and, *143,* 143
  Charles' Law and, *144,* 144
  chemical changes in, 149-150, *151,*
    151, 152, 489
  definition of, **135**
  density of, 362
  elasticity of, 362
  electric force and, 77
  elements and, 164
  heat and, *222,* 222-225
  magnetic field and, 137
  particle model of, *135,* 135
  physical changes in, *147,* 147-148,
    *148,* 150, 151
  properties of, 136-138, *138,* 165
  radiant energy and, *215,* 215
Measuring. *See also* SI unit
  acceleration, *40,* 40, 66
  calculations and, 15-16
  converting units and, 15
  definition of, **4**
  density, *11, 13,* 13
  depth of ocean, 401
  electric current, 269-271, *270, 271*
  electricity's power, 279, 280
  energy, 108, 279
  force, 56, 57, 85
  garment sizes, *16,* 16
  heat, 209
  heat transfer, 216-217, 236
  in kilometers, *413,* 413-414
  kinetic energy, 47, 209
  length, *11, 12,* 12
  in light-years, 413
  mass, *11, 13,* 13
  momentum, 67
  motion, 34
  power, 109
  pressure, 85
  properties of matter, 137
  radiation dose, 563
  as science process skill, 4
  scientific notation and, 14
  shopping and, *16,* 16

sound waves frequency, 368
speed, 34
temperature, *11, 14,* 14, 210
time, *11,* 14
volume, *11, 12,* 12
weight, 13
work, 108
Mechanical advantage (M.A.), **113,**
  *113,* 118, *119,* 119
Mechanical efficiency, **114,** 115
Mechanical energy, *122,* 122, 125,
  584
Mechanical engineering, 21, 114
Mechanics, 24
Medium
  definition of, **335**
  energy transfer and, 335
  interaction of waves and, 348
  longitudinal waves and, *337,* 337,
    342
  refraction of waves and, 351
  sound waves and, 361, *363,* 363,
    *387,* 387
  transverse waves and, *336,* 336,
    342
Melody, *391,* 391
Melting point, **224,** *224*
Mendeleev, Dmitri, 183-185
Meniscus, 12
Mental model, 9
Mercury, 165, 189
Mercury oxide (HgO), 500
Metabolic rate, 556
Metallic bonds, 469, **481,** *481*
Metalloids
  antimony, *196,* 196
  arsenic, *196,* 196
  in periodic table, *186-187,* 187
  properties of, 194
Metallurgy, **614,** *614*
Metals. *See also specific types of*
  *metals*
  activity series of, 501
  alkali, *186, 191,* 191, 475
  alkaline earth, *186, 191,* 191, 475
  alloys of, *176,* 176, *193,* 193, 515
  ancient technology and, 25
  atoms and, 190
  as conductors, 192, 263
  density of, 362
  ductibility of, 189
  elasticity of, 362
  machinists and, 190
  malleability of, 137, 189, *481,* 481
  metallurgy and, *614,* 614
  in periodic table, 186, *187,* 187
  photo sensitive, 411
  properties of, 189-190
  rare-earth, *187,* 187, *192,* 192, 475
  resistance of, 271
  specific heat of, *216,* 216
  transition, *192,* 192
Meter (m), *11,* **12**

Methane ($CH_4$), *540,* 540, *607*
Methanol, *542,* 542, 592
Michelson, Albert Abraham, 413
Microbalance, making, 26
Microprocessors, **322**
Microscopes, *451,* 451, 454
Microwave oven, *421,* 421
Microwaves, 419, *421,* 421
Middle ear, **386**
Mid-ocean, *89*
Milk of magnesia, 191, 502, 524
Millimeter (mm), **12**
Mining, 626
Mirrors
  concave, *443,* 443
  convex, *443,* 443
  definition of, **442**
  lasers and, *455,* 455
  microscopes and, *451,* 451
  plane, *442,* 442
  in super telescopes, 444
Mitochondria, *555*
Mixtures. *See also* Suspensions; *spe-*
  *cific types of mixtures*
  compounds and, 174
  definition of, **174**
  properties of, 175
  in synthesis reactions, 500
  types of, *176,* 176
Models
  of atoms, 157-160, 162
  of light, 410
  making, 99, 162, 325, 570
  particle, *135,* 135
  of radioactive decay, making, 570
  types of, 9
Modem, 325
Molecular compounds, **170,** *170*
Molecules
  covalent bonds and, 478-479
  designer, *470,* 470
  in motion, 209, 210
  sticky, 482
Momentum, **67**
Monomer, **609**
Moon, *76,* 76
Morse, Samuel F. B., 315
Moseley, Henry, 185
Moths, 403
Motion. *See also* Acceleration; Speed
  accelerated, 64-66, *65,* 67
  in ancient history, 37
  average speed and, 35
  changes in, *45,* 45
  in circle, *43,* 43, *68,* 68
  constant speed and, 35
  energy of, *45,* 45-49
  equal and opposite force and, 70-
    71, *71*
  first law of, 60
  frames of reference and, *31-32,* 31-
    33, 37
  friction and, 61-62

gas mileage and, 69
inertia and, 60-61
measuring, 34
molecules in, 209, 210
momentum and, 67
objects in, *61,* 61
projectile, *58,* 58
relativity and, 37
second law of, 64, 66, 69
solution rate and, 518
space-time and, 37
third law of, 70, *71,* 71
of waves, 338
Mountains, *86*
Mouse, computer, 320, *323,* 323
Movable pulley, *119,* 119
Movement. *See* Motion
Moving fluids, *97,* 97
Music, *390,* 390-393, *391,* 394, *395*
Musical instruments, *390,* 390, 392-393, 394, 397

 Natural gas, 586, 587, 605, 606
Nearsightedness, *439,* 439, 447
Negative acceleration, *40,* 40-41
Negative electric charge, 257-258, *258,* 259, 266
Negative terminal, 274, 275
Negative-type (n-type) semiconductor, 312
Neon (Ne), *197,* 197, 435
Neon light, 435
Neptunium (Np), 188
Networks, computer, 319, 325
Network solids, 480
Neutral electric charge, 257, 258, 266
Neutralization, 527, 529
Neutrons, **160,** 162, 188, 257, *571*
Newton meter (Nm), 108
Newton, Sir Isaac
first law of motion and, 60
newtons and, 56
second law of motion and, 65, 66
third law of motion and, 70, 71
universal gravitation law and, 76
Newtons (N), **56,** 57, 85
Nitric oxide, 500
Nitrogen (N)
boiling point of, *223,* 223
in earth's atmosphere, *164*
formula for compounds of, *171*
importance of, 196
ions, *475,* 475
nonmetal group of, *196,* 196
oxide and, 500
Nitrogen group of nonmetals, *196,* 196
Noble gases, *197,* 197, 198
Noise, 394-395, *395*
Noise pollution, 388, *396,* 396
Nonmetals
boron group of, *195,* 195

carbon group of, *195,* 195
gases and, 194
halogens, *197,* 197
hydrogen, 197, 198
ions and, 194
nitrogen group of, *196,* 196
noble gases, *197,* 197, 198
oxygen group of, 196
in periodic table, 186, *187,* 187
properties of, 194
Nonrenewable resources, *596,* 596
Northern lights (aurora borealis), *291,* 291
North Pole, 290
n-type (negative-type) semiconductors, 312
Nuclear chemistry. *See* Radioactivity
Nuclear energy, 123
Nuclear fission
definition of, **571**
fission reactors and, *572,* 572
fusion-reaction projects and, 574
nuclear fusion and, 573
nuclear power plants and, 573
nuclear waste and, 574
process, *571,* 571
Nuclear force, *78,* 78
Nuclear fusion, **573**
Nuclear medicine, 569
Nuclear power, *587,* 587
Nuclear power plants, 573
Nuclear waste disposal
methods of, *627,* 627
nuclear fission and, 574
problem of, 78, 527, 589
safety of, *574,* 574
Nucleus. *See also* Nuclear fission
of atom, *159,* 160
definition of, **159**
in electron cloud model of atoms, 160
parts of, 160
radioactive decay and, changes in, 565
of radioactive element, *562,* 562
radioactivity and, *562,* 562, 565
in Rutherford's model of atoms, 159
of uranium-235, 571
Nutrients, 476
Nylon polymers, 543

*O* Observing, **3**
Ocean
depth of, 401
pressure, *88-89,* 88-89
sound waves and, 398
tidal power and, 593
waves, *338,* 338, *339,* 339
Odor, 136, 544
Oersted, Hans Christian, 293, 300
Ohm (OHM), 271
Ohm, George, 271

Ohm meter, *271,* 271
Ohm's law, 271
Oil. *See also* Petroleum
drilling for, 597
formation of, 605
as fossil fuel, 586, 587, 589
shale, 592
shortage of, 589
spills, 624
steam pressure and, 584
transport of, 626
Opaque objects, **423,** *423*
Operating-system software, 324
Opposite force, 70-71, *71*
Optical fiber, **457**
Opticians, 449
Optic nerve, **438,** *438*
Ores, **192**
Organic compounds, **537,** 538-539
Organizing, **5**
Ouabain, 172
Outer ear, **386**
Output devices, computer, 323
Ovens, *214,* 214, *421,* 421
Overtones, **391**
Oxide, 500
Oxygen (O)
covalent bonds and, *479*
in earth's atmosphere, *164*
helium and, 199
hydrogen and, 169, *171,* 171
nonmetal group of, *196,* 196
in water, *467,* 467
Oxygen group of nonmetals, *196,* 196
Ozone, 243, 623
Ozone layer, *87,* 498, *498*

*P* Packaged programs, 324
Packaging liquids, *146,* 146
Pagoda, *347,* 347
Paint, *427,* 427
Parallel circuits, *277,* 277
Particle accelerators, *22,* 22, 567
Particle model of matter, **135,** *135*
Particles
light, 411
magnetic effect of, 291
of matter, *22,* 22, *135,* 135
movement of, 142, 143
size of, 518
transmutation of elements and, 562
Passive solar heating system, *235,* 235
Peanut butter, 526
Pectin, 524
Percussion instruments, 393
Period, **186,** *186-187*
Periodic, **183**
Periodic table
alkali metals in, *186, 191,* 191
alkaline earth metals in, *186, 191,* 191

description of, *186-187*, 186
development of modern, 183-185
metalloids in, *186-187*, 187
metals in, 186, *187*, 187
nonmetals in, 186, *187*, 187
Permanent magnets, 289, 302
Permanents, hair, 151
Perspiration, *240*, 240
PET, *613*, 613
Petrochemicals. *See also* Plastics
  definition of, **609**
  dyes and, 611
  pharmaceuticals and, 611
  properties of, *609*, 609-612
  solvents and, 612
  synthetic fibers and, *609*, 609, 611
Petroleum. *See also* Oil
  deposits of, *606*, 606
  formation of, 605
  refining, 607
  reserves, *606*, 606
  temperature and, *607*, 607
pH, **529**-530, *530*, *531*, 531
Pharmaceuticals, 611
Pharmacy, 172-173, *173*
Phases of matter
  gases, *140*, *142*, 142-144
  heat and, *222*, 222-224, *223*, *224*
  liquids, *140*, *141*, 141
  plasma, 145
  solids, *140*, *141*, 141
Phenolphthalein, 530
Phosphorus (P), *196*, 196
Photochemical smog, 623
Photoelectric effect, **411**-412, *412*
Photons, **409**, *409*
Photosynthesis
  cell respiration and, *555*
  chemical reactions of, *552-553*, 552-553
  definition of, **552**
  light for, 554
  process of, *552-553*, 552-553
Physical changes in matter, **147**-148, *147*, *148*, 150, 151
Physical science
  branches of, 21
  careers in, 24
  definition of, **21**
  tools of, *22*, 22-23, *23*
Physics, **21**, 24
Physiology, 24
Pictures, dots used to make, 321
Pigments, *427*, 427
Pistons, 244
Pitch, **367**-368, *368*, 391
Plane mirrors, **442**, *442*
Planetary model of atoms, 159
Plasma, **145**, *145*, 476
Plastics
  biodegradable, 612
  components of, 609
  as conductors, 273

electrons in, 273
as insulators, 137, 263
as matrix, 618
polymers and, 543, 610, *611*
polystyrene, 610
PVC, 610
recycling, *613*, 613
uses of, 543, 610
Plutonium, 587
Polarized sunglasses, *411*, 411
Polarized waves, **410**
Pollution
  air, 248, **621**, 623
  chemical, 625
  noise, 388, *396*, 396
  runoff, 625
  thermal, 625
  water, 628
Polonium-214, 568
Polyatomic ions, **480**, *480*
Polymers
  carbon compounds and, 541
  definition of, **541**, 609
  plastics and, 543, 610, *611*
  properties of, changing, 620
  starches and, 546
  synthetic, 543
Polynesian boat design, 94
Polystyrene plastics, 610
Polyvinyl chloride (PVC) plastics, 610
Porcelain, 616
Pore, 240
Positive acceleration, 40
Positive electric charge, 257-258, *258*, 259, 266
Positive terminal, 274
Positive-type (p-type) semiconductor, 312
Potassium chloride, *501*, 501
Potassium hydroxide, 528
Potassium nitrate, *501*, 501
Potential energy, **46**, 47, 48
Pottery, ceramic, 616, 617
Power
  of appliances, *279*, 279
  definition of, **109**
  of electricity, *279*, 280
  measuring, 109
  work and, 109
Power grid, *585*
Power plants, 584
Precipitate, 490, 501
Precipitation, 624
Predicting, **4**
Pressure. *See also* Fluid pressure
  air, *85*, 85-87, *86-87*, *98*, 98
  airplane design and, 99
  atmospheric, *86-87*, 86-87
  definition of, **85**
  flight and, *98*, 98-99
  fluid movement and, *97*, 97
  kite flying and, *102*, 102
  measuring, 85

particle movement and, 142, 143
solubility and, 519
steam, 584
water, *88-89*, 88-89
Printing, four-color, *428*, 428
Prism, *417*, 417
Products, **495**, *495*
Programs, computer, *324*, 324
Projectile motion, *58*, 58
Promethium (Pm), 188
Propane ($C_3H_8$), 169, 171
Proteins, **548**, *548*
Protons
  atomic number and, 161
  in chlorine, *472-473*, 472-473
  definition of, **159**
  force of attraction and, 258
  force of repulsion and, 258
  mass number and, 162
  in nucleus, 160
  in Rutherford's model of atoms, 159
  in sodium, *472-473*, 472-473
p-type (positive-type) semiconductors, 312
Pulley, **119**, *119*
Pupil, **437**, *438*, 438
PVC (polyvinyl chloride) plastics, 610

 Quality-control chemists, 507
Quality of sound, *370*, 370

Radiant heating, *233*, 233
Radiation. *See also* Radioactivity
  chlorofluorocarbons and, 243
  definition of, **215**, 561
  heat transfer and, *215*, 215
  on human body, 569
  measuring dose of, 563
  solar, *215*, 215, *218-219*, 218-219
  x-rays and, *561*, *569*, 569
Radiation detectors, *564*, 564, 569
Radiation dose, 563
Radiators, *212*, 212, *232*, 232
Radioactive decay
  alpha, *566*, 566
  artificial, 571
  beta, *566*, 566
  carbon-14 dating and, *568*, 568
  definition of, **565**
  gamma, *566*, 566
  model of, making, 570
  nucleus and, changes in, 565
  process of, 571
  rate of, 568
  transmutation of elements and, 567
  of uranium-238, *567*, 567, 568
Radioactive elements, *562*, 562
Radioactive isotopes, 161, **563**, *563*, 569
Radioactivity. *See also* Nuclear waste

disposal; Radiation
definition of, **561**
discovery of, 561
elements and, *562,* 562
nucleus and, *562, 562,* 565
of promethium, 188
radiation detection and, *564,* 564
radiation doses and, 563
radioactive isotopes and, *563,* 563
Radios, 316
Radiotelescopes, *23,* 23
Radio waves, 419
Rare-earth metals, *187,* 187, **192,** *192,* 475
Rarefaction, *337,* 337, 360, *361*
Reactants, **494**-495, *495,* 501, 502
Reaction rate, 505
Real images, 446
Recording, **5**
Recordings, *317,* 317, 318-319
Rectifiers, **310**
Recycling, *600,* 600, *613,* 613, 624
Red glass, 524
Reflected rays, **441**
Reflecting telescopes, *453,* 453
Reflection. *See also* Mirrors
definition of, **349**
internal, 457
of light waves, 424, *441,* 441
of sound waves, *372,* 372-373, *373,* 379, 380
in water, *441,* 441
of waves, *349,* 349
Refracting telescopes, *453,* 453
Refraction. *See also* Lenses
definition of, **351**
of light waves, 424, *445,* 445
of sound waves, *375,* 375
water and, *445,* 445
of waves, *351,* 351
Refrigerants, **241,** 242, 243
Refrigeration technicians, 241
Refrigerators, 241, *242,* 242
Relativity, 37
Renewable resources, *596,* 596
Rennin, 508
Repulsion, force of, *258,* 258
Research group, *10,* 10
Reservoirs, 586
Resistance (R), **271**
Resistance force, *117,* 117-118, *118,* *119,* 119
Resistors
in compact disk player, 317
definition of, **274**
electric circuit and, 274, *275*
in integrated circuits, 313
overloading electric circuits and, 281
as poor conductors, 271
Resonance, **368,** *377,* 377-378
Respiration, **554**-555, *555*
Respirometers, *556,* 556

Retina, 426, **438,** *438*
Risk-benefit analysis, 597
Rocket fuel, 72
Rocks, 148, 150
Rods, 426, 438
Rolling friction, *62,* 62
Rubber, 263
Ruby crystal laser, *455*
Rumford, Count (Benjamin Thompson), 210
Runoff pollution, 625
Rutherford, Ernest, 159
Rutherford's model of atoms, 159
R-value, **236**

**S** Saccharin, *470,* 470
SAD (Seasonal Affective Disorder), 414
Safety
electricity, *6, 281,* 281-282
eye goggles and, 440
laboratory, *6,* 6
nuclear power plants and, 573
of nuclear waste disposal, *574,* 574
Salt, iodized table, 175, 191, 529
Saturated hydrocarbons, **541**
Saturated lipids, 547
Saturated solutions, 520, 521
Saxophone, 393
Scale model, 9
Scent, 136, 544
Science. *See also* Materials science; Physical science
ancient technology and, 24-25
applied, 21
careers in, 24
communities, *10,* 10
experiments, *7,* 7
fact in, 9
graphs and, 20
laboratory safety and, *6,* 6
law in, 9
models in, 9
process skills, 3-5, *4, 5*
scientific methods and, *8,* 8, *9*
shopping and, *16,* 16
theory in, 9
Science process skills, 3-5, *4, 5*
Scientific communities, *10,* 10
Scientific law, 9
Scientific methods, **8,** *8, 9*
Scientific notation, **14**
Scientific theory, 9
Scientific units. *See* SI
Sclera, **437**
Screws, **116**
Scrubbers, 623
Sea level, *86,* 92
Seasonal Affective Disorder (SAD), 414
Seasoning mix, 175
Seat belts, 67

Second class levers, 117
Second (s), *11,* 14
Seismographs, *347*
Selenium (Se), *196,* 196
Semiconductors, 194, **312**-313, *312,* *313*
Series circuits, *276,* 276
Ships, *95,* 95
Shopping, *16,* 16
Short-circuit, 281
Shutter, *452*
Sight-impaired people, *440,* 440
Silicon (Si), 194, *195,* 195, 312
Silicon carbide, 619
Silicon dioxide ($SiO_2$), 169, 171
Silicon nitride, 619
Silt, *522,* 522
Silver, 189
Silver chloride, *501,* 501
Silver nitrate, *501,* 501
Simple machines, **116**-119, *116, 119*
Single-replacement reactions, 499, **501,** *501*
SI unit (*Système International d'Unités*). *See also* Measuring
for circuit, 270
definition of, **11**
for density, *13,* 13
for energy, 108, 279
for force, 56
for length, *11, 12,* 12
for mass, *11, 13,* 13
for power, 279
prefixes in, 11
for resistance, 271
for temperature, *11, 14,* 14
for time, *11,* 14
for voltage, 270
for volume, *11, 12,* 12
Skid-mark evidence, *44,* 44
Slag, 615
Sliding friction, *62,* 62
Slip rings, *302,* 302
Smart cards, *314,* 314
Smog, *509,* 509, **623**
Smoke detector, 188
Soap bubble, 178
Soda, 617
Sodium-24, 569
Sodium (Na), *166, 472-473,* 472-473
Sodium chloride (NaCl)
antacids and, 502
formula for compound of, 171
ionic bonds and, *472-473,* 472-473
properties of, 169
sulfuric acid and, 501
Sodium hydroxide, 502, 528, 530
Sodium sulfate, 501
Sodium-vapor light, 435
Soft contact lenses, 448, 449
Software, computer, **324,** *324,* 325
Soft water, 177, 477
Solar cells, **590,** *590*

Solar energy, *552-553,* 552-553
Solar heating systems, 234-235, *235*
Solar hot-dog cookers, 595
Solar power, 247, *590,* 590, 595
Solar-powered engines, 247
Solar radiation, *215,* 215, *218-219,* 218-219
Solar system, *74-75, 74, 76*
Solids
  amorphous, 141
  definition of, **141**
  elements as, 165
  expansion of, 225
  ionic, 474, 476
  network, 480
  as phase of matter, 140, *141,* 141
Sols, **524**
Solubility, **519,** *519,* 520-521
Solute, **515,** 516
Solution chemistry. *See* Solutions
Solution rate, 518
Solutions
  air as, 515
  basic, 528
  concentrations of, 520-521
  definition of, **515,** *515*
  insolubility and, 520-521
  kitchen, 521
  properties of, *525*
  saturated, 520, 521
  solubility and, *519,* 519, 520-521
  solution rate and, 518
  supersaturated, 520, 521
  types of, 515-516, *516*
  unsaturated, 520, 521
  water as solvent and, *517,* 517
Solvents, **515,** 516, *517,* 517, 612
Sonar, *398,* **400**-401, *400-401*
Sonogram, **399,** *399*
Soot, *138,* 138
Sound. *See also* Sound technology;
  Sound waves
  control, *379,* 379
  decibels and, *367,* 367
  Doppler effect and, *369,* 369
  hearing and, 365, *385,* 385-388
  intensity of, *366,* 366
  music and, *390,* 390-393, *391,* 394, *395*
  noise and, 388-389, *389,* 394-395, *395*
  pitch and, 367-368
  quality of, *370,* 370
  sound-effect machines and, 371
Sound barrier, *364,* 364
Sound-effects machines, 371
Sound energy, 365
Sound recordings, *317,* 317-318
Sound technology
  animal echolocation, 402-403
  hearing aids, *404,* 404
  sonar, *398, 400-401,* 400-401
  ultrasound, *398,* 398-399

Sound waves
  air and, *387,* 387
  definition of, **359**
  diffraction of, *374,* 374
  frequency of, *368,* 368, *387,* 387
  interference of, *376,* 376-377
  medium and, *387,* 387
  medium and, different, *363,* 363
  music, *395,* 395
  noise, *395,* 395
  ocean and, 398
  reflection of, *372,* 372-373, *373,* 379, 380
  refraction of, *375,* 375
  resonance of, *377,* 377-378
  sound barrier and, *364,* 364
  sources of, *359,* 359
  speed of, 361-363, *362, 363, 387,* 387
  temperature and, *362,* 362, *375,* 375
  travel of, *360-361,* 360-361
  of tuning fork, struck, *366,* 366
  water and, *387,* 387
  wavelength of, 374
Southern lights (aurora australis), 291
Space
  edge of, *87*
  frames of reference in, *33,* 33
  planets in, *74-75, 74, 76*
Space shuttle, *619,* 619
Space-time, 37
Spark plugs, 616
Specific heat, **216,** *216*
Spectroscope, *22,* 22
Speed
  average, 35
  of balloon rocket, 50
  changes in, 39
  constant, 35, 37
  definition of, **34**
  of earth's rotation, 38
  kinetic energy and, 47
  of light waves, 37, 300, 361, *413,* 413-414
  measuring, 34
  of sound waves, 361-363, *362, 363, 387,* 387
  of waves, 345
Sphalerite, 192
Spray cans, 243, 498, 524
Stability of chemical bonds, *469,* 469
Starches, 546
Static discharge, 264
Static electricity. *See also* Electric charge
  conduction and, *262,* 262
  conductors and, *263,* 263
  electroscope and, *261,* 261, *262*
  fabric softeners and, 266
  friction and, *258,* 262
  hair conditioner and, 266
  induction and, *262,* 262
  insulators and, *263,* 263

  lightning and, 261, *264-265,* 264-265
  static build-up and, 261, 261-263, *262, 263*
Steam engines, 246, 246-247
Steam heating, *233,* 233
Steam pressure, 584
Steel, 95, 193, *615,* 615
Sticky substances, 482
Stone hand ax, *25,* 25
Stoves, *583,* 583, 594
Stringed instruments, 392
Strip mining, 626
Strong force, 160
Strontium (Sr), *166*
Strychnine, 172
Subatomic particles, 158, 160, 163
Submarine, 95
Subscript, **171,** *171,* 497
Substituted hydrocarbons, **542,** *542*
Sucrose, *470,* 470
Sugars, *470,* 470, 546
Sulfur (S), 165, *196,* 196, 500
Sulfuric acid, 501
Sunglasses, polarized, *411,* 411
Supersaturated solutions, 520, 521
Super telescopes, 444
Surface area, 505
Surfing, *339,* 339, 341
Suspensions, **522**-523, *523,* 524, *525.*
  *See also specific types of suspensions*
Sweat, *240,* 240
Sweeteners, *470,* 470
Symbols, 494
Synthesis reactions, 499, **500,** *500*
Synthetic elements, 188
Synthetic fibers, *609,* 609, 611
Synthetic fuels, 592
Synthetic polymers, 543
*(Système International d'Unités). See* SI
Systemize, **3**

 Tacoma Narrows Bridge (United States), 378
Tar sands, 592
Technology, 24-25. *See also specific technologies*
Telegraphs, *315,* 315
Telephones, *316,* 316
Telescopes, 444, 447, *453,* 453
Televisions (TVs), 318-319
Temperature
  absolute zero and, 211
  Celsius scale, *211,* 211
  definition of, **209**
  of human body, 125
  Kelvin scale, *211,* 211
  measuring, *11, 14,* 14, 210
  particle movement and, 142, 144
  petroleum and, *607,* 607
  reaction rate and, 505

solubility and, 519
solution rate and, 518
sound waves and, *362,* 362, *375,* 375
Temperature inversion, **622**
Terminal velocity, 57-58
Texture, 136, 165
Thallium (Tl), *195,* 195
Theory, 9
Thermal expansion, **225**
Thermal pollution, **625**
Thermocouples, *268,* 268
Thermogram, *125,* 125
Thermometer, *14,* 14, 210, *211,* 211
Thermostat, *231,* 231, 240
"Thin-film" solar technology, 590
Thioglycolic acid, 151
Third class levers, 118
Thompson, Benjamin (Count Rumford), 210
Thomson, J. J., 158
Thomson's model of atoms, 158
Thorium-234, 567
Three Mile Island (United States), 572
Three-way electric plug, *281,* 281
Thrust, 98-**99**
Thunder, 361
Thyroid gland, 563
Tidal power, 593
Timbre, **370**
Time, *11,* 14
Tin (Sn), *195,* 195
Toxic wastes, 627. *See also* Nuclear waste disposal
Trace elements, 167
Tracers, 569
Transformers, *303,* 303, *585*
Transistors, **313,** *313*
Transition metals, **192,** *192*
Translucent objects, **423,** *423*
Transmutation of elements, **567**
Transparency, 136, *423,* 423
Transparent objects, **423,** *423*
Transuranium elements, 188
Transverse waves, **336**-337, *336, 342,* 342-343, *353,* 353
Trench, *89*
Triple covalent bond, 539
Trough, **336,** *336*
True north, 290
Trumpet, 393
Tumors, 569
Tungsten-halogen lights, 435, 436
Tuning forks, *366,* 366
Turbines, **247**-248, *584,* 591
TVs (televisions), 318-319
Two-pulley system, *119,* 119

*U*
Ultrasound, **398**-399, *398*
Ultraviolet radiation, 498
Ultraviolet rays, 418, **420,** 436
Unbalanced chemical equations, *496,* 496

Unbalanced force, 70-71, *71*
UNIVAC (Universal Automatic Computer), 322
Universal Automatic Computer (UNIVAC), 322
Universal forces
definition of, **73,** *73*
electric, *77,* 77
gravitational, 73-74, *74-75, 76,* 76
magnetic, *77,* 77, 287
nuclear, *78,* 78
Unsaturated hydrocarbons, **541**
Unsaturated lipids, 547
Unsaturated solutions, 520, 521
Uranium, 188, 587
Uranium-235, 571, 572
Uranium-238, *567,* 567, 568

*V*
Vacuum, 87
Vacuum tubes, **310**-311, *310, 311,* 315, 322
Valence electrons, *468*
Vanilla extract, 521
Variable, **7**
VCRs (video cassette recorders), 315, 318-319
Velocity. *See also* Acceleration
of car, determining, *44,* 44
change in, 39, 41
definition of, **34**
terminal, 57-58
wind, *34,* 34
Vertebrae, 538
Vibrations, 360, 378
Video cassette recorders (VCRs), 315, 318-319
Video electronic devices, *318,* 318-320
Videophones, *458,* 458
Video recordings, *318,* 318-320
Vinegar, 521, 527
Violin, 392
Viperfish, 89
Virtual images, **442,** 447, 454
Virtual reality, *324,* 324
Visible electromagnetic spectrum, *417,* 417-418, *418*
Vision
color, 426
correcting, *448,* 448-449, *449*
eye and, *437,* 437-438, *438*
loss of, 440
path of light and, 439
problems, *439,* 439
Vitamins, 549-550, *550*
Volt (V), 270, 271, 279
Voltage, **267, 270,** *270,* 271, 279, 303
Voltmeter, *270,* 270, 297
Volume
buoyancy and, *92,* 92
measuring, *11, 12,* 12
as property of matter, 136

*W*
Washing soda, 477
Water
in active solar heating system, *235,* 235
boiling point of, *211,* 211, *223,* 223
calcium oxide and, 500
as compound, 169
as conductor, 263, 282
decomposition of, *500,* 500
energy of falling, *49,* 49
as energy source, 584, 586
fire on, 628
flow rate of, 270
fluoride in, 172
freezing point of, *211,* 211, 224
hard, 177, 477
in hot-water heating system, *232,* 232
in human body, 125
hydrogen in, *467,* 467
oxygen in, *467,* 467
pollution, 628
pressure, *88-89,* 88-89
quality, 624-625, *625*
reflection in, *441,* 441
refraction and, *445,* 445
soft, 177, 477
softener, 477
as solvent, *517,* 517
sound waves and, *387,* 387
in steam heating system, *233,* 233
synthesis of, *500,* 500
waves on surface of, 340
Watt (W), **109,** 279
Watt-hour, 279
Waveforms, *353,* 353-354
Wavelength
of electromagnetic waves, *417,* 417
of lasers, 455
of light waves, 425
of sound waves, 374
of waves, **343,** *343*
Waves. *See also* Light waves; Sound waves
amplitude of, *344,* 344, *352*
barriers to, *353,* 353
behavior of, *341,* 341
breakwaters and, 353
characteristics of, 342-345
definition of, **335**
diffraction of, *350,* 350
earthquakes and, 345, 347
electromagnetic, *416,* 416-417
energy and, *348,* 348
energy transfer and, 335-337
frequency of, *344,* 344
gamma waves, *420,* 420
infrared rays, *420,* 420
interactions of, *348,* 348
interference of, *352,* 352
light, *410,* 410
longitudinal, **337,** *337,* 342-343, *343*

aves, 419, *421,* 421

of, *338,* 338

an, *338,* 338, *339,* 339

parts of, *342-343*

polarized, 410

properties of, *341,* 341

radio, 419

reflection of, *349,* 349

refraction of, *351,* 351

speed of, 345

surfing and, *339,* 339, 341

transverse, *336,* 336-337, *342,* 342-343, *353,* 353

ultraviolet rays, 420

water surface and, 340

waveforms and, computer models of, *353,* 353-354

wavelength of, *343,* 343

X-rays, *420,* 420

Weather, *218-219,* 218-219

Weathering processes, *148,* 148

Weatherizing, 237

Weather vane, *34*

Wedge, **116**

Weight, 13

Wet cells, 267, *268,* 268

Wheel and axle, **118**

Wind, *34,* 34

Wind generators, *591,* 591

Wind instruments, 392-393

Windmill, *122,* 122

Wind tunnel, *23,* 23

Wood-burning stove, *583,* 583

Work

  conditions for, *107,* 107-108, *108*

  definition of, **107**

  energy and, 122, 126

  force and, 107, 108

  input, 114

  measuring, 108

  output, 114

  power and, *109,* 109

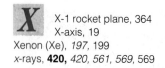

X-1 rocket plane, 364

  X-axis, 19

Xenon (Xe), *197,* 199

x-rays, **420,** *420, 561, 569,* 569

*y*-axis, 19

  Yeager, Chuck, 364

Yield sign, *495,* 495

Zeolites, 477

# Acknowledgments

## Photographs

**Title Page** i Robert L. Dunne/Bruce Coleman Inc.; i-L Ken Karp*; i-C Bill Ross/AllStock-TR Ellis Herwig/Stock, Boston

**Contents** iii Don Carroll/The Image Bank; ivBL Phil Degginger/Bruce Coleman Inc.; ivCL Lee Boltin; ivTR Ken Karp*; vBL GHP Studio*; vBR Ken Karp*; vi-vii Ken Karp*; viBL Ted Levin/Earth Scenes; viTC David Parker/Science Photo Library/ Photo Researchers; viTL Jeff Hornbaker; viiBC Louis Bencze/AllStock; viiBR Stanley Breeden/DRK Photos; viiiBR Robert Winslow/Tom Stack & Associates; viiiBL GHP Studio*; viiiCL Science Photo Library/Photo Researchers; viiiTL Dan McCoy/Rainbow; ixBL Nick Pavloff*; ixBLC The Granger Collection; ixBR GHP Studio*; ixBRC The Granger Collection; ixTR Robert Shafer/Tony Stone Worldwide; xi Agence Vandystadt/Allsport; xiiB National Museum of American History/Smithsonian Institution; xiiT Elliott Smith*; xiii Ken Karp*; xivC James E. Lloyd/Animals, Animals; xivL Ken Karp*; xivR GHP Studio*

**Unit 1** xvi-1 Nuridsany & Perennou/Photo Researchers

**Chapter 1** 2 John Cancalosi/Peter Arnold, Inc.; 3B GHP Studio*; 3C GHP Studio*; 4B Ken Karp*; 5 Ken Karp*; 10 Stacy Pick/Stock, Boston; 12L GHP Studio*; 12R Ken Karp*; 13L Ken Karp*; 13R Ken Karp*; 14 Ken Karp*; 21 James A. Sugar/Woodfin Camp & Associates; 22B CERN/Science Photo Library/Photo Researchers; 22C Kodansha/The Image Bank; 22T Richard Nowitz/Phototake; 23B Takeshi Takahara/Photo Researchers; 23C T. J. Florian/Rainbow; 23TL Ken Eward/Science Source/Photo Researchers; 23TR Jean Claude Revy/Phototake; 25L Erich Lessing/Art Resource; 25R Lee Boltin; 26 Ken Karp*

**Chapter 2** 30 © Roger Ressmeyer/Starlight; 31B W. Eastep/The Stock Market; 31T W. Eastep/The Stock Market; 34B Gabor Demjen/Stock, Boston; 34T Elliott Smith*; 36 John Eastcott-Yva Momatiuk/DRK Photos; 39 Agence Vandystadt/Allsport; 41 Vince Streano/The Stock Market; 42 Anna & Manot Shah/Animals, Animals; 43T Michael J. Howell/Stock, Boston; 45 Steve Elmore/Tom Stack & Associates; 46 Eberhard Grames-Bilderberd/The Stock Market; 47B John Gillmoure/The Stock Market; 49B John Running/Stock, Boston; 49T Z. Leszczynski/Earth Scenes; 50 Ken Karp*

**Chapter 3** 54 John M. Roberts/The Stock Market; 55 Elliott Smith*; 59 David Madison; 60 Elliott Smith*; 61 Elliott Smith*; 62B GHP Studio*; 62L Tony Duffy-Priscilla Rouse/Allsport; 62TR Stephen Hilson/AllStock; 63 Ken Karp*; 67 Calspan for the National Highway Traffic Safety Administration; 70 NASA; 71B Focus on Sports; 72 Bill Ross/AllStock; 77B Craig Davis/Sygma; 77T Wes Thompson /The Stock Market; 78B Robert Winslow/Tom Stack & Associates; 78C Hank Morgan/Rainbow; 78T Richard Nowitz/The Stock Market; 79 L. Steinmark/Custom Medical Stock Photo; 80 Ken Karp*

**Chapter 4** 84 Phototake; 88L Bob Abraham/The Stock Market; 88R Mike Severns/Tom Stack & Associates; 89L Doug Perrine/DRK Photos; 89R Dr. Paul A. Zahl/Photo Researchers; 91 Kevin Schafer-Martha Hill/AllStock; 93 Ken Karp*; 94 Jack Fields/Photo Researchers; 95 Robert Azzi/Woodfin Camp & Associates; 96 Ken Karp*; 97B Elliott Smith*; 97T Elliott Smith*; 98 Paul Chauncey/The Stock Market; 100B Wayne Lankinen/DRK Photos; 100R Keith H. Murakami/Tom Stack & Associates; 101L Michael Fogden/Bruce Coleman Inc.; 101R A.E. Zuckerman/Tom Stack & Associates; 102B GHP Studio*; 102C GHP Studio*; 102T GHP Studio*

**Chapter 5** 106 Bernard Van Berg/The Image Bank; 107 Elliott Smith*; 108 Elliott Smith*; 109L Charles Gupton/AllStock; 109R Elliott Smith*; 113 GHP Studio*; 114 Nick Pavloff*; 120T GHP Studio*; 123T; NASA; 124B GHP Studio*; 124C GHP Studio*; 124T GHP Studio*; 125 Don Carroll/The Image Bank; 126 Ken Karp*; 130-131 Ken Karp*

**Unit 2** 132-133 Masa Uemura/AllStock

**Chapter 6** 134 Manfred Kage/Peter Arnold, Inc.; 135 NASA; 136BCL Erich Lessing/Art Resource; 136BL Lee Boltin; 136BR Erich Lessing/Art Resource; 136CRB Ken Karp*; 136CRT Janice Sheldon*; 136TL Phil Degginger/Bruce Coleman Inc.; 137BC Lee Boltin; 137BR Ken Karp*; 137L Ken Karp*; 137TC Ken Karp* 137TR; Stephen Frisch*; 138C Ken Karp*; 138L Fred Ward/Black Star; 138R GHP Studio*; 139C Joe Bator/The Stock Market; 139L Karl Hartmann-Sachs/Phototake; 139TR Fred Ward/Black Star; 141CR Ken Karp*; 141L Karl Hartmann-Sachs/Phototake; 142B GHP Studio*; 145 NASA; 146 GHP Studio*; 147 D. P. Hershkowitz/Bruce Coleman Inc.; 148C L. L. T. Rhodes/Earth Scenes; 149B James E. Lloyd/Animals, Animals; 149L Colin Milkins/Oxford Scientific Films/Earth Scenes; 149R Steve Elmore/The Stock Market; 150 Lawrence Migdale*; 151T CNRI-Science Photo Library/Photo Researchers; 152 Ken Karp*

**Chapter 7** 156 Bryan Peterson/The Stock Market; 158L GHP Studio*; 158R GHP Studio*; 159L GHP Studio*; 159R GHP Studio*; 163 David Parker-Science Photo Library/Photo Researchers; 165BC Ken Karp*; 165BR Tui De Roy/Bruce Coleman Inc.; 165R GHP Studio*; 165TC GHP Studio*; 165TR Wayland Lee*; 166B Ken Karp*; 166BC Ken Karp*; 166CT Ken Karp*; 166T Ken Karp*; 168B Ken Karp*; 168C Ken Karp*; 168T Ken Karp*; 169BC GHP Studio*; 169L Stephen Frisch*; 169R Runk-Schoenberger/Grant Heilman Photography; 169TC Breck P. Kent/Earth Scenes; 170B Ken Karp*; 170T Ken Karp*; 172 Elliott Smith*; 173 Bob Daemmrich/Stock, Boston; 174B Ken Karp*; 174C Ken Karp*; 174T Ken Karp*; 175BL Ken Karp*; 175C Ken Karp*; 175R Ken Karp*; 175TL Ken Karp*; 176C Farrell Grehan/Photo Researchers; 176L Ken Karp*; 176R GHP Studio*; 178 Ken Karp*

**Chapter 8** 182 Brenda Tharp; 188 Yoav Levy/Phototake; 189 GHP Studio*; 190 Nick Pavloff*; 191BL Ken Karp*; 191BR Cindy Lewis; 191TL Ken Karp*; 191TR GHP Studio*; 192BL Joseph Nettis/Photo Researchers; 192BR Stacy Pick/Stock, Boston; 192TL Ken Karp*; 192TR Phototake; 193 Seth Joel/Woodfin Camp & Associates; 194 Dan McCoy/Rainbow; 195BL Stephen Frisch*; 195BR GHP Studio*; 195TL GHP Studio*; 195TR Breck P. Kent/Earth Scenes; 196BL Ken Karp*; 196BR Ken Karp*; 196TL GHP Studio*; 196TR NASA; 197BL CNRI/Phototake; 197BR Ellis Herwig/Stock, Boston; 197TL Elliott Smith*; 197TR Ted Mahieu/The Stock Market; 199 David Lawrence/The Stock Market; 200 Ken Karp*; 204-205 M. Angelo/Westlight

**Unit 3** 206 GHP Studio*; 206-207 Gerald & Buff Corsi/Tom Stack & Associates

**Chapter 9** 208 Chuck O'Rear/Westlight; 209 David Madison/DUOMO; 210 Tim Davis*; 216 Ken Karp*; 219B Salmoiraghi/The Stock Market; 219T Gerald & Buff Corsi/Tom Stack & Associates; 221 Ken Karp*; 225C Ken Karp*; 225L Robert Mathena/Fundamental Photographs; 225R Ken Karp*

**Chapter 10** 230 Phillip A. Harrington/Fran Heyl Associates; 236B Anne Dowie*; 236T Anne Dowie*; 238 Ken Karp*; 241 Nick Pavloff*; 247 Greg Vaughn/Tom Stack & Associates; 252-253 GHP Studio*; 254 T. J. Florian/Rainbow; 254-255 Cameron Davidson/Bruce Coleman Inc.

**Chapter 11** 256 Bob O'Shaughnessy/The Stock Market; 257 Ken Karp*; 258B Ken Karp*; 258TL Ken Karp*; 258TR Ken Karp*; 260 Ken Karp*; 261 GHP Studio*; 263L GHP Studio*; 263R GHP Studio*; 267 Ken Karp*; 270L Ken Karp*; 270R Ken Karp*; 271 Ken Karp*; 272 Nick Pavloff*; 275B Ken Karp*; 275T Ken Karp*; 276 Ken Karp*; 277 Ken Karp*; 281B Stephen Frisch*; 281C Stephen Frisch*; 281T Stephen Frisch*

**Chapter 12** 286 CNRI-Science Photo Library/Photo; Researchers 287; GHP Studio*; 288 Ken Karp*; 289B The Granger Collection; 289T The Granger Collection; 291 NASA; 292B GHP Studio*; 292CL Bill Ross/Westlight; 292CR W. Cody/Westlight; 292T Linda K. Moore/Rainbow; 298 Chromosohm/Sohm/AllStock; 299 Ken Karp*; 300 Rich Buzzelli/Tom Stack & Associates; 304 GHP Studio*

**Chapter 13** 308 David Parker-Science Photo Library/Photo Researchers; 309 Elliott Smith*; 313BL Ken Karp*; 313BR David Parker-Science Photo Library/Photo Researchers; 313R David Parker-Science Photo Library/Photo Researchers; 313T Ken Karp*; 314T

...rt/Woodfin Camp & Associates; 321 Ken Karp*; 322 ...mann; 324 Peter Menzel/Stock, Boston; 330-331 GHP Studio*

**Unit 5** 332 Ken Karp*; 332-333 Frank Siteman/Rainbow

**Chapter 14** 334 W. Maehl/AllStock; 336 Ken Karp*; 339 Jeff Hornbaker; 340 Ken Karp*; 341 Steve Lissau/Rainbow; 346 Roy Giles/Tony Stone Worldwide; 347B Tony Stone Worldwide; 347T Charles O'Rear/Westlight; 348 Jonathan Blair/Woodfin Camp & Associates; 350 Baron Wolman; 351L Ken Karp*; 353 Baron Wolman; 354L Dick Luria-Science Source/Photo Researchers; 354R Pix Elation/Fran Heyl Associates

**Chapter 15** 358 Mark Richards*; 359 Tim Davis*; 364 Tony Stone Worldwide; 367C GHP Studio*; 367L GHP Studio*; 367R GHP Studio*; 370L Anne Dowie*; 370R Anne Dowie*; 376 Baron Wolman; 377L Ken Karp*; 377R Runk-Schoenberger/Grant Heilman Photography; 379 Lawrence Manning/Tony Stone Worldwide; 380 Ken Karp*

**Chapter 16** 384 © Lennart Nilsson from `Behold Man', Little, Brown & Co., Boston; 385 Doug Menuez/Stock, Boston; 388 Robert Shafer/Tony Stone Worldwide; 389 Gabe Palmer/The Stock Market; 390C Ken Karp*; 390L Ken Karp*; 390R Mark Richards*; 392B Anne Dowie*; 392R Andrea Brizzi/The Stock Market; 392TL Ken Karp*; 393C Anne Dowie*; 393L Ken Karp*; 393R Ken Karp*; 397 Ken Karp*; 398 Martin Rogers/Stock, Boston; 399 Howard Sochurek/The Stock Market; 401 Rod Catanach/Woods Hole Oceanographic Institute; 402TL Kelvin Aitken/Peter Arnold, Inc.; 402TR Stephen J. Krasemann/DRK Photos; 403B Dwight R. Kuhn/DRK Photos; 403R Stanley Breeden/DRK Photos; 403TL Stephen Dalton/Photo Researchers

**Chapter 17** 408 A.M. Rosario/The Image Bank; 410 Kodansha/The Image Bank; 415 Ken Karp*; 417 Runk-Schoenberger/Grant Heilman Photography; 420B David Pollack/The Stock Market; 420C Stuart L. Craig Jr./Bruce Coleman Inc.; 420T NASA; 422 Louis Bencze/AllStock; 423C Ken Karp*; 423L Ken Karp*; 423R Ken Karp*; 424C Ken Karp*; 424L Anne Dowie*; 425 John Livzey/AllStock; 426L Ken Karp*; 426R Ken Karp*; 427 Giraudon/Art Resource; 428 Lawrence Migdale*

**Chapter 18** 432 Michael Furman/The Stock Market; 433 Mary Clay/Tom Stack & Associates; 434BL Robert L. Dunne/Bruce Coleman Inc.; 434BR Wallace Kirkland/Animals, Animals; 434L Ken Karp*; 434TC Ken Karp*; 435CB Spencer Grant/Stock, Boston; 435CR Kent Knudson/Stock, Boston; 435L Ken Karp*; 435TR Don & Pat Valenti/DRK Photos; 440 Elliott Smith*; 441 Don & Pat Valenti/DRK Photos; 443B Ken Karp*; 443T Ken Karp*; 445 Phillip A. Harrington/Fran Heyl Associates; 446 Ted Levin/Earth Scenes; 447 Ken Karp*; 448L Anne Dowie*; 448C Anne Dowie*; 448R Anne Dowie*; 449B Ken Karp*; 449T Harry Pulschen/Custom Medical Stock Photo; 450 Ken Karp*; 451 Ken Karp*; 456R Yoav Levy/Phototake; 456T Philippe Plailly/Science Photo Library/Photo Researchers; 457BR Doug Armand/Tony Stone Worldwide; 457R Chuck O'Rear/Woodfin Camp & Associates; 458 Chuck O'Rear/Woodfin Camp & Associates; 462 Ken Karp*; 462-463 Renee Lynn*

**Unit 6** 464 Stephen Frisch*; 464-465 GHP Studio*

**Chapter 19** 466 William McCoy/Rainbow; 467 Ken Karp*; 469 Dr. A. Lesk, Laboratory of Molecular Biology-Science Photo Library/Photo Researchers; 471 Craig Aurness/Woodfin Camp & Associates; 474R OMIKRON/Science Source/Photo Researchers; 478 Anne Dowie*; 481 GHP Studio*; 483L Marty Cordano/DRK Photos; 483R Pat O'Hara/DRK Photos; 484 Ken Karp*

**Chapter 20** 488 Craig Aurness/ Westlight; 489B GHP Studio*; 489T GHP Studio*; 490B Ken Karp*; 490CL Ken Karp*; 490R GHP Studio*; 490TC Ken Karp*; 492B Ken Karp*; 492T Richard Pasley/Stock, Boston; 498 NASA; 499 Stephen Frisch*; 503 Ken Karp*; 505B Ken Karp*; 505CR Ken Karp*; 505TL Elliott Smith*; 505TR Ken Karp*; 507 Anne Dowie*; 508 John Colwell/Grant Heilman Photography; 510 Ken Karp*

**Chapter 21** 514 Jon Brenneis/Photo 20-20; 515 Holt Studios/Earth Scenes; 516 Elliott Smith*; 517 Ken Karp*; 518C GHP Studio*; 518CL Ken Karp*; 518R Ken Karp*; 518TL Ken Karp*; 519 Elliott Smith*; 521 Bohdan Hrynewych/Stock, Boston; 522 Tom Till/DRK Photos; 524B Charles Derby/Photo Researchers; 524T Dan McCoy/Rainbow; 525 Seth H. Goltzer/The Stock Market; 527 Elliott Smith*; 528 Ken Karp*; 529 Ken Karp*; 532 Ken Karp*

**Chapter 22** 536 J. Gross, Biozentrum-Science Photo Library/Photo Researchers, Inc.; 537 John Gerlach/DRK Photos; 538 Anne Dowie*; 542 GHP Studio*; 544 Ken Karp*; 545 Mike King/Tony Stone Worldwide; 546 GHP Studio*; 547 GHP Studio*; 548 GHP Studio*; 549 Anne Dowie*; 555 Science Photo Library/Photo Researchers; 556 Anne Dowie*

**Chapter 23** 560 Patrice Loiez, CERN/Science Photo Library/Photo Researchers; 561 Shopper/Stock, Boston; 564C Photo Researchers; 564T Dan Budnik/Woodfin Camp & Associates; 565 Art Resource; 569B Biophoto Associates/Science Source/Photo Researchers; 569T Biophoto Associates/Photo Researchers; 570 Ken Karp*; 573 Zefa-Streichan/The Stock Market; 574 Jeff Zaruba/The Stock Market; 578-579 Chuck O'Rear/Westlight; 578C GHP Studio*; 578T GHP Studio*; 579 GHP Studio*

**Unit 7** 580 Mark Sherman; 580-581 Barry L. Runk/Grant Heilman Photography

**Chapter 24** 582 Dan McCoy/Rainbow; 583 C. H. Currier/The Bettmann Archive 586; James H. Carmichael/Bruce Coleman Inc.; 587 Jan Staller/The Stock Market; 589 Gabe Palmer/The Stock Market; 590B Dewitt Jones/Woodfin Camp & Associates; 590T Bernard Pierre Wolff/Photo Researchers Inc.; 591B Kunio Owaki/The Stock Market; 591T Torin Boyd; 592B Robert Frerch/Woodfin Camp & Associates; 592C Greg Vaughn/Tom Stack & Associates; 592T Simon Fraser/Science Photo Library/Photo Researchers Inc.; 593 Sepp Seitz/Woodfin Camp & Associates; 595 Ken Karp*; 599 Jim Pickerell/Westlight; 600 Heartland All Species Project

**Chapter 25** 604 Lisl Dennis/The Image Bank; 605B Tom Stack/Tom Stack & Associates; 605C Eric Grave/Phototake; 609B GHP Studio*; 609T GHP Studio*; 610B GHP Studio*; 610D GHP Studio*; 610L GHP Studio*; 610R GHP Studio*; 611C GHP Studio*; 611L Stephen Frisch*; 611R GHP Studio*; 612 GHP Studio*; 613 GHP Studio*; 616BL GHP Studio*; 616C Geoffrey Clifford/Woodfin Camp & Associates; 616CL GHP Studio*; 616R Tim Davis*; 617 Stephen Trimble/DRK Photos; 618B Ron Kimball; 618C Herb Charles Ohlmeyer/Fran Heyl Associates; 619 NASA; 620 Ken Karp*; 621 NASA; 623B Marc Muench/AllStock; 623T M. Gottschalk/Westlight; 624BL Gary Braasch/AllStock; 624C David M. Dennis/Tom Stack & Associates; 624R Gary Milburn/Tom Stack & Associates; 624TL Tom Walker/AllStock; 625L Tom Carroll/Phototake; 626B Thomas Kitchin/Tom Stack & Associates; 626R Tom Bean/AllStock; 626T Ray Pfortner/Peter Arnold, Inc.; 627T Matt McVay/Black Star; 628C Robert Winslow/Tom Stack & Associates; 628T Ivan Massar/Black Star; 632 GHP Studio*; 632-633 GHP Studio*

* Photographed expressly for Addison-Wesley, Inc.

## *Science and Literature*

**Unit 1** From *The Boy Who Reversed Himself* by William Sleator. Copyright © 1986 by William Sleator. Used by permission of Dutton Children's Books, a division of Penguin Books USA Inc.

**Unit 2** From *Invitation to the Game* by Monica Hughes. Copyright © 1990 by Monica Hughes. Reprinted by permission of HarperCollins Publishers, HarperCollins Publishers Ltd., Toronto and Reed Consumer Books.

**Unit 3** From *Child of the Owl* by Laurence Yep. Copyright © 1977 by Laurence Yep. Reprinted by permission of HarperCollins Publishers.

**Unit 4** From *Genie With The Light Blue Hair* by Ellen Conford. Copyright © 1989 by Conford Enterprises Ltd. Used by permission of Bantam Books, a division of Bantam Doubleday Dell Publishing Group, Inc.

**Unit 5** From *Blue Tights* by Rita Williams-Garcia. Copyright © 1988 by Rita Williams-Garcia. Reprinted by permission of Penguin Books USA Inc.

**Unit 6** From "Mother and Daughter," *Baseball in April and Other Stories* by Gary Soto. Copyright © 1990 by Gary Soto. Reprinted by permission of Harcourt Brace and Company.

**Unit 7** Reprinted with permission of Macmillan Publishing Company from *M.C. Higgins, The Great* by Virginia Hamilton. Copyright © 1974 by Virginia Hamilton.